FINANCIAL STATEMENT ANALYSIS

PRENTICE-HALL SERIES IN ACCOUNTING
Charles T. Horngren, Editor

AUDITING: AN INTEGRATED APPROACH, 3/E
Arens/Loebbecke

KOHLER'S DICTIONARY FOR ACCOUNTANTS, 6/E
Cooper/Ijiri

INTERMEDIATE ACCOUNTING, 2/E
Danos/Imhoff

FINANCIAL STATEMENT ANALYSIS, 2/E
Foster

FINANCIAL ACCOUNTING: PRINCIPLES AND ISSUES, 3/E
Granof

COST ACCOUNTING: A MANAGERIAL EMPHASIS, 5/E
Horngren

INTRODUCTION TO FINANCIAL ACCOUNTING, 2/E
Horngren

INTRODUCTION TO MANAGEMENT ACCOUNTING, 6/E
Horngren

CPA PROBLEMS AND APPROACHES TO SOLUTIONS,
VOLUME I, 5/E
Horngren/Leer

ADVANCED MANAGEMENT ACCOUNTING
Kaplan

FUND ACCOUNTING: THEORY AND PRACTICE, 2/E
Lynn/Freeman

A NEW INTRODUCTION TO FINANCIAL ACCOUNTING, 2/E
May/Mueller/Williams

AUDITING PRINCIPLES, 5/E
Stettler

BUDGETING, 4/E
Welsch

FINANCIAL STATEMENT ANALYSIS

Second Edition

George Foster

Stanford University

Prentice-Hall, Englewood Cliffs, New Jersey 07632

Library of Congress Cataloging-in-Publication Data

Foster, George (date)
    Financial statement analysis.

    Includes bibliographies and index.
    1. Financial statements.   I. Title.
HF5681.B2F64   1986   657'.3   85-28112
ISBN 0-13-316317-2

Editorial/production supervision and
    interior design: Joe O'Donnell Jr.
Cover design: Wanda Lubelska Design
Manufacturing buyer: Ray Keating

Printed in the United States of America

10   9   8

ISBN 0-13-316317-2   01

PRENTICE-HALL INTERNATIONAL (UK) LIMITED, *London*
PRENTICE-HALL OF AUSTRALIA PTY. LIMITED, *Sydney*
PRENTICE-HALL CANADA INC., *Toronto*
PRENTICE-HALL HISPANOAMERICANA, S.A., *Mexico*
PRENTICE-HALL OF INDIA PRIVATE LIMITED, *New Delhi*
PRENTICE-HALL OF JAPAN, INC., *Tokyo*
PRENTICE-HALL OF SOUTHEAST ASIA PTE. LTD., *Singapore*
EDITORA PRENTICE-HALL DO BRASIL, LTDA., *Rio de Janeiro*
WHITEHALL BOOKS LIMITED, *Wellington, New Zealand*

CONTENTS

PREFACE

This book provides an intensive study of financial statement analysis, seeking to describe and explain:

- The demand and supply forces underlying the provision of financial statement data,
- The properties of numbers derived from financial statements,
- The key aspects of decisions that use financial statement information, and
- The features of the environment in which these decisions are made.

The perspective adopted is that readers who have a solid grasp of these four factors are in a strong position to exploit the richness of the information contained in many financial statements as well as to appreciate fully the limitations of that information.

Two key features of the first edition that were received with much enthusiasm by reviewers and adopters of the text were the explicit linkage to the research literature and the emphasis placed on empirical evidence. Both features have been retained in this edition. Each chapter contains much discussion of and many references to research on the topics covered. At the end of each chapter is a section titled ''Some General Comments'' that includes discussion of unresolved issues in existing research, analysis of future research directions, or discussion of individual studies. One objective of this book is to increase the reader's appreciation of the important role that research has played and will continue to play in the analysis of financial statement information.

Empirical evidence is emphasized in this book more than is customary in financial statement analysis texts. Many issues in financial statement analysis can be resolved only at an empirical level. It is important that students be exposed to examples of these situations and be able to evaluate critically the existing evidence. Considerable new evidence is presented in this edition on the properties of financial statement data. This evidence relates to the distributional properties of financial ratios, correlations between financial statement numbers, and cross-sectional and time-series properties of financial statement numbers.

The term "financial statement" in the title of this book is used to mean a statement that contains financial information. It is not used exclusively with respect to balance sheets, income statements, or statements of changes in financial position. These three statements form a subset (albeit an important one) of the many financial statements that are the subject of analysis. Indeed, an emerging trend is the vast array of disclosures occurring outside the body of the traditional financial statements included in interim and annual reports. With the increased use of computer-based analysis and the availability of large, highly disaggregated data bases, it is likely that much of financial statement analysis will take place without direct access to traditional financial statements such as the balance sheet. In part due to this development, Chapter 3 of this edition contains a new appendix on "Considerations in Using Computerized Financial Statement Data Bases."

This textbook is aimed at both MBA or master's graduate students and senior students in undergraduate accounting, finance, or business programs. It should also be of interest to investment and credit analysts. This edition was pretested in graduate or undergraduate programs at Duke University (by W. Ricks), University of California at Davis (by P. Griffin), University of Washington (by G. Biddle), Washington University (by M. Pincus), and Stanford University (myself). It assumes familiarity with the material covered in introductory accounting, finance, and statistics courses. Unavoidably, some chapters are more difficult than others. Users of the first edition reported that the chapter on "Time-Series Analysis of Financial Statement Information" caused the most difficulty. I have restructured this chapter (and several others) so that the highly technical materials are now included as appendices. An instructor's manual is available for faculty adopting the text.

MAJOR CHANGES IN SECOND EDITION

This book contains the following major changes from the first edition:

1. Increased recognition is given to the multiple parties demanding financial statement information and to the diverse decision contexts in which that information is used. A new chapter on "The Demand for Financial Statement Information" (Chapter 1) has been added that discusses individual parties such as

investors, managers, employees, and lenders and the potential conflicts among them. Corporate restructuring decisions (mergers, divestitures, etc.) are given more detailed attention in a new chapter on "Corporate Restructuring and Financial Information" (Chapter 13).

2. Increased emphasis is given to the incentives facing suppliers of financial statement information. New chapters on "The Supply of Financial Statement Information" (Chapter 2) and "Financial Statement Numbers and Alternative Accounting Methods" (Chapter 5) have been added. Supply-side incentives are also discussed in sections covering line-of-business reporting (in Chapter 6) and management's timing of revenues and expenses and their accounting representation (in Chapter 7). This increased recognition of supply-side incentives provides insight into why the set of information placed in the public domain is not always the most timely or unbiased subset of that available to internal parties.

3. Increased attention is paid to the activities of investment and credit analysts and the sources of information available to them. A new chapter has been added on "Forecasting Financial Statement Information" (Chapter 8). Conversations with analysts and examination of their reports indicated that forecasting is one of their most important tasks. New coverage is given to research-based commercial services available to investment and credit analysts. For example, Chapter 10 provides discussion of the BARRA risk estimation service while Chapter 15 discusses the Zeta Services, Inc., financial distress analysis service.

4. Increased attention is paid to international aspects of financial statement analysis. A section on issues to be considered in making international comparisons of financial ratios has been added to Chapter 6. The text contains reference to non-U.S.– as well as U.S.–based examples and evidence in most chapters. One format adopted to capture this broadened international focus is tables summarizing data from each of several countries: Table 1.1 on investor rankings of information sources in each of three countries, Table 6.4 on fiscal year ends in each of six countries, Table 10.6 on firm-size portfolio returns in each of four countries, Table 14.1 on firms that rate debt securities in each of five countries, and Table 15.10 on financial profiles of failed and nonfailed firms in each of five countries.

ACKNOWLEDGMENTS

Many people have provided criticisms and comments that were helpful in preparing this revision. Especially detailed comments on the published version of the first edition were provided by R. Bowen, D. Emanuel, O. Joy, R. Officer, T. O'Keefe, and K. Schipper. M. Yoshino and the Security Analysts Association of Japan provided a meticulous review of the book during the Japanese translation of the first edition. Very useful feedback on a preliminary outline to revise the first edition was given by N. Dopuch, R. Dukes, P. Griffin, C. Horngren, J. Ketz, R. Leftwich, J. Liberman, and R. Vigeland. Constructive comments and assistance on drafts of individual chapters of this edition were provided by E. Altman, M. Barron, G. Biddle, W. Buffett, W. Buijink, E. Dimson, P. Dodd, R. Freeman, P. Griffin, R. Halderman, R. Ingram, M. Jegers, L. Lookabill, W. Ricks, S. Schaefer, W. Sharpe, and S. Zeff. J. Magliolo and T. Shevlin assisted with developing the new empirical evidence presented in this edition. I am especially grateful to the seven people who provided detailed comments on the complete manuscript: P. Brown, G. Clinch, E. Hubbard, M. Pincus, T. Shevlin, D. Shores, and D. Then. My greatest intellectual debt is due to my parents who (among other things) instilled in me a strong work ethic and an optimistic outlook and to the following academics who have been especially influential in my development: R. Ball, W. Beaver, P. Brown, R. Chambers, J. Demski, N. Dopuch, C. Horngren, and B. Lev. Dean R. Jaedicke at Stanford University helped create an environment in which individuals attempting to integrate research and teaching were made to feel highly valued citizens.

During the several years that I have worked on this revision I have been fortunate to have the assistance of the following very competent, as well as good-humored, typists: Teri Bush, Jeannette Ochoa, Margaret Russ, Yuri Sasaki, Alice Sheehan, and Cheryl Webster. Julie Warner of Prentice-Hall provided much encouragement during the revision of this book. Joe O'Donnell, Jr. handled the production of this book in a very efficient way. My thanks to all the above people.

George Foster

1

THE DEMAND
FOR FINANCIAL STATEMENT
INFORMATION

1.1 INTRODUCTION

What is observed in financial statements is the product of a diverse set of demand and supply forces. This chapter discusses demand-side forces and how they affect the content of financial statements or the timing of their release. Supply-side forces are discussed in Chapter 2.

Parties demanding financial statement information include (A) shareholders, investors, and security analysts; (B) managers; (C) employees; (D) lenders and other suppliers; (E) customers; and (F) government regulatory agencies. These parties will demand financial statement information to facilitate decision making, to facilitate the monitoring of management, or to interpret contracts or agreements that include provisions based on such information.

1.2 PARTIES DEMANDING FINANCIAL STATEMENT INFORMATION

A. Shareholders, Investors, and Security Analysts

Shareholders and other investors are major recipients of the financial statements of corporations. These parties range from individuals with relatively limited resources to large, well-endowed institutions such as insurance companies and mutual funds. The decisions made by these parties include not only which shares to buy, retain, or sell, but also the timing of the purchases or sales of those shares. Typically, these decisions will have either an *investment focus* or a *stewardship focus*; in some cases, both will occur simultaneously.

In an *investment focus*, the emphasis is on choosing a portfolio of securities that is consistent with the preferences of the investor for risk, return, dividend yield, liquidity, and so on. The information required for this choice can vary significantly. To illustrate, consider approaches aiming to detect mispriced securities by a fundamental analysis approach as opposed to a technical analysis approach. A fundamental analysis approach examines firm-, industry- and economy-related information; financial statements play a major role in this approach. An important aspect is predicting the timing, amounts, and uncertainties of the future cash flows of the firm. In contrast, technical analysis aims to detect mispriced securities by examining trends in security prices, security trading volume, and other related variables; financial statement information typically is not examined. (See Chapters 9 and 12 for further discussion.)

In both the fundamental and technical approaches, priority is placed on detecting mispriced securities. In some other contexts, investors may assume that they have no superior insight about the future prospects of a firm relative to that already implicit in the current security price. This assumption does not preclude the use of financial statement information. One important use could be to estimate or predict firm specific variables such as risk and dividend yield. The purpose of this estimation is to match the chosen portfolio with the investor's preferences and to minimize the transaction costs associated with maintaining a portfolio with this match over time.

In decisions with a *stewardship focus,* the concern of shareholders is with monitoring the behavior of management and attempting to affect its behavior in a way deemed appropriate. Management has considerable discretion concerning the use and disposition of a firm's resources. It can make decisions that divert these resources from existing shareholders, leaving them with only a "corporate shell." The existence of this potential conflict has created incentives for

- Contracts or agreements to be written between management and the firm that better align the interests of management and shareholders (e.g., the issuance of stock options as part of the compensation contracts between management and the firm or the use of the earnings to shareholders' equity ratio rather than total sales to decide the size of a bonus pool)
- Information to be presented by management and other parties that discloses how management has used the resources under its control (e.g., the issuance of interim and annual financial statements to shareholders).

When predicting the timing, amounts, and uncertainties of future cash flows of the firm, the past track record of management in relation to the resources under its control can be a critical variable.

The analysis undertaken for decisions by shareholders and investors can be done by those parties themselves or by intermediaries such as security analysts and investment advisors. These intermediaries can also act as a pressure group on management and other bodies (e.g., regulatory agencies) that influences the timing or content of information provided to external parties. Note, however, that these intermediaries can have different rankings for financial statement variables than the investors for whom the information analysis is conducted. For example, investors may support the mandatory disclosure of management earnings forecasts, whereas security analysts may oppose this disclosure because it competes with their own activities and reduces the areas where the items included in analyst reports are the direct result of their own information analysis.

B. Managers

One source of the demand for financial statement information by managers arises from contracts that include provisions based on financial statement variables. One example is management incentive contracts. To illustrate, consider the following provision in the senior management incentive plan of Pabst Brewing Company:

> The Program for key management salaried employees is based upon pre-established corporate goals for return on invested capital and sales. Participants in the Program

are eligible to receive from 10% to 100% of base salaries, depending upon performance of the Company and the participant against the pre-determined goals. Awards
under the Program will not be made unless the Company is profitable for the year
in question and no awards are to be made unless a minimum of 70% of the corporate
goals for return on invested capital and sales has been achieved. The (current) corporate goals for the program components are a 7.25% pre-tax return on invested
capital and barrels of beer shipped of 12,875,000. Individual job performance of participants is determined by the Chief Executive Officer and recommended to the Personnel Policy Committee of the Board of Directors.[1]

The Pabst plan has an explicit linkage to the firm's financial statements. In other
cases, there may be implicit (but still very strong) linkages between compensation
and financial statement variables such as earnings, earnings per share, or the
earnings to shareholders' equity ratio.

When structuring agreements between the firm and other entities, management may include contractual terms based on financial statement variables. For
instance, in a joint partnership agreement, one firm may agree to be the operating
partner, to be reimbursed on a cost-plus basis for operating expenditures, and to
share in the earnings of the partnership on an agreed percentage basis. It is not
unusual in these cases for the joint partners to hire an accounting firm to audit
the financial statements of the partnership. The important point (as regards this
chapter) is that the partners have, by the way they formed their partnership,
created a derived demand for financial statement information.

Managers also utilize financial statement information in many of their financing, investment, or operating decisions. A financial statement-based variable,
such as the current debt-to-equity ratio or the interest coverage ratio, is frequently
important in deciding how much long-term debt to raise. The financial statements
of other firms can also be used in management decisions. For instance, when
deciding where to redirect the resources of a firm, the financial statements of
other firms can show areas where high profit margins are currently being earned.

C. Employees

The demand for financial statements by employees can arise from several
motivations. Employees have a vested interest in the continued and profitable
operations of their firm; financial statements are an important source of information about current and potential future profitability and solvency. Employees
can also demand financial statements to monitor the viability of their pension
plans.

In some cases, employee interest is magnified by contracts between employees and the company being based on variables included in financial statements. Consider the contract written between the United Auto Workers (UAW)
and the Ford Motor Company in the early 1980s:

The Plan requires a minimum 2.3% pre-tax return on sales before any profits are
shared. After the minimum return is reached, the Total Profit Share is equal to the

sum of the following calculations:

10% of profits above the minimum 2.3% return on sales, but below a 4.6% return on sales;

plus 12.5% of profits above a 4.6% return on sales but below a 6.9% return on sales;

plus 15% of profits above a 6.9% return on sales.

Note that the payouts are cumulative—i.e., each step of the calculation is added to the next step—and that the profit sharing percentages increase as the return on sales increases. To illustrate:

Assume:

$$
\begin{aligned}
\text{Profits} &= \$1.8 \text{ billion} \\
\text{Sales} &= \$36 \text{ billion} \\
\text{Return on Sales} &= \$1.8 \text{ billion}/\$36 \text{ billion} \\
&= 5.0\%
\end{aligned}
$$

Minimum Return:

$$.023 \times \$36 \text{ billion} = \$828 \text{ million}$$

Total Profit Share:

$$
\begin{aligned}
.10 \times (.046 \times \$36 \text{ billion} - .023 \times \$36 \text{ billion}) &= \$\ 82.8 \text{ million} \\
\text{plus } .125 \times (\$1,800 \text{ million} - \$1,656 \text{ million}) &= \underline{\$\ 18.0 \text{ million}} \\
& \underline{\$100.8 \text{ million}}
\end{aligned}
$$

Profits represent the earnings of all of Ford's U.S. operations with two exceptions: Ford Aerospace (including a new sister subsidiary, Ford Electronics and Refrigeration Corporation) and Ford Land.

Profits are measured before income taxes in the case of consolidated manufacturing operations, and after income taxes for unconsolidated non-manufacturing subsidiaries such as Ford Motor Credit. Profits are also calculated before supplemental compensation payments to Ford executives, profit sharing payments under this and all other profit sharing plans, extraordinary items of income or expense, and gains or losses from the disposal of operations.

Sales are for the same U.S. operations covered by the profits definition, except that revenues from unconsolidated subsidiaries are excluded from the calculation.

All of the calculations and underlying sales and profit data are to be certified by a firm of independent certified public accountants. Ford is also required to respond to requests from the Union for information supporting such calculations.[2]

In this case, employees of Ford (or their representatives) clearly have a vested interest in monitoring financial statement-based variables such as profits and sales.

D. Lenders and Other Suppliers

In the ongoing relationship that exists between suppliers and a firm, financial statements can play several roles. Consider the relationship between a firm and the suppliers of its loan capital, for example, a bank. In the initial loan-granting stage of the relationship, financial statements typically are an important item. Indeed, many banks have standard evaluation procedures that stipulate that information relating to liquidity, leverage, profitability, and so on be considered when determining the amount of the loan, the interest rate and the security to be requested. If the decision to grant a loan is made, the terms of that loan may contractually stipulate that financial statement variables be an important factor in determining the nature of the ongoing relationship. Many bank loans include bond covenants that, if violated, can result in the bank restructuring the existing loan agreement; see Castle (1980). Consider the following statement in the 1984 Annual Report of Clark Equipment Company:

> Under agreements entered into in 1984 between Clark and lenders to Clark Equipment Overseas Finance Corporation (CLEO), Clark is obligated to maintain CLEO's minimum capital base at $15.0 million and CLEO's debt to equity ratio at 10 to 1. Clark has also agreed to maintain CLEO's ratios of earnings to fixed charges at 1.05 times fixed charges.[3]

One effect of incorporating such covenants into the loan agreement is to create a demand by the bank for successive financial statements of the firm.

In some cases, the loan agreement will make the level of interest or principal repayments contingent upon financial statement–based variables. Consider the following clause in an agreement between Superscope (a company engaged in the marketing and distribution of audio home entertainment products) and its lenders:

> The restructured $9.9 million in debt will be payable over 10 years at the rate of $1 million per year at the end of the third through the eighth year and $2 million in the ninth and tenth years. Interest accrues for the first three years only to the extent of 25% of net pre-tax income up to a market rate. Thereafter, interest will accrue at a minimum rate of 5% up to a market rate, but not to exceed 40% of consolidated pre-tax income. . . . Dividends on common stock under the new bank agreement are restricted until such time as Superscope is paying a market rate of interest on the restructured bank debt.[4]

The lenders in this agreement clearly have an incentive not only to demand the financial statements of Superscope but also to monitor the accounting methods used by them to compute "net pre-tax income." Another example similar to the Superscope example is the income bonds issued by a small subset of firms. The payment of interest on these bonds is contingent upon the amount of the issuing corporation's reported accounting income; see McConnell and Schlarbaum (1981) for further discussion.

E. Customers

The relationships between a firm and its customers can extend over many years. In some cases, these relationships take the form of legal obligations associated with guarantees, warranties, or deferred benefits. In other cases, the long-term association is based on continued attention to customer service.

Customers have a vested interest in monitoring the financial viability of firms with which they have long-term relationships. This interest is likely to increase when concerns develop about possible bankruptcy. Consider the example of Lykes Corp., a major U.S. steel manufacturer. In the late 1970s, LTV made a takeover bid for Lykes Corp. Due to past agreements with the Justice Department, LTV had to gain specific approval for the Lykes merger. LTV argued that Lykes was a "failing company" and that the benefits from merging with LTV outweighed any antitrust considerations. The use of this "failing company" argument, however, raised the possibility of Lykes' customers and suppliers terminating their relationships should the merger not be approved. *The Wall Street Journal* reported that "most worrisome to those close to the merger is the possibility of a panicky reaction among Lykes' suppliers, customers or lenders in the days and weeks after a negative decision. . . . A longtime customer says it already has reduced its orders sharply so that it doesn't depend on the company as the single source for any products."[5] The financial statements of the firm represent one source of information that customers and suppliers can use to make inferences about the viability of the firm.

F. Government/Regulatory Agencies

Demands for financial statement information by government/regulatory agencies can arise in a diverse set of areas such as

- Revenue raising, for example, for income tax, sales tax, or value-added tax collection
- Government contracting, for example, for reimbursing suppliers paid on a cost-plus basis or for monitoring whether companies engaged in government business are earning excess profits
- Rate determination, for example, deciding the allowable rate of return that an electric utility can earn
- Regulatory intervention, for example, determining whether to provide a government-backed loan guarantee to a financially distressed firm.

Financial statement information is but one input into such decisions. Political factors also may be equally if not more important in some cases; for example, in determining whether to approve a government-backed loan guarantee, the policy platform of the party in power and the electoral areas suffering unemployment if the distressed firm becomes bankrupt may be critical factors.

G. Other Parties

The set of parties that make demands on corporations is open-ended. Diverse parties such as academics, environmental protection organizations, and other special interest lobbying groups approach corporations for details relating to their financial and other affairs. Many corporations do make concerted efforts to respond to some of the requests that come from these parties.

1.3 CONFLICTS AMONG DIVERSE PARTIES

Actions taken by one or more of the parties discussed in Section 1.2 can result in wealth redistributions among these parties. For example,

- Shareholders' wealth may decrease, but managers' wealth may increase when a firm makes a large acquisition at an excessive price. Larger firms often pay higher salaries to management.
- Shareholders' wealth may increase by the payment of a large dividend that decreases the assets available as security for the creditors of the firm.
- Shareholders' wealth may increase when an electric utility regulatory body approves a large rate increase that results in customers paying higher utility bills.

The foregoing are but three areas where the interests of shareholders, management, workers, suppliers, customers, and government may conflict. Jensen and Smith (1985) provide an overview of issues in this area.

Recognizing the existence of these and similar conflicts increases our understanding of two important factors associated with the demand for financial statement information:

1. Each party will *not* have similar rankings as to the items to be disclosed in financial statements or the timing of those disclosures. Individual parties typically will oppose the disclosure of certain items that may adversely affect their own self-interest. For instance, management and shareholders of a bank will likely oppose full and prompt disclosure of "problem loans" on the grounds that it could cause a "run" on the deposits of the bank. In contrast, the depositors of the bank may have a preference for early rather than late disclosure of such "problem loans."

2. Financial statements may perform an important role in the mechanisms used to monitor potential wealth redistributions between parties. For instance, the provision of audited financial statements is one mechanism by which shareholders monitor potential wealth redistribution actions by management.

The existence of conflicts among the parties cited in Section 1.2 has been recognized by courts for many years. For example, Dewing (1953, pp. 1360–1361) describes a 1910 legal case involving a conflict between the income bondholders and the shareholders of Central of Georgia Railway. For interest to be paid to the income bondholders, the reported profits of Central of Georgia had to exceed a stipulated amount. The interest payments were noncumulative. The income bondholders alleged that Central of Georgia understated reported earnings in 1907 to avoid making interest payments. The Court upheld the income bondholders' claim. It found that Central of Georgia (1) had failed to recognize as earnings "the earnings of a subsidiary steamship line that should have been paid to the railroad," (2) had set aside an "excessive reserve for unadjusted claims on lumber freight," and (3) had been incurring excessive maintenance costs (costs "well above those of other southern railroads and far above the average for the country as a whole"). The Court restated the earnings of Central of Georgia and required it to make retroactive interest payments to the income bondholders.

Contracts between individual parties in some cases explicitly recognize the ability of one party to appropriate wealth from other parties. As noted earlier, lenders typically include covenants in loan agreements that restrict the ability of the borrower to make decisions that can significantly reduce his or her ability to repay the loan principal and accrued interest. As a second example, consider the employee profit sharing agreement signed in 1982 between the UAW and Mack Trucks Inc. (a 41-percent-owned subsidiary of Renault, the French automobile maker). The agreement stipulated that profits are for continuing operations, specifically excluding profits or losses from discontinued operations. The agreement also stipulated that Mack Trucks' profits from U.S. operations were to be calculated before any corporate administrative expenses assessed by its parent. The effect of these stipulations is to restrict the ability of the management of Mack (and Renault) to reduce the reported profits of Mack via charges associated with discontinued operations or via an increase in the corporate administrative expense charged to the Mack operation.

The existence of conflicts of interest does not mean that each party necessarily will take actions that disadvantage other parties. For instance, conflicting parties first may seek ways to make their interests congruent. However, at an empirical level, a model predicting that individual behavior will be guided by vested self-interest appears to have considerable explanatory power (especially relative to competing models). The advice given by an Australian state premier (Jack Lang) to a (then) novice politician is of interest in this regard: "In the race of life always back self-interest . . . you know it will be trying."

1.4 FACTORS AFFECTING DEMAND
FOR FINANCIAL STATEMENT INFORMATION

The demand for financial statement information is derived from the improvement in decision making or monitoring that arises with its use. Factors that determine whether such an improvement is expected to occur include (A) the potential of the information to reduce uncertainty and (B) the availability of competing information sources.

A. Potential of the Information to Reduce Uncertainty

An important element in many decisions is uncertainty. For instance, there may be uncertainty over the future profitability of a firm, the quality of its management, or the ability of a supplier to fulfill obligations under a warranty agreement. In this context, there are two related issues:

1. What level of uncertainty is faced by the decision maker and what are the expected gains from reducing it?
2. What role can financial statement information play in revising beliefs about uncertainty?

In some situations, financial statement analysis can play an important role in revising such beliefs. Assume that a lender wishes to forecast the profitability of a loan applicant that is in a relatively stable industry and a presumption of continuity of management appears to be reasonable. In this context, the past and current profitability record can be a very useful starting point when forecasting profitability over the life of the proposed loan.

In other situations, uncertainty may arise from sources about which financial statements provide little insight. When investing in oil and gas exploration partnerships, a major area of uncertainty is in the geological structure of the exploration leases; this information is not typically reported in financial statements. Similarly, the major area of uncertainty in many start-up ventures relates to the feasibility of new technologies and the market acceptance of products not yet developed; again, corporate financial statement information provides little insight into these areas. However, even in such contexts as oil and gas exploration and start-up ventures, financial statements can play an indirect role. The quality and reputation of management is a critical variable in such partnerships and ventures. The financial statements of prior activities with which the management has been associated can be a useful input into assessing their "past track record." Section 1.5 discusses results from an empirical study by Wolfson (1985) that concludes that "reputation effects are at work in the market" (p. 124).

B.   Availability of Competing Information Sources

Financial statement information is one of many information sources available to the parties outlined in Section 1.2. Other sources include (1) company-oriented releases such as dividend releases and production reports, (2) industry-oriented releases such as new wage contracts with unions, and (3) economy-oriented releases such as money supply announcements. There are several grounds on which financial statements may have a comparative advantage over these competing sources:

1. Financial statement information is *more directly related* to the variable of interest. Consider a contract written between the buyer and seller of a service business. Due to differences of opinion between buyers and sellers about the future earnings, many such contracts include a provision that bases part of the consideration on a percentage of future earnings as earned. In this case, financial statements have a comparative advantage vis-à-vis other information sources as they report the variable of direct interest to the parties to the contract.
2. Financial statement information is a *more reliable* information source. One

rationale for reliability could be the existence of auditors to certify the financial statements presented by management. A second rationale is that external parties may perceive that statements pertaining to (say) new products could have a relatively higher public relations content vis-à-vis information included in financial statements.

3. Financial statement information is a *lower-cost* information source. In most jurisdictions, firms do not charge individual users when providing financial statements. In contrast, many external agencies charge fees (at times not inconsiderable) to access data bases that they make commercially available.

4. Financial statement information is a *more timely* information source. In some cases, management can reduce the value of information provided by competing sources such as outside agencies by making prompt release of budget information, information on the impact of new events for the firm, and so forth. In general, the potential for financial statement information being more timely is greater with financial releases that pertain to future years (for example, earnings forecasts) than with audited financial statements that pertain to the current and past years. For most items included in audited financial statements, timeliness is not likely to be a source of comparative advantage.

The notion of competing information sources is important in assessing the role of financial statement information in monitoring decisions. As noted in Section 1.2, the issuance of interim and annual financial statements is one means by which shareholders can monitor management behavior. However, there are many other monitoring devices available. The board of directors, corporate lenders, and security analysts all potentially can provide information about management behavior. Nonfinancial information such as physical production reports and market share details may also be used to monitor management. Within a firm itself, individual managers can serve as monitors for each other. Given this setting, financial statements will be used only where they are a cost-effective means of monitoring. Note that in most cases the choice is not one monitoring device to the exclusion of others. Rather, the choice will concern the appropriate mix of the many monitoring devices available.

It is important to recognize that no single source has a monopoly over the information that can be used in decisions. Attempts by any source to expand or contract its activities can affect the demand for information provided by other sources. For instance, a decision by a firm to release audited market value data pertaining to all its properties can reduce the demand for security analysts to estimate such figures independently.

1.5 SOME GENERAL COMMENTS*

1. Many research studies have reported the results of interviews or questionnaires with one or more classes of the parties demanding financial statement

* This section (and similarly titled ones in subsequent chapters) discusses research that relates to the issues previously raised in the chapter.

information. An illustrative study is Chang, Most, and Brain (1983). A questionnaire survey was sent to individual investors, institutional investors, and financial analysts in the United States, United Kingdom, and New Zealand. Views were elicited on both "the importance which the three groups placed on financial statements as a source of information for investment decisions and also on the perceived usefulness of this information source" (p. 64). Respondents were asked to assess the importance they placed on each of the questionnaire items on a five-point scale. Using the average score on this five-point scale, the sources of information can be ranked from most important to least important. Panel A of Table 1.1 reports results for the ranking of information sources. Corporate annual reports

TABLE 1.1 Rankings by Individual Investors, Institutional Investors and Financial Analysts in United States (U.S.), United Kingdom (U.K.), and New Zealand (N.Z.)

Sources and Items Ranked in Questionnaires	Individual Investors			Institutional Investors			Financial Analysts		
	U.S.	U.K.	N.Z.	U.S.	U.K.	N.Z.	U.S.	U.K.	N.Z.
A: Information Sources									
Corporate annual reports	1	3	3	1	1	2	1	2	1
Corporate interim reports	—	—	—	—	—	—	4	4	2
Stockbroker's advice	4	2	2	4	2	1	—	—	—
Advisory services	3	5	5	2	5	3	5	8	8
Newspapers and magazines	2	1	1	3	4	5	8	5	7
Proxy statements	5	4	4	5	3	4	7	7	6
Corporate press releases	—	—	—	—	—	—	6	6	4
Prospectuses	—	—	—	—	—	—	2	3	5
Communications with management	—	—	—	—	—	—	3	1	3
Advice of friends	6	6	6	6	6	6	—	—	—
Tips and rumors	7	7	7	7	7	7	—	—	—
B: Corporate Annual Report Items									
Balance sheet	3	3	3	2	1.5	3	2	2	2
Income statement	1	2	2	1	1.5	1	1	1	1
Statement of changes in financial position	4	4	4	3	3	2	3	3	5
Summary of operations: 5–10 years	2	1	1	5	8	4	6	9	3
Management's discussion of operations	6	5	5	9	6	5	8	5	4
Sales and income by product line	5	6	6	7	7	6	4.5	4	7
President's letter	10	7	7	10	9	7	10	8	6
Auditor's report	9	9	10	8	10	10	9	10	10
Accounting policies	8	8	8	6	4	8	4.5	6	9
Other footnotes	7	10	9	4	5	9	7	7	8

SOURCE: Chang, Most, and Brain (1983), pp. 66, 68, 70, 74, 76, and 77.

are the source with the most consistently high ranking of importance. Panel B of Table 1.1 reports the rankings for ten items included in annual reports. The income statement is the item with the most consistently high ranking of importance.

The reliability of inferences drawn from such studies about the demands of individual participants is contingent (in part) upon how severe the methodological problems with survey research are perceived to be. For instance, non-response bias is a common problem; see Stinchcombe, Jones, and Sheatsley (1981); Kalton (1983); and Omura (1983). The response rates in the Chang, Most, and Brain (1983) study ranged from 21.3% for U.K. individual investors to 43.4% for N.Z. financial analysts. The setting in this study was hypothetical; no costs were associated with the provision of information from the various sources and the incentives of individual respondents to misrepresent their preferences were not explicitly considered. The approach adopted in this book is that, notwithstanding these limitations, such survey research can be a useful part of a broader research program into the demand for financial statement information by the diverse parties discussed in Section 1.2.

2. Differential disclosure arises when there are differences in the content (or timing) of information provided to individual recipients. Examples include

- Major lenders receiving information that is more detailed and updated more frequently than that provided to shareholders
- Bond rating agencies being provided with more details about individual product profit margins than is disclosed in annual reports
- Venture capitalists receiving more details about new product development and research and development projects than is disclosed to other external parties.

Part of the information given "private" or "selective" distribution to these parties may result in a competitive disadvantage if given wider distribution; for example, the public disclosure of R&D budgets by a high-technology start-up company could enable competitors to use this information to better target their own R&D budgets. By selectively disclosing this information to only a subset of parties, the firm is attempting to gain the benefits of increased disclosure (access to more capital or borrowing at a lower rate) while reducing the costs (competitive disadvantage) associated with unrestricted disclosure to all parties. (A useful introduction to the economics literature in this area is in Grossman, 1981).

One important benefit from recognizing the existence of "private" or "selective" disclosure is that the decision/actions of parties receiving such disclosures themselves can be informative. Consider the following:

- A decision by a rating agency to assign a rating higher than the expected rating, given its annual report disclosures
- A decision by a venture capitalist with a long and impressive track record to invest heavily in a new venture.

Both decisions convey information that may not be discernable from the public disclosures made by a firm. Changes in the security prices of firms can also be a signal about the "private" information held by selected parties. Subsequent chapters of this book illustrate how such information can be utilized in applied decision contexts such as financial distress prediction and credit decisions.

3. One mechanism for increasing the reliability of information, in the light of possible conflicts of interest among managers, shareholders, and bondholders, is the hiring of an external auditor. Chow (1982) presents evidence on whether variables perceived to be associated with the magnitude of such conflicts could predict the decision to hire or not hire an external auditor. The sample comprised firms traded on the New York Stock Exchange and over the counter in 1926 (a period when there was no externally imposed audit requirements by regulatory bodies). It was hypothesized that

- The higher the proportion of debt in a firm's capital structure, the higher is the probability that the firm voluntarily engages an external auditor. This hypothesis is based on the proposition that as the proportion of debt in a firm's capital structure increases, shareholders have a greater incentive to transfer wealth from the bondholders, and thus bondholders have a greater incentive to hire an external auditor.
- The greater the number of different accounting measures in a firm's debt convenants, the higher the probability that the firm voluntarily engages an external auditor.

Results for a sample of 110 firms with an external auditor's report included in its 1926 annual reports and 55 firms with no auditor's report supported both propositions (at statistically significant levels):

Variable	Firms with Auditors' Reports	Firms Without Auditors' Reports
1. Mean debt-to-equity ratio	.136	.064
2. Mean number of debt covenants based on accounting measures	1.518	.909

The conclusion was that a major reason for hiring an external auditor "is to help control the conflict of interests among firm managers, shareholders, and bondholders. Leverage and the number of accounting-based covenants are predicted to increase the probability that a firm will voluntarily hire external auditing" (p. 287).

4. In many ventures with a high degree of uncertainty, the reputation of management is a critical factor. Wolfson (1985) presents evidence on the importance of reputation effects in the pricing of oil and gas tax-shelter programs. These programs are limited partnerships in which a general partner makes operating decisions pertaining to oil-drilling activities. The hypothesis was that "limited

partners will be willing to pay a premium to participate in a program if, other things equal, the general partner's past performance suggests above-average success in finding oil'' (p. 112). The following data from an industry trade source (*The Stanger Register*) was used to test for reputation effects: (a) a "net return rating" (NRR) measure that was a proxy for the price charged to buy into a partnership and (b) a "total expected return ratio" (ERR) that was a proxy for the track record of the general partner in finding and marketing oil and gas. The ERR variable was calculated by *Stanger* using (a) information in the financial statements of prior partnerships operated by the general manager(s) of the new partnership (e.g., cash distributions to limited partners and partnership net working capital) and (b) estimates of "undiscounted escalated future net revenues" from the proved oil and gas reserves of the partnerships. For a sample of 27 oil and gas limited partnerships, Wolfson found a significant correlation between the general partner's past track record and the price charged to enter a new partnership—the better the past track record, the higher the price charged. The conclusion was that "reputation effects are at work in the market" (p. 124).

1.6 SUMMARY

1. Demands for financial statements arise from a diverse set of parties. Each party has its own focus of attention, and it is unlikely that all parties will unanimously agree on (say) a ranking of items to be disclosed by firms. When predicting the information demands of individual parties (and their behavior), the vested self-interest of the party is an important consideration.

2. Financial statement information is only a subset of the information demanded by parties. Examples of other information demanded include the structure of management contracts, the types of employee training programs, the assets pledged as security for bank loans, and the safety record of products sold. Information about the reputation of management is often a critical item in many decisions using financial information.

3. Financial statement information can serve several roles. One role is to revise beliefs about the uncertainty in investment and credit decisions. Another role is to serve as an observable on which contracts are written. In many cases, financial statements will be serving several different roles at the same time.

NOTES

1. Schedule 14D-9 of Pabst Brewing Company, filed with Securities and Exchange Commission, November 3, 1982, p. 1.

2. UAW-Ford Profit Sharing Plan (undated), pp. 1–4.
3. 1984 Annual Report, Clark Equipment, p. 26.
4. Letter to Shareholders, Superscope Inc., October 24, 1980, p. 3.
5. *The Wall Street Journal*, May 24, 1978.

QUESTIONS

QUESTION   1.1:   Conflict Between Parties and Financial Statement Information

Shareholders can take actions that are at variance with the interests of corporate lenders such as banks and insurance companies. To reduce the likelihood of such actions, lending agreements typically will include loan covenants. In some cases, these convenants are written on financial statement-based variables. For example, Alaska Airlines stated in a recent annual report that "Some of the Company's debt agreements contain provisions which require the Company to maintain specified levels of equity and cash flow coverage and limit capital expenditures and additional indebtedness. The Company is also prohibited from paying cash dividends on capital stock or redeeming or repurchasing capital shares under certain restrictions." In other cases, covenants are written on nonfinancial statement–based variables. For example, the covenants of one oil and gas exploration company (Juniper Petroleum) are "related primarily to engineering projections of revenues from its producing properties"; the covenants of another oil and gas company (Houston Oil and Minerals) include provisions based on "the discounted present value of mortgaged estimated proved oil and gas reserves."

REQUIRED

1. Give examples of actions shareholders can take that are at variance with the interests of corporate lenders. (Assume that management and shareholders are the same party.)
2. What factors should be considered by a corporate lender in deciding whether to write loan covenants relating to financial statement- or nonfinancial statement-based variables?
3. Give examples of actions management can take that are at variance with the interests of shareholders.
4. What forces or mechanisms might serve to reduce potential conflicts between (a) shareholders and corporate lenders and (b) management and shareholders?

QUESTION   1.2:   Profit Sharing, Ownership Sharing, and the Demand
                   by Employees for Financial Statements of Eastern Airlines

One motivation for employees demanding financial statements is the existence of profit-sharing agreements between the company and its employees. Consider

Eastern Airlines, a major U.S. airline. Table 1.2 presents selected financial statement data over the 19X1–19X10 period. (Salaries, wages, and benefits were only
disclosed in the 19X6–19X10 period.) After the net loss of $89 million in 19X2,
employees agreed to a voluntary wage freeze that saved the company $32 million
in 19X3. In 19X4 Eastern proposed a variable earnings program (VEP). Under
this plan, "all employees subject 3.5% of their earnings to the achievement of a
corporate profit target equal to two cents on the revenue dollar." The 3.5% of
wages withheld would be returned (with a bonus) to employees at year's end if
the profit target was achieved through normal operations. VEP was a five-year
undertaking, and on July 1, 19X4, with the majority of representatives of organized
labor agreeing, it was implemented.

In its 19X4 Annual Report, Eastern reported that "the Company's wage and
salary expense was approximately $6.0 million less than it would have been had
VEP not been in effect"; no VEP payment was made to employees that year. In
its 19X5 Annual Report, Eastern noted

> Employees participating in our innovative VEP and profit-sharing plan shared in (our)
> good return. The Company not only paid out the 3.5 percent of base salaries placed
> under VEP toward our minimum profit goal of 2 cents on each sales dollar, but also
> paid an additional 1.2 percent in VEP incentive payments.

In 19X5 wage and salary costs were $9.8 million more because of VEP. In the
19X6–19X9 period, Eastern did not make any VEP payments. It reported that
VEP reduced wage and salary costs by $22.8 million in 19X6, by $37.3 million in
19X7, by $40.6 million in 19X8, and by $37.7 million in 19X9. The 19X9 Annual
Report stated that "The Company has reached a tentative agreement with the
International Association of Machinists and Aerospace Workers (the IAM) to
terminate VEP and to create an alternative program involving the borrowing by
Eastern of amounts withheld and repayment thereof with interest at a rate not in
excess of 10 percent per annum."

TABLE 1.2 Eastern Airlines: Selected Financial Data ($ Millions)

Financial Item	19X1	19X2	19X3	19X4	19X5	19X6	19X7	19X8	19X9	19X10
Operating revenues	$1,530	$1,624	$1,826	$2,036	$2,380	$2,629	$3,152	$3,387	$3,406	$3,608
Salaries, wages, and benefits	N.D.	N.D.	N.D.	N.D.	N.D.	1,131	1,274	1,347	1,386	1,574
Operating profit (loss)	71	2	78	34	97	111	2	(50)	(19)	(100)
Interest expense	66	51	41	40	75	84	110	141	178	236
Income before extraordinary items	9	(54)	34	35	67	58	(42)	(66)	(75)	(184)
Net income (loss)	12	(89)	45	35	67	58	(17)	(66)	(75)	(184)
Total assets	1,407	1,290	1,301	1,244	1,909	2,453	2,816	2,935	3,225	3,758
Shareholders' equity	340	251	299	384	441	441	435	350	255	177
Market capitalization	62	81	166	122	211	193	182	146	192	233
S&P 500 Index	67	89	107	94	95	107	134	122	139	164

N.D. – Not disclosed.

In late 19X10 the employees of Eastern agreed to accept wage reductions in return for stock of Eastern. The 19X10 Annual Report noted that "salaries and wages in 19X10 will be reduced in varying amounts from 18% to 20%, and the employees will work with the Company to achieve productivity improvements. The Company has then agreed to issue 12 million shares of Common Stock" to its employees. In 19X10, the IAM, as part of its negotiations, requested access to Eastern's books. The IAM insisted that the books be audited by a third party. This third party was comprised of a Wall Street investment banker retained by Eastern and two researchers retained by the IAM. The team concluded that Eastern's financial position was indeed precarious. The IAM then expressed a willingness to accept a pay cut in return for an equity interest and some say in management decisions.

REQUIRED

1. Even if no Variable Earnings Program (VEP) existed, what incentives exist for the employees of Eastern to monitor its published financial statements?

2. What are the pros and cons to employees of adopting the VEP?

3. What factors should be considered in deciding the financial statement-based variables to include in a VEP-type agreement, for example, operating revenues, operating profit, net income, the ratio of operating profit to operating revenues, or the ratio of net income to shareholders' equity?

4. Why might employees of Eastern prefer a stock ownership plan to a profit-sharing contract such as the VEP?

5. Most companies have strongly opposed unions or their representatives investigating the financial records underlying their financial statements. Why? Given this opposition, why might Eastern have agreed to outside parties investigating its records?

QUESTION   1.3:   Accounting Information Needs of Loan Officers
                    for Large-Public versus Small-Private Loan Applicants

An important class of users demanding financial statement information is loan evaluation officers. Stanga and Tiller (1983) report the results of a questionnaire study on how loan officers "evaluate the importance" of 40 information items using the following scale:

0 = Not important
1 = Slightly important
2 = Moderately important
3 = Very important
4 = Extremely important

The object of the study was to "compare the informational needs of bank loan officers who make lending decisions that involve large public companies with the informational needs of loan officers who make lending decisions that involve small private companies'' (p. 63). Two versions of a pretested questionnaire were used. The two versions were identical in all respects except that one version had a large-company context while the other had a small-company context. The large-company questionnaire requested respondents to make a decision involving a public industrial company, defined as one whose operations are relatively large, usually with total revenues greater than $125 million, and whose securities are traded in a public market. The small-company questionnaire called for a decision involving a private industrial company, defined as one whose operations are relatively small, usually with total revenues of less than $5 million, and whose securities are not traded in a public market. The respondents were asked to assume that

- They were dealing with a typical new customer in a context of relatively tight money
- The customer was applying for a term loan that is significant in dollar amounts but considerably less than the respondent's legal lending limit
- The dollar amounts of all 40 questionnaire items were significant
- Each questionnaire item pertained to the company's most recent fiscal year, unless otherwise stated.

Respondents also were reminded that information has a cost; therefore, if a loan officer asks a company to disclose information that is too costly to provide, the company may seek other lending sources.

The large-public-company questionnaire was sent to the chief commercial loan officers from each of the 200 largest banks in the United States. The small-private-company questionnaire was sent to the 200 chief commercial loan officers who represent each of the U.S. banks that are ranked in size from 1,001 to 1,200. The response rates were 55.5% for the large-public-company questionnaire and 59.5% for the small-private-company questionnaire.

Results for a subset of the 40 items in the questionnaire are presented in Table 1.3. Also included in Table 1.3 is the result of a significance test (Mann-Whitney) for whether the mean importance score differs between the two groups. Out of the 40 items in the full questionnaire, only 10 had means that were significantly different. The conclusion was that "the fact that thirty of the forty tests (75%) were not significant suggests that the two survey groups have substantially similar (although not identical) needs for the information items included in the questionnaire'' (p. 68).

REQUIRED

1. What problems arise in conducting questionnaire-based research? Are these problems addressed in the Stanga and Tiller study?
2. What explanations are there for the low number of items (ten) for which the mean response for the large-public-company group differs from the mean response for the small-private-company group?

TABLE 1.3 Ranking of Importance of Financial Statement Items for Companies by Commercial Loan Officers

Financial Statement Items	Mean of Large-Public Group	Mean of Small-Private Group	Significance Test for Difference in Means
A. Conventional GAAP			
1. Sales revenue	3.604	3.555	N.S.
2. Cost of goods sold	3.541	3.395	N.S.
3. Net income	3.856	3.857	N.S.
4. Property, plant, and equipment	3.279	3.294	N.S.
5. Summary of accounting methods	3.225	2.983	S.
6. Changes in accounting principles	3.550	3.269	S.
7. Cash provided by operations	3.460	3.395	N.S.
8. Capital leases	2.685	2.252	S.
B. Managements' Forecasts			
1. Forecasted sales revenue	3.288	3.101	S.
2. Forecasted net income	3.396	3.294	N.S.
3. Amount of financing planned	3.505	3.378	N.S.
C. Constant Dollar Data			
1. Cost of goods sold	2.198	2.235	N.S.
2. Depreciation	2.126	2.076	N.S.
D. Current Cost Data			
1. Cost of goods sold	1.991	2.177	N.S.
2. Depreciation	2.000	2.008	N.S.
3. Income from continuing operations	2.036	2.252	N.S.

Key: 0 = Not important; 1 = slightly important; 2 = moderately important; 3 = very important; 4 = extremely important.
N.S. – Not significantly different at the .05 level.
S. – Significantly different at the .05 level.
SOURCE: Stanga and Tiller (1983, Table 1), pp. 66–67.

3. Do you agree with the following? "The conclusion of the study is that the information needs of bank loan officers do not differ substantially between large-public companies and small-private companies" (p. 69). What alternative approaches could be used to gain evidence on this issue?

REFERENCES

CASTLE, G. R. "Term Lending—A Guide to Negotiating Term Loan Covenants and Other Financial Restrictions." *Journal of Commercial Bank Lending* (November 1980): 26–39.

CHANG, L. S., K. S. MOST, and C. W. BRAIN. "The Utility of Annual Reports: An International Study." *Journal of International Business Studies* (Spring/ Summer 1983): 63–84.

CHOW, C. W. "The Demand for External Auditing: Size, Debt and Ownership Influences." *The Accounting Review* (April 1982): 272–291.

DEWING, A. S. *Financial Policy of Corporations*. New York: The Ronald Press, 1953.

GROSSMAN, S. J. "An Introduction to the Theory of Rational Expectations Under Asymmetric Information." *Review of Economic Studies* (October 1981): 541–559.

JENSEN, M. C., and C. W. SMITH. "Stockholder, Manager, and Creditor Interests: Applications of Agency Theory." In E. I. Altman and M. G. Subrahmanyam, (eds.), *Recent Advances in Corporate Finance* (Homewood, Ill.; Dow-Jones Irwin; 1985), pp. 93–131.

KALTON, G. *Compensating for Missing Survey Data*. Ann Arbor: Survey Research Center, University of Michigan, 1983.

McCONNELL, J. J., and G. G. SCHLARBAUM. "Returns, Risks, and Pricing of Income Bonds, 1956–76 (Does Money Have an Odor?)." *The Journal of Business* (January 1981): 33–63.

OMURA, G. S. "Correlates of Item Nonresponse." *Journal of the Market Research Society* (October 1983): 321–330.

STANGA, K. G., and M. G. TILLER. "Needs of Loan Officers for Accounting Information from Large Versus Small Companies." *Accounting and Business Research* (Winter 1983): 63–70.

STINCHCOMBE, A. L., C. JONES, and P. SHEATSLEY. "Nonresponse Bias for Attitude Questions." *Public Opinion Quarterly* (Fall 1981): 359–375.

WOLFSON, M. A. "Empirical Evidence of Incentive Problems and Their Mitigation in Oil and Gas Tax Shelter Programs," in J. W. Pratt and R. J. Zeckhauser (eds.), *Principals and Agents: The Structure of Business* (Boston, Mass.; Harvard Business School Press; 1985), pp. 101–125.

2

THE SUPPLY
OF FINANCIAL STATEMENT
INFORMATION

2.1 INTRODUCTION

This chapter focuses on factors that affect the supply of financial statement information provided to external parties. Emphasis is placed on regulatory and market forces that affect the content of financial reports or the timing with which these reports are released. Figure 2.1 presents an overview of the parties discussed in this chapter. Financial reports are part of a broader set of firm disclosures that range from verbal qualitative responses to shareholder questions at annual meetings to written quantitative communications, such as physical production reports and mineral exploration reports, as well as financial reports. Management has considerable discretion over the content and timing of the many diverse public disclosures it makes. These disclosures can be partial substitutes for each other with the result that expansion (or contraction) in one form of disclosure can affect the supply of information provided in other forms. Interaction between the parties in Figure 2.1 is one important theme of this chapter. A second important theme is that the set of financial statement and other information placed in the public domain is not always the most timely nor is it necessarily an unbiased subset of that available to internal parties.

FIGURE 2.1 Factors Affecting Information Set Available to External Parties

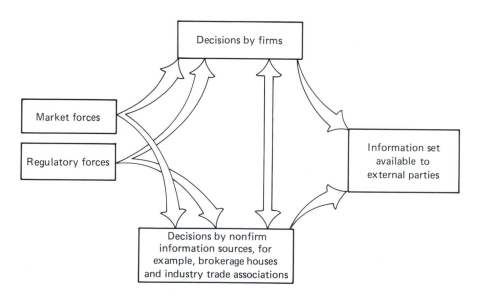

2.2 REGULATORY FORCES AND THE SUPPLY OF FINANCIAL STATEMENT INFORMATION

A common feature of the financial reporting environment in many countries is the existence of public sector-based regulatory forces that affect the disclosure decisions of firms and other entities. In some cases, specific legislation governing the content of financial reports exists, such as the Companies Acts in many British Commonwealth countries. In other cases, legislation associated with corporate taxation is an important determinant of the content of financial statements, as in Germany, Japan, and Sweden. In yet other cases, decisions by government regulatory bodies exert an important influence, as with the Securities and Exchange Commission (SEC) in the United States. This section describes the existing institutional framework for financial reporting in the United States. The concern is with illustrating how regulatory forces operate rather than with presenting specific details of the current set of specific regulations.

A. Institutional Framework in the United States

Figure 2.2 presents an overview of some key players in the existing institutional framework. Four levels are distinguished:

- *Level One* consists of the executive, legislative, and judicial branches of the U.S. government. The executive and legislative branches can exert influence in a proactive way. The judicial branch exerts influence via its rulings.
- *Level Two* includes governmental regulatory bodies such as the SEC and the Department of the Treasury.
- *Level Three* includes private sector regulatory bodies such as the Financial Accounting Standards Board (FASB), the American Institute of Certified Public Accountants (AICPA), and the New York Stock Exchange (NYSE).
- *Level Four* includes lobbying groups that attempt to influence decisions made by parties in Levels One, Two, or Three. These groups range from enduring organizations (such as the Financial Analysts Federation and the Financial Executives Institute) to organizations that are disbanded when an issue is decided (such as "The Committee to Permit Small Producers to Compete in Energy Exploration," a lobbying group that was formed in 1977 and disbanded in 1978).

All four levels influence financial reporting decisions made by firms. For this reason, the existing framework in the United States is best viewed as a "joint" effort between the public sector institutions in Levels One and Two and the private sector institutions in Levels Three and Four.

Level One bodies typically do not promulgate standards relating to corporate financial statements. Rather, these bodies delegate the power to make such standards to the Level Two and Level Three bodies. However, the Level One bodies

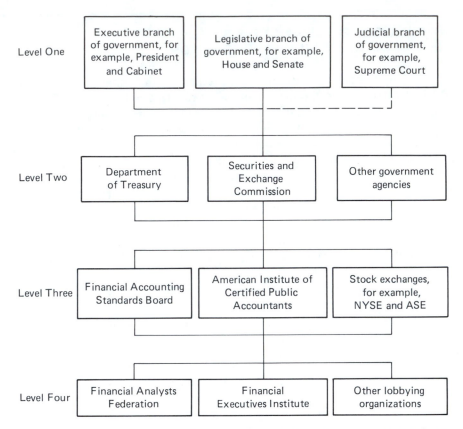

FIGURE 2.2 Institutional Framework Governing Financial Reporting in the United States

have the ability to recentralize this power. The investment tax credit scenario in the 1970s illustrates this observation. Congress instituted the investment tax credit to stimulate investment in capital assets. The two main accounting alternatives for the investment tax credit are the deferral method (the tax benefits affect reported income over the life of the purchased asset) and the flowthrough method (the tax benefits affect reported income in the year the asset is purchased). In October 1971, the Accounting Principles Board (APB)—the private sector body that preceded the FASB—issued an exposure draft supporting the deferral method. Horngren (1972) provides the following details on the chain of events:

1. The APB did not issue its exposure draft of October 22, 1971, until receiving two written commitments. The SEC said it would support the APB position, and the Department of the Treasury indicated that it "will remain neutral in the matter."

2. The Senate Finance Committee issued its version of the 1971 Revenue Act on November 9. In response to lobbying, the Committee clearly indicated that companies should have a free choice in selecting the accounting treatment of the new credit.

3. On November 12, Treasury sent a letter to the chairman of the Senate Finance Committee that stated: "Since any change in the pre-existing well-established financial accounting practice might operate to diminish the job-creating effect of the credit, the Treasury Department strongly supports a continuation of the optional treatment."

4. Congress then cut the ground out from under the APB and the SEC by passing legislation that stated that "no taxpayer shall be required, without his consent, to use . . . any particular method of accounting for the credit."

5. The APB's unanimous denunciation of congressional involvement was issued on December 9, 1971. (p. 10)

The APB's denunciation was shared by many accountants who had the mistaken impression that a Level Three organization (that is, the APB) had the ultimate authority to issue standards on financial reporting issues. The investment tax scenario and several subsequent scenarios, for example, marketable equity securities (see Horngren, 1973), have illustrated that the Level Three organizations in Figure 2.2 operate in the same way that the middle managers of a decentralized firm operate; that is, they frequently have considerable discretion but, in the final play, little real authority.

A second example of interaction between the parties in Figure 2.2 is the accounting for oil and gas exploration cost issue. The two main accounting alternatives are successful efforts (which employs a narrow definition of the cost center used to capitalize exploration costs) and full cost (which employs a broad definition of the cost center). The following events transpired in the 1975–1978 period:

1. In the February–November 1975 period, the House of Representatives debated an energy bill that vested responsibility in the SEC for developing uniform accounting standards for oil and gas companies. The bill permitted the SEC to prescribe accounting practices by rule after consultation with the FASB. In October 1975, the FASB added to its agenda a project entitled "Financial Accounting and Reporting in the Extractive Industries."

2. In July 1977, the FASB issued an Exposure Draft of *FASB Statement No. 19* that indicated that it supported the successful-efforts method of accounting for exploration costs. Many small exploration companies using the full-cost method would have been affected by the FASB proposal. In December 1977, the FASB formally adopted the successful-efforts method in *FASB Statement No. 19*. Intense lobbying efforts were made by full-cost oil and gas companies to have *FASB Statement No. 19* rescinded by the FASB or overruled by a party in Levels One or Two of Figure 2.2.

3. In February 1978, the Department of Energy held a public hearing to assess the effect of *FASB Statement No. 19* on the ability of oil and gas companies to raise capital and on oil and gas exploration and development activity.

4. In March–April 1978, the SEC held public hearings to discuss the effects of *FASB Statement No. 19*.

5. In August 1978, the SEC overruled *FASB Statement No. 19* and announced its own "reserve recognition" accounting requirements.

One accounting firm has concluded that "when push comes to shove, the velvet glove cloaking the iron fist of SEC oversight rapidly disintegrates, making those repeated assertions of reliance on private-sector leadership in setting accounting standards sound somewhat hollow."[1]

The SEC is a government regulatory body set up with the passage of the Securities Act of 1934. The regulations issued by the SEC cover both the form and content of financial statements as well as the timing with which financial information must be placed in the public domain. As an illustration, consider the disclosures required under Form 8-K filings with the SEC. The purpose of this report is to encourage timely disclosure of "incipient problems." Form 8-K must be filed by companies with the SEC within ten days after the close of a month in which one or more events such as the following occur: "acquisition or disposition of assets," "extraordinary item charges and credits," "other material changes and credits to income of an unusual nature" and "material provisions for loss."

The most detailed regulations covering the content of financial statements come from the FASB, a seven-member board that issues standards governing the financial reports released by publicly held firms. The standards issued cover both (1) the accounting methods used (for inventories, fixed assets, leases, and the like) and (2) the disclosures made by firms (for example, line-of-business reporting for multiactivity firms).

Another private sector body regulating the flow of financial information from publicly traded firms to external parties is the stock exchange listing the firm's securities. For instance, the New York Stock Exchange *Company Manual* includes the following requirement for firms listed on this exchange:

> A Corporation whose securities are listed on the New York Stock Exchange, Inc., is expected to release quickly to the public any news or information which might reasonably be expected to materially affect the market for those securities. (p. A-18)

Announcements of annual and interim earnings, dividends, acquisitions, and mergers are examples of items designated "for immediate release." In some cases, the NYSE will temporarily halt trading in a security to provide a period for public evaluation of the announcement. Other stock exchanges also have regulations that relate to financial disclosures. Differences across the various exchanges in the United States exist, with the result that firms have the option of deciding on some aspects of the regulatory regime under which they will operate.

B. The Influence of Regulatory Forces

The influence of regulatory forces is difficult to isolate as other factors also affect financial reporting decisions by firms (see Sections 2.4 and 2.5). However, in some cases strong evidence exists that specific disclosures are best explained as the result of a regulatory mandate. Consider the terms managers use in annual reports when describing the following FASB or SEC mandated disclosures:

- SEC Mandate for Replacement-Cost Disclosures

  I strongly urge all . . . stockholders to join with me in ignoring the one-sided story on replacement-cost accounting made mandatory by current accounting rules of the SEC. It is truly expensive hogwash.   (Mapco)

- FASB Mandate for Constant-Dollar and Current-Cost Disclosures

  The company has serious reservations as to whether the required supplemental financial information is appropriate for measuring the impact of inflation on a utility regulated, as Pacific Gas and Electric is, on a cost-of-service basis. This information is presented solely because it is required to be presented. It should be clearly understood that the required information is complicated, difficult to understand, and because of the permitted subjectivity inherent in developing this prescribed information, unwarranted comparisons and inferences may result.   (Pacific Gas and Electric)

- SEC Mandate for Reserve Recognition Accounting (RRA) for Proved Reserves of Oil and Gas Companies

  Management believes that the results of oil and gas producing activities calculated on the basis of RRA are misleading and should not be relied upon in evaluating the company or its performance. . . . The revenue and cost projections should not be construed as realistic estimates of future cash flows, nor should the present value figures be interpreted as representing market value or value to the company. The information presented in these disclosures is not meaningful or useful to company management in making investment and operating decisions.   (Superior Oil)

It is difficult to imagine management presenting such statements to accompany disclosures that it was voluntarily releasing to external parties. The SEC or FASB regulatory mandate appears to explain best the decision by the firms noted to supply this information externally.

In some cases, regulatory bodies set boundaries on the disclosures firms make rather than prescribe a specific form of behavior. Consider the timing of the information released. The SEC mandates that firms file their 10Ks within 90 days after the end of the fiscal year; however, firms have the option of filing any time within this 90-day period. Consider also the content of the information released. The FASB requires multiactivity firms to disclose segment data pertaining to revenues and earnings; however, firms have the flexibility to decide if they are a multiactivity firm and how to group their individual activities into segments.

Decisions by regulatory bodies also can have an effect on the information production activities of nonfirm information sources. Some effects of changes in U.S. life insurance financial reporting standards illustrate this point. Starting in 1973, life insurance companies were required to report their underwriting results using generally accepted accounting principles (GAAP). Prior to this date, most firms reported underwriting results using the accounting principles prescribed by state insurance commissioners. These principles—termed statutory principles—differed from GAAP in two main respects:

1. Costs of writing new policies were expensed in the first year of the policy rather than being amortized over the life of the policy.
2. The interest rate assumptions used in computing policy reserves were below the returns insurance companies earned on their investments.

Prior to 1973, various bodies (for example, Standard & Poor's and A. M. Best) adjusted the statutory earnings of life insurance companies for differences (1) and (2) noted above. The resultant earnings numbers—termed adjusted earnings—were provided to subscribers of the investment services of these firms. Since 1973, however, these bodies have stopped reporting their own adjusted earnings estimates. They now report the GAAP numbers provided in the annual reports of insurance companies. Thus, the effect of the 1973 life insurance reporting requirements has been to transfer the source of (and presumably the costs of preparing) GAAP earnings numbers from several information intermediaries to life insurance companies.

2.3   EVIDENCE OF VOLUNTARY
OR NONREGULATORY MANDATED DISCLOSURES

There are many pieces of evidence to suggest that factors other than regulatory mandates influence the supply of financial statements. Consider the following:

1. Financial statements were publicly released by firms well before the formation of the major regulatory forces currently influencing financial reporting. The SEC was formed in the 1930s. Private sector bodies associated with the accounting profession are a product of the twentieth century. Yet, financial statements dating back to the eighteenth and nineteenth centuries exist for some U.S. firms. For instance, the Bank of New York issued a "Statement of Condition" as early as 1784. As a second example, the annual reports issued in the nineteenth century by U.S. railroads were especially detailed. The 1874 Annual Report of the Atchison, Topeka, and Santa Fe Railroad Co. was 49 pages in length and included a balance sheet, an annual income statement that reported monthly earnings and operating expenses by activity (passenger, freight, mail, express, and miscellaneous), an auditor's report, and an "estimate of earnings and expenses for fiscal year 1875." More comprehensive evidence on voluntary disclosure prior to regulatory mandates is in Benston (1969) and Morris (1984).

2. Financial statements are voluntarily issued by entities not under the jurisdiction of the SEC. For instance, Days Inns of America, Inc., is a privately held company operating in the lodging industry. Each year since 1976 it has vol-

untarily issued a detailed annual report. The 1983 Annual Report includes an income statement, a statement of changes in financial position, a balance sheet with both historical cost and current value figures, an auditor's report, a report from a real estate appraiser to certify the current value figures, and a five-year statement of forecasted income and stockholders' equity. Many municipalities in the United States also issued financial statements despite there being no mandate by a regulatory body to release this information.

3. Some firms issue financial statements at more frequent time intervals than is mandated by regulatory bodies. For example, both the SEC and NYSE mandate U.S. companies file quarterly reports; some companies, however, voluntarily release monthly interim reports.

4. Some firms release considerably more information in their financial statements than is mandated by regulatory bodies. For instance, companies in Australia and the United Kingdom are not required to disclose the market values of their properties; however, a considerable number of companies report such information in their annual reports. A subset of hotel chains in the United States (for example, Holiday Inns, Hilton Hotels and Marriott) also voluntarily report this information in their annual reports.

2.4 MARKET FORCES AND THE SUPPLY OF FINANCIAL STATEMENT INFORMATION

The voluntary disclosures discussed in Section 2.3 are more likely the result of market forces rather than regulatory-based forces. This section discusses three market forces affecting the content or timing of financial statement disclosures: (A) the capital market, (B) the labor market, and (C) the corporate control market.

A. Capital Market Forces

Firms compete with each other in the capital market on many dimensions. These dimensions include:

- The instrument offered—equity securities, preferred securities, bank loans, and so on
- The terms of the instrument offered—the taxation status of dividend payments, convertibility features of debt, the interest rate on loans, the security offered to lenders, and so on
- The distribution of expected returns from each instrument.

Market forces will exert pressure on firms and other capital raisers to provide financial information that relates to the foregoing factors. To illustrate, consider the municipal bond market. At the time of the New York City financial crisis in the mid-1970s, municipalities were not required to present annual financial statements to bondholders. One newspaper article noted that subsequent to the crisis, there was increased market pressure for more disclosure of municipal finances. The article noted that "whatever the law says . . . bond analysts say the market itself will encourage improved disclosure. A municipality standing on its legal rights to keep mum will pay a penalty—higher borrowing costs."[2]

Standard & Poor's Corporation (1980) sponsored a research firm to conduct a market survey on municipal accounting. Interviews were conducted among 200 underwriters, dealers, dealer banks, and institutional investors.

> Results show that the market may already be imposing penalties in the form of higher interest costs where accounting and financial reporting are substandard.
>
> To assess the size of the penalty, S&P looked to one of its units which regularly prices about $20 billion of tax-exempt bonds for investment trusts. Based on views obtained there, plus contact with underwriters and market makers who set interest costs on new issues, research shows penalties may average 0.125 to 0.25 percentage points.
>
> On a typical $100 million issue of bonds with a 10-year average life, that equals a penalty of $1,250,000 to $2,500,000 over the issue's average life.   (p. 3)

Standard & Poor's noted that in 1980 it withdrew the rating on San Francisco's bonds "because of the lack of timely financial reporting" (p. 2).

Two important features of the capital market are

1. There is uncertainty about the quality of the product. For instance, some firms that issue bonds subsequently default on their interest and principal repayments. Some firms that raise equity finance subsequently go into bankruptcy, with equity owners receiving no distributions. At the other extreme, some firms turn out to be highly profitable, pay their bond interest and principal repayments on schedule, and simultaneously provide shareholders with substantial capital appreciation.

2. There is a cost of being perceived as a "lemon" (as in the used car market); see Akerlof (1970). This cost could be in the form of paying higher interest rates on a bank loan, having very stringent conditions placed on the loan, or offering an equity issue that raises less money.

Given the uncertainty about product quality and the cost of being perceived as a "lemon," firms have an incentive to supply the set of information that they believe will enable them to raise capital on the best available terms. In some cases, there can be incentives to make "overly optimistic" (possibly false or "misleading") representations in their financial statements. At least four mechanisms exist to reduce the likelihood of such misrepresentations in financial statements:

1. *The reputation of the firm.* Firms typically make several equity or debt issues over time, and they are interested in maintaining their credibility with the financial community. A short-run gain due to a financial misrepresentation could prove to be very costly in subsequent visits to the capital market. One

security analyst made the following comment after a firm (Warner Communications) made a dramatic downward revision in earnings two weeks after a company visit by the analyst: "I would stay away from the stock. It seems like there are still a lot of worms in the can." *The Wall Street Journal* made the following comment on Prime Computer: "Prime's credibility on Wall Street is in tatters because of forecasts this year. Twice the company revised downward earlier forecasts of quarterly results. 'Three strikes and they're out,' says a security analyst at Morgan Stanley."[3]

2. *The reputation of management.* Individual managers have a vested interest in maintaining their own credibility. Statements by managers with low credibility are likely to be heavily discounted. In addition, the labor market for managers is likely to penalize individuals who are not perceived to be reliable in their dealings with external parties.

3. *Third-party certification.* Institutions or individuals supplying capital to firms often require third parties to "verify" the representations made by management. These third parties include external auditing firms, investment bankers, and underwriting firms. Each of these third parties serves many clients and likewise has a strong interest in maintaining its reputation with the financial community.

4. *Legal penalties.* Most jurisdictions have civil or criminal penalties for attempts to defraud external parties via the issuance of false or misleading financial representations.

The system of checks and balances implicit in these mechanisms helps to add to the reliability of financial statements placed in the public domain.

B. Labor Market Forces

If left unrestricted, management could make decisions that significantly reduce the value of the equity or debt components of the firm. Consider the following instances:

- Management sells all the assets of the firm, distributing the cash proceeds as dividends to equityholders and leaving debtholders with a "corporate shell"

- Management reinvests all the assets of the firm in high-variance projects that redistribute wealth from debtholders to stockholders (due to debtholders sharing in large losses but not in large gains)

- Managers pay themselves salaries many times what their counterparts in other firms are earning for comparable jobs, thus reducing the value of both the equity and debt components.

In Chapter 1 we noted that the equity- and debtholders have a vested interest in reducing the propensity of management to take such actions. Management also can have an incentive to signal to the capital market that it will not take such actions. These incentives arise from labor market forces. Managers who are unwilling to agree to constraints being placed on their behavior or mechanisms being put into place to monitor their actions may not be hired, or if they are hired, they may be paid a relatively low salary. A manager who perceives that he or she has the ability to increase the market value of the firm significantly may be willing to accept a contract that restricts his or her main sources of discretionary compensation to those items where there is congruence between the manager's interests and those of the shareholders. Labor market forces can arise from both external sources (for example, via changes in the marketability of executives to other firms) and internal sources (for example, via changes in promotion prospects, salary, and perquisites).

The mechanisms available to monitor management include financial statements and third-party certification (for example, by an independent auditor) of those statements. Third-party certification is likely to be viewed by the external labor market as increasing the reliability of inferences drawn from financial statements about the quality of management. Higher-quality management has an incentive to institutionalize mechanisms that facilitate their being distinguished in the labor market from lower-quality management. Where third-party certification is mandated, higher-quality management may have an incentive to add additional monitoring bodies, for example, an audit committee of its board of directors.

C. Corporate Control Market Forces

Managers appear to value very highly their ability to control the financing, investment, and operating decisions of firms. Attempts by external parties to take this control from existing management often encounter stiff opposition. The financial press contains many examples of (1) takeover battles between existing management and an unfriendly suitor or (2) proxy fights between a coalition of the existing management and a subset of shareholders vis-à-vis another subset of shareholders. One tactic that managements can use in such battles (or in an attempt to preempt such battles) is to release financial information that they perceive will increase the likelihood of their retaining control.

Two examples illustrate this factor. One example concerns the release of information pertaining to the market values of individual assets owned by the firm. The following disclosure was made at an annual meeting of South Australian Brewing Holdings:

> Last year I made reference to the existence, at that time, of a certain amount of speculative comment to the effect that "The Brewing Company was about to be taken over." . . . I reported that the directors intended to take steps to determine, as nearly as practicable, the present value of the Group's freehold properties and the plant and equipment used in its modernised and expanded Southwark Brewery.
>
> A detailed examination of the factors relevant to making such an assessment was duly carried out by senior members of the Group's professional staff. . . . This information enabled the directors to present this year's Balance Sheet on a much more informative basis. . . . The Group's shareholders' funds (are now) shown at the much more realistic figure of $91 million, compared with $58.5 million a year earlier.[4]

The second example concerns the speed with which the first quarter results of a U.S. brewing company were published. In 1981, Pabst Brewing Company reported its first annual loss ($23.536 million) in over 20 years. Pabst released the first quarter's results for 1981 (a loss) 15 days after the end of the quarter. In the ten years prior to 1981, results were announced an average of 12 days after the end of the fiscal quarter. However, in early 1982, management was embroiled in an acrimonious proxy battle for control of Pabst and released the results just six days after the end of the first quarter. This release included the following comment:

> We are pleased to report that for the first quarter of 1982 Pabst has returned to profitability. For the three months ended March 31, 1982, Pabst had pre-tax income of $2,712,000 compared to a pre-tax loss of $3,063,000 in the same period last year. We attribute these results to the programs and the effective leadership of William F. Smith, Jr., since becoming President and Chief Executive Officer last September.[5]

The preceding examples are notable if only for their nonsubtlety. In fact, many firms adopt concerted public relations campaigns aimed at promoting the image that management is both capable and responsive to shareholder interests.

2.5   COSTS ASSOCIATED WITH DISCLOSURE

One factor that management consistently cites as important in disclosure decisions is the costs associated with those disclosures. These costs include (A) collection and processing costs, (B) litigation costs, (C) political costs, (D) competitive disadvantage costs, and (E) additional constraints on management decisions.

A.   Collection and Processing Costs

Collection and processing costs include the costs borne by both the preparers and the users of financial data. Little systematic evidence exists as to the magnitude of these costs. The limited numerical information that is available mostly relates to the estimated costs of complying with regulatory mandates and should be viewed as "approximate at best." One example is the costs that firms estimated they would incur in complying with the Line of Business Report Program proposed in the 1970s by the Federal Trade Commission (FTC). Nine companies surveyed by the General Accounting Office (GAO) estimated initial start-up costs ranging from $350,000 to $1,800,000 and annual maintenance costs ranging from $95,000 to $325,000. In contrast, the FTC reported to the GAO that respondents would incur initial costs of from $10,000 to $20,000 per firm to set up the program and from $5,000 to $10,000 in succeeding years to maintain it. Benston (1984) analyzed differences between these estimates and concluded that the FTC "tends to underestimate costs severely. Principally, the agency does not recognize that a company must prepare data that can withstand hostile scrutiny; inexpensively pre-pared estimates will not do . . ." (p. 123). (The FTC undoubtedly would respond that companies "tend to overestimate costs severely.") A second example of collection and processing costs is the Perry and Searfoss (1982) memorandum on the time 10 companies reported it took to prepare the *FASB Statement No. 33* constant dollar and current costs disclosures in their 1981 annual reports. Table 2.1 contains a summary of these time estimates; the range was from 100 hours to 4,800 hours.

Even less information is available about the processing costs borne by users of financial statement information. For newly disclosed items that are reasonably complex, these costs may well be quite considerable.

B. Litigation Costs

Legal suits against the firm or its managers are an ever-present threat in today's litigious society. In some cases, this threat can operate to reduce disclo-sure. For instance, one argument against voluntary disclosure of earnings fore-casts is that ex post they may turn out to be overly optimistic; investors then may use the incorrect forecast as one basis to sue management to obtain reimbursement for a drop in the price of their equity investment. In other cases, the threat of litigation can promote disclosure. As an example, assume that external parties such as security analysts make estimates of firm-oriented variables that manage-ment views as "without foundation." The prompt public release of a corrective statement can reduce the potential losses to shareholders or reduce the potential exposure of the firm and its management in subsequent litigation. (An example of a firm providing additional information to "correct" what it believed were misleading allegations is Telex Corporation; see Anderson and Pincus, 1984.)

TABLE 2.1 Estimated Time (Hours) Required to Comply with FASB No. 33 Constant Dollar and Current Cost Mandated Disclosures

Case	Nature of Business	1981 Revenues ($ Billions)	Estimated Hours to Comply
1	Retailer	2.70	100
2	Hospital and laboratory supplies	2.87	4,800
3	Aeronautics	1.34	1,600–3,200
4	Truck trailer manufacturer and automotive	2.30	300–400
5	Transportation equipment and diversified	4.70	1,700
6	Consumer food products	.66	600–700
7	Electronics	4.90	400
8	Metal and glass containers, packaging	1.53	500–1,000
9	Consumer food, manufacturing, and restaurant	3.40	400
10	Retailing (supermarkets)	3.00	250

SOURCE: Perry and Searfoss (1982).

C. Political Costs

Governments have the power to expropriate wealth from corporations and redistribute it to other parties in society. Financial reports represent one source of information that governments can use to choose firms or industries that will be singled out. The "excess profits" tax imposed on U.S. oil companies in the late 1970s was stimulated, in part, by the sizable dollar amounts that oil companies reported as profit increases in several years prior to the legislation. Consider the following comment:

> "Pornographic" was the way oil profits were described by James G. Archuleta, a spokesman for the Oil, Chemical and Atomic Workers Union. He added that the industry "certainly cannot plead poverty" when the union starts negotiating new contracts later this year.
>
> House Speaker Thomas "Tip" O'Neill called the increased earnings "sinful" and "an absolute and utter disgrace." The House responded by reversing an earlier vote and killing a measure removing price controls on gasoline.
>
> Senator John Durkin said the profits "border on the criminal" and called for a Watergate-type investigation of oil firms.
>
> Consumer advocate Ralph Nader seized the opportunity to call for creation of a national energy corporation to exploit oil, natural-gas and coal resources on public land.
>
> President Carter wasted no time in using the profit reports as a springboard for a renewed campaign to ram through Congress a strong "windfall profits" tax on oil-company revenues to soak up some of the money resulting from decontrol of crude-oil prices and price hikes by the Organization of Petroleum Exporting Countries. He threatened to take "punitive" action against oil firms if Congress fails to get "tough" with the industry.[6]

In this environment, firms may choose accounting methods that they perceive will reduce the likelihood of large profit increases being reported in any one year.

Political cost considerations can also influence the disclosure decisions of firms. Firms may disclose certain information items if they provide evidence that the arguments used by those wishing to appropriate wealth from them are invalid. Firms also can choose to aggregate items in such a way that their political cost exposure is reduced. Assume that a multiactivity firm acquires a firm over the objections of the Justice Department on the grounds that the acquired firm is a "failing company." (The "failing company" doctrine is a valid legal defense to an otherwise anticompetitive merger.) If the acquired company has a significant turnaround, the acquiring company may wish to keep this information confidential. By grouping the results of the acquired business with those of an existing segment, the firm can increase the difficulty the Justice Department faces in any subsequent follow-up of the profitability of the "failing company."

D.   Competitive Disadvantage Costs

A common argument presented against disclosure is the cost incurred when competitors use the disclosures to their own advantage. One sensitive area in this connection is information about research and development and new products. Firms that perceive that they have an advantage over competitors in these areas face difficult decisions when raising new capital. Unless they provide some information pertaining to the R&D or new products, the capital market is less likely to support a new share offering. Yet, if they provide detailed information, they may reduce the lead time with which competitors learn about developments within the company. A second sensitive area is with disclosure of advertising budgets. Schlitz Brewing Company made the following comment at an annual meeting: "As a matter of policy, we do not announce advertising budgets in advance because it's information our competitors would like to have." Competitive disadvantage costs can also arise if labor unions and other suppliers are able to use the financial disclosures to improve their bargaining power and hence to increase the relative cost structure of the firm.

The motivations behind disclosure or nondisclosure are diverse, and in some cases the stated motivations appear less than convincing. This is especially true for many appeals to the competitive disadvantage notion. Consider the use of this notion by A. H. Belo Corporation (owner of *The Dallas Morning News*) against a minority shareholder proposal that it become a publicly listed company. A financial newspaper commented,

> The company maintains that publishing information required of public companies by the SEC would put it at a severe competitive disadvantage, since the data would be available to its main competitor, *The Dallas Times Herald*, which is owned by Times Mirror Co., Los Angeles. Belo maintains that because it is significantly smaller than Times Mirror, financial disclosures required by the SEC would reveal too much of its inner workings. Times Mirror owns several major papers and can group its newspaper financial data for reporting purposes. By contrast, *The Dallas Morning News* is the only major newspaper property of Belo.[7]

On at least the revenue side, the Times Mirror Company already can use competing information sources to learn considerable information about *The Dallas Morning News*. This paper is a member of the Audit Bureau of Circulations that publishes very detailed unit circulation figures on *The Dallas Morning News* every six months. The advertising rates of the paper are readily available to an external party in a booklet titled "Retail Advertising Rates." The list of advertising clients is available at the cost of a subscription to the paper. In short, these competing sources of information are considerably more detailed and cover more facts than does the "sales" figure required in the 10-K of a publicly listed company.

Firms in any industry typically have a rich network of information sources on what their competitors are doing. Given this network, it would be difficult to support an argument that increased disclosure of many items in financial reports would cause a major competitive disadvantage. However, several key items could well fall in this category. Examples include (1) a breakdown of major customers and (2) forecasts of gross margin, income, or sales by individual lines of business.

E. Constraints on Managerial Behavior

One set of disclosure costs reported to be important by some managers is the constraints that arise (or are perceived to arise) when specific disclosures are made. For example, when an earnings-per-share forecast is publicly released at the start of a fiscal year, there is pressure for managers to take actions during the year that result in the actual earnings-per-share being closer rather than farther away from the forecast. Managements may reject opportunities that maximize firm value but that would result in the actual earnings-per-share diverging considerably from the publicly released earnings-per-share forecast. As a second example, when a company publicly releases its corporate objectives (for example, earnings-per-share growth rate of 15%), pressures may be placed on managers to reject firm value-increasing projects that have projected short-run earnings inconsistent with the publicly stated corporate objectives.

2.6 SOME GENERAL COMMENTS

1. The main arguments for public sector-based regulation of financial reporting are

(a) Market forces will lead to an "inefficient" resource allocation, given some economic standard of efficiency. The economics literature has for some time focused on conditions where the market solution results in non-Pareto resource allocations (termed "market failures"). For instance, there has been considerable argument that because of the inability effectively to exclude the nonpurchasers of patents, warrants, and so on, there will be underinvestment in research and development; see Arrow (1962). There has also been a related concern in the accounting literature that because of the inability to exclude nonpurchasers, there will be underproduction of information by firms; see Gonedes and Dopuch (1974). Although it has been documented that market failures may occur with respect to information production, it is far from obvious that a policy body such as the SEC or the FASB can regulate information production so as to achieve an efficient allocation of resources; see Leftwich (1980) for further discussion.

(b) Market forces will lead to an "inequitable" resource allocation, given some ethical standard of equity or fairness. Issues regarding fairness appear important in proposals by the SEC in the 1970s to mandate disclosure of earnings forecasts (Burton, 1974):

> At the same time as many companies announced their projections publicly, a number of others communicated their expectations to a select few. . . . While the overwhelming majority of such efforts were done in good faith, the end

> result was lack of knowledge as to what forecasts were those of management as opposed to those of analysts working independently. In a few cases there was evidence of *selective disclosure* to institutional investors interested in the stock and *unfair use* of such insider information.   (p. 86, emphasis added)

Clearly, value judgments are involved in deciding what is an "undesirable" or "unfair" use of inside information. What an external investor might consider an "undesirable" use of inside information, a corporate official might think is very "desirable."

The question of whether the foregoing arguments are sufficient to justify the existing degree of regulation is an extremely difficult one to structure, let alone answer. Examples of debate over, and evidence relating to, regulation of accounting standards include Benston (1982), Merino and Neimark (1982), Chow (1983), and Cooper and Keim (1983). Much work in the industrial organization literature has empirically examined arguments used to justify intervention in market forces by regulatory bodies such as the SEC, the Interstate Commerce Commission, the Federal Communications Commission, and the Civil Aeronautics Board. At present, the evidence suggests that these arguments are often based on isolated cases of alleged "inefficiency" or "inequity" or on overestimates of the ability of government agencies to achieve set goals.

2. Political costs are those associated with the government expropriating wealth from corporations and redistributing it to other parties in society. Interesting work is currently being undertaken on factors that are correlated with differences across firms in their political costs. It is frequently argued that firm size is an important variable affecting political cost exposure; for example, Watts and Zimmerman (1978) argue that "the magnitude of the political costs is highly dependent on firm size. Even as a percentage of total assets or sales, we would not expect a firm with sales of $100 million to generate the same political costs (as a percentage of sales) as a firm with $10 billion of sales" (pp. 182–183).

To gain evidence on whether political costs are associated with firm size, Zimmerman (1983) examined the association between effective corporate tax rates and firm size. Using the Compustat data base, tax rates for the following five firm size categories (based on sales) were examined:

  I. Largest 50 firms
 II. Firms in 75–100% size category (excluding those in I)
III. Firms in 50–75% size category
 IV. Firms in 25–50% size category
  V. Firms in smallest to 25% size category

One variable examined was the ratio of taxes paid to operating cash flows. Results for selected years in the 1972–1981 period were:

Firm Size Categories

Year	I (largest firms)	II	III	IV	V (smallest firms)
1972	.161	.120	.134	.138	.139
1974	.195	.132	.136	.137	.137
1976	.169	.129	.136	.140	.131
1978	.178	.130	.137	.133	.133
1979	.158	.127	.134	.128	.127
1980	.168	.110	.118	.119	.123
1981	.154	.108	.113	.119	.133

Two inferences drawn from this and several other data sets were (a) the largest 50 firms have the highest corporate tax rates, and (b) average tax rates do not increase strictly with firm size, but rather are better approximated as a step function (largest 50 firms in one step and all other firms in the other step). Zimmerman (1983) concluded that "effective tax rates are partial measures of the firm's political costs and hence provide evidence on the association between firm size and political costs. . . . Corporate tax rates are associated with firm size, thereby supporting the previous use of firm size as a proxy for a firm's political costs" (p. 144). (A puzzle in the Zimmerman results is why, given the higher effective tax rates, the largest 50 firms do not reduce their size via spinoffs, return of capital to shareholders, etc.)

One implication from studies arguing that political cost is an important variable in disclosure decisions (and accounting method decisions—see Chapter 5) is that management will attempt to reduce these costs via changes in the content or timing of their disclosures; for example, they may not separately disclose profitability of government contracting from the profitability of other activities. Note that the assumption underlying these studies is that politicians and other regulators do not have the ability or the incentive or the resources necessary to obtain the information not disclosed by firms via competing information sources.

3. There is a growing body of evidence on the timing of firm disclosures and factors associated with differences in that timing across firms. For example, Chambers and Penman (1984) examined a sample of 1,000 NYSE firms over the 1970–1976 period. It was found that "the reporting lag times (the number of days between the end of the fiscal period and the earnings announcement) of firms in the sample are quite regular and predictable. For the representative firm, the standard deviation of reporting lag times for interim reports is three to four calendar days, and one week for annual reports" (p. 45). Kross and Schroeder (1984) report similar results for a sample of 297 New York and American stock exchange firms over the 1977–1980 period. Table 2.2 presents median reporting lags for firms in 15 SIC two-digit industries. Some industry patterns in reporting lags are apparent; for example, the banking industry consistently is one of the earliest

TABLE 2.2 Median Reporting Lags in Calendar Days for Selected Industries, 1971–1982

SIC Two-Digit Code	Industry Title	Interim Earnings	Annual Earnings
10	Metal/mining	21	31
20	Food and kindred products	19	34
23	Apparel and other finished products	24	45
26	Paper and allied products	15	26
29	Petroleum refining	19	22
33	Steel (primary metal industries)	17	26
36	Electrical and electronic machinery	18	35
40	Railroad transportation	16	19
45	Air transportation	18	28
49	Electric, gas services	19	23
56	Apparel and accessory stores	25	40
60	Banking	11	12
65	Real estate	28	51
70	Hotels/lodging	22	41
78	Motion pictures	27	59

SOURCE: S. Penman, the University of California at Berkeley, unpublished.

industries to report interim and annual results after the end of the fiscal quarter or year. Another finding related to the timing of earnings reports is that reporting lags are longer for small firms than for large firms. Zeghal (1984) reported the following for a sample of 1,402 firms on the NYSE and ASE in the 1973–1975 period:

Firm Size (market capitalization)	Reporting Lag	
	Median	Mean
Small (less than $20 million)	39	40
Medium ($20 million to $132 million)	30	32
Large (greater than $132 million)	26	28

One explanation Zeghal (1984) offered for this result was "the advantages that large firms enjoy in producing information and particularly financial and accounting information" (p. 308).

Both Chambers and Penman (1984) and Kross and Schroeder (1984) report that goods news and bad news releases are not symmetrically distributed around their expected announcement date. To illustrate, Kross and Schroeder computed

a. *The unexpected timing of earnings releases.* The reporting dates of each firm were used to develop a predicted announcement date for each earnings release. Using this predicted date and the actual announcement date, individual announcements were ranked from the earliest to the latest, where earliest/latest refers to the firm for which the actual reporting date preceded/ came after the expected reporting date by the most number of days.

b. *The earnings surprise factor associated with each interim and annual release.* Using both the past series of earnings and the capital market reaction to each earnings announcement, releases were classified according to whether they conveyed good news or bad news.

After correlating (a) and (b), it was found that firms with good news to announce are more likely to report it earlier than their expected reporting date, whereas firms with bad news are more likely to announce it after their expected reporting date. One explanation for this is that management systematically suppresses the release of negative information. A (partial) alternative explanation is that bad news releases are associated with audit delays. (This audit delay story does not explain the early release of good news.)

Patell and Wolfson (1982) also examined the good news/bad news issue, focusing on the intraday timing of corporate disclosures of earnings and dividends. Using information on "the exact timing (hour and minute) of announcements in relation to the hours of operation of the major stock exchanges," evidence was presented on "the 'market wisdom' that good news is released during trading while bad news is held until after the market closes" (p. 509). (This "market wisdom" on the timing of corporate announcements is consistent with "political wisdom." A communications assistant to a U.S. president stated: "It was one of the first things I learned when I arrived in Washington. If you've got some news that you don't want to get noticed, put it out Friday afternoon at 4 P.M.") The Patell-Wolfson sample included approximately 1,000 earnings and dividend announcements released by 96 firms during 1976, 1977, and 1979. The findings supported the "market wisdom," especially for the earnings announcements. For example, only 10.7% of announcements reporting earnings increases were released after trading. In contrast, 34.6% of announcements reporting earnings decreases were released after trading. The authors stressed that these results "should not be interpreted as indicating that firms are trying to 'hide' bad news by releasing it after the close of trading. Virtually all such announcements . . . are fully reported in the following (business) day's *Wall Street Journal.* . . . Managements (may be) attempting to provide a natural no-trading period for the dissemination and evaluation of news releases, and . . . they employ this strategy more frequently when they have less favorable news to report" (pp. 510, 525).

4. There is increasing recognition that firms that disclose nonmandated items are not a random sample. Evidence relating to three disclosure areas illustrates this nonrandom finding:

- *Funds statements.* In an early study of voluntary disclosure, Anton (1954) reported that "one in every three large companies presents funds statements to stockholders regularly," whereas the comparable statistic for small companies is "one in twenty" (p. 622).

- *Management earnings forecasts.* Ruland (1979) examined the characteristics of firms voluntarily reporting earnings forecasts by management in the 1968–1973 period. He reported that "earnings variability is lower for reporting firms" than for a sample of nonreporting firms and that "the reporting firms tended to be larger than the nonreporting firms" (p. 200). Waymire (1985) further examined this issue and likewise concluded that "firms which issue earnings forecasts more frequently are characterized by less volatile earnings processes relative to firms which issue such projections on an infrequent basis" (p. 1).

- *Line-of-business disclosure.* Salamon and Dhaliwal (1980) examined the characteristics of multiactivity firms voluntarily reporting line-of-business disclosures in the late 1960s. One finding was that "diversified firms which voluntarily disclosed segmental sales and earnings data are significantly larger than the diversified firms which did not voluntarily disclose such data" (p. 561).

The variable most consistently reported as significant in studies examining differences across firms in their disclosure policy is firm size. An unresolved issue is explaining the underlying factor(s) that this firm size variable represents; for example, is it due to (a) larger firms attempting to reduce political costs, or (b) larger firms having lower competitive disadvantage costs associated with their disclosures, or (c) larger firms having lower information production costs? Increases in our understanding of which of the foregoing or other factors is important would make it easier for users of financial statement information to draw inferences from the voluntary disclosures (and nondisclosures) of firms.

One explanation for specific voluntarily disclosed items that is given limited recognition in the academic literature is the influence of dominant individuals. The evidence supporting this explanation is typically of an anecdotal kind. For example,

- A company president promoted the inclusion of inflation-adjusted income figures in the annual report prior to their being mandated. These figures were used to support an argument in the president's letter to shareholders against taxation on historical cost figures.

- A chief executive officer who perceived that his company was being ignored by security analysts promoted the voluntary inclusion in the annual report of a very detailed set of forecasted income figures broken down by lines of business. The annual report was distributed to security analysts with a questionnaire soliciting their reaction to the new disclosures.

Research on the dominant individual explanation for specific unusual disclosures in annual reports is very sparse. Although the anecdotes often make entertaining stories, it is unclear just how descriptively valid they are or how representative the dominant individual explanation is of other disclosure decisions.

2.7 SUMMARY

1. The factors that affect the content or timing of financial statement disclosures include (a) regulatory forces, (b) market forces, and (c) the costs associated with those disclosures. When using financial statement information, it is important to recognize that factors such as (a), (b), and (c) can result in the set of information placed in the public domain not always being the most timely or an unbiased subset of that available to internal parties.

2. Financial statement information is a subset of the many disclosures firms and other reporting entities release to external parties. The content and timing of the nonfinancial disclosures can affect the usefulness of financial statement information to external parties.

3. There are both regulatory and market penalties to firms and managers that adopt a policy of financial misrepresentation. Alternative information sources may be used as a check on possible misrepresentation in financial statement disclosures.

NOTES

1. Price Waterhouse, *Accounting Events and Trends* (June/July 1983), p. 2.
2. *The Wall Street Journal*, January 6, 1975.
3. *The Wall Street Journal*, July 18, 1983.
4. Address by the Chairman of Directors, *S. A. Brewing Holdings Limited*, June 19, 1981.
5. Corporate Release, *Pabst Brewing Company*, April 5, 1982.
6. Excerpted from *U.S. News & World Report* issue of Nov. 15, 1979. Copyright, 1979, U.S. News & World Report, Inc.
7. *The Wall Street Journal*, December 29, 1978.

QUESTIONS

QUESTION 2.1: Voluntary Public Disclosure of Key Financial Objectives: McCormick & Company

Many firms develop key financial objectives to guide their internal decision making. A small subset of these firms publicly discloses such objectives voluntarily to external parties. McCormick & Company, a diversified specialty food company, has for some time included such information in its annual reports. Objectives pertaining to at least nine variables have been reported in one or more of its annual reports in the seven-year period (termed 19X1 to 19X7) covered in this question. In 19X7 McCormick had sales of $743 million ($329 million from the grocery products division, $157 million from food service, $131 million from industrial products, $36 million from packaging, and $90 million from international).

Panel A of Table 2.3 summarizes the financial objectives reported in each year of the 19X1–19X7 period. Panel B presents the actual values of all variables (and several additional items) as reported in the annual report for that year in the 19X1–19X8 period. The 19X1 Annual Report noted that "management regularly reviews these objectives to confirm their validity. As conditions change within our business and the investment and capital markets, management may find it advisable to adjust these objectives. . . . Management monitors performance against these objectives on a rolling five-year basis, as well as for each year."

Disclosure of Capital Expenditure Budgets

Each year over the 19X1–19X7 period, McCormick also provided details in its annual reports about projected capital expenditures. The following (in millions of dollars) was disclosed in the respective annual reports:

Disclosed in 19.X Annual Report	One-Year-Ahead Projection	Two-Year-Ahead Projection (Aggregate)	Five-Year-Ahead Projection (Aggregate)
19X1	$12	$29	$ 76
19X2	9	29	84
19X3	24	51	109
19X4	17	N.D.	105
19X5	19	N.D.	120
19X6	42	N.D.	N.D.
19X7	26	N.D.	N.D.

N.D.–Not disclosed in that year's Annual Report.

The actual capital expenditures reported by the company (in millions of dollars) were

19X2	19X3	19X4	19X5	19X6	19X7	19X8
$14	$18	$25	$26.5	$22.4	$37.2	$31.3

When making the projections in 19X1, McCormick noted that "the largest amount of the expenditures over the next five years will be allocated to the Food Service/ Industrial Sector." In 19X2, McCormick broke up the $84 million projected five-year capital expenditures into $27 million to grocery products, $46 million to food

TABLE 2.3   McCormick & Company Financial Data

A. Stated Financial Objectives Reported in 19.X Annual Report							
Financial Variable	*19x1*	*19x2*	*19x3*	*19x4*	*19x5*	*19x6*	*19x7*
1 Annual sales growth	15%	15%	15%	N.D.	N.D.	N.D.	N.D.
2 Unit sales increase	N.D.	N.D.	N.D.	N.D.	10%	10%	10%
3 Growth in net income	16%	15%	15%	N.D.	N.D.	N.D.	N.D.
4 Net income margin	N.D.	N.D.	N.D.	N.D.	5%	5%	5%
5 Return on average assets employed	12.5%	12.5%	12.5%	15%	15%	15%	15%
6 Return on equity	N.D.	N.D.	N.D.	18–20%	18–20%	18–20%	18–20%
7 Total debt to total capital	35–40%	35–40%	35–40%	35–40%	35–40%	35–40%	35–40%
8 Current ratio (minimum objective)	2 to 1	2 to 1	2 to 1	2 to 1	2 to 1	2 to 1	N.D.
9 Dividend payout	27–30%	27–30%	27–30%	27–30%	27–30%	27–30%	27–30%

B. Actual (Realized) Value of Variable Reported in 19.X Annual Report								
Financial Variable	*19x1*	*19x2*	*19x3*	*19x4*	*19x5*	*19x6*	*19x7*	*19x8*
1 Annual sales growth	17%	13%	14%	20%	25%	9%	3.5%	6.1%
2 Unit sales increase	12%	5%	6%	7%	16.8%	5.2%	3.5%	6.1%
3 Growth in net income	28%	13%	16%	(24%)*	127%	(17%)*	61%	36%
4 Net income margin	4.0%	4.0%	4.2%	2.5%	4.5%	3.5%	5.4%	6.9%
5 Return on average assets employed	11.1%	10.6%	11.2%	10.3%	15.4%	15.6%	16.3%	17.7%
6 Return on equity	15.2%	14.9%	15.5%	10.9%	19.6%	14.1%	20.6%	23.1%
7 Total debt to total capital	33.8%	32.7%	37.2%	43.5%	32.7%	32.3%	25.8%	36.7%
8 Current ratio	2.6	2.5	2.1	2.3	1.8	1.6	1.6	1.4
9 Dividend payout	30%	28%	29%	42%	28%	39%	27%	26%
10 Sales ($ millions)	355	400	457	548	660	718	743	788
11 Net income ($ millions)	14.8	16.7	19.4	14.8	29.9	25.0	40.1	54.6
12 Shareholders' equity (book value $ millions)	109	121	135	132	174	187	216	244
13 McCormick market capitalization ($ millions)	179	170	227	214	242	331	362	399
14 S&P 500 Index	94	95	107	134	122	139	164	164
15 Annual inflation rate (CPI)	6.8%	7.4%	10.9%	13.6%	10.6%	6.6%	3.2%	4.2%

* Brackets mean a decrease in the variable.
N.D. – Not disclosed in that year's Annual Report.
SOURCE: McCormick & Company annual reports.

service/industrial, $10 million to international, and $1 million to miscellaneous. In 19X3, McCormick did not break up the $109 million projected five-year expenditure, noting only that "the largest amount will be allocated to food service and industrial activities." In 19X4 McCormick stated that the $105 million projected amount would be "for maintenance and expansion of existing businesses," and in 19X5 it reported that the $120 million five-year projection was "almost all for increased capacity and cost reduction projects in existing businesses." In its 19X6 to 19X8 annual reports, McCormick only disclosed details of its one-year-ahead projected capital expenditures.

REQUIRED

1. Why might McCormick voluntarily disclose key financial objectives in its annual reports over the 19X1–19X7 period? What are the pros and cons of disclosing this information?

2. How successful was McCormick in meeting its key financial objectives over the 19X2 to 19X8 period? (Assume that a financial objective reported in, say, the 19X2 Annual Report relates to the 19X3 fiscal year and subsequent years.)

3. One variable that McCormick did not cite as a key financial objective was earnings per share. What are the limitations to management or shareholders of using this variable as a key financial objective?

4. Comment on McCormick's voluntary disclosure of capital expenditure projections. (Such information is rarely disclosed by firms.)

5. Over the 19X1–19X7 period, McCormick changed (a) the set of financial objectives disclosed in any one year and (b) the breakdown of projected capital expenditures. Why might these changes have been made?

6. In what firms or industries might you expect to see nondisclosure to external parties of key financial objectives? In what firms or industries might you expect to see nondisclosure to external parties of projected capital expenditures? Explain.

QUESTION   2.2:   Earnings Forecast Disclosure Policy
                              at the Allen Group

In 19X1 new management was installed at The Allen Group, and the company was reorganized into four operating subsidiaries along product groupings:

Automotive, Diagnostic, Service, and Automation

Automotive Accessories

Special Vehicles and Equipment

Electronic and Industrial Components

The new management established a firm policy with regard to forecasting earnings: "The company would make no public forecasts of earnings and would refuse to discuss forecasts of third parties or to indicate probable ranges for earnings levels.'' The company stated (retrospectively in 19X5) that it adopted this policy for several reasons:

> First, management did not feel, nor does it now feel, that the making of public forecasts should be the duty of management. We view management's role as one of responsibility for the operation of the business in the long-term interest of stockholders and we see many dangers in too strong a commitment to achieving an arbitrary short-term earnings target.
>
> Second, while Allen's management realizes the importance of near-term earnings in today's investment climate, it believes that this factor alone is a poor guide to the investment merits of a company and that a focus of attention on this single element tends to discourage analysis of many more important factors. The record and ability of the management group, the vitality of the company's markets and the strength of its position within them, the soundness of the company's objectives and strategies, the strength of its financial position, and the degree of commitment of the company's people to achieving their goals are all basic factors that should be examined and weighed closely.
>
> Third, it was felt that a policy of not making public earnings forecasts would ultimately encourage those analysts who wished to formulate an earnings projection to undertake an in-depth investigation of all of Allen's business areas.
>
> And, finally, while your management did not believe that making and achieving forecasted earnings results was the only way to secure the confidence of Wall Street and the investing public, we were acutely aware of the dangers associated with the failure to achieve forecasts. During this period in which The Allen Group was undergoing substantial change in business commitments, in personnel, in organization and in business philosophy and style, it was extremely difficult to make reliable forecasts of short-term earnings progress.

During 19X4, management reconsidered its forecast policy ''in light of changing company circumstances. Opinions from a broad spectrum of the investment community were sought in the course of that reevaluation.'' This review led to a policy reversal. Beginning in 19X5, management commenced publishing earnings forecasts. The Allen Group provided the following reasons for this change in policy:

> During the past year, it became increasingly clear that our policy has not had the desired result on our relations with stockholders and the investment community. The principal difficulty has stemmed from the fact that while management has refused to discuss earnings, the analysts have been forced by prevailing custom in the investment community to issue earnings estimates. Since analysts follow companies that tend to excite their imagination and are captive to the necessity of making forecasts, and since management has been optimistic in its assessment of Allen's future, without referring to earnings prospects, the result has often been an excess of enthusiasm in the prediction of earnings for The Allen Group.
>
> In each of the last three years, forecasts prepared by a wide spectrum of analysts made at the beginning of the year proved, when actual results were known, to be quite wide of the mark. The outstanding example occurred in early 19X4 when an investment advisory firm published a forecast, without our prior knowledge, that Allen's earnings would reach $2 per share in 19X4—an extremely high forecast to anyone who really knew the company, but one which had a dramatic, temporary impact on stock price and trading. Repeated attempts were made, both verbally and

in writing, to have the forecast lowered, but we were unable to have the number reduced in a meaningful manner.

This repeated excess of enthusiasm on the part of the investment community tended to create several problems for Allen's management and for its stockholders. In a rather curious way, our management's refusal to discuss earnings, instead of focusing a concentration on the more fundamental issues, seems to have discouraged it. Embarrassed by their beginning-of-the-year optimism, some analysts have asked management, "Why are you falling short of our estimate of earnings?" instead of focusing their attention on the dramatic progress that has been made in many areas. Unhappily, because forecasts are a convenient yardstick, many stockholders have used the overly optimistic forecasts of others as a measure of the company's progress. We also have found a few instances where individuals refused to acknowledge the source of these forecasts, with the result that management has been questioned anyway, notwithstanding continuing gains in sales, earnings and return on equity.

For the stockholder, the impact has been felt in three ways. First, to the extent that excessive earnings forecasts have interfered with a proper communication of Allen's progress, stockholder values have undoubtedly suffered.

Second, bullish forecasts, in certain instances, have had an effect on short-term stock price movements that has clearly operated to the disadvantage of many Allen stockholders. Following the $2-per-share investment advisory service forecast mentioned earlier, for example, the number of trades and number of shares traded of Allen stock quadrupled, and in a nine-day period, the stock moved from the low $20s to $30—a price change of approximately 40%. Similarly, when the same service reversed its position some months later, our stock trading again increased dramatically and the price dropped sharply. In this rapid up-and-down movement, many stockholders were undoubtedly abused.

Finally, all stockholders have not had access to the same information at the same time because independent forecasts usually reach only a small portion of the total group. A recent study by the Financial Analysts Federation asked whether all investors had access to forecasts on a timely basis. Results of the study showed that 57% of the analysts have access to outside forecast information while only 14% of investors are able to obtain this information.

Table 2.4 presents the EPS forecasts made by The Allen Group over the 19X5–19X15 period. The company has a December 31 fiscal year end. Table 2.4 also presents additional data from the annual report of each year.

With the exception of years 19X7, 19X14, and 19X15, all initial forecasts for each year were released in March. In March 19X7, the company noted:

The present economic environment, with its great uncertainties as to GNP levels, auto and truck production, inflation, consumer spending and government anti-recession and energy policies, has made accurate forecasting impossible.

The $0.78 forecast for 19X7 was issued on August 4.

In March 19X14, the company included the following in its "Special Report to Stockholders."

We continue to believe that our forecasts are beneficial to stockholders. . . . However, we recognize there are times, such as those we are currently experiencing, when external conditions are so unsettled and unclear that a meaningful forecast is not

TABLE 2.4 The Allen Group Financial Data, 19X1–19X15

Year	Forecasted EPS ($)	Actual EPS ($)	Net Sales ($ millions)	Net Income ($ millions)	Price-Earnings Ratio of Allen Group	Median Price-Earnings Ratio of Compustat Firms
19X1	N.D.	0.36	98	1.2	36.7	14.2
19X2	N.D.	0.69	112	3.0	13.0	13.8
19X3	N.D.	0.87	123	3.6	11.7	14.8
19X4	N.D.	0.89	149	3.8	12.6	13.2
19X5	1.01 to 1.05	1.03	197	4.5	4.7	7.5
19X6	1.07 to 1.18	0.81	218	3.5	3.4	4.9
19X7	0.78	0.83	227	3.6	7.8	6.9
19X8	1.42 to 1.73	1.44	263	6.5	6.0	8.0
19X9	1.68 to 1.82	1.76	280	7.9	6.5	7.4
19X10	1.87 to 2.05	1.90	301	8.5	5.3	6.8
19X11	2.18 to 2.36	2.21	343	10.2	5.8	6.8
19X12	2.45 to 2.73	1.84	348	8.8	8.3	7.8
19X13	1.95 to 2.36	1.72	363	8.7	7.9	7.4
19X14	N.D.	(2.32)	315	(11.8)	(5.6)	9.5
19X15	0.95	1.03	352	6.2	25.0	10.8

N.D. – Not disclosed.
Note: The forecasted EPS and actual EPS series have been adjusted for stock splits and stock dividends.

possible. An earnings forecast for the year made in this volatile environment would have little value and could undermine the discipline we have brought to this program. Accordingly, we will characterize the general outlook for each of our business segments but will defer a specific forecast until the economic environment is more clearly discernable.

No earnings forecast was issued for 19X14. The company stated (in 19X15) that during the "course of 19X14, we regularly provided updates on the developing trends in our business. In our Third Quarter Report, we indicated the likelihood of reporting a loss for the year, along with the possibility of special charges that were under consideration."

In March 19X15, The Allen Group reported

The volatile economic conditions that prevailed in 19X14 led us to the judgment that it was unrealistic to make an earnings forecast. For the same reason, that is the policy we will follow in 19X15.

The $0.95 forecast for 19X15 was released in "a special letter to shareholders" in September of that year.

REQUIRED

1. Comment on the reasons The Allen Group gave for not releasing forecasts in the 19X1–19X4 period. What other reasons might motivate nondisclosure of forecasts?

2. Comment on the reasons The Allen Group gave for voluntarily releasing forecasts in 19X5. What other reasons might motivate disclosure of forecasts?

3. In its 19X4 deliberations, The Allen Group considered a third option (other than forecasting or not forecasting). This option was to "attempt to 'guide' security analysts and others in the making of their so-called 'independent' forecasts." What are the pros and cons of this option?

4. How would you evaluate the accuracy of The Allen Group's forecasts over the 19X5–19X15 period? What problems may arise in this evaluation? (For those who wish to compute forecast error measures, a reading of Section 8.3.A of Chapter 8 may be useful.)

5. Would you expect security analysts to support an SEC mandate that all companies publicly release earnings forecasts?

QUESTION   2.3:   Financial Reporting and the Case for Government Regulation

An ongoing debate concerns the appropriate role of public sector regulation of financial reporting. Consider the following argument by Robert Chatov in a debate on "Should the Public Sector Take Over the Function of Determining Generally Accepted Accounting Principles?":

> As our debate topic implicitly and too accurately recognizes, the private sector presently determines generally accepted accounting principles, which is not what was intended by the Congress that passed the 1933 Securities Act and the 1934 Securities Exchange Act. Those acts explicitly authorized development of corporate financial reporting rules in the public sector, and that is where they ought to be formulated today. Whether one favors development of corporate financial reporting rules by the private or the public sector depends upon how one feels about the relative importance of three distinct, frequently contradictory objectives of corporate financial reporting. The three objectives are corporate reporting, investor evaluation and government planning.
>
> *Corporate Reporting.* To permit the corporation to present the financial information it considers most conducive to its corporate purposes.
>
> *Investor Evaluation.* To provide investors (broadly defined) with information on a particular corporation, or with data sufficient to permit comparison of two or more corporations, even in different industries.
>
> *Government Planning.* To provide the basis for a wide range of macroeconomic public policy decisions, such as forecasting the effect of inventory changes, capital investment, R & D expenditures, corporate profitability, etc., on economic activity, and in addition, to allow measurement of competition in different markets; and for the SEC to implement the directive of the securities acts to eliminate speculation in the financial markets that negatively affects the nation's economic health.
>
> These three objectives are mutually exclusive in today's atmosphere of private-sector control of the development of corporate financial reporting rules. I am aware that this is a strong statement but I have deliberately left out any qualifiers like "probably" or "potentially" before "mutually exclusive." Today only the first objective is being approximated. Investor information is inadequate because of the undecipherability of corporate statements, attributable in part to the Security and Exchange Commis-

sion's advocated footnote disclosure policy, which was originated in 1935. Secondly, because of the multitude of accounting alternatives available to corporations in reporting their financial position, we have a lack of standardization of accounting conventions within industries no less than between industries. The result is that average investors are clearly incapable of deciphering corporate financial reports, sophisticated investors and financial institutions are similarly disadvantaged, and the government is presented with a mass of data which when aggregated is substantially meaningless. For example, can anyone assert that aggregated corporate profits really mean anything, except to indicate the state of mind of the corporate sector? . . .

The objective most likely to be satisfied (by the FASB) is that of permitting corporations to show those things which they would most like to show, and to devote itself to a continuing avoidance of really controversial issues. This is to be expected, and one ought not to be upset about it. But there ought to be better ways of doing things. My contention is that the public sector has the major interest in, and the responsibility for, developing rules for corporate financial reporting. Because of the tradition in the SEC towards having the private sector develop rules of corporate financial reporting, and because developing an intelligible set of corporate financial rules is a scholarly undertaking, not suited to a government agency, I do not recommend that the SEC take over this function.

I suggest that what is needed is a national commission to develop a comprehensive accounting code for industrial corporations within the United States. You may shudder with horror at my assertion that this accounting code ought to provide several things: (1) it ought to provide for uniformity in accounting treatment; (2) it ought to provide the elimination of alternative treatments of accounting; (3) it ought to provide for comparability among the financial reports of different corporations, which should result if the first two objectives are met. Only in this way will investors be able to rely upon corporate financial reports and upon making comparisons between them. Only in this way will the government have reliable financial information which it will be able to appraise on the basis of knowing specifically what is in the reports and their aggregations. And only in this way can we look forward to intelligent and meaningful public policy decisions to be made by government, based on consistent, aggregatable corporate financial data.

REQUIRED

1. What are the main arguments Chatov presents for (a) having accounting principles set within the public sector and (b) having a national commission to develop a comprehensive code for industrial corporations within the United States? What other arguments might be offered to support Chatov's proposals?

2. Do you agree with Chatov that "the private sector presently determines generally accepted accounting principles"?

3. What arguments could be made for having a private sector regulatory body determine generally accepted accounting principles?

4. The only two options discussed by Chatov are a public sector regulatory body or a private sector regulatory body. A third option is to have no regulatory body and to let the "invisible hand" of the marketplace determine the accounting methods used and the corporate disclosures made by firms. What are the pros and cons of this third option?

REFERENCES

AKERLOF, G. "The Market for 'Lemons': Quality Uncertainty and the Market Mechanism." *Quarterly Journal of Economics* (August 1970): 488–500.

ANDERSON, J. A., and M. PINCUS. "Market Efficiency and Legal Liability: Some Extensions and an Illustration." *Accounting and Business Research* (Spring 1984): 169–181.

ANTON, H. R. "Funds Statement Practices in the United States and Canada." *The Accounting Review* (October 1954): 620–627.

ARROW, K. J. "Economic Welfare and the Allocation of Resources for Invention." In *The Rate and Direction of Economic Activity: Economic and Social Factors*, pp. 609–625. Princeton, N.J.: National Bureau of Economic Research, 1962.

BALL, R., and G. FOSTER. "Corporate Financial Reporting: A Methodological Review of Empirical Research." *Studies of Current Research Methodologies in Accounting: A Critical Evaluation*, supplement to *Journal of Accounting Research* (1982): 161–234.

BENSTON, G. J. "The Value of the SEC's Accounting Disclosure Requirements." *The Accounting Review* (July 1969): 515–532.

BENSTON, G. J. "An Analysis of the Role of Accounting Standards for Enhancing Corporate Governance and Social Responsibility." *Journal of Accounting and Public Policy* (Fall 1982): 5–17.

BENSTON, G. J. "The Costs of Complying with a Government Data Collection Program: The FTC's Line of Business Report." *Journal of Accounting and Public Policy* (Summer 1984): 123–137.

BURTON, J. "Forecasts: A Changing View From The Securities and Exchange Commission." In P. Prakash and A. Rappaport, eds., *Public Reporting of Corporate Financial Forecasts*. New York: Commerce Clearing House, 1974.

CHAMBERS, A. E., and S. H. PENMAN. "Timeliness of Reporting and the Stock Price Reaction to Earnings Announcements." *Journal of Accounting Research* (Spring 1984): 21–47.

CHATOV, R. "Should the Public Sector Take Over the Function of Determining Generally Accepted Accounting Principles." *The Accounting Journal* (Spring 1977): 117–123.

CHOW, C. W. "Empirical Studies on the Economic Impacts of Accounting Regulations: Findings, Problems and Prospects." *Journal of Accounting Literature* (Spring 1983): 73–109.

COOPER, K., and G. D. KEIM. "The Economic Rationale for the Nature and Extent of Corporate Financial Disclosure Regulation: A Critical Assessment." *Journal of Accounting and Public Policy* (Fall 1983): 189–205.

FOSTER, G. "Externalities and Financial Reporting." *The Journal of Finance* (May 1980): 521–533.

GONEDES, N. J., and N. DOPUCH. "Capital Market Equilibrium, Information Production, and Selected Accounting Techniques: Theoretical Framework and Review of Empirical Work." *Studies on Financial Accounting Objectives: 1974*, supplement to *Journal of Accounting Research:* 48–129.

HORNGREN, C. T. "Accounting Principles: Private or Public Sector?" *The Journal of Accountancy* (May 1972): 37–41.

HORNGREN, C. T. "The Marketing of Accounting Standards." *The Journal of Accountancy* (October 1973): 61–66.

KROSS, W., and D. A. SCHROEDER. "An Empirical Investigation of the Effect of Quarterly Earnings Announcement Timing on Stock Returns." *Journal of Accounting Research* (Spring 1984): 153–176.

LEFTWICH R. "Market Failure Fallacies and Accounting Information." *Journal of Accounting and Economics* (December 1980): 193–211.

MAUTZ, R. K., and W. G. MAY. *Financial Disclosure in a Competitive Economy.* New York: Financial Executives Research Foundation, 1978.

MERINO, B. D., and M. D. NEIMARK. "Disclosure Regulation and Public Policy: A Sociohistorical Reappraisal." *Journal of Accounting and Public Policy* (Fall 1982): 33–57.

MORRIS, R. D. "Corporate Disclosure in a Substantially Unregulated Environment." *Abacus* (June 1984): 52–86.

NEW YORK STOCK EXCHANGE, *Company Manual* (NYSE, updated).

PATELL, J. M., and M. A. WOLFSON. "Good News, Bad News, and the Intraday Timing of Corporate Disclosures." *The Accounting Review* (July 1982): 509–527.

PERRY, R., and J. SEARFOSS. "Eleven Companies' Approach to Changing Prices as of December 31, 1981." Memorandum to FASB by Perry and Searfoss of Touche Ross, 1982.

RULAND, W. "The Time Series of Earnings for Forecast Reporting and Nonreporting Firms." *Journal of Business Finance and Accounting* (Summer 1979): 187–201.

SALAMON, G. L., and D. S. DHALIWAL. "Company Size and Financial Disclosure Requirements with Evidence from the Segmental Reporting Issue." *Journal of Business Finance and Accounting* (Winter 1980): 555–568.

STANDARD & POOR'S. "Who's Watching the Books?" *Standard & Poor's Perspective.* New York: S&P, 1980, 1–6.

VANGERMEERSCH, R. *Financial Reporting Techniques in 20 Industrial Companies Since 1861.* Gainesville: University Presses of Florida, 1979.

WATTS, R. L. "Corporate Financial Statements, A Product of the Market and Political Process." *Australian Journal of Management* (April 1977): 53–75.

WATTS, R. L., and J. L. ZIMMERMAN. "Towards a Positive Theory of the Determination of Accounting Standards." *The Accounting Review* (January 1978): 112–134.

WAYMIRE, G. "Earnings Volatility and Voluntary Management Forecast Disclosure." *Journal of Accounting Research* (Spring 1985): 268–295.

ZEGHAL, D. "Firm Size and the Informational Content of Financial Statements." *Journal of Financial and Quantitative Analysis* (September 1984): 299–310.

ZIMMERMAN, J. L., "Taxes and Firm Size." *Journal of Accounting and Economics* (August 1983): 119–149.

3

FINANCIAL STATEMENT ANALYSIS: INTRODUCTORY TECHNIQUES

3.1 INTRODUCTION

Financial statement analysis includes the study of relationships within a set of financial statements at a *point in time* and with trends in these relationships *over time*. This chapter outlines several techniques that have been developed for these tasks. In subsequent chapters, further analysis of these and other techniques is presented. Financial statement and other information relating to G. Heileman Brewing Company and three other U.S. brewing companies will be used to illustrate these techniques.

The U.S. brewing industry, as of 1984, included six companies that accounted for over 90% of U.S. sales—Anheuser-Busch, Miller Brewing, Stroh Brewing, G. Heileman Brewing, Adolph Coors, and Pabst Brewing. Of these six companies, Heileman experienced the most rapid growth rate in the 1964–1983 period. A major part of this growth came from the acquisition of other brewing companies and the acquisition of the brands or plants of other brewing companies. In this chapter the financial statements of Heileman will be compared with Busch, Coors, and Pabst. All four are publicly held companies with at least 80% of their sales from brewing activities. (Miller Brewing is a subsidiary of Philip Morris and accounts for less than 25% of the sales of Philip Morris. Stroh Brewing is a privately held company.)

Many comparative financial statement exercises of the kind presented in this chapter access computerized data bases rather than the actual annual reports of the companies examined. The appendix to this chapter discusses issues that arise when using computerized data bases.

3.2 CROSS-SECTIONAL TECHNIQUES

Two frequently discussed cross-sectional techniques of financial statement analysis are (A) common-size statements and (B) financial ratio analysis. This section illustrates the use of these techniques in the analysis of Heileman vis-à-vis Busch, Coors, and Pabst.

A. Common-Size Statements

One impetus to the development of the common-size statement came from the problems in comparing the financial statements of firms that differ in size. Suppose that Company A (Heileman) has long-term debt of $95.719 million and that Company B (Pabst) has long-term debt of $76.810 million. Due to possible size differences between the two companies, it would be misleading to always infer that A was more highly leveraged than B. One way of controlling for size differences is to express the components of the balance sheet as a percentage of total assets (liabilities + equity) and the components of the income statement as a percentage of total revenues. The derived statements are termed common-size statements. For instance, in 1983 Heileman had total assets (liabilities and equities) of $530.301 million, while Pabst had total assets (liabilities and equities) of

TABLE 3.1   Common-Size Financial Statements

A. Common-Size Balance Sheets, 1983				
	Heileman	*Busch*	*Coors*	*Pabst*
Assets				
Cash and marketable securities	4.0%	5.0%	10.2%	2.3%
Accounts receivables	7.1	6.6	6.3	10.0
Inventories	21.3	6.9	11.2	26.2
Other current assets	1.2	2.2	3.7	1.2
Properties plant and equipment	64.2	74.0	67.7	56.1
Other assets	2.2	5.3	.9	4.2
	100.0%	100.0%	100.0%	100.0%
Liabilities + Equity				
Accounts payable	15.9%	7.6%	5.4%	22.2%
Other current liabilities	10.0	9.1	9.7	20.6
Long-term debt	18.0	22.2	.0	31.5
Capital leases	.0	.0	.0	1.3
Other long-term liabilities	.0	.0	.9	2.0
Deferred credits	11.0	13.2	9.6	7.2
Minority preferred shareholders	.0	7.1	.0	.0
Shareholders' equity	45.1	40.8	74.4	15.2
	100.0%	100.0%	100.0%	100.0%

B. Common-Size Income Statements, 1983				
	Heileman	*Busch*	*Coors*	*Pabst*
Revenues				
Sales	99.4%	99.8%	99.1%	99.6%
Other revenues	.6	.2	.9	.4
	100.0%	100.0%	100.0%	100.0%
Expenses and Net Income				
Excise taxes	13.1%	9.3%	10.5%	14.1%
Cost of goods sold	61.7	61.7	57.5	67.7
Marketing, general, and administrative	16.5	18.3	17.7	16.1
Interest expense	.7	1.2	.1	1.2
Other expense	.0	.3	1.8	.1
Taxation, current	2.2	2.0	4.0	(.3)
Taxation, deferred	1.5	2.0	1.3	.7
Net income	4.3	5.2	7.1	.4
	100.0%	100.0%	100.0%	100.0%
Total assets ($ million)	$ 530	$4,330	$1,156	$244
Total revenues ($ million)	1,334	6,671	1,254	804

$243.915 million. Their respective common-size balance sheets show

Heileman: Long-term debt of 18.0% ($95.719/$530.301)
Pabst: Long-term debt of 31.5% ($76.810/$243.915)

Table 3.1 illustrates the 1983 common-size balance sheets and income statements of Heileman, Busch, Coors, and Pabst. All four companies have a December 31 fiscal year.

Several inferences can be drawn from Table 3.1. Coors has (1) the highest percent in cash-related assets (10.2%), (2) the lowest percent of long-term debt (.0%), and (3) the highest percent of net income from each dollar of revenue (7.1%). In contrast, Pabst has (1) the lowest percent in cash-related assets (2.3%), (2) the highest percent of long-term debt (31.5%), and (3) the lowest percent of reported net income from each dollar of revenue (.4%). Both Heileman and Busch fall between the extremes of Coors and Pabst on each of these three factors.

The percentages in Table 3.1 will reflect accounting method-induced (historical cost) differences as well as financing-investment-operating differences across the four companies. For instance, one explanation for the percentage of Busch's total assets in properties, plant, and equipment (74.0%) being higher than Heileman (64.2%) is that Busch has a higher proportion of plant that has been built at more recent construction costs.

B. Financial Ratio Analysis

The most widely discussed cross-sectional technique is a comparison of ratios across firms. Numerous individual ratios have been proposed in the literature. The following seven categories and ratios within each category are meant to be illustrative rather than exhaustive. The seven categories are (1) cash position, (2) liquidity, (3) working capital/cash flow, (4) capital structure, (5) debt service coverage, (6) profitability, and (7) turnover. Further discussion of methods for grouping financial ratios into categories is in Chapter 4.

Cash Position

Cash and marketable securities form an important reservoir that the firm can use to meet its operating expenditures and other cash obligations when and as they fall due. The ratios that have been used when comparing the relative cash positions of different firms include

- $$\frac{\text{Cash } + \text{ marketable securities}}{\text{Current liabilities}}$$

- $$\frac{\text{Cash } + \text{ marketable securities}}{\text{Sales}}$$

- $$\frac{\text{Cash } + \text{ marketable securities}}{\text{Total assets}}$$

The higher each of these ratios, the higher the cash resources available to the firm.

Brewing Industry Ratios.   Table 3.2 presents the three ratios of the four brewing companies. Across all three ratios there is a consistent ranking of companies: Coors has the highest cash position, then Busch, then Heileman, and then Pabst with the lowest cash position. An important additional item in interpreting the ratios is revolving credit agreements with lenders. Two of the companies report sizable amounts of cash available under these agreements. Busch has $1 billion and Heileman $75 million as the unused components of their respective revolving credit agreements; the cash and marketable securities items in their balance sheets are $218.4 million for Busch and $21.258 million for Heileman. One motivation for both companies having such sizable amounts available is to be able to make a cash acquisition without any delays due to the arranging of finance. (The three cash position ratios typically do not incorporate unused amounts under revolving credit agreements in the computation of the ratio itself.)

Liquidity

Liquidity refers to the ability of a firm to meet its short-term financial obligations when and as they fall due. The cash position ratios discussed capture one dimension of liquidity. Two additional liquidity ratios that are frequently used are

- $$\text{Quick ratio} = \frac{\text{Cash} + \text{short-term marketable securities} + \text{accounts receivables}}{\text{Current liabilities}}$$

- $$\text{Current ratio} = \frac{\text{Current assets}}{\text{Current liabilities}}$$

Both ratios extend the assets in the numerator of the cash position ratios to include items that potentially can be converted into cash. The quick ratio includes accounts receivable. (Cash + short-term marketable securities + accounts receivables are often called the "quick assets.") The current ratio also includes in the numerator items such as inventories and prepaid expenses. The higher both the ratios, the higher the liquidity position of the firm.

TABLE 3.2 Cash Position Financial Ratios, 1983

	Heileman	Busch	Coors	Pabst
$\dfrac{\text{Cash} + \text{marketable securities}}{\text{Current liabilities}}$	.15	.30	.68	.05
$\dfrac{\text{Cash} + \text{marketable securities}}{\text{Sales}}$	.02	.03	.10	.01
$\dfrac{\text{Cash} + \text{marketable securities}}{\text{Total assets}}$	.04	.05	.10	.02

TABLE 3.3 Liquidity Ratios, 1983

	Heileman	Busch	Coors	Pabst
Quick assets / Current liabilities	.43	.69	1.10	.29
Current assets / Current liabilities	1.30	1.24	2.08	.93

Brewing Industry Ratios.   Table 3.3 presents the 1983 quick and current ratios of the four brewing companies. The only change from the inferences drawn previously is that the liquidity rankings of Busch and Heileman are switched when the current ratio is used; this is in part due to the relatively high inventory holdings of Heileman, causing its current ratio to exceed its quick ratio by a sizable amount.

The use of different asset and liability valuation methods across firms means that a less than literal interpretation of the numerical magnitude of each firm's current or quick ratio is appropriate. Consider inventory valuation methods. While all four brewing companies use the "lower of cost or market" method, they differ with regard to the methods used to determine cost:

Heileman: LIFO (last in, first out) 49%, FIFO (first in, first out) 51%
   Busch: LIFO for brewing inventories, FIFO for food inventories
   Coors: LIFO
   Pabst: Moving average basis

The effect of using alternative valuation rules is sometimes reported in the footnotes or supplemental disclosures included in annual reports. For instance, each of the four firms reports the current cost of inventories in its supplemental disclosures (as required by *FASB Statement No. 33*). Using these data, the current ratio can be computed using a consistent inventory valuation method across all four companies:

	Heileman	Busch	Coors	Pabst
Current ratio (historical cost for inventory)	1.30	1.24	2.08	.93
Current ratio (current cost for inventory)	1.35	1.39	2.43	.93

The effect of using current cost for inventories is to change the ranking between Heileman and Busch on the current ratio. Busch now has a higher current ratio than does Heileman; the difference, however, appears minimal.

Working Capital/Cash Flow

Increasing attention is being paid to the cash-generating ability of firms. While most firms do not directly report cash flow information in their annual reports, inferences about cash flow can be gained by adjusting the reported net income figure for the noncash items in its computation. Table 3.4 presents a set

TABLE 3.4 Computation of Working Capital from Operations and Cash Flow From Operations for Heileman ($000s)

A. Working Capital From Operations (WCO)		
Net Income		$ 56,969
Additions		
1. Depreciation, amortization, and depletion expense	$23,494	
2. Amortization of intangibles and deferred charges	0	
3. Amortization of discount on bonds payable	0	
4. Amortization of premium on bond investments	0	
5. Additions to deferred investment tax credits	0	
6. Increase in deferred income taxes payable	20,104	
7. Pro rata share of reported losses in excess of cash dividends recognized from unconsolidated stock investments under the equity method	0	
8. Minority interest in consolidated subsidiaries' net income	0	
9. Losses from nonoperating items	0	
		$ 43,598
Subtractions		
1. Amortization of deferred credits	0	
2. Amortization of premium on bonds payable	0	
3. Amortization of discount on bond investments	0	
4. Amortization of deferred investment tax credit	0	
5. Decrease in deferred income taxes payable	0	
6. Pro rata share of reported income in excess of cash dividends recognized from unconsolidated stock investments, under the equity method	0	
7. Minority interest in consolidated subsidiaries' net loss	0	
8. Gains from nonoperating items	0	
		$ 0
Working capital from operations		$100,567
B. Cash Flow From Operations (CFO)		
Working capital from operations		$100,567
Additions		
1. Decrease in accounts receivable	10,740	
2. Decrease in inventory	0	
3. Decrease in prepaid expenses	0	
4. Increase in accounts payable	27,076	
5. Increase in accrued expenses	0	
		$ 37,816
Subtractions		
1. Increase in accounts receivable	0	
2. Increase in inventory	14,883	
3. Increase in prepaid expenses	1,526	
4. Decrease in accounts payable	0	
5. Decrease in accrued expenses	8,279	
		$ 24,688
Cash flow from operations		$113,695

of adjustments outlined by Gombola and Ketz (1983) to compute "working capital from operations" and "cash flow from operations." Financial ratios that incorporate these two concepts include

- $$\frac{\text{Working capital from operations}}{\text{Sales}}$$

- $$\frac{\text{Working capital from operations}}{\text{Total assets (average)}}$$

- $$\frac{\text{Cash flow from operations}}{\text{Sales}}$$

- $$\frac{\text{Cash flow from operations}}{\text{Total assets (average)}}$$

The average total assets figure in the ratios typically is calculated as the equally weighted average of the opening and closing total asset figure for the fiscal period. Where seasonal patterns occur, a moving average based on quarterly data, or even monthly data if available, may be used. The higher each of the ratios, the larger the working capital or cash flow generated by the firm in its operations. The ratios could be extended to include changes in working capital or cash flow from nonoperations activities, for example, the use of cash to repurchase the shares of the firm.

The reader is cautioned that the terms "working capital" and "cash flow" have been used differently in many diverse contexts. There is neither consistency in their usage in annual reports nor agreement in the literature as to their definitions. The usage of these terms in Table 3.4 is but one of several available to an analyst. For example, an alternative to the Table 3.4 meaning of "working capital" focuses on the difference between current assets and current liabilities. One should always determine the precise meaning of such terms when examining a specific annual report or a specific research article. See Hicks and Hunt (1981) for a collection of papers in this area.

An alternative approach to cash flow analysis is to make projections of the amounts and timing of future cash inflows and outflows; these projections can then be summarized in a budgeted cash flow statement. In some internal applications, a daily budget may be prepared. One use of such a statement is in decisions about the investment of available cash resources.

Brewing Industry Ratios. Table 3.5 presents the foregoing ratios for each brewing company. For each of these ratios, Heileman is in the middle ground, with Busch/Pabst having the highest/lowest working capital and cash flow generated for each dollar of sales or total assets. One important benefit of a higher cash flow per dollar of sales or total assets is the greater flexibility it permits a firm in its financing, investment, or operating decisions; for example, Busch and Heileman have a greater flexibility than does Pabst in decisions about the ex-

TABLE 3.5 Working Capital from Operations and
Cash Flow from Operations Ratios, 1983

	Heileman	Busch	Coors	Pabst
Working capital from operations / Sales	.076	.157	.138	.034
Working capital from operations / Total assets (average)	.195	.254	.159	.082
Cash flow from operations / Sales	.086	.156	.138	.042
Cash flow from operations / Total assets (average)	.220	.253	.158	.103

pansion or modernization of plant, the reduction of long-term debt, the repurchase of shares, or the payments of dividends.

Capital Structure

Capital structure ratios provide insight into the extent to which nonequity capital is used to finance the assets of the firm. Some representative ratios are

- $$\frac{\text{Long-term liabilities}}{\text{Shareholders' equity}}$$

- $$\frac{\text{Current liabilities + long-term liabilities}}{\text{Shareholders' equity}}$$

The higher each of these ratios, the higher the proportion of assets financed by nonshareholder parties. Which components to include in the numerator or denominator of the ratios depend on how one defines liabilities and shareholders' equity. Unfortunately, there is not general agreement in the accounting literature or in published financial reports on the precise distinction between liabilities and equity. For example, the decision to classify deferred taxes as an equity item rather than as a liability can cause marked changes in the two ratios when the dollar magnitude of this item is large (e.g., integrated oil and gas companies). Section 3.5 contains further discussion of classification issues when computing these and other financial ratios.

An important issue when computing the capital structure ratios is the treatment of obligations under leasing contracts. FASB reporting rules require that a subset of lease obligations (termed "capital leases") be reported as a liability on the balance sheet. The ratios computed in this chapter treat these capital lease obligations as a long-term liability. However, the items classified as capital leases are only a subset of those covered by lease and lease-related financing. Firms typically prefer to keep such items off the balance sheet and may structure specific financing transactions so that they do not give rise to liabilities as defined by the FASB's (SEC's, etc.) existing rules.

Brewing Industry Ratios. The two capital structure ratios for the four brewing companies are reported in Table 3.6. Deferred taxes are treated as part of shareholders' equity when computing these ratios. Both Heileman and Busch have capital structures that are between the extremes of Pabst (which relies very heavily on debt financing) and Coors (which relies only on outside financing for current liabilities). The amount of lease financing reported in the annual reports of these four companies is relatively minor.

Debt Service Coverage

Debt service coverage refers to the ability of an entity to service from its operations interest payments that are due to nonequity suppliers of capital. Two ratios useful in making inferences about coverage are

- $\dfrac{\text{Operating income}}{\text{Annual interest payments}}$

- $\dfrac{\text{Cash flow from operations}}{\text{Annual interest payments}}$

Operating income typically is calculated as revenue less cost of goods sold and marketing and general administrative expenses (and, in the case of brewing companies, less excise taxes). Annual interest payments in both financial ratios refer to the interest payments made to the nonequity suppliers of capital (irrespective of whether the borrower expenses or capitalizes those interest payments). The higher these ratios, the greater the ability to service interest payments to external parties. Debt service coverage ratios can be based on interest payments to external loan capital providers, or they can be extended to include payments to other providers of capital, for example, by including payments on leasing contracts in the denominator of the two coverage ratios.

Brewing Industry Ratios. Table 3.7 presents the foregoing two financial ratios for the four brewing companies. Given Coor's corporate policy of minimal long-term debt, computation of coverage ratios for that company provides limited insights. (Chapter 4 discusses computation and interpretation issues arising with

TABLE 3.6 Capital Structure Ratios, 1983

	Heileman	*Busch*	*Coors*	*Pabst*
Long-term liabilities / Shareholders' equity	.32	.36	.01	1.55
Current and long-term liabilities / Shareholders' equity	.78	.64	.19	3.46

TABLE 3.7 Debt Service Coverage Ratios, 1983

	Heileman	*Busch*	*Coors*	*Pabst*
Operating income / Annual interest payments	7.49	6.29	85.92	1.38
Cash flow from operations / Annual interest payments	7.87	9.35	95.44	3.39

financial ratios when the denominator approaches zero.) Both Heileman and Busch evidence much greater ability to service their interest payments on long-term debt than does Pabst.

Profitability

Profitability refers to the ability of a firm to generate revenues in excess of expenses. When making comparisons across firms (or over time), it is useful to control for differences in their resource base. The following three ratios illustrate alternative ways of expressing relative profitability.

- $$\frac{\text{Net income}}{\text{Revenues}}$$

- $$\frac{\text{Net income}}{\text{Shareholders' equity (average)}}$$

- $$\frac{\text{Net income}}{\text{Total assets (average)}}$$

The net income-to-revenue ratio indicates how much net income is earned from each dollar of revenue. The net income to shareholders' equity ratio (sometimes shortened to return on equity ratio) measures the efficiency with which common shareholders' equity is being employed within the firm. The net income-to-total assets ratio measures the efficiency with which total assets are employed within the firm. The higher each of these ratios, the more profitable the firm in a relative sense. The numerator of the ratios is usually net income available to common shareholders (i.e., after preferred dividend payments). In some cases, interest payments (net of tax benefit) are added back to net income in the net income-to-total assets ratio to control better for capital structure differences across firms or over time. As with the capital structure ratios, the net income-to-shareholders' equity ratio requires one to define debt and equity, for example, when deciding whether to include or exclude deferred tax from the denominator.

Brewing Industry Ratios. Table 3.8 presents the ratios for the four brewing companies. Coors earns the highest net income from each revenue dollar, followed by Busch, Heileman, and Pabst. Using the net income-to-shareholders' equity

TABLE 3.8 Profitability Ratios, 1983

	Heileman	Busch	Coors	Pabst
Net income / Revenues	.043	.052	.071	.004
Net income / Shareholders' equity (average)	.215	.161	.097	.025
Net income / Total assets (average)	.110	.085	.083	.011

(ROE) ratio and the net income-to-total assets (ROA) ratio, Heileman is the most profitable, followed by Busch, Coors, and Pabst. Deferred taxes are included in the denominator when computing the ROE ratio.

The ratios reported in Table 3.8 reflect historical cost accounting-induced differences as well as financing-investment-operating differences across the four companies. Using the current cost disclosures mandated by *FASB Statement No. 33*, one can calculate the effect of restating (1) inventory, (2) cost of goods sold, (3) plant and equipment, and (4) depreciation for differences between current cost and historical cost. To illustrate, compare the 1983 net income-to-shareholders' equity ratio under historical cost and current cost valuation measures:

Net Income to Shareholders' Equity

	Heileman	Busch	Coors	Pabst
Historical cost	.215	.161	.097	.0248
Current cost	.065	.085	.039	.0003

Part of Heileman's strategy since 1960 has been to expand via the acquisition of the brands and brewing plants of other companies. Many of the plants acquired are included in the primary (historical cost–based) financial statements of Heileman at amounts well below their current construction cost (even after adjusting for efficiency differences between old and new plant). The drop in Heileman's 1983 net income-to-shareholders' equity ratio from .215 (historical cost) to .065 (current cost) illustrates how reported profitability is, in part, a function of the accounting methods employed.

Turnover

Various aspects of the efficiency with which assets are utilized can be gleaned from turnover ratios as well as from several of the previously examined ratios. One such ratio is the total asset turnover ratio:

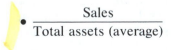

$$\frac{Sales}{Total\ assets\ (average)}$$

This ratio indicates how many times annual sales cover total assets. In examining this ratio, it is important also to examine the related net income-to-sales ratio. Firms may trade off an increase in the total asset turnover ratio for a decrease in the net income-to-sales ratio.

A second turnover ratio is the accounts receivable turnover ratio:

$$\frac{\text{Sales}}{\text{Accounts receivable (average)}}$$

As accounts receivable pertain only to credit sales, it is often recommended that the numerator include only credit sales. In many cases, however, total sales are used due to a breakdown of cash and credit sales not being provided in published annual reports. By dividing 365 by the accounts receivable turnover ratio, one obtains an estimate of the average collection period of credit sales.

A third turnover ratio is the inventory turnover ratio:

$$\frac{\text{Cost of goods sold}}{\text{Inventory (average)}}$$

The magnitude of this ratio can be affected markedly by inventory valuation rules. For instance, for firms experiencing increasing raw material prices and increasing inventory levels, the use of LIFO typically will result in higher inventory turnover ratios vis-à-vis the ratios computed with the FIFO valuation method.

Brewing Industry Ratios.   The foregoing three ratios for the four brewing companies are reported in Table 3.9. For both the accounts receivable and inventory turnover ratios, Heileman is between the industry extremes; for example, its inventory turnover ratio of 8.97 lies between those for Busch (13.56) and Coors (7.27). The reasons an analyst should consider in explaining these differences across firms include (1) more efficient inventory policies, (2) a shorter production cycle for beer requiring a lower work-in-process inventory, (3) nonbeer activities of each firm having different inventory holding patterns, and (4) differential accounting valuation methods for inventory. To illustrate possibility 4, the supple-

TABLE 3.9   Turnover Ratios, 1983

	Heileman	*Busch*	*Coors*	*Pabst*
$\dfrac{\text{Sales}}{\text{Total assets (average)}}$	2.57	1.62	1.15	2.45
$\dfrac{\text{Sales}}{\text{Accounts receivable (average)}}$	39.17	25.26	18.01	35.28
$\dfrac{\text{Cost of goods sold}}{\text{Inventory (average)}}$	8.97	13.56	7.27	8.54

mental current cost disclosures (from *FASB Statement No. 33*) can be used:

	Heileman	*Busch*	*Coors*	*Pabst*
	LIFO 49%	LIFO 75%	LIFO 100%	Moving
	FIFO 51%	FIFO 25%		average
Historical cost	8.97	13.56	7.27	8.54
Current cost	8.26	10.28	4.88	8.54

The decline in turnover, when inventory is valued at current cost, is most marked for the two companies using LIFO as the primary valuation method (i.e., Busch and Coors). Pabst reports the same inventory figure for both historical cost and current cost, and hence both show the same inventory turnover ratio.

3.3 TIME-SERIES TECHNIQUES

This section illustrates the use of trend statements and financial ratios to gain insight into a firm's performance over time.

A. Trend Statements

Constructing trend statements involves choosing one year as a base and then expressing the statement items of subsequent years relative to their value in the base year. As a convention, the base year is given a value of 100. Consider the sales item in successive income statements of Heileman (in millions of dollars):

1980	*1981*	*1982*	*1983*
$840.784	$931.940	$1,000.567	$1,325.632

Choosing 1980 as the base year, the 1981 sales item in the trend statement becomes 110.8: ($931.940/$840.784) × 100.

Trend statements for selected items in the income statements of Heileman over the 1980–1983 period are presented in Table 3.10. Also presented in trend statement format is the number of barrels of beer sold each year by Heileman. One feature apparent from Table 3.10 is that marketing, general, and administrative expenses have increased at a faster rate than have both sales and cost of goods sold. Total beer sold by all companies in the 1980–1983 period has been relatively constant (flat?); total U.S. consumption in barrels increased less than 4% in this period (see Table 3.13). Increased marketing is one means that Heileman has used to increase its market share. A second feature apparent from Table 3.10 is that dollar value of beer-related sales has increased 62.8% over the 1980–1983 period, whereas the number of barrels of beer sold has increased only 32.2%. By

TABLE 3.10 Trend Statement of Selected
Items of Heileman, 1980–1983

	1980	1981	1982	1983
Total $ sales	100	110.8	119.0	157.7
Beer-related $ sales	100	111.3	119.8	162.8
Cost of goods sold	100	111.9	118.4	155.9
Marketing, general, and				
administrative expenses	100	112.5	130.7	176.1
Net income	100	116.0	131.6	164.3
Barrels of beer sold	100	105.2	109.4	132.2

dividing the dollar amount of beer sales each year by the barrels of beer sold, the price received per barrel can be calculated:

1980	1981	1982	1983
$56.01	$59.24	$61.32	$68.95

Thus, over the 1980–1983 period, the two main factors underlying Heileman's sales increase has been a 23% increase in price per barrel and a 32% increase in barrels of beer sold.

Factoring out the dollar sales series into price and quantity components can be especially insightful in industries where marked changes in price or quantity can occur over relatively short time periods; for example, variations in the dollar sales series of gold, silver, and copper companies are often highly correlated with changes in the world prices for these metals.

B. Financial Ratio Analysis

Analysis of time-series trends in financial ratios is another technique used in financial statement analysis. In some cases, this analysis is relatively heuristic; for example, an analyst may attempt to extrapolate a general trend based on (say) the current ratio over the past four years. In other cases, a more systematic analysis is made of the past sequence of the series. Chapter 7 discusses quantitative models that can be used in the time-series analysis of accounting numbers.

Table 3.11 presents selected financial ratios of Heileman over the 1980–1983 period. Several of these ratios reflect the acquisition by Heileman in December 1982 of a 68% interest in Pabst Brewing Company and a related March 1983 transaction in which Heileman traded its 68% interest for three Pabst brewing plants and six brands. (This transaction was motivated by antitrust considerations.) To finance the acquisition of the Pabst shares, Heileman increased its long-term debt from $53.795 million in 1981 to $170.530 million in 1982. During 1983, it reduced its year-end long-term debt to $95.719 million. The increase in the long-term liabilities-to-shareholders' equity ratio in 1982 and the decrease in the 1983

TABLE 3.11 Selected Financial Ratios of Heileman, 1980–1983

	1980	*1981*	*1982*	*1983*
Cash and marketable securities / Total assets	.11	.14	.06	.04
Current assets / Current liabilities	1.38	1.83	1.68	1.30
Working capital from operations / Sales	.069	.075	.080	.076
Long-term liabilities / Shareholders' equity	.30	.30	.73	.32
Operating income / Annual interest payments	13.38	14.35	13.87	7.49
Net income / Shareholders' equity (average)	.257	.236	.216	.215
Sales / Accounts receivable (average)	33.97	41.10	37.70	39.17
Cost of goods sold / Inventory (average)	8.25	8.53	9.03	8.97

operating income-to-interest payments ratio are influenced by these transactions. (An alternative data presentation to Table 3.11 uses a trend statement format with the 1980 value of each ratio reset at 100.)

C. Variability Measures

An approach that is gaining popularity in the literature is to compute variability measures for financial ratios and other variables over time. One object is to expand beyond one fiscal year the information contained in a single ratio measure. For example,

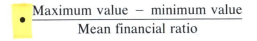

$$\frac{\text{Maximum value} - \text{minimum value}}{\text{Mean financial ratio}}$$

Table 3.12 presents this measure for the net income-to-revenue ratio of the four brewing companies over the 1974–1983 period. Heileman has the lowest variability in its net income-to-revenue ratio while Pabst has the highest variability.

TABLE 3.12 Net Income-to-Revenue Ratio, 1974–1983

Year	Heileman	Busch	Coors	Pabst
1974	.026	.035	.070	.033
1975	.027	.041	.094	.031
1976	.044	.031	.105	.043
1977	.045	.041	.094	.030
1978	.046	.041	.072	.015
1979	.041	.060	.078	.012
1980	.041	.045	.063	.015
1981	.043	.049	.048	(.029)
1982	.045	.055	.038	.004
1983	.043	.052	.071	.004
$\dfrac{\text{Max} - \text{Min}}{\text{Mean}}$	.50	.64	.92	4.50

3.4 COMBINING FINANCIAL STATEMENT AND NONFINANCIAL STATEMENT INFORMATION

Financial statements are only a subset of the information an analyst can examine. This section illustrates how information from the product and the capital markets can be combined with financial statement data.

A. Product Market Information

An analysis of product market information provides insight into market share shifts. Table 3.13 presents market share statistics (based on barrels sold) for the six major U.S. brewing companies and total consumption over the 1980–1983

TABLE 3.13 Market Share and Consumption Data for U.S. Brewing Industry, 1980–1983

Company	1980	1981	1982	1983
Busch	28.2%	30.0%	32.4%	32.9%
Miller	21.1	22.2	21.5	20.4
Stroh/Schlitz	13.9	12.9	12.6	13.2
Heileman	7.5	7.7	7.9	9.5
Coors	7.8	7.3	6.5	7.5
Pabst	8.5	7.4	6.7	7.0
Other companies	13.0	12.5	12.4	9.5
	100.0%	100.0%	100.0%	100.0%
Total consumption (millions of barrels)	177.9	181.9	182.4	183.8

SOURCE: Weingarten of Goldman, Sachs & Co. [1984], p. 6.

period. In this period of relatively constant total consumption, Busch has increased from 28.2% to 32.9% share of the market while Heileman has increased from 7.5% to 9.5% share of the market. The other four major brewing companies have each decreased in market share over the 1980–1983 period as has the share held by other companies (e.g., Falstaff Brewing, Genesee Brewing, and Pittsburgh Brewing).

Another use of barrelage information is expressing the operating profits on a per-barrel basis. For companies with nonbrewing activities, operating profit information from line-of-business disclosures in annual reports rather than from the consolidated income statement is appropriate for this computation:

1983 Operating Profit per Barrel			
Heileman	*Busch*	*Coors*	*Pabst*
$5.93	$10.74	$10.84	$1.07

These figures document the sizable differences across brewing companies in their relative operating profits. (Further discussion of factors to be considered in using line-of-business information can be found in Chapter 6.)

In other industries, product market information also can be important in the financial analysis of corporations. For example, the room occupancy rate is the key variable in the lodging industry. A similar statistic in the airline industry is the load factor (percentage of available seats occupied). Given the sizable fixed costs in both these industries, increases in occupancy rates/load factors above break-even points can result in large percentage increases in net income.

B. Capital Market Information

Capital markets access a broad set of information. By examining changes over time in market capitalization (market price per equity share × number of common shares outstanding), insight can be gained about changes in the consensus expectation of the relationship between future and current profitability. The price-to-earnings (PE) ratio is a frequently used figure in this analysis:

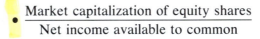

$$\bullet \quad \frac{\text{Market capitalization of equity shares}}{\text{Net income available to common}}$$

Other things being equal, the higher the price-to-earnings ratio, the higher the expected future income relative to the current reported income. Table 3.14 presents price-to-earnings ratios for the four brewing companies over the 1980 to 1983 period; the market price per share as of December 31 for each year is used as the numerator. Chapter 12 discusses two alternative scenarios for companies with high price-to-earnings ratios in a single year (such as Pabst's 1982 ratio of 63.83): (1) current reported income is temporarily depressed, or (2) growth in the future income series over several subsequent years is expected. (PE ratios are

TABLE 3.14 Capital Market Information, 1980–1983

Company	1980	1981	1982	1983
A. Price-to-earnings ratio				
Heileman	8.39	7.97	11.52	13.86
Busch	7.30	8.60	10.84	8.68
Coors	8.59	7.07	10.68	7.94
Pabst	9.65	(5.39)	63.83	12.81
B. Dividend payout				
Heileman	.22	.23	.23	.21
Busch	.26	.24	.23	.31
Coors	.15	.20	.26	.14
Pabst	.26	(.14)	1.22	.00

sometimes computed as EP ratios, one motivation being that the EP format is less likely to have extreme values due to the denominator approaching zero.)

A second capital market variable frequently discussed in the literature is the dividend payout ratio:

$$\bullet \quad \frac{\text{Dividends paid}}{\text{Net income}}$$

Table 3.14 also presents this information for the four brewing companies over the 1980–1983 period. It is difficult to make unequivocal inferences from the magnitude of the dividend payout. Diverse reasons for a low dividend payout include (1) management expects to encounter substantial cash flow problems from existing operations, or (2) management perceives it has future investment prospects that earn greater than the cost of capital, or (3) the firm has attracted a clientele of investors preferring minimal dividend income (e.g., due to taxation motivations).

3.5 SOME GENERAL COMMENTS

1. An important trend in financial reporting is an increase in the amount of information included in annual reports but not incorporated in the primary financial statements. In part, this increase is due to regulatory mandates. For example,

- Constant-dollar and current-cost information is provided as a supplement to the historical cost/GAAP numbers by many firms in order to comply with *FASB Statement No. 33*
- Estimates of the value of proved oil and gas reserves is provided as supplementary information by oil and gas companies in order to comply with *SEC Accounting Series Release No. 253*.

There is also an increasing amount of information disclosed in the footnotes to financial statements, for example, employee pension plans, lease commitments, and revolving credit agreements. There is considerable diversity across firms in the format and detail of these disclosures. Computer data bases, such as Compustat and Value Line, include only a subset of supplemental disclosures made by firms in their annual or interim reports. One consequence is that analysts who do not use the actual annual and interim reports may exclude information potentially important to their decisions.

2. Many classification and definitional issues need to be addressed when computing financial ratios. These issues are especially difficult when computing debt-to-equity ratios. Even when a firm has only one class of equity and one class of long-term debt, the classification of deferred taxes arises. Note that different users can adopt different classifications. For example, a bank loan officer may classify deferred taxes as part of debt, whereas an investor may classify deferred tax as part of equity.

The growing complexity of so-called hybrid securities has increased the gray areas that arise when computing debt-to-equity ratios. Urbancic (1980) illustrates the effect that different classification rules for redeemable preferred stock has on debt-to-equity ratios of 30 companies issuing such stocks. The average increase in the total liabilities-to-shareholders' equity ratio was 23.4% when preferred stock was included as a liability rather than as an equity.

3. Another factor increasing gray areas when computing debt-to-equity ratios is the growing diversity of off-balance-sheet financing methods, for example, captive and project financing arrangements, throughput arrangements, take-or-pay contracts, and limited partnerships; see Landsittel and Stewart (1983). Greene (1980) describes this trend: "The basic drives of man are few: to get enough food, to find shelter and to keep debt off the balance sheet" (p. 59). The level of disclosure about these forms of financing is highly variable. External analysts often will have to employ very heuristic adjustments when estimating the debt-to-equity ratios of companies making extensive use of off-balance-sheet financing. In some cases, external analysts exclude many of these off-balance-sheet items from their computations. This exclusion could be due to (a) a conscious decision that they are not debt in the same sense as (say) a long-term bank loan, (b) data non-availability, or (c) oversight ("out of sight, out of mind").

The motivations for off-balance-sheet financing need not be the same across each specific form of such financing. For example, there may be risk sharing and taxation motivations for using limited partnerships while project financing arrangements might lower the cost of loan borrowing. A commonly alleged motivation is to avoid the appearance of a "lower-quality balance sheet." The suggested rationales include (a) the avoidance of analysts making unfavorable relative comparisons when major competitors make extensive use of off-balance-sheet financing and (b) the avoidance of credit rating agencies downgrading the company's credit rating. At present, the literature is long on anecdotes (e.g., as to the extreme lengths to which management will go to avoid transactions qualifying as "debt") and short on detailed research analysis.

Firms that rate debt securities report that they go to considerable lengths to incorporate off-balance-sheet items into their rating decisions. For example, Standard & Poor's (1983) reports the following:

Off-balance-sheet items that are factored into the leverage analysis include:
—Operating leases
—Pension obligations
—Debts of joint ventures and unconsolidated subsidiaries
—Guarantees
—Take-or-pay contracts and obligations under throughput and deficiency agreements
—Receivables that have been factored or transferred.

S & P uses various methodologies to determine the proper capitalized value for each of the off-balance-sheet items. In general, the relevance of the activity financed to the mainstream business of the organization and the likelihood of its need for financial support are key considerations. Thus, debt of joint ventures which are sound, stand-alone credits may be viewed as a much less onerous liability than capitalized operating rents. (p. 22)

Rating agencies can request confidential information from firms and thus can be in a better position than many external analysts in incorporating off-balance-sheet items into their decisions.

4. Financial ratios are frequently referred to in published annual reports. Gibson (1982b) made a study of the annual reports of 100 U.S. companies in the *Fortune* 500 listing of industrial firms. Using the financial ratio categories of liquidity, debt, and profitability, he reported that the following ratios were most frequently cited. (Reprinted with permission of the *CPA Journal,* Copyright 1982, New York State Society of Certified Public Accountants.)

	Frequency of Appearance
Liquidity	
Current ratio	47
Debt ratios	
Debt to capital	23
Debt to equity	19
Profitability	
Return on equity	62
Profit margin	58
Return on capital	21

Gibson reported consistency in the way companies computed the current ratio but inconsistency in the other ratios cited. For instance, the profit margin ratio was computed in eight separate ways, the two most frequent being net income-to-sales (40 mentions) and income from continuing operations-to-sales (6 mentions).

Williamson (1984) examined whether financial ratios cited by firms in their annual reports were more favorable than are those of firms not citing them. Using a sample of 141 *Fortune* 500 companies, the ratios cited by each company were noted. Focusing on 11 of these ratios, Williamson found that for eight, the citing and nonciting firms had values that statistically were not significantly different. For the three with significant differences (return on equity, current ratio, and return on sales), firms citing them had higher values than those not citing them in their annual reports. The conclusion was that "selective reporting by *Fortune* 500 companies does occur for some ratios" (p. 298). In a related study of 25 annual reports, Frishkoff (1981) concluded that "if a ratio was 'good' or had 'shown improvement,' reference at least in the CEO letter was far more likely" (p. 46). This evidence about selective reporting by firms is far from overwhelming. However, it underscores the necessity for users of annual reports to be ever alert to the possibility that the "vested self-interest" of management can affect either the content or the timing of financial disclosures made to external parties.

5. Several questionnaire-based studies have examined the relative importance managerial respondents give to individual financial ratios and/or variables. A representative study is Walsh (1984), where "the primary purpose was to learn the preferences of a representative group of chief executive officers and other senior executives concerning the ratios and other financial indicators that they use regularly for various types of decision making" (p. 3). Questionnaires were sent to the CEOs of 500 of the *Fortune* 1000 industrial companies and 50 firms in service industries. A total of 101 usable survey responses was received. Respondents were asked to note the "decision-making activities" in which individual ratios were used. These activities were grouped into the following categories:

- Planning, budgeting, and goal setting (PBGS)
- Evaluating investment proposal (EIP)
- Appraising performance of managers and units (APMU)
- Awarding incentive compensation (AIC)
- Other

Table 3.15 summarizes a subset of the responses. Ratios relating to return on investment were the most frequently mentioned by the respondents. Executives were also asked to rank individual ratios and/or variables in terms of overall importance in their decisions. Walsh (1984) concluded that based on "the number of times that each indicator was ranked first in importance, return on investment and absolute net earnings receive the most such mentions" (p. 11). Gibson (1982a) also used a questionnaire approach when surveying the opinions of the controllers of companies listed in *Fortune*'s 500 largest firms. The conclusion was that "financial officers rated profitability ratios as the most significant" (p. 19).

Due to the many methodological problems associated with questionnaire-based research, considerable care needs to be taken when drawing inferences from these and similar studies. A specific limitation is that neither questionnaire elicited responses about how financial ratios are used in specific management decisions. Both studies, however, do highlight that internal management is an

TABLE 3.15 Financial Ratios and Their Application in Managerial Decision-Making Situations: Number of Individual Ratio Mentions by Respondents

Category of Ratio/Variable	PBGS	EIP	APMU	AIC	Other	Total
1. Return on investment (6 ratios)	154	128	84	81	2	449
2. Absolute net earnings (1)	81	64	74	69	2	290
3. Debt ratios (2)	140	80	5	2	4	231
4. Inventory turnover (1)	71	26	76	31	0	204
5. Net profit margin (1)	70	44	57	29	0	200
6. Accounts receivable turnover (1)	61	21	67	25	2	176
7. Earnings per share (1)	64	29	14	38	1	146
8. Liquidity ratios	88	29	11	1	8	137

PBGS – Planning, budgeting, and goal setting.
EIP – Evaluating investment proposals.
APMU – Appraising performance of managers and units.
AIC – Awarding incentive compensation.
SOURCE: Walsh (1984, Table 3): pp. 8–9.

important user of financial statement information. To date, the published literature on financial statement analysis has focused largely on external users and has given inadequate attention to managerial users.

6. Cash flow-related variables are the subject of much interest to management and to external parties. Many studies have approximated cash flow from operations as "net income plus depreciation and amortization" or "net income plus depreciation and amortization plus deferred tax." An appealing feature of these approximations is their simplicity. A drawback is that they exclude many items that can affect cash flow. Increasing attention is now being given in business practice and in the published literature to developing more refined measures of cash flow. Table 3.4 has outlined a set of adjustments that Gombola and Ketz (1983) use to estimate cash flow from operations. Bowen, Burgstahler, and Daley (1984) report results on the distribution of the coefficient of determination (R^2) between the changes (Δ) in pairs of the following variables for a sample of 324 Compustat firms:

- Net income before extraordinary items (NIBEI)
- Net income before extraordinary items plus depreciation (NIDPR)
- Net cash flow (NCF) as calculated by a set of adjustments similar to those outlined in Table 3.4

A separate regression between changes in pairs of the three variables was run for each firm over the 1971–1981 period. The mean and median R^2 of these regressions across the sample of firms were

	Mean R^2	Median R^2
ΔNIBEI and ΔNIDPR	.98	.94
ΔNIBEI and ΔNCF	.13	.20
ΔNIDPR and ΔNCF	.15	.21

The conclusion was that adding back depreciation and amortization to net income to approximate "cash flow" yields a series highly correlated with the original net income series. However, when more refined adjustments to derive a cash flow measure are made, the resultant series is much less correlated with the original net income series. The evidence is consistent with these more refined net cash flow measures capturing a different aspect of a firm's financial attributes than would a profitability measure such as net income.

3.6 SUMMARY

1. This chapter outlined several techniques used in the analysis of financial statement information, for example, common-size statements, financial ratios, and trend statements. These techniques are best viewed as data reduction devices. Subsequent chapters present a more detailed examination of the properties of financial statement information, for example, evidence on the distribution of financial ratios (Chapter 4), the effect of using alternative accounting methods (Chapter 5), industry differences in financial ratios (Chapter 6), and issues in modeling the time-series behavior of financial variables (Chapter 7).

2. Users of financial statements should recognize that management can affect the timeliness of the information provided or its representativeness of the underlying information set. For instance, management may have a bias to present that subset of information that shows its performance in the best possible light. Similarly, firms may provide minimal information about their off-balance-sheet financing in an attempt to have external parties underestimate the underlying financial risk exposure of the firm. As discussed in Chapters 1 and 2, users of financial statements often can access competing information sources to supplement (and validate) information provided by management.

APPENDIX 3.A   CONSIDERATIONS IN USING COMPUTERIZED FINANCIAL STATEMENT DATA BASES

Users of financial statement information often have the option of accessing standardized computer data bases that contain a large number of items for a broad cross section of firms; for example, the Compustat service of Standard & Poor's includes over 100 annual financial statement items each year for over 2,500 U.S. firms. Much of the research discussed in this book has utilized Compustat or similar data bases rather than accessing the annual and interim reports of individual companies. Similar services are available in other countries, for example, the Australian Graduate School of Management file for Australian companies and the MicroEXSTAT file for European and Australian companies. A major benefit of these computer data bases is the saving in time and other resources when conducting a study. Many years of observations from large numbers of firms are readily available to an analyst. These benefits, however, do not come cost free. This appendix describes some potential limitations of using computer data bases without an accompanying analysis of the underlying annual or interim reports. The focus is on those data bases that extract information from annual or interim reports rather than provide a full on-line presentation of the report. Gale (1982) discusses the latter.

Data Base May Exclude Currently Surviving Firms

Many computer data bases are developed by commercial organizations whose decisions about the inclusion/exclusion of companies are based on marketing considerations. Large publicly held corporations that are actively traded typically are the highest priority for inclusion in data bases that are to be sold to security analysts and other members of the investment community. Firms that may be excluded include those (1) small in size, (2) not actively traded, or (3) privately held.

In any single project, an analyst should be aware of the choice criterion underlying selection of the firms in the computerized data base being used. Where firms excluded from that data base are important to the inferences drawn from a study, resources should be devoted to including a sample of the excluded firms.

Data Base May Exclude Nonsurviving Firms

Several data bases delete firms when they have been acquired by other firms, have entered bankruptcy, or have gone private. In some projects, these firms can be important; for example, a study of industry profitability over a ten-year period would overstate actual profitability if it excluded firms that went bankrupt over this period. The Compustat annual industrial tape includes only current publicly held firms. (However, Standard & Poor's does market a data base called the "research file" that contains histories of companies that have been dropped from the files in the post-1970 period.) Whether data bases having a survivorship criterion are "biased" (as opposed to being just incomplete) is an empirical issue. For example, security return data files based on surviving firms will omit merged firms (which may have sizeable *increases* in security returns at the time of the merger) as well as bankrupt firms (which may have sizable *decreases* in security returns at the time of the bankruptcy); see McElreath and Wiggins (1984) for evidence on the number of firms in these two and other categories.

Data Base May Not Contain Most Recent Data

In some data bases, time lags exist between the publication of data by a firm and (1) its provision to the organization developing the summary data base, or

(2) the inclusion of the data in the summary data base, or (3) its provision to clients. The result is that the data base will not contain the most recent data for each firm. Note that the increasing availability of on-line data bases is reducing delays due to restriction 3.

Data Base May Exclude Items for Firms Included

The available standardized computer data bases typically include only a subset of the information in a firm's annual report, its interim report, or its other disclosures. Items that are more likely to be excluded are those for which there are only a subset of firms disclosing (e.g., earnings forecasts included in an annual report) or for which the presentation of a standardized format is difficult (e.g., details of bond covenant restrictions).

A related problem occurs when data bases have a single coding category that is insufficient to capture the information in the underlying annual or interim report. Consider a coding for the inventory valuation method (e.g., FIFO = 1, LIFO = 2, average cost = 3, etc.) of the following three firms: Firm A (100% LIFO), Firm B (51% LIFO, 49% FIFO), and Firm C (34% LIFO, 33% FIFO, 33% average cost). All three would be coded in the data bases as LIFO inventory firms. The inventory coding in most data bases typically is for only the major inventory method. Inevitably there will be a loss of information when firms with multiple inventory methods are given a single coding.

Data Base May Classify Financial Statement Items Inconsistently Across Firms

This limitation can arise from several sources. One source is that not all firms adopt a consistent set of financial statement categories in their annual or interim reports; for example, Firm A reports cash separately from marketable securities while Firm B reports cash and marketable securities as one item. Individuals constructing data bases typically will have a standard set of rules for treating these problems; for example, they will include Firm B's marketable securities in the cash category with 0 reported for its marketable securities category.

A second source of inconsistency arises from differences across firms in the classification of items. For example, Firm A includes overhead expenses in the "cost of goods sold" category while Firm B includes overhead in its "marketing, general, and administrative expense" category. Often there will be insufficient information for an outside party to place A and B on a uniform treatment of overhead expenses.

Data Base May Contain Recording Errors

Recording errors are inevitable in the construction of any large financial statement data base, for example, due to numbers being entered incorrectly or being entered in the wrong category. Techniques that can be used to locate such errors include

1. Checking if accounting definitions are satisfied. For example,

   Assets = Liabilities + equities

   Cost of goods sold = Opening inventory + purchases − closing inventory

   One benefit of separately collecting aggregate numbers such as total assets and total revenues in a data base, in addition to the individual components of those aggregates, is their use in locating recording errors in either the components or the aggregate numbers.

2. Checking if known relationships between financial ratios are satisfied. For example, if the quick ratio > the current ratio, or the long-term debt-to-equity ratio > the total debt-to-equity ratio, the possibility of recording errors should be investigated.

3. Checking data plots or printouts visually to locate any outliers followed by an investigation into the cause(s) of each outlier. Suppose that a printout of total revenues (in millions of dollars) showed

1980	1981	1982	1983
$100.67	$110.84	$12.641	$141.26

   One explanation for the 1982 figure is a misplaced decimal point with the actual revenue number being $126.41 million. (Other explanations also exist, for example, a strike.)

4. Merging two independently collected data bases and examining instances where both data bases do not report identical numbers for the same items. Given that many recording errors arise from random lapses in the attention span of individuals, it is highly unlikely that two separate data bases will contain the same recording errors.

5. Sampling a subset of the items in the data base and comparing them with the numbers in the annual or interim reports. This approach is especially useful for items the analyst expects will not readily fit into a standardized format.

Studies that examine errors and classification problems in some widely used financial statement data bases include San Miguel (1977), Vasarhelyi and Yang (1983), and Stone and Bublitz (1984). Related research on security-return data bases includes Beedles and Simkowitz (1978), Rosenberg and Houglet (1974), and Bennin (1980).

QUESTIONS

QUESTION 3.1: Accounting Data and Public Policy Debate:
Alternative Profitability Measures for Land Developers

Accounting data frequently are used in debates in the public arena. Consider the following debate on Canadian land development companies in *The Calgary Herald*. The first article was titled "Building Goliaths' Pre-tax Returns Averaged 35 Cents to the Dollar":

> The biggest players in Calgary's land development and housing game rank among the 10 largest real estate corporations in Canada. And three of the four busiest developers here—locally based Nu-West Development Corporation, Carma Developers Ltd., and Vancouver-based Daon Development Corporation—can credit their impressive assets to profits turned here (in Calgary).
>
> According to a federal-provincial study on Canada's real estate price boom, released by Toronto lawyer David Greenspan last fall, rapid price increases across the country between 19X4 and 19X7 gave the country's largest developers huge profits—an average pre-tax return of 35 cents on every dollar invested by shareholders.
>
> In 19X1, when Nu-West became a public company, its land holdings totalled 760 acres, all in Calgary, and its assets were worth $18.6 million. Now it has more than 26,000 acres in four Canadian provinces and four of the "sun belt" states—and has assets worth $732.5 million. Total revenues for the company have jumped from $18 million in 19X1 to $4 billion last year (19X10)—an average increase of 40 percent a year.[1]

A subsequent issue of *The Calgary Herald* included the following "Letter to the Editor" from the president (Ralph Scurfield) of Nu-West Development Corporation:

> Congratulations on *The Herald's* excellent series about housing in Calgary. A better understanding of the factors affecting the housing industry should allow our community to make better decisions—decisions that hopefully will allow us to manage Calgary's explosive growth more effectively and efficiently.
>
> I believe Calgarians have generally been well and efficiently served by the building and development industry. We all know that business must have profits to survive. Our shareholders, investors, bankers and creditors won't allow us to stay in business unless we do. *The Herald's* article states in a headline that ". . . pre-tax returns average 35 cents to the dollar." Fortunately, it is explained later in the article that this refers to return on shareholders' investment, not return on sales dollar.
>
> The return on shareholders' investment analysis is only one test of the industry, and one that falls far short of telling the whole story. The development industry operates with very large pools of borrowed funds which result in significantly increased risk to the investor. At the same time, he should be able to earn on his investment. Certainly one wouldn't expect to invest funds in development to earn a maximum 10 percent return when money can be invested virtually risk-free in a government bond

[1] *The Calgary Herald* (July 31, 1979).

TABLE 3.16   Nu-West Development Corporation, Fiscal Years December 31, 19X6–19X10 (consolidated figures as reported in $ millions)

	19X6	*19X7*	*19X8*	*19X9*	*19X10*
1. Total revenues	97	143	216	319	408
2. Cost of revenue and operating expenses	82	116	182	272	350
3. Interest	3.6	5.1	10.8	18.8	26.3
4. Depreciation	.4	.5	1.1	1.7	2.0
5. Amortization	.1	.2	.3	.4	.5
6. Income from operations	12.3	21.3	21.2	25.9	28.8
7. Income taxes	6.4	10.7	10.1	13.4	13.5
8. Net income before the undernoted	5.9	10.6	11.1	12.4	15.1
9. Dividends from marketable securities	—	—	—	.9	1.8
10. Equity in net income of affiliates[1]	1.7	3.3	5.2	6.2	9.9
11. Minority interest	—	—	—	—	.3
12. Net income	7.6	14	16.3	19.4	27.1
13. Total assets	139	187	365	483	733
14. Shareholders' equity	24	37	51	75	109
15. Long-term debt	39	59	158	221	333

[1] Full-line description is "Equity in net income, after income taxes, of Carma Land Developers Ltd. and other affiliates." The book value of Nu-West's investment in Carma Developers in 19X10 was $30 million (market value of the investment was $54 million). Nu-West's equity in the revenues of its affiliates is not included in the above "total revenue" figures. Including this item would result in "combined revenues" of 19X6—$109 million, 19X7—$164 million, 19X8—$247 million, 19X9—$360 million, 19X10—$467 million.

or a bank account at approximately that same rate. To attract money to a risk business, somewhat higher potential returns on investment are required.

Because of the highly leveraged nature of the development business, more appropriate tests for examining the performance of the development industry are return on assets and margin on operations. Nu-West Development Corporation Ltd., which employed average assets of $608,000,000 during 19X10, earned an after-tax return of 6.8 percent on those investments. On Nu-West's 19X10 sales of $408,000,000, it earned a net margin of 3.7 per cent, or less than 4 cents profit for every dollar of sales. Our 19X10 earnings expressed as a percentage of sales were almost identical to the average over the past 10 years, and perhaps slightly better than that of the competitive building and development industry as a whole.

Clearly, a 4 percent profit on the sale of a product that often represents years from the initiation of land acquisition to completion of the final home is not excessive, and obviously total elimination of our profit from land development and home sales would have little impact on housing prices. Profits are not the cause of high prices; your recent series of articles touches on several other factors that probably are.

In closing, I would like to point out that regretfully our total revenues for 19X10 did not reach the $4 billion noted in the fourth of your articles; the correct number is $408,000,000. We hope that some day we will be able to report multi-billion dollar sales.[2]

Table 3.16 presents financial data for Nu-West over the 19X6 to 19X10 period.

[2] *The Calgary Herald* (August 8, 1979).

REQUIRED

1. The letter from Scurfield refers to the following profitability measures:
   a. Net income to revenues
   b. Net income to average shareholders' equity
   c. Net income to average total assets

   Compute these ratios for Nu-West over the 19X7–19X10 period.

2. In reporting Nu-West's 19X10 net margin on revenues of 3.7%, Scurfield used the $15.1 million figure for the numerator (item 8 in Table 3.16). What arguments could be advanced for using this figure rather than the 19X10 net income figure of $27.1 million?

3. Do you agree with Scurfield that "because of the highly leveraged nature of the development business, more appropriate tests for examining the performance of the development industry are return on assets and margin on operations"? Give reasons.

4. The Greenspan report referred to by *The Calgary Herald* used pretax profits. In his letter, Scurfield used after-tax profits. What are the pros and cons of using either measure when examining profitability?

5. What consequences might ensue if politicians decide that Nu-West and other land developers are earning excessive profits?

QUESTION 3.2: Financial Statement Analysis of General Foods and General Mills

General Foods and General Mills are two large consumer food companies. Table 3.17 summarizes information from their successive annual reports over the 19X1–19X5 period; these data are "as reported" for each year. General Foods classifies its lines of business in 19X5 as packaged grocery products (44% of sales), grocery coffee (27%), processed meats (18%), and food service and other (11%). General Mills classifies its lines of business in 19X5 as consumer foods (49% of sales),

TABLE 3.17 Financial Data of General Foods and General Mills (in millions of dollars)

	General Foods					General Mills				
	19X1	*19X2*	*19X3*	*19X4*	*19X5*	*19X1*	*19X2*	*19X3*	*19X4*	*19X5*
Assets										
1. Cash and marketable securities	$ 178	$ 309	$ 163	$ 285	$ 277	$ 39	$ 39	$ 33	$ 58	$ 66
2. Accounts receivable	669	759	900	938	906	374	391	409	468	551
3. Inventories	1,003	904	1,124	1,035	1,097	543	611	661	633	662
4. Prepaid expenses	100	46	67	56	66	30	34	156	199	112
5. Properties, plant, and equipment	931	1,004	1,394	1,546	1,615	747	921	1,054	1,198	1,229
6. Other assets	96	107	213	449	471	279	305	389	388	239
	$2,977	$3,129	$3,861	$4,309	$4,432	$2,012	$2,301	$2,702	$2,944	$2,859

TABLE 3.17   (*Continued*)

	General Foods					General Mills				
	19X1	*19X2*	*19X3*	*19X4*	*19X5*	*19X1*	*19X2*	*19X3*	*19X4*	*19X5*
Liabilities and Equity										
7. Accounts payable	$ 332	$ 380	$ 360	$ 327	$ 390	$ 325	$ 323	$ 409	$ 410	$ 478
8. Accrued (current) expenses	715	548	855	1,015	855	245	416	639	712	668
9. Long-term debt	255	391	731	736	750	378	349	332	464	363
10. Capital leases	0	0	0	0	0	0	0	0	0	0
11. Other long-term liabilities	85	81	147	163	180	20	26	43	42	49
12. Deferred taxes	110	119	142	196	217	25	42	46	89	77
13. Shareholders' equity	1,480	1,610	1,626	1,872	2,040	1,019	1,145	1,233	1,227	1,224
	$2,977	$3,129	$3,861	$4,309	$4,432	$2,012	$2,301	$2,702	$2,944	$2,859
Revenues										
14. Sales	$5,960	$6,601	$8,351	$8,256	$8,600	$4,170	$4,852	$5,312	$5,551	$5,601
15. Other revenues	52	43	60	71	86	0	0	0	0	0
Total Revenues	$6,012	$6,644	$8,411	$8,327	$8,686	$4,170	$4,852	$5,312	$5,551	$5,601
Expenses and net income										
16. Cost of goods sold (including depreciation)	$3,675	$4,006	$5,197	$5,117	$5,263	$2,660	$3,036	$3,195	$3,251	$3,299
17. Marketing, general and administrative	1,828	2,120	2,590	2,551	2,704	1,146	1,384	1,636	1,832	1,849
18. Interest expense	39	47	142	124	145	49	58	75	59	61
19. Other expense	0	0	64	0	0	0	0	0	0	0
20. Taxation, current	215	153	130	157	229	144	161	169	133	177
21. Taxation, deferred	(1)	64	67	90	27	3	17	12	32	(12)
22. Net income	$ 256	$ 254	$ 221	$ 288	$ 318	$ 168	$ 196	$ 225	$ 244	$ 227
23. Earnings per share	$5.12	$5.14	$4.47	$5.73	$6.10	$3.37	$3.90	$4.46	$4.89	$4.98
Miscellaneous										
24. Depreciation and amortization	$ 78	$ 89	$ 131	$ 133	$ 156	$ 81	$ 100	$ 113	$ 128	$ 133
25. Dividends paid	97	109	109	115	125	64	72	82	93	96
26. Market capitalization	1,299	1,631	1,656	2,100	2,427	1,390	1,744	1,990	2,830	2,290
27. Inventory, current cost	1,002	876	1,117	1,044	1,130	614	694	756	715	743
28. Properties, plant, and equipment, current cost	1,578	1,658	2,080	2,075	2,220	1,198	1,447	1,650	1,757	1,761
29. Cost of goods sold, current cost	3,853	4,054	5,296	5,178	5,344	2,698	3,083	3,266	3,314	3,335
30. Depreciation, current cost	140	157	198	200	208	112	132	151	164	167
31. Revolving credit line	524	940	546	652	499	103	190	408	406	280
Other										
32. Shares outstanding (000s)	49,962	49,421	49,432	51,862	52,046	49,870	50,357	49,897	49,870	45,802
33. Consumer price index	100	112	122	128	132	100	112	122	128	132

restaurants (19%), toys (14%), fashion (10%), and specialty retailing and other (8%).

Extracts from Annual Reports of General Foods

19X1: "We aim to increase real earnings growth per share at least as much as the median of competitive performance over time. We also aim to achieve an overall after-tax return on invested capital of no less than 15 percent."

19X2: "We have added two operating goals: (1) We must generate profitable and enduring volume growth in each sector that is greater than the growth of the aggregate market. . . . (2) We must accelerate our asset investment rate in new and existing businesses."

19X3: "An important step we took was the acquisition of Oscar Mayer [leader in the processed meat industry], the largest in General Foods' history [cost of acquisition $470 million; 19X3 sales of Oscar Mayer $1,358 million]."

19X4: "General Foods' business objectives . . . We seek to increase the value of our shareholders' investment by attaining increases over time in earnings at an annual rate of three to five percent in excess of inflation, while earning a return on investment of at least 15 percent."

19X5: "Earnings from acquisitions have not yet grown sufficiently to provide return on investment at or above General Foods' objective of 15 percent. Despite the short-term dilutive effect from these investments, return on investment is well above our cost of capital and has added value to the company and to our shareholders' investment."

Extracts from Annual Reports of General Mills

19X1: "For our shareholders, our objective will be to maximize the long-term return on their investment. This past year, we revised upward our goal for return on average shareholders' equity from a minimum 17% to 19% by 19X5. We believe this goal is reasonable and attainable. From a performance standpoint, it should place General Mills in the top quartile of major corporations as measured by the Standard and Poor's 400 Industrial and other similar indices."

19X2: "The most important long-range financial goals are the achievement of a 19 percent return on average stockholders' equity by 19X5, average five-year growth in earnings per share of 14 percent and the maintenance of a strong balance sheet— approximately two-thirds equity and one-third debt. We plan to continue our policy of regular dividend increases equal to the long-term rate of increase in earnings per share. . . . Our basic business strategy is to emphasize internal growth, selectively adding acquisitions and new ventures with high potential."

19X3: "Our specific numerical return on equity (ROE) goal will change with changing inflation expectations. However, our goal to be in the top quartile is a long-term objective. Our dividend goal is to approximate the long-term rate of earnings per share growth within a payout rate of 35 to 40 percent of earnings."

19X4: "Our earnings per share growth objective is to exceed the rate of inflation by 6 percentage points on average over a five-year period."

19X5: "Our overall commitment remains the same—to maximize shareholder value by performing in the top quartile of large United States corporations. Our specific goals are:

A minimum of 19 percent return on equity;

Earnings per share growth averaging 6 percentage points greater than inflation over five years;
Increasing dividends in line with the long-term growth in earnings per share;
Maintaining a strong balance sheet.''

Additional Information

1. General Foods and General Mills both use the straight-line method of depreciation. General Foods reports inventories ''at the lower of cost (principally average) or market for financial reporting purposes.'' No information is provided as to the numerical effect of using alternative inventory valuation methods. General Mills reports that ''inventories are valued at the lower of cost or market.'' Both the LIFO and FIFO methods are used by General Mills:

	19X1	19X2	19X3	19X4	19X5
Component valued at LIFO	$204	$189	$220	$219	$263
Component valued at FIFO	339	422	441	414	399
	$543	$611	$661	$633	$662

General Mills reported the following amounts for inventory had FIFO been used consistently for all components:

19X1	19X2	19X3	19X4	19X5
$603	$685	$736	$713	$742

2. The net income for General Foods includes no nonoperating gain or loss on all years except 19X3 when it had a $21 million nonoperating loss associated with a provision for discontinued operations. The net income for General Mills includes no nonoperating item in 19X1 and 19X2; associated with an asset redeployment program, it had a nonoperating loss of $34 million in 19X3 and nonoperating gains of $3 million in 19X4 and $8 million in 19X5.

3. For working capital from operations calculations, assume zero entries for the following items for General Foods and General Mills in Table 3.4: additions (items 2–5, 7–8) and subtractions (items 1–4, 6–7).

4. General Foods and General Mills are included in Value Line's ''Food Processing Industry'' grouping of firms. Summary data for the ''Food Processing Industry'' over the 19X1–19X5 period are

	19X1	19X2	19X3	19X4	19X5
Sales ($ millions)	92,676	97,951	111,725	111,451	115,666
Net profit ($ millions)	3,102	3,677	3,962	4,076	4,410
Long-term debt to					
net worth ratio	.36	.33	.34	.33	.31
Average annual PE ratio	7.4	6.8	7.3	8.1	9.7

REQUIRED

1. What inferences can be made about the cash position, liquidity, cash flow, capital structure, debt service coverage, profitability, and turnover of General Foods vis-à-vis General Mills from the data in Table 3.17?

2. How do the results of General Foods and General Mills in the 19X1–19X5 period compare with their published financial goals? Where insufficient information is provided for a specific goal, state this in your answer.

3. Only a small subset of firms publicly discloses specific (numeric) details of their financial goals. What are the pros and cons of voluntarily disclosing this information?

4. Comment on the following argument by Gibson and Boyer (1980, pp. 82–84) for the SEC or FASB to issue authoritative guidelines on the computation and reporting of financial ratios in annual reports:

> Successful financial statement analysis should include the computation and interpretation of financial ratios. . . . There is a need for standard ratios and financial reporting of such ratios. This position is supported by the fact that there are alternative methods of computation, confusion over ratio labels and lack of information for ratio computation. . . . There are clear and misleading inconsistencies in published annual reports in the computing of numerous financial ratios. The lack of uniformity limits the comparability desired in financial statement analysis. . . . The absence of standardization also allows companies to present ratios most favorable to their position.

> There should be standard meanings concerning how these ratios were computed. The SEC and the FASB should accept the same role in this area as they do for financial statements in general. Standard meanings of ratios should be determined and selected ratios should be reported as part of the footnotes. An attempt should be made, when feasible, to have all companies report the same ratios. . . . Authoritative guidelines would not restrict statement analysis, but, rather, would enhance this art.

QUESTION 3.3: Financial Magazines, Computerized Data Bases, and Published Financial Statement Information

After several years of service with a well-known financial magazine, you are called into the editor's office. You are to be responsible for the financial surveys regularly included in the magazine. Your predecessor had developed a computerized data base that was updated on a quarterly (or annual) basis. Your name will appear in bold print at the bottom of each of the following surveys:

1. Directory of the Largest 500 U.S. Industrial Companies.

2. Directory of the Largest 500 U.S. Non-Industrial Companies. The current year's issue comprises three 100-company rankings (of the largest diversified financial, diversified service, and commercial banking companies) and four 50-company rankings (of the largest life insurance, retailing, transportation, and utility companies).

3. Directory of the Largest 100 U.S. Private Industrial Companies.

4. Directory of the Largest 100 U.S. Private Non-Industrial Companies.

5. Directory of the Largest 500 Non-U.S. Industrial Companies.

6. Directory of the Largest 500 Non-U.S. Non-Industrial Companies.

7. The 100 Fastest Growing U.S. Companies.

8. The Big Winners and the Big Losers—the 50 most profitable companies in the world and the 50 least profitable (heaviest losses) in the world.

9. Annual and Quarterly Scoreboards—showing sales, profits, margins, and price-to-earnings ratios for a broad cross section of U.S. firms.

The editor stresses that the prestige of the magazine is closely tied to publicity the financial surveys have generated. It is essential that the surveys be both accurate and up-to-date. Errors and nontimely data are simply unacceptable. As you are leaving, you are handed the following "Letters to the Editor" and "Corrections" published in several competing magazines:

1. "In your May 3 issue you incorrectly reported NVF Co.'s net income as $440,000, a figure that was actually NVF's sales from discontinued operations. The correct net income figure is $21,987,000.

   "Because of the error, a table you printed of changes in profits showed NVF as having the largest decrease among the 500 companies—97%. In fact, NVF's profits increased 52%."

2. "Your October 25 issue states that profits at Consolidated Papers were down 62% for the third quarter. This may be technically correct, but an important footnote was omitted. Effective September 30, the company closed its Appleton (Wisc.) sulfite pulp mill. The closing costs were $11.05 million on a pretax basis, or $6.2 million after income taxes, and were charged to earnings for the third quarter. This reduced after-tax income to $4.6 million, the figure shown in your table. Earnings without the closing costs were $10.8 million, compared with $12 million a year ago—a decline of only 10%."

3. "In your Mutual Fund issue, you reported that the annual expenses per $100 for State Street Investment Corp. were 4.97%. The correct figure is 0.497%. This error indicates that our expense ratio is among the highest in the industry when, in fact, it is among the lowest."

4. "The loss reported by our company (Del Webb) in first quarter was $300,000, not $300 million. Actually, results were improved over first quarter and were better than anticipated because of our turnaround efforts and better than expected performance by contracting and hotel/casino operations."

5. "The per-share earnings of MGM/UA are listed in your April 30 issue as 19X1, $3.13; 19X2, $1.40. The company was formed in September 19X1 and was listed (NYSE) December 19X1, with a pro forma year's (19X1) earnings of $1.01. The $1.40/share earnings for 19X2 is accurate.

   "You state the indicated dividend rate is $0.20/share, with a payout rate of 14% of earnings. Our declared dividend for 19X2 was $0.85 ($0.60 regular and $0.25 special), which represented a 60% payout of our $1.40 earnings."

6. "[A table that appeared in your magazine] lists Masonite Corp. as the worst stock market performer among the S&P 400 leading industrials. This is totally inaccurate. In truth, Masonite shareholders have enjoyed a 32% increase in the value of their holdings, not a 59.7% decrease, during the period Aug. 6 to Oct. 8.

   "During that time, Masonite transferred its timberlands to its shareholders as part of a plan of partial liquidation. This was reported in [your magazine's] Sept. 13 issue. As a result of a 3-for-1 reverse stock split that was effected as a part of the plan, and the issuance of units in Timber Realization Co., now traded over the counter, the Masonite shareholder who held 300 shares of Masonite stock on Aug. 6 (worth $7,200) had, as of Oct. 8, 100 shares of Masonite stock (worth $2,900) plus 300 units of Timber Realization (worth $6,600). Total value of his holdings was $9,500 on Oct. 8 vs. $7,200 on Aug. 6. That's a 32% increase in value.

"Not only was the plan fully explained in our proxy statement of Aug. 4, but it was also discussed in your own article in the Sept. 13 issue."

7. Correction: "By failing to take account of a stock split, the directory misstated some of Hillenbrand Industries' data. The earnings per share were $0.51 in 19X1, $1.54 in 19X10, and $1.78 in 19X11. The 19X1–19X11 growth rate—13.3%—ranked 90th among the 500" (published survey reported growth rate of 5.73% with rank of 234).

8. Correction: "Based on information provided by the company, the 500 directory misstated Exxon's return on equity. The correct figure is 16.9%" (published survey reported 7.8%).

REQUIRED

1. What size and growth measures would you consider using in the above surveys? What measures for the winners and losers survey would you consider using? What criteria would you use to decide the subset of measures to present?

2. What problems would you expect to encounter in collecting and reporting the information to be included in the above surveys?

3. Categorize the types of errors cited in the "Letters to the Editor."

4. Outline the procedures you would employ to ensure that each financial survey is both accurate and up to date. (Remember the dictum, "Errors and nontimely data are simply unacceptable.")

REFERENCES

BARRON, M. "The MicroEXSTAT Financial Statement Analysis System." (Working paper) London: London Business School, 1984.

BEEDLES, W. L., and M. A. SIMKOWITZ. "A Note on Skewness and Data Errors." *The Journal of Finance* (March 1978): 288–292.

BENNIN, R. "Error Rates in CRSP and COMPUSTAT: A Second Look." *The Journal of Finance* (December 1980): 1267–1271.

BOWEN, R. M., D. BURGSTAHLER, and L. A. DALEY. "Empirical Evidence on the Relationships Between Earnings, Cash Flow, and Cash Flow Surrogates." Working paper: University of Washington, Seattle, 1984.

FRISHKOFF, P. *Reporting of Summary Indicators: An Investigation of Research and Practice.* Stamford, Conn.: FASB, 1981.

GALE, A. P. "Computerized Research: An Advanced Tool." *The Journal of Accountancy* (January 1982): 73–84.

GIBSON, C. H. "How Industry Perceives Financial Ratios." *Management Accounting* (April 1982a): 13–19.

GIBSON, C. H. "Financial Ratios in Annual Reports." *The CPA Journal* (September 1982b): 18–29.

GIBSON, C. H., and P. A. BOYER. "The Need for Disclosure of Uniform Financial Ratios." *The Journal of Accountancy* (May 1980): 78–86.

GOMBOLA, M. J., and J. E. KETZ. "A Note on Cash Flow and Classification Patterns of Financial Ratios." *The Accounting Review* (January 1983): 105–114.

GREENE, R. "The Joys of Leasing." *Forbes* (November 24, 1980), 59.

HICKS, B. E., and P. HUNT. *Cash Flow Accounting.* Sudbury, Canada: Laurentian University, 1981.

LANDSITTEL, D. L., and J. E. STEWART. "Off-Balance-Sheet Financing: Commitments and Contingencies." In S. Davidson and R. L. Weil, eds., *Handbook of Modern Accounting,* 3rd ed., pp. 26.1–26.24. New York: McGraw-Hill, 1983.

MCELREATH, R. B., and C. D. WIGGINS. "Using the COMPUSTAT Tapes in Financial Research: Problems and Solutions." *Financial Analysts Journal* (January–February 1984): 71–76.

ROSENBERG, B., and M. HOUGLET. "Error Rates in CRSP and Compustat Data Bases and Their Implications." *The Journal of Finance* (September 1974): 1303–1310.

SAN MIGUEL, J. G. "The Reliability of R & D Data in Compustat and 10-K Reports." *The Accounting Review* (July 1977): 639–641.

STANDARD & POOR'S. *Credit Overview: Industrial Ratings.* New York: S&P, 1983.

STONE, M., and B. BUBLITZ. "An Analysis of the Reliability of the FASB Data Bank of Changing Price and Pension Information." *The Accounting Review* (July 1984): 469–473.

URBANCIC, F. R. "Reporting Preferred Stock: Debt or Equity?" *Mergers and Acquisitions* (Spring 1980): 15–20.

VASARHELYI, M. A., and D. C. H. YANG. "Financial Accounting Databases: Methodological Implications of Using the Compustat and Value Line Databases." Working paper: Columbia University, New York, 1983.

WALSH, F. J., *Measuring Business Performance.* New York: The Conference Board, 1984.

WEINGARTEN, J. M. "The Brewing Industry." New York: Goldman Sachs, 1984.

WILLIAMSON, R. W. "Evidence on the Selective Reporting of Financial Ratios." *The Accounting Review* (April 1984): 296–299.

4

FINANCIAL STATEMENT NUMBERS: SOME EMPIRICAL ISSUES AND EVIDENCE

4.1 INTRODUCTION

When using financial statement numbers, it is important to recognize

1. The assumptions underlying alternative summary measures (such as the ratio form)
2. The empirical properties of both the underlying numbers and the summary measures.

Failure to consider these issues can result in the drawing of erroneous inferences, the use of inappropriate statistical tools, or the collection of data that are redundant. This chapter discusses topics related to both (1) and (2), for example, assumptions made when using financial ratios to control for firm size, the distributional properties of financial statement variables, and the correlation and comovement between alternative financial ratios. Subsequent chapters present further discussion and evidence on these issues. For example, Chapter 5 presents evidence on the correlation between financial statement numbers when alternative accounting methods are used. Chapter 6 presents evidence on industry differences in the distribution of financial ratios and on the importance of industry and economy factors in the behavior of accounting numbers over time. Chapter 7 presents evidence on time-series properties of variables such as earnings, earnings per share, and return on equity.

4.2 ASSUMPTIONS OF RATIO ANALYSIS

The most common mode in which financial statement data are summarized is the ratio form. Motivations for examining data in ratio form include

1. To control for the effect of size differences across firms or over time
2. To make the data better satisfy the assumptions underlying statistical tools such as regression analysis (for example, homoscedastic disturbances)
3. To probe a theory in which a ratio is the variable of interest
4. To exploit an observed empirical regularity between a financial ratio and the estimation or prediction of a variable of interest (for example, the risk of a security or the likelihood of a firm declaring bankruptcy).

Controlling for the effect of size differences is the most frequently cited motivation for analyzing data in ratio form.

An important assumption underlying the use of ratios as a control for size differences is strict proportionality between the numerator and the denominator.

This strict proportionality is assumed both in comparisons of ratios across firms at a point in time and in comparisons of the ratios of firms over time. Consider the earnings-to-sales ratio. The strict proportionality assumption implies that

$$E = p \cdot S \tag{4.1}$$

where p is the proportionality factor. Panel A of Figure 4.1 plots equation (4.1) for alternative values of p. Panels B to D plot several contexts in which (4.1) is not descriptive. Two conditions are represented in panels B to D, neither of which implies a strictly proportional relation between earnings and sales:

1. The existence of a constant or an intercept term. One rationale for a negative constant term is the existence of fixed costs, which implies a loss at zero sales level. One rationale for a positive constant term in the earnings-sales relation is an income source (for example, interest income on cash investments) not related to sales.

2. The existence of a nonlinear relation between earnings and sales, for example, due to economies of scale.

FIGURE 4.1 Earnings-to-Sales Relationships

A. Proportionality Without Constant

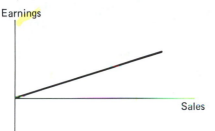

C. Non-proportionality Without Constant

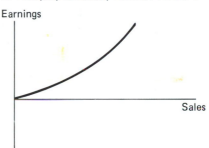

B. Proportionality With Constant

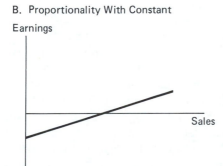

D. Non-proportionality With Constant

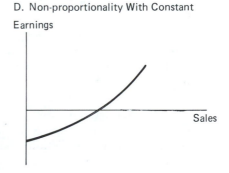

The plots in Figure 4.1 assume a two-variable model:

$$\text{Earnings} = f(\text{Sales}) \qquad \textbf{(4.2)}$$

A more general model posits that differences in earnings across firms or over time are a function of multiple variables.

$$\text{Earnings} = f(\text{Sales}, \text{\# of employees}, \text{\# of plants}, \dots, \text{etc.}) \qquad \textbf{(4.3)}$$

The model in equation (4.3) could be linear or nonlinear. Clearly, the strict proportionality relationship in (4.1) is but one of many possible relationships that can exist between earnings and sales. It is important that an analyst recognize this situation rather than cavalierly assume that variables in ratio form automatically control for size differences across firms or over time.

Sales is but one measure that can be used to control for the effect of size differences across firms. Other measures include total assets, shareholders' equity, market capitalization, and the number of employees. Typically, there will not be theoretical support to guide the choice among the size measures. In this context, the analyst can gain empirical support by plotting the numerator against alternative size measures and choosing the measure that best satisfies the strict proportionality assumption.

A second approach to checking visually for proportionality is to plot values of the ratio for alternative values of the denominator. For example, for the profit-to-total assets ratio, values of the ratio for alternative total-asset size categories could be examined. Proportionality implies that the value of this ratio across total asset size categories would be similar. In the limit, a line linking values of the ratio would be parallel to the horizontal axis.

Rationales for Nonratio Analysis

The foregoing discussion focused on relational assumptions implicit in the ratio approach to controlling for the effect of size differences across firms or over time. Where the proportionality assumption is not descriptive, using statistical tools like linear or nonlinear regression analysis can be a more fruitful way to analyze the data.

There are also economic rationales for not restricting the analysis to data in ratio form. Even where the proportionality assumption is appropriate, controlling for firm size differences via the use of ratios can result in the loss of important information. Consider the prediction of corporate failure. Chapter 15 discusses empirical research on this topic. A common finding in this literature is that the frequency of failure is considerably higher for smaller than for larger firms. This finding implies that firm size is an important variable to include in a corporate failure prediction model. Yet, if data in only ratio form were examined, firm size would be precluded from being a variable in the model.

4.3   COMPUTATION ISSUES IN CALCULATING RATIOS

Computation or interpretation problems can arise with financial ratios in a variety of contexts. This section considers problems associated with (A) negative denominators and (B) "extreme" (outlier) observations.

A.   Negative Denominators

Assume that an analyst is examining the profitability of firms in an industry and encounters a firm having negative shareholders' equity. The use of this observation as the denominator in the earnings-to-shareholders' equity ratio can result in a ratio that has no obvious interpretation. Various possibilities exist in this context.

1. Delete the observation from the sample. This procedure is frequently adopted. For example, Robert Morris Associates (1983) adopts this procedure when computing the "profit before taxes to tangible net worth" ratio in its *Annual Statement Studies.*

2. Examine reasons for the negative denominator and make subsequent adjustments. For example, if it is due to assets being understated, an asset revaluation can result in the revised estimate of shareholders' equity being positive. (Asset understatement obviously can also exist for firms with positive shareholders' equity. Consistency would argue for revaluation for all firms in the sample.)

3. Use an alternative ratio that captures some aspects of profitability, for example, return on total assets or earnings to sales. Rarely is the denominator in either of these ratios negative.

The advent of computerized financial statement analysis means that analysts typically access the summary ratios rather than the components of those ratios. This situation is not without problems. Consider a computer printout that reports the net income-to-shareholders' equity ratio of Firm X as 16% and Firm Y as 14%. Underlying the 16% and 14% are the following components:

	Firm X	Firm Y
Net income	− $4 million	$28 million
Shareholders' equity	− $25 million	$200 million

Clearly, this example illustrates the importance of adding checks in a computer program, where possible, to flag situations such as that for Firm X. (In many data bases, such as Compustat and Value Line, the components are available and these checks can be made.)

B. Outlier Observations

Section 4.4 presents evidence on the distribution of financial ratios. For a subset of the ratios examined in that section, the highest three observations (and the mean and the median) are

Ratio	Highest	Second Highest	Third Highest	Mean	Median
Cash and marketable securities Current liabilities	1,129.50	31.41	31.39	1.30	.28
Long-term liabilities Shareholders' equity	273.31	27.00	26.53	.91	.40
Operating income Interest payments	2,863.50	2,713.00	1,350.50	8.55	1.43
Market capitalization Net income	1,975.00	1,787.50	1,650.00	19.20	10.79

Are these observations outliers or do they represent an extreme state of the underlying characteristic? An outlier is "an observation which appears to be inconsistent with the remainder of that set of data. The phrase 'appears to be inconsistent' is crucial. It is a matter of subjective judgment on the part of the observer whether or not he picks out some observation for scrutiny" (Barnett and Lewis, 1978, p. 4).

There are several steps in deciding whether observations such as those just reported are outliers. A useful first step is to determine if the extreme observation arises due to computation reasons. For example,

- Is the extreme value due to a recording error? This is a frequent source of outlier observations. The most direct approach is to compare the numbers underlying the computation of the financial ratio with those reported in the annual report. (Typographical errors do occur in annual reports, but they are relatively rare.) The appendix to Chapter 3 outlines additional approaches available to detect recording errors in computerized data bases.

- Is the extreme value due to the denominator of the ratio approaching zero in a particular year? Values of the ratio in prior years can provide useful evidence in deciding if this situation exists.

A useful second step is to examine accounting classification, accounting method, and economic or structural change as reasons for the extreme observations.

- *Accounting classification.* For example, the inclusion in net income of a large write-down for a plant closing can cause an outlier in the earnings-to-sales ratio. One approach to detecting this is to compare (1) operating earnings to sales, (2) earnings before interest and taxes to sales, and (3) earnings to sales. If a firm is an outlier observation for only (3), then the likelihood of the outlier being due to an accounting classification is considerably increased.

- *Accounting methods*. For example, an extreme times interest-earned ratio may be due to the existence of "off-balance-sheet" financing.
- *Economic*. For example, all other firms could be capital intensive while the firm with the "extreme" ratio could be labor intensive due to relatively cheap labor in the area in which it is located. These differences could give rise to marked differences across firms in profit margin ratios when sales volume expands quickly.
- *Structural change*. For example, a merger can cause outlier observations, especially for ratios comparing balance sheet or income items postmerger with those same items premerger.

The alternatives available to an analyst when faced with extreme observations (not arising from recording errors) include

- Deleting the extreme observation on the grounds that it represents a "true outlier"
- Retaining the extreme observation on the grounds that it represents an extreme state of the underlying characteristic
- Making adjustments for the economic or accounting factors believed to cause the extreme observation, for example, by imputing the interest payments associated with the "off-balance-sheet" financing
- "Winsorizing" the sample, for example, changing the value of the extreme observation to the value of the nearest observation not viewed as "suspect"
- "Trimming" the sample by deleting the top *N* and the bottom *N* observations.

These alternatives recognize that the causes of extreme values are varied and that a systematic consideration of computation, accounting, economic, and structural change factors facilitates a more reasoned judgment as to their handling in financial statement applications. (Extreme values occur in many data analysis exercises. A useful introduction to statistical procedures for handling them is in Barnett and Lewis, 1978.)

4.4 THE DISTRIBUTION OF FINANCIAL STATEMENT NUMBERS

A. Importance of Distribution Evidence

Examples of decision areas in which evidence on the distribution of financial statement numbers is important include

- A bank lending decision in which an analyst wishes to determine where on the industry distribution a loan applicant's financial ratio lies
- A corporate strategy decision where the focus is on the upside potential from moving the earnings-to-sales ratio of a business unit from the bottom 10% of its industry to the top 10%.

- A decision in an audit engagement about the design of a sampling approach to estimate the financial characteristics of a population (for example, the number of observations to sample and the use of a random sampling approach or a stratified sampling approach).
- A decision about what statistical tools to use when analyzing financial statement data. The statistics and econometrics literatures contain a wide variety of tools with differing assumptions about the distribution of the data being analyzed. For instance, normality is assumed when a *t* test is used to assess the significance of individual variables in ordinary least squares regression. In contrast, tools such as *probit* and *logit* that are used to predict firm classifications in financial distress prediction applications require different distributional assumptions.

Evidence on the distribution of financial statement numbers can also be a stimulus to subsequent research that promotes better understanding of the properties of financial statement data. For instance, a repeated finding that industries with low concentration ratios have greater intraindustry dispersion in profitability ratios than do those with high concentration ratios could prompt research in the industrial organization literature that aims to explain this empirical regularity.

B. Focus on Normality

Much of the analysis of the distribution of financial statement numbers examines whether a normal distribution can be used to describe those numbers. Given that numerous other distribution forms exist (for example, gamma and exponential), why focus on the normal distribution? One reason is that the normal distribution has the appealing property that knowledge of only two statistics (the mean and the standard deviation) is sufficient to characterize the whole normal distribution. Thus, given only the mean and the standard deviation of the turnover ratio of the brewing companies in Chapter 3, the statistical significance of deviations from the mean can be determined if the distribution of that ratio is normally distributed.

A second reason for focusing on normality is that many of the statistical tools available for analyzing financial statement data are based on the assumption that the data are normally distributed. Statisticians and econometricians have found the tractability of working with normally distributed variables to be highly appealing. (It is important to note, however, that considerable research is being conducted on statistical tools appropriate for nonnormally distributed variables.)

Despite the attractions of working with normally distributed variables, reasons exist for expecting nonnormality for many financial ratios. If the strict proportionality assumption in equation (4.1) does not hold between the numerator and the denominator of the financial ratio, then skewness in the distribution can occur; see Section 4.6 and Barnes (1982) for further discussion. Some financial ratios have technical limits that prevent a normal distribution from being a literal description; for example, the current ratio has a technical lower limit of zero, whereas the normal distribution will include negative values. A similar example is the total debt-to-total assets ratio, which has both a technical lower limit of zero and a technical upper limit of one. Some financial ratios have economic limits that may result in fewer observations in either the lower or upper end of the distribution than under the normal distribution; for example, firms in the same industry may have fewer observations in the upper end of the distribution of the accounts receivable turnover ratio than under a normal distribution due to common pressure from customers to retain a minimum payment period of at least (say) one month.

What If Normality Is Rejected?

Assume that an analyst decides that a normal distribution is not descriptively valid for the data being examined. The options available include the following:

1. *Impose normality on the data.* This can be achieved by ranking all the observations in the data examined and then converting these ranks to points on a standardized normal distribution. Note that if you use the converted financial ratios to develop a predictive model, data not used in the initial conversion will have to be rescaled according to where they fit on the underlying distribution for the initial sample.

2. *Attempt to transform the data such that a normal distribution assumption is descriptive* (for example, via the use of a logarithmic transformation). Section 4.4 illustrates that use of this transformation does reduce the violations from normality for several financial ratios. When considering this option, it is important to keep in mind the economic meaning of the transformed data. For instance, when the logarithmic transformation is used, the transformed variables give less weight to equal percentage changes in a variable where the values are larger than when they are smaller; that is, there is less difference between a $1 billion- and a $2 billion-size firm than there is between a $1 million- and a $2 million-size firm. An issue that arises with the logarithmic transformation (and several others, such as the square root transformation) is that the distribution is undefined for negative values. One option in this situation is to shift the entire distribution to the right so that all observations are positive. A limitation of this option is that one extreme observation (the most negative) will affect the shape of the distribution imposed on all other observations. A second option when faced with negative observations is to use a transformation for which negative values are defined, for example, the power transformation.

3. *Attempt to impose normality by resetting extreme observations to less extreme values* (this is called winsorizing the data). An example would be to reset all times interest earned ratios below the .02 percentile and above the .98 percentile to the values of the .02 percentile and the .98 percentile, respectively.

4. *Attempt to impose normality by deleting observations that deviate most from normality* (this is called trimming the sample). The Frecka and Hopwood (1983) study described in Section 4.4.D illustrates the use of this

alternative for 11 financial ratios. This alternative has a major drawback in applied decision contexts. Suppose that a credit-scoring model were built for a subsample of data satisfying normality. A banker who turned away potentially good credit applicants because their ratios were not normally distributed (and hence would not meet the specifications required for using the credit-scoring model) would likely have a short list of clients (and a short banking career).

5. *Recognize nonnormality without attempting to identify the specific nonnormal distribution.* For example,

- *Data analysis*—examine the fractiles or percentiles of the distribution rather than focusing only on the mean and standard deviation. In some contexts, complete enumeration of the distribution may be adopted.

- *Statistical tool choice*—use nonparametric statistics that are so-called "distribution free" in their assumptions (or at least do not assume normality).

- *Inference drawing*—if tools such as ordinary least squares (OLS) regression are used, do not draw inferences from the results that are contingent on the normality assumption. For instance, the OLS estimates of the model coefficients are still unbiased with nonnormal data, but they are not necessarily the maximum likelihood estimates of the population values.

6. *Identify the specific nonnormal distribution form that characterizes the data of interest.* This identification could be based on (a) an analysis of the sample evidence, (b) prior evidence available, or (c) an economic analysis of the distribution of the ratio.

When examining the distribution of financial statement numbers, it is important to remember that one rarely expects that the distribution of any sample will exactly correspond to that implied by any one theoretical distribution. Indeed, in small samples (say, 20 to 30 observations), it is often very hard, due to sampling variation, to identify the underlying distribution. If one were to start with a prior belief that the underlying distribution was normal (due to, say, published evidence and economic reasoning), one would only look for systematic and substantial deviations from normality in the sample evidence before concluding that normality was not a workable description of the underlying distribution.

C. Aspects of Distributions

Some important features of distributions will be illustrated by reference to the 1983 total debt (current liabilities and long-term liabilities, CL & LTL) to shareholders' equity (SE) ratio of 63 firms in the SIC four-digit "crude oil and gas" industry (1311). (Chapter 6 contains a discussion of SIC and other industry classification schemes.)

Central Tendency

The central tendency of a distribution can be measured by several statistics. One statistic is the median, which is computed by ranking the observations from the highest (51.038) to the lowest (.065) and choosing that ratio that is midway on the distribution; the median of the 63 observations is .98. The equal-weighted mean (Y_1), another measure of central tendency, is computed as follows:

$$\hat{Y}_1 = \frac{\sum\limits_{i=1}^{N} X_i}{N} \tag{4.4}$$

$$= 3.46$$

where X_i is the debt-to-equity ratio of the ith firm and N is the number of observations.

Dispersion

Another feature of a distribution is its dispersion. The standard deviation (γ_2)—a common measure of dispersion—is estimated as follows:

$$\hat{Y}_2 = \sqrt{\frac{\sum\limits_{i=1}^{N} (X_i - \hat{Y}_1)^2}{N - 1}} \tag{4.5}$$

$$= 7.92$$

If the debt-to-equity ratio were normally distributed, knowledge of Y_1 and Y_2 would be sufficient to generate the whole distribution. For instance, approximately two-thirds of the distribution would lie within one standard deviation of the mean. A related measure of dispersion is the *variance*. This measure is estimated as the square of the standard deviation ($\hat{Y}_2^2 = 62.67$).

Figure 4.2 presents a plot of the distribution of the 63 total debt-to-equity ratios. The theoretical normal distribution with a mean of 3.46 and a standard deviation of 7.92 is also plotted on Figure 4.2. The actual distribution does not have the familiar bell-shaped curve of the theoretical normal distribution.

Skewness

A skewed distribution departs from the bell-shaped curve of the normal distribution in either the upper or lower parts of the distribution. The actual distribution in Figure 4.2 is blunt on the left and has a long tail pointing to the right. Evidence of positive skewness appears present. A common measure of this

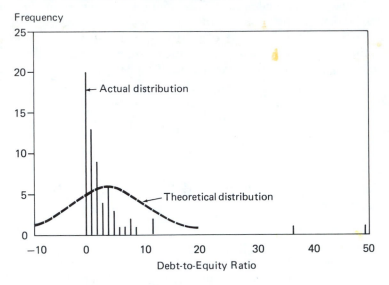

FIGURE 4.2   Distribution of Total Debt-to-Shareholders' Equity Ratio for Crude Oil and Gas Industry (1311)

is the skewness coefficient (Y_3):

$$\hat{Y}_3 = \frac{\dfrac{\sum\limits_{i=1}^{N} (X_i - \hat{Y}_1)^3}{\hat{Y}_2^3}}{N} \tag{4.6}$$

$$= 4.58$$

where $\hat{Y}_2$ is the estimated standard deviation of the total debt-to-equity ratio. For a normal distribution, $Y_3 = 0$. For samples of 20 to 100 observations, a benchmark for suspecting positive skewness is $Y_3 > +.5$; the benchmark for suspecting negative skewness is $Y_3 < -.5$.

Kurtosis

A common test for normality is to compare the sample distribution in the tails with the distribution under the theoretical normal distribution.

One statistic used in this comparison is the kurtosis coefficient (Y_4):

$$\hat{Y}_4 = \frac{\dfrac{\sum\limits_{i=1}^{N} (X_i - \hat{Y}_1)^4}{\hat{Y}_2^4}}{N} - 3 \tag{4.7}$$

$$= 22.37$$

The kurtosis coefficient provides evidence on whether the distribution is more or less *fat-tailed* than would be expected from the normal distribution. For a normal distribution, $Y_4 = 0$. A convenient rule of thumb for suspecting violations from normality is $Y_4 < -1$ or $Y_4 > +1$. A Y_4 of 22.37 is consistent with the debt-to-equity ratio not being well approximated by a normal distribution.

Studentized Range

Another measure of the dispersion is the *studentized range* (S.R.). This statistic is the ratio of the sample range (largest observation minus smallest observation, $51.038 - .065$) to the sample standard deviation (7.92):

$$\text{S.R.} = \frac{X_{\max} - X_{\min}}{\hat{Y}_2}$$

(4.8)

$$= 6.44$$

This statistic tends to be "large" for fat-tailed distributions. A rule of thumb for suspecting the underlying distribution to have fat tails when using 50 and 100 sample observations is a studentized range greater than 6.0 and 6.5, respectively.

Fractiles of the Distribution

Useful insights into the distribution of a variable can often be obtained from the fractiles of the distribution. Computing such fractiles involves ranking the sample observations from highest to lowest and observing the actual (or implied) values at various percentiles on the distribution. The deciles of the distribution (the .9, .8, . . . , .2, .1 fractiles) of the debt-to-equity ratio are

	Deciles								
	.1	*.2*	*.3*	*.4*	*.5*	*.6*	*.7*	*.8*	*.9*
Debt-to-equity	.17	.34	.50	.74	.98	1.33	2.74	3.70	7.21

The .25 (.44) and .75 (3.14) fractiles are referred to as the lower and upper quartiles of the distribution; the difference between the .75 fractile and the .25 fractile is termed the interquartile range (2.70). As noted previously, the .5 fractile (.98) is the median.

D.   Published Evidence on Distributions

A growing number of studies report distribution evidence on financial ratios. Some representative studies are

1. Deakin (1976), who examined the distribution of 11 financial ratios for U.S. manufacturing firms over the 1953–1973 period, for example, current assets-to-sales, working capital-to-total assets, cash flow-to-total debt, net income-to-total assets, and total debt-to-total assets. The conclusion was that "it

would appear that assumptions of normality for financial accounting ratios would not be tenable except in the case of the total debt (TD) to total assets (TA) ratio. Even for TD/TA, the assumption would not hold for the most recent data observations. . . . However, it does appear that normality can be achieved in certain cases by transforming the data" (pp. 95–96).

2. Ricketts and Stover (1978), who examined the distribution of 11 financial ratios of U.S. banks over the 1965–1974 period. A distinctive feature of this paper was the focus on firms in a single industry as opposed to the more typical analysis of firms from a broad cross section of industries. The conclusion was that "a normality assumption could not be rejected for most of the commercial bank ratios examined" (p. 123). The only financial ratios to exhibit departures from normality included "at least one item from the income statement," for example, the provision for loan losses-to-operating expense ratio and the net income-to-total capital ratio.

3. Frecka and Hopwood (1983), who examined the same 11 financial ratios as Deakin (1976) for the 1950–1979 period. The focus was on the effect of outliers on the distribution properties of financial ratios. Outliers were identified using both skewness and kurtosis tests. They concluded, "Our results indicate that, by deleting outliers, normality or approximate normality can usually be achieved for our population of manufacturing firms and for specific industry groupings. Furthermore, the procedure results in large reductions in relative variances and increases the stability of variances over time" (p. 2). One interesting finding in this study was the relatively small number of observations that had to be deleted for some ratios to achieve considerable reductions in the skewness and kurtosis measures. For instance, out of 1,156 firm observations examined for 1979, the number of outliers identified for a subset of financial ratios were

Ratio	Outliers in Left Tail	Outliers in Right Tail	% Classified as Outliers
1. Current assets-to-sales	0	6	.5
2. Working capital-to-sales	1	6	.6
3. Current ratio	0	57	4.9
4. Cash flow-to-total debt	12	67	6.8
5. Net income-to-total assets	51	10	5.3
6. Total debt-to-total assets	14	1	1.3

The definition of an outlier in this study was based on statistical criteria. Accounting classification, accounting method, economic, or structural change sources of outliers were not separately examined.

4. Bougen and Drury (1980), who examined the distribution of seven financial ratios for over 700 U.K. companies in 1975 (return on invested capital, profit margin, borrowing to shareholders' funds, current ratio, quick ratio, inventory turnover, and debtor turnover). The conclusion was that "the U.K. evidence seems to indicate non-normality caused by varying degrees of skewness and the existence of extreme outliers" (p. 46). A normal distribution was rejected as descriptive for each of the seven ratios examined.

5. Buijink and Jegers (1984), who examined distribution properties of 11 fi-

nancial ratios for a large sample of Belgian companies over the 1977–1981 period. An interesting result is that given ratios (or ratio/transformation combinations) exhibit persistency in the aspects of their distribution (for example, positive skewness) over each year of the 1977–1981 period.

Evidence on the dispersion and symmetry of the distribution of financial ratios is presented in many trade and government publications. For example, the .25, .50, and .75 fractiles of the distribution of financial ratios for many industries are presented in the annual editions of Dun & Bradstreet's *Key Business Ratios* and Robert Morris Associates' *Annual Statement Studies*. Table 4.1 presents evidence on the symmetry of three financial ratios for 140 manufacturing industries reported in Robert Morris Associates (1983). For each industry and for each ratio, the difference between the upper quartile (UQ) and the median (M) was compared with the difference between the median (M) and the lower quartile (LQ):

(UQ-M) > (M-LQ) is consistent with positive skewness.

(UQ-M) < (M-LQ) is consistent with negative skewness.

For all three ratios in Table 4.1, more industries exhibit positive skewness than negative skewness. Positive skewness is most marked for the ratio of earnings before interest and taxes to interest, and it is least marked for the ratio of profit before taxes to tangible net worth.

E. Some Additional Evidence

To gain additional insight into the distributions of financial variables, the deciles of the distributions of the following were computed. The data base com-

TABLE 4.1 Symmetry of Distributions of Financial Ratios for 140 Manufacturing Industries in Robert Morris Associates, 1983

Financial Ratio	*Positive Skewness* $(UQ - M) > (M - LQ)$	*Symmetric* $(UQ - M) = (M - LQ)$	*Negative Skewness* $(UQ - M) < (M - LQ)$
Current assets / Current liabilities	88.5%	8.6%	2.8%
Earnings before interest and taxes / Interest	95.0%	0%	5.0%
% Profit before taxes / Tangible net worth	61.4%	0%	38.6%

UQ – Upper quartile.
 M – Median.
LQ – Lower quartile.
Copyright 1983 by Robert Morris Associates.

prised all firms with 1983 data on the annual industrial Compustat tape:

Cash Position

1. (Cash + marketable securities)/Current liabilities, (C + MS)/CL
2. (Cash + marketable securities)/Sales, (C + MS)/S
3. (Cash + marketable securities)/Total assets, (C + MS)/TA

Liquidity

4. Quick assets/Current liabilities, QA/CL
5. Current assets/Current liabilities, CA/CL

Working Capital/Cash Flow

6. Working capital from operations/Sales, WCO/S
7. Working capital from operations/Total assets (average), WCO/TA
8. Cash flow from operations/Sales, CFO/S
9. Cash flow from operations/Total assets (average), CFO/TA

Capital Structure

10. Long-term liabilities/Shareholders' equity, LTL/SE
11. (Current and long-term liabilities)/Shareholders' equity, (CL + LTL)/SE

Debt Service Coverage

12. Operating income/Interest payments, OI/INT
13. Cash flow from operations/Interest payments, CFO/INT

Profitability

14. Net income, NI
15. Earnings per share, E.P.S.
16. Net income/Sales, NI/S
17. Net income/Shareholders' equity (average), NI/SE
18. Net income/Total assets (average), NI/TA

Turnover

19. Sales/Total assets (average), S/TA
20. Sales/Accounts receivable (average), S/AR
21. COGS/Inventory (average), COGS/INV

Capital Market

22. Price per share/EPS, PE
23. Dividend per share/EPS, DIV. PAYOUT

Firm Size

24. Total assets, TA
25. Sales, S
26. Market capitalization, MKT. CAP.

The deciles of the distribution for each variable are presented in Table 4.2. Positive/negative skewness is indicated when the difference between the .9 (.8, .7, .6) decile and the .5 decile exceeds/is less than the difference between the .5 decile and the .1 (.2, .3, .4) decile. Several variables exhibit evidence of marked positive skewness, for example, cash position, liquidity, capital structure, debt service coverage, and firm size. The skewness (γ_3), kurtosis (γ_4), and studentized range (S.R.) statistics were also computed for each variable in Table 4.2. For all but 3 (EPS, NI/S, and NI/SE) of the 26 variables in Table 4.2, statistically significant evidence (at the .01 level) of positive skewness was found. For all 26 variables, statistically significant evidence of a fat-tailed distribution was found.

Approaches Available to Reduce Departures From Normality

Section 4.3 discussed several approaches that may reduce the departures from normality. To illustrate these, the effect of using two alternative approaches for the following three financial ratios is presented:

- Current assets/current liabilties
- (Current + long-term liabilities)/shareholders' equity
- Sales/accounts receivable

1. *Trimming the sample.* For illustrative purposes, the top and bottom 1% and 2% of observations were successively trimmed. The results are in Table 4.3. The term "raw ratios" in Table 4.3 refers to the original or nontransformed ratio. Not surprisingly, trimming substantially reduces the observed departures from normality when the full sample is examined.

2. *Transforming the (raw) financial ratios.* Two commonly used transformations for a positively skewed distribution are the natural logarithmic transformation and the square root transformation:

$$T_i^L = \ln(X_i)$$
$$T_i^S = \sqrt{X_i}$$

These results are also in Table 4.3. Both transformations reduce the observed departures from normality when the (raw) financial ratios are examined.

The three ratios presented all have positive observations for each firm in the distribution. For other ratios, firms with negative observations (and zero observations with the logarithmic transformation) would have to be deleted (or recentered) when using the two transformations. For some ratios, a sizable percentage of the distribution falls in this category; for example, approximately 15%

TABLE 4.2 Deciles of Distribution of Financial Ratios/Variables: All Industries, 1983

Financial Ratio/Variable	Deciles of Distribution									Number of Observations
	.1	.2	.3	.4	.5	.6	.7	.8	.9	
1. (C + MS)/CL	.04	.08	.13	.19	.28	.39	.56	.80	1.30	1,744
2. (C + MS)/S	.01	.02	.03	.04	.06	.10	.14	.22	.74	1,968
3. (C + MS)/TA	.01	.02	.03	.05	.07	.10	.13	.18	.24	1,969
4. QA/CL	.55	.74	.88	1.02	1.15	1.32	1.52	1.81	2.47	1,675
5. CA/CL	.98	1.21	1.42	1.67	1.91	2.19	2.50	2.94	3.80	1,865
6. WCO/S	.00	.03	.05	.06	.08	.10	.12	.16	.25	1,778
7. WCO/TA	.00	.05	.07	.08	.10	.12	.14	.16	.18	1,766
8. CFO/S	−.02	.02	.04	.06	.08	.10	.13	.16	.24	1,636
9. CFO/TA	−.02	.03	.06	.08	.10	.12	.14	.17	.21	1,636
10. LTL/SE	.03	.12	.20	.29	.40	.53	.72	.96	1.51	1,961
11. (CL + LTL)/SE	.35	.52	.67	.82	.98	1.18	1.41	1.81	3.06	1,887
12. OI/INT	−.79	.11	.43	.95	1.43	2.01	2.94	4.74	9.83	2,069
13. CFO/INT	−.80	.72	1.70	2.69	3.84	5.12	7.13	10.24	17.81	1,570
14. NI ($ millions)	−4	1	2	5	11	20	34	67	163	2,165
15. E.P.S.	−.72	.17	.74	1.17	1.62	2.12	2.66	3.49	4.73	2,159
16. NI/S	−.04	.01	.02	.03	.04	.05	.07	.09	.18	2,162
17. NI/SE	−.09	.02	.06	.09	.10	.12	.14	.17	.22	1,959
18. NI/TA	−.03	.01	.02	.03	.04	.05	.07	.08	.11	2,150
19. S/TA	.18	.42	.65	.91	1.11	1.29	1.49	1.76	2.22	2,151
20. S/AR	3.53	4.49	5.24	5.94	6.68	7.31	8.37	10.18	16.28	1,704
21. COGS/INV	1.92	2.59	3.25	3.97	4.63	5.51	7.31	9.99	18.79	1,614
22. PE	−4.02	6.00	7.65	9.13	10.79	12.45	14.53	18.54	27.16	2,140
23. DIV. PAYOUT	.00	.00	.00	.17	.27	.35	.44	.57	.75	2,154
24. TA ($ millions)	30	58	106	176	303	547	1,109	2,355	5,164	2,167
25. S ($ millions)	26	59	112	185	295	466	786	1,495	3,458	2,166
26. MTK. CAP. ($ millions)	16	35	66	111	177	273	476	833	1,630	2,146

SOURCE: Computed from 1983 Compustat annual industrial file.

TABLE 4.3 Alternative Approaches to Reducing Departures from Normality in the Distribution of Financial Ratios

	Skewness Coefficient	Kurtosis Coefficient	Studentized Range	Number of Observations
Current assets				
Current liabilities				
Raw ratios, full sample	43.00	1,851.42	43.20	1,865
Raw ratios, top and bottom (1% trimmed)	1.54	3.15	6.37	1,829
Raw ratios, top and bottom (2% trimmed)	1.24	1.73	6.13	1,791
Square root transformation	32.05	1,243.78	40.21	1,865
Logarithmic transformation	.71	10.51	16.87	1,865
Current + long-term liabilities				
Stockholders' equity				
Raw ratios, full sample	29.31	925.47	34.58	1,887
Raw ratios, top and bottom (1% trimmed)	4.82	31.09	10.53	1,851
Raw ratios, top and bottom (2% trimmed)	3.05	12.20	7.96	1,813
Square root transformation	11.72	226.87	24.27	1,887
Logarithmic transformation	− .06	6.82	13.94	1,887
Sales				
Accounts receivable				
Raw ratios, full sample	7.21	64.72	14.27	1,704
Raw ratios, top and bottom (1% trimmed)	5.28	31.37	9.47	1,670
Raw ratios, top and bottom (2% trimmed)	4.74	24.89	8.75	1,636
Square root transformation	4.28	22.54	10.23	1,704
Logarithmic transformation	1.41	5.06	9.21	1,704

SOURCE: Computed from 1983 Compustat annual industrial file.

of firms in Table 4.2 have operating income-to-interest expense ratios with negative or zero values.

4.5 CORRELATIONS AND COMOVEMENTS BETWEEN FINANCIAL STATEMENT NUMBERS

The number of financial ratios one can compute from financial statements is obviously very high. Even within each of the main categories of ratios described in Chapter 3, there is a minimum of at least three or four different ratios proposed in the literature. In general, the number of ratios to compute in each category will depend on the specific decision context being considered. One important factor will be the extent to which the ratios in each category overlap in the information they provide. A useful first step in examining this issue is to compute the correlation and comovement between various ratios in each category. In Section 4.5.A, we shall examine the correlation between financial ratios of firms at a point in time; that is, it is a cross-sectional analysis. In Section 4.5.B, we shall examine the extent to which financial ratios of one firm move together over time; that is, it is a time-series analysis.

A. Cross-Section Correlation

Cross-sectional correlations between financial ratios are important when using such ratios in a statistical model. Consider a multiple regression model. One extreme case is where two ratios are the only independent variables and these two ratios happen to be perfectly collinear. In this case, one would not be able to compute estimates of the coefficients of the model. (This is due to the technical requirement that the matrix be invertible.) A less extreme case is where two ratios in a model are highly (but less than perfectly) correlated. In this case, problems exist in assessing the significance of individual variables in the multiple regression model. One consequence of multicollinearity between independent variables is that it is difficult to disentangle the influence of each variable. Moreover, the coefficients on the individual variables are sensitive to the number of observations used to estimate the model. A small change in the number of observations examined can often lead to a marked change in the estimated coefficients of the model.

The evidence in Section 4.4 indicated that the distribution of many financial ratios is nonnormal. This evidence has implications when examining the correlation between financial ratios at a point in time. The two main statistics for examining the correlation between two variables are (1) the Pearson moment correlation statistic and (2) the Spearman rank correlation statistic. The Pearson statistic is appropriate if the distribution of the two variables is approximately normal. In contrast, the Spearman statistic does not assume any specific distribution for the two variables. Due to the evidence in Section 4.4, the Spearman statistic is used in this section.

The Spearman rank correlation coefficient is calculated as

$$r_s = 1 - \frac{6 \sum d_i^2}{N^3 - N} \tag{4.9}$$

where d_i is the disparity in rankings of the two variables and N is the number of observations.

Consider computing the correlation between the 1983 current ratios and quick ratios for seven of the U.S. brewing companies discussed in Chapter 3:

Company	Current Ratio (CR_i)	Quick Ratio (QR_i)	Rank of CR_i	Rank of QR_i	d_i	d_i^2
Genesee	2.285	1.617	1	2	1	1
Falstaff	2.282	1.671	2	1	1	1
Adolph Coors	1.931	1.096	3	3	0	0
G. Heileman	1.298	.429	4	6	2	4
Anheuser-Busch	1.242	.695	5	5	0	0
Pittsburgh	1.040	.757	6	4	2	4
Pabst	.927	.287	7	7	0	0
						10

$$r_s = 1 - \frac{6 \times 10}{7^3 - 7} = .82$$

A Spearman rank correlation of .82 for seven observations is significant at the .05 level.

A high correlation between financial ratios used in a regression model does not necessarily mean that one wants to delete ratios from the model. The regression model might be specified by some theory (for example, of corporate failure), and a model excluding certain specified ratios may not be a test of the descriptive validity of the theoretical model. Note also that techniques have been developed by econometricians to improve the estimation of coefficients when multicollinearity is present; see Johnston (1984, pp. 239–259).

Even if one is concerned with building a parsimonious model, deleting financial ratios from the model is not the only alternative open to an analyst. For instance, a statistical tool such as factor analysis can be used prior to estimating the regression model. This tool aims at capturing the information contained in many variables and representing that information by a smaller number of derived variables; see Green (1978). In some contexts, there need be no requirement that all independent variables be uncorrelated with each other. If the concern is with explaining variations in the dependent variable, then including two correlated ratios may well explain more variation than using either of the ratios as a single independent variable. If the concern is with predicting the dependent variable, including two correlated ratios also can be justified.

B. Time-Series Comovement

Financial ratios are also used to assess changes in the liquidity, profitability, and so on of firms over time. As with cross-sectional tools, the issue arises of how many ratios to examine in such time-series assessments. One approach to gaining evidence on this issue is to examine the extent to which financial ratios move together over time. Consider the current and quick ratios of the seven brewing companies. The 1982 and 1983 values and the sign of the change (Δ) from 1982 to 1983 is

Company	CR_i 1982	CR_i 1983	QR_i 1982	QR_i 1983	ΔCR_i	ΔQR_i
Genesee	1.864	2.285	1.277	1.617	+	+
Falstaff	2.484	2.282	1.600	1.671	−	+
Adolph Coors	2.252	1.931	1.135	1.096	−	−
G. Heileman	1.586	1.298	.686	.429	−	−
Anheuser-Busch	1.071	1.242	.410	.695	+	+
Pittsburgh	.936	1.040	.631	.757	+	+
Pabst	1.254	.927	.504	.287	−	−

In six out of seven cases, the sign of the change in the current ratio is the same as the sign of the change in the quick ratio. The comovement measure is thus .86 (6/7); a measure of 1(0) indicates perfect positive (negative) comovement in the *sign* of the financial variable changes. (Another approach to examining the extent to which financial ratios move together is to conduct a correlation test similar to that in Section 4.5.A in a time-series context.)

C. Some Additional Evidence

Using the 1983 Compustat tape, correlations and comovements for the financial ratios/variables in the nine categories discussed in Section 4.4 were calculated. The correlation evidence was based on data for 1983 with the sample size for the pairwise correlations ranging from 1,536 to 2,165. The comovement evidence was based on data for 1978 to 1983 (that is, 1978–79, 1979–80, . . . , 1982–83) with the sample size for the pairwise comovements ranging from 7,744 to 11,272.

Results are presented in Table 4.4 for correlations and comovements *within* each of the nine categories of financial ratios. The numbers below the diagonal are the Spearman rank correlations for 1983. The numbers above the diagonal are the comovement measures for the 1978–1983 period. Results are presented in Table 4.5 for correlations and comovements of representative ratios *across* different categories.

In general, the correlations and comovements of ratios *within* each category are higher than the correlations and comovements of representative ratios *across* different categories. For example, cross-sectional correlation between the quick ratio and the current ratio is .790, and their time-series comovement is .833. In contrast, the correlation of the current ratio and the net income-to-shareholders' equity ratio is .110, and their comovement is .489. The turnover and the capital market categories have the lowest within category correlations between individual ratios. These two categories have also been reported to be relatively heterogeneous in prior studies.

TABLE 4.4 Correlations and Comovements Within Categories of Financial Ratios[1]

Cash position	(C + MS)/CL	(C + MS)/S	(C + MS)/TA		
(C + MS)/CL	**	.881	.901		
(C + MS)/S	.869	**	.911		
(C + MS)/TA	.908	.836	**		

Liquidity	QA/CL	CA/CL			
QA/CL	**	.833			
CA/CL	.790	**			

Working capital/Cash flow	WCO/S	WCO/TA	CFO/S	CFO/TA	
WCO/S	**	.849	.588	.585	
WCO/TA	.660	**	.563	.594	
CFO/S	.716	.436	**	.943	
CFO/TA	.545	.631	.820	**	

Capital structure	LTL/SE	(CL + LTL)/SE			
LTL/SE	**	.777			
(CL + LTL)/SE	.803	**			

Debt Coverage	OI/INT	CFO/INT			
OI/INT	**	.626			
CFO/INT	.682	**			

Profitability	NI	EPS	NI/S	NI/SE	NI/TA
NI	**	.884	.803	.796	.819
EPS	.820	**	.782	.811	.815
NI/S	.598	.597	**	.833	.867
NI/SE	.570	.617	.694	**	.899
NI/TA	.491	.486	.678	.869	**

Turnover	S/TA	S/AR	COGS/INV		
S/TA	**	.713	.706		
S/AR	.486	**	.637		
COGS/INV	.204	.370	**		

Capital market	PE	DIV. PAYOUT			
PE	**	.745			
DIV. PAYOUT	.275	**			

Firm size	TA	S	MKT. CAP		
TA	**	.820	.686		
S	.891	**	.672		
MKT. CAP.	.864	.869	**		

SOURCE: Computed from 1983 Compustat annual industrial file.
[1] Spearman rank correlations below diagonal which is marked **; agreement in sign of annual change above diagonal.

TABLE 4.5   Correlations and Comovements Between Representative Financial Ratios of Different Categories[1]

	$\dfrac{C + MS}{TA}$	$\dfrac{CA}{CL}$	$\dfrac{CFO}{S}$	$\dfrac{LTL}{SE}$	$\dfrac{OI}{INT}$	$\dfrac{NI}{SE}$	$\dfrac{S}{TA}$	PE	TA
(C + MS)/TA	**	.605	.650	.497	.560	.531	.488	.514	.493
CA/CL	.423	**	.508	.557	.538	.489	.472	.517	.458
CFO/S	.206	− .016	**	.469	.532	.528	.469	.503	.469
LTL/SE	− .337	− .446	− .132	**	.406	.519	.491	.504	.471
OI/INT	.256	.339	.241	− .591	**	.769	.579	.434	.495
NI/SE	.257	.110	.186	− .154	.700	**	.676	.383	.510
S/TA	.013	.209	− .450	− .219	.369	.239	**	.456	.508
PE	.111	.281	.162	− .226	.432	.201	.221	**	.557
TA	− .087	− .367	.261	.172	− .057	.097	− .338	− .133	**

SOURCE: Computed from 1983 Compustat annual industrial file.
[1] Spearman rank correlations below diagonal which is marked **; agreement in sign of annual change above diagonal.

4.6   SOME GENERAL COMMENTS

1. There is growing recognition of the strict proportionality assumption implicit when using financial ratios as a control for size differences across firms. Two influential articles are Lev and Sunder (1979) and Whittington (1980). For some ratios, there are theoretical reasons for questioning this strict proportionality assumption. Consider the implications for the inventory turnover ratio of using the economic order quantity (EOQ) inventory model outlined in many textbooks:

$$q = \sqrt{\frac{2C_p D}{C_s}} \tag{4.10}$$

where q = the economic order quantity
  C_p = the cost of placing an order
  D = the expected demand for the period
  C_s = the cost of storing one unit of inventory for the period
Holding C_p and C_s constant, there is a nonlinear relationship between q and D. Assume an industry in which the only difference across firms is the scale of their operations and one in which there is a proportional relation between sales (demand) and cost of goods sold. In this industry, the EOQ model would predict the second derivative between inventory holdings and sales to be negative. To illustrate, assume C_p = \$100 and C_s = \$5 per unit. Then, when

$$D = 100 \quad q = 63.24$$
$$D = 200 \quad q = 89.44$$
$$D = 300 \quad q = 109.54$$
$$D = 400 \quad q = 126.49$$

The optimal order quantity, when computed by the EOQ model, varies with the square root of periodic demand and not in linear proportion to this demand. The implication of adopting this EOQ model is that the relationship between the numerator and denominator of the inventory turnover ratio is nonlinear.

This EOQ model is but one normative model of inventory choice. It assumes that demand is known with certainty and that management is concerned only with one period ahead. The management science literature is replete with models that vary these and other assumptions. The actual inventory holdings of firms may not appear as predicted by (4.10) for several reasons; for example, (a) management uses a different inventory model in its decisions because the assumptions of the EOQ model are not descriptive, or (b) the assumptions are descriptive but management makes nonoptimal inventory decisions. Using (4.10) to explain differences across firms in their inventory holdings or their inventory turnover ratios would run into some thorny empirical problems. Most firms have numerous products, and data may not be available to an external analyst at the individual product level. The analyst also needs to estimate C_p, C_s, and D for each firm—not a trivial task in itself.

2. Detailed empirical evidence on the descriptive validity of the strict proportionality assumption is limited. McDonald and Morris (1984) probed this assumption for four financial ratios: current assets/sales, current assets/current liabilities, cash flow/total debt, and total debt/total assets. If strict proportionality between the numerator (X) and the denominator (Y) of a ratio exists, the intercept term in the following relation will be zero:

$$X_i = c + p \cdot Y_i + e_i \qquad \qquad \textbf{(4.11)}$$

where c is the intercept term and p is the responsiveness coefficient. Ordinary least squares was used to estimate (4.11) for both (a) 126 U.S. firms drawn from 126 separate four-digit SIC industries and (b) 113 U.S. firms from one four-digit industry (utilities). The motivation for McDonald and Morris examining both (a) and (b) was "to test the ratio method in its traditional application to intra-industry data and its more general extension to heterogeneous data" (p. 92). For the heterogeneous sample, the intercept was significantly different from zero for three of the four ratios; only for the total debt-to-total assets ratio was the intercept insignificantly different from zero. In addition, the residuals from (4.11) exhibited both skewness and kurtosis. It was concluded that these results were "not surprising, given that traditional analysis has long recognized that ratios do not have similar distributional characteristics across various industries" (p. 94). For the homogeneous industry sample, the intercept term was not significantly different from zero across any of the four ratios. Moreover, the "presence of nonnormalities is substantially reduced using the ratio specification" (p. 95); the "ratio specification" is the simple X/Y form traditionally found in the literature. The conclusion was that the "ratio method proved to be consistently superior to alternative (OLS) specifications for the intraindustry sample. . . . (These) findings provide strong empirical support for simple ratio analysis in its traditional form"

(p. 96). The generalizability of these conclusions to other single-industry samples is an open issue.

3. Empirical work on the distribution of financial ratios typically has examined which of two worlds exists: (a) ratios are normally distributed, or (b) ratios are nonnormally distributed. A more appealing approach is to expand the distributions examined so that more insight is gained into what distribution might be descriptive rather than the (seemingly) inevitable conclusion that the normal distribution is not descriptive. McLeay (1984) discusses the use of a maximum likelihood approach in this connection. A related approach is adopted by Buckmaster and Saniga (1984). These authors describe their methodology as follows:

> This study examines cross-sectional distribution forms for forty-one common financial ratios of large industrial firms classified according to a system of frequency curves proposed by Karl Pearson. . . . He represented the probability density function as a solution to a single differential equation with parameters depending upon the central moments, and expressed in terms of the population variance, the population skewness and the population kurtosis. (p. 3)

The aim of the analysis was to classify ratio distributions into shapes such as those in Figure 4.3. Forty-one financial ratios over the 1969–1978 period were examined. The conclusion was "that for 164 or 40.0% of the 410 years (41 ratios × 10 calendar years) reported, a J-shape distribution provides the best fit. The most striking feature . . . is the relative frequency of the J, Reverse J, Skewed and U-shaped distributions (97% of the total). . . . Departures from normality appear to be the rule for financial ratio distributions" (p. 8). This exploratory data approach provides little economic interpretation. However, prior research in this area is very much in this tradition. The benefit of the Buckmaster and Saniga approach is the increase in the informativeness of the results. For example, the conclusion is that "the current ratio has a J-shaped distribution" rather than the conclusion of most prior research that the current ratio does "not have a normal distribution."

An important but little researched area is the determinants of the distributions of financial ratios. Potential candidates include firm size, industry, and calendar year. Several trade associations publish yearly summary financial statement data, cross-categorized by firm size and industry; the implication is that homogeneity of financial statement relationships is increased by controlling for these two variables.

4. Evidence is presented in Chapter 6 that financial ratios and other variables move together over time due to the influence of economy and industry-related factors. This evidence suggests that tests for normality or other distribution forms should take account of these sources of cross-sectional commonalities. For instance, tests for normality could use residuals from a regression of firm ratios on economy and industry factors; these residuals might better satisfy the independence assumption implicit in the many tests used in the existing literature.

FIGURE 4.3 Shapes of Financial Ratio Distributions

Distribution	Shape	Characteristics
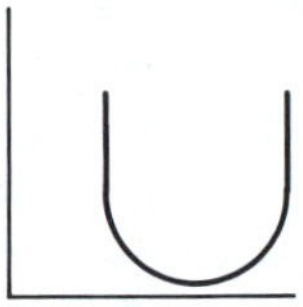	U	Unbounded both sides
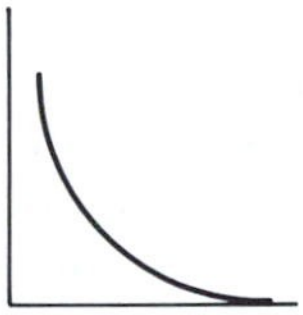	J	Right side bounded
	Reverse J	Left side bounded
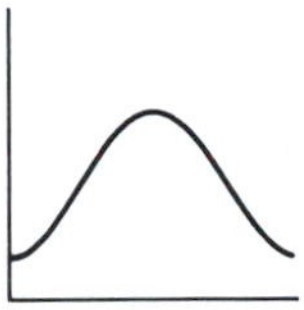	Normal	Unbounded both sides
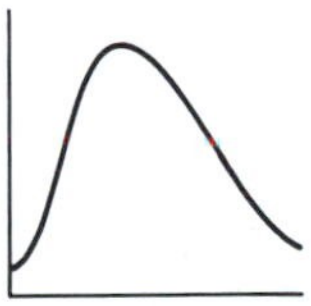	Skew	Unbounded both sides
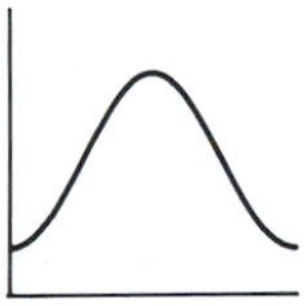	Symmetric	Unbounded both sides
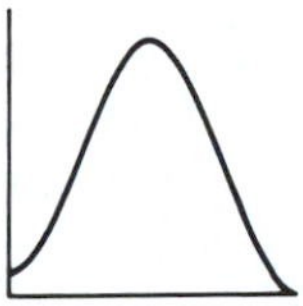	Regular (cocked-hat)	One side bounded

Source: Buckmaster and Saniga (1984): p. 12.

These commonalities also imply that one cannot invoke the central limit theorem as justification for assuming financial ratios are normally distributed. This theorem states that sums of N independent and identically distributed random variables will approximate a normal distribution as N becomes large. There are two important provisos in this theorem. First, the random variables are independent. As noted, due to economy and industry commonalities, this condition does not appear to be a descriptively valid one for many financial ratios. The second condition is that the random variables be identically (although not normally) distributed. Inasmuch as an identical distribution of a ratio across firms is a special case, there appears little economic rationale for expecting this special case to hold. At a minimum, differences across industries as regards concentration, barriers to entry, and so forth, may well mean that the distributions of a ratio across industries are not identical. In short, an appeal to the central limit theorem for assuming normality of financial ratio distributions is of questionable validity.

5. A growing body of evidence is accumulating concerning how the traditional categories of financial ratios (liquidity, leverage, profitability, and turnover) correspond to empirical relationships observed between these ratios. Gombola and Ketz (1983) is an illustrative study. These authors computed 58 financial ratios for 783 manufacturing firms over the 1971–1980 period. Then for each year, factor analysis was applied to the 58 financial ratios. Factor analysis takes correlations between combinations of these ratios and constructs new variables (called factors) that represent a more parsimonious description of the original set of variables; see Green (1978) and Jackson (1983). The aim is to express the (maximal) amount of information in the original variables by a reduced set of factors. Gombola and Ketz derive eight such factors. (With factor analysis, it is the researcher who decides the label to describe each factor.) These eight factors and the ratio with the highest correlation with each factor are

1. *Cash position:* cash/current debt
2. *Cash flow:* cash flow/assets
3. *Cash expenditures:* cash/cash expenditures
4. *Financial leverage:* total debt/net worth
5. *Return on investment:* income/equity
6. *Inventory intensiveness:* cost of goods sold/inventory
7. *Return on sales:* working capital from operations/sales
8. *Capital intensiveness:* current assets/total debts.

Gombola and Ketz reported that there was "considerable time-series stability" over the 1971–1980 period in the foregoing eight factors. One insight from this research is that cash flow and cash position ratios have different correlation structures than do the ratios traditionally grouped under the liquidity category. A second insight is that the turnover ratio category is a relatively heterogeneous one.

Factor analysis can, if used in an uncritical manner, become brute empiricism in the extreme. However, when used with recognition of its limitations (for example, the potential excessive reliance on factors suggested by data) and of the judgment calls necessary in its application (for example, how many separate factors to identify and what the labels of those factors should be), it can be a useful addition to the tools used in financial statement analysis. A useful discussion of the limitations of brute empiricism, alternatively known as data mining, data grubbing, or fishing, is in Lovell (1983).

4.7 SUMMARY

1. There is a diverse set of motives for examining financial data in a ratio format, including (a) controlling for size differences across firms or over time, (b) facilitating drawing of inferences from statistical analysis, (c) probing a theory in which a financial ratio is a variable of interest, and (d) exploiting observed empirical regularities between financial ratios and the estimation or prediction of variables of interest. Underlying one or more of these motivations are assumptions about the empirical properties of financial ratios, for example, strict proportionality between the numerator and the denominator or normality of the ratio distribution. An analyst should examine whether specific assumptions are descriptive of the financial data of interest.

2. Computational or interpretational problems are frequently encountered when examining data in ratio form. The possible causes of these problems are many, and an analyst should consider them before deciding how to handle them. For instance, the causes of extreme observations include factors such as recording errors, accounting classification, accounting method, and economic and structural change.

3. There is considerable evidence that many financial ratios are not well described by a normal distribution. When faced with nonnormally distributed data, the options available are many, for example, imposing normality on the data, using a transformation to better approximate normality, winsorizing the sample, trimming the sample, or using statistical tools that are more appropriate to the nonnormal distribution.

4. There is considerable evidence that specific financial ratios within many of the various categories (e.g., cash position, capital structure, and profitability) are often highly correlated with each other and have a high degree of comovement over time. This evidence is consistent with a smaller set of ratios being able to capture much of the information contained in the numerous financial ratios that can be calculated.

QUESTIONS

QUESTION 4.1: Financial Ratios and the Proportionality Assumption

A major motivation for examining financial data in ratio form is to control for the effect of size differences across firms or over time. Two important issues in regard to this motivation are

A. Given that alternative size measures are available, how does one decide the appropriate denominator for the financial ratio?
B. For a given size measure, is there a strict proportionality relationship between the numerator and denominator of the ratio?

Part A. Alternative measures of firm size include (1) sales, (2) total assets, (3) number of employees, (4) book value of shareholders' equity, and (5) market capitalization. Assume that the following correlations (Spearman rank) hold between pairwise combinations of (1) to (5) for a sample of the 1,000 largest (using sales) U.S. industrial companies:

	Sales	Assets	Employees	Book Value
Assets	.940			
Employees	.898	.887		
Book value	.907	.965	.861	
Market capitalization	.737	.832	.737	.880

REQUIRED

1. How would this information be useful in deciding the size measure to convert a financial variable to a ratio format?
2. What other information would you collect when deciding the appropriate denominator for a financial ratio?
3. Comment on the following: "When measuring profitability in ratio format, the choice of the denominator should be based on how the ratio is to be used: for product market applications, use sales; for public policy, use total assets; for labor market applications, use number of employees; for investment applications, use market capitalization."

Part B. Robert Morris Associates, in its *Annual Statement Studies,* presents median financial ratios for four firm-size categories, based on total assets:

    I. $0 to 1 million
   II. $1 to 10 million
  III. $10 to 50 million
  IV. $50 to 100 million

In addition, the median is presented for I, II, III, and IV combined in the "All" category. Using this information, preliminary evidence on the strict proportionality assumption can be gathered for the following two ratios reported in *Annual Statement Studies*:

- % Profit before taxes to total assets
- Sales to total assets

Table 4.6 presents the industry medians for these two ratios across the total asset categories for six manufacturing, three wholesaling, and five retailing industries.

REQUIRED

1. How might the strict proportionality assumption implicit in the use of the financial ratio format to control for size differences be violated? How would you test for these violations?
2. Do either or both of the two ratios in Table 4.6 violate the strict proportionality assumption?
3. What motivations, other than controlling for size differences, are there for examining data in ratio form?

QUESTION 4.2: Distribution of Industry Financial Ratios

Robert Morris Associates (RMA) in its *Annual Statement Studies* presents details of the lower quartile (.25 percentile), median (.50 percentile), and upper quartile (.75 percentile) of 16 financial ratios for a broad cross section of four-digit industries. Table 4.7 presents distribution data (LQ, M, and UQ) for 15 manufacturing industries for the following three ratios:

- Quick ratio
- Net sales/accounts and notes receivables
- (Profit before taxes/tangible net worth) × 100

RMA (a national association of U.S. bank loan and credit officers) states that "the individual firm financial reports used in the *Statement Studies* are not selected by any random or statistically reliable method. RMA member banks voluntarily submit the raw data they have available each year."

REQUIRED

1. Summarize the data in Table 4.7 into the Table 4.1 format, showing the percentage for each ratio with positive skewness, symmetry, and negative skewness in their distributions. What factors may explain the skewness percentages for each of the three financial ratios?
2. One approach to presenting distribution statistics of financial ratios is to rank observations from the lowest to highest and then determine the lower and upper quartiles. Another approach is to rank ratios from the strongest

TABLE 4.6 Industry Median Financial Ratios and Firm Size

Industry and SIC Code	% Profit Before Taxes to Total Assets					Sales to Total Assets				
	I	II	III	IV	ALL	I	II	III	IV	ALL
A. Manufacturing										
1. Plastic Products (3079)	5.4	5.7	5.0	2.0	5.4	2.4	1.9	1.6	1.4	2.0
2. Valves & Pipe Fittings (3494)	8.1	5.7	11.2	14.2	9.0	2.3	1.6	1.5	1.2	1.5
3. General Industrial Machinery (3561)	7.2	5.2	5.3	3.8	5.3	2.3	1.8	1.4	1.3	1.8
4. Electronic Computing Equipment (3573)	5.7	7.8	12.1	15.2	8.6	2.2	1.6	1.3	1.1	1.5
5. Radio & T.V. Transmitting Equip. (3662)	3.3	12.6	10.9	9.5	10.2	2.2	1.8	1.4	1.2	1.6
6. Electronic Components & Acces. (3671)	10.7	8.7	7.2	9.9	9.3	2.4	1.8	1.4	1.2	1.8
B. Wholesalers										
1. Heavy Commercial Equipment (5084)	3.5	2.6	2.5	-0.7	2.9	2.9	2.3	1.8	1.7	2.5
2. General Groceries (5141)	4.2	5.5	4.6	9.7	5.1	5.0	5.0	6.3	6.7	5.3
3. Fuel Oil (5172)	3.0	3.8	4.2	2.9	3.4	6.6	6.2	4.1	5.5	6.1
C. Retailing										
1. Road Machinery Equipment (5082)	3.0	1.1	0.3	-3.7	1.0	2.2	1.6	1.5	1.4	1.6
2. Department Stores (5311)	6.7	3.8	5.0	7.2	5.0	2.2	2.0	2.3	2.3	2.1
3. Groceries & Meats (5411)	7.8	5.3	7.1	8.4	6.9	6.4	6.4	5.9	5.1	6.2
4. Restaurants (5812)	6.6	7.9	7.4	13.2	7.3	3.4	2.4	1.8	1.7	2.8
5. Restaurants—Fast Foods (5812)	9.0	7.1	5.6	5.7	8.2	3.0	2.5	1.7	1.6	2.6

KEY: I = $0 to $1 million in total assets; II = $1 to $10 million; III = $10 to $50 million; IV = $50 to $100 million.

SOURCE: Robert Morris Associates [1983], copyright 1983

NOTE: Interpretation of Statement Studies figures: "RMA recommends that *Statement Studies* data be regarded only as general guidelines and not as absolute industry norms. There are several reasons why the data may not be fully representative of a given industry:

(1) The financial statements used in the *Statement Studies* are not selected by any random or statistically reliable method. RMA member banks voluntarily submit the raw data they have available each year, with these being the only constraints: (a) The fiscal year-ends of the companies reported may not be from April 1 through June 29, and (b) their total assets must be less than $100 million.

(2) Many companies have varied product lines; however, the *Statement Studies* categorize them by their primary product Standard Industrial Classification (SIC) number only.

(3) Some of our industry samples are rather small in relation to the total number of firms in a given industry. A relatively small sample can increase the chances that some of our composites do not fully represent an industry.

(4) There is the chance that an extreme statement can be present in a sample, causing a disproportionate influence on the industry composite. This is particularly true in a relatively small sample.

(5) Companies within the same industry may differ in their method of operations which in turn can directly influence their financial statements. Since they are included in our sample, too, these statements can significantly affect our composite calculations.

(6) Other considerations that can result in variations among different companies engaged in the same general line of business are different labor markets; geographical location; different accounting methods; quality of products handled; sources and methods of financing; and terms of sale.

For these reasons, RMA does not recommend the *Statement Studies* figures be considered as absolute norms for a given industry. Rather the figures should be used only as general guidelines and in addition to the other methods of financial analysis. RMA makes no claim as to the representativeness of the figures printed in this book."

TABLE 4.7 Distribution Statistics for Financial Ratios of Selected Industries

Industry and SIC Code	Number of Firms	Quick Ratio			Sales/Receivables			% Profit Before Taxes to Tangible Net Worth		
		LQ	M	UQ	LQ	M	UQ	LQ	M	UQ
1. Paint, varnish, and lacquer (2851)	136	.8	1.1	1.7	6.8	8.1	10.7	3.2	11.0	23.6
2. Plastic materials (2821)	126	.6	.9	1.3	7.0	8.3	10.7	6.4	15.4	30.7
3. Bread and bakery products (2051)	108	.5	.8	1.3	13.1	17.0	27.0	8.0	22.1	47.3
4. Dairy products (2021)	124	.5	.8	1.1	12.9	16.9	22.5	6.8	17.3	31.2
5. Meat packing (2011)	134	.6	1.0	1.6	19.0	24.7	29.1	2.9	13.0	29.1
6. Wood furniture (2511)	129	.5	.8	1.4	7.0	8.9	13.9	.1	13.3	28.5
7. Millwork (2431)	142	.5	.8	1.7	7.0	9.3	12.6	−7.1	11.1	22.8
8. Sawmills (2421)	167	.2	.5	1.0	10.6	14.6	23.9	−18.8	3.5	10.7
9. Radio and T.V. transmitting equipment (3662)	166	.7	1.0	1.8	5.0	6.2	8.6	8.8	22.1	46.0
10. Construction equipment (3531)	117	.4	.7	1.7	6.0	8.3	13.6	−13.5	5.1	14.1
11. Electronic computing equipment (3573)	178	.7	1.1	1.9	4.6	5.6	7.2	3.8	21.3	39.7
12. General industrial equipment (3561)	411	.6	1.0	1.6	5.7	7.4	10.2	1.3	13.9	29.1
13. Machine shop repair (3599)	550	.6	.9	1.5	6.7	8.7	11.8	−5.5	12.3	28.1
14. Iron and steel foundries (3321)	147	.6	1.1	1.9	7.4	9.6	13.3	−13.5	4.0	18.3
15. Nonferrous fabricated products (3499)	183	.6	1.0	1.6	6.4	8.2	10.9	−3.6	11.6	27.7

LQ – Lower quartile (.25 percentile).
M – Median (.5 percentile).
UQ – Upper quartile (.75 percentile).

SOURCE: Robert Morris Associates (1983), Copyright 1983. Table 4.6 includes a note by RMA on the "Interpretation of *Statement Studies* Figures," which should be read when using the RMA data.

to the weakest; for example, the current ratio is ranked from the highest (strongest) to the lowest (weakest), whereas, the debt-to-equity ratio is ranked from the lowest (strongest) to the highest (weakest). What problems may arise in deciding what is the "strongest" ratio and what is the "weakest" ratio as opposed to deciding what is the lowest and what is the highest?

3. When computing the profit before taxes-to-tangible net worth ratio, what alternatives might RMA consider when tangible net worth is reported on a financial statement as negative?

4. A recent empirical study examined whether financial ratios were normally distributed. Phase 1 examined an economywide sample of 1,000 firms from ten industries. Phase 2 examined separately the ten industries comprising the economy sample. It was found that the normality assumption was more likely to be rejected for the economywide sample than for each of the ten separate industry subsamples. What factors could explain this result? What problems arise in testing whether financial ratios are better described by a normal distribution at the industry level than at the economy level?

QUESTION 4.3: Outliers and the Distribution of Financial Ratios

Tests for whether a normal distribution describes the distribution of a financial ratio are sensitive to the number and magnitude of extreme observations. Frecka and Hopwood (1983) report results using two alternative approaches to "reducing" the effect of extreme observations:

1. Use of a square root transformation.
2. Use of an "outlier removal" approach—"outliers are removed until skewness or kurtosis is no longer significant" (p. 119). This approach is applied independently to each financial ratio distribution examined.

They report (in figure 3, p. 124) the following statistics for the quick ratio (quick assets/current liabilities):

Distribution Statistic	Raw Data	Square Root Transformation of Ratio, All Observations	Square Root Transformation, "Outliers" Removed
Mean (Y_1)	1.361	1.102	1.062
Variance (Y_2^2)	10.884	.146	.042
Skewness (Y_3)	31.630	13.325	.176
Kurtosis (Y_4)	1,048.444	317.146	3.335
Number of observations	1,156	1,156	1,113

The most extreme quick ratio in the sample was 110.6.

REQUIRED

1. How successful are the foregoing two approaches in transforming the quick ratio such that its distribution is better approximated by a normal distribution?

2. Comment on the following argument by Frecka and Hopwood (1983):

   > Once the outliers are removed, the distribution does not appear to depart from normality in any extraordinary fashion. Since it is well-known that most statistical tests are robust with respect to mild departures from normality, normality may be an "accurate enough" approximation for many decision applications (p. 123).

3. Do you agree with the following criticisms of the "outlier approach":

   > The first criticism is that it is difficult to see how "suspicious observations" can exist when the financial statements from which the observations are calculated are carefully drawn up. The second criticism is that ratios are often interdependent and that to discard observations on one ratio should logically lead to elimination of seemingly normal observations calculated from the same financial statement on the interdependent ratios. For example, given a Debt-to-Equity Ratio of, say, 1 and a certain level of current assets, even an extreme Current Ratio due to a very low level of current liabilities will coincide with a perfectly innocent-looking Long-Term Debt-to-Equity Ratio. However, if the outlying CR is suspect, why not then the LTDE ratio?

4. Assume that you develop a quantitative model for a lending institution to monitor changes in the financial solvency of its clients. The quick ratio is one of the variables you wish to include in the model. What are the pros and cons of the two approaches used by Frecka and Hopwood to deriving a distribution of the quick ratio that is better approximated by the normal distribution?

5. In the lending decision context, what other alternatives to handling extreme observations exist?

QUESTION   4.4:   Correlations and Comovements Between Financial Ratios

There is substantial evidence that financial ratios are correlated in cross-sectional contexts and comove in time-series contexts. Tables 4.4 and 4.5 have presented empirical evidence that relates to both within category and between category correlations and comovements.

REQUIRED

1. What factors could account for the observed correlations and comovements in Table 4.4? Compare and contrast the correlations/comovements observed for financial ratios within each of the nine categories in Table 4.4.

2. Compare and contrast the correlations/comovements reported in Table 4.4 with those in 4.5.

3. What inference would you draw if the correlation and comovement measures for selected pairs of financial ratios in Table 4.5 exceeded .9?

4. Evaluate the following argument:

> This presence of collinearity is both a blessing and a curse for financial ratio analysis. It means that only a small number of financial ratios are needed to capture most of the information that ratios can provide, but it also means that this small number must be selected very carefully. A selection of collinear ratios that are related to a dependent variable in the same fashion would obscure and possibly worsen the results of multivariate analyses. It is clear that large numbers of financial ratios cannot be computed willy-nilly in an analysis. The collinearity of these ratios requires that a careful and parsimonious selection be carried out.

REFERENCES

BARNES, P. "Methodological Implications of Non-Normally Distributed Financial Ratios." *Journal of Business Finance and Accounting* (Spring 1982): 51–62.

BARNETT, V., and T. LEWIS. *Outliers in Statistical Data*. New York: John Wiley, 1978.

BEECHER, A., M. EZZAMEL, and C. MAR-MOLINERO. "On the Distributional Properties of Financial Ratios in Small Samples—A Cross-Sectional Analysis," working paper. University of Southampton, U.K., 1984.

BEEDLES, W. L., and M. A. SIMKOWITZ. "A Note on Skewness and Data Errors." *The Journal of Finance* (March 1978): 288–292.

BIRD, R. G., and A. J. McHUGH. "Financial Ratios—An Empirical Study." *Journal of Business Finance and Accounting* (Spring 1977): 29–45.

BOUGEN, P. D., and J. C. DRURY. "U.K. Statistical Distributions of Financial Ratios, 1975." *Journal of Business Finance and Accounting* (Spring 1980): 39–47.

BUCKMASTER, D., and E. SANIGA. "Distribution Forms of Financial Accounting Ratios: Pearson's Taxonomy and Empirical Identification," working paper. University of Delaware, Newark, 1984.

BUIJINK, W., and M. JEGERS. "Cross-Sectional Distributional Properties of Financial Ratios in Belgian Manufacturing Industries: Some Empirical Evidence," working paper. University of Antwerp, Belgium, 1984.

CHEN, K. H., and T. A. SHIMERDA. "An Empirical Analysis of Useful Financial Ratios." *Financial Management* (Spring 1981): 51–60.

DEAKIN, E. B. "Distributions of Financial Accounting Ratios: Some Empirical Evidence." *The Accounting Review* (January 1976): 90–96.

FRECKA, T. J., and W. S. HOPWOOD. "The Effect of Outliers on the Cross-Sectional Distributional Properties of Financial Ratios." *The Accounting Review* (January 1983): 115–128.

GOMBOLA, M. J., and J. E. KETZ. "Financial Ratio Patterns in Retail and Manufacturing Organizations." *Financial Management* (Summer 1983): 45–56.

GREEN, P. E. *Analyzing Multivariate Data*. Hinsdale, Ill.: Dryden Press, 1978.

HORRIGAN, J. O. "Some Empirical Bases of Financial Ratio Analysis." *The Accounting Review* (July 1965): 558–568.

HORRIGAN, J. O. "Methodological Implications of Non-Normally Distributed Financial Ratios: A Comment." *Journal of Business Finance and Accounting* (Winter 1983): 683–689.

JACKSON, B. B. *Multivariate Data Analysis*. Homewood, Ill.: Richard D. Irwin, 1983.

JOHNSTON, J. *Econometric Methods,* 3rd ed. New York: McGraw-Hill, 1984.

LEV, B., and S. SUNDER, "Methodological Issues in the Use of Financial Ratios." *Journal of Accounting and Economics* (December 1979): 187–210.

LOVELL, M. C. "Data Mining." *The Review of Economics and Statistics* (February 1983): 1–12.

MCDONALD, B., and M. H. MORRIS. "The Statistical Validity of the Ratio Method in Financial Analysis: An Empirical Examination." *Journal of Business Finance and Accounting* (Spring 1984): 89–97.

MCLEAY, S. "A Likelihood Approach to the Statistical Modelling of Financial Ratios," working paper. University of Lancaster, U.K., 1984.

RICKETTS, D., and R. STOVER, "An Examination of Commercial Bank Financial Ratios." *Journal of Bank Research* (Summer 1978): 121–124.

ROBERT MORRIS ASSOCIATES. *Annual Statement Studies*. Philadelphia: RMA, 1983.

POHLMAN, R. A., and R. D. HOLLINGER. "Information Redundancy in Sets of Financial Ratios." *Journal of Business, Finance and Accounting* (Winter 1981): 511–528.

WHITTINGTON, G. "Some Basic Properties of Accounting Ratios." *Journal of Business Finance and Accounting* (Summer 1980): 219–232.

5

FINANCIAL STATEMENT NUMBERS AND ALTERNATIVE ACCOUNTING METHODS

5.1 INTRODUCTION

The numbers reported in financial statements are a function, in part, of the accounting methods chosen by the firm. This chapter discusses (1) issues and evidence associated with accounting method choice and (2) options available to analysts when faced with diversity in accounting methods. The pros and cons of individual accounting issues such as changing prices, foreign currency translation, and pension obligations will not be discussed. These individual issues are examined in detail in textbooks for corporate financial reporting or intermediate accounting courses.

Change and experimentation in accounting method choice are common events. New lines of business can be started by firms that have their own idiosyncratic accounting problems (for example, cable television). New business practices can develop that raise previously unaddressed accounting issues (for example, leveraged leasing). New economic phenomena can occur that were not contemplated when the existing accounting methods were chosen (for example, floating foreign exchange rates). The many pressures for accounting change place a premium on understanding accounting method choice at a more basic level than is typically found when the pros and cons of a specific set of accounting alternatives are discussed.

5.2 REPORTED NUMBERS AND ACCOUNTING METHODS: AN INTERACTIVE PERSPECTIVE

The numbers reported in financial statements are affected by firm-oriented, industry, and economy factors. Figure 5.1 presents an overview of this perspective. The four firm-oriented factors (neither mutually exclusive nor collectively exhaustive) illustrated in Figure 5.1 are:

1. *Mix of business.* For example, will the firm operate in a single line of business (LOB), a vertically integrated set of businesses, a horizontally integrated set of businesses, a set of technology related businesses, or a diversified (conglomerate) set of businesses?

2. *Financing decisions.* For example, will finance be raised by equity, bank loans, public debt, leasing, or R&D partnerships? And will bank loans be at a variable or a fixed rate of interest?

3. *Operating decisions.* For example, what mix of products will be manufactured, what level of wages will be paid, what level of inventory will be held, and how much will be spent on discretionary items like research and development and exploration?

FIGURE 5.1 Interactive Perspective of Accounting Method Choice

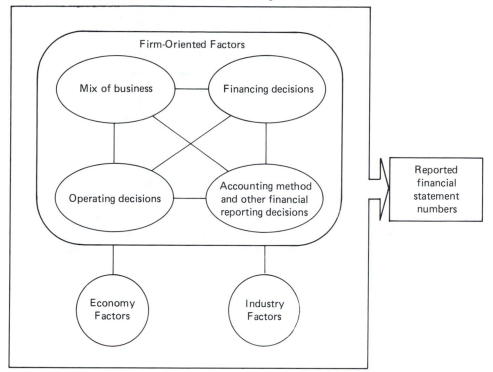

4. *Accounting method and other financial reporting decisions.* For example, what asset and liability rules will be adopted from the available options, what rules will be adopted for revenue and expense recognition, and what items will be classified as extraordinary?

The importance of firm-oriented, industry, and economy factors in explaining the numbers reported in financial statements is discussed in this and subsequent chapters. Evidence presented in Chapter 6 indicates that for a sample of 315 U.S. firms, industry and economy factors, on average, jointly explain 43% of the change in annual net income of individual firms.

Why an Interactive Perspective?

Figure 5.1 portrays accounting method choice (and other financial reporting decisions) as affecting and being affected by the other three firm-oriented factors (mix of business, financing decisions, and operating decisions) and by industry and economy factors. There is considerable evidence to support this interactive perspective. Consider FASB decisions in the leasing area. Abdel-khalik (1981) reported results of a study on the economic consequences of *FASB Statement No. 13* (Accounting for Leases). This FASB statement outlined criteria to distinguish between capital leases (which had to be reported as a liability on the balance sheet) and operating leases. One finding was that a majority of companies surveyed were structuring the terms of new lease contracts to avoid capitalization; that is, the financing decisions of a firm were affected by their balance sheet representations. The many creative (and not-so-creative) efforts of the investment banking industry to structure other forms of off-balance-sheet financing (for example, project financing) is also consistent with the interactive perspective in Figure 5.1.

Statements made by management concerning FASB decisions in the foreign exchange translation area also support the interactive perspective. Systematic survey evidence by Evans, Folks, and Jilling (1978) found an interaction between *FASB Statement No. 8* (Accounting for the Translation of Foreign Currency Transactions and Foreign Currency Financial Statements) and the forward contracts entered into by multinationals. Based on interviews with "corporate treasury personnel at sixteen of the largest U.S. industrial companies," Andrews (1983–84) reports a similar interaction finding with the successor to *FASB Statement No. 8*, that is, *FASB Statement No. 52* (Foreign Currency Translation).

5.3 FACTORS AFFECTING ACCOUNTING METHOD CHOICE

This section outlines a variety of factors that management may consider when making accounting method choices. These factors are not mutually exclusive, and in any one choice several may be simultaneously considered.

A. Compliance with Regulatory Mandates

Many firms cite compliance with the accounting standards issued by regulatory bodies when explaining changes in their accounting methods:

- Du Pont adopted Statement of Financial Accounting Standards No. 34, "Capitalization of Interest Cost". . . . As a result, interest cost was included in plants and properties and interest on borrowing was reduced. (Du Pont)
- The Company adopted the percentage of completion method of income recognition for its marine construction contracts. . . . The change was adopted to better reflect the progress and performance of contract work in the marine construction operations and to conform with criteria contained in The Statement of Position "Accounting for Performance of Construction-Type Contracts" issued by the American Institute of Certified Public Accountants. (McDermott Incorporated)

When faced with a regulatory mandate, compliance need not be the only option available to the firm. For instance, the firm may choose to receive a qualified audit opinion relating to noncompliance with a FASB standard. Another option is for the firm to become privately owned; mandates by regulatory bodies, such as the FASB or the SEC, do not apply to privately owned firms.

B. Consistency with the Accounting Model

A major segment of the accounting literature posits that the choice between alternative methods should be based on accounting model notions such as matching costs with revenues, conservatism, and objectivity. Statements given by management in annual reports at the time of voluntary accounting changes make frequent reference to these notions:

- The change (from FIFO to LIFO) was made to achieve a better matching of current costs with revenues.   (International Minerals and Chemical Corp)
- The change (from LIFO to FIFO) was made . . . because the impact of technology on the cost of inventory results in a more proper matching of current cost with current revenue utilizing FIFO.   (Keithley Instruments)

The president of Comserv gave, to a financial reporter, the following rationale for the company's expensing rather than capitalizing the costs associated with software development:

> Conservatism of accounting is the only basis on which we should defend our position. We should leave our creativity to our software development and not the way we account for it.

Intermediate accounting textbooks focus heavily on accounting model notions when discussing the pros and cons of individual accounting method alternatives.

C. Presentation of Economic Reality or Truth

Terms such as "economic reality" and "truth" often are used by management either when explaining an accounting change or criticizing a mandated accounting method. Consider the following statements by firms opting for early adoption of *FASB Statement No. 52* over *FASB Statement No. 8* in the foreign currency translation area:

- We believe the adoption of FASB No. 52 will eliminate much of the non-economic volatility that has plagued the earnings reports of companies with international operations such as ours.   (Bundy Corporation)
- The earnings now more clearly present a true indication of the economic operating realities of the company.   (Emhart)
- The company has adopted the new standard because it more appropriately reflects the economic realities of managing a multinational company.   (Hercules)

Operational definitions of terms such as "economic reality" and "truth" have remained elusive. There appears to be little similarity in the many contexts in which management uses these terms to justify their accounting method decisions.

D. Comparability with Other Firms in the Same Industry

The desire to achieve comparability with other firms in the industry is often cited as an important factor in accounting method choice. For example,

- The change was made principally to conform with the predominant depreciation method used by other companies in the (sugar production and real estate) industries. (Alexander and Baldwin)
- In order to achieve greater comparability with the accounting practices of other companies in the industry, the Company changed its method of accounting for finance costs it incurs on dealer receivables transferred with recourse to finance companies. (Hesston Corporation)

The reason why intraindustry uniformity in accounting methods is important is not always made explicit by management. Comments made in the financial press typically argue that management perceives the existence of a mechanistic relationship between reported earnings and the company's stock price. The belief is that the capital market adopts a fixed earnings multiple for all firms in the same industry, irrespective of the accounting methods used to compute reported earnings. (Subsequent chapters of this book will provide evidence on whether the capital market reacts to reported earnings in the mechanistic way that appears implicit in many statements by corporate management.)

E. Economic Consequences to the Firm

The choice of accounting method can influence the market value of the firm's equity or debt securities in at least five (overlapping) ways:

Taxation Expense Influence

Where there is a link between the accounting methods used for financial reporting and those used for tax reporting, firms can affect their corporate tax exposure via accounting method choice. Under several U.S. laws passed in the late 1930s, a firm that uses the LIFO inventory method for tax reporting also has to use LIFO for financial reporting. This law gives firms the option of reducing taxation payments by accounting method changes: firms that expect inventory levels to increase (decrease) and the purchase prices of inventory to increase (decrease) can reduce expected taxation payments (in present value terms) by switching from FIFO to LIFO (LIFO to FIFO). Management statements in annual reports at the time of inventory accounting changes frequently cite the cash flow benefits of the change. One company gives the following estimate of the dollar magnitude of the tax savings:

> When it became evident that we had entered a long-term high inflation period, Dayco shifted to the LIFO method of valuing domestic inventories. . . . Taxing authorities permit us to deduct the LIFO provision on our tax returns. We believe that a dollar saved in taxes is as good for our shareholders as a dollar earned (after taxes) from operations.
>
> We have estimated the net present value of the tax benefits to Dayco from using LIFO. To do this, we used the very conservative assumptions of:

An average annual projected LIFO tax benefit of $1,500,000 plus the existing tax savings of $24,471,000, and

An average after-tax rate of return of 8 percent.

The present tax benefit, combined with the estimated future tax benefit discounted at 8 percent, yields a value to the Corporation in today's dollars of approximately $43,221,000 or $7.22 per share. This represents approximately 32 percent of our current book value.   (Dayco Corporation)

Given that many of the factors that influence inventory decisions will be common to all firms in the industry, industry patterns in inventory choice are to be expected. (Section 5.4 provides further discussion.)

Data Collection and Operating Cost Influence

Accounting alternatives can differ in their data collection and operating costs. For instance, reporting land and buildings at historical cost is less costly than is reporting land and buildings at current market values where these market values are updated annually and certified by an external valuer. Similarly, using group depreciation rates for broad categories of plant and equipment is less costly than is using a separate depreciation rate for each individual item of plant and equipment.

Operating cost issues also are an important factor in inventory decisions. One factor in minimizing taxation under LIFO, when faced with increasing purchase prices per unit, is maintaining a constant or increasing (physical) level of inventories. When purchase prices are increasing, a reduction in inventory levels can cause the firm to "dip into" lower-costed inventory layers; this results in higher reported earnings and thus higher taxation payments. One means of avoiding this situation is for a firm to make purchases such that a reduction in inventory does not occur; see Biddle (1980) for evidence consistent with this proposition. This strategy can result in higher operating expenses due to increased storage costs and more money tied up in inventory. Note that in this context, the inventory accounting method choice can involve a trade-off between taxation minimization and higher operating expenses.

Financing Cost Influence

An example where financing costs can be influenced by accounting method choice is in the bank lending area. Assume that a firm has borrowed from a bank and that, as part of the lending agreement, a covenant is written on the times interest earned ratio. If the lending agreement does not specify the accounting methods under which the covenant is to be interpreted, management may make an accounting change to avoid technical violation of the covenant. The financing cost impact of this decision will be influenced by the actions the bank would have taken had a violation occurred; for example, the bank may have forced a renegotiation of the loan at a higher interest rate. Not surprisingly, firms do not state that avoidance of a loan covenant violation is the reason for making an accounting change. However, the financial press and other external parties have cited it as a factor in some individual cases. For instance, *The Wall Street Journal* in the 1970s raised the possibility that a revenue recognition change enabled Pan American to avoid violating some "critical covenants or financial tests in its current bank loan agreement." The change, which related to revenue estimation from advance ticket sales, increased monthly revenue by $28.3 million in a month that earnings (after the change) were reported as $19.3 million.

Political and Regulatory Cost Influences

Governments and regulatory agencies have the power to transfer wealth from firms to other parties. Firms may attempt to affect such wealth redistributions via their accounting method choice. For example, consider the debate over retirement, replacement, and betterment (RRB) versus depreciation accounting for railroads and the perceived effect of the choice on the rail rates set by the Interstate Commerce Commission. Under RRB accounting, the costs of track replacements are expensed in the period in which the costs are incurred; this method was widely adopted by railroads up to 1982. In 1983, the Interstate Commerce Commission required railroads to use depreciation accounting for these costs; this method allocates these costs over their expected lives. The effect was to increase the reported incomes of many railroads. *The Wall Street Journal* noted that railroad executives "fear that the new bookkeeping could hinder railroads' efforts to secure federal approval of proposed rate increases and could force some lines to pay higher state income and property taxes."

In addition to their effect on rate regulation, reported profits can affect the perception of politicians as to a firm's "ability to pay" additional taxes. In this situation, management may choose accounting methods that they perceive will minimize their exposure to additional taxation. For instance, accounting alternatives that allocate "gains" over several years may be preferred to those that result in the "gains" being reported as profit in a single year. Similarly, historical cost rules for natural resources, such as oil and gas and timber, may be preferred to the use of market value rules that typically report firms as having more resources under their control. (See Chapter 2 for further discussion of political costs.)

Wealth Redistribution Among Claimants

Financial statement numbers are often the basis by which wealth is distributed among various parties, for example, in profit sharing agreements with workers and in "earn-out" provisions associated with acquisitions. In this context, accounting method choice may affect the amounts individual parties receive. For instance, assume that Company A acquires Company B and part of the acquisition consideration is a percentage of the earnings of Company B in the following three years. The management of Company A has an incentive to adopt accounting alternatives that expense items in the next three years as opposed to alternatives that capitalize costs and expense them over a longer time horizon.

F.   Economic Consequences to Management

Management's wealth may be affected by accounting method choice in several ways. Many executive compensation packages *explicitly* include bonus plans or stock option plans in which financial statement-based variables are a key component. For instance, some plans define the bonus pool to be a percentage of reported earnings. Other plans base the award of stock option units on the return on equity of the firm vis-à-vis the average return on equity of a "key competitor" group of firms. In this context, management has the potential to affect their compensation by choosing accounting methods that are perceived to increase the present value of their compensation package. Even if there is no explicit link between financial statement variables and an executive compensation plan, an *implicit* link could result in management considering this factor in accounting method choice.

As with the bond-covenant-violation motivation discussed in Section 5.3.E, management is unlikely to state that maximization of their compensation is a factor in their accounting method decisions. However, external commentators have long recognized this possibility. For instance, Lindhe (1963) made a study of firms that switched from straight-line to accelerated depreciation in the 1950s. His conclusions included the following: "Profit sharing could be a deterrent to adoption of accelerated depreciation . . . , since adoption could reduce profits use as a basis for profit-sharing plans. In some industries, firms with high rates of profit-sharing tend to use straight-line depreciation, while those with lower rates use accelerated depreciation. Changes in profit-sharing rates sometimes were followed by a change in depreciation policy. Since the motives of the decision-makers are in question, there is no true way of resolving the cause of the action" (p. 145).

Management may also perceive that accounting method choices can affect the likelihood of a takeover, or the cost of a takeover. For instance, reporting higher current profits may be perceived as increasing the acquisition cost of the firm (and potentially decreasing the likelihood of acquisition) if management believes that acquiring firms use a mechanical multiplier of reported earnings in their acquisition analysis.

G.   Overview Comments

1. The six factors just discussed are not mutually exclusive. For instance, the regulatory mandate may be justified in terms of the accounting model view or the economic reality view. The economic consequences to the firm and the economic consequences to management views can be congruent if man-

agement's incentives are structured to maximize the value of the firm (for example, via the use of stock options for an all-equity financed firm). Note, however, that in any one accounting method decision, these factors may not all operate in the same direction. For example, to reduce political costs an income-decreasing method may be preferred, whereas to increase executive compensation an income-increasing method may be preferred.

2. Evidence on the existence or relative importance of the six factors comes from a variety of sources, for example, statements by management in annual reports, questionnaire responses by management, submissions by management to accounting regulatory bodies, comments made in the financial press, and studies in the empirical and analytical academic research literatures. Section 5.7 discusses several of these forms of evidence.

3. Several of the factors cited as important in Sections 5.3.A–F assume that other parties do not automatically make adjustments to neutralize the effect of any accounting change. Consider the argument that management can increase compensation by making an accounting change that will increase the available bonus pool. Management compensation schemes typically include a provision giving a compensation committee discretion to make adjustments to the plan. For senior executives, this committee often includes outside directors. When an accounting change is made, the compensation committee could automatically adjust the bonus pool formula such that the increase in reported earnings is offset by a lower percentage being allocated to the bonus pool. Similarly, consider the argument that rate regulators will set higher rates if firms choose accounting alternatives that report lower profits. This assumes rate regulators do not have the ability nor the incentive to make adjustments to examine how reported profits would appear under alternative accounting methods.

4. Figure 5.2 outlines several perspectives on accounting method choice. Most

FIGURE 5.2 Alternative Perspectives on Accounting Method Choice

		Number of Accounting Issues (Inventory, Depreciation, etc.) Simultaneously Considered	
		Single issue at a time focus	Multiple issues simultaneously considered
Number of Periods That Financial Statement and Other Impacts of Choice Considered	Current period only	I	II
	Multiple periods	III	IV

discussions in annual reports and in the accounting literature focus on I in Figure 5.2; that is, they focus on a single accounting issue at a time and consider its financial statement and other effects for only a single (that is, the current) period. Alternative perspectives, focusing on multiple issues or on multiple periods, are more complex; see Amershi, Demski, and Wolfson (1982) for a discussion. Ultimately, it is an empirical issue as to which perspective in Figure 5.2 is most descriptive of accounting method choice by firms.

5.4 ACCOUNTING METHOD DIFFERENCES: EVIDENCE OF SYSTEMATIC PATTERNS

There is considerable evidence of systematic patterns in the accounting methods chosen by firms. This section presents a subset of this evidence. (A further discussion of the evidence and related topics is in Section 5.7.)

A. Profiles of Firms Using Different Accounting Alternatives

Industry membership is one variable that explains differences across firms in their accounting method choice. Early recognition of this variable is in Gilman (1939). He observed that while cost-based inventory valuation methods were used by companies in most industries, market-based methods were used by both gold-mining companies and meat-packing companies. One rationale offered for this industry difference was the greater difficulty of allocating joint costs to individual products in both these industries. (Joint products were perceived to be more common in these industries than in many other industries.)

Industry patterns have also been noted for the adoption of the LIFO (last-in, first-out) inventory method. Butters and Niland (1949) noted heavy use of LIFO by oil and gas firms. In a more recent study, Biddle (1980) also reports an industry factor in LIFO choice. Biddle examined firms that adopted LIFO vis-à-vis firms in the same four-digit industry that did not adopt LIFO. He reported that "in several industries (for example, chemicals and glass) nearly all the Compustat firms were either already using LIFO to some extent or simultaneously adopted LIFO" (p. 251). Table 5.1 presents data on the 1983 inventory valuation methods used by Compustat firms for a select set of industries. Note, for example, the predominant use of FIFO (first-in, first-out) inventory accounting by computer firms, LIFO by retailers, and average cost by air transportation firms. The data in Table 5.1 reinforce prior findings that differences across firms in accounting method choice are correlated with differences in their industry membership.

A related approach to examining factors associated with different accounting method usage is to present profiles of financial and other characteristics of firms adopting different methods. For example, Foster (1980) examined the profiles of oil and gas firms using full-cost vis-à-vis those using successful-efforts when accounting for exploration costs. The main difference between these two methods

TABLE 5.1 Inventory Valuation Usage of Selected Four-Digit SIC Code U.S. Industries, 1983

SIC Industry Title and Code	Number of Firms Using				Total No. of Firms
	FIFO	LIFO	Average Cost	Other	
A. FIFO Predominant					
Telegraph and telegraph apparatus (3661)	9	0	3	0	12
Computers: mini and micro (3681)	8	1	1	1	11
Perfumes and cosmetics (2844)	9	3	2	0	14
Apparel and other finished goods (2300)	23	9	2	3	37
Radio and T.V. transmitting equipment (3662)	20	6	0	7	33
B. LIFO Predominant					
Retail, department stores (5311)	1	14	0	1	16
Retail, drugs and proprietary stores (5912)	1	10	1	0	12
Knitting mills (2250)	1	9	0	1	11
Chemicals and allied products (2800)	3	14	0	0	17
Blast furnaces and steel works (3310)	2	24	4	0	30
Retail, grocery stores (5411)	7	21	1	1	30
C. Average-Cost Predominant					
Air transportation (4511)	1	0	19	0	20
Natural gas transmission (4922)	0	2	10	0	12
Telephone communication (4811)	4	0	14	0	18

SOURCE: Computed from 1983 Compustat annual industrial file.

is the broadness of the cost center used to accumulate exploration costs: full-cost accounting uses a broader cost center (for example, the United States), whereas successful-efforts uses a narrower cost center (for example, a geological area such as the north slope of Alaska). Full-cost accounting enables companies to capitalize the costs of dry holes in one area and write them off against the revenues from successful holes in other areas; full-cost accounting can result in higher reported earnings for companies with rapidly expanding exploration budgets and lower reported earnings for companies with rapidly declining exploration budgets. Foster reported the following differences between 49 full-cost firms and 34 successful-efforts firms:

	Full-Cost Firms Median	*Successful-Efforts Firms Median*
1. Gross revenues	$95.6 million	$900.6 million
2. Market capitalization	$87.5 million	$537.7 million
3. Debt-to-equity ratio	.416	.213
4. Interest expense-to-revenue ratio	.040	.012
5. Dividend yield	.007	.026

Full-cost firms are smaller and more highly leveraged and have lower dividend yields. Related to this finding is the adoption of successful-efforts by each of the ten largest integrated oil and gas companies based in the United States.

B. Profiles of Firms Making Accounting Changes

Studies examining the characteristics of firms making accounting changes have consistently reported that these firms are not a random sample. Three representative studies are

- Ball (1972) reported that in the five years prior to the accounting change, a sample of firms making 267 changes had experienced relative declines in their security prices.
- Bremser (1975) reported that a sample of 80 firms reporting discretionary accounting changes exhibited "a poorer pattern or trend of EPS than a random sample of companies with no reported accounting changes during the same period" (p. 572).
- Archibald (1976) reported that the majority of firms switching back from accelerated depreciation to straight-line depreciation were exhibiting "unfavorable net income performance" vis-à-vis a benchmark net income measure for each firm's industry. The conclusion was that "the positive effect of the switchback on subsequent net income statements appears to be a strong motivation to managements under pressure to improve their earnings reports" (p. 69).

Evidence consistent with the foregoing studies is in Schwartz's (1982) analysis of the accounting changes made by 163 firms identified as exhibiting financial distress. Each firm was matched with an "apparently healthy firm" from the same industry and of approximately the same size; "industry and size were used as pairing criteria because these factors may have a bearing on reporting decisions as well as on the incidence of failure among firms" (p. 40). The finding was that "distressed firms collectively made nearly twice as many material changes, but over four times as many material positive (for example, increasing current net income) changes" (p. 41).

The consistent finding in each of the above is that firms voluntarily changing accounting methods have underperformed, either in stock price performance or in profitability, relative to a random sample of all firms or relative to a sample of firms not making accounting changes. (One area where several studies have reported results different from those noted above is for firms adopting LIFO; see Chapter 11 for further discussion.)

C. Evidence From International Comparisons

In several areas, there is diversity in the predominant accounting methods adopted by firms in different countries. Survey evidence, based on an analysis of 1,000 published annual reports from 24 different countries, is presented in

TABLE 5.2 Accounting Method Differences Across Countries (based on predominant method used in annual reports examined)

Country	Accounting for Long-Term Investments: Less than 20% Ownership Cost Method?	Accounting for Long-Term Investments: 21–50% Ownership Equity Method?	Both Domestic and Foreign Subsidiaries Consolidated	Deferred Taxes Recorded When Accounting Income Isn't Equal to Taxable Income	Financial Leases (Long-Term) Capitalized
United States	Yes	Yes	Yes	Yes	Yes
Canada	Yes	Yes	Yes	Yes	Yes
United Kingdom	Yes	Yes	Yes	Yes	No
West Germany	Yes	No	No	Yes	No
France	Yes	Yes	Yes	Yes	No
Netherlands	No	Yes	Yes	Yes	No
Switzerland	Yes	No	Yes	No	No
Sweden	Yes	No	Yes	No	No
Finland	No	No	No	No	No
Japan	Yes	No	Yes	Yes	No
Australia	Yes	No	Yes	Yes	No
South Africa	Yes	No	Yes	Yes	No

SOURCE: Choi and Bavishi (1983, Exhibit 3): 66–67.

Choi and Bavishi (1983). The number of company annual reports examined for several countries was relatively small, so the inferences drawn about the predominant method used may be subject to considerable sampling error. Table 5.2 presents a subset of the findings in this study for five accounting areas in twelve different countries. Other areas (in addition to those in Table 5.2) where there was considerable diversity across countries in accounting method choice included accounting for inflation and foreign currency translation.

Differences across countries that may be important in understanding the accounting-method diversity in Table 5.2 include the role of government and private-sector regulatory bodies, the link between the accounting methods used for taxation and those used for financial reporting, and the broadness and depth of the capital market. It is only recently that serious attention has been paid to explaining intercountry diversity in accounting-method choice (as opposed to simply documenting its existence).

5.5 ACCOUNTING METHOD DIVERSITY AND INTERFIRM COMPARISONS

A frequent criticism of corporate financial reporting is the diversity in accounting methods used by firms. Diversity in accounting method choice, it is claimed, implies noncomparability of the numbers derived from the financial statements of different firms. The position taken in this book is a less extreme one. We argue that an analyst should consider at least three options when faced with interfirm diversity in accounting methods:

Option 1. Do not make adjustments to the reported financial numbers of firms. There could be several motivations for adopting this option:

- Firms have rationally selected their accounting methods to best represent their underlying economic attributes
- Insufficient information is available to make adjustments that the analyst would view as reliable
- The decision context in which the financial numbers are being used is insensitive to the choice of accounting method by firms.

Option 2. Make adjustments, using information provided by the firm, so that all firms are on a uniform set of accounting methods. This information could be in footnotes, management's discussion of results, and so on; see Section 5.5.A.

Option 3. Make adjustments, using approximating techniques, so that all firms are on a uniform set of accounting methods. Section 5.5.B provides an example of an approximating technique plus a discussion of its accuracy.

A. Adjustments Using Company-Based Estimates

In some cases, sufficient information is provided by the company for an external analyst to use a set of accounting methods other than those adopted in the primary financial statements. Consider the provision of supplemental financial statements using alternative accounting methods. Early instances of such disclosure were voluntary. For example, starting in 1954, Indiana Telephone Corporation voluntarily disclosed general price-level-adjusted financial statements in addition to the mandated historical cost-based statements. More recently, regulatory bodies have mandated such disclosures of companies in countries such as the United Kingdom and the United States. These disclosures permit external analysts to compare companies on an alternative set of accounting methods other than those provided in the primary financial statements. In some cases the supplemental disclosures may reduce the interfirm diversity in accounting methods encountered when using the primary statements. Consider *FASB Statement No. 33*, which mandates that U.S. companies report current cost supplemental information. Companies that use different inventory methods in their primary statements (LIFO, FIFO, average cost, etc.) all use a uniform method (current cost) in their *FASB Statement No. 33* supplemental disclosures. (Note, however, that if firms differ in the methods used to estimate current cost, uniformity in accounting method across firms may be more in form than in substance.)

Another example of disclosure of the numerical effect of alternative accounting method choice is inventory valuation. LIFO firms typically disclose in a footnote the amount by which their inventory valuation would have differed had FIFO been used. In some cases, these amounts can be substantial. Consider

General Electric, which uses LIFO as its predominant inventory valuation method for financial reporting. Using information in General Electric's income statement and in the footnotes, the following can be derived for a recent five-year period (in millions of dollars):

	19X1	19X2	19X3	19X4	19X5
Inventories (as reported) using LIFO	$3,343	$3,461	$3,029	$3,158	$3,670
Inventories using FIFO	5,583	5,926	5,295	5,310	5,697

Biddle and Martin (1985) provide discussion of the tax consequences of LIFO/FIFO differences such as those above for General Electric.

B. Adjustments Using Approximating Techniques

Considerable effort has been devoted to developing approximating techniques that estimate the financial statement numbers reported with alternative accounting methods. A sizable body of literature exists on techniques to estimate the effect of general price-level changes; examples include Petersen (1973), Davidson and Weil (1975), and Parker (1977). An interesting comparison of the adjustment techniques used in these three papers is in Ketz (1978). A summary comparison of the models in these papers is in Table 5.3. Each adjustment technique combines (1) company-provided information and information about the general price level, with (2) assumptions about the turnover of assets and liabilities and the pattern of revenues and expenses during the year. Each of the models in Table 5.3 can be used to obtain estimates of the general price-level-adjusted financial statements of one or more firms.

Evidence on the "accuracy" of the Davidson-Weil model in Table 5.3 is in Walther (1982). The sample was 459 U.S. companies. General price-level adjusted (GPLA) estimates based on the Davidson-Weil model were compared with the *FASB Statement No. 33* amounts disclosed by these firms in their 1979 annual reports. The finding was that "the Davidson-Weil model estimate of historical cost/constant dollar cost of goods sold was in excess of reported amounts by an average of 0.54%, the model estimate of historical cost/constant dollar depreciation expense exceeded reported amounts by an average of 13.73%, and the model estimate of the purchasing power gain/loss exceeded reported amounts by an average of 68.3%" (p. 376). Note that the *FASB Statement No. 33* disclosures of many firms were based on approximating techniques themselves. Hence, this evidence may shed more light on the similarity of approximating techniques than on the "correctness" of either one.

Each of the three models in Table 5.3 (and other examples of approximating techniques) has an underlying similarity. Each technique makes simplifying assumptions (for example, that inventory additions accrue uniformly throughout the year) for one of two reasons:

1. The nonavailability of data
2. The desire to obtain a "cost-effective" adjustment technique.

TABLE 5.3 Comparison of Models Available to Approximate General Price-Level–Adjusted Financial Statements

Item	Petersen	Davidson-Weil	Parker
Overall philosophy	Theoretical	Theoretical	Practical
Inventory			
FIFO	Turnover rate	Date of average purchase Increase: add average purchases of year	Number of days purchased in ending inventory
LIFO	Regress inventory over time	Decrease: date at two years	Develop LIFO layers
Weighted average	Regress inventory over time	Use ratio of COGS to COGAS	Use ratio of ending inventory to COGAS
Depreciation			
Straight line	Composite age	Composite age	Composite age
Sum of the years' digits	Composite sum of the years' digits	Age-reducing factors	Adjust like straight line
Double declining balance	Composite double declining balance	Age-reducing factors	Adjust like straight line
Ongoing items	Arithmetic mean	Geometric mean	Geometric mean
Isolated items	Specific weighting by user	Specific weighting by user	Specific weighting by model
Monetary gain or loss	Equity change	Based on average balance of monetary items	Based on average balance of monetary items
Owners' equity	Total assets − total debt	Total assets − total debt	Total assets − total debt

SOURCE: Ketz (1978, Table 1): 953.

Attempts to evaluate the usefulness of a particular technique solely by looking at the reasonableness of its simplifying assumptions ignore the importance of also examining the decision context in which the adjustment technique is to be used. Indeed, for some internal decisions, adjustment techniques may be used even where a more refined analysis could be made. For instance, management may wish to evaluate how the existing compensation plan would operate with an alternative set of accounting methods. It may decide that use of adjustment techniques is "cost effective" for its evaluations vis-à-vis a more detailed analysis done either by the firm's own accounting department or by an external auditing firm.

5.6 ALTERNATIVE ACCOUNTING METHODS AND FINANCIAL VARIABLES

In this section, two issues relating to the effect of alternative accounting methods on financial ratios and other financial variables will be discussed:

1. What is the effect on computed financial ratios of all firms consistently using accounting method A vis-à-vis all firms consistently using method B?
2. What is the effect on computed financial ratios if a subset of firms uses accounting method A while another subset uses method B?

A. Uniformity and Financial Variables

The effect on financial statement numbers of alternative accounting methods will be illustrated by reference to the accounting for changing prices issue. Considerable information exists about the correlation between historical cost-based income numbers and current cost- or constant dollar- (general price-level) based income numbers. Beaver and Landsman (1983), using information in the *FASB Statement No. 33* supplementary disclosures, reported correlations between subsets of the following income numbers:

HC: Historical cost earnings (earnings available for common before extraordinary items)

CC: Current-cost earnings from continuing operations

CD: Constant-dollar earnings from continuing operations

CC-PP: Current-cost purchasing power earnings (purchasing power gains/losses on monetary items are added to/subtracted from current cost earnings)

CD-PP: Constant-dollar purchasing power earnings (purchasing power gains/losses on monetary items are added to/subtracted from constant dollar earnings).

For a sample of 323 firms in 1980 and 297 firms in 1981, the following correlations were found:

	1980	*1981*
HC and CC	.71	.70
HC and CD	.69	.63
HC and CC – PP	.73	.71
HC and CD – PP	.73	.64
CC and CC – PP	.82	.84
CD and CD – PP	.83	.87

These correlations are consistent with the various income measures overlapping in the information they provide about the underlying profitability of the firm.

An interesting extension of the foregoing and similar evidence is to examine economy, industry, and firm factors that affect the magnitude of these correlations. Ketz (1983) reports that for a sample of 119 companies over the 1962–1980 period, correlations between historical cost- and constant-dollar- (including purchasing power gains or losses) based earnings numbers were affected by the inflation rate; for example,

Highest Correlations Between Historical Cost and Constant-Dollar Earnings			*Lowest Correlations Between Historical Cost and Constant-Dollar Earnings*		
Year	*Correlation*	*Inflation Rate*	*Year*	*Correlation*	*Inflation Rate*
1962	.999	1.2%	1974	.439	12.2%
1964	.999	1.2	1969	.695	6.1
1965	.999	1.9	1980	.738	12.4

Firm-specific factors, such as fixed asset intensity and financial leverage, also are potentially important factors that may affect the correlation between historical cost earnings and current-cost or constant-dollar earnings.

B. Diversity and Financial Variables

The second issue to be discussed arises when a subset of firms uses accounting alternative A (say, straight-line depreciation) and another subset uses alternative B (say, accelerated depreciation). Some argue that diversity in accounting method is a major limitation of conventional accounting. Several factors need to be considered on this diversity issue. The context in which the financial data are used is *one factor*. Suppose that an analyst were only interested in ranking companies in terms of a leverage ratio. If the use of diverse accounting rules did not change the ranking of companies vis-à-vis what they would have been if uniform accounting rules had been used, then the diversity in accounting rules in this context would pose no problem. A *second factor* is the availability of methods to adjust reported numbers to reduce such diversity. Section 5.5 of this chapter illustrates the use of company-based information and approximating techniques to make adjustments for accounting method differences. Where the decision context is highly sensitive to the accounting methods used, strong economic incentives may exist for the decision maker to employ these adjustment techniques. A *third factor* is the availability of competing information sources. For example, estimates of cash flow for a broad cross section of firms are available from several brokerage firms.

In many decisions, accounting information is but one of many information sources used. The existence of "noise" in the accounting inputs used in a decision may cause increased reliance on other sources. (Note that in cases where the interpretation of clauses in contracts is based on *reported* financial statement numbers, the second and third factors noted may not be operative. In this context, parties to the contract can reduce the problems associated with accounting method diversity by specifying the accounting methods on which the financial statement numbers are to be computed.)

Some insight into the accounting method diversity topic is in the Dawson, Neupert, and Stickney (1980) study. The focus was on the correlation between (1) variables based on reported financial statement numbers and (2) variables derived after converting the reported numbers to those based on a uniform set of accounting methods. The sample was 96 firms randomly selected from the largest 250 industrial U.S. firms. Adjustments for the following five accounting methods were made:

1. *Inventory* with all firms converted to a FIFO basis—73 firms required adjustment

2. *Depreciation* with all firms converted to an accelerated method—80 firms required adjustment

3. *Consolidation* of wholly owned subsidiaries—23 firms required adjustment, primarily for the consolidation of captive finance or insurance subsidiaries

4. *Pension obligations* recognized as liabilities, with separate analyses recognizing (a) the unfunded prior service obligation and (b) the excess of vested benefits over pension fund assets—66 firms disclosed an unfunded prior service obligation, while 60 firms reported an excess of vested benefits over pension fund assets

5. *Deferred tax* accounting effects eliminated from the financial statements of all companies (that is, assuming that deferred taxes had never been recognized).

Table 5.4 presents the correlation between the as reported and the restated numbers for (1) to (5) individually and when (1) to (5) are simultaneously made. The higher the correlation, the less likely it was assumed that inferences drawn from

TABLE 5.4 Correlation Between Financial Ratio/Variable Based on As Reported Numbers and Financial Ratio/Variables Derived Using Uniform Accounting Method for All Companies

Financial Ratio or Variable	Adjustments Made for						
	FIFO (1)	Accelerated Depreciation (2)	Consolidation of Subsidiary (3)	Prior Service Obligation (4a)	Vested Pension Benefits (4b)	Deferred Taxes (5)	Combined (1) – (5)
Current ratio	.944	*	.911	*	*	.944	.815
Total liabilities/total equities	.993	.997	.848	.832	.925	.981	.743[1]/.800[2]
Interest coverage	.999	.999	.995	*	*	.999	.994
Net income	.996	.994	*	*	*	.987	.995
Profit margin	.994	.989	.986	*	*	.982	.975
Return on equity	.994	.987	*	.955	.986	.916	.896[1]/.914[2]
Return on assets	.995	.993	.929	*	*	.976	.909
Asset turnover	.998	.997	.891	*	*	.999	.877
Receivables turnover	*	*	.431	*	*	*	.431
Inventory turnover	.944	*	*	*	*	*	.944

* Ratio not affected by this adjustment.
[1] Combined, including unfunded prior service obligation.
[2] Combined, including unfunded vested benefits.
SOURCE: Dawson, Neupert, and Stickney (1980, Table 1): 40.

financial ratios would be affected by accounting method diversity. (Clearly this assumption is a simplification.) The highest correlations were for the inventory, depreciation, and deferred tax adjustments; the authors concluded that "except in the case of some capital-intensive firms in the steel and petroleum industries, the benefits of adjusting net incomes and financial statement ratios for differences in accounting method hardly seem worth the effort" (p. 42). Adjustments associated with pension obligations, and especially consolidation of subsidiaries, resulted in lower correlations between the as reported and the restated numbers: "the potential bias in the data from not consolidating can be substantial, particularly when a significant portion of the parent's sales are funneled through the subsidiary—as occurs frequently in the automobile, farm equipment and industrial equipment manufacturing industries" (p. 42).

5.7 SOME GENERAL COMMENTS

1. The perspective adopted in this book is that accounting method decisions *interact* with other key firm decisions such as mix of business, financing, and operating decisions. An alternative perspective is that accounting methods are a filter that transforms the cash flow and other results of a fixed set of business mix-financing-operating decisions into reported financial numbers such as earnings and assets:

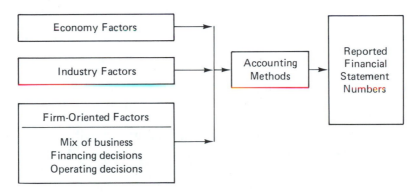

This "filter perspective" is a common one in the accounting literature. For instance, the adjustment techniques discussed in Section 5.5.B implicitly adopt a filter perspective. These techniques make adjustments from method X to method Y on the assumption that the business mix-financing-operating decisions are unaffected by the change from X to Y. With this assumption, a mechanical set of adjustment rules that is independent of the users of the data can be adopted.

2. Insight into the factors underlying accounting method choices can be gained from several sources, for example,

A. Statements by management about the factors important in their choices

B. Submissions by management to accounting policy bodies

C. Analysis of variables correlated with the accounting methods adopted by firms.

Research has been conducted on each of these sources.

A. Statements by Management.   These statements can be made at the time of accounting changes, in private interviews, or via mail questionnaires. Early examples of this approach include Butters and Niland (1949) on inventory valuation and Lindhe (1963) on depreciation. Factors said to be important include

- Taxation savings
- Administrative complexity
- Expected effect on the price of the company's stock
- Industry practice
- Management compensation effects
- Restrictions on dividend distributions
- Fear of excess profits taxation.

A more recent example is Granof and Short (1984). The following question was mailed to the chief financial officers of 380 firms using FIFO or weighted average as their predominant inventory method: "Why has your firm not adopted LIFO as its primary inventory method?" One motivation for this question was a financial press comment that "many firms have voluntarily paid tens of millions of dollars in additional income taxes by continuing to use FIFO rather than switching to LIFO." Granof and Short received 213 usable responses ranging from "a few words to two-page letters." Table 5.5 presents a summary of the responses. The conclusion was that "there are many legitimate economic reasons for the use of inventory methods other than LIFO" (p. 332) and that "the dollar amount of the benefits to those that switch may be substantially less than is widely believed" (p. 333).

Studies such as Butters and Niland (1949), Lindhe (1963), and Granof and Short (1984) are helpful in identifying factors that may be important in accounting method choice. However, several caveats should be considered when interpreting the results. One limitation arises from the possibility that management may not honestly communicate its knowledge. For instance, there can be incentives to disguise true motives such as a desire to manipulate a management compensation plan or to avoid a bond covenant violation. A second limitation is the potential for management to rationalize past decisions (especially when questions relate to their motives). Third, there is the problem of deciding who in an organization makes a specific disclosure decision; no single manager may be able to describe accurately the actual management decision process.

One factor that has been reported as important in several interview/questionnaire studies is the influence of a key individual (for example, the chairman or president or even a major shareholder). Consider the following anecdote that

TABLE 5.5 Why Companies Reject LIFO? Explanations Given by Chief Financial Officers

Categorization of Responses	% of Firms Citing Factor
1. No expected tax benefits • No immediate tax payments to be made (e.g., due to either carryforward tax losses or credits) • Declining prices (e.g., in electronics, meat-packing, steel, and drug industries) • Immaterial inventory • Inventory used in long-term projects or in equipment held for lease	73%
2. Regulatory or other restrictions LIFO deemed inappropriate by most rate-making authorities	12
3. Excessive cost • High administrative costs • Problems of managing cash flow owing to involuntary liquidations	20
4. Other adverse consequences • Lower reported earnings • Trigger disputes with IRS	11

SOURCE: Granof and Short (1984, Table 1, p. 327). Reprinted by permission from the *Journal of Accounting Auditing and Finance,* Summer 1984. Published by Warren, Gorham and Lamont, Inc., 210 South St., Boston, MA. Copyright © 1984. All Rights Reserved.

Archibald (1976) reported:

> One treasurer flatly stated that an influential shareholder demanded the firm not show a relative decrease, and that the accountants were obliged to figure a way out of the problem. The depreciation change was the easiest and the most obvious. (p. 72)

Such anecdotes are difficult to verify. However, they do highlight the difficulties faced by researchers in developing models that explain decisions by management about accounting method choice.

B. Submissions to Accounting Policy Bodies. Accounting policy bodies frequently solicit the opinions of firms potentially affected by their decisions. Typically a small subset of firms make written submissions. Examples of studies examining these submissions are Watts and Zimmerman (1978) on general price-level accounting and Dhaliwal (1982) on the interest cost capitalization issue. The dependent variable in these studies was a support/oppose classification of the submission sent by individual firms in relation to the FASB's Discussion Memorandum on each issue. Independent variables examined included firm size, the existence of a management incentive scheme, and the debt-to-equity ratio. Both papers reported that firm size was a significant factor in classifying firm submissions. For instance, Watts and Zimmerman (1978) reported that "the larger firms are more likely to favor GPLA (if earnings decline). This finding is consistent with our (political cost) argument since the larger firms are more likely to be subjected to governmental interference and, hence, have more to lose than smaller corporations" (p. 131). The most significant variable in Dhaliwal (1982) was debt-to-equity: "highly leveraged firms would be expected to oppose an accounting change which reduces reported earnings or equity, or increases the volatility of reported earnings. The results . . . are consistent with this hypothesis" (pp. 263–264).

Some thorny research design issues arise in this area, and the results can be highly sensitive to variations from the specific design reported in some studies. For instance, McKee, Bell, and Boatsman (1984) reexamined the Watts-Zimmerman (1978) sample of 34 Discussion Memorandum (DM) submissions using alternative classification methods and alternative variable measures. An additional sample of 70 Exposure Draft (ED) submissions of GPLA were also examined. (The FASB issues a DM prior to its voting on the recommended accounting method; an ED is issued after a first round of voting and is a tentative statement of the FASB's position on an issue.) The conclusion was that the Watts-Zimmerman results "deteriorate" significantly. "The theory fails to classify correctly a disturbingly large number of observations, particularly in the ED sample. . . . A model which predicts that all submissions will be unfavorable produces superior classificatory success" (p. 658).

Examining firm submissions reduces several of the problems encountered when examining management statements. For instance, ex-post rationalization by management is less of a problem when examining firm submissions. However, other problems can become more critical. There is the unresolved issue of how firms see their submissions affecting the decisions of the regulatory body. For example, is it via a voting mechanism? In this case, positive submissions costs, when associated with the low likelihood of influencing outcomes, can result in there not being a one-to-one correspondence between firms' interests and their submissions. Moreover, there is a problem of generalization; for example, Watts and Zimmerman (1978) only could examine 34 DM submissions from unregulated firms when the population of such firms affected was potentially over 2,000.

C. Variables Correlated with Accounting Method Choice. A growing literature employs either cross-sectional or time-series analysis in which the dependent variable is the accounting method adopted and the independent variables are factors hypothesized as determinants of accounting method choices by firms: for example, Bowen, Noreen, and Lacey (1981) on the decision to capitalize or expense interest costs associated with capital expenditures; Lilien and Pastena (1982) on the choice of full-cost versus successful-efforts made by oil and gas companies; Daley and Vigeland (1983) on the decision to capitalize or expense research and development expenditures; and Morse and Richardson (1983) on the decision to switch to LIFO. The independent variables examined in these and similar studies included firm size, the existence of a profit sharing plan for management, leverage and interest coverage ratios, industry concentration, and a manager- versus an owner-controlled firm variable. A reliable body of evidence has not emerged from this literature, in part due to the severe methodological problems associated with this research; see Ball and Foster (1982), Holthausen and Leftwich (1983), and Kelly (1983).

One of the most interesting approaches in this literature is in Zmijewski and Hagerman (1981). Four accounting alternatives (depreciation, inventory, investment tax credit, and pension cost amortization) were simultaneously examined. The hypothesis is that management chooses a portfolio of accounting methods rather than examines each issue in isolation. (Unfortunately, using a model with six independent variables, the authors were not able to improve upon the predictions of a model that assumed that a firm will always be in the most commonly adopted composite accounting-method category for their sample.)

3. Accounting method choices are frequently made in areas outside the domain of regulatory bodies such as the FASB or the SEC. For example, accounting method choices are made

- By private companies when reporting to their shareholders
- In private lending agreements between companies and their long-term lenders (banks, insurance companies, etc.)
- In employee profit sharing agreements
- In executive compensation agreements for senior management
- By management in internal resource allocation decisions and when evaluating the efficiency and effectiveness of their individual activities or of their employees.

By observing the choices made in these contexts, insight into the perceived benefits and costs of individual accounting methods can be gained; see Leftwich (1983).

A particularly rich source of evidence about the perceived costs and benefits of alternative accounting methods is in the internal accounting systems used by management. Seed (1981) examines this evidence in an analysis of managerial uses of constant-dollar and current-cost information. Table 5.6 presents an extract from the results of a questionnaire. Seed reported widespread nonadoption of constant-dollar or current-cost accounting in the internal systems of the U.S. firms surveyed. McCosh and Howell (1983), in a study of 32 U.K. firms, report a similar finding: "only one-third used any part of formal current-cost accounting, and only one in six based its performance targets on the current-cost accounting income concept" (p. 200).

4. Accounting regulatory bodies could take one of several extremes when issuing accounting standards relating to accounting method alternatives:

a. Issue a broad set of standards stating the qualities of financial information required (for example, relevance, reliability, and timeliness) but not prescribe a detailed set of accounting methods to be used.

TABLE 5.6 Managerial Uses of Constant-Dollar or Current-Cost Information

Question	Regularly Applied	Plan to Apply	Is Not Applied	No Answer
Business unit performance is measured in constant dollars?	24.5%	9.2%	64.5%	1.8%
Business unit performance is routinely compared with CPI or other indices?	16.0	5.3	75.9	2.8
Fixed assets are restated on a current cost basis for internal performance measurement?	6.4	9.9	81.9	1.8
Business unit profits are restated on current costs basis for internal performance measurement?	7.5	8.5	81.2	2.8
Actual results are compared with price-level-adjusted flexible budget?	6.7	5.0	84.8	3.5
Management incentive compensation is based on inflation-adjusted performance measurements?	11.3	5.0	80.5	3.2

SOURCE: Seed (1981, pp. 238–239). Reprinted from the October 1981 issue of *Management Accounting*. Copyright by the National Association of Accountants.

    b. Issue a detailed set of guidelines that prescribes how each individual transaction or event is to be reported in financial statements. (This approach is akin to the level of detail found in many tax codes.)

As a generalization, accounting regulatory bodies have adopted a middle ground between (a) and (b) with a trend over time toward more reliance on (b). One stated motivation for increasing recourse to (b) is the role that vested self-interest plays in the financial reporting decisions of individual firms. The chairman of the FASB made the following comments in this regard (Kirk, 1984):

> There is an (important) force at work that causes standard setters to be rule writers. In a recent speech I commented that the gentleman's game of golf requires a set of rules—in fact, a very detailed set. Of course you and I do not read or need those rules because we play every shot as it lays. It is because of those "other guys" that we have the rules. Nor do you and I search for ways to keep debt off the balance sheet or research and development costs and executive stock compensation off the income statement. We know the broad principle that liabilities should be in the balance sheet and expenses in the income statement. We know that substance must triumph over form. We don't need rules to tell us what is right, and we know that some things are wrong even if there is no rule that prohibits them. The problem is that those "other guys" do not view the game the same way we do. . . . . There always will be people who read the rules for what they say, not for what they intend. As long as such behavior is not considered professionally unethical, the rulemakers will have to act if the financial reporting game is to remain credible. (pp. 15, 17).

Several of the factors outlined in Section 5.3 as affecting accounting method choice explicitly recognize the role of vested self-interest of either the firm or management (see Sections 5.3.E and 5.3.F). No matter how detailed the set of rules issued by accounting policy bodies, creative managers or their advisors will find means of structuring transactions that do not give rise to reported expenses or reported liabilities even though, in spirit, expenses or liabilities exist. This is but one of several reasons why the disclosures in annual reports need not represent either a complete or an unbiased representation of the underlying transactions and events affecting the firm.

5.8 SUMMARY

1. Accounting method choice is an important factor affecting reported financial statement numbers. The perspective taken in this chapter is that the accounting method choice interacts with decisions concerning the mix of business, financing, and operating aspects of the firm.

2. Increasing recognition is being given to the economic consequences to the firm and the economic consequences to management factors affecting accounting method choice. At present, security analysts, financial commentators, and academics are better able to list factors such as taxation benefits, political costs, and executive compensation than to develop models that reliably predict how the foregoing (and possibly other) factors interact to produce the set of accounting methods chosen by individual firms.

3. There is considerable evidence of self-selection by firms in their accounting method choices. Industry similarities and firm-size similarities have been documented. In addition, firms making voluntary accounting changes typically have experienced lower profitability and lower stock price performance in the period prior to the change.

4. The existence of differences across firms in their accounting methods does not, in itself, preclude analysts from making interfirm comparisons of financial statement variables. The availability of supplemental information provided by firms and of approximating techniques partially reduces potential problems arising from interfirm diversity in accounting method choice.

QUESTIONS

QUESTION 5.1:   Lease Accounting and Leverage Ratios of Airline Companies

Accounting for leases is a topic that has generated much controversy. The issues considered (and reconsidered) by regulatory bodies typically include

1. Should all, a subset, or no leases be classified as liabilities (and hence placed on the balance sheet)? The answer to this question is frequently "a subset." For example, the International Accounting Standards Committee in *Accounting for Leases* (1982) concludes that "finance leases" (sometimes called "capital leases") should be included on the balance sheet whereas "operating leases" need not be reflected on the balance sheet.

2. If only a subset of leases is to be included on the balance sheet, what criteria should be used to distinguish this subset? As an example, *FASB Statement No. 13* (Accounting for Leases) states that leases meeting any of the following criteria should be capitalized and accounted for as assets and liabilities (*capital* leases) on the balance sheet:

   a. Ownership is transferred to the lessee by the end of the lease

   b. There is a bargain (less than fair value) purchase option

   c. The lease term is 75% or more of the leased property's estimated economic life

   d. The present value of the minimum lease payments is 90% or more of the fair value of the leased property.

3. What level of detail should a regulatory body provide so that companies that have capital leases in substance cannot avoid reporting them on their balance sheet by changes in their appearance or form? The FASB has resorted to an increasing level of detail in the lease area, in part due to the considerable efforts by firms and investment bankers to develop forms of financing that are not technically classified as "capital leases."

4. When changes in lease accounting are made by regulatory bodies, how quickly should companies be required to comply with those regulations? One reason given for having an extended transition period is the problem that companies may have with restrictive covenants in their existing loan agreements. A newspaper article at the time of a proposal to expand the number of leases to be included on the balance sheet commented

   > The airlines are highly concerned about any modification of accounting methods which would outlaw "off-balance-sheet" financing as currently practiced. One of the immediate consequences would be possible technical violations of covenants in earlier loan agreements. Such agreements must be interpreted under existing accounting rules and not under those in effect when the leases were incurred. The required modification or reopening of previous loan agreements likely would entail higher interest charges or other elements more costly to the borrower.

The airline industry is one of the largest users of lease financing. Table 5.7 summarizes information pertaining to lease and other forms of financing reported on the balance sheets of U.S.-based airline companies. Total long-term debt in Table 5.7 includes capitalized lease obligations but excludes future obligations on operating leases.

TABLE 5.7 U.S. Airline Companies Selected Financial Data ($ millions)

Company	Current Liabilities	Capitalized Lease Obligations	Total Long-Term Debt (Inc. C.L.O)	Deferred Tax	Shareholders' Equity	Operating Income	Interest Expense	Rent Expense for Operating Leases
Aloha	$ 23	$ 23	$ 75	$ 6	$ 22	$ 32	$ 7	$ 2
American	1,438	785	1,512	131	1,300	281	152	103
Delta	744	0	1,092	437	897	(207)	93	65
Eastern	965	871	2,319	187	130	(100)	250	160
Frontier	137	38	210	27	189	(19)	22	22
Hawaiian	29	27	105	0	13	4	15	10
Muse	23	0	84	0	66	5	9	3
Northwest	376	0	100	260	854	69	8	36
Ozark	108	6	55	21	113	2	7	9
PSA	135	37	431	39	181	(1)	59	13
Pan Am	1,126	257	1,103	0	432	51	153	129
Piedmont	205	178	513	30	279	60	42	25
Southwest	48	32	159	63	315	68	12	8
TWA	879	467	1,102	4	526	(66)	114	70
UAL (United)	1,934	619	1,311	261	1,399	216	195	103
US Air	277	69	332	94	613	128	30	42
Western	263	113	438	10	57	(56)	55	38

REQUIRED

1. Compute the long-term debt-to-equity ratios of the airlines in Table 5.7 with

    a. Lease obligations excluded from the balance sheet

    b. Lease obligations included as long-term debt on the balance sheet

    Would the alternative accounting treatments of lease obligations affect inferences you might make about the relative indebtedness of each airline?

2. The airline industry (and airline construction industry) has been a strong opponent of the inclusion of leases on the balance sheet. What economic (and other) arguments may motivate this opposition? What are the benefits (and costs) of so-called off-balance-sheet financing?

3. Comment on the following statement by the vice-president of finance of a truck rental company:

    > Capital leases have to be carried on a company's balance sheet as assets and liabilities, but operating leases do not. Operating leases are accounted for as expenses. Consequently, operating leases provide considerably greater financial benefits. Companies will show a better return on assets and a lower debt-to-equity ratio. Asset turnover also will be higher. The lease payments are fully deductible.

    How would the inclusion of the rental expense for operating leases with the interest expense (vis-à-vis use of interest expense alone as the denominator) affect the coverage ratio of the airlines in Table 5.7?

4. It was stated in the cited newspaper article that one consequence of recognizing future lease obligations as a liability would be "technical violations of covenants in loan agreements." Why would an airline company agree to a set of covenants in loan agreements that can be violated by accounting changes as well as economic changes in the airline's financial ability? How could a company make its bond indenture agreements less vulnerable to violations arising from accounting changes mandated by regulatory bodies?

5. The newspaper article also noted that "the required modification or reopening of previous loan agreements likely would entail higher interest charges and other elements more costly to the borrower." What options has a lender when a lendee violates a loan covenant due to a mandated accounting change? What factors would a lender consider when choosing between these options?

QUESTION 5.2: Hilton Hotels: Accounting Alternatives for Properties and Land

Hotel chains hold sizable amounts of their assets in property and land. Under historical cost–based accounting methods, changes in the value of this property and land are not recognized unless those properties or land are sold. Several hotel chains voluntarily disclose information about the appraised or market values of these assets in their annual reports. This case examines disclosures made by Hilton Hotels Corporation over an eight-year period (termed 19X1 to 19X8). The current market value concept that Hilton employs for "operating properties and management and franchise fees" is based on "the present values of the respective net income streams generated." The current market value of "investments in unconsolidated affiliates is the estimated present value of future income streams minus debt."

As of 19X8, the company (1) operated 13 hotels that were wholly owned or leased, (2) operated 13 hotels that were partially owned and managed, (3) managed 23 hotels, (4) managed three hotel-casinos, and (5) had 194 hotels franchised.

19X1, 19X2, and 19X3 Annual Reports

These annual reports called "attention to the fact that the market value of Hilton's hotel properties was substantially greater than the book value shown on the financial statements." In footnotes, Hilton provided the following information (in millions of dollars):

	Historical Cost			*Current Market Value*		
	19X1	*19X2*	*19X3*	*19X1*	*19X2*	*19X3*
Net property of Hilton subsidiaries	237	253	305	467	496	818
Net property of Hilton proportional share of 20–50% owned companies	134	154	157	251	278	362

The 19X1 Annual Report stated that "current market value was arrived at by calculating the present worth of estimated future income streams accruing to the owner utilizing rates of return ranging from 9 to 12 percent, and various terms of financing, and conditions of sale and profitability factors with respect to individual properties." This method is referred to by some appraisal companies as the "income approach to fair market value." As an example, the value of one Hilton property was based on a ten-year horizon period. The future annual revenues and future expenses for the property were predicted and then used to calculate the "most probable net operating income and pre-tax cash flow to be generated by the property." An estimate of the residual value of the property at the end of the tenth year was also made. The discount rate was that yield "which would attract a prudent investor to a property with comparable degrees of risk, non-liquidity and management burdens." In the two years prior to 19X1, Hilton had noted that the current market value greatly exceeded the book value of property but had not provided estimates of the difference.

19X4 Annual Report

Starting in 19X4, Hilton reported current-cost and constant-dollar supplemental information to comply with *FASB Statement No. 33:*

> The objective (of current cost) is to reflect the effect of changes in the specific prices (also referred to as "current costs") of the resources actually used in the Company's operations. Current costs of property and equipment were based on replacement

cost appraisals. . . . The (constant-dollar) method provides data adjusted for "general inflation" using the Consumer Price Index. The objective of this approach is to provide financial information in dollars of equivalent value or purchasing power.

Table 5.8 (lines 14–17) summarizes these disclosures for stockholders' equity and net income. Hilton argued that "current-value measurements" were more relevant than current-cost or constant-dollar measurements to meeting the distinctive features of income-producing properties: "Management believes that presentation

TABLE 5.8 Hilton Hotels Financial Data 19X1–19X8 ($ millions)

	19X1	19X2	19X3	19X4	19X5	19X6	19X7	19X8
Historical cost basis								
1. Current assets	$ 83	$117	$159	$ 190	$ 207	$ 213	$ 196	$ 267
2. Investments and other assets	108	114	117	124	127	148	217	282
3. Property and equipment	218	281	314	324	362	455	525	550
4. Total assets	409	512	590	638	696	816	938	1,099
5. Total liabilities	178	293	297	249	238	284	370	465
6. Stockholders' equity	231	219	293	389	458	532	568	634
7. Net income	31	40	68	99	106	113	83	113
Current market value basis								
8. Current assets	N.D.	N.D.	N.D.	190	207	213	196	268
9. Investments	N.D.	N.D.	N.D.	398	473	514	525	589
10. Property and equipment	N.D.	N.D.	N.D.	1,243	1,500	1,691	1,697	1,859
11. Total assets	N.D.	N.D.	N.D.	1,831	2,180	2,418	2,418	2,716
12. Total liabilities	N.D.	N.D.	N.D.	249	238	284	370	465
13. Stockholders' equity	N.D.	N.D.	N.D.	1,582	1,942	2,134	2,048	2,251
Current cost/specific price basis								
14. Stockholders' equity	N.D.	N.D.	N.D.	712	848	1,083	1,182	1,295
15. Net income	N.D.	N.D.	N.D.	75	93	94	62	53
Constant dollar basis								
16. Stockholders' equity	N.D.	N.D.	N.D.	755	894	1,058	1,235	1,308
17. Net income	N.D.	N.D.	N.D.	75	86	91	60	59
Other data								
18. Average consumer price index	100.0	106.5	114.6	127.5	144.8	159.8	169.6	175.0
19. Market capitalization of equity	299	293	508	822	1,112	1,012	1,147	1,522
20. Standard & Poor's 500 index	107	94	95	107	134	122	139	164
21. Shares outstanding (millions)	13.1	11.3	22.8	26.0	26.3	26.6	26.7	26.7

N.D.–Not disclosed.

of the current values of Company assets is the most significant information which can be presented." For the first time, Hilton in 19X4 included in its annual report a "Condensed Consolidated Statement of Assets—Current Value Basis." Table 5.8 (lines 8–13) summarizes these disclosures. Outside appraisal companies provided the "fair market appraisals of the Company's major wholly owned and 20% to 50% owned properties."

19X5, 19X6, 19X7, and 19X8 Annual Reports

In each year, Hilton continued reporting a "Condensed Consolidated Statement of Assets—Current Value Basis" as well as the current-cost and constant-dollar disclosures mandated by *FASB Statement No. 33*. The following statement in the 19X7 Annual Report reflects Hilton's ongoing preference for current market value measures:

> The (current cost and constant dollar) disclosures deal exclusively with the impact of inflation and do not represent any measure of current value. It is obvious, however, that changes in the values of assets are brought about by forces other than inflation— operating performance, property maintenance practices and competition also have a very direct bearing on property values and capital growth. While inflation affects directly the cost of new assets acquired each year, neither the timing nor the magnitude of changes in inflation indices satisfactorily coincide with changes in total hotel property values.
>
> The only medium which duly reflects all changes occurring in asset values is market value. Additionally, because hotels are generally held for investment as well as operating purposes, market values are critical factors in measuring economic performance.

Changes in Current Value Revaluation Equity

The difference between stockholders' equity using current market value and stockholders' equity using historical cost was termed revaluation equity. Hilton provided the following details of changes in components of revaluation equity over the 19X4–19X8 period:

	19X4	19X5	19X6	19X7	19X8
Balance, January 1	$ 895	$1,193	$1,483	$1,601	$1,479
Increase					
Unconsolidated affiliates	57	71	26	(61)	28
Marketable securities	2	—	(5)	5	3
Operating properties and others	211	188	62	(113)	123
Management and franchise agreements	28	31	35	47	22
Property transactions	—	—	—	—	(38)
Total	298	290	118	(122)	138
Balance, December 31	$1,193	$1,483	$1,601	$1,479	$1,617

The company noted that the decline in 19X7 was associated with a "protracted recession that brought about a decline in business, leisure and international travel as well as a reduction in the Nevada gaming market, . . . Increases in average rates were insufficient to maintain recent profit margins."

Disclosures by a Competitor

Starting in 19X6, Holiday Inn voluntarily disclosed fair market value estimates for net tangible assets when calculating shareholders' equity: "The principal method used to estimate the fair market value was the discounted cash flow technique, which reflects the present value of future cash flows. This is a widely accepted valuation method and one of the methods the company uses to evaluate prospective investments." The 19X6, 19X7, and 19X8 disclosures were (in millions of dollars):

	19X6	19X7	19X8
Shareholders' equity (fair market value)	$1,860	$2,500	$2,700

Other information (in millions of dollars) pertaining to Holiday Inn includes

	19X4	19X5	19X6	19X7	19X8
Historical cost					
Net income	$ 71	$ 108	$ 137	$ 97	$ 124
Shareholders' equity	627	708	772	943	1,040
Total Assets	1,227	1,680	1,815	1,708	1,937
Current cost					
Net income	N.D.	65	88	51	76
Shareholders' equity	N.D.	1,351	1,513	1,592	1,720
Constant dollar					
Net income	48	76	99	65	94
Shareholders' equity	918	1,155	1,311	1,392	1,486
Market capitalization of equity (year end)	576	865	859	820	1,775

N.D.–Not disclosed.

REQUIRED

1. Describe Hilton's current-value method. Compare and contrast it with the historical-cost, current-cost, and constant-dollar methods used by Hilton in its primary financial statements or its supplemental disclosures.

2. Illustrate how Hilton's current-value, current-cost, and constant-dollar disclosures can be used in financial ratio analysis? (At a minimum, compute the ratio of total liabilities to stockholders' equity and the ratio of net income to stockholders' equity. Use year-end values of the denominator in both ratios.)

3. Comment on the following criticism of the current-value method: "Current-value estimates based on future cash flows have no place in the accountant's measure of the current period's earnings. These estimates are subjective at

best, involving many hypothetical assumptions that inevitably will turn out to be incorrect. Moreover, they are likely to produce earnings numbers that vary significantly from year to year.''

4. What factors might explain Hilton's voluntary disclosure of current-value information in 19X1 and its expanded disclosures starting in 19X4? What factors might explain Holiday Inn's voluntary disclosure of current-value information starting in 19X6?

5. What factors might explain the difference between the market capitalization of equity and the value of stockholders' equity (using the current-value accounting method) for Hilton and Holiday Inn?

QUESTION 5.3: Energy Reserves Group: Accounting Method Choice

Energy Reserves Group (ERG) is engaged in the exploration for and the production and sale of oil and natural gas. The primary financial statements are based on the historical cost method. Table 5.9 presents summary financial and operating

TABLE 5.9 Energy Reserves Group, 19X1–19X8

Financial and Operating Data	19X1	19X2	19X3	19X4	19X5	19X6	19X7	19X8
A. *Primary Financial Statement Disclosures ($ millions)*								
1. Total revenues	60	71	76	102	149	175	160	142
2. Earnings before extraordinary items/ discontinued operations	3.7	6.6	(.1)	14.4	13.9	(22.6)	9.7	12.6
3. Net earnings	5.6	10.4	.3	15.1	13.9	(22.6)	(14.5)	12.6
4. Reported interest expense	1.0	1.1	2.8	7.0	11.6	23.9	22.5	25.3
5. Capital expenditures	39	46	53	67	86	162	93	28
6. Stockholders' equity	76	85	84	94	112	91	160	173
7. Total assets	113	141	162	204	256	357	502	470
8. Properties, plant, and equipment	94	120	137	158	201	282	431	414
B. *Operating Disclosures Production (net interest)*								
9. Crude oil produced (million barrels)	4.01	3.85	3.55	3.21	3.22	3.41	3.27	3.08
10. Average sale price per barrel	$9.56	$10.95	$11.79	$19.80	$31.76	$35.78	$31.66	$29.25
11. Natural gas produced (billion cubic feet)	26.16	26.10	25.51	24.09	23.35	22.48	21.08	17.38
12. Average sale price (thousand cubic feet)	$0.63	$0.92	$1.12	$1.34	$1.60	$1.87	$2.27	$2.49
Estimated Net Proven Reserves								
13. Oil (million barrels)	25.86	23.17	23.35	23.15	23.78	27.36	25.30	29.23
14. Gas (billion cubic feet)	235.14	242.12	272.08	263.20	228.16	238.49	237.54	239.16
C. *Capital Market Data*								
15. ERG market capitalization of equity ($ millions)	92	114	167	468	881	491	174	175
16. Standard & Poor's 500 Index	107	94	95	107	134	122	139	164

information relating to the 19X1 and 19X8 period. Extracts from selected annual reports, and details of other events, in this eight-year period are presented in the paragraphs that follow.

19X1 Annual Report: The "Summary of Significant Accounting Policies" noted that ERG used a form of successful-efforts accounting for its oil and gas exploration expenditures.

19X2: In 19X2, the FASB (in *FASB Statement No. 19*) proposed that all oil and gas companies use successful-efforts accounting. The FASB's version of successful-efforts followed that used by ERG with minor exceptions. Many oil companies of similar size to ERG used full-cost accounting. One study estimated that for a sample of 45 full-cost companies, adoption of the FASB's successful-efforts method would reduce their 19X2 reported income by an average of 27 percent.

19X3 Annual Report: ERG noted that its 19X3 reported earnings were "impacted by its use of the conservative 'successful-efforts' method . . . [there was] a 46 percent increase in exploration expenses, including dry holes, and a 51 percent increase in exploration and development drilling expenditures." In 19X3 the FASB, under pressure from the SEC, withdrew its proposal that full-cost companies be required to change to the successful-efforts method of accounting. In the same year, the SEC issued two releases relevant to oil and gas accounting. The first release (ASR 253) outlined the requirement that companies report the "future net revenues" and "present value" (using a 10% discount rate) of proved reserves. (These disclosures, termed "Reserve Recognition Accounting," are examined in Question 13.1.) The second release (ASR 257) required companies using successful-efforts to conform to the specific guidelines outlined in FASB 19.

19X4 Annual Report: ERG announced that it "revised its method of successful-efforts accounting to conform" with the requirements of *FASB Statement No. 19*. The principal change was "the expensing of all geological and geophysical costs as incurred." The effect of this revision was to increase 19X4 reported net earnings by $2.4 million.

19X5 Annual Report: The footnotes to the financial statements noted the following accounting change: "The Company adopted effective January 1, 19X5, FASB Statement No. 34 which requires the capitalization of interest costs as part of the historical cost of acquiring certain assets when a period of time is required to make them ready for their intended use. Prior to 19X5, all interest was expensed as incurred. Adoption of this revised standard decreased 19X5 interest expense by $800,000 and increased 19X5 net earnings by $400,000 ($0.01 a share) over what would have been otherwise reported. Since *FASB Statement No. 34* may only be applied prospectively, no interest has been capitalized for years prior to 19X5."

19X6 Annual Report: The letter to shareholders stated that "total dry hole costs in 19X6 were $29.1 million compared with $8.7 million in 19X5. Under the method of accounting utilized by ERG ('successful efforts'), these dry hole costs are charged against 19X6 earnings. . . . In our view, and that of most oil analysts, a more valid comparison (of companies using diverse accounting methods) is one based on increases in asset value and oil and gas reserves.''

19X7 Annual Report: The letter to shareholders included the following comments: ''We have discontinued our minerals and mining operations and have provided a reserve for future losses upon disposition of minerals and mining assets. . . . After considerable thought and discussion, we adopted the full-cost method of accounting for oil and gas properties. The primary difference between the full-cost method and the successful-efforts method previously followed by the Company is that costs of exploratory dry holes, geological and geophysical expenses, and exploration overhead expenses which were previously charged to expense as incurred, are now capitalized and amortized based on the Company's estimated proved reserves. Although reported earnings are not and have not been our goal, and we continue to believe that growth in net present value and cash flow are the best measures of an exploration and production company's performance, in times of uncertainty investors tend to look to reported earnings and balance sheet strength in making investment decisions. Also, the great majority of publicly held exploration and production companies to which ERG is compared follow the full-cost method of accounting. If financial statement comparisons are important to investors and creditors, we believe it to be in the best interest of our shareholders to place ERG in a more competitive position by using the predominant accounting method.'' The 19X7 reported net loss of $14.5 million was *after* a $24.2 million loss from discontinued operations.

The ''Five-Year Financial and Operating Summary'' included data ''restated to reflect the change to the full-cost method of accounting'' for years 19X3 to 19X6 as well as 19X7 (in millions of dollars):

	19X3	19X4	19X5	19X6	19X7
Earnings before discontinued operations	$ 12.7	$25.1	$28.2	$21.0	$ 9.7
Net earnings	11.0	21.9	21.1	7.3	(14.5)
Stockholders' equity	116	139	163	173	160
Total assets	226	289	357	492	502
Properties, plant, and equipment	N.D.	N.D.	N.D.	417	431

N.D.–Not disclosed.

The footnotes to the financial statements stated that the effect of the change in accounting principle was to increase ''Earnings from Continuing Operations'' by $21.2 million in 19X7. The effect of the change on ''Net earnings'' was to reduce the 19X7 loss by $42.7 million. The footnotes also stated that ''the company believes that the full-cost method is predominant among those companies with which it must compete for capital and that the new method will improve the ability of investors and lenders to compare the company's performance with its competitors.''

19X8 Annual Report: The footnotes to the financial reports stated that after the discontinuance of the mineral and mining operations in 19X7, no interest costs were capitalized in 19X8. ERG reported the following "as reported" data over the 19X5 to 19X7 period:

	19X5	*19X6*	*19X7*
Total Interest Cost	$12.4	$28.7	$23.8
Net Interest Capitalized	.8	4.8	1.3
Reported Interest Expense	11.6	23.9	22.5

REQUIRED

1. Outline the accounting changes made by ERG in the 19X1–19X8 period. What evidence is there of the numerical effect of these changes? What is their impact on computed financial ratios?

2. What factors did ERG cite as important when making each change? What other factors may have influenced ERG's change in 19X7?

3. ERG cited industry comparability as a major factor in its 19X7 decision to adopt full-cost accounting. Outline specific areas where ERG's management might believe its "competitive position" would be improved by the adoption of full-cost accounting.

4. At approximately the same time ERG switched from the successful-efforts method to the full-cost method, Kaneb Services made the following announcement:

   The company changed from the full-cost to the successful-efforts method of accounting for its oil and gas operations. The company's management feels that adoption of the successful-efforts accounting method will produce reported operating results which more accurately reflect the current level of Kaneb's exploration and production activities.

   How would you explain these different accounting method switches by ERG and Kaneb?

REFERENCES

ABDEL-KHALIK, A. R. *The Economic Effects on Leases of FASB Statement No. 13, Accounting for Leases.* Stamford, Conn.: FASB, 1981.

AMERSHI, A. H., J. S. DEMSKI, and M. A. WOLFSON. "Strategic Behavior and Regulation Research in Accounting." *Journal of Accounting and Public Policy* (Fall 1982): 19–32.

ANDREWS, M. D. "FASB 52: Corporate Response and Related Foreign Exchange Market Effects." *Federal Reserve Bank of New York Quarterly Review* (Winter 1983–84): 69–70.

ARCHIBALD, T. R. "Some Factors Related to the Depreciation Switchback." *Financial Analysts Journal* (September–October 1976): 67–73.

BALL, R. J. "Changes in Accounting Techniques and Stock Prices." *Empirical Research in Accounting, Selected Studies*, Supplement to *Journal of Accounting Research* (1972): 1–38.

BALL, R., and G. FOSTER. "Corporate Financial Reporting: A Methodological Review of Empirical Research." *Studies of Current Research Methodologies in Accounting: A Critical Evaluation*, Supplement to *Journal of Accounting Research* (1982): 161–234.

BEAVER, W. H., and W. R. LANDSMAN. *Incremental Information Content of Statement 33 Disclosures*. Stamford, Conn.: FASB, 1983.

BIDDLE, G. C. "Accounting Methods and Management Decisions: The Case of Inventory Costing and Inventory Policy." *Studies on Economic Consequences of Financial and Managerial Accounting: Effects on Corporate Incentives and Decisions*, Supplement to *Journal of Accounting Research* (1980): 235–280.

BIDDLE, G. C., and R. K. MARTIN. "Tax-Cutting Inventory Management," *Midland Corporate Finance Journal* (Summer 1985): 33–40.

BOWEN, R. M., E. W. NOREEN, and J. M. LACEY. "Determinants of the Corporate Decision to Capitalize Interest." *Journal of Accounting and Economics* (August 1981): 151–179.

BREMSER, W. G. "The Earnings Characteristics of Firms Reporting Discretionary Accounting Changes." *The Accounting Review* (July 1975): 563–573.

BUTTERS, J. K., and P. NILAND. *Effects of Taxation: Inventory Accounting and Policies*. Cambridge, Mass.: Harvard University Press, 1949.

CHOI, F. D. S., and V. B. BAVISHI. "International Accounting Standards: Issues Needing Attention." *The Journal of Accountancy* (March 1983): 62–68.

DALEY, L. A. and R. L. VIGELAND. "The Effects of Debt Covenants and Political Costs on the Choice of Accounting Methods: The Case of Accounting for R&D Costs." *Journal of Accounting and Economics* (December 1983): 195–211.

DAVIDSON, S., and R. L. WEIL. "Inflation Accounting: What Will General Price Level Adjusted Income Statements Show?" *Financial Analysts Journal* (January–February 1975): 27–31, 70–84.

DAWSON, J. P., P. M. NEUPERT, and C. P. STICKNEY. "Restating Financial Statements for Alternative GAAPs: Is It Worth the Effort?" *Financial Analysts Journal* (November–December 1980): 38–46.

DHALIWAL, D. S. "Some Economic Determinants of Management Lobbying for Alternative Methods of Accounting: Evidence from the Accounting for Interest Costs Issue." *Journal of Business Finance and Accounting* (Summer 1982): 255–265.

EVANS, T. G., W. R. FOLKS, and M. JILLING. *The Impact of Statement of Financial Accounting Standards No. 8 on the Foreign Exchange Risk Management Practices of American Multinationals*. Stamford, Conn.: FASB, 1978.

FOSTER, G. "Accounting Policy Decisions and Capital Market Research." *Journal of Accounting and Economics* (March 1980): 29–62.

GILMAN, S. *Accounting Concepts of Profit*. New York: The Ronald Press, 1939.

GRANOF, M. H., and D. G. SHORT. "Why Do Companies Reject LIFO?" *Journal of Accounting, Auditing and Finance* (Summer 1984): 323–333.

HOLTHAUSEN, R. W., and R. W. LEFTWICH. "The Economic Consequences of Accounting Choice: Implications of Costly Contracting and Monitoring." *Journal of Accounting and Economics* (August 1983): 77–117.

INTERNATIONAL ACCOUNTING STANDARDS COMMITTEE. *Accounting for Leases*, IAS 17. London: IASC, 1982.

KELLY, L. "Positive Theory Research: A Review." *Journal of Accounting Literature* (Spring 1983): 111–150.

KETZ, J. E. "The Validation of Some General Price Level Estimating Models." *The Accounting Review* (October 1978): 952–960.

KETZ, J. E. "Are Constant Dollar Disclosures Informative?" *Financial Analysts Journal* (March–April 1983): 52–55.

KIRK, D. J., "Reality and Rules: Can Financial Reporting Learn from the Game of Golf?" Address before Financial Executives Institute, Freeport, Grand Bahama, 1984.

LEFTWICH, R. "Accounting Information in Private Markets: Evidence from Private Lending Agreements." *The Accounting Review* (January 1983): 23–42.

LILIEN, S., and V. PASTENA. "Determinants of Intra Method Choice in the Oil and Gas Industry." *Journal of Accounting and Economics* (December 1982): 145–170.

LINDHE, R. "Accelerated Depreciation for Income Tax Purposes—A Study of the Decision and Some Firms Who Made It." *Journal of Accounting Research* (Autumn 1963): 139–148.

McCOSH, A. M., and S. D. HOWELL. "Planning and Control Systems and Their Evolution During Inflation." In D. Cooper, R. Scapens, and J. Arnold, eds., *Management Accounting Research and Practice*, London: I.C.M.A., 1983, pp. 199–264.

McKEE, A. J., T. B. BELL, and J. R. BOATSMAN. "Management Preferences over Accounting Standards: A Replication and Additional Tests." *The Accounting Review* (October 1984): 647–659.

MORSE, D., and G. RICHARDSON. "The LIFO/FIFO Decision." *Journal of Accounting Research* (Spring 1983): 106–127.

PARKER, J. E. "Impacts of Price-Level Accounting." *The Accounting Review* (January 1977): 69–96.

PETERSEN, R. J. "Interindustry Estimation of General Price-Level Impact on Financial Information." *The Accounting Review* (January 1973): 34–43.

SCHWARTZ, K. B. "Accounting Changes by Corporations Facing Possible Insolvency." *Journal of Accounting, Auditing and Finance* (Fall 1982): 32–43.

SEED, A. H. *The Impact of Inflation on Internal Planning and Control.* New York: National Association of Accountants, 1981.

WALTHER, L. M. "A Comparison of Estimated and Reported Historical Cost/ Constant Dollar Data." *The Accounting Review* (April 1982): 376–383.

WATTS, R. L., and J. L. ZIMMERMAN. "Towards a Positive Theory of the Determination of Accounting Standards." *The Accounting Review* (January 1978): 112–134.

ZEFF, S. A. "'Intermediate' and 'Advanced' Accounting: The Role of 'Economic Consequences.'" *The Accounting Review* (October 1980): 658–663.

ZMIJEWSKI, M. E., and R. L. HAGERMAN. "An Income Strategy Approach to the Positive Theory of Accounting Standard Setting/Choice." *Journal of Accounting and Economics* (August 1981): 129–149.

6

CROSS-SECTIONAL ANALYSIS OF FINANCIAL STATEMENT INFORMATION

6.1 INTRODUCTION

Financial statement data are often used in a comparative mode, such as

- Cross-sectional applications: comparisons of one entity with other entities at the same point in time
- Time-series applications: comparisons of one entity at different points in time.

This chapter examines issues that arise in cross-sectional analysis. Issues that arise in time-series applications are discussed in Chapter 7.

Cross-sectional analysis is used in many areas. The following are illustrative:

1. Valuation analysis for mergers or acquisitions where the financial statements of other firms are used to make inferences about the relative under- or overvaluation of a target company or division
2. Management performance evaluation and executive compensation where one input is the profitability of the firm compared to a benchmark set of firms operating in the same competitive environment
3. Prediction of financial distress using models based on firms in the one industry
4. Public policy decisions about excess profits tax legislation where one input is the profitability of firms in one industry compared to that of firms in other industries.

The issues discussed in this chapter are important in these and other cross-sectional uses of financial statement data.

6.2 CRITERIA USED TO SELECT COMPARABLES

Many decision contexts using cross-sectional analysis compare entities that are "similar" in at least one attribute. The following illustrate alternative approaches to defining "similar" entities:

1. *Similarity on supply side.* Firms may be grouped on the basis of having similar raw materials, similar production processes, similar distribution networks, and so on. This supply-side focus is used in the Enterprise Standard Industrial Classification (SIC) scheme for defining industries; the main factors considered are "physical or technological structure" and "homogeneity of production." The Enterprise SIC scheme aims to classify whole enterprises into two-, three-, and four-digit industries. A two-digit classification is the broadest definition of an industry; a four-digit classification is the narrowest definition. Consider the

two-, three-, and four-digit SIC industry groups in which Anheuser-Busch and G. Heileman Brewing are included. The two-digit code title (20) is "food and kindred products." The three-digit code title (208) is "beverages." The four-digit code title (2082) is "malt beverages." (A narrower classification scheme is available for products. For instance, the five-digit code for the products of these firms includes 20821 for "Canned Beer & Ale," 20822 for "Bottled Beer & Ale," 20823 for "Beer in Bulk," and 20824 for "Malt Liquor.")

Many information services use variants of the SIC approach when classifying firms into industry groupings. For instance, Standard & Poor's, in compiling the Compustat tape, uses the Enterprise SIC firm classifications as its basic source and then makes adjustments where it thinks those classifications are out of date (for example, due to recent acquisitions or divestitures).

2. *Similarity on demand side.* This approach emphasizes "similar" in terms of end-product similarity and the perceptions of customers as to the substitutability of products. Although the focus of demand-side comparisons typically is at the product level, comparisons can be made between companies producing similar products. The comparison can have a short-run perspective (for example, which firms produce brands that will compete with our products next period?) or a longer-run perspective (which firms will offer a range of services comparable to our range in five years' time?).

3. *Similarity in capital market attributes.* From an investment perspective, stocks that have similar attributes such as risk, price-to-earnings ratios, or market capitalization may be of interest. For instance, an investor who wishes to invest in small companies may rank firms on market capitalization and then invest in the bottom 10% of stocks so ranked.

4. *Similarity in legal ownership.* An important managerial use of cross-sectional analysis is in allocating resources between different subsidiaries (or lines of business). These subsidiaries may be quite diverse in terms of both supply-side and demand-side characteristics. Their similarity arises from being owned by the same set of shareholders. Ratios such as return on capital employed and cash flow per sales dollar can be important inputs in these managerial resource allocation decisions.

In some cross-sectional applications, the comparison set may include firms that are similar on several criteria. For instance, Robert Morris Associates (1983), in its *Annual Statement Studies*, publishes data cross-classified according to industry similarity using a supply-side focus and firm size. The data are based on the financial statements of loan applicants at banks that voluntarily report such data to Robert Morris Associates. Dun & Bradstreet uses a similar format in its industry norm studies; data for 14 "key business ratios" are presented for SIC four-digit industries with a breakdown based on a size criterion. Some trade associations also present comparative data using several criteria. For instance,

Lisciandro's (1983) analysis of the motor carrier industry for the American Trucking Association is broken down according to three classes of general freight carriers based on gross revenue. They are then cross-categorized along geographical bases, for example, New England, Rocky Mountain, and Pacific. The presentation of these subcategories is based on the assumption that the comparison of a carrier with similar-sized companies operating in the same geographical area is likely to yield the most meaningful inferences about relative profitability, liquidity, and so on.

6.3   AGGREGATION OPTIONS IN CROSS-SECTIONAL ANALYSIS

When comparing the ratios of a firm with those of a comparable set of firms, the analyst has various options as to how to aggregate the ratios of those firms:

1. Use a single summary measure of central tendency, for example, median, equally weighted mean, or value weighted mean

2. Use both a measure of central tendency and a measure of dispersion, for example, the median and the interquartile range (.75 percentile − .25 percentile) or the mean and the standard deviation

3. Use summary measures such as percentiles or fractiles of the distribution of the ratios

4. Use both the rank and the ratio of each firm.

The following example illustrates the computation of equal- and value-weighted industry earnings-to-common equity ratios. Consider an industry with three firms:

	Firm A	Firm B	Firm C
Earnings available for common	$240	$860	$1,400
Common equity, book value	$1,200	$8,600	$20,000
Earnings-to-common equity ratio	20%	10%	7%
Common stock outstanding, market value	$2,000	$10,000	$20,000

The equal-weighted industry average is

$$\tfrac{1}{3} (20\% + 10\% + 7\%) = 12.33\%$$

Computation of a value-weighted index requires choice of a weighting scheme. Two alternatives are illustrated:

1. Weighted by the book value of common equity (denominator of ratio):

$$\left(\frac{\$240}{\$1,200} \times \frac{\$1,200}{\$29,800} \right) + \left(\frac{\$860}{\$8,600} \times \frac{\$8,600}{\$29,800} \right) + \left(\frac{\$1,400}{\$20,000} \times \frac{\$20,000}{\$29,800} \right)$$

$$= \frac{\$240 + \$860 + \$1,400}{\$29,800} = 8.39\%$$

2. Weighted by the market value of common stock outstanding:

$$\left(\frac{\$240}{\$1,200} \times \frac{\$2,000}{\$32,000}\right) + \left(\frac{\$860}{\$8,600} \times \frac{\$10,000}{\$32,000}\right) + \left(\frac{\$1,400}{\$20,000} \times \frac{\$20,000}{\$32,000}\right)$$

$$= \left(20\% \times \frac{\$2,000}{\$32,000}\right) + \left(10\% \times \frac{\$10,000}{\$32,000}\right) + \left(7\% \times \frac{\$20,000}{\$32,000}\right) = 8.75\%$$

The arithmetic and value-weighted mean (and the standard deviation statistic) can be very sensitive to extreme observations. If an analyst wishes to use these as summary measures, it is important to plot the individual observations at least to be aware if extreme observations occur in the sample.

Assume that an analyst at Miller Brewing Company (a subsidiary of Philip Morris with divisional operating revenues of $2.936 billion) is examining inventory turnover in the U.S. brewing industry. Data for the seven publicly listed companies in 1983 are

Firm	COGS/Inventory	COGS (000s)	Inventory (000s)
1. Adolph Coors	7.27	$ 720,152	$ 99,051
2. G. Heileman	7.79	822,100	105,505
3. Pabst	8.54	543,552	63,654
4. Genesee	10.78	111,608	10,355
5. Falstaff	12.02	50,044	4,164
6. Pittsburgh	12.64	34,356	2,718
7. Anheuser-Busch	13.56	4,113,200	303,300
		$6,395,012	$588,747

The median ratio is 10.78, the equal-weighted mean is 10.37, and the value-weighted mean (weighted by the denominator of the ratio) is 10.86. In this illustration, there are sufficiently few firms to present the complete distribution. One benefit is that an analyst can then select those subsets that are considered of special interest (for example, due to size similarities, the analyst at Miller Brewing may be especially interested in Anheuser-Busch).

The information reported in many trade sources and in industry association publications typically does not enable complete enumeration of the distribution. For instance, industry data published by Dun & Bradstreet and Robert Morris Associates include only the quartiles of the distribution of each ratio. However, the increasing availability of computerized data bases means that complete enumeration, or at least distribution statistics such as deciles, is now frequently available to external analysts. As a general rule, disaggregated approaches are to be preferred if the costs of accessing and processing the data are minimal.

6.4   DATA AVAILABILITY ISSUES IN CROSS-SECTIONAL ANALYSIS

Many difficult problems can arise in the data collection phase of a cross-sectional analysis project. Where there are no readily available solutions to these problems, considerable caution should be employed when making inferences from cross-sectional data.

A. Nonavailability of Data

A frequently encountered problem is that data are not available for the entities of interest. Reasons for nonavailability include

1. The entity is owned by a multiactivity company that provides limited financial disclosures relating to the entity; for example, it is not disclosed as a separate line of business.
2. The entity is privately held and does not publicly release financial statement information. (Indeed, one motivation for remaining private could be to avoid regulatory mandates to publish such information. In some cases, third parties may make estimates of individual financial statement items such as sales and net earnings. However, these estimates will not be certified by the company or its auditors.)
3. The entity is owned by a foreign company (foreign government, etc.) that provides limited financial disclosures.

Consider an analyst who wishes to examine the profitability of firms in the U.S. frozen potato industry. In the early 1980s, there were ten major participants in this industry. Table 6.1 outlines these participants and the problems of obtaining financial statements for them. Not one of the ten participants is a publicly held, single-line-of-business (LOB) enterprise. Five are privately held, none of which

TABLE 6.1 Data Availability in the U.S. Frozen Potato Industry

Parent Company	Company Name in Frozen Potato Industry	Data Availability
1. Simplot	Simplot	Company is privately held.
2. Amfac	Lamb-Weston	Amfac does not report LOB data for Lamb-Weston.
3. H. J. Heinz	Ore-Ida	Heinz does not report LOB data for Ore-Ida.
4. Carnation	Carnation	Carnation does not report LOB data for frozen potato activities.
5. Chef Ready	Chef Ready	Company is privately held.
6. Rogers Walla Walla	Rogers Walla Walla	Company is privately held.
7. Consolidated Foods	Idaho Frozen Foods	Consolidated does not report LOB data for Idaho.
8. U&I	Gourmet Foods	U&I does not report LOB data for Gourmet.
9. Western Idaho Potato Producers	Western Idaho Potato Producers	Company is privately held.
10. Prosser Pack	Prosser Pack	Company is privately held.

makes a practice of distributing its financial statements to external parties. The other five are owned by multiactivity firms, none of which separately reports frozen potato activities as a single line of business. An external analyst has very few options when faced with an industry such as frozen potatoes. The limited availability of financial statement data effectively may preclude cross-sectional analysis as a meaningful exercise.

Table 6.2 shows a useful approach to gaining insight into how representative of the industry are the firms with available data. (The focus in Table 6.2 is on domestic firms.) The cleanest inferences about industry profitability, leverage, and so on are from firms in the category of single-activity firms with available financial statement data. The next section of this chapter discusses issues that arise in using the line of business disclosures of firms in categories B and C in Table 6.2.

TABLE 6.2 Format for Assessing the Representativeness of Financial Statement Data Available for Firms in an Industry with Illustration from Domestic U.S. Brewing Industry, 1983

Domestic Firms	*U.S. Brewing Industry*
A. Single-activity firm with financial statements available	Pabst Brewing ($800 million sales) Genesee Brewing ($186 million sales) Falstaff Brewing ($66 million sales) Pittsburgh Brewing ($58 million sales)
B. Multiactivity firm with major activity in relevant SIC code; financial statements available	Anheuser-Busch ($5,532 million beer sales out of $6,659 million sales) Heileman Brewing ($1,210 million beer sales out of $1,326 million sales) Adolph Coors ($1,079 million beer sales out of $1,242 million sales)
C. Multiactivity firm with major activity not in relevant SIC code; financial statements available, including LOB disclosure for relevant activity	Miller Brewing ($2,936 million operating revenues; subsidiary of Philip Morris with $12,976 million operating revenues of which $9,095 is from tobacco sales) Iroquois Brands ($46 million sales for Alcoholic Beverage division out of total sales of $156 million; Nutritional Products division has sales of $90 million)
D. Multiactivity firm with major activity not in relevant SIC code; financial statements available, but no LOB disclosure for relevant activity	——
E. Privately held firm with no financial statements available (third party estimates of individual items sometimes available)	Stroh Brewing ($1,522 million sales*) C. Schmidt Brewing ($204 million sales*) General Brewing ($128 million sales*)

* Sales estimates taken from *Ward's Directory* (1984): p. 54.

In some countries, there may be few domestically based competitors. Inferences about a firm's efficiency will be facilitated by including in the analysis firms based in other countries. An extreme example is Singapore Airlines. This is the only airline based in Singapore. Inferences about its efficiency are facilitated by comparing its financial and operating performance with carriers such as British Airways, Malaysian Airlines, Pan American, and Qantas. Issues that arise in international cross-sectional comparisons of financial ratios are discussed in Section 6.7.

Data Pertaining to Privately Held Companies

Some privately held companies are relatively large. Table 6.3 presents a list of the ten largest (using dollar sales) publicly held and the ten largest privately held U.S. corporations. In some industries, privately held companies hold major market shares. A factor increasing the importance of privately held companies is the "going private" phenomenon (see Chapter 13).

A subset of privately held companies voluntarily publishes financial statements. The motivations for such voluntary disclosure could be many. For instance, the privately held company may be expanding via franchising, and each

TABLE 6.3 Largest Publicly Held and Privately Held U.S. Companies

Company Name	1983 Sales: ($ billion)	Major Line of Business
Publicly Held		
1. Exxon	$88.6	Oil and gas
2. General Motors	74.6	Motor vehicles
3. Mobil	54.6	Oil and gas
4. Ford Motor	44.5	Motor vehicles
5. International Business Machines	40.2	Computers
6. Texaco	40.1	Oil and gas
7. E. I. DuPont	35.4	Chemicals and oil and gas
8. Phibro Salomon	29.8	Trading and financial services
9. Amoco	27.6	Oil and gas
10. Chevron	27.3	Oil and gas
Privately Held		
1. Cargill	$28.6	Grain
2. Mocatta Metals	26.5	Bullion dealers
3. Continental Grain	15.8	Grain
4. Koch Industries	14.0	Oil and mining
5. Bechtel Group	13.6	Engineering services
6. Apex Oil	5.4	Petroleum distribution
7. USA Petroleum	4.0	Oil and gas extraction
8. Mars	4.0	Candy
9. United Parcel Service	3.5	Package delivery
10. Coral Petroleum	2.8	Petroleum refining

SOURCE: *Fortune*, April 30, 1984, and June 11, 1984, for publicly held companies; *Town and Country*, August 1984, for privately held companies.

potential franchisee could use the published financial statements in loan applications to banks, insurance companies, and so on. Another motivation could be that the privately held company is planning a public issue and is seeking to establish an ongoing relationship with security analysts.

Industry associations often publish aggregate data based on financial statements provided by their members. Privately held companies that are members of the association typically are "guaranteed" that only aggregate industry data will be reported so that firm identification of their ratios, and so on, will not be possible. Notwithstanding these guarantees, not all firms in an industry belong to their relevant trade association, and not all members agree to provide financial statements to their association. The result is that industry or trade association data can be highly variable in terms of its representativeness.

B. Nonsynchronous Reporting Periods

There is considerable diversity across firms in their fiscal year reporting periods. Table 6.4 presents fiscal breakdowns for the annual reports of companies in the United States, Australia, Belgium, Japan, New Zealand, and the United Kingdom. December is the most common fiscal year end in the United States, Belgium, and the United Kingdom; March is the most common fiscal year end in Japan and New Zealand; June is the most common fiscal year end in Australia. Not all companies use an end-of-month cutoff for their fiscal year, and not all have the same number of calendar days in each fiscal year. For example, Barron (1984) reports that a small subset of U.K. companies close their fiscal year on a particular day of the week; the result is that the number of calendar days for a

TABLE 6.4   Fiscal Year Breakdown of Companies

Month Fiscal Year Ends	United States	Australia	Belgium	Japan	New Zealand	United Kingdom
January	4.4%	.5%	.8%	2.2%	1.1%	4.4%
February	2.0	1.0	.4	3.7	1.1	2.4
March	3.5	4.2	2.6	54.9	44.7	20.4
April	2.0	1.3	.5	4.9	2.8	4.3
May	1.7	1.6	.3	4.5	1.6	1.5
June	7.6	71.3	4.5	1.6	20.6	6.4
July	2.8	3.7	.4	.9	5.6	2.8
August	2.3	1.2	.4	1.1	2.2	1.7
September	6.6	3.7	2.8	6.8	6.1	8.8
October	2.8	.9	.6	2.8	5.9	3.5
November	2.2	1.0	.9	7.9	1.1	2.8
December	62.1	9.6	85.8	8.7	7.2	41.1

SOURCES: United States (Compustat tape); Australia (P. Dodd); Belgium (W. Buijink and M. Jegers); Japan (Nakamura and Terada, 1984); New Zealand (Mercantile Gazette, 1984); United Kingdom (M. Barron, 1984). U.S. data are for 1983, Australian for 1983, Belgian for 1982, Japanese for 1983, New Zealand for 1983, and United Kingdom for 1981.

fiscal year will oscillate over time. Some industry patterns are observable for fiscal year ends. For example, January 31 is the predominant date chosen by most U.S. retailing companies.

When all firms in the sample do not have comparable fiscal year ends, problems can arise in making inferences about (say) relative profitability or relative firm size. For instance, Firm X with a December 31 fiscal year may appear more profitable than Firm Y with a September 30 fiscal year, because the most recent three months were in an expanding phase of the economy whereas the comparable three months of the prior year were in a recessionary phase of the economy. In some cases, adjustments can be made to place firms with noncomparable fiscal years onto comparable reporting periods. In the example, given quarterly reporting, the calendar year earnings of Firm Y can be determined by adding the October–December quarter of the current year and subtracting the comparable period of the prior year. An amusing illustration of this problem occurred in 1978. In November 1978, Coopers & Lybrand announced that its revenues for the fiscal year ending September 30 were $595 million. The headline of its press release read "Coopers & Lybrand reports highest CPA revenues"; the firm stated it was "the largest annual volume reported by an accounting firm." *Forbes* magazine subsequently carried an article entitled "The new champion: Coopers & Lybrand." Peat, Marwick & Mitchell fired back a response that its recently reported revenues of $585.9 million were for a June 30 fiscal year and that had it used the same September 30 fiscal year end, it would have reported revenues of "over $603 million."

When making comparisons across companies from different countries, the nonsynchronous data problem can be severe. Countries differ in fiscal year reporting patterns (see Table 6.4) and also differ in the periodicity of interim reporting. Many British Commonwealth countries, for instance, report on a half-yearly (semiannual) rather than a quarterly basis.

C. Nonuniformity in Accounting Methods

In many samples of firms, diversity in accounting method choice is encountered. Chapter 5 discussed factors that may explain these differences across firms. An important conclusion of that chapter is that firms can have substantive reasons for adopting different accounting methods. In this situation, nonuniformity of accounting methods across firms does not necessarily imply noncomparability of financial statement–based ratios. However, if an analyst decides that uniformity of accounting methods is desirable, one of several options can be adopted:

1. Restrict the sample of firms to only those that adopt uniform accounting methods
2. Use company-provided information to adjust the reported numbers to those derived using the alternative method (see Section 5.5.A)

3. Use approximating techniques to adjust the reported numbers to those derived using the alternative method (see Section 5.5.B).

Note that in some decision contexts, nonuniformity in accounting method choice will not pose a problem; for example, if the concern is restricted to explaining differences across firms in their inventory turnover ratios, differences in their lease accounting methods will not be a problem.

6.5 LINE-OF-BUSINESS INFORMATION

The importance of multiactivity firms means that cross-sectional analysis of firms in specific industries often will use line-of-business (LOB) information presented in annual and interim reports.

A. Incentives of Firms to Disclose Line-of-Business Data

The argument typically given for investors demanding LOB data relates to assessment of the risks, returns, and growth prospects of each of the individual activities. If individual activities differ in these aspects, LOB data potentially can highlight this fact. Notwithstanding this argument, many multiactivity firms provided limited LOB disclosures prior to their being mandated by regulatory bodies. The arguments used by firms against increased disclosure emphasized "competitive disadvantage" issues. Consider the following responses by several U.S. firms to SEC and FASB proposals that detailed line-of-business data be disclosed as well as a breakdown of sales by country and by major class of customer:

- The reporting of segment information would tend to hamper continued earnings and growth prospects. The competitive position of the enterprise would be endangered by providing information which, when evaluated, would invite additional competitive pressures, encourage supplier militancy, and provide indications of the enterprise's strategy. Reporting of segment information would place limits on management's desire to undertake activities involving a high risk since they would avoid a position which could invite criticism of their actions; yet risk-taking is essential to business. Disclosure of segment information would give big money a clear advantage over small business and the small investor by revealing highly profitable lines of business. (Harsco Corporation)

- We object to the disclosure of financial data by country or groups of countries. We are of the opinion that this type of data would be more beneficial to our competition than to the general users of financial data. This is especially true in those countries or geographical areas where we might not be as diversified as we are in the United States. In these cases the data disclosed could be quite specific, thereby, jeopardizing our competitive situation.   (Uniroyal, Inc.)

Regulatory bodies typically have allowed multiactivity firms discretion in presenting LOB data. For instance, U.S. firms have considerable discretion over key aspects such as

1. Whether the firm views itself as a multiactivity or single-activity entity
2. How the individual activities are to be grouped into individual lines of business
3. How intersegment transfers are to be priced when calculating the sales and profits of individual lines of business
4. How allocations of interest costs and shared resources are to be made across individual lines of business.

When using LOB data in cross-sectional analysis, it is important to recognize that firm choices on (1) to (4) are likely to be made, taking into account competitor accessibility to the disclosures. An external analyst may find the LOB disclosures of limited "value" precisely because that is what the disclosing firm was attempting to achieve in its decisions on (1) to (4).

B. Structural and Organizational Change Implications

When using LOB data, it is important to recognize factors that can affect the reported numbers (over and above changes in the underlying profitability of the individual activities). These include

- *Acquisitions.* When a new firm is acquired, decisions have to be made as to whether the new firm should be shown as a separate LOB or have its individual activities allocated across the existing LOBs. Allocation is often adopted, especially when a motivation for the merger is to capture operating synergies between a firm's current activities and those of the firm acquired.
- *Divestitures.* Divested activities are not always restricted to activities comprising a single LOB. Where they form only part of a single LOB or they span several LOBs, the divestiture can prompt a firm to reexamine its existing groupings. The result can be a consolidation of several existing groupings or a realignment of the groupings of continuing activities.
- *Organization changes.* Changes in the organization structures of firms can occur for many reasons other than acquisitions and divestitures, for example, to gain a better focus of operations on end-product markets, to reduce duplication of corporate overhead, and to reduce internal disputes between interrelated divisions. These organization shifts may result in changes in the LOB groupings that can be readily derived from the internal reporting system.
- *Changes in the internal reporting system.* The profit and sales figures reported for individual LOBs are a function, in part, of the transfer-pricing methods used and the interest and overhead-expense-allocation methods employed. Over time, firms can make changes in these methods to (say) promote goal congruence within the firm and to make division managers more aware of the cost of money. A consequence can be changes in the LOB profit and sales figures reported in externally released financial statements.

Where major changes occur in LOB reporting, firms generally will alert the reader to them. In some cases, changes are made in LOB reporting without accompanying comments in the annual report. A comparison of LOB data in successive annual reports often can be an effective way of becoming aware of potential changes.

6.6 INDUSTRY COMPARISONS OF FINANCIAL RATIOS

An important assumption of industry ratio analysis is that significant differences in the distributions of industry ratios exist. If, for example, the distribution of the current ratio of each industry were the same, there would be little point in separately examining deviations of a firm's current ratio from its industry average. Comparison of a firm's ratio with the economy average would be sufficient in this situation. This section provides evidence on industry differences in financial ratios. Prior to presenting this evidence, alternative definitions of the industry notion are discussed.

A. Definition of an Industry

There is no single definition of "industry" that is universally accepted. Alternative approaches include focus on one or more of the following attributes:

- Similarity in raw material usage
- Similarity in production process
- Similarity in end product as perceived by consumers
- Similarity in end consumer group.

Early research in this area was conducted by economists specializing in industrial organization. Bain (1952) argued that "ideally, an industry is a group of products of firms which are perfect substitutes for each other to a common group of buyers and which are very poor substitutes for all other products in the economy" (p. 24). More recent research has focused on ways of operationalizing the product substitutability notion and of setting limits on the geographical area that can be defined as a "single market." For instance, Stigler and Sherwin (1983) propose using parallel *product* price movements as the criteria in deciding the definition of a market: "If we find parallel price movements, the loci of the prices are in the same market. If we find significant nonparallel price movements, the loci of the prices are *not* in the same market unless the discordance in movements can be traced to changes in transportation costs" (p. 2).

Research in the marketing and corporate strategy literatures has also discussed the industry notion, with the focus expanding beyond the substitutability notion. For instance, financial products such as checking facilities, credit cards, insurance, and security transactions are viewed by some corporate strategy researchers as comprising a single industry (''financial services''). These individual products need not be viewed as close substitutes by the consumer; the focus here is on the range of services that have the common denominator of being ''financial'' in nature.

B. Sources of Information about Firms in an Industry

Several sources of information can be used in determining the firms to include in an industry:

1. A published coding or classification of firms into individual industries, for example, the SIC codes or the Value Line classifications for U.S. companies, the SEIC codes for U.K. companies, and the STATEX codes for Australian companies.

2. Firms mentioned by security analysts and other sources as competing in the same market. The list of firms could be based on a citation analysis of the research reports of a chosen set of security analysts.

3. Results of a project in which firms are grouped into industries based on their empirical commonalities. Techniques such as factor analysis and cluster analysis could be used to determine the relevant grouping of firms; see Jackson (1983) for a description of these techniques. King (1966) and Meyers (1973) illustrate this approach for commonalities based on similar comovements of security returns. Bourgeois, Haines, and Sommers (1980) discuss this approach for commonalities based on product-demand factors.

Most industry-based applications use published classifications, in part due to their ready availability and their (apparent) objectivity. However, it is important to verify that the basis of the chosen categorization is consistent with the purpose of the data analysis and that the codings reflect recent ownership changes (that is, via acquisitions or divestitures).

C. Evidence of Industry Differences

The most comprehensive data base of U.S. firms is the Compustat tape, which focuses on supply-side similarities in operationalizing the industry notion. Table 6.5 presents evidence on the extent of numerical differences in the median financial ratios/variables of 15 SIC four-digit industries. These industries are those for which there were more than 20 firms available on the 1983 Compustat annual tape. The 12 financial ratios are

1. Cash and marketable securities/total assets, $(C + MS)/TA$
2. Current assets/current liabilities, CA/CL
3. Cash flow from operations/sales, CFO/S
4. Long-term liabilities/stockholders' equity, LTL/SE
5. Operating income/interest payments, OI/INT
6. Net income/stockholders' equity, NI/SE
7. Sales/total assets, S/TA

TABLE 6.5 Median Financial Ratios for Selected Four-Digit SIC Industries, 1983

SIC Code	Industry Title (manufacturing)	$\frac{(C+MS)}{TA}$	$\frac{CA}{CL}$	$\frac{CFO}{S}$	$\frac{LTL}{SE}$	$\frac{OI}{INT}$	$\frac{NI}{SE}$	$\frac{S}{TA}$	$\frac{S}{AR}$	$\frac{COGS}{INV}$	PE	$\frac{DIV.}{PAY.}$	TA $
1311	Oil, crude producers	.042	1.34	.430	.56	.74	.054	.28	3.61	5.98	12.50	.00	189
2300	Textile apparel manufacturing	.065	2.90	.054	.27	2.68	.131	1.77	6.37	3.20	9.22	.12	80
2600	Paper and applied products	.021	1.87	.086	.46	1.14	.058	1.02	9.16	7.06	14.38	.42	1,488
2830	Drugs	.147	2.10	.114	.15	3.97	.200	1.07	5.56	2.37	12.92	.34	961
2911	Petroleum refining	.057	1.23	.118	.37	1.69	.085	1.21	9.41	11.71	8.67	.45	4,109
3310	Steel and blast furnaces	.030	1.86	.036	.53	-.71	-.084	1.08	7.03	4.47	-3.49	.00	398
3560	General industrial machinery	.098	2.49	.080	.35	.26	.010	1.13	5.02	3.04	12.59	.00	110
3662	Radio and T.V. transmitting equipment	.121	2.62	.114	.10	5.24	.119	1.29	5.61	3.03	17.31	.14	105
3679	Electronic components	.128	2.98	.075	.14	2.68	.105	1.20	6.00	3.20	22.27	.13	66
4511	Air transport	.057	1.02	.063	1.41	-.35	-.062	1.10	10.82	28.46	-.88	.00	1,035
4924	Natural gas	N.C.	.99	N.C.	.73	1.06	.095	1.37	N.C.	N.C.	7.38	.68	181
4931	Electric and other services	N.C.	1.04	N.C.	.86	1.46	.114	.48	N.C.	N.C.	6.58	.69	1,498
5411	Retail food chains	.074	1.50	.024	.63	2.07	.136	4.47	89.43	11.29	10.27	.25	268
6312	Life insurance	.006	N.C.	N.C.	.04	4.29	.093	.32	8.23	N.C.	8.32	.35	2,514
6798	Real estate investment trusts	.030	N.C.	N.C.	.36	1.75	.112	.16	N.C.	N.C.	10.80	.87	77

N.C. – Not calculated.
SOURCE: Computed from 1983 Compustat annual industrial file.

8. Sales/accounts receivable, S/AR
9. Cost of goods sold/inventory, COGS/INV
10. Price-to-earnings ratio, PE
11. Dividend payout, DIV. PAY.
12. Total assets, TA ($ millions)

The results in Table 6.5 are consistent with there being sizable differences across a subset of industries in their financial ratios.

One of the most challenging areas of research in accounting and other business disciplines is explaining differences such as those documented in Table 6.5. Section 6.8 discusses several studies in this area.

6.7   INTERNATIONAL COMPARISONS OF FINANCIAL RATIOS

In many situations, analysts are concerned with comparing the financial statements of companies from different countries. Issues that arise in international comparisons of financial ratios include

1. Differences in the set of accounting principles adopted in each country
2. Differences in taxation rules adopted in each country and in the relationship between the accounting principles used for tax and those used for financial reporting
3. Differences in the financing, operation, and other business arrangements in each country
4. Differences in the cultural, institutional, and the political environment in each country.

It is important to consider these factors before making inferences based on observed differences in the financial ratios of companies.

An interesting paper in this area is the Choi, Hino, Min, Nam, Ujiie, and Stonehill (1983) study of the financial ratios of Japanese, Korean, and U.S. firms. The initial data examined were based on aggregate statistics for large samples of manufacturing enterprises as collected by the Bank of Japan, the Bank of Korea, and the Federal Trade Commission. Some representative results for the 1976–1978 period are

	Japan (976 firms)	Korea (354 firms)	United States (902 firms)
Current ratio	1.15	1.13	1.94
Total debt to total assets	.84	.78	.47
Times interest earned	1.60	1.80	6.50
Inventory turnover	5.00	6.60	6.80
Average collection period	86 days	33 days	43 days
Profit margin	.013	.023	.054
Return on total assets	.012	.028	.074

The conclusion was that "Japanese and Korean companies generally appear less liquid, solvent, efficient, or profitable than their U.S. counterparts" (p. 115).

The authors then matched a Japanese and a U.S. firm for each of ten industries (for example, Fuji Photo and Kodak) and a Korean and a U.S. firm for each of eight industries (for example, Daewoo and Whittaker). One issue Choi et al. (1983) examined was whether differences in accounting principles explained the observed differences in the financial ratios of firms in the same industry in different countries: "to minimize the apples and oranges problem, an attempt was made to conform Japanese and Korean financial statements to U.S. GAAP" (p. 119). For the ten Japanese firms, the authors concluded: "No significant difficulties were encountered" (p. 119) in making the restatements. It was found that "accounting restatements do have some effects on paired-ratio differences. In most instances, however, these effects are not appreciable because significant ratio differences remain" (p. 119). Making restatements for the eight Korean firms "proved troublesome. To begin, consolidation of group accounts, taken for granted in the United States, is rarely practiced in Korea. . . . Because of nondisclosure, elimination of intercompany profits was impossible as was computation of minority interest and reversal of (several other) major accounting differences" (p. 119). (For example, R&D is expensed in the United States but is capitalized in Korea.)

The final issue Choi et al. (1983) examined was whether the observed differences in financial ratios could be explained by "cultural and institutional dimensions of the Japanese and Korean business environments" (p. 119). For instance, factors cited as important for the observed differences in leverage ratios included

- The shallow nature of the equity market in Korea vis-à-vis the U.S. equity market
- The strong interdependence between banks and corporate firms in Japan and Korea resulting in "long-term debt assuming the characteristics of preferred stock" (p. 123).

At this stage, research has not progressed beyond a listing of potential "institutional, cultural, political and tax considerations." Yet to be attempted is the more difficult task of explaining how much of observed financial ratio difference is due to such factors, as opposed to (say) an efficiency difference between companies in different countries.

6.8   SOME GENERAL COMMENTS

1. A small set of studies has presented empirical evidence relating to the homogeneity of firms classified into different industry groups. Sudarsanam and Taffler (1984) examined a sample of over 250 U.K. firms that were each classified into one of 14 codes of the (London) Stock Exchange Industrial Classification

(SEIC) system. The SEIC codes were "established by a committee of actuaries, investment managers and stockbrokers. . . . The economic criteria for classification . . . would appear to be predominantly output- or end-product-based" (p. 2). The model used to predict the SEIC industry code of a firm was

$$I_i = f(X_{ij}, \ldots, X_{in}) \tag{6.1}$$

where

I_i = SEIC industry coding of firm i

X_{ij} = financial statement variable j of firm i

The 14 manufacturing industries examined were chosen to represent a "wide spectrum of product characteristics, production technology and maturity," for example, building materials, general food manufacturing, and general chemicals. The final model for (6.1) included six independent variables (X_{ij}'s):

- Accounts receivable payment period
- Accounts receivable/inventory
- Earnings before interest and taxes/sales
- Wages/total assets
- Accounts receivable/accounts payable
- Sales/fixed assets.

These variables were chosen using an empirical search that initially included "18 financial ratios chosen so as to reflect a broad range of important characteristics relating to the economic, financial and trade structure of industries" (p. 6).

Discriminant analysis was used to estimate (6.1). (The appendix to Chapter 14 provides a description of discriminant analysis.) *If* the independent variables in (6.1) reflect industry differences, and *if* there is homogeneity of firms *within* each industry and heterogeneity across the 14 industries, (6.1) will classify a high percentage of the firms into their correct industry codings. By chance, approximately 7% of the firms (that is, 1 out of 14 industries) will be classified into their correct SEIC industry coding. The model in (6.1) was able to classify correctly 30.45% of the firms into their four-digit SEIC industry grouping:

> The more homogeneous groups are Food, Clothing and Chemicals with an average of over 40% of their firms correctly classified. The most heterogeneous are Textiles, Metallurgy and Footwear with 15% or fewer firms correctly classified. The significant overall classification result appears attributable to the substantial homogeneity exhibited by about half of the sample industries, the other half being quite heterogeneous. The SEIC may be said to have achieved partial success in creating groups of firms homogeneous with respect to their substantive economic attributes.   (p. 13)

The authors then grouped the 14 industries into four meta industries (processing, engineering, textiles, and food); (6.1) was reestimated with the dependent variable being the meta-industry classification of firm i. The model in (6.1) was able to classify 69.7% of the firms into their four meta-group industry classifications, compared to approximately 29% being correctly classified by chance alone.

The foregoing research probes the important issue of the homogeneity of firms classified into different industry groupings. The approach adopted can be extended using alternative industry coding schemes, additional independent variables, and classification techniques other than discriminant analysis. In addition, one could examine the effect that diversification by firms into multiple lines of business has on the predictive ability of models like (6.1). Such extensions would provide extra insight into the robustness and descriptive validity of the industry classifications schemes available to users of financial statement information.

2. The evidence presented in Chapters 4 and 6 is consistent with differences across firms and across industries in their relative profitability. Academics from several disciplines have sought to explain these differences. Early economics research argued that in perfect markets under certainty, the rates of return of all firms and all industries would be the same. Many authors have attempted to explain differences in accounting profitability measures by relaxing either the certainty assumption or the perfect market assumption. Relaxing the certainty assumption, Stigler (1963) hypothesized that differences in accounting rates of return could be explained by differences in business risk; risk-averse entrepreneurs would require higher rates of return in industries in which there is higher business risk, and vice versa. Empirical research has not provided strong support for this hypothesis. Bowman (1980) examined the correlation between the mean return on equity (ROE) and the variance of ROE for 387 companies from 11 industries in the 1972–1976 period. The Stigler hypothesis would predict a positive correlation. In 10 of the 11 industries examined, the correlation was negative. Marsh and Swanson (1984) reexamined this issue. They examined firms in 13 industries over the 1963–1981 period. In only 2 industries (machinery and textile mills) was there a significant correlation (both positive) between average ROE and the variance of ROE; 8 industries had positive correlations, and 5 had negative correlations. On balance, these studies (and their many predecessors) have not been able to shed much new light on why firms differ in their relative profitability.

The economics profession has devoted much effort to probing imperfect market-related explanations for differences in firm or industry profitability, for example, by analyzing correlations between profitability and variables proxying for industry concentration or barriers to entry. This literature was especially active in the 1950s and 1960s. Weiss (1971) surveyed over 30 studies from this era; many reported a significant (albeit small) positive relationship between profitability and industry concentration. Recent research has (in part) been motivated by the availability of more detailed information on the line of business profitability of firms. Ravenscraft (1983) is an illustrative study. The data base was 3,186 line-of-business disclosures to the Federal Trade Commission (along four-digit FTC categories) by 258 manufacturing companies in 1975. The methodology employed was regression analysis with the ratio of operating income to sales as the dependent variable and combinations of 23 variables measuring industry structure attributes as the independent variables. Ravenscraft reported that "the most important variables are the positive effect of higher-capacity utilization and industry growth, with the positive effect of market share running a close third" (p. 25). Among the insignificant correlations was a measure of industry concentration: "The results do not support the hypothesis that the simple linear four-firm concentration variable is a proxy for the ability to collude. A positive relationship between profitability and concentration does not appear in the regression" (p. 26). This study is typical of many in this literature; it is heavily data driven, with theory playing a small role in variable choice or model specification. At this stage, it is difficult to find even a single variable across the numerous economic studies in this area that has consistently exhibited a significant ability to explain cross-sectional differences in firm or industry profitability.

3. The determinants of interfirm and interindustry profitability are also the focus of research in the business strategy and marketing literatures. Much of this research can be characterized as data exploration exercises. Correlations between variables such as return on equity, profit margin, advertising expenditures, and market share have been reported. In an early example of this research, Buzzell, Gale, and Sultan (1975) examined the PIMS (profit impact of market strategies) data base, which includes profitability information on individual "business units" of firms. This information is voluntarily provided by firms associated with the Marketing Science Institute:

> Each business is a division, product line, or other profit center within its parent company, selling a distinct set of products or services to an identifiable group or groups of customers, in competition with a well-defined set of competitors.   (p. 105)

Buzzell, Gale, and Sultan report that they identified "37 key profit influences, of which one of the most important is market share. . . . On the average, a difference of 10 percentage points in market share is accompanied by a difference of about 5 points in pretax ROI" (p. 97). Pretax ROI was measured as "pretax operating profits" divided by "the sum of equity and long-term debt." Explanations offered for this correlation between market share and pretax ROI included "economies of scale," "market power," and "quality of management." A more recent example of this research is the Phillips, Chang, and Buzzell (1983) study of the "effects of product quality on direct costs and business unit return on investment (ROI)" (p. 26). Using the PIMS data base, these authors examined segment data in six types of business (consumer durables, consumer nondurables, capital goods, raw and semifinished materials, components, and supplies). The following finding is illustrative of their results: "The data support the view that achieving a low relative-cost position is one way to earn supranormal returns, since cost position is a significant determinant of ROI in all businesses except consumer durables"   (p. 38).

At present, well-developed theories do not exist as to how variables such as advertising, cost structure, market share, and product quality affect profitability. The most promising advances will likely come (in the short run) from careful econometric research in which considerable attention is paid to data quality and the construction of research designs discriminating between competing hypotheses. Anterasian (1984) provides a good overview of these issues.

4. The evidence presented in Table 6.5 shows sizable differences across industries in their financial leverage as measured by the long-term liability-to-stockholders' equity ratio. Similar evidence is in Bowen, Daley, and Huber (1982) and Bradley, Jarrell, and Kim (1984). Explanations advanced for these differences include the following.

Taxes and Bankruptcy Cost. Given the tax deductibility of interest on debt, there are benefits from debt financing that are not available from equity financing. However, the use of debt financing increases the risk of bankruptcy due to the possibility of operating profit being insufficient to cover interest payments. Under this explanation, differences across industries in their leverage ratios would be due to differences in (a) tax rates and (b) in the cost of bankruptcy and the probability of bankruptcy under alternative debt-to-equity levels.

Managerial Signaling. This explanation posits that management possesses superior information to that held by external parties and uses its capital structure decisions to signal this superior information; for example, it may choose a higher debt-to-equity structure if it perceives that the capital market is underestimating its future earnings potential. To apply at the interindustry level, this explanation would posit that information differences between internal and external parties are industry related.

Key Personality. This explanation posits that the philosophies of key individuals such as the chairman or president play an important role in determining a firm's capital structure. Business periodicals often contain such anecdotes. For example, *Business Week* noted that Adolf Coors Company, controlled by the Coors family, "refuses to borrow money—a family tradition." An Adolph Coors release in 1984 noted that "we are hopeful we could finance (a new brewery costing $500 million) from internally generated resources. We may go into debt somewhat, but we do not believe in leveraging."

Little progress has been made in testing the descriptive validity of these and other explanations. Myers (1984) concludes that "we know very little about capital structure. We do not know how firms choose the debt, equity or hybrid securities they issue" (p. 575). The result is that users of financial statements have few reliable theories to explain cross-sectional differences across firms in their capital structure or interest coverage ratios.

5. Interesting issues relating to cross-sectional analysis arise in the design of relative performance executive compensation contracts. These contracts base part of an executive's compensation on the performance of a firm (or division) relative to the performance of a comparable set of firms. As an example, the performance plan adopted by Chemical New York Corporation includes a component based on its return on assets as compared with a competitor group of

eleven of the largest bank holding companies in the country. Among the issues that arise with relative performance plans are (a) choice of the time period of the plan, (b) choice of the comparison set of firms, and (c) choice of the variable used to measure performance. Many of the issues discussed in this chapter are relevant to these choices.

Executive compensation represents one of the most active and vibrant areas of business research; the Winter 1985 issues of the *Midland Corporate Finance Journal* and Volume 7 (1985) of *Journal of Accounting and Economics* are both devoted to this topic. One example of research in this area is Larcker's (1983) analysis of the association between performance plan adoption and corporate capital investment. Two samples of firms were examined. One sample comprised 25 firms that had adopted a performance plan in the 1971–1978 period. The second sample was selected by matching each firm from the first sample with another firm in the same industry and of similar size that had not adopted a formal performance plan. The capital investment patterns of the two samples were examined. It was reported that "firms adopting performance plans (relative to similar nonadopting firms) experience a statistically significant growth in capital investment" (p. 4). Explanations for this finding discussed by Larcker included the incentive effects of performance plans, the tax consequences of these plans, and the effect of confounding events. An overview of research in this area is in Lambert and Larcker (1985).

6.9   SUMMARY

1. Cross-sectional comparisons of the financial statements of firms and other entities require choices about the set of comparables. This choice can be based on a variety of criteria, for example, similarity on supply side, demand side, capital market attributes, or legal ownership.

2. Data availability issues are a frequent problem in many cross-sectional comparisons of financial statement information. The existence of multiactivity firms, privately held firms, and nondomestic firms means that the available data may not be representative of the set of firms of interest to an analyst.

3. Firms have considerable discretion over the reporting of line-of-business information, for example, how individual activities are grouped and how intersegment transfers are priced. The possibility that competitors will use the LOB information to the disadvantage of the disclosing firm serves as a constraint against some firms providing highly disaggregated LOB information.

4. The traditional focus of cross-sectional financial statement analysis is at the industry level. Support for this focus comes from the evidence in Section 6.6 of differences across industries in their financial ratios. At present there are very few reliable theories or models that explain the observed differences in industry financial ratios.

APPENDIX 6.A   INDUSTRY AND ECONOMY INFLUENCES ON FINANCIAL STATEMENT NUMBERS

It is commonly argued that changes in the earnings and other financial series of firms are influenced by industry and economy factors. Such statements are commonplace in annual reports, especially when management is explaining earnings declines:

- CNA Financial Corporation experienced generally satisfactory results, considering the strong negative pressures affecting both the economy and the industries in which it does business.   (CNA Financial Corporation)

- We, together with most American businesses, are now suffering from the eighth postwar recession—and it's a lulu! Most secondary financing companies are especially affected. One does not have to be a financial genius to see that our profit spread is detrimentally affected by such market forces.   (Oxford First Corporation)

In this appendix, we present evidence, via the following index models, on the importance of industry and economy factors:

$$\Delta X_{i,t} = \alpha + \beta_1 \Delta X_{I,t} \tag{6.A.1}$$

$$\Delta X_{i,t} = \alpha + \beta_1 \Delta X_{M,t} \tag{6.A.2}$$

$$\Delta X_{i,t} = \alpha + \beta_1 \Delta X_{I,t} + \beta_2 \Delta X_{M,t} \tag{6.A.3}$$

where

Δ = a first-differenced operator

$X_{i,t}$ = financial variable of firm i in period t

$X_{I,t}$ = industry index (value weighted) for financial variable in period t (other firms in firm i's four-digit SIC industry)

$X_{M,t}$ = economy index (value weighted) for financial variable in period t

Equations (6.A.1) to (6.A.3) were estimated for firms in all SIC four-digit industries with ten or more firms on the 1983 Compustat tape. Data covering the 1964–1983 period were used.

Prior research using the foregoing models include Brown and Ball (1967), Gonedes (1973), Magee (1974), and Lev (1980). Evidence from these studies supports (1) the use of value-weighted indexes for $X_{I,t}$ and $X_{M,t}$ when examining financial ratios and variables and (2) the estimation of index models in first differences (Δ's) rather than levels in order to reduce econometric problems associated with autocorrelation. Value-weighted indexes have the advantage of being less affected by the extreme observations that can occur with some financial variables.

Panel A of Table 6.6 presents the (adjusted) R^2 and Durbin-Watson (D.W.) statistic for the first-differenced net income variable. A separate regression is run for each firm, and then distribution statistics for the R^2 and the D.W. statistics over the 315 firms are calculated. The mean R^2 for (6.A.1) is .36, indicating that

TABLE 6.6 Industry and Economy Influences on First-Differenced Financial Variables, 1964–1983

Financial Variable	R^2 Industry (6.A.1)	R^2 Economy (6.A.2)	R^2 Industry and Economy (6.A.3)	D.W. Industry (6.A.1)	D.W. Economy (6.A.2)	D.W. Industry and Economy (6.A.3)	No. of Firms	No. of Industries
A. Net Income								
Means	.36	.17	.43	2.13	1.70	2.08	315	15
.1 Fractile	.02	.00	.08	1.19	.71	1.24		
.3 Fractile	.15	.02	.25	1.80	1.29	1.75		
.5 Fractile	.31	.07	.42	2.18	1.73	2.14		
.7 Fractile	.51	.20	.60	2.52	2.09	2.39		
.9 Fractile	.75	.51	.77	2.88	2.56	2.84		
B. Financial Ratios								
Means								
(C + MS)/TA	.18	.06	.22	2.24	2.18	2.29	198	12
CA/CL	.13	.08	.19	2.42	2.39	2.45	286	13
CFO/S	.25	.14	.35	2.59	2.45	2.49	158	10
LTL/SE	.16	.10	.21	2.10	2.12	2.19	249	11
OI/INT	.31	.17	.37	2.00	2.01	2.15	239	10
NI/SE	.23	.15	.30	2.24	2.20	2.24	258	12
S/TA	.34	.18	.41	1.90	1.77	1.98	299	14
S/AR	.27	.13	.32	1.92	2.01	2.02	142	9
COGS/INV	.27	.17	.33	1.86	1.87	1.97	124	8
PE	.39	.26	.46	2.38	2.37	2.42	275	13
DIV. PAY.	.16	.12	.25	2.39	2.37	2.36	303	15
TA	.34	.31	.45	1.54	1.61	1.74	323	15

SOURCE: Computed from 1983 Compustat annual industrial file.

an industry variable explains (on average) 36% of the variation in the change in net income for the 315 firms. The mean R^2 for (6.A.2) is .17, indicating that an economy variable explains 17% of the variation in the change in net income for the 315 firms. The joint explanatory power of the industry and economy variables is .43 (these two variables are collinear). The mean Durbin-Watson statistics for (6.A.1), (6.A.2), and (6.A.3) are consistent with autocorrelation in the residuals not being a serious econometric problem.

Panel B of Table 6.6 presents the mean R^2 and Durbin-Watson for (6.A.1), (6.A.2), and (6.A.3) for the 12 financial ratios/variables outlined in Section 6.6.C. The mean R^2 ranges from

1. .13 (CA/CL) to .39 (PE) for the industry variable index model
2. .06 ((C + MS)/TA) to .31 (TA) for the economy variable index model
3. .19 (CA/CL) to .46 (PE) for the industry and economy variable index model.

On balance, the results in Table 6.6 provide strong support for both industry and economy movements being important variables in explaining firm movements in financial variables.

There are considerable interindustry differences in the importance of industry and economy influences on financial variables. Table 6.7 presents the mean R^2 and Durbin-Watson of (6.A.1), (6.A.2), and (6.A.3) for 15 four-digit SIC industries for the net income variable. Industry factors are strongest in the paper and allied products (2600), petroleum refining (2911), and steel and blast furnace (3310) four-digit industries. These three industries also have the highest R^2s when

TABLE 6.7   Industry Breakdown of Industry and Economy Influences on First-Differenced Net Income Series, 1964–1983

Industry Title	Four-Digit SIC Code	Mean R^2 Industry (6.A.1)	Mean R^2 Economy (6.A.2)	Mean R^2 Industry and Economy (6.A.3)	Mean D.W. Industry (6.A.1)	Mean D.W. Economy (6.A.2)	Mean D.W. Industry and Economy (6.A.3)	No. of Firms
1. Crude petroleum and natural gas	1311	.23	.14	.35	2.06	1.79	1.98	18
2. Paper and allied products	2600	.60	.49	.61	1.93	1.87	1.99	15
3. Drugs	2830	.26	.14	.40	1.71	1.54	1.68	16
4. Petroleum refining	2911	.54	.37	.60	2.12	1.93	2.01	28
5. Steel and blast furnaces	3310	.53	.35	.58	2.02	2.03	2.07	17
6. General industrial machinery and equipment	3560	.29	.23	.44	2.14	1.86	2.21	12
7. Radio and T.V. transmitting equipment	3662	.17	.14	.29	1.77	1.50	1.69	14
8. Electronic components	3679	.37	.32	.44	2.12	2.15	2.08	10
9. Trucking	4210	.42	.21	.48	2.04	1.91	2.12	12
10. Air transportation	4511	.15	.12	.25	2.21	1.88	2.06	16
11. Electric services	4911	.39	.08	.47	2.45	1.48	2.31	61
12. Natural gas distribution	4924	.11	.13	.21	2.07	2.09	2.10	17
13. Electric and other service combinations	4931	.45	.06	.51	2.38	1.37	2.27	47
14. Retail, grocery stores	5411	.17	.09	.26	1.77	1.49	1.62	10
15. State banks, Federal Reserve System	6022	.25	.05	.30	2.31	1.59	2.21	22
Totals		.36	.17	.43	2.13	1.70	2.08	315

SOURCE: Computed from 1983 Compustat annual industrial file.

the economy variable is separately included (6.A.2) and when both the industry and economy variables are included (6.A.3).

The industry index in (6.A.1) and (6.A.3) captures movements in the primary activity of each firm. An interesting extension would be to include multiple-industry indexes when examining multiactivity firms. Several commercial services now provide such multiple indexes in their list of commercial products. (See Chapter 10 for description of the BARRA service.)

Industry and economy factors are but two variables that can be included in index models. Consider the following statement in the annual report of Phelps Dodge, a major copper-producing company:

> Economic conditions have been particularly hard on a number of industries that are major markets for our copper and copper products. . . . The result has been clearly reflected in copper prices. Our price for copper began the first quarter (of last year) at $1.06 a pound, and rose briefly to $1.44. From there it has declined steadily to . . . $0.75 today. . . . To place this decline in the perspective of our earnings, at current production rates, each one-cent change in the price of copper, annualized, affects our net earnings by $3 to $4 million.

Variables representing commodity price changes for oil, gold, silver, copper, and so on, can explain sizable percentages in the variation of the earnings of natural resource companies. The index models in (6.A.1) to (6.A.3) potentially could be expanded to include such variables.

QUESTIONS

QUESTION 6.1: Cross-Sectional Comparison of the Profitability of Japanese and U.S. Motor Vehicle Companies

The president of a Japanese motor vehicle company reads a research paper that concludes that "Japanese companies generally appear less efficient or profitable than their U.S. counterparts." He finds this conclusion counterintuitive. As his research assistant, you are requested to examine the summary data published in the most recent edition of *Fortune*'s listing of the 500 largest U.S. industrial companies and the 500 largest non-U.S. industrial companies. The data are presented in Table 6.8.

REQUIRED

1. Your first task is to compute industry measures for the net income-to-stockholders' equity ratio. You are requested to compute the following for both Japan and the United States:
    a. Equal-weighted average
    b. Value-weighted average (weighted by stockholders' equity)

TABLE 6.8 Financial Data of Japanese and U.S. Motor Vehicle Companies

Company	Sales ($ millions)	Total Assets ($ millions)	Net Income ($ millions)	Stockholders' Equity ($ millions)
Japanese				
Toyota Motor	$22,182	$13,414	$ 950	$ 7,874
Nissan Motor	19,232	14,909	331	5,477
Honda Motor	10,166	6,114	409	2,452
Mazda Motor	5,846	3,276	110	845
U.S.				
General Motors	$74,582	$45,694	$3,730	$20,767
Ford Motor	44,455	23,869	1,867	7,545
Chrysler	13,240	6,772	701	1,143
American Motors	3,566	1,724	(1)	134

Are the inferences about the relative profitability of the Japanese and U.S. motor vehicle industries affected by the use of (a) or (b)? Which one would you prefer to use in the assignment?

2. As a second approach, you compare the net income-to-stockholders' equity ratio of *individual* Japanese and *individual* U.S. firms. Present the results using the comparison format you think most informative. What inferences would you draw from this comparison?

3. What additional factors would you consider before making inferences about the relative profitability of Japanese and U.S. motor vehicle companies?

QUESTION 6.2: Cross-Sectional Comparison of the Profitability
of U.S. Oil Companies Using Entity and Subentity (Segment) Data

The president of Shell Oil received both good news and bad news in the mail that had accumulated during his vacation. The good news was that for the second year in a row he was named "Best Manager" by *The Wall Street Monitor*; this award was based on a survey of security analysts specializing in oil and gas stocks. Included in an article discussing the award was the information in Table 6.9. The eight companies in Table 6.9 are the eight largest publicly held oil and gas companies in the United States (using sales as the size criterion).

The bad news was a newspaper article reporting that Atlantic Richfield (ARCO) was considerably more profitable than Shell in both its upstream (exploration and production) and downstream (transportation, refining, and marketing) activities. The article then raised questions about the basis on which the "Best Manager" award was made. The journalist used information from the segment disclosures of ARCO and Shell in their most recent annual reports. Table 6.10 presents these disclosures. The following information is also disclosed in the annual reports of these two companies.

TABLE 6.9   Financial Data of Integrated U.S. Oil and Gas Companies

Company	Revenues ($ millions)	Interest Expense ($ millions)	Net Income ($ millions)	Total Assets ($ millions)	Stockholders' Equity ($ millions)	Net Income / Revenues
Exxon	$94,734	$749	$4,978	$62,963	$29,443	.053
Mobil	58,998	814	1,503	35,072	13,952	.025
Texaco	41,147	181	1,233	27,199	14,726	.030
Amoco	29,494	371	1,868	25,805	12,440	.063
Chevron	29,182	75	1,590	24,010	14,106	.054
Gulf Oil	28,887	196	978	20,964	10,128	.034
ARCO	26,279	344	1,548	23,282	10,888	.059
Shell Oil	19,883	238	1,633	22,169	11,359	.082

ARCO: "Oil and gas operations comprise the exploration for and the development and production of crude oil, natural gas liquids and natural gas. The Fuels segment includes the refining, transportation and marketing of petroleum products. Inter-segment sales/transfers are made at prices approximating current market values." Intersegment sales were (in $millions)

Oil and gas	$5,366
Fuels	
Refining and marketing	580
Transportation	573
Minerals	—
Materials	312
	$6,831

SHELL: "Exploration and Production includes oil and gas exploration and production. Oil Products includes the transportation, refining and marketing business. . . . Income taxes are allocated to segments on the basis of contributions to taxable income reduced by investment tax credits based on qualified capital expenditures for each segment. Intersegment transfers (are based on) estimated market-related values." Intersegment transfers were (in $millions)

Oil and gas exploration and production	$5,152
Oil products	1,292
Chemical products	162
	$6,606

Both ARCO and Shell derive over 90% of their revenue from U.S. operations.

REQUIRED

1. Do the data in Table 6.9 support the conclusion that Shell is the most profitable of the large oil and gas companies? What additional information would you collect in making inferences about the relative profitability of large companies in the oil and gas industry?
2. Do the data in Table 6.10 support the newspaper journalist's conclusion that ARCO was considerably more profitable than Shell in both its upstream and

TABLE 6.10 Segment Disclosures of Atlantic Richfield (ARCO) and Shell Oil ($ millions)

A. Atlantic Richfield

Segment	Sales and Other Operating Revenues	Segment Earnings	Total Assets
Oil and gas	$ 6,686	$2,566	$ 9,184
Fuels			
Refining and marketing	20,600	474	2,526
Transportation	1,223	781	2,718
Minerals	396	(139)	1,800
Materials			
Chemicals	2,550	64	2,603
Metals	1,146	(125)	2,132
Other operations	167		2,319
Elimination of intersegment amounts	(6,831)		
Unallocated expenses and other operations		(604)	
Interest		(344)	
Income taxes		(1,125)	
Total	$25,937	$1,548	$23,282

B. Shell Oil

Segment	Oil and Gas Exploration and Production	Oil Products	Chemical Products	Other	Total
Total revenue	$ 6,587	$16,053	$3,395	$291	$19,720
Costs and operating expense	3,030	15,444	3,068	313	15,249
Depreciation, amortization	1,076	180	197	(48)	1,405
Operating profit	$ 2,481	$ 429	$ 130	$ 26	$ 3,066
Interest expense, capitalized leases	0	1	0	0	1
Corporate expense, allocated	54	43	32	4	133
Income tax expense, allocated	1,070	163	35	(15)	1,253
Equity in net income (loss) of others	(29)	(16)	—	11	(34)
Segment net income	$ 1,386	$ 238	$ 63	$ 26	$ 1,713
Nonallocated costs	—	—	—	—	80
Net income	—	—	—	—	$ 1,633
Identifiable assets	$12,824	$ 4,138	$3,759	$645	$22,169

downstream activities? What additional information would you collect in making inferences about the profitability of these two business segments of ARCO and Shell?

3. Both ARCO and Shell derive over 90% of their net income from U.S. operations. In contrast, Exxon derives less than 50% of its net income from U.S. operations. What problems (additional to those discussed in part 2) would arise in comparing the profitability of the upstream U.S. activities and the downstream U.S. activities of Exxon with those of ARCO and Shell?

4. What factors might ARCO, Shell, and Exxon consider when deciding the specific amount and format of information disclosed about their individual business segments and about their geographic segments?

QUESTION 6.3 Industry Inventory Turnover Ratios and Industry Characteristics

Differences across industries in their median or mean inventory turnover ratios appear to be both sizable and systematic. Gupta and Huefner (1972) examined inventory turnover "ratios at a macro level for broad industry classes, seeking a correspondence between the accounting numbers and basic attributes" (p. 77). They examined the 1967 inventory turnover ratios of 20 manufacturing industries, defined according to the two-digit SIC code. They classified the industries into the following four groups, based on similarities in their inventory turnover ratios:

Group	Industry	Inventory Turnover	Group Mean
I	Petroleum	12.35	11.55
	Printing	11.62	
	Food	10.67	
II	Paper	7.93	6.77
	Motor vehicles	7.68	
	Stone, clay, and glass	7.06	
	Chemicals	6.72	
	Lumber and wood	6.49	
	Furniture and fixtures	6.35	
	Apparel	6.32	
	Leather	6.30	
	Fabricated metal	6.09	
III	Primary metal	5.61	4.98
	Textile	5.58	
	Rubber and plastic	5.57	
	Electrical equipment	4.95	
	Scientific instruments	4.83	
	Machinery	4.39	
	Transportation equipment	3.94	
IV	Tobacco	2.18	2.18

The industries in each group were then examined to see if they exhibited common characteristics. They noted the following:

(1) Product life. Industries producing a product with a very short life may be expected to have low inventories and a high turnover. Short life may be due to rapid obsolescence (as in the case of newspapers) or perishability (as in the case of some food products).

(2) Holding costs. High costs of holding inventories are a second factor that would be expected to result in low inventories and a high turnover. The short-product-life situation is one factor that would contribute toward high holding costs. In some

industries, physical holding costs are very high. This is especially true in the petroleum industry, where specialized storage facilities are required.

(3) Production period. Industries with a long production period may be expected to have high inventories and a low turnover. This has been particularly true in the tobacco industry where a long aging process has been common. (pp. 87–88)

The conclusion was that "financial ratios can represent underlying industry characteristics" (p. 90).

Robert Morris Associates (1983) presents the median industry turnover ratio (cost of sales/inventory) for 140 different manufacturing industries. The 12 highest industry median inventory turnover ratios are

Line of Business	Industry Median Ratio
Meat packing	27.4
Newspapers, publishing and printing	23.5
Dairy products	20.5
Typesetting	20.1
Bread and other bakery products	17.4
Ready-mixed concrete	16.8
Canned and cured fish and seafoods	14.9
Coating, engraving, and allied services	13.3
Commercial printing (lithographic)	13.3
Petroleum refining	13.3
Bookbinding and miscellaneous related work	12.6
Bottled and canned soft drinks	12.3

The 12 lowest industry median inventory turnover ratios are

Line of Business	Industry Median Ratio
Men's work clothing	3.4
Valves and pipe fittings	3.4
Hat manufacturers	3.3
Radios, T.V., and phonographs	3.3
Wines, distilled liquor, and liqueurs	3.3
Industrial instruments for measurement, display, and control	3.2
Jewelry, precious metals	3.2
Sporting and athletic goods	3.2
Electronic computing equipment	3.1
Engineering, laboratory, scientific, and research instruments	3.0
Farm machinery and equipment	2.6
Instruments for measuring and testing of electricity	2.5

REQUIRED

1. What evidence is there that the characteristics outlined by Gupta and Huefner help to discriminate between industries with high turnover ratios and those with low turnover ratios in the Robert Morris Associates survey?

2. Can you determine any other characteristics that discriminate between the two groups of industries? Give reasons.

3. Evaluate the Gupta-Huefner approach of examining whether there is a correspondence between financial ratios and underlying industry characteristics.

4. Describe an alternative approach of examining whether there is a correspondence between financial ratios and underlying industry characteristics.

QUESTION 6.4: Strategy Consulting and Industry Distributions of Financial Ratios

Multicorp is a diversified multiactivity firm, operating in eight lines of business (using SIC industry codes). The former chairman and founder of the company was characterized in the press as strong on acquisition activity but weak on integration of those businesses once acquired. Current sales exceed $2 billion, but earnings have not been above $40 million in any of the last five years. The current return on equity is .072, which is approximately half the mean for all firms in the economy. The eight lines of business (and their respective SIC codes) are

- Textile mill products (2200)
- Apparel and other finished products (2300)
- Paper and allied products (2600)
- Drugs (2830)
- General industrial machinery and equipment (3560)
- Radio and T.V. transmitting equipment (3662)
- Electronic components (3679)
- Motor vehicle parts (3714)

Multicorp contacts a well-known consulting firm—Strategic Horizons Group (SHG)—to make a presentation on the potential gains from the implementation of management systems that could substantially increase the operating efficiency and effectiveness of individual business units. The first part of the SHG presentation (a multicolored slide show, of course) outlined three "Components of Business Profitability":

- *Strategic factors*, for example, relative product quality, relative market share, and growth of served market
- *Operating effectiveness*, for example, effectiveness of labor utilization and effectiveness of working capital usage
- *Transitory factors*, for example, business cycle, weather conditions, problems of union relations, and technological problems or breakthroughs.

SHG then presented the data in Table 6.11 pertaining to the eight industries in which Multicorp operates. ROE was measured as net income divided by the average book value of shareholders' equity. The industry distribution data were based on all firms with available data on the most recent version of the *Compustat tape*. The ROE figures for each division of Multicorp were supplied by Multicorp; long-term debt was allocated to each division based on the percentage of the total book value of fixed assets attributable to that division.

One theme of the SHG presentation was that many of the Multicorp divisions had substantial upside potential, as indicated by the gains attainable by moving the division's ROE above the .70 fractile of the industry distribution. After the presentation, the board of directors decides to hire SHG. However, several of the directors had prior negative experiences with consulting firms. They proposed that SHG initially work with only two divisions and develop a track record of success.

REQUIRED

1. What computational and other issues arise in calculating the ROE measures for the firms in each four-digit industry and for each division of Multicorp? How might these issues be important when interpreting the results in Table 6.11?

2. What factors could explain differences in the dispersion (say, .9 fractile − .1 fractile) of ROE across the eight industry groupings in Table 6.11?

3. What factors could explain the difference between the ROE of each Multicorp division and the .7 fractile ROE of its respective industry?

4. The directors recommend that SHG be hired as a consultant to the divisions in the 2830 (drugs) and 3560 (general industrial machinery and equipment) industries. These two have the largest difference between the .7 fractile industry ROE and the ROE of the Multicorp division. Do you agree with this choice? What factors would you consider when choosing the division(s) for which SHG will be a consultant?

TABLE 6.11   ROE for Industry and Multicorp

SIC Industry Code	No. of Firms in Industry	Fractiles of Industry ROE Distribution					Multicorp Division's ROE
		.1	.3	.5	.7	.9	
2200 Textile	28	− .135	.027	.073	.108	.150	.126
2300 Apparel	41	− .187	.068	.121	.185	.250	.021
2600 Paper	22	.042	.099	.130	.158	.177	.104
2830 Drugs	29	.039	.176	.208	.253	.343	.046
3560 Machinery	31	.017	.099	.134	.168	.229	− .040
3662 Radio and T.V.	33	.042	.126	.151	.193	.216	.052
3679 Electronics	19	− .076	.038	.137	.185	.218	.021
3714 Motor vehicle parts	25	− .064	.041	.114	.157	.194	.178

REFERENCES

ANTERASIAN, C. "Disentangling Rival Hypotheses Among Marketing Expenditures, Market Share and Profitability," working paper. Stanford University, Stanford, Calif., 1984.

AYANIAN, R. "Advertising and Rate of Return." *Journal of Law and Economics* (October 1975): 479–506.

BAIN, J. S. *Price Theory*. New York: Wiley, 1952.

BAREFIELD, R. M., and G. L. HOLMSTROM. *Disclosure Criteria and Segment Reporting*. Gainesville: University Presses of Florida, 1979.

BARRON, M., "Some Empirical Evidence on the Year-End Dates of Larger British Companies," working paper. London Business School, 1984.

BAVISHI, B., F. CHOI, and H. SHAWKY. *Analyzing the Financial Ratios of the World's 1000 Leading Industrial Companies*. New York: Business International, 1981.

BOURGEOIS, J., G. H. HAINES, and M. S. SOMMERS. "Defining an Industry." In D. B. Montgomery and D. R. Wittink, eds., *Market Measurement and Analysis*. Cambridge, Mass.: Marketing Science Institute, 1980: 120–133.

BOWEN, R. M., L. A. DALEY, and C. C. HUBER. "Evidence on the Existence and Determinants of Inter-Industry Differences in Leverage." *Financial Management* (Winter 1982): 10–20.

BOWMAN, E. H. "A Risk/Return Paradox for Strategic Management." *Sloan Management Review* (Spring 1980): 17–31.

BRADLEY, M., G. A. JARRELL, and E. H. KIM. "On the Existence of an Optimal Capital Structure: Theory and Evidence." *The Journal of Finance* (July 1984): 857–878.

BROWN, P., and R. BALL. "Some Preliminary Findings on the Association Between the Earnings of a Firm, Its Industry, and the Economy." *Empirical Research in Accounting: Selected Studies*, Supplement to *Journal of Accounting Research* (1967): 55–77.

BUZZELL, R. D., B. T. GALE and R. G. M. SULTAN. "Market Share—A Key to Profitability." *Harvard Business Review* (January–February 1975): 97–106.

CHOI, F. D. S., H. HINO, S. K. MIN, S. O. NAM, J. UJIIE, and A. I. STONEHILL. "Analyzing Foreign Financial Statements: The Use and Misuse of International Ratio Analysis." *Journal of International Business Studies* (Spring/Summer 1983): 113–131.

GONEDES, N. J. "Properties of Accounting Numbers: Models and Tests." *Journal of Accounting Research* (Autumn 1973): 212–237.

GUPTA, M. C., and R. J. HUEFNER. "A Cluster Analysis Study of Financial Ratios and Industry Characteristics." *Journal of Accounting Research* (Spring 1972): 77–95.

JACKSON, B. B. *Multivariate Data Analysis*. Homewood, Ill.: Richard D. Irwin, 1983.

KING, B. F. "Market and Industry Factors in Stock Price Behavior." *The Journal of Business* (January 1966): 139–190.

LAMBERT, R. A., and D. F. LARCKER. "Executive Compensation, Corporate Decision-Making and Shareholder Wealth: A Review of the Evidence." *Midland Corporate Finance Journal* (Winter 1985): 6–22.

LARCKER, D. F. "The Association Between Performance Plan Adoption and Corporate Capital Investment." *Journal of Accounting and Economics* (April 1983): 3–30.

LEV, B. "On the Use of Index Models in Analytical Review by Auditors." *Journal of Accounting Research* (Autumn 1980): 524–550.

LISCIANDRO, P. *1982 Financial Analysis of the Motor Carrier Industry*. Washington, D.C.: American Trucking Association, 1983.

MAGEE, R. P. "Industry-Wide Commonalities in Earnings." *Journal of Accounting Research* (Autumn 1974): 270–287.

MARSH, T. A., and D. S. SWANSON. "Risk-Return Tradeoffs for Strategic Management." *Sloan Management Review* (Spring 1984): 35–49.

MERCANTILE GAZETTE OF N.Z. *The New Zealand Company Register*. Christchurch, N.Z.: MG Publications, 1984.

MEYERS, S. L. "A Re-Examination of Market and Industry Factors in Stock Price Behavior." *The Journal of Finance* (June 1973): 695–705.

MILLER, M. H. "Debt and Taxes." *The Journal of Finance* (May 1977): 261–275.

MOHR, R. M. "The Segmental Reporting Issue: A Review of Empirical Research." *Journal of Accounting Literature* (Spring 1983): 39–71.

MYERS, S. C. "The Capital Structure Puzzle." *The Journal of Finance* (July 1984): 575–592.

NAKAMURA, T., and N. TERADA. "The Size Effect and Seasonality in Japanese Stock Returns," working paper. Nomura Research Institute, Japan, 1984.

PHILLIPS, L. W., D. R. CHANG, and R. D. BUZZELL. "Product Quality, Cost Position and Business Performance: A Test of Some Key Hypotheses." *Journal of Marketing* (Spring 1983): 26–43.

RAVENSCRAFT, D. J., "Structure-Profit Relationships at the Line of Business and Industry Level." *Review of Economics and Statistics* (1983): 22–31.

ROBERT MORRIS ASSOCIATES, *Annual Statement Studies 1983*. Philadelphia: RMA, 1983.

STIGLER, G. J. *Capital and Rates of Return in Manufacturing Industries*. Princeton, N.J.: Princeton University Press, 1963.

STIGLER, G. J., and R. A. SHERWIN. "The Extent of the Market," working paper. University of Chicago, December 1983.

SUDARSANAM, P. S., and R. J. TAFFLER. "Industrial Classification in U.K. Capital

Markets: A Test of Economic Homogeneity,'' working paper. University of Leeds, England, 1984.

Ward's Directory of 51,000 Largest U.S. Corporations. Petaluma, Cal.: Baldwin H. Ward Publications, 1984.

WEISS, L. "Quantitative Studies in Industrial Organization." In M. D. Intrilligator, ed., *Frontiers of Quantitative Economics*, Amsterdam: North-Holland, 1971: 362–411.

7

TIME-SERIES ANALYSIS OF FINANCIAL STATEMENT INFORMATION

7.1 INTRODUCTION

This chapter examines issues associated with describing and explaining the behavior over time of financial series such as earnings, sales, and return on equity. This topic is important for several reasons. One reason is the key role that forecasts play in many decision contexts, for example, in equity valuation models used in investment decisions and in valuation approaches used in acquisition or divestiture decisions. Forecasts based on time-series analysis are an important source of data in such decisions. Time-series analysis exploits any systematic patterns in the behavior of a series over time when forecasting subsequent values of that series. Time-series analysis can also be important in the subsequent evaluation of forecasts and in the revision of existing models used in forecasting. For instance, such analysis may indicate that a macroeconomic variable is an important determinant of periodic changes in earnings but is not built into the model currently used for forecasting. A detailed discussion of forecasting issues may be found in Chapter 8.

Time-series analysis is also important in many nonforecasting contexts such as

- Performance evaluation of management where a key concern is what percentage of the earnings change is due to nonfirm-oriented factors
- Examining allegations that management is "manipulating" earnings to (say) avoid violating restrictive convenants in a bank loan agreement
- Designing a "profit-sharing" component of an executive compensation plan where a central concern is risk sharing between management and other parties associated with the firm
- Management decisions on alternative accounting methods where an important factor is the time-series variability in the reported earnings series
- Litigation where allegations of excess profits have been made and the concern is to explain the sources of a reported earnings series
- Litigation where business operations have been disrupted by a fire or a strike and estimation must be made of the earnings that would "normally" have occurred.

Many of the issues discussed in this chapter arise in the foregoing and similar contexts.

7.2 ISSUES IN ANALYZING FINANCIAL TIME-SERIES DATA

This section outlines several data quality issues that are important in time-series analysis of financial data.

A. Structural Change Issues

Many of the statistical computations performed on financial statement data assume that the time series is stationary. A time series is stationary when its basic statistical properties (for example, mean and variance) remain constant over time; see Appendix 7.A for further discussion. Structural change can cause this assumption to be (at best) of questionable validity. Structural change can result from factors such as

1. Changes due to government deregulation
2. Changes in competition, either from other products or from new firms
3. Developments in technology that substantially change cost-volume-profit relationships
4. Acquisitions or divestitures.

There are two offsetting considerations when one suspects structural change. For estimation efficiency, a large sample size is preferred. In a time series, this means going back over a long period of time. However, the farther one goes back in time, the more one expects factors such as (1) to (4) to be encountered. Visual analysis will often identify possible structural change problems. In addition, statistical analysis can be used to test formally for equality of (say) the subperiod variances of the series examined (see Ali and Thalheimer, 1983).

Suppose an analyst concludes that structural change exists with the available time series. What then? An important step is to determine its cause(s). As an illustration, consider the revenue and net income series of DuPont over the 1972–1983 period. During this period, a merger took place that had a marked effect on both series. In August 1981, DuPont merged with Conoco, Inc. Table 7.1 presents the "as reported" financial series of these two firms. If one were building a time-series model in mid-1981 to forecast the 1981, 1982, and 1983 revenue and net income figures, knowledge of the merger would likely lead to an inference of structural change for DuPont. Several options could be adopted in this context.

Option One. Combine the DuPont and Conoco series for the premerger period and build a time-series model on this combined series. There are several implicit assumptions with this option. One is that there were no profitable transactions between DuPont and Conoco prior to the merger; the profits on all such transactions would be eliminated once the two firms are merged. Another assumption is that DuPont does not have to incur additional interest expense due to borrowings necessary to acquire control of Conoco. A third assumption is that there are no synergies associated with the merger. A fourth assumption is that in the period being forecast, there will not be any divestitures of existing activities of the two firms.

Option Two. Combine the DuPont and Conoco series for the premerger period and make adjustments for the Option One assumptions deemed not descriptive. This option was partially adopted for the 1980 and 1981 years in footnote

TABLE 7.1 Conoco and DuPont Net Income and Revenue Series

Year	Conoco ($ millions)		DuPont ($ millions)	
	Net Income	Revenue	Net Income	Revenue
1971	96	3,122	357	4,371
1972	176	3,696	414	4,948
1973	220	4,491	586	5,964
1974	302	7,344	404	6,910
1975	326	7,666	272	7,222
1976	456	8,352	459	8,361
1977	381	9,052	545	9,435
1978	451	9,872	787	10,584
1979	815	13,083	939	12,572
1980	1,026	18,766	716	13,652
1981	—	—	1,401[a]	23,092[a]
1982	—	—	894	33,604
1983	—	—	1,127	35,769

[a] The 1981 results for DuPont include the operations of Conoco from August 1, 1981 through December 31, 1981.

15 of the 1981 Annual Report of DuPont. This footnote reported a series of adjustments when presenting "pro forma combined results of operations . . . giving effect to the acquisition of Conoco as though it had occurred January 1, 1980":

> The results are based on the purchase accounting adjustments recognized in consolidating Conoco, and reflect additional interest expense as if borrowings incurred in connection with acquisition had been outstanding from the beginning of each year at the interest rates that would have been applicable to the borrowings during these periods. Sales would have been $33.0 billion (1981) and $29.6 billion (1980), after elimination of Conoco's exchanges of crude oil of $2.4 billion and $2.1 billion, respectively. . . . Net income . . . would have been $1,634 million (1981) and $1,301 million (1980).

Option Three. Ignore the Conoco premerger series and focus exclusively on the DuPont series. While this option may appear "simplistic" in this case, it is often taken with many firms on the assumption that the merger is immaterial, relative to the size of the surviving firm.

Option Four. Examine only the postmerger series of DuPont. This option is not feasible in 1981, as no postmerger observations are yet available.

None of the preceding options may appear satisfactory when the limitations of each are examined in isolation. However, the time-series analyst is faced with choosing among such imperfect options. Moreover, the options available with other forms of structural change may be even more constrained. In some cases, the only effective options are to ignore the structural change or to use a time period for model identification that is considerably shorter than the available data set.

Restated Accounting Data

The data presented in Table 7.1 were the "as reported" figures for each year for Conoco and DuPont. Annual reports sometimes include restated figures for prior years to show the results "as if" the present entity existed in prior years. One complication with restated data arises when an entity engages in acquisitions and divestitures on a frequent basis. Consider an analyst seeking to obtain an extended time series for Fuqua Industries as it existed at the end of 1981. The 1979–1981 annual reports of Fuqua provide the following restated data for sales from continuing operations (in millions of dollars):

Year	Sales as Reported in 1979 Annual Report	Sales as Reported in 1980 Annual Report	Sales as Reported in 1981 Annual Report
1975	$ 471	—	—
1976	525	$ 300	—
1977	620	361	$316
1978	1,533	1,217	666
1979	2,018	1,600	686
1980	—	1,590	655
1981	—	—	707

Over the 1975–1981 period, Fuqua's restructuring activities included acquisitions, divestitures, and a corporate spinoff. Note that there are three figures for sales from continuing operations for each of the years 1977, 1978, and 1979. Moreover, the 1975 and 1976 restated figures do not relate to Fuqua as it existed at the end of 1981. There are no easy answers to obtaining "appropriate" figures for 1975 and 1976. One possibility is to restrict the number of years examined to those that relate to the existing entity (that is, only use the disclosures from the 1981 Annual Report).

B. Accounting Method Changes

The time periods used in time-series modeling of accounting data typically have ranged from 10 to 50 years for annual data and 5 to 15 years for interim data. Even over a 5-year period, it is a rare firm that has not made at least one change in its accounting methods. As discussed in Chapter 5, these changes could be voluntary or mandated by a regulatory body.

The options available in time-series analysis when accounting changes occur include the following:

Option One. Do not make any adjustment on the assumption that the change is immaterial or that the change is an appropriate response by management to (say) a shift in the underlying business environment.

Option Two. Retain all observations in the time series but make adjustments so that a consistent set of accounting rules is used over the time series. Chapter 5 outlines several adjustment approaches that could be adopted, for example, via the use of footnote information or approximation techniques based on external data.

Option Three. Examine only those observations in the time series that are derived from the same set of accounting methods. This option could well result in only one year's observations if there are frequent changes mandated by regulatory bodies or voluntarily made by management.

C. Accounting Classification Issues

Firms have considerable flexibility over the timing of many events and in the classification used to represent those events in the financial statements. An analyst may wish to adopt a different pattern of timing or classification of events than is represented in the financial statements. Given access to disaggregated data, the analyst can go behind the reported figures and classifications used.

Consider the accounts of F & M Schaefer Corporation, an eastern regional U.S. brewing company. When it went public in 1968, Schaefer operated three breweries—two in New York State (Albany and Brooklyn) and one in Maryland (Baltimore).

- In 1972 a new plant in Pennsylvania (Lehigh Valley) began operations. The 1972 Annual Report noted that "our manufacturing costs were out-of-line with competition, as our capacity, with Lehigh Valley coming on-stream, far exceeded our requirements. To correct this situation, we closed our Albany brewery." The 1972 income statement included an extraordinary charge of $5.4 million related to the "closing of the Albany brewery and brewery operations."

- In 1975 the company closed its Brooklyn brewing plant. The annual report stated that it was "economically obsolete and inefficient compared with larger, automated, high-speed plants that have been erected by brewers over the last few years." The 1975 income statement included a separate line item of $26.1 million related to closing of the Brooklyn plant. The item was *not* treated as an extraordinary income item.

- In 1978 the Baltimore brewery was closed. The 1978 income statement included a separate line item of $7.7 million called "provision for plant closing." This item was *not* treated as an extraordinary income one. The 1978 income statement also included a separate line item of $50.7 million for "write-off of goodwill." The goodwill first appeared in the accounts in 1968 when Schaefer went public.

Assume that an analyst wished to build a time-series model for Schaefer's net income-before-extraordinary-items series. Summary "as reported" data for Schaefer over the 1968–1980 period are presented in Table 7.2. (In 1981, Schaefer was acquired by the Stroh Brewery Company.) There is no necessary reason why the definition of extraordinary items used in the financial statements has to be adopted by an analyst. For instance, the line items associated with the brewery closings in 1972, 1975, and 1978 could be classified consistently rather than 1972

TABLE 7.2   F & M Schaefer Corporation, 1968–1980 ($ millions)

Year	Operating Profit	Net Income Before Extraordinary Items	Net Income	Stockholders' Equity	Reported Goodwill	Market Capitalization of Equity
1968	$13.5	$ 3.8	$ 3.8	$36.9	$50.7	$62.4
1969	16.6	5.6	5.6	43.9	50.7	94.2
1970	17.1	5.8	5.8	50.7	50.7	49.5
1971	14.3	4.3	4.3	55.0	50.7	30.4
1972	4.7	(1.0)	(6.4)	48.6	50.7	16.3
1973	9.3	1.0	1.0	49.6	50.7	6.9
1974	10.0	6.8	6.8	50.3	50.7	4.4
1975	(1.4)	(32.5)	(33.1)	17.3	50.7	5.3
1976	8.7	.7	1.4	18.6	50.7	13.2
1977	7.7	.5	.9	19.6	50.7	8.6
1978	(1.0)	(63.1)	(63.1)	(43.9)	.0	5.4
1979	2.3	(4.7)	(4.7)	(48.6)	.0	6.0
1980	4.2	.6	3.8	(16.2)	.0	10.5

being classified as extraordinary and 1975 and 1978 as nonextraordinary. In addition, after observing the complex nature of the items in the net income-before-extraordinary-items (NIBE) series in Table 7.2, the analyst may seriously consider modeling the operating profit series separately from the other items in the NIBE series. Though the financial statements of Schaefer report that the $50.7 million goodwill write-down occurred in 1978, the management of Schaefer had considerable flexibility in both the timing and amount of this write-down. Prior to 1978, however, an analyst was not constrained to include the goodwill item in the computation of total assets, shareholder's equity, and so on. (Similarly, the capital market was likewise not constrained to recognize the reported goodwill.) Given the separate disclosure of the goodwill item, alternative treatments could be adopted by external analysts.

D.   Treatment of Extreme Observations

The time-series tools described in Appendix 7.A can be very sensitive to extreme observations that can occur with financial series such as net income and net income-to-shareholders' equity. Empirically, extreme observations (those that diverge most from the prior time series) are more likely to be negative than positive. Table 7.3 presents the most negative net income figure in each year of the 1970–1983 period for firms on the 1983 Compustat tape. An analyst has several options when extreme observations occur. One option is to do nothing in the belief that the extreme value represents a phenomenon that may recur on an ongoing basis in the forecast period. Large losses appear to be an ongoing phenomenon in some industries, for example, airlines, motor vehicles, and steel. Another option is to adjust the reported loss to a less extreme value. There are

TABLE 7.3   The Champion Money Losers Hall of Fame: Largest Loss Reported Each Year in 1970–1983 Period

| Year | Net Income Before Extraordinary Income | | Net Income After Extraordinary Income | |
	Company	Dollar Amount (millions)	Company	Dollar Amount (millions)
1970	Lockheed Corp.	−$86	Northwest Industries	−$227
1971	Occidental Petroleum	−48	Anaconda Company	−356
1972	Grumman Corp.	−70	Boise Cascade	−170
1973	Eastern Airlines	−51	Marcade Group	−67
1974	CNA Financial Corp.	−190	CNA Financial Corp.	−216
1975	Chrysler Corp.	−207	Singer Co.	−451
1976	Cook International	−82	Cook International	−81
1977	Bethlehem Steel	−448	Bethlehem Steel	−448
1978	Massey Ferguson	−257	Brascan Ltd.	−325
1979	Chrysler Corp.	−1,097	Chrysler Corp.	−1,126
1980	General Motors Corp.	−763	General Motors Corp.	−716
1981	International Harvester	−636	Chrysler Corp.	−475
1982	Ford Motor Company	−658	Ford Motor Company	−658
1983	Dome Petroleum	−884	Dome Petroleum	−888

several motivations for making such adjustments. One is that the underlying cause of the extreme value is expected to recur but that its severity is overrepresented by the numerical value of the observation. Another motivation is that the cause (say, a fire or a strike) of the extreme value is not expected to recur in subsequent periods. (See Chapter 4 for further discussion of extreme observations.)

7.3   TIME-SERIES ANALYSIS APPROACHES

At least three approaches to analyzing time-series data can be used:

1. *Economic.* This can involve both ex ante hypothesizing about systematic patterns expected in the time-series data and ex post analysis of causal factors underlying the behavior of the time series.

2. *Visual.* This involves plotting the data and then visually examining the plot for any systematic patterns.

3. *Statistical.* This involves using statistical tools such as an autocorrelogram (a table of autocorrelation coefficients) to detect systematic patterns in the data.

These three approaches are not mutually exclusive. For instance, an economic approach can suggest systematic patterns that the visual or statistical approaches might confirm. Moreover, the visual and statistical approaches can reinforce each other in identifying systematic patterns in the time series. Consider the quarterly financial data of Dayton-Hudson Corporation, a U.S. retailing firm. Table 7.4 contains the revenue, net earnings, and net earnings-to-revenue series of Dayton-Hudson over the 1975–1983 period. The fiscal year end is January 31; the first quarter covers February through April; the fourth quarter covers November through January. Figure 7.1 contains plots of the data. Based on a visual analysis, a strong seasonal pattern is apparent in the data. The fourth quarter in every year has the highest revenue and the highest net earnings. The percentage of annual revenues reported in the fourth quarter ranges between 32% and 35%; the percent of annual net earnings reported in the fourth quarter ranges between 51% and 61%. Economically, this fourth quarter seasonality is not surprising. This quarter includes the Christmas period, which is the most active buying season during the year. A second systematic pattern in the Dayton-Hudson series is the increase in the levels of the revenue and net earnings series. Over the period

TABLE 7.4   Quarterly Data of Dayton-Hudson Corporation

Year	First Quarter	Second Quarter	Third Quarter	Fourth Quarter
	Revenues ($ millions)			
1975	$ 337	$ 389	$ 415	$ 552
1976	386	421	459	633
1977	427	479	530	734
1978	567	651	704	1,041
1979	657	743	822	1,163
1980	757	855	993	1,429
1981	977	1,097	1,195	1,674
1982	1,123	1,242	1,363	1,933
1983	1,372	1,545	1,660	2,387
	Net Earnings ($ millions)			
1975	$ 2.7	$ 7.3	$10.7	$ 30.6
1976	6.6	8.3	15.1	35.7
1977	8.1	11.4	18.4	43.0
1978	11.6	3.6	23.0	60.2
1979	14.4	17.6	29.9	64.6
1980	16.7	15.2	33.5	81.3
1981	26.8	18.1	32.1	96.4
1982	21.8	26.3	38.9	119.7
1983	22.7	36.1	44.5	142.2
	Net Earnings/Revenues			
1975	.008	.019	.026	.055
1976	.017	.020	.033	.056
1977	.019	.024	.035	.059
1978	.020	.006	.033	.058
1979	.022	.024	.036	.056
1980	.022	.018	.034	.057
1981	.027	.016	.027	.058
1982	.019	.021	.029	.062
1983	.017	.023	.027	.060

FIGURE 7.1 Quarterly Net Earnings-to-Revenue Series of Dayton-Hudson Corporation, 1975–1983

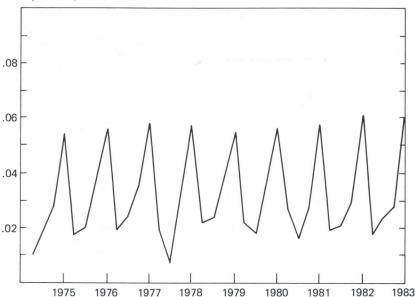

covered, there has been over a 400% increase in both the revenue and net earnings series. This increase is due to several factors: (1) an increase in the scale of operations via new store expansion and increase in the sizes of existing stores, (2) acquisition of other retailing chains, and (3) inflation causing an increase in nominal revenues and nominal net earnings.

A sizable segment of the literature aims to identify systematic statistical patterns in time-series financial data. These systematic patterns are then modeled and can be exploited for forecasting purposes. As yet, little attempt has been made to provide an economic rationale for the statistical models examined. Appendix A of this chapter discusses several key notions (stationarity, differencing, random walk model, and autocorrelation) that are central to a discussion of this literature. Appendix B presents a step-by-step example of statistical modeling using the Box-Jenkins univariate time-series methodology. Appendix C highlights the major findings of statistical research on the time-series properties of financial statement data.

7.4 ECONOMIC ANALYSIS OF TIME-SERIES DATA

Economy, industry, and firm-oriented factors can affect reported financial statement numbers. This section discusses firm-oriented factors. Economy and industry factors were discussed in Chapter 6.

A. Causal Factor Analysis

Four important categories of management decisions that can affect the time series of reported financial statement numbers are

1. *Mix of business decisions*. For example, will the firm operate in a single line of business (LOB), a vertically integrated set of businesses, a horizontally integrated set of businesses, a set of technology-related businesses, or a diversified (conglomerate) set of businesses? For instance, a single-LOB firm typically will have a more variable earnings time series than a multiple-LOB firm, in part due to the earnings changes of individual businesses offsetting each other with a multiple-LOB firm. In some instances, a firm can reduce the variability of its reported earnings by divesting an activity that has the potential to show sizable losses in any one year; for example, Transamerica, an insurance and financial services company, divested its movie studio business (United Artists) the year after it reported a $29 million write-down associated with one movie (*Heaven's Gate*).

2. *Financing decisions*. For example, will money be raised via leasing, bank loans, equity securities, and so on; will bank loans be at a variable or a fixed rate of interest; and will stock be repurchased? For instance, by choosing fixed interest rate loans, firms can better insulate their reported earnings series from variability due to movements in interest rates.

3. *Operating decisions*. For example, what mix of products will be manufactured, what level of wages will be paid, what level of inventory will be held, how much will be spent on discretionary items such as research and development and exploration, and how will commodities be purchased? For instance, by using forward markets, firms can hedge their net incomes against risks of price fluctuations for their commodity purchases.

4. *Financial reporting decisions*. For example, what asset and liability rules will be adopted from the available options, what rules will be adopted for revenue and expense measurement, and what items will be classified as extraordinary? For instance, by using full-cost as opposed to successful-efforts accounting, oil- and gas-producing companies can reduce the potential of individual dry holes to decrease reported net income in a single year.

Attempts in annual reports to quantify in detail the relative impact of each of the foregoing (and possibly other) factors are rare. The disclosures by Monsanto in Table 7.5 illustrate one attempt to capture some of the factors noted. The company summarized the 19X3 versus 19X2 comparison as "income improved, higher volumes and reduced costs offset lower selling prices." In times of changing prices, information on volume, prices, and product mix can provide much insight.

B. Seasonality

An understanding of the factors underlying the reported financial statement numbers can facilitate the drawing of inferences from those numbers. As an illustration, assume that an analyst has observed strong evidence of seasonal

TABLE 7.5   Monsanto: Explaining Yearly EPS Changes

Analysis of Changes in EPS Better (Worse)	19X2 vs. 19X1	19X3 vs. 19X2
Selling prices	$2.30	$(1.25)
Sales volume and mix	(3.96)	2.22
Raw material prices	2.77	0.22
Other manufacturing costs	(1.31)	0.22
Divestitures	(2.01)	(0.20)
Nonmanufacturing expenses	(1.13)	(0.33)
Operating income	$(3.34)	$0.88
Interest expense	0.31	(0.23)
Interest income	(0.08)	0.17
All other income and expenses	(0.28)	0.31
Effective tax rate	0.40	(0.09)
Extraordinary items	0.58	0.23
Shares outstanding	(0.30)	(0.28)
Change in earnings per share	$(2.71)	$0.99

patterns in the reported interim earnings and sales series of a firm. Possible sources of this seasonal pattern include

1. *Event date induced.* Christmas-related buying plays a major role in retailers having a strong seasonal pattern in their quarterly data. Seasonality is also observed for B. Manischewitz Company, a maker of Jewish foods; the February–April quarter (including Passover week) typically has over 45% of annual sales and over 80% of earnings.

2. *Weather induced.* Soft drink and beer sales typically are highest in the hottest times of the year, whereas demand for electricity and gas is typically highest in the coldest times of the year.

3. *Reporting cycle induced.* Firms with no seasonality induced by (1) or (2) can appear to have seasonal patterns if they follow a nonuniform interim reporting cycle. For example, Wometco has a 12-week, 12-week, 12-week, 16-week reporting cycle; it is not surprising that the fourth quarter typically has the highest sales and net earnings.

Assume that in one year, no evidence of seasonality is observed for a company with a prior history of seasonality. An analyst with an understanding of factors such as (1), (2), and (3) could make an informed judgment about the likelihood of this nonseasonality persisting. For example, if the sales by electric utilities were significantly down one winter, a useful statistic to examine is the number of days in the period with subzero temperatures. Indeed, several utility companies report this statistic in their annual report and refer to it when explaining year-to-year changes in operating results.

Two opposing theories for the computation of interim net income for firms with seasonality are the integral theory and the discrete theory. Under the *integral theory,* each interim period is treated as an integral part of the fiscal year. A forecast is made at the start of each fiscal year of annual sales, advertising costs, fixed costs, and so on; these costs are then allocated to each interim period based on the predicted (or actual) sales of each interim period. Results for the fourth quarter will include an adjustment for differences between predicted and actual sales or costs. Under the *discrete theory*, each interim period is treated as an independent reporting period. What is spent in the interim period for advertising, fixed costs, and so on, is recorded as an expense of that period. Income taxes for each interim period are typically estimated using the integral theory. There is considerable diversity regarding the reporting of other costs by firms with seasonal patterns in their revenues or expenditures.

C. Ex Post Analysis versus Ex Ante Analysis

The factors that can affect the reported earnings series are both numerous and diverse. When attempting to model a subset of these factors, it is useful to distinguish between ex post analysis (understanding what happened) and ex ante analysis (forecasting what will happen). Ex post hindsight is usually keener than foresight. For ex post purposes, the set of causal factors examined can be relatively large. While the analyst faces uncertainty about how the causal factors interact and their relative importance, typically the actual values of the causal factors will be available (for example, economy factors such as GNP, industry factors such as the price of minerals, and firm-specific factors such as the number of units shipped). In contrast, the actual values of such causal factors will not be available in an ex ante context. In some cases, there may be even more uncertainty about the future values of the causal factors than about the future values of reported earnings. An analyst may have little insight into how to forecast these causal factors. The result is that the models used for forecasting generally will incorporate few causal factors (in the limit, none) and can appear relatively naive from an economic viewpoint.

7.5 EARNINGS MANAGEMENT, SMOOTHING, AND THE BIG BATH

A common perspective in the financial press is that management "manages" or "smooths" the behavior of reported earnings over time. At one level, these statements are hardly newsworthy. As noted in Section 7.4, management makes decisions about the mix of its businesses, financing options, and operating activities; all these decisions can affect the time-series behavior of reported earnings. At another level, the "earnings management" or "smoothing" statements are more newsworthy. The assertion is that management "manipulates" the reported numbers. Phrases such as "cooking the books" and "paper entrepreneurialism" adequately convey the pejorative connotation associated with this perspective.

A. Areas of Potential Management Intervention

There are many areas where management can deliberately misrepresent the timing, amount, or intent of transactions or events in the financial statements. For example,

1. Sales related
   a. Timing of invoices (for example, moving a sale made in the next period to the current period by backdating the invoice)
   b. Phony orders (for example, reporting a sale to a nonexistent customer this period and reversing it the next period)
   c. Downgrading products (for example, classifying nondamaged goods as damaged to make sales to a customer at a lower than normal price)
2. Expense related
   a. Splitting invoices (for example, having a supplier split a single purchase order into several orders with invoice dates in more than one accounting period)
   b. Recording prepayments as expenses (for example, recording advertising prepayments as expenses of the period in which the payment is made).

In many other instances, management can use the large amount of discretion it has to time expense recognition, even though no fraud, falsification of the records, or circumvention of the internal control system is involved. For example,

- Banks have considerable discretion as to the timing and amount of losses on loan portfolios (that is, when a bad loan is classified as bad)
- Oil and gas companies have considerable discretion as to the timing and amount of exploration costs to be expensed in any one year (that is, when a dry hole is classified as dry).

Management can also engage in substantive transactions to affect the reported financial statement numbers. For example, research and development or exploration budgets can be cut in the second half of a fiscal year when it appears that reported annual earnings will fall below internal or external expectations.

B. Legal and Regulatory Decisions

There is a gray area between the extremes of earnings management (via business practices that are beyond reproach) and earnings manipulation (via cooking the books/paper entrepreneurialism). An analysis of judicial and regulatory decisions is one way to gain insight into the practices that some parties view as being beyond the gray and into the "cooking the books" area.

One example of questionable accounting and management practices is McCormick and Company, a diversified specialty U.S. food company with products sold in over 80 countries. This case focused on the "inflation" of the current earnings of McCormick's Grocery Products Division (GPD). The Audit Board of McCormick conducted an investigation of alleged "earnings inflation." The following extracts are taken from the Form 8-K McCormick filed with the SEC on May 27, 1982:

> The Company has followed a decentralized management philosophy, in which each of its operating units, of which the Grocery Products Division (GPD) is the largest, has substantial autonomy and its own administrative, manufacturing, accounting and marketing staff. Management at corporate headquarters sets policy, monitors performance, conducts planning and carries out overall financial policies.
>
> **Improper Accounting Practices**
>
> **Deferral of Expenses.** The principal improper accounting practice found was the deferral of recognition of certain expenses by delaying payments to a later period and not accruing for the expense in the earlier period.
>
> With respect to certain customer allowances, payments were authorized by means of a promotional authorization form signed and approved by six different GPD officials. The form, as originally conceived, was used to justify real promotional allowance programs. A variation of the form prepared for certain customer allowances during the investigation period was fictitious. Beginning in 1978 expense information was deliberately understated by GPD personnel on the form to avoid expense accruals.
>
> The marketing function at GPD effectively controlled the accounting for most marketing expenses, with the concurrence and assistance of the GPD controller and other accounting personnel. Accordingly, it was possible for the marketing function to schedule payment of customer allowances in a manner which permitted it flexibility and enabled it to be responsive to the perceived need for additional profit in any particular period. In 1980 and 1981, deductions taken by customers were delayed in internal processing at GPD, resulting in the improper deferral of recognition of expense.
>
> The second largest area of expense deferral was advertising. Much of this deferral was done with the cooperation of GPD's advertising agency which, at GPD's request, delayed billings until a subsequent period. In other instances, GPD personnel altered invoices to conceal earlier dates and, finally, in many instances invoices were simply held until later periods.
>
> **Sales.** For more than 25 years, GPD and one of its predecessors, the McCormick Division, had recognized as sales goods which were picked and staged, although not shipped, at the end of a period. This practice was not in accordance with generally accepted accounting principles. The amounts of goods picked and staged but not shipped at year-end 1977, 1978 and 1979 were in the range of $1,000,000; however, in 1980 the amount increased to $3,600,000 (less than 2% of GPD sales).
>
> GPD picked and staged goods after midnight on the last day of a fiscal period on a number of occasions. This failure to cut off sales was not proper.
>
> GPD personnel reportedly persuaded certain carriers to accept merchandise for shipment before they would have, in the ordinary course of business, and to hold such merchandise for future delivery in order to increase sales within the reporting period of such early acceptance. In other instances, dates on shipping documents were reportedly altered to reflect sales in an earlier period.
>
> **Raw Material Inventory at Corporate.** The investigation in this area focused principally on certain practices related to the management of the black pepper inventory which is conducted by the Corporate purchasing function and accounted for on a LIFO basis. Among the practices used to avoid booking black pepper at year-end

were the exchanging of one type of contract for another with an agreement to pay extra consideration for the delay, requesting vendors to postdate invoices and, in some instances, taking black pepper into inventory when invoices were paid rather than when the risk of loss had shifted to the Company. The adjustment for these purchases affected the LIFO calculation at the end of 1978, 1979 and 1980.

Conclusions

There are a number of factors which special counsel believes contributed to the improper accounting practices at GPD. First, during the period investigated, GPD came under increasing profit pressure. The demands by Corporate for continued high profit performance were viewed by GPD as unrealistic, and there was a general belief among those interviewed at GPD that Corporate knew or must have known that the goals could not be reached without deferring payments.

Second, there was a team spirit at GPD which led persons to participate in practices which they knew to be wrong.

Third, the accounting function within the Company and GPD was not given the same emphasis that was given other functions.

In its 1981 Annual Report, McCormick provided restatements for the 1977–1981 (third quarter) period. Table 7.6 summarizes these disclosures. The McCormick case is but one of a number of documented instances of what has been labeled as "middle-management book cooking." Other examples are cited in Treadway (1983).

C. The Big Bath

One phenomenon associated with earnings management appears under several labels, for example, "the big bath," "the clean sweep," "clearing the decks," and "housekeeping." The underlying theme is that once management encounters a loss year, additional steps are taken to add to the magnitude of the loss, for example, by further writing down of assets or by creating provisions for possible future losses. The result is a sizable decrease in the current year's reported income and, it is hoped, an increase in the income that will be reported in subsequent years. The support for this phenomenon is based more on anecdotes cited in the financial press than on systematic research. Examples from the financial press of quotations from "unnamed" executives include

- We had one single big write-off that we decided we should take. Once we decided on that, we tended to throw some other stuff in with it.
- So we get shellacked this time around. By making it a little worse, we can guarantee an improved income picture in the future. Why not get some benefit out of an existing fiasco?

In one of the few systematic studies in this area, Copeland and Moore (1972) reported that "the bath phenomenon does exist, (but) it is less frequent than some observers estimated" (p. 68). One interesting finding was that firms that had a "significantly higher proportion of discretionary accounting decisions" were more likely to be undergoing changes in top management. There are several explana-

TABLE 7.6 McCormick and Company as Reported and Restated Data ($ millions)

	1977	1978	1979	1980
Net sales as previously reported	$355.151	$400.357	$457.165	$547.966
Net reduction resulting from restatement	5.469	8.270	13.668	20.365
Net sales as restated	$349.682	$392.087	$443.497	$527.601
Net income as previously reported	14.816	16.735	19.430	14.840
Correction of accounting for certain customer allowances and sales	(.919)	(2.366)	(1.117)	(2.184)
Correction of accounting for advertising and other expenses	(.458)	.218	(.284)	(1.067)
Income tax effect	.676	1.099	.680	1.607
Net income as restated	$14.115	$15.686	$18.709	$13.196

	1981			
	1st Qtr	2nd Qtr	3rd Qtr	4th Qtr
As previously reported				
Net sales	$134.491	$154.435	$166.684	*
Gross profit	50.251	52.508	56.385	*
Net income	3.509	3.788	4.952	*
As restated				
Net sales	$131.995	$157.002	$166.703	$204.117
Gross profit	46.674	55.660	56.682	77.394
Net income	3.879	3.612	4.940	17.493

*"As previously reported" and "As restated" amounts are identical.
SOURCE: McCormick and Company, Form 8-K (May 27, 1982).

tions for this result; for example, (1) prior management was overly optimistic about items such as inventory values, or (2) new management is laying the "accounting foundations" for future years showing an increase in reported income.

7.6 SOME GENERAL COMMENTS

1. The literature on earnings manipulation/income smoothing is both sizable and spreads across many publication outlets. Examples of this literature include:

(a) Articles in the financial press. The titles/subtitles of two such articles aptly convey their underlying themes: (i) "Slick Accounting Ploys Help Many Companies Improve Their Income: By Proper or Improper Means, They 'Manage' Earnings For the Desired Effect" and (ii) "Manipulating Profits: How It's Done.

Executives rarely have to violate the law to put a gloss on dreary earnings. Accepted accounting principles leave ample room for those who want to fudge the numbers." In a related vein, a former member of the FASB commented: "[Executives have developed a] two-platoon system—an offensive unit to penetrate holes in GAAP for a bottom-line score, and a defensive unit to plug the holes and hold the line."

(b) Individual case studies that examine the financial accounts of a firm over an extended time period. Examples are in audit board reports from companies (for example, H. J. Heinz, 1980, and McCormick and Company, 1982) and in the proceedings of legal cases brought by the SEC against individual companies.

(c) Empirical research studies examining large samples of firms that probe the hypothesis that management attempts to smooth the reported earnings series. Ronen and Sadan (1981) summarize over 30 such studies. The main development in this research has been increasing recognition of the many ways management can affect the reported earnings series, for example, via transactions with suppliers and creditors, via decisions regarding discretionary expenditure items like R&D and exploration budgets, via the accounting methods adopted, and via the classification of expenditures as ordinary or extraordinary. There has not been a similar development in analytical models or research designs to handle this increasing recognition of the very complex environment empirical researchers face in this area.

The academic research literature has not been able to provide strong evidence that income smoothing behavior is widespread. However, the problems of research in this area, rather than the limited nature of such behavior, could well explain the limited evidence documenting its existence. Note also that management may attempt to "smooth earnings" but be unsuccessful. For instance, an attempt to transfer income from subsequent "good years" to what management perceives to be a current "bad year" assumes the existence of subsequent "good years." For a subset of firms this assumption is doubtful at best. (See Chapter 15 on "Financial Distress Analysis.") In this case, transferring income to the current year could well increase rather than decrease the variability in the reported earnings series.

2. A diverse set of motives for earnings manipulation/income smoothing behavior has been posited. For example,

- To promote an external perception that the company is low risk (where reported earnings variability is believed to be a critical factor in risk assessment)
- To convey information relevant to the prediction of future earnings
- To maintain satisfactory industrial relations
- To minimize taxation
- To promote an external perception of competent management
- To increase the compensation paid to management.

Until recently, very few attempts have been made to probe the descriptive validity of one or more of the preceding motivations. Healy (1985) represents one of the first detailed attempts to document the importance of the management compensation motive. The data base comprised 94 companies for which details of their management bonus contracts could be obtained. Healy conducted tests that compared the sign of the accrual component of reported earnings with the sign of the accrual that was hypothesized to be in management's self-interest, as reflected in the bonus contract. An accrual was defined as "the difference between reported earnings and cash flow from operations" (p. 86). By examining the bonus contract of each firm, Healy distinguished cases where management was predicted to have (a) an incentive to select income-decreasing discretionary accruals (that is, when the bonus plan's upper or lower bounds were binding) or (b) an incentive to select income-increasing discretionary accruals (that is, when the bonus plan's bounds were not binding). Although not all tests showed significant results, the overall tenor of the findings supported bonus-plan incentives as a factor in management decisions about accruals: "There is a greater incidence of negative accruals when the upper and lower bounds in the bonus contracts are binding" (p. 99).

The question examined in Healy (1985) and related research assumes that managements may take actions that maximize their own vested self-interest at the expense of shareholder interest. It is likely that such management would also take actions that make their self-interest maximizing behavior difficult for other parties (including an outside researcher) to detect. Partly for this reason, studies in this area will probably *not* report consistently significant evidence of earnings manipulation/income smoothing behavior.

7.7 SUMMARY

1. Much of financial statement analysis involves describing and explaining time-series patterns in data. When making this analysis, some potentially severe data quality problems can arise, for example, due to structural changes, accounting method changes, and the existence of extreme observations. This chapter does not provide "cookbook solutions" to such problems. The aim is a more modest one, that is, to sensitize those who conduct time-series analysis to the existence of such problems and some of the possible ways they can be handled.

2. Management can affect the time-series behavior of reported financial statement numbers via their mix of business, financing, operating, and accounting method decisions. There is a gray area between the extremes of earnings management (by business practices that are beyond reproach) and earnings manipulation (by cooking the books/paper entrepreneurialism).

3. The most impressive advances in knowledge about the time-series behavior of financial statement numbers has come from statistical time-series modeling. Appendix 7.C provides a detailed discussion of these advances. For the

annual earnings series, the random walk model has been identified as a robust mean/median univariate time-series model. For the interim earnings series, models incorporating both seasonal and between seasonal quarter patterns have been found to capture mean/median patterns in time-series behavior. Over time, more advances in the statistical time-series part of the literature are likely. These advances could arise from developments in the statistics literature itself, from improvements in computer capabilities, or from the availability of more extensive or more reliable data bases.

APPENDIX 7.A   STATISTICAL TOOLS FOR TIME-SERIES ANALYSIS

This appendix discusses (1) the stationarity concept; (2) differencing as a means of reducing nonstationarities; (3) submartingales, martingales, and random walks; (4) autocorrelation functions; and (5) sampling variation and model identification.

Stationarity

A time series is stationary when its basic statistical properties (for example, mean and variance) remain constant over time. Consider the net income, revenues, and net income-to-revenue series of a soft drink company over a ten-year period (in $ millions):

Year	Net Income	Revenues	Net Income/Revenues
19X1	$197	$2,425	.081
19X2	237	2,773	.085
19X3	262	2,928	.089
19X4	306	3,228	.095
19X5	337	4,013	.084
19X6	394	4,488	.088
19X7	404	5,475	.074
19X8	440	5,699	.077
19X9	510	5,921	.086
19X10	558	6,429	.087
Mean	365	4,338	.085

Neither the net income nor the revenue series is stationary as they exhibit no affinity for their respective means of $365 million and $4,338 million. Both series move farther away from their means in the 19X6–19X10 period. In contrast, the net income-to-revenues series exhibits an affinity over time for its mean of .085. For a stationary series, the mean can be calculated and be equally applicable to any subset of the time series. For a nonstationary time series, different subperiods will have different means. Although a mean statistic can be computed for a nonstationary series, it is not a meaningful measure of the central tendency of the entire time series.

Many time-series tools require the calculation of a single variance for a series. A series that has a constant variance is sometimes called a homogeneous variance series. Over extended time periods, financial series such as earnings and sales can exhibit an increasing level of variability (associated with the level of the series increasing, due to inflation, reinvestment of earnings, or acquisition). In this context, a technique such as examining logarithms of the financial series can result in the constant variance assumption being better satisfied by the data analyzed. (This technique is only appropriate for financial series with positive numbers.)

In many cases, some adjustment to time-series financial data will be necessary to attain a stationary series. As illustrated in Section 7.2 of this chapter, nonstationarity can arise due to acquisitions. In this context, achieving a stationary series may require analysis of only the postmerger firm, or the combining (with adjustments) of the time series of the two firms in the years prior to their merger. Another approach that has proved useful in reducing nonstationarities in many time series is differencing.

Differencing

Differencing a time series requires choice of a differencing interval. Let $(X_t, X_{t+1}, \ldots, X_{t+n})$ be the series to be examined. This nondifferenced series is frequently called the "levels." A first-differenced series reflects changes in consecutive observations:

$$(X_{t+1} - X_t), \quad (X_{t+2} - X_{t+1}), \ldots (X_{t+n} - X_{t+n-1})$$

A second-differenced series is calculated as:

$$(X_{t+2} - X_{t+1}) - (X_{t+1} - X_t), \quad (X_{t+3} - X_{t+2}) - (X_{t+2} - X_{t+1}), \ldots$$

Consider the net income time-series example used previously in this appendix. The levels, first- and second- differenced series, are

Year	Levels	First Differences	Second Differences
19X1	$197	—	—
19X2	237	$40	—
19X3	262	25	$15
19X4	306	44	19
19X5	337	31	-13
19X6	394	57	26
19X7	404	10	-47
19X8	440	36	26
19X9	510	70	34
19X10	558	48	-22
Mean	365	40	1

The first-differenced series shows more evidence of stationarity than does the levels series; that is, the first-differenced series shows more affinity for its mean value of 40 than the levels series does for its mean value of 365.

Seasonal differencing is often used in time-series contexts. This involves choosing a differencing interval that corresponds to the frequency of the seasonal cycle. For example, if seasonality is calendar-year related, fourth differencing would be used with quarterly data and twelfth differencing with monthly data. Appendix 7.B illustrates the use of seasonal differencing when modeling the quarterly net income-to-sales ratio series of Marshall Field and Company.

Submartingales, Martingales, and Random Walks

A submartingale time-series model can be described by

$$X_t = \phi X_{t-1} + \delta + e_t \tag{7.A.1}$$

where $\phi = 1$ and $\delta \geq 0$. A martingale model can be described by (7.A.1) with $\phi = 1$ and $\delta = 0$. If additionally the $(e_t, e_{t+1}, \ldots, e_{t+n})$ series is independently and identically distributed, (7.A.1) is a random walk model. The model in (7.A.1) portrays the time series as a stochastic process. This means that the sequence of observations evolves through time according to some probability law, in marked contrast to a sequence evolving through time in a deterministic pattern.

Autocorrelation Function

This function displays the autocorrelation structure of a time series up to a specified lag. The jth-order autocorrelation coefficient measures the extent to which the X_t and X_{t+j} observations move together. If a higher (lower) than average observation tends to be followed by another higher (lower) than average observation j periods later, the X_t and X_{t+j} observations are said to be positively autocorrelated. If a higher (lower) than average observation tends to be followed by a lower (higher) than average observation j periods later, the X_t and X_{t+j} observations are negatively autocorrelated. The jth order autocorrelation coefficient is estimated as

$$r_j = \frac{\dfrac{1}{T-j} \displaystyle\sum_{t=1}^{T-j} (X_t - \overline{X})(X_{t+j} - \overline{X})}{\gamma^2} \tag{7.A.2}$$

where $\overline{X}$ is the mean of the stationary series, γ^2 is the variance of the stationary series, and T is the number of observations. The range of r_j is from -1 to $+1$.

A theoretical property of the first-differenced series of a stationary random walk model is

$$r_j = 0 \text{ for all } j = 1 \text{ to } n \tag{7.A.3}$$

where n is the number of autocorrelations that can be computed with the series. Testing whether a series behaves as a random walk involves estimating the r_j's for the actual series and comparing them with the theoretical predictions of the random walk model. The following autocorrelations were estimated for the first-differenced net income series of Abbott Laboratories over a 21-year period (that is, they are based on 20 first-differenced observations):

r_1	r_2	r_3	r_4	r_5
$-.133$	$.113$	$.072$	$-.229$	$.039$

Even if a random walk model is a "true" description of the underlying time-series model for Abbott, one does not expect that the estimated autocorrelations in any finite sample will all be exactly zero.

Significance tests are often very useful in deciding if the estimated auto-correlations are statistically different from zero. The standard error (SE) of each r_j is calculated as follows:

$$SE(r_j) \approx \sqrt{\frac{1}{T - j}} \qquad (7.A.4)$$

given that the underlying series has $r_j = 0$ for all lags. A general rule of thumb is that r_j is significantly different from zero if the sample estimate is more than two standard errors from zero. If the sample r_j is no more than two standard errors from zero, one cannot reject (at a 95% confidence level) the null hypothesis that the population $r_j = 0$. For estimating $SE(r_1)$ of Abbott, $T = 20$, $j = 1$; hence $SE(r_1) = .229$. Thus, even though the sample estimate of $-.133$ for r_1 is not zero, one cannot reject the hypothesis that the underlying r_1 of Abbott is zero. A similar conclusion applies to r_2 through r_5 in the example. This autocorrelation evidence is consistent with Abbott's net income series in this 21-year period being well described by the random walk model.

Sampling Variation and Model Identification

An important part of statistical time-series analysis involves comparing sample autocorrelations with those implied by specific time-series models. In many applications using financial statement data, the stationarity assumption will limit the time series to a small number of observations (covering a relatively short time period). With small samples, model identification is a difficult task. Consider the following model:

$$X_t = \phi X_{t-1} + e_t \qquad (7.A.5)$$

with a "true" value of $\phi = .5$. In any one sample of observations generated by this model, it is quite possible to observe sample estimates of ϕ different from .5. To illustrate this, 100 X_t values were simulated for (7.A.5) and from the last 30 simulated values estimated the sample autocorrelations up to lag 8. This was repeated ten times. Table 7.7 has the results of this experiment. The theoretical model that generated the data implies $r_1 = .5$, $r_2 = .25$, $r_3 = .125$, and so on.

TABLE 7.7 Theoretical Autocorrelations and Sample Autocorrelations for Ten Independent Realizations of $T = 30$: $X_t = .5X_{t-1} + e_t$

	Autocorrelation Coefficients							
	r_1	r_2	r_3	r_4	r_5	r_6	r_7	r_8
Theoretical Model	.50	.25	.125	.062	.031	.016	.008	.004
Sample 1	.537	.140	−.042	−.129	−.026	−.071	−.210	−.213
Sample 2	.139	−.024	.286	.010	−.214	−.033	.074	−.191
Sample 3	.498	.172	.047	−.083	−.216	−.213	−.108	−.128
Sample 4	.491	.165	.063	−.051	−.016	.038	.071	.096
Sample 5	.388	.178	.142	.137	.216	−.085	.018	−.076
Sample 6	.582	.055	−.276	−.222	−.005	−.008	−.142	−.264
Sample 7	.503	.295	.173	.096	.272	.089	.036	−.120
Sample 8	.459	.173	.336	.571	.506	.119	.037	.201
Sample 9	.145	.313	−.057	−.101	.034	−.174	−.085	−.218
Sample 10	.429	.175	−.144	−.131	−.227	−.183	−.156	.063

Note, however, that the sample estimates of r_1 ranged from .139 to .582. Similarly, the sample estimates of r_2 ranged from −.024 to .313. That is, the sample estimate of r_j from a finite sample can be very different from that implied by the underlying time-series model. Note that in many situations one does not obtain ten independent realizations of 30 observations of a specific firm. One obtains one set of observations and must infer the model from the sample and other available information. The patterns of r_1 to r_8 for the ten realizations in Table 7.7 suggest that with small samples, it is quite difficult to identify anything but a crude approximation of the underlying time-series model.

APPENDIX 7.B BOX-JENKINS TIME-SERIES MODELING

The Box-Jenkins (1976) methodology is being applied to financial statement data with increasing frequency. This appendix illustrates the univariate time-series methodology using the interim net income-to-sales (NI/S) ratio of Marshall Field and Company (a retail department store chain). Data for the 1960–1975 period are reported in Table 7.8. A step-by-step approach is outlined to structure the exposition. Computer programs are now available to automate model identification, estimation, and forecasting. Hopwood (1980) describes one such automated program.

Step One: Plot the data. This step serves several important functions. First, one can check for possible errors/outliers in the data (for example, due to a misplaced decimal point). Second, one can check for evidence of structural change in the series being examined (for example, due to a merger or a change in lines of business). Third, one can check for evidence of possible nonstationarity in the series. (Appendix 7.A discusses the importance of stationarity.) Figure 7.2 plots the NI/S series over the 1960–1973 period. (The 1974 and 1975 observations will be used to illustrate forecasting with Box-Jenkins models.) The strong seasonal pattern in the data is readily apparent in Figure 7.2.

Step Two: *Compute autocorrelations.* The autocorrelations for the levels of the series are

r_1	r_2	r_3	r_4	...	r_8	...	r_{12}	...	r_{16}
$-.04$	$-.53$	$-.11$	.88	...	.76	...	.66	...	.56

Note the strong evidence of a seasonal pattern in the data. A common technique used to take seasonality into account is to difference the series at seasonal intervals, that is, derive a new series: $(Z_t - Z_{t-4}), (Z_{t-1} - Z_{t-5}) \ldots$. The autocorrelations for this new series are

r_1	r_2	r_3	r_4	...	r_8	...	r_{12}	...	r_{16}
.52	.26	.05	$-.07$	...	$-.09$	...	$-.05$	...	$-.11$

Step Three: *Preliminary model identification.* This step involves identifying possible Box-Jenkins models consistent with the data being analyzed. This entails,

TABLE 7.8 Quarterly Net Income-to-Sales Ratio of Marshall Field and Company, 1960–1975

Year	First Quarter	Second Quarter	Third Quarter	Fourth Quarter
1960	.019	.020	.037	.062
1961	.020	.023	.040	.060
1962	.023	.022	.037	.059
1963	.018	.019	.038	.058
1964	.025	.029	.051	.062
1965	.029	.034	.054	.065
1966	.035	.035	.049	.065
1967	.029	.038	.050	.065
1968	.026	.032	.046	.061
1969	.030	.035	.044	.056
1970	.019	.029	.042	.057
1971	.021	.028	.038	.064
1972	.021	.028	.041	.070
1973	.024	.028	.036	.062
1974	.023	.029	.036	.053
1975	.006	.026	.036	.054

FIGURE 7.2 Quarterly Net Income-to-Sales Series of Marshall Field and Company, 1960–1975

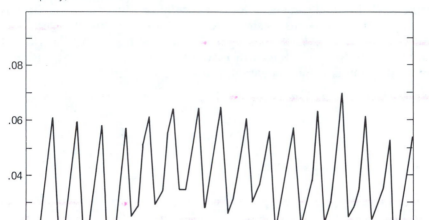

among other things, a comparison of the sample autocorrelations with the theoretical autocorrelation pattern of particular autoregressive moving average models. The pattern of autocorrelations reported suggests an autoregressive model of order 1—termed AR(1)—in the seasonally differenced series

$$X_t = \phi_1 X_{t-1} + \delta + e_t \tag{7.B.1}$$

where $X_t = Z_t - Z_{t-4}$. The theoretical autocorrelation function of this model, assuming that the sample r_1 of .52 is the population value, is

r_1	r_2	r_3	r_4	...	r_8	...	r_{12}	...	r_{16}
.52	.27	.14	.07	...	.01	...	.00	...	.00

As noted in Appendix 7.A, one does not expect an exact correspondence between the sample autocorrelation function and any theoretical autocorrelation function. In this example, the correspondence between the theoretical autocorrelation function and the sample function is quite high, given the sample size of 52 observations.

Step Four: Model estimation. For the preliminary model identified in Step Three, estimates of its parameters are next obtained. Using a commercially available Box-Jenkins package for estimation, the following model resulted:

$$X_t = .555 X_{t-1} + e_t \tag{7.B.2}$$

This model was estimated with the constant (δ) term in (7.B.1) suppressed to zero. When the model was (initially) estimated with the constant included, the sample estimate of δ was insignificantly different from zero.

Step Five: Diagnostic checking.   Several checks can be made on the adequacy of the model estimated in Step Four. One check is the significance of the coefficients of the estimated model. The coefficient on the autoregressive term is significant at conventional levels ($t = 4.57$). Another check on the estimated model is whether its residuals are random (white) noise. The aim of Step Four is to obtain a model with the e_t series being serially uncorrelated. If this series is not serially uncorrelated, there is additional information in the series that can be exploited in forecasting. The autocorrelations of the residuals from (7.B.2) are

r_1	r_2	r_3	r_4	...	r_8	...	r_{12}	...	r_{16}
.00	.07	$-.05$	$-.18$	...	$-.07$	...	$-.03$	...	.03

This evidence is consistent with the AR(1) model, in the seasonally differenced series, being a descriptively valid one.

Step Six: Forecasting.   The 1974 and 1975 quarterly observations withheld from the model identification time period are now used to illustrate forecasting. The estimated model is

$$X_t = .555X_{t-1} + e_t$$

where $x_t = Z_t - Z_{t-4}$. An equivalent form of the estimated model is

$$Z_t - Z_{t-4} = .555(Z_{t-1} - Z_{t-5}) + e_t \tag{7.B.3}$$

For forecasting Z_t, this model becomes

$$E(Z_t \mid Z_{t-1}, \ldots) = Z_{t-4} + .555(Z_{t-1} - Z_{t-5}) \tag{7.B.4}$$

Thus, the one-step-ahead (quarter) forecast for the 1974 first quarter NI/S ratio is

$$E(Z_{1974,1}) = Z_{1973,1} + .555(Z_{1973,4} - Z_{1972,4})$$
$$= .024 + .555 \times (.062 - .070) = .020$$

The actual values of one-step-ahead forecasts and the forecast errors (that is, the actual minus the forecast value) for 1974 and 1975 are

Year, Quarter	Actual	Forecast	Forecast Error (Actual–Forecast)
1974, 1	.023	.020	$+.003$
1974, 2	.029	.027	$+.002$
1974, 3	.036	.037	$-.001$
1974, 4	.053	.062	$-.009$
1975, 1	.006	.018	$-.012$
1975, 2	.026	.020	$+.006$
1975, 3	.036	.034	$+.002$
1975, 4	.054	.053	$+.001$

Note how the Box-Jenkins model has incorporated seasonal patterns into its one-step-ahead forecasts.

APPENDIX 7.C   STATISTICAL ANALYSIS OF FINANCIAL STATEMENT DATA

This appendix highlights the major findings of statistical research on the time-series properties of financial statement data. First, annual earnings and then interim earnings (where seasonality issues arise) are discussed. This is followed by a discussion of financial ratios and the several research directions found in the literature.

Annual Earnings: Mean/Median Analysis

The typical approach in mean/median studies is to compute autocorrelation coefficients for each firm and then to present the mean or median results for all firms in the sample. Assume that the following autocorrelations were found for the first-differenced earnings series of five firms:

	r_1	r_2	r_3	r_4	r_5
Firm A	.27	.21	.18	.04	−.16
Firm B	−.33	−.16	.20	.16	.08
Firm C	−.13	−.10	−.08	.10	−.12
Firm D	.41	.16	.11	.02	.12
Firm E	.08	.18	−.16	.06	−.14

The mean and median autocorrelation functions would show

	r_1	r_2	r_3	r_4	r_5
Mean	.060	.058	.050	.076	−.044
Median	.080	.160	.110	.060	−.120

There are several reasons why mean/median results for large samples of firms are important. The first reason relates to sampling error. The number of annual earnings observations that are available on machine-readable sources is not large. For instance, the Compustat annual industrial file includes data for only 20 years. Such small data bases mean that the sampling error, when attempts are made to identify and estimate the time-series models of individual firms, is quite large. By aggregating the results over many firms, it is hoped that there is a reduction in this sampling error. A second reason for examining mean/median results is the use that such information can play in forming prior probabilities of the time-series models for individual firms. That is, one can combine prior information from

TABLE 7.9   Distribution of Autocorrelation Coefficients
for First-Differenced Net Income and First-Differenced EPS, 1964–1983

Distribution Statistic	Autocorrelation Coefficients							
	Net Income				Earnings per Share			
	r_1	r_2	r_3	r_4	r_1	r_2	r_3	r_4
Mean	−.011	−.023	−.055	−.021	−.135	−.068	−.072	−.046
.1 Decile	−.418	−.323	−.307	−.232	−.416	−.304	−.303	−.248
.3 Decile	−.203	−.156	−.176	−.104	−.265	−.177	−.175	−.126
.5 Decile	−.023	−.038	−.068	−.030	−.142	−.079	−.075	−.052
.7 Decile	.158	.095	.044	.057	−.022	.025	.017	.023
.9 Decile	.406	.292	.222	.194	.152	.180	.163	.164

SOURCE: Computed from 1983 Compustat annual industrial file.

mean/median studies with the information contained in the sample autocorrelation of an individual firm to form a revised probability of the appropriate time-series model. In the case of recently formed firms, such prior information could be critical, as there may be only three or four years of firm-specific annual data available as sample evidence.

Empirical Evidence

Research in this area has a long history. Early work was reported by Little (1962) for U.K. companies and by Ball and Watts (1972) for U.S. companies. Little (1962) examined the correlation between successive growth rates in the earnings of U.K. firms over the 1951–1959 period. The conclusion was that "the work done on correlating past and future growth . . . strongly suggested that the true relationship was rather random" (p. 408). Ball and Watts (1972) used three different kinds of tests when examining a sample of U.S. Compustat firms over the 1947–1966 period: (1) a runs test, which examines if the sign of successive changes in earnings is independent, (2) an analysis of autocorrelation coefficients, and (3) a forecasting test in which alternative time-series models were ranked in terms of the mean absolute error of the one-year-ahead forecasts. The same inference arose from each test; that is, the net income and earnings per share (EPS) series could be described by a model closely resembling a random walk.

Evidence from a more recent time period for U.S. firms also supports the random walk finding. Table 7.9 presents autocorrelation distribution statistics for the first differences in the net income series and for the first differences in the EPS series. The sample is 1,265 Compustat firms over the 1964–1983 period. The mean autocorrelation for the first-differenced net income series is

r_1	r_2	r_3	r_4
−.011	−.023	−.055	−.021

Compare this finding with the mean autocorrelations Ball and Watts (1972) report for Compustat firms over the 1947–1966 period:

r_1	r_2	r_3	r_4
$-.030$	$-.040$	$.006$	$-.007$

Both sets of autocorrelations are not significantly different from the theoretical autocorrelations implied by a random walk model. (The random walk model implies that $r_j = 0$ for all j for the first-differenced series.) There is small evidence of negative autocorrelation for the EPS change series in both the Table 7.9 results (mean $r_1 = -.135$) and the Ball and Watts (1972) results (mean $r_1 = -.200$). However, an autocorrelation of $-.200$ implies only 4 percent explanatory power for an autoregressive predictive model. Note that the .1 and .9 decile values for r_1 to r_4 in Table 7.9 all seem different from zero. This does not necessarily mean that the time series implied by the mean/median results does not adequately describe these .1 and .9 decile firms. With 19 observations (successive earnings changes) for each firm, some dispersion across firms' *sample* autocorrelations is to be expected even if a random walk model describes the underlying time series of net income or EPS for each firm.

The result that, on average, annual reported earnings or EPS can be well described by a random walk model is one of the most robust empirical findings in the financial statement literature. In addition to the U.K. and U.S. evidence noted, similar results have been reported for other countries. For example, Whittred (1978) reports that "successive changes in the reported earnings of Australian corporations are essentially independent and well approximated by a random walk" (p. 198). Caird and Emanuel (1981) report a similar finding for a sample of New Zealand companies.

Annual Earnings: Individual Firm Analysis

Much of financial statement analysis is concerned with evaluating individual firms. A natural question is whether the mean/median results reported in the prior subsection also apply to individual firms. Two approaches have been adopted to address this question: (a) individual-firm-model versus single-model analysis and (b) sample partitioning or stratification analysis.

Individual-Firm-Model versus Single-Model Analysis

This approach identifies and estimates time-series models for each individual firm and then compares their forecasts with those from a single ("premier") model. The single model typically used is the random walk model suggested by the mean-median results. Two major conclusions emerge from this approach. First, a sizable number of firms reject a random walk model as being descriptive of their past time series. For instance, Watts and Leftwich (1977) report that for over half the firms in their sample, they can "reject the null hypothesis that the estimated process is no different from a random walk at the .05 level" (p. 263). The second major conclusion is that attempts to exploit these departures from a random walk model for forecasting purposes have met with limited success. Watts and Leftwich (1977) summarize their forecast results: "If any conclusion is to be drawn, it must be that the random-walk model predicts 'better' than the identified models according to the sum of ranks based on squared (forecast) errors" (p. 267). Albrecht, Lookabill, and McKeown (1977) report a similar result: "We found little difference in the predictive accuracy of the random-walk model and the best fitted Box-Jenkins models" (p. 242). These results highlight the frequent finding in this literature that there need not be a one-to-one mapping between the model that best describes the time series in a past period and the model that produces the most accurate forecast in a future time period.

One explanation for the forecasting results is the problem posed by structural change over a 20-or-more-year period for time-series analysis of individual firms. This problem manifests itself in inefficiently estimated firm-specific Box-Jenkins models and poor forecasting results for subsequent observations of the changed firm. A related explanation is that the random walk model only uses the most recent year's earnings when forecasting; extreme observations arising from divestitures, plant closings, accounting changes, and so on, are quickly dropped from the data set used for forecasting vis-à-vis the data set used for forecasting with the individual firm-identified Box-Jenkins models (especially moving average models).

Sample Partitioning or Stratification Analysis

This approach hypothesizes instances where departures from a random walk are predicted and then partitions (or stratifies) a sample to focus on those instances. At present there is no well-developed theory to guide the partitioning approach. At an empirical level, at least one "successful" form of partitioning has been reported. This partitioning is based on the magnitude of the earnings change in the prior period. Firms that have "large" changes in measured accounting income behave in a manner different from that implied by a random walk model. A representative study is Brooks and Buckmaster (1980), which examined a sample of U.S. Compustat firms over the 1955–1974 period. "Large" changes were detected by dividing the yearly earnings change by the standard deviation of such changes in past years and then ranking the resultant standardized changes; "large" changes were defined as those observations in either tail of the distribution. The conclusion was that "a firm with a large relative increase in income is generally followed by two or more periods when the firm underperforms the average or most likely outcome. Likewise, a firm with a large relative decrease in income generally outperforms the average or most likely outcome for two or more periods following the large decrease" (p. 451). This result has been reported in other studies, for example, Beaver, Lambert, and Morse (1980) and Freeman,

Ohlson, and Penman (1982). At an empirical level, it appears to be a relatively robust result.

The Brooks and Buckmaster (1980) and related results do not necessarily conflict with the mean/median results. The latter, as their name implies, are "average" results and need not be descriptive of any single firm. The Brooks and Buckmaster findings are based on a systematic partitioning of the sample to facilitate an empirical search for departures from the random walk model. Although such departures have been identified, they comprised no more than 10% of their sample. It is interesting to note that Brooks and Buckmaster report that a random walk model best explains "the time-series behavior of an *unpartitioned* set of individual firm income series" (p. 450) for their sample.

Interim Earnings: Mean/Median Analysis

Quarterly accounting data provide a much larger data base for identifying time-series models than do annual accounting data. It is partly this enlarged data base that has led to intensive statistical analysis of the time-series properties of quarterly data. An enlarged data base, other things being equal, means more observations to identify and estimate the parameters of specific models. Other things, however, are not equal. At a minimum, issues of seasonality occur in using quarterly data.

Table 7.10 presents distribution evidence of autocorrelations for the interim net income series of 1,813 Compustat firms. The time period covered is the first quarter of 1975 to the fourth quarter of 1983. For each firm, the autocorrelations for several combinations of first differencing (d) and seasonal differencing (D) were computed:

$$1.\ d = 1, D = 0$$
$$2.\ d = 0, D = 1$$

Seasonal differencing involves four periods (quarters) per seasonal cycle. If a random walk model adequately describes quarterly earnings, the sample autocorrelations for the $d = 1, D = 0$ (that is, first differences in quarterly earnings) combination would all be insignificantly different from zero. The mean autocorrelations, for the $d = 1, D = 0$ combination are

r_1	r_2	r_3	r_4	r_5	r_6	r_7	r_8
$-.309$	$-.070$	$-.135$	$.281$	$-.131$	$-.042$	$-.098$	$.208$

These results provide evidence of seasonality in quarterly earnings changes ($r_4 = .281$ and $r_8 = .208$). A random walk model does not adequately describe the time-series behavior of first-differenced quarterly earnings. The mean autocorrelations for the $d = 0, D = 1$ combination are

r_1	r_2	r_3	r_4	r_5	r_6	r_7	r_8
$.371$	$.183$	$.038$	$-.221$	$-.069$	$-.048$	$-.038$	$-.045$

TABLE 7.10 Distribution of Autocorrelation Coefficients for First-Differenced and Seasonally Differenced Quarterly Net Income Series, 1975–1983

Distribution Statistic	Autocorrelation Coefficients							
	r_1	r_2	r_3	r_4	r_5	r_6	r_7	r_8
A. First-Differenced								
Mean	−.309	−.070	−.135	.281	−.131	−.042	−.098	.208
.1 Decile	−.564	−.451	−.449	−.070	−.408	−.368	−.376	−.094
.3 Decile	−.418	−.206	−.228	.081	−.218	−.145	−.163	.030
.5 Decile	−.313	−.065	−.105	.248	−.108	−.040	−.065	.167
.7 Decile	−.193	.060	−.007	.456	−.019	.066	.007	.345
.9 Decile	−.054	.293	.116	.708	.096	.264	.109	.596
B. Seasonally Differenced								
Mean	.371	.183	.038	−.221	−.069	−.048	−.038	−.045
.1 Decile	.046	−.035	−.197	−.472	−.301	−.264	−.238	−.253
.3 Decile	.249	.082	−.065	−.350	−.159	−.133	−.112	−.127
.5 Decile	.399	.172	.032	−.241	−.068	−.045	−.036	−.046
.7 Decile	.530	.276	.131	−.113	.020	.037	.037	.031
.9 Decile	.654	.420	.282	.053	.158	.157	.156	.160

SOURCE: Computed from 1983 Compustat annual industrial file.

An r_1 of .371 implies that a random walk model does not adequately describe the seasonally differenced interim earnings series. The autocorrelation evidence implies that quarterly earnings in time t arc not only related to quarterly earnings in time $t - 4$ but also to quarterly earnings reported between time $t - 1$ and $t - 5$.

The foregoing mean/median results suggest that quarterly earnings have (1) a seasonal component and (2) an adjacent quarter-to-quarter component. There is debate in the literature over a representative model to reflect these mean/median patterns. The competing alternatives all involve seasonal differencing of the series. The debate centers on whether (1) an autoregressive model (Foster, 1977), (2) a moving average model (Watts, 1975; Griffin, 1977), or (3) a combined autoregressive moving average model (Brown and Rozeff, 1979) best captures the other systematic patterns in the data. The existing evidence supports (3) when the criterion is which model best forecasts future quarterly earnings or quarterly EPS. Bathke and Lorek (1984) examined the quarterly earnings per share series of 240 firms; the 1962–1974 period was used to identify and estimate time-series models, while the 1975–1977 period was used to test the forecasting ability of each model. In each of the four fiscal quarters, the time-series model identified in Brown-Rozeff (1979) provided the most accurate forecasts. Another finding in this study was that the fourth fiscal quarter had higher forecast errors than the first three quarters: "These results are suggestive of a fourth-quarter 'dumping' process by which accruals and deferrals on an interim basis are brought into correspondence with the annual figures. This phenomenon evidently induces a random shock or noise component in the quarterly EPS time-series which may impede the modeling process'' (p. 168).

Interim Earnings: Individual Firm Analysis

Similar to annual earnings, research has examined whether the mean/median results reported in the prior subsection also apply to individual firms.

Individual-Firm-Model versus Single-Model Analysis

This approach has compared individual firm-identified models for interim earnings with those of a single (''premier'') model. The premier models analyzed have included those discussed in Watts (1975), Foster (1977), Griffin (1977), and Brown-Rozeff (1979). The results are remarkably similar to those for annual earnings. First, a sizable number of firms reject the chosen mean/median model as being descriptive for the past reported quarterly earnings time series. Second, attempts to exploit these departures from the mean/median model for forecasting purposes have met with limited success. For instance, Collins and Hopwood (1980) reported that for a sample of 50 firms, ''the best performing model was the premier model suggested by Brown and Rozeff, followed by the model individually identified by each firm'' (pp. 397–398). Hopwood and McKeown (1981) report a similar finding for a sample of 267 Compustat firms.

TABLE 7.11   Median Autocorrelation Coefficients for Levels and First Differences of Selected Financial Statement Ratios or Variables, 1964–1983

Financial Ratio or Variable	Autocorrelation Coefficients								No. of Firms
	Levels				First Differences				
	r_1	r_2	r_3	r_4	r_1	r_2	r_3	r_4	
(C + MS)/TA	.422	.159	.031	−.015	−.172	−.082	−.060	−.026	1,148
CA/CL	.462	.236	.090	.035	−.207	−.090	−.053	−.003	1,172
CFO/S	.012	−.045	−.061	−.051	−.369	−.048	−.010	−.022	1,250
LTL/SE	.609	.340	.152	.024	−.049	−.070	−.047	−.041	1,074
OI/INT	.556	.252	.079	−.003	.013	−.096	−.057	−.022	981
NI/SE	.480	.141	−.001	−.049	−.093	−.119	−.081	−.052	1,075
S/TA	.652	.371	.172	.065	.043	−.087	−.083	−.064	1,201
S/AR	.592	.292	.130	−.003	−.019	−.094	−.038	−.057	954
COGS/INV	.603	.331	.170	.068	−.022	−.126	−.061	−.019	912
PE	.433	.226	.167	.087	−.217	−.117	.004	.028	1,135
DIV. PAY	.295	.087	.019	−.007	−.289	−.003	−.021	−.008	1,184
TA	.780	.610	.441	.296	.250	.085	.009	−.008	1,295

SOURCE: Computed from 1983 Compustat annual industrial file.

Sample Partitioning or Stratification Analysis

Not all firms have a seasonal pattern in their interim earnings series. Table 7.10 includes the following decile evidence for r_4 and r_8 of the first-differenced series:

	Deciles				
	.1	.3	.5	.7	.9
r_4	−.070	.081	.248	.456	.708
r_8	−.094	.030	.167	.345	.596

Subsets of firms exhibit no significant evidence of seasonality, while other firms report strong evidence of seasonality. Lorek and Bathke (1984) report that these differences can be exploited in time-series analysis. Using a sample of 240 Compustat firms, they identify 29 nonseasonal firms. They then document that for these 29 firms the so-called premier models (which assume seasonality) result in reduced levels of forecast accuracy.

Financial Ratios: Some Additional Evidence

At present, there is little published evidence on the time-series behavior of financial ratios. The following analysis was conducted to gain some preliminary evidence on this issue. Autocorrelations for the following 12 financial ratios or variables were computed for all firms with available data on the Compustat tape.

1. Cash and marketable securities/total assets, (C + MS)/TA
2. Current assets/current liabilities, CA/CL
3. Cash flow from operations/sales, CFO/S
4. Long-term liabilities/stockholders' equity, LTL/SE
5. Operating income/interest payments, OI/INT
6. Net income/stockholders' equity, NI/SE
7. Sales/total assets, S/TA
8. Sales/accounts receivable, S/AR
9. Cost of goods sold/inventory, COGS/INV
10. Price-to-earnings ratio, PE
11. Dividend payout, DIV. PAY.
12. Total assets, TA

Autocorrelations were computed for both the levels of each series and for the first differences. The time period covered was 1964 to 1983 (except for CFO/S, which used 1971 to 1983 due to data availability limitations). Table 7.11 presents the median autocorrelations. Focusing on the first-differenced series, it appears that a random walk model could describe the median behavior of several series (for example, OI/INT and COGS/INV). As expected, the TA series exhibits nonstationarity in the levels; a combination of inflation, reinvestment, and merger activity has caused the level of the total assets series of many firms to increase over the 1964–1983 period.

Some General Comments

1. Many studies reporting evidence on the time-series properties of financial statement data access data bases with a "survivorship bias"; that is, only firms currently surviving are included in the analysis. The effect of this restriction is difficult to predict, in part due to the diverse reasons for nonsurvival of firms, for example, acquisition or merger, bankruptcy, and voluntary dissolution. Ball and Watts (1979) provide evidence that samples of survived firms do not differ markedly in their autocorrelations from random samples of firms. They reported results for the following three samples:

- Sample A: 25 firms randomly selected from Moody's *Industrial Manual* for 1917 and 1966; thus, each firm was required to have survived at least 50 years.
- Sample B: 25 firms randomly selected from Moody's *Industrial Manual* for 1917; thus, there is no survivorship bias.
- Sample C: 25 firms randomly selected from Moody's *Industrial Manual* for 1966; thus, no survivorship bias exists.

The mean autocorrelations of the first-differenced annual EPS series for the three samples are

	r_1	r_2	r_3	r_4
Sample A	− .16	− .05	.01	− .02
Sample B	− .14	− .06	.04	.03
Sample C	− .17	− .05	.08	− .01

The conclusion was that "the average correlogram for first differences in firms' EPS is not noticeably altered by a relatively severe sample selection bias" (pp. 203–204).

2. Studies examining the time-series statistical properties of financial statement data have focused primarily on the reported historical cost net income or EPS series. A small but growing literature is examining how accounting alternatives other than those employed by the firm affect the time-series model identified for firms. Hillison, Hopwood, and Lorek (1983) provide results on the effect of general price-level adjustments (GPLA) on quarterly earnings for 24 firms in the U.S. airline industry. The conclusion was that GPLA transformations "did not substantially alter the time-series properties of quarterly earnings data" (p. 363).

Two areas where accounting alternatives potentially can cause sizable changes in the variability of the reported time series are foreign currency translation and marketable equity securities. Accounting alternatives that include in the income statement period-by-period changes in foreign exchange rates, or capital market values for marketable securities, typically will have a more variable reported income series vis-à-vis alternatives that do not recognize such changes in the computation of reported income.

QUESTIONS

QUESTION 7.1: Earnings Management at H. J. Heinz

The net income series of many large food companies exhibit considerable predictability in their growth. For example, over a nine-year period H. J. Heinz reported that net income before income tax steadily rose from $75 million in 19X1 to $204 million in 19X9. In year 19X9 of this period, general counsel of Heinz became aware of allegations about the internal control and financial reporting in one of its divisions. The Audit Committee of the board of directors engaged an outside law firm and an accounting firm to fully investigate these and related allegations. In 19X10, Heinz filed with the SEC a "Report of Audit Committee to the Board of Directors: Income Transferral and Other Practices."

The report concluded that during years 19X1 to 19X9 certain Heinz "affiliates" (divisions) "engaged in the practices of improperly accounting for income and expense items and sales, which had the effect of transferring income between fiscal years." Table 7.12 presents a summary of the restatements to reported sales and net income made by the company in 19X10.

TABLE 7.12 H. J. Heinz Income Transferral Practices ($000s)

Year	Total Net Income Before Tax Before Restatement	Improper Recognition of Expenses	Improper Recognition of Sales	Other Practices	Increase (Decrease) Net Income Before Tax	Total Net Income Before Tax After Restatement	% Effects of Restatement
(1)	(2)	(3)	(4)	(5)	(6)	(7)	(8)
19X1	$ 75,381	$ 513	—	—	$ 513	$ 75,894	.7%
19X2	80,995	1,814	$1,968	—	3,782	84,777	4.5
19X3	92,250	4,250	309	$1,364	5,923	98,173	6.0
19X4	116,525	(2,476)	(1,527)	615	(3,388)	113,137	(3.0)
19X5	127,633	111	1,815	(877)	1,049	128,682	.8
19X6	154,936	4,139	1,294	(268)	5,165	160,101	3.2
19X7	168,731	(734)	2,872	(671)	1,467	170,198	.9
19X8	199,547	(8,888)	(7,085)	(396)	(16,369)	183,178	(8.9)
19X9	203,823	(76)	354	233	511	204,334	.3

One set of restatements was due to prior "improper recognition of advertising and market research expenses. These practices generally resulted in an overstatement of expenses in the year in which the item was expensed and a comparable understatement of expenses in a succeeding year when the previously expensed amount was recovered." The percentage of total advertising and market research expenses improperly recognized ranged from 10.8% in 19X3 to 0.2% in 19X5. Examples included

- In 19X3, Heinz USA (HUSA) solicited $2 million of invoices from an advertising agency for services that would be rendered in 19X4. Such invoices were recorded as expenses in 19X3.

- Questionable invoices were recorded as expense in the current fiscal year with an intent that the amounts thereof would be recovered in the form of cash refunds or services in subsequent years. During the 19X1–19X9 period, ten vendors furnished questionable invoices to HUSA.

Another set of restatements was due to "improper recognition of sales. Certain affiliates recorded sales in a fiscal period other than the period in which such sales should have been recorded." The percentage of total sales improperly recognized ranged from 0.0% in 19X1 to 1.3% in 19X2 (and 1.1% in 19X9). Examples included

- In 19X2 to 19X5, the report stated that HUSA's books "may have been kept open for a period of time after year end, or documents may have been misdated to include additional sales in those years."

- In 19X6 and 19X7, HUSA made attempts to "shut off sales by halting shipments in order to limit income in such years. Instructions were given to distribution centers not to make shipments in the last few days of those fiscal years. As a practical matter, however, this was difficult to accomplish and, in some cases, the customers' orders were actually shipped prior to the end of the fiscal year and the paperwork was altered or misdated to record the sales in the succeeding fiscal year."

- In 19X6 and 19X7, HUSA deferred processing vendor credits through its accounting system in the year in which they were received and recorded them in the succeeding fiscal year.

The largest item in the "Other practices" column of Table 7.12 related to transactions with a bean wholesaler:

- In 19X2, HUSA entered into forward contracts to purchase navy beans. When the price of navy beans increased in 19X3, HUSA "entered into a four-stage purchase/sale/repurchase/resale agreement with a bean wholesaler pursuant to which the profit to be realized by HUSA as a result of the arrangement ($1.364 million) was to be paid to HUSA in three equal installments in 19X4. HUSA recorded $1.364 million as income for 19X4. The net effect was to transfer the $1.364 million from 19X3 to 19X4. One motivation cited for this transaction was that Wage and Price Controls (existing in 19X3) were to be dropped in 19X4.

Background on H. J. Heinz

H. J. Heinz's organizational structure consists of its world headquarters located in Pittsburgh and affiliates, which, in the 19X1–19X10 period, were "largely self-sufficient enterprises conducting business with their own operating officers and managements." Heinz operated as a highly decentralized organization.

During the 19X1–19X10 period, Heinz publicly stated that its objective was to seek an increase in company earnings at a steady and consistent rate; for example, "the Company's financial objectives are a compound growth rate in earnings per share of 10% to 12% per year." The Audit Board report noted that world headquarters used "budgets to monitor the operations of Affiliates. . . . If any of the reports showed an unexpected variance, immediate inquiry was made of the Affiliate concerned, seeking the reason for such variance. If there was to be any shortfall in the expected results of a particular Affiliate, other Affiliates might be encouraged to show extra profit, which could be accomplished by various means, including the reduction of discretionary expenses. The overall aim was to meet the projected consolidated earnings goals. Predictability was the watchword, and surprises were to be avoided."

The company maintained a management incentive program (MIP). In 19X10, 225 employees were covered by this program, which included "the corporate officers, the senior World Headquarters personnel and the officers and senior personnel of most of the Affiliates. Goals were stated in terms of a 'fair' goal of a certain earnings figure and a higher 'outstanding' goal. . . . The emphasis of the MIP program was on the achievement of short-term [earnings] results, that is, one year." The amount paid to each MIP participant represented a significant portion (in some cases 40%) of total compensation. Several of the income transferral practices were designed to ensure that the divisions met, but did not substantially exceed, their profit targets, since each year's goals were based on the previous year's results. A long-term incentive plan (based on a moving three-year cycle) was used for 19 persons (as of 19X10); participation was limited to "World Headquarters senior management and the presidents or managing directors of the largest Affiliates." These 19 individuals also participated in the MIP program.

REQUIRED

1. Compare and contrast the "earnings management activities" at Heinz with those of McCormick (described in the Section 7.5.B of this chapter).

2. What factors may have motivated the "income transferral and other practices" documented in the Heinz Audit Board report? Distinguish between the motivations of (a) management at the affiliate level and (b) senior management at world headquarters.

3. The Audit Board report stated "there is no evidence that any employee of [Heinz] sought or obtained any direct personal gain in connection with any

of the transactions or practices described in this Report." Do you agree with this statement?

4. The reaction to the H. J. Heinz, McCormick, and similar disclosures has been mixed. One SEC commissioner stated he could think of "no activity which can do greater damage to investor confidence than financial statement fraud. Those who would profit from 'cooked books' are few compared to the number of people who are harmed." In contrast, the financial press has quoted business executive reaction as including "the amounts involved are typically immaterial," "nobody loses," and the "high pressure for results is business as usual." Discuss these various reactions.

QUESTION 7.2: Modeling Annual Time-Series Data: Caterpillar Tractor and Inland Steel

Table 7.13 presents the following data for both Caterpillar Tractor Co. and Inland Steel Company covering the 1928–1983 period: net income, sales, and net income-to-sales. Also included in Table 7.13 is the consumer price index for the 1928–1983 period.

Caterpillar Tractor is the world's largest producer of earthmoving equipment. Major markets include road building, mining, logging, agriculture, petroleum, and general construction. Products include tractors, scrapers, graders, compactors, loaders, off-highway trucks and pipe layers. The company also makes diesel and turbine engines and lift trucks. In 1982 and 1983, Caterpillar suffered the largest losses in its history. In explaining these results, they reported a 32% decline in physical sales volume in 1982 and a further 13% decline in physical sales volume in 1983. The lower sales were said to result from "depressed economic conditions in many countries" and "lower price levels realized because of intense competition for the available business and the effects of the stronger U.S. dollar." Included in Caterpillar's loss for 1983 was a "nonrecurring pretax charge of $112 million" for the estimated costs of plant closing; this was part of "actions taken to reduce excess manufacturing capacity and overhead costs." Value Line in 1984 reported the following aggregate information for 18 companies (including Caterpillar) in their "Machinery (Construction and Mining) Industry" group (in millions of dollars):

	1980	1981	1982	1983
Net income	$ 1,115	$ 1,202	$ 83	$ (239)
Sales	20,360	22,046	18,094	14,644

Inland Steel is the fourth largest steel producer in the United States. Major markets include steel service centers, transportation, industrial, and construction. Major products include sheet and strip steel, steel bars, and plate steel. The company also maintains a steel service center operation, a construction products group, and a housing subsidiary. In 1982 and 1983, Inland Steel suffered the largest losses in its history. The 1982 Annual Report noted that "the national economic shock which persisted throughout 1982 precipitated a new full-scale depression for the steel industry." Raw steel production for Inland Steel was 8.1 million tons in 1981, 5.2 million tons in 1982, and 6.3 million tons in 1983; capacity utilization was 86.6% in 1981, 55.6% in 1982, and 67.8% in 1983. Value Line in 1984 reported that following aggregate information for six companies (including Inland Steel) in their "Steel (Integrated) Industry" group (in millions of dollars):

	1980	1981	1982	1983
Net income	$ 1,086	$ 2,112	$ (1,301)	$ (1,423)
Sales	39,886	43,472	40,224	37,203

REQUIRED

1. What systematic patterns are apparent in the reported net income, sales, and net income-to-sales series of (a) Caterpillar and (b) Inland Steel over the 1928–1975 period?

2. How might the inflation index (CPI) be used in modeling the time series of Caterpillar or Inland Steel? What are the pros and cons of incorporating the CPI index into the modeling?

3. Assume you are asked in 1976 to develop time-series models to predict the one-year-ahead net incomes of Caterpillar and Inland Steel. What factors would you consider in deciding the number of observations used to identify and estimate the time-series model?

4. Assume you are asked in 1984 to develop time-series models to predict the 1985 and 1986 net incomes of Caterpillar and Inland Steel. How would you treat the 1982 and 1983 observations of each firm?

5. In August 1984, a security analyst at Value Line made the following forecasts of net income and sales for 1984 and 1985 (in millions of dollars):

	Caterpillar		Inland Steel	
Year	Net Income	Sales	Net Income	Sales
1984	$ 30	$7,030	$ 60	$3,650
1985	336	8,300	100	4,050

Why might these predictions be more accurate than time-series models that predict both annual net income and sales will follow a random walk (that is, the 1984 and 1985 values are predicted to be the same as the 1983 value of each respective series)?

QUESTION 7.3: Time-Series Properties of Net Income and Sales of Computer Companies

Ramona Sharp is a security analyst specializing in the "computers and peripherals" industry. While attending an "alumni reunion" day, she hears one of her former professors discussing research on the time-series properties of reported net income. The professor focuses on mean/median results for a broad cross

TABLE 7.13 Caterpillar Tractor and Inland Steel: Annual Financial Data, 1928–1983

Year	Caterpillar Tractor			Inland Steel			Inflation CPI (1983 = 1.000)
	Net Income ($ millions)	Sales ($ millions)	Net Income / Sales	Net Income ($ millions)	Sales ($ millions)	Net Income / Sales	
1928	$ 8.7	$ 35	.249	$ 9.3	$ 64	.145	.184
1929	12.4	52	.238	11.7	69	.170	.182
1930	9.1	45	.202	6.5	52	.125	.182
1931	1.6	24	.067	1.3	32	.041	.169
1932	(1.6)	13	−.123	(3.3)	15	−.220	.152
1933	.4	14	.029	0.2	28	.007	.137
1934	3.8	24	.158	3.7	40	.093	.141
1935	6.2	36	.172	9.4	63	.149	.145
1936	10.2	54	.189	12.8	99	.129	.147
1937	10.6	63	.168	12.7	111	.114	.150
1938	3.2	48	.067	4.9	74	.066	.152
1939	6.0	58	.103	10.9	115	.095	.149
1940	7.8	73	.107	14.5	142	.102	.149
1941	7.7	102	.075	14.8	203	.073	.150
1942	7.0	142	.049	10.7	190	.056	.167
1943	7.6	171	.044	10.8	204	.053	.180
1944	7.3	242	.030	10.2	221	.046	.185
1945	6.5	231	.028	9.9	217	.046	.190
1946	6.1	128	.048	15.6	218	.072	.194
1947	13.5	189	.071	29.9	315	.095	.229
1948	17.5	218	.080	38.6	393	.098	.253
1949	17.2	255	.067	25.0	346	.072	.256
1950	29.2	337	.087	38.0	403	.094	.251
1951	15.8	394	.040	34.4	519	.066	.271
1952	22.7	481	.047	23.8	458	.052	.282

Year						
1953	20.6	438	.047	33.9	576	.059	.284
1954	25.9	407	.064	41.3	533	.077	.287
1955	36.0	533	.068	52.5	660	.080	.285
1956	55.5	686	.081	53.0	727	.073	.286
1957	40.0	650	.062	58.9	764	.077	.295
1958	32.2	585	.055	47.9	656	.073	.305
1959	46.5	742	.063	45.1	705	.064	.309
1960	42.6	716	.059	47.1	747	.063	.313
1961	55.8	734	.076	54.7	725	.075	.318
1962	61.9	827	.075	52.5	760	.069	.320
1963	77.3	966	.080	56.1	808	.069	.324
1964	129.1	1,217	.106	71.1	874	.081	.330
1965	158.5	1,405	.113	68.4	968	.071	.333
1966	150.1	1,524	.098	64.5	1,054	.061	.340
1967	106.4	1,473	.072	52.8	992	.053	.351
1968	121.6	1,707	.071	75.8	1,074	.071	.363
1969	142.5	2,002	.071	58.7	1,216	.048	.380
1970	143.8	2,128	.068	52.3	1,195	.044	.403
1971	128.3	2,175	.059	47.8	1,254	.038	.424
1972	206.4	2,602	.079	65.9	1,470	.045	.439
1973	246.8	3,182	.078	83.1	1,829	.045	.455
1974	229.2	4,082	.056	148.0	2,450	.060	.497
1975	398.7	4,964	.080	83.3	2,107	.040	.556
1976	383.2	5,042	.076	104.1	2,388	.044	.593
1977	445.1	5,849	.076	87.8	2,682	.033	.624
1978	566.3	7,219	.078	158.3	3,248	.049	.666
1979	491.6	7,613	.065	131.1	3,635	.036	.729
1980	564.8	8,598	.066	29.7	3,256	.009	.830
1981	578.9	9,154	.063	57.3	3,755	.015	.928
1982	(179.9)	6,469	−.028	(133.1)	2,808	−.047	.963
1983	(345.2)	5,424	−.064	(52.3)	3,046	−.017	1.000

section of over 1,200 U.S. firms. The mean/median autocorrelations for first differences in annual net income (computed using 20 years of data for each firm) were

	r_1	r_2
Mean	$-.011$	$-.023$
Median	$-.023$	$-.038$

The professor concludes that, on average, the time series of first differences in reported net income can best be described by a random walk model.

Sharp's professor also reports the following mean/median results for the first-differenced sales series of over 1,200 U.S. firms for the same 20-year period:

	r_1	r_2
Mean	.236	.068
Median	.256	.046

On returning to her office, Sharp reads the following in a survey of growth companies:

> A recent computer screening of nearly 6,000 publicly traded stocks has turned up 53 stocks sharing at least two outstanding characteristics: Earnings have increased for at least seven consecutive fiscal years at an average annual rate of 45% or more and earnings continued to rise in the latest reporting period.

Three companies Sharp follows are on this list—Apple Computer, Commodore International, and Wang Laboratories. Table 7.14 presents financial data for these companies for the most recent seven years. Sharp computes the first- and second-order autocorrelations (r_1 and r_2, respectively) for the first-differenced (Δ) sales and the first-differenced (Δ) net income series:

	(Δ) Sales		(Δ) Income	
	r_1	r_2	r_1	r_2
Apple Computer	.441	.112	.392	$-.121$
Commodore International	.189	$-.039$	.179	$-.051$
Wang Laboratories	.246	$-.019$	.400	$-.010$

Several of these autocorrelations did not appear similar to those reported by her former professor.

REQUIRED

1. Reconcile the correlations for Apple, Commodore, and Wang with the mean/median autocorrelations reported by Sharp's professor.

2. These companies are often referred to as growth companies by security analysts. One variable that analysts consider before applying this term to a

TABLE 7.14 Apple Computer, Commodore, and Wang: Financial Time Series for Sales and Net Income ($ millions)

	19X1	19X2	19X3	19X4	19X5	19X6	19X7
Apple Computer							
Sales	$ .8	$ 7.9	$ 47.9	$117.1	$ 334.8	$ 583.1	$ 982.8
Net income	.1	.8	5.1	11.7	39.4	61.3	76.7
Commodore							
Sales	46.2	50.2	71.1	125.6	186.5	304.5	681.2
Net income	1.5	3.4	6.0	16.2	24.9	40.6	88.0
Wang							
Sales	198.1	321.6	543.3	856.4	1,159.3	1,538.0	2,184.7
Net income	15.5	28.6	52.1	78.1	107.1	152.0	210.2

company is its compound annual growth rate in earnings or sales. This growth rate is calculated via the following formula:

$$\frac{x}{y} = (1 + g)^n$$

where x = earnings (sales) of nth year
y = earnings (sales) of base year
g = compound growth rate
n = number of years excluding base year

Estimate the compound annual growth rate in earnings and in sales of each of the three companies over the 19X1–19X7 period. What limits may exist to the companies continuing these growth rates?

3. Sharp believes that structural change might be a problem in this industry. She reads the following comments by an analyst colleague:

> Getting a fix on this industry has never been easy. Over the past year confidence in technology issues has been shaken badly. Concerns are manyfold: the ability of companies to fund the rising research and development budgets required by shorter product life cycles and the threat of a technological breakthrough on the part of a competitor; the difficulties of getting state-of-the-art wares to the market; confusion about the relative prospects of mainframes, minis, and microcomputers in the ongoing evolutionary process toward distributed data processing and office automation; and the omnipresence of IBM, which is making good on its promises to be the producer of lowest cost and to participate in all computer markets.

How might Sharp decide whether structural change is a problem in this industry? What are its implications for statistical time-series analysis?

4. What alternatives to statistical time-series analysis might be used to analyze the financial data of firms in this industry?

QUESTION 7.4: Accounting Alternatives and the Time Series of Interim Earnings

Grace Bond is a retail chain that has over 50 stores, primarily located in upscale suburban malls. As part of a diversification program, Grace Bond took a 30% interest in Discount Unlimited (DU); the other 70% was publicly held. Discount was a rapidly growing retail chain that sold items to a low- to middle-income clientele. For the first ten years of its investment in Discount Unlimited, Grace Bond included in its reported earnings only dividends paid by Discount Unlimited. Excluded from Grace Bond's reported earnings over this period were capital gains or losses on its investment as reflected in year-to-year changes in Discount Unlimited's market capitalization. (Also excluded was Grace Bond's equity in the reported earnings of Discount Unlimited.)

The financial vice-president of Grace Bond hears that an accounting regulatory body is considering mandating that all companies include gains and losses on marketable equity securities as a component of their reported earnings. The financial vice-president collects the following interim data from the past ten years:

1. Quarterly EPS as reported by Grace Bond
2. Adjustment that would be made to Grace Bond's reported EPS if quarterly

TABLE 7.15 Grace Bond: Alternative Quarterly Per Share Series

Year & Quarter	(1) As Reported EPS	(2) DU's Capital Gains	(3) (1) + (2) Combined	Year & Quarter	(1) As Reported EPS	(2) DU's Capital Gains	(3) (1) + (2) Combined
19X1: Q1	.21	.32	.53	19X6: Q1	.35	−.08	.27
Q2	.30	−1.13	−.83	Q2	.46	1.86	2.32
Q3	.40	−1.51	−1.11	Q3	.74	−.61	.13
Q4	1.21	.89	2.10	Q4	1.97	−1.27	.70
19X2: Q1	.18	.05	.23	19X7: Q1	.41	1.16	1.57
Q2	.31	−3.30	−2.99	Q2	.47	−.91	−.44
Q3	.37	3.26	3.63	Q3	.56	2.63	3.19
Q4	1.20	−.98	.22	Q4	1.49	−1.27	.22
19X3: Q1	.26	.00	.26	19X8: Q1	.37	.23	.60
Q2	.35	.04	.39	Q2	.43	1.33	1.76
Q3	.41	−.13	.28	Q3	.50	−.45	.05
Q4	1.16	.74	1.90	Q4	1.80	−.43	1.37
19X4: Q1	.30	.35	.65	19X9: Q1	.53	.47	1.00
Q2	.35	−.19	.16	Q2	.57	−.31	.26
Q3	.44	−.48	−.04	Q3	.73	−.17	.56
Q4	1.67	−.80	.87	Q4	2.24	.69	2.93
19X5: Q1	.44	.54	.98	19X10: Q1	.39	.30	.69
Q2	.41	−.25	.16	Q2	.55	−2.41	−1.86
Q3	.57	.26	.83	Q3	.52	1.07	1.59
Q4	1.96	2.98	4.94	Q4	2.22	−.92	1.30

fluctuations in the aggregate market value of their stock investment in Discount Unlimited were to be included in EPS

3. Adjusted quarterly EPS (sum of 1 and 2).

Table 7.15 presents these three series for Grace Bond over the 19X1–19X10 period.

REQUIRED

1. Compare and contrast the reported EPS time series (1) with the adjusted EPS time series (3).
2. Assume that you were building a model to predict the adjusted EPS time series (3). What factors would you consider in choosing between
   a. Modeling series 1 and series 2 separately and then combining the separate predictions for 1 and 2?
   b. Modeling series 3 and making a prediction for 3 from this model?
3. The financial vice-president strongly opposes the adjusted series (3) being mandated by the accounting regulatory body. He argues that use of the adjusted series "will result in a significant distortion in our quarterly and annual earnings statements, and will result in a situation in which the figure designated as net earnings will become the least useful figure in the Statement of Earnings." Why might the financial vice-president make this argument? What external parties might he believe would be misled by the adjusted series?
4. Several research studies have reported that the fiscal quarter with the most "unexpected variation" in reported earnings is the fourth quarter. What factors might explain this finding?

REFERENCES

ALBRECHT, W. S., L. L. LOOKABILL, and J. C. McKEOWN. "The Time-Series Properties of Annual Earnings." *Journal of Accounting Research* (Autumn 1977): 226–244.

ALI, M. M., and R. THALHEIMER. "Stationarity Tests in Time Series Model Building." *Journal of Forecasting* (July–September 1983); 249–257.

BALL, R., and G. FOSTER. "Corporate Financial Reporting: A Methodological Review of Empirical Work." *Studies on Current Research Methodologies in Accounting: A Critical Evaluation,* Supplement to *Journal of Accounting Research* (1982): 161–234.

BALL, R., and R. WATTS. "Some Time Series Properties of Accounting Income." *Journal of Finance* (June 1972): 663–681.

BALL, R., and R. WATTS. "Some Additional Evidence on Survival Biases." *Journal of Finance* (March 1979): 197–206.

BATHKE, A. W., and K. S. LOREK. "The Relationship Between Time-Series Models and the Security Market's Expectation of Quarterly Earnings." *The Accounting Review* (April 1984): 163–176.

BEAVER, W., R. LAMBERT, and D. MORSE. "The Information Content of Security Prices." *Journal of Accounting and Economics* (March 1980): 3–28.

BOX, G. E. P., and G. M. JENKINS. *Time-Series Analysis: Forecasting and Control,* rev. ed. San Francisco: Holden-Day, 1976.

BROOKS, L. D., and D. A. BUCKMASTER. "First-Difference Signals and Accounting Income Time-Series Properties." *Journal of Business Finance and Accounting* (Autumn 1980): 437–454.

BROWN, L. D., and M. S. ROZEFF. "Univariate Time-Series Models of Quarterly Accounting Earnings per Share: A Proposed Model." *Journal of Accounting Research* (Spring 1979): 179–189.

CAIRD, K. G., and D. M. EMANUEL. "Some Time-Series Properties of Accounting Income Numbers." *Australian Journal of Management* (December 1981): 7–15.

COLLINS, W. A., and W. S. HOPWOOD. "A Multivariate Analysis of Annual Earnings Forecasts Generated from Quarterly Forecasts of Financial Analysts and Univariate Time-Series Models." *Journal of Accounting Research* (Autumn 1980): 390–406.

COPELAND, R. M., and M. L. MOORE. "The Financial Bath: Is It Common?" *MSU Business Topics* (Autumn 1972): 63–69.

FOSTER, G. "Quarterly Accounting Data: Time-Series Properties and Predictive-Ability Results." *The Accounting Review* (January 1977): 1–21.

FREEMAN, R. N., J. A. OHLSON, and S. H. PENMAN. "Book Rate-of-Return and Prediction-of-Earnings Changes: An Empirical Investigation." *Journal of Accounting Research* (Autumn 1982): 639–653.

GRIFFIN, P. A. "The Time-Series Behavior of Quarterly Earnings: Preliminary Evidence." *Journal of Accounting Research* (Spring 1977): 71–83.

HEALY, P. M. "The Effect of Bonus Schemes on Accounting Decisions," *Journal of Accounting and Economics* (April 1985): 85–107.

HEINZ, H. J. "Report of Audit Committee to the Board of Directors," May 6, 1980.

HILLISON, W. A., W. S. HOPWOOD, and K. S. LOREK. "Quarterly GPLA Earnings Data: Time-Series Properties and Predictive Ability Results in the Airlines Industry." *Journal of Forecasting* (October–December 1983): 363–375.

HOPWOOD, W. S. "On the Automation of the Box-Jenkins Modeling Procedures: An Algorithm with an Empirical Test." *Journal of Accounting Research* (Spring 1980): 289–296.

HOPWOOD, W. S., and J. C. MCKEOWN. "An Evaluation of Univariate Time-Series Earnings Models and Their Generalization to a Single-Input Transfer Function." *Journal of Accounting Research* (Autumn 1981): 313–322.

LEV, B. "Some Economic Determinants of Time-Series Properties of Earnings." *Journal of Accounting and Economics* (April 1983): 31–48.

LITTLE, I. M. D. "Higgledy Piggledy Growth." *Bulletin of the Oxford Institute of Economics and Statistics* (November 1962): 387–412.

LOREK, K. S., and A. W. BATHKE. "A Time-Series Analysis of Nonseasonal Quarterly Earnings Data." *Journal of Accounting Research* (Spring 1984): 369–379.

McCORMICK & COMPANY. "Form 8-K," filed with SEC, May 27, 1982.

RONEN, J., and S. SADAN. *Smoothing Income Numbers.* Reading, Mass.: Addison-Wesley, 1981.

"Slick Accounting Ploys Help Many Companies Improve Their Income," *The Wall Street Journal,* June 20, 1980.

TREADWAY, J. C. "Cooked Books: No New Recipes," remarks to the Securities Law Committee of the Federal Bar Association. Washington, D.C., March 2, 1983.

WATTS, R. L. "The Time-Series Behavior of Quarterly Earnings," working paper. University of Newcastle, 1975.

WATTS, R. L., and R. W. LEFTWICH. "The Time Series of Annual Accounting Earnings." *Journal of Accounting Research* (Autumn 1977): 253–271.

WHITTRED, G. P. "The Time-Series Behaviour of Corporate Earnings." *Australian Journal of Management* (October 1978): 195–202.

WORTHY, F. S. "Manipulating Profits: How It's Done." *Fortune* (June 25, 1984): 50–54.

8

FORECASTING FINANCIAL STATEMENT INFORMATION

8.1 INTRODUCTION

Financial forecasts are made or used by many parties including security analysts, lending institutions, and management:

- *Security Analysts:* Forecasts of earnings and other variables are included in almost all reports by security analysts. These forecasts range from short term (for example, one quarter or one year ahead) to long term (for example, five-year earnings growth rates).
- *Lending Institutions:* The loan procedures followed at many financial institutions include a forecast of an applicant's or client's earnings and cash flows over the term of a loan.
- *Management:* An important management activity is corporate strategy analysis, an integral part of which is forecasting the cash flow or earnings implications of alternative combinations of financing, investment, and operating decisions. Another management activity is corporate disclosure, which includes decisions about whether to publicly release forecasts of earnings.

This chapter discusses issues related to the preparation and evaluation of forecasts of financial statement information by the foregoing and other parties.

8.2 ALTERNATIVE FORECASTING APPROACHES

Table 8.1 outlines one classification scheme of forecasting approaches.

1. *Mechanical versus Nonmechanical Approaches.* In a mechanical approach to forecasting, the data inputs are combined in a prespecified way such that, given the same data base and the chosen model, the same forecast will always be made. One example is a model that forecasts earnings ($X_{i,t}$) to be an equally

TABLE 8.1 Classification of Forecasting Approaches

	Univariate	*Multivariate*
Mechanical	Moving average models Box-Jenkins univariate models	Regression models Box-Jenkins transfer function models Econometric models
Nonmechanical	Visual curve extrapolation	Security analyst approach

weighted average of the past five year's earnings:

$$E(X_{i,t}) = \frac{1}{5} \sum_{n=1}^{5} X_{i,t-n} \tag{8.1}$$

A second example is a regression model that forecasts the earnings of a firm via forecasts of two independent variables related to economy ($X_{M,t}$) and industry ($X_{I,t}$) factors:

$$E(X_{i,t}) = \alpha + \beta_1 \cdot E(X_{M,t}) + \beta_2 \cdot E(X_{I,t}) \tag{8.2}$$

In a nonmechanical approach, there is no prespecified link between the data examined and the forecast made. For instance, an analyst may incorporate a judgmental factor into a forecast, and this factor can reflect an ever-changing mix of economic inputs.

2. *Single-Variable (Univariate) versus Multiple-Variable (Multivariate) Approaches.* A univariate approach examines only one variable when forecasting. The five-year moving-average model in equation (8.1) is a univariate model as only the past sequence of one variable (earnings) is used to develop a forecast. With a multivariate approach, more than one variable is used when forecasting. The regression model in (8.2) is a multivariate model, as both economy and industry variables are used to develop an earnings forecast for a firm.

Examples of Forecasting Approaches

Each of the four cells in Table 8.1 contains approaches that have been used to forecast financial statement variables:

Univariate/Mechanical. The equally weighted moving average model in (8.1) is one example of this approach. A variant is a weighted moving-average model:

$$E(X_{i,t}) = .7X_{i,t-1} + .2X_{i,t-2} + .1X_{i,t-3} \tag{8.3}$$

These models are frequently outlined in many financial statement analysis and investment texts. These texts, however, rarely provide statistical or economic justifications for the particular model examined or its chosen parameters. Another example of this approach to forecasting is Box-Jenkins univariate time-series analysis. One distinctive feature of this approach is that a systematic *statistical analysis* of the financial series is made when choosing a forecasting model. Appendix 7.B illustrates this approach in modeling the quarterly net income-to-sales series of Marshall Field.

Univariate/Nonmechanical. A typical example of this approach is a "freehand" extrapolation of a time-series plot of earnings. Heuristic adjustment of the past earnings series for so-called nonrecurring items when forecasting future values is also a variant of this approach.

Multivariate/Mechanical. One class of examples of this approach is based on systematic statistical analysis. The index models described in the appendix to Chapter 6 are a special case of a more general class of multivariate models termed "transfer function" models. Applications of transfer function modeling in the financial statement area are increasing (for example, Hopwood, 1980). They offer the advantage over single-variable models of being able to incorporate more of the factors that may affect the time-series behavior of earnings and other series. Large-scale econometric models are also examples of this approach. Forecasts are obtained from these models by the simultaneous solution of an equation system, after historical values of endogenous and exogenous variables and projected future values of exogenous variables have been provided. (An endogenous variable is one for which the projected value is determined by the econometric model. An exogenous variable is one for which the projected value is determined independently of the econometric model.) Most work on building such econometric models has been done at the economy or industry level; an important advantage of this approach is that interrelationships among variables can be considered. Work on econometric models of individual firms is relatively less developed.

Multivariate/Nonmechanical. Security analysts typically adopt this approach to forecasting earnings. Many quantitative and qualitative information sources are consulted, for example, macroeconomic forecasts, industry trade association reports, annual and interim reports, company visits, and interviews with management. The weights placed on individual sources can vary from forecast to forecast for the one company and across companies at any one point in time. Although a description of the basic assumptions underlying an earnings forecast is often included in an analyst's report, the linkage between these assumptions and the specific forecast is rarely provided. (In some cases, no such linkage may even exist.) Figure 8.1 presents a listing of the numerous factors one security analyst institution considers in its earnings growth forecasts.

As with most classification schemes, specific forecasting approaches may have elements of more than one of the categories in Table 8.1. For example, Box-Jenkins time-series models are mechanical only after the chosen model is identified and estimated. (While computer algorithms now exist to mechanically identify and estimate models, the algorithms themselves have to be chosen.) As a second example, in the multivariate econometric model approaches, predictions of exogenous variables may be based on nonmechanical forecasts made by individual economists. (Further discussion of alternative forecasting approaches is in Wheelwright and Makridakis, 1984.)

8.3 CRITERIA TO EVALUATE FORECASTS

At a general level, a better quality forecast is one that leads to a better quality decision being made. Given this perspective, a detailed evaluation of the

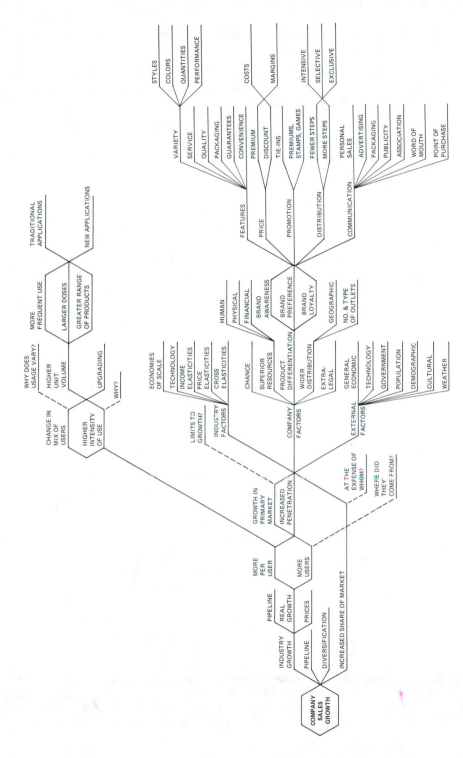

Figure 8.1 Estimating Growth: A Security Analyst's Approach
Source: Wertheim & Co., Inc., Member of New York Stock Exchange, Inc.

quality of forecasts will require analysis of the specific decision context in which a forecast is to be used. Illustrative contexts include

- An investment context where the aim is to detect misvalued securities
- An investment context where the aim is to maintain a well-diversified portfolio with a specific risk level
- A credit lending context where the aim is to balance higher interest payments against the likelihood of bankruptcy
- A divestiture context where the aim is to forecast the future earnings to be derived from the division of a company.

At present, little research has been conducted into how attributes of forecasts, such as their accuracy and timeliness, are differentially valued in diverse decision contexts such as those just outlined. Typically, forecasts are evaluated in the research literature using the error measures described in the following subsections. However, it is important to keep in mind that these error measures may not adequately describe the loss function implicit in a specific investment, credit, divestiture, or other decision. In particular, the potentially critical attribute of timeliness of a forecast (for example, does the forecast only reflect information already impounded in security prices?) is not captured by these error measures.

A. Forecast Error Measures

In this section, forecast error measures are described. The first set of measures focuses on the dispersion of forecasts, whereas the second set examines the bias of forecasts.

Dispersion

Two commonly used measures of the dispersion of forecast errors are the mean absolute error (MABE) and the mean square error (MSE):

$$\text{MABE}_i = \frac{1}{N} \sum_{t=1}^{N} \mid X_{i,t} - E(X_{i,t}) \mid \qquad (8.4)$$

$$\text{MSE}_i = \frac{1}{N} \sum_{t=1}^{N} [X_{i,t} - E(X_{i,t})]^2 \qquad (8.5)$$

where

$X_{i,t}$ = the realization of the forecast variable in period t for firm i
$E(X_{i,t})$ = the forecast of the variable in period t for firm i
N = the number of forecasts examined

The larger the MABE (MSE) measure, the larger the magnitude of forecast errors in the period examined. The MABE measure gives equal weighting to all forecast errors (which is consistent with a linear loss function). The MSE measure gives greatest weight to large forecast errors (which is consistent with a quadratic loss function). When used in relation to forecasting, accuracy typically refers to dispersion of forecast errors; the lower the dispersion measure, the more accurate the forecast is said to be.

When the error measures in (8.4) and (8.5) are averaged across firms, a few large firms can dominate the summary statistic. The use of deflated error measures is one means of reducing scale effects from the inclusion of large firms. (The discussion in Chapter 4 on the assumptions underlying the use of ratios to control for scale differences across firms or over time is also pertinent to the issues raised in this section.) The variables that can be used to deflate the forecast errors of each firm include

1. A measure of the level of the series being forecast, for example, $X_{i,t}$ or $E(X_{i,t})$. Use of either deflator results in a percentage forecast error measure.
2. A measure of the variability of the series being forecast, for example, the average absolute value of past changes in the series being forecast.
3. A variable that is of interest in the decision context in which the forecast is to be used, for example, the market capitalization of the firm.

When $X_{i,t}$ or $E(X_{i,t})$ is used as the deflator in (8.4) or (8.5), the error measure can be undefined (when the denominator is zero). When $X_{i,t}$ or $E(X_{i,t})$ is negative, the interpretation of the error measure is less than obvious. Both these problems typically do not arise, or are encountered less frequently, when the latter two classes of deflators are used.

Bias

A forecast is said to be unbiased if the expected value of the forecast error is zero. A measure that provides evidence on bias is the average error (AVE):

$$\text{AVE}_i = \frac{1}{N} \sum_{t=1}^{N} (X_{i,t} - E(X_{i,t})) \tag{8.6}$$

Forecasts errors of differing signs are allowed to cancel each other out in (8.6). The concern of the AVE is not with each individual forecast error but rather with the average error over all forecasts.

Note that when $X_{i,t} - E(X_{i,t})$ is negative in (8.6), deflation by $X_{i,t}$ when it is also negative will result in a positive forecast error measure. Brown, Foster, and Noreen (1985, p. 59) report that this situation arises in approximately 2% of the cases examined. Most research avoids this situation by either deleting these observations from the sample examined or by deflating the forecast error by the absolute value of $X_{i,t}$.

The discussion on outlier observations in Section 4.3.B is relevant to the interpretation of forecast error measures, especially those in deflated form. For example, outliers can arise when $X_{i,t}$ is used as the deflator and values of $X_{i,t}$ approach zero. The published literature has adopted a diverse set of approaches in such situations, for example, (1) winsorizing the sample, (2) trimming the sample, (3) deleting observations for which the denominator is less than a minimum amount (say, $0.20 when forecasts of EPS are examined), or (4) examining median rather than mean error measures. (Additional discussion of outliers in a forecasting context is in Levenbach, 1982.)

Illustration of Forecast Error Measures

Consider the following earnings series (in millions) of a firm over a ten-year period:

Year 1	Year 2	Year 3	Year 4	Year 5
$10.800	$11.640	$12.720	$12.480	$13.750

Year 6	Year 7	Year 8	Year 9	Year 10
$14.260	$13.760	$12.240	$12.280	$10.860

Assume that the following two models are used to forecast one-year-ahead earnings:

$$E(X_{i,t}) = X_{i,t-1} \tag{8.7}$$

$$E(X_{i,t}) = \frac{1}{5} \sum_{n=1}^{5} X_{i,t-n} \tag{8.8}$$

For year 6, (8.7) predicts earnings to be $13.750. The error measures for (8.7) are

	$X_{i,t} - E(X_{i,t})$	$|X_{i,t} - E(X_{i,t})|$	$[X_{i,t} - E(X_{i,t})]^2$
Year 6	.510	.510	.2601
Year 7	− .500	.500	.2500
Year 8	− 1.520	1.520	2.3104
Year 9	.040	.040	.0016
Year 10	− 1.420	1.420	2.0164

Based on the foregoing for (8.7), and the comparable forecast errors for (8.8), the following were computed:

	AVE	MABE	MSE
(8.7)	− .578	.798	.9677
(8.8)	− .360	1.468	2.5342

Using these error measures, (8.7) yields forecast errors with lower dispersion measures (MABE and MSE) but with a more negative bias (AVE) than (8.8).

The major advantage of these error metrics is their computational simplicity. The major disadvantage is that they may not capture the loss function in a specific decision context. However, attempts can be made to develop guidelines about the decision contexts in which one type of error metric better captures the loss function. Moreover, the error metrics can be modified if it is found that none adequately captures the loss function. For instance, in a competitive bidding context for a government contract, the penalty from overestimating cost may be significantly higher than the penalty from underestimating cost (particularly, if reimbursement is on a cost-plus basis). In this context, a firm with past experience in cost estimation may want to use a quadratic loss function for overestimates and a linear loss function for underestimates.

Forecasts made at any one time (especially by external parties) typically will be for the entity as existing at that particular moment. Over time, however, corporations can engage in significant restructuring such that the realizations of the variables forecast pertain to a substantially different entity. This restructuring could include takeovers, mergers, and divestitures. When interpreting error metrics, it is important to examine if such restructurings have occurred before making inferences about a forecaster or a forecast model having a "poor" track record. A related problem arises when analysts forecast earnings per share based on an assumed amount of stock remaining outstanding and a corporation subsequently buys back a significant number of outstanding stock.

B. Forecast Horizon Issues

In some decision contexts, the concern is with forecasting a sequence of future observations at the one point in time. The error metrics just discussed can be readily applied in this context. Consider earnings-per-share forecasts for each year of a five-year horizon made by three analysts. The forecasts are all made at the start of year 1:

	One Year Ahead (Year 1)	Two Years Ahead (Year 2)	Three Years Ahead (Year 3)	Four Years Ahead (Year 4)	Five Years Ahead (Year 5)
Analyst A	$1.40	$1.75	$2.15	$2.75	$3.00
Analyst B	1.80	2.50	3.20	4.20	5.50
Analyst C	1.55	2.00	2.60	3.70	4.60

The actual earnings-per-share results were

Year 1	Year 2	Year 3	Year 4	Year 5
$1.64	$2.15	$2.69	$3.37	$4.00

Use of the following percent error measure

$$\frac{\text{Actual EPS} - \text{Forecast EPS}}{\text{Actual EPS}} \times 100 \qquad (8.9)$$

for each year being forecast (at the start of year 1) yields:

	One Year Ahead	Two Years Ahead	Three Years Ahead	Four Years Ahead	Five Years Ahead
Analyst A	14.6%	18.6%	20.1%	22.8%	25.0%
Analyst B	−9.8	−16.3	−19.0	−24.6	−37.5
Analyst C	5.5	7.0	3.3	−9.8	−15.0

Several observations can be drawn from these data:

1. Analyst A consistently underestimates actual earnings, and the percentage error increases the farther one moves away from the forecast date. Analyst B consistently overestimates actual earnings, and the percentage error also increases the farther one moves away from the forecast date.

2. Using a percentage absolute error criterion (which ignores the sign of the above forecast errors), Analyst C dominates Analysts A and B in each year of the five-year forecast horizon. In general, there will not always be an individual analyst (or forecasting model) that dominates all other analysts (or models). In this case, the decision maker faces the difficult issue of how to weight the forecast errors of different years over the forecast horizon. The decision context in which the forecasts will be used should guide the appropriate set of weights. For instance, one approach that is consistent with a multiyear equity valuation model (see Chapter 12) is to weight the forecast errors of earlier years in the horizon more heavily than those of later years.

3. The example also facilitates the discussion of consensus forecasts. A consensus forecast represents the "average" forecast of individual forecasters. Alternative ways of computing the consensus include the median of the individual forecasts, the equally weighted mean, and a weighted mean (where the weights could reflect, say, the individual forecaster's past track record in forecasting accuracy). Weighting each analyst equally in the example gives the following consensus forecasts and percentage error rates:

	One Year Ahead	Two Years Ahead	Three Years Ahead	Four Years Ahead	Five Years Ahead
Consensus forecast	$1.58	$2.08	$2.65	$3.55	$4.37
% Forecast error	3.7%	3.3%	1.5%	−5.3%	−9.3%

For each year of the forecast horizon, the consensus forecast in this example outperforms each individual forecaster. In Section 8.6, evidence on the properties of consensus forecasts is presented.

Survey research by Moizer and Arnold (1982) and Arnold, Moizer, and Noreen (1983) indicates that most security analysts claim to have a multiyear horizon. This evidence is based on the response by security analysts to a question concerning the horizon used in their earnings forecasts:

Forecast Horizon	American Security Analysts (102 responses)	British Security Analysts (200 responses)
Up to 3 months	1%	1%
4–6 months	0	2
7–12 months	15	22
13–24 months	27	49
2–3 years	36	19
4–5 years	12	
Greater than 5 years	7	4
No forecast	2	3

Some 84% of American security analysts and 75% of British security analysts reported using a forecast horizon longer than 12 months ahead.

8.4 PROPERTIES OF SECURITY ANALYST FORECASTS

Security analyst forecasts of earnings can be obtained from both (1) primary sources—the reports issued by individual analysts—and (2) secondary sources—the reports of services that collect and distribute earnings forecasts made by analysts at many institutions. Examples of secondary sources include (a) Lynch, Jones and Ryan's Institutional Brokers Estimate System (IBES), (b) Standard & Poor's The Earnings Forecaster, and (c) Zacks Investment Research's Icarus Service.

Figure 8.2 presents an extract from the IBES Monthly Summary Data Book of Lynch, Jones and Ryan. Figure 8.3 presents an extract from the monthly report of The Icarus Service of Zacks Investment Research, Inc. Both IBES and Icarus collect from individual security analysts details of their earnings-per-share forecasts for one year ahead (FY1) and two years ahead (FY2) and their estimate of a five-year earnings-per-share growth rate. Subscribers to these services can access data relating to individual companies and to individual security analysts. In addition, each service reports "summary data" based on (1) aggregates of individual analysts for each firm and (2) aggregates of individual analysts for all firms in an industry.

A. Forecast Revision Evidence

Research on security analyst forecast revisions has found several results that appear relatively robust.

1. In any one calendar month, only a minority of security analysts will report a revision of their earnings forecasts. For instance, Brown, Foster, and Noreen (1985) report that over the 1976–1980 period, the individual security analysts in

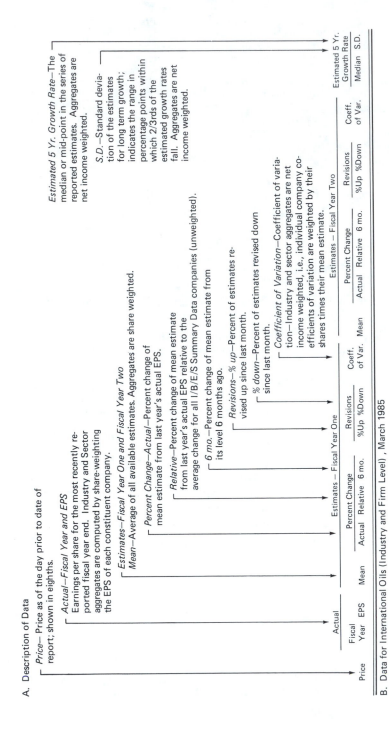

A. Description of Data

Price— Price as of the day prior to date of report; shown in eighths.

Actual—Fiscal Year and EPS
Earnings per share for the most recently reported fiscal year end. Industry and Sector aggregates are computed by share-weighting the EPS of each constituent company.

Estimates—Fiscal Year One and Fiscal Year Two
Mean—Average of all available estimates. Aggregates are share weighted.

Percent Change—Actual—Percent change of mean estimate from last year's actual EPS.

Relative—Percent change of mean estimate from last year's actual EPS relative to the average change for all I/B/E/S Summary Data companies (unweighted).

6 mo.—Percent change of mean estimate from its level 6 months ago.

Revisions—% up—Percent of estimates revised up since last month.

% down—Percent of estimates revised down since last month.

Coefficient of Variation—Coefficient of variation—Industry and sector aggregates are net income weighted, i.e., individual company coefficients of variation are weighted by their shares times their mean estimate.

Estimated 5 Yr. Growth Rate—The median or mid-point in the series of reported estimates. Aggregates are net income weighted.

S.D.—Standard deviation of the estimates for long term growth; indicates the range in percentage points within which 2/3rds of the estimated growth rates fall. Aggregates are net income weighted.

B. Data for International Oils (Industry and Firm Level), March 1985

| | | Actual | | Estimates — Fiscal Year One | | | | | | | Estimates — Fiscal Year Two | | | | | | | Estimated 5 Yr. Growth rate | |
| | | | | | Percent Change | | | Revisions | | | | Percent Change | | | Revisions | | | | |
Sector/Industry/Company	Price	Fiscal Year	EPS	Mean	Actual	Relative	6 mo.	%Up	%Down	Coeff. of Var.	Mean	Actual	Relative	6 mo.	%Up	%Down	Coeff. of Var.	Median	S.D.
INTERNATIONAL OILS			5.77	6.23	8.1	0.86	-4.8	5	26	5.4	6.87	19.1	0.79	-1.8	5	5	6.6	7	3
CHEVRON CORP	34-1	12/84	4.48	4.69	4.6	0.83	-15.5	3	24	8.1	5.82	30.0	0.86	NA			16.1	7	4
EXXON	49-2	12/84	6.77	6.84	1.1	0.80	-0.1	14	20	3.9	7.47	10.3	0.73	NA			2.7	7	3
MOBIL CORP	29-5	12/84	3.12	3.54	13.4	0.90	-18.4		36	9.8	4.20	34.6	0.89	NA			12.4	7	3
ROYAL DUTCH PETE	54-0	12/83	9.59	11.12	16.0	0.92	3.4	12	4	5.5	11.61	21.0	0.80	-1.1	8	8	4.6	7	3
SHELL TRANS&TRAD	33-7	12/83	5.79	7.00	20.9	0.96	1.2			1.5	7.41	28.0	0.85	-2.9			7.1	10	1
TEXACO	35-2	12/84	4.45	4.61	3.7	0.82	-17.5		42	10.1	4.93	10.9	0.74	NA			6.1	7	3

FIGURE 8.2 Extract from Monthly Summary Report of the IBES Service
Source: Lynch, Jones, and Ryan, *IBES Monthly Summary Data* (New York, NY).

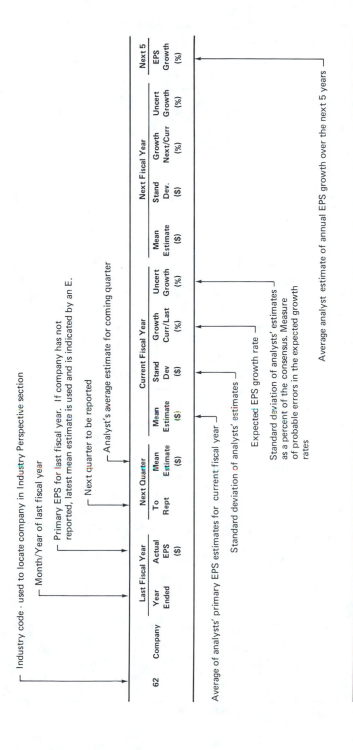

A. Description of Data

Industry code - used to locate company in Industry Perspective section

Month/Year of last fiscal year

Primary EPS for last fiscal year. If company has not reported, latest mean estimate is used and is indicated by an E.

Next quarter to be reported

Analyst's average estimate for coming quarter

| | | Last Fiscal Year | | Next Quarter | | Current Fiscal Year | | | | Next Fiscal Year | | | | Next 5 |
		Year Ended	Actual EPS ($)	To Rept	Mean Estimate ($)	Mean Estimate ($)	Stand Dev ($)	Growth Curr/Last (%)	Uncert Growth (%)	Mean Estimate ($)	Stand Dev. ($)	Growth Next/Curr (%)	Uncert Growth (%)	EPS Growth (%)
62	Company													

Average of analysts' primary EPS estimates for current fiscal year

Standard deviation of analysts' estimates

Expected EPS growth rate

Standard deviation of analysts' estimates as a percent of the consensus. Measure of probable errors in the expected growth rates

Average analyst estimate of annual EPS growth over the next 5 years

B. Data for Companies

| Company | Last Fiscal Year | | Next Quarter | | Current Fiscal Year | | | | Next Fiscal Year | | | | Next 5 |
	Year Ended	Actual EPS ($)	To Rept	Mean Estimate ($)	Mean Estimate ($)	Stand Dev ($)	Growth Curr/Last (%)	Uncert Growth (%)	Mean Estimate ($)	Stand Dev ($)	Growth Next/Curr (%)	Uncert Growth (%)	EPS Growth (%)
AMERICAN MTRS C	12/84	0.04	MAR	−0.03	0.24	0.24	N/A	99.2	−0.34	0.09	N/A	26.1	N/A
CHRYSLER CORP	12/84	11.75	MAR	4.08	12.34	1.50	4.9	12.1	9.13	3.66	−25.9	40.1	11.1
FORD MTR CO	12/84	15.79	MAR	4.53	14.20	1.46	−10.0	10.2	12.31	4.63	−13.3	37.5	8.0
GENERAL MOTORS	12/84	14.22	MAR	4.19	14.99	1.37	5.4	9.1	13.63	3.94	−9.1	28.9	8.4

FIGURE 8.3 Extract from Monthly Summary Report of the Icarus Service
Source: Zacks Investment Research, Inc., *The Icarus Service* (Chicago, Illinois).

the IBES data base had the following average monthly revisions statistics (expressed in relative frequency terms):

	Forecasts of One-Year-Ahead EPS (FY1)	Forecasts of Two-Year-Ahead EPS (FY2)
Downward revisions (↓)	.102	.074
No change (0)	.772	.838
Upward revisions (↑)	.126	.088
	1.000	1.000

Possible explanations for the large number of observations in the "no change" category for each month include (1) most analysts follow a large number of securities and do not have the time to do a detailed analysis of each company each month, and (2) only a small set of stocks in any one month have significant unexpected information releases that prompt analysts to revise their forecasts.

Buchenroth and Jennings (1984) present evidence on the relative frequency of changes in weekly consensus earnings-per-share forecasts reported in the Icarus data base. The results cover the 1978–1983 period for a sample of 805 firms with calendar year fiscal year ends; the average number of analysts per firm ranged from three in 1978 to eight in 1982. The consensus measure examined was the mean of the individual analyst forecasts. Data were presented for each of one- to eight-quarter-ahead forecasts: "The quarters-ahead classification denotes the maximum time ahead of the forecast. Thus, the eight-quarter-ahead forecast denotes forecasts which range from 24 months to 21 months and a day prior to the year-end; and the one-quarter-ahead forecast classification includes forecasts 1–90 days prior" (p. 8). Results are presented in Table 8.2. The authors concluded that "as the forecast horizon lengthens, there are fewer small weekly changes in the (weekly consensus earnings forecast) and more large changes" (p. 8).

2. When analysts forecast earnings per share for each of several years of a forecast horizon, there is positive correlation in the sign of contemporaneous forecast revisions across years of the horizon. Brown, Foster, and Noreen (1985) report evidence on individual security analysts at Wells Fargo Investment Advisors. In the 1977–1980 period, these analysts forecast earnings-per-share for

TABLE 8.2 Relative Frequency of Weekly Changes in Security Analyst EPS Forecasts: Icarus Data Base

Size of Change	Quarters Ahead							
	8	7	6	5	4	3	2	1
0%	.781	.831	.826	.842	.836	.863	.837	.854
0–5%	.072	.109	.112	.117	.130	.087	.102	.104
5–10%	.022	.023	.017	.016	.003	.013	.014	.015
10–25%	.026	.015	.012	.012	.011	.010	.013	.012
>25%	.091	.022	.033	.013	.020	.027	.034	.015

SOURCE: Buchenroth and Jennings (1984, Table 4): p. 8.

each year of a five-year forecast horizon. The relative frequency of a revision (in any single month) for each year of the forecast horizon is:

	Year 1 (FY1)	Year 2 (FY2)	Year 3 (FY3)	Year 4 (FY4)	Year 5 (FY5)
Downward revisions (↓)	.093	.076	.054	.046	.041
No change (0)	.794	.838	.870	.876	.886
Upward revisions (↑)	.113	.086	.076	.078	.073

Consider now the relative frequency of a revision for year 2 (year 3, year 4, year 5) given a revision for year 1 *in the same month*:

$$FY2 \downarrow \mid FY1 \downarrow = .574 \qquad FY3 \downarrow \mid FY1 \downarrow = .412$$
$$FY4 \downarrow \mid FY1 \downarrow = .350 \qquad FY5 \downarrow \mid FY1 \downarrow = .321$$

$$FY2 \uparrow \mid FY1 \uparrow = .616 \qquad FY3 \uparrow \mid FY1 \uparrow = .503$$
$$FY4 \uparrow \mid FY1 \uparrow = .484 \qquad FY5 \uparrow \mid FY1 \uparrow = .454$$

One consequence of this positive correlation in contemporaneous forecast revisions across years of the horizon is reduction of the incremental information content of forecast revisions in the later years of the horizon (given access to the forecast revisions in the early years of the horizon).

B. Forecast Error Evidence

Much research has been conducted on the properties of forecast errors made by security analysts. The most consistent finding in the literature is that the magnitude of the forecast error made by security analysts is reduced as the announcement month of the earnings per share being forecast is approached. Table 8.3 presents from the Brown, Foster, and Noreen (1985) study the behavior of the mean absolute forecast error in months -22, -18, -14, -10, -6, and -2, where month 0 is the month in which the actual earnings per share is announced. The data base is consensus earnings-per-share forecasts as reported by IBES for approximately 500 U.S. firms over the 1976–1980 period. The absolute forecast error is computed four ways:

1. Undeflated
2. Deflated by the average absolute change in earnings per share over the 1976–1980 period
3. Deflated by security price at end of forecast month
4. Deflated by actual earnings per share.

Two means are reported in Table 8.3: (1) mean based on all observations and (2) truncated mean computed by excluding the ten most extreme negative and the ten most extreme positive observations. The motivation for including the truncated mean is that the effect of large observations on general patterns in the data is reduced. Figure 8.4 presents the .9, .7, .5, .3, and .1 fractiles of the distribution for the absolute forecast error deflated by the average absolute change in earnings per share over the 1976–1980 period. Analysis of fractiles is another way of minimizing the effect that extreme observations can have on general patterns in the data. Both Table 8.3 and Figure 8.4 report a similar pattern. Security analyst earnings-per-share forecasts become more accurate as the announcement month of the actual earnings-per-share is approached. This result is not surprising. For instance, during the -8- to -1-month period, analysts are able to observe interim earnings-per-share figures that comprise a part of the annual earnings per share being forecast. A second explanation for this increase in accuracy (and reduction in dispersion) is the expansion of information available to analysts about the conditions that will prevail for the remainder of the horizon period left to forecast. These results pertain to forecasts made in the 1976–1980 period. Crichfield, Dyckman, and Lakonishok (1978) present similar results for forecasts made in the 1967–1976 period.

What are the sources of security analyst earnings forecast errors? Interesting evidence on this issue is presented by Elton, Gruber, and Gultekin (1984). For a sample of IBES firms, they examined how much of the forecast error is due to (1) "the inability of analysts to predict what earnings per share will be for the economy (actually for the total of firms in our sample)," (2) "the analysts' misestimating the differential performance of individual industries," and (3) "the inability to predict how each firm will differ from its industry average" (p. 356). The percentage decomposition for forecasts made in selected months for a sample of December 31 fiscal-year firms in the 1976–1978 period was

Forecast Month	Economy Component	Industry Component	Firm Component
March	2.4%	36.2%	61.4%
June	2.7	29.4	67.9
September	2.7	26.5	70.8
December	.8	15.5	83.7

The conclusion was that "the vast majority of error in forecasting arises from misestimates of industry performance and company performance" (p. 358).

C. Security Analysts versus Time-Series Models

The two most accessible sources of earnings forecasts are security analysts and mechanical (typically univariate time-series) models. Table 8.4 summarizes the pros and cons of both approaches. Many studies have examined the relative accuracy of earnings-per-share forecasts made by security analysts and univariate time-series models. The dominant finding in studies conducted over the past decade is that security analysts provide more accurate forecasts than time-series models. A comprehensive study is Brown, Griffin, Hagerman, and Zmijewski (1984). The sample was 233 firms over the 1975–1980 period. Analyst forecasts contained in *The Value Line Investment Survey* were compared with forecasts made by three univariate Box-Jenkins time-series models. An important strength

TABLE 8.3 Mean Absolute Forecast Error: Effect of Length of Forecast Horizon for Firms in IBES Data Base

Error Measure	Month Relative to Month Actual EPS Announced					
	−22	−18	−14	−10	−6	−2
A. | *Actual–forecast* |						
Mean	1.08	.94	.81	.65	.46	.25
Truncated mean	.94	.84	.73	.59	.41	.22
B. $\dfrac{\mid Actual\text{–}forecast \mid}{\text{Average absolute change in EPS}}$						
Mean	1.14	.99	.83	.65	.47	.27
Truncated mean	1.11	.97	.81	.64	.46	.26
C. $\dfrac{\mid Actual\text{–}forecast \mid}{\text{Security price}} \times 100$						
Mean	4.69	4.44	4.35	3.53	2.57	1.56
Truncated Mean	3.97	3.88	3.69	2.96	2.10	1.18
D. $\dfrac{\mid Actual\text{–}forecast \mid}{\text{Actual}}$						
Mean	.39	.43	.33	.23	.18	.10
Truncated mean	.26	.27	.22	.18	.13	.08

SOURCE: Brown, Foster, and Noreen (1985, Table 3.9): p. 56.

FIGURE 8.4 Deciles of Distribution of Mean Absolute Forecast Error (Deflated by Average Absolute Change in EPS): Effect of Length of Forecast Horizon for Firms in IBES Data Base

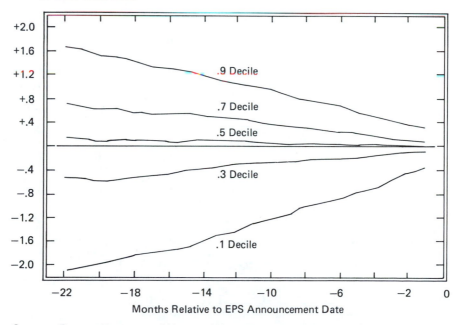

Source: Brown, Foster, and Noreen (1985, Figure 3.2): p. 44.

TABLE 8.4 Pros and Cons of Security Analyst and Univariate Time-Series Model Approaches to Forecasting

---

SECURITY ANALYST APPROACH TO FORECASTING
Pros

1. Ability to incorporate information from many sources.
2. Ability to adjust to structural change immediately.
3. Ability to update continually as new information becomes available.

Cons

1. High initial setup cost and high ongoing cost to monitor numerous variables, make company visits, and so on.
2. Heavy dependence on the skills of a single individual.
3. Analyst may have an incentive not to provide an unbiased forecast (e.g., due to pressure to conform to consensus forecasts).
4. Analyst may be manipulated by company officials (at least in the short run).

UNIVARIATE TIME-SERIES MODEL APPROACH TO FORECASTING
Pros

1. Ability to detect and exploit systematic patterns in the past series.
2. Relatively low degree of subjectivity in the forecasting (especially given the availability of computer algorithms to identify and estimate models).
3. Low cost and ease of updating.
4. Ability to compute confidence intervals around the forecasts.

Cons

1. Limited number of observations available for newly formed firms, firms with structural change, and so on.
2. Financial statement data may not satisfy distributional assumptions of time-series model used.
3. Inability to update forecasts between successive interim or annual earnings releases.
4. Difficulty of communicating approach to clients (especially the statistical methodology used in identifying and estimating univariate models).

TABLE 8.5 Univariate Box-Jenkins Models versus Value Line Security Analyst Forecasts of Quarterly EPS: Mean Absolute Forecast Error

Forecast Horizon	Forecast Model	Fiscal Quarter Being Forecast			
		First	Second	Third	Fourth
One Quarter Ahead	Box-Jenkins #1	.259 (3)	.263 (3)	.288 (2)	.309 (3)
	Box-Jenkins #2	.268 (4)	.268 (4)	.302 (4)	.322 (4)
	Box-Jenkins #3	.251 (2)	.253 (2)	.294 (3)	.302 (2)
	Value Line	.234 (1)	.214 (1)	.221 (1)	.217 (1)
Two Quarters Ahead	Box-Jenkins #1	.307 (3)	.319 (3)	.300 (3)	.305 (2.5)
	Box-Jenkins #2	.316 (4)	.327 (4)	.324 (4)	.316 (4)
	Box-Jenkins #3	.306 (2)	.318 (2)	.299 (2)	.305 (2.5)
	Value Line	.267 (1)	.276 (1)	.264 (1)	.246 (1)
Three Quarters Ahead	Box-Jenkins #1	.332 (2)	.325 (3)	.291 (2)	.343 (4)
	Box-Jenkins #2	.335 (3)	.336 (4)	.301 (4)	.337 (3)
	Box-Jenkins #3	.342 (4)	.321 (2)	.300 (3)	.332 (2)
	Value Line	.291 (1)	.300 (1)	.252 (1)	.299 (1)

SOURCE: Brown, Griffin, Hagerman, and Zmijewski (1984): p. 33.

of the study was the detailed analysis of different forecast horizons and different fiscal quarters being forecast. Table 8.5 presents the mean absolute forecast error for the Value Line security analyst forecasts and for the following three univariate time-series models:

> Box-Jenkins 1: Moving-average model in seasonally differenced series, as discussed in Watts (1975) and Griffin (1977)
>
> Box-Jenkins 2: Autoregressive model in seasonally differenced series, as discussed in Foster (1977)
>
> Box-Jenkins 3: Combined autoregressive, moving-average model in seasonally differenced series, as discussed in Brown and Rozeff (1979).

Each absolute forecast error is deflated by the absolute value of actual earnings, and any value of the error measure above 100% is reset to 100%. The rankings for each forecast horizon/fiscal quarter are also presented in Table 8.5. The striking result is that the Value Line security analyst forecast is more accurate than each of the three Box-Jenkins models on all 12 forecast horizon/fiscal quarter combinations. A second result in Table 8.5 is that the mean absolute forecast error for a given forecast model/fiscal quarter being forecast is an increasing function of the horizon length; for example, two-quarter-ahead forecasts have higher absolute forecast errors than do one-quarter-ahead forecasts.

There are several potential explanations for security analysts producing more accurate forecasts than univariate time-series models:

1. Analysts have a timing advantage over forecasts made by time-series models. In many research studies, the security analyst forecasts examined were made *after* the release of the most recent observation of interim or annual earnings. Given the continual flow of information about firms, analysts can incorporate information about events occurring after the release of the most recent earnings figure. Brown et al. (1984) report that analysts are able to improve their forecasts over time. However, they find that when analysts' forecasts made *prior* to the release of the most recent earnings figure used by the time-series model are examined, the analysts' forecasts "are at least as accurate as time-series model forecasts" (p. 23).

2. Analysts have access to a broader information set than just the past time-series used by the univariate models. For instance, analysts can also access information about macroeconomic forecasts, the competitive structure of a firm's industry, events such as acquisitions or divestitures, and so on. An interesting study providing some support for this factor is Collins and Hopwood (1980). These authors concluded that Value Line analysts had "means and standard deviations of forecast errors lower than those generated" (p. 397) by four univariate Box-Jenkins models. They then analyzed the extreme forecast errors in their sample and concluded that "analysts generated outliers that were lower both in number and degree than the univariate models. Investigation into the economic events that were the underlying causes of these outliers (for example, a strike) generally indicated that

analysts were more capable of incorporating the effects of these economic events as the events became known. The univariate models tended to lag in reaction until the effects of these economic events were incorporated in reported earnings'' (p. 402).

8.5 PROPERTIES OF MANAGEMENT FORECASTS

Forecasts of earnings, sales, or other variables that are publicly released by management differ from those issued by security analysts on several dimensions:

1. Management forecasts are released by only a subset of firms, whereas, security analyst forecasts typically are available for a broad cross section of firms. Some firms that are tracked by a large number of security analysts have an explicit policy of prohibiting the external release of management forecasts.

2. Firms releasing management forecasts typically release only one forecast each year, whereas security analysts publish revisions of their forecasts throughout the year.

3. Management forecasts are not always issued as point estimates. Phrases such as "earnings will be at least $X" and "earnings are expected to show adverse comparisons with the prior year" are used in some corporate releases.

Most management forecasts are for one-year-ahead aggregate earnings or earnings per share, with limited accompanying documentation of the assumptions underlying the forecast. In a small subset of cases, firms provide more disaggregated information. Figure 8.5 presents an extract from the 1983 Annual Report of Masco Corporation. Masco presents forecasts of a five-year growth rate for sales, plus a five-year cash flow forecast; also disclosed are key assumptions used in the forecasts. Masco's annual report has won awards for "excellence in financial reporting" from organizations such as the Financial Analysts Federation and *Financial World*.

A. Characteristics of Firms Voluntarily Disclosing Forecasts

Firms that publicly release management forecasts do not appear to be a random sample of all firms. Several studies have examined the characteristics of firms disclosing forecasts vis-à-vis firms not publicly disclosing such forecasts or a random sample of firms. One consistent finding is that disclosing firms have a less variable earnings (or earnings-per-share) series. For instance, Imhoff (1978) examined a sample of 92 firms disclosing forecasts and a "random sample of (100) non-forecast firms" (p. 842). For each of four earnings series (net income, net income before extraordinary items, operating income, and earnings per share) the forecast firms had lower earnings variability. Waymire (1985) further explored

FIGURE 8.5 Management Forecast Disclosure by Masco Corporation

FIVE-YEAR FORECAST

We have included in this annual report a sales forecast for each of our major product lines and operating groups for 1988.

While we recognize that long-term forecasts are subject to many variables and uncertainties, our experience has been that our success is determined more by our own activities than by the performance of any industry or the economy in general. In addition, the balance and diversity of our products and markets have been such that a shortfall in expected performance in one area has been largely offset by higher than anticipated growth in another.

Although variations may occur in the forecast for any individual product line, we have a relatively high level of confidence that our overall five-year growth forecast is achievable.

ASSUMPTIONS USED IN FORECAST

1. Average 2-3 percent annual real growth in GNP.
2. Average inflation 5-7 percent.
3. Present tax structure to continue.
4. No change in currency exchange rates.
5. No acquisitions.
6. No additional financing.
7. Dividend payout ratio 20 percent.
8. Four percent after-tax return on investment of excess cash.
9. No exercise of stock options.

FIVE-YEAR CASH FLOW FORECAST

(In Thousands)	1984-1988
Net Income	$ 850,000
Depreciation	280,000
	1,130,000
Working Capital	(230,000)
Note Payments	(280,000)
Capital Expenditures	(260,000)
Dividends	(170,000)
Net Cash Change	190,000
Beginning Cash, 1-1-84	210,000
Cash, 12-31-88	$ 400,000

SALES GROWTH BY PRODUCTS

(In Thousands)

	Sales Forecast		Actual Sales		
	5-Year Growth Rate 1984-1988	1988	5-Year Growth Rate 1979-1983	1983	1978
Products for the Home and Family	14%	$1,225,000	16%	$ 638,000	$308,000
Products for Industry	16%	875,000	9%	421,000	278,000
Total Sales	15%	$2,100,000	13%	$1,059,000	$586,000

SALES GROWTH BY SPECIFIC MARKETS AND PRODUCTS [1][2]

(In Thousands)

	Forecast		Actual		
	5-Year Growth Rate 1984-1988	1988	5-Year Growth Rate 1979-1983	1983	1978
Masco Faucet Sales [3]	15%	$490,000	9%	$243,000	$155,000
Faucet Industry Sales-Units	7%	35,000	(5)%	25,000	32,000
Masco Market Share-Units	2%	38%	5%	34%	27%
Housing Completions	4%	1,700	(4)%	1,400	1,700
Independent Cold Extrusion Industry Sales	13%	$580,000	1%	$310,000	$290,000
Masco Cold Extrusion Sales [3]	14%	$170,000	5%	$ 88,000	$ 70,000
Truck Production	7%	3,400	(8)%	2,400	3,700
Auto Production	4%	8,200	(6)%	6,800	9,200
Masco Auto Parts Sales	13%	$210,000	8%	$113,000	$ 76,000

(1) Excludes foreign sales.　(2) Industry data Masco estimates.　(3) Includes foreign sales.

Source: 1983 Annual Report of Masco Corporation, p. 42.

this issue in an analysis of 466 forecasts of annual earnings per share by company executives that were reported in *The Wall Street Journal*. The sample was partitioned into "repeat forecasters" (more than one management forecast in the 1968–1973 period) and "non-repeat forecasters" (only one management forecast in the 1968–1973 period). Using several variability measures, it was found that "firms which issue earnings forecasts more frequently are characterized by less volatile earnings processes relative to firms which issue such projections on an infrequent basis" (p. 1).

Another variable examined is firm size. Most studies have reported that disclosing firms are typically larger than nondisclosing firms; for example, "comparison of net asset sizes revealed a median size of $396 million for reporting firms as opposed to only $133 million for the nonreporting group" (Ruland, 1979, p. 194). The time-series variability and size differences between firms disclosing and not disclosing management earnings forecasts need not be independent. For instance, if larger firms typically have more lines of business than smaller firms, their lower earnings variability could reflect the diversification effect of these multiple lines of business.

Not only are there systematic differences between disclosing and nondisclosing firms, but there also appear to be systematic differences between the times when disclosing firms release and do not release forecasts. Disclosing firms appear more likely to release forecasts when they have "good news" to convey than when they have "bad news." For instance, Penman (1980) examined a sample of 737 cases where management issued forecasts of annual earnings per share in the 1968–1973 period. Using both monthly and daily security return data surrounding these 737 forecasts, Penman examined whether the returns of voluntary disclosing firms are, on average, higher than those for the market as a whole. The finding was that "forecasting firms, on average, enjoy 'good times' during the three months on either side of the forecast date (as well as) on the day of the forecast announcement" (p. 155).

B. Forecast Error Evidence

Many studies report summary statistics pertaining to the accuracy of management forecasts. A representative study is Hagerman and Ruland (1979). The source was management forecasts that were reported in the "December, January, and February *Wall Street Journal* editions for the five-year period beginning in December 1968" (p. 173). The forecast horizon period ranged from 8 to 14 months. The variable examined was earnings per share before extraordinary items. Summary statistics are

	.25 Fractile	*.5 Fractile*	*.75 Fractile*
Absolute forecast error (%)	2.4%	7.4%	22.9%

The authors also reported a significant correlation between the length of the forecast horizon and the accuracy of management forecasts (that is, the accuracy of management forecasts increases as the horizon is reduced).

One issue not yet examined in detail is whether the distribution of management forecast errors depends on the context in which the forecast is released. For instance, are management forecasts issued at the time of a hostile takeover bid for the company more likely to be optimistic compared to forecasts issued at the annual company meeting? Similarly, are management forecasts issued at the time of a leveraged buyout likely to be pessimistic compared to forecasts issued when the firm is making an all-equity takeover bid for another company?

C. Management versus Security Analysts

Management forecasts potentially can incorporate internal information such as future production plans and advertising budgets. An interesting issue is whether management forecasts are more accurate than those made by security analysts. Survey research has reported that one rationale cited by management for voluntarily forecasting is to "improve" the forecasts made by security analysts; see Lees (1981). Two illustrative studies are Hassell and Jennings (1984) and Waymire (1984). Hassell and Jennings (1984) examined a sample of 116 management forecasts of earnings per share made over the 1979–1982 period. These forecasts were compared to analyst consensus forecasts reported in Zacks Investment Company's Icarus Service; consensus analyst forecasts were collected both before and after the week of the management forecast (termed week 0). Forecast accuracy was measured as

$$\frac{\text{Forecasted EPS} - \text{Actual EPS}}{|\text{Actual EPS}|}$$

All firms in the sample had positive actual earnings per share. A Wilcoxon signed rank test was used to compare the relative accuracy of the management forecast in week 0 with security analyst consensus forecasts in the weeks surrounding week 0. Table 8.6 presents the Z statistic for this test (approximately normally distributed) in the -4-week to $+12$-week period surrounding the week of the management earnings forecast. A negative (positive) Z score in Table 8.6 means that the consensus analyst forecast is less (more) accurate than the management forecast released in week 0. The results in Table 8.6 are consistent with consensus analyst forecasts prior to, and at the time of, the release of the management forecast being less accurate than the management forecast. In the weeks subsequent to week 0, security analyst consensus forecasts become progressively more accurate than the management forecast. Waymire (1984) also reports a similar finding for a sample of 425 management forecasts of earnings per share made in the 1970–1973 period. One explanation for this result is that management has

TABLE 8.6 Relative Accuracy of Security Analyst Consensus EPS Forecast (Icarus Data Base) Relative to Management EPS Forecast Released in Week Zero

Week Relative to Management Forecast Announcement Week	Median Security Analyst Forecast Error	Median Management Forecast Error	Z Statistic for Difference Between Security Analyst Forecast Error and Management Forecast Error
− 4	.106	—	− 4.83**
− 3	.109	—	− 4.79**
− 2	.102	—	− 4.65**
− 1	.104	—	− 4.63**
0	.097	.065	− 4.37**
+ 1	.093	—	− 3.70**
+ 2	.077	—	− 2.83**
+ 3	.073	—	− 2.29*
+ 4	.071	—	− 1.91
+ 5	.063	—	− .80
+ 6	.062	—	− .09
+ 7	.055	—	1.44
+ 8	.057	—	1.90
+ 9	.051	—	2.58**
+10	.042	—	4.51**
+11	.035	—	5.63**
+12	.026	—	6.14**

* Significant at .05 level.
**Significant at .01 level.
SOURCE: Hassell and Jennings (1984, Tables 2–3): pp 27–28.

access to nonpublic information and that they use their earnings forecasts as a means of publicly communicating this information.

Schreuder and Klaassen (1984) conducted a related study using 53 forecasts of a "representative" sample of companies listed on the Amsterdam Stock Exchange and 124 forecasts provided by members of the Dutch Financial Analysts Federation. A key feature of the study was that the management forecasts were "confidential internal" forecasts. Both revenue and profit forecasts were examined. The conclusion was that for revenue forecasts "all prediction errors are smaller for management than for the analysts, although the differences are not very impressive" (p. 72); for the profit series, "management and analysts did not differ very much in their forecasting characteristics" (p. 73).

Several difficult issues arise when making comparisons between security analyst and management forecasts:

1. The loss function facing management and security analysts when forecasting need not be the same.
2. Analysts and management derive reciprocal benefits from interacting with each other. There are incentives on both sides to communicate information, even when "insider trading" laws exist. The result is that an external researcher finds it difficult to discriminate among competing explanations for

a finding of no difference in forecast errors; for example, (a) neither management nor analysts have a comparative advantage in forecasting, or (b) management has significant superiority in forecasting but shares its forecast (and possibly its assumptions) with analysts without ''publicly'' releasing that forecast.

3. Management has the ability to influence the variable being forecast via its financing, operating, or production decisions and may have strong economic incentives (for example, compensation plan effects) to have the firm report a particular level of earnings. In contrast, security analysts cannot take such actions to make their forecasts more accurate.

8.6 GAINS FROM AGGREGATING INDIVIDUAL FORECASTS

This section discusses evidence on the gains from aggregating forecasts made by individual security analysts and by aggregating forecasts made by different forecasting approaches.

A. Aggregating Over Individual Forecasters

For many economic series, forecasts are available from numerous individual forecasters. An important finding in several different contexts is that consensus forecasts are more accurate than the individual forecasts underlying the consensus. Much research in this area has examined macroeconomic forecasts. A representative study is Zarnowitz (1982), which examined the forecasts of 79 individuals participating in surveys made by the National Bureau of Economic Research and the American Statistical Association. Variables covered in the surveys included percentage changes in nominal and real GNP, the implicit price deflator and consumer expenditures for durable goods. The accuracy of individual forecasters was compared with the group average forecast. The conclusion was

> The group mean forecasts from a series of surveys on the average over time are more accurate than most of the corresponding sets of individual predictions. This is a strong conclusion, which applies to all variables and predictive horizons covered and is consistent with evidence for different periods and from other studies. . . . No single individual forecaster has been observed to earn a long record of superior overall accuracy, and indeed nothing in the present study would encourage us to expect any individual to reach this elusive goal. (pp. 20, 21)

One explanation for this result is that the forecast errors made by individual economists are less than perfectly correlated, and in the process of aggregation, many of the individual economist errors cancel each other out.

Related research has been conducted using security analyst forecasts of earnings per share. Coggin and Hunter (1982–1983) used the IBES data base in a comparison of analyst consensus (arithmetic mean) forecasts, individual analyst forecasts, and the forecasts of three univariate time-series models. For a sample of 149 firms in 1978 and 180 firms in 1979, the ranking in terms of mean squared percentage error was

	1978	1979
Analyst consensus	1	1
Individual analyst	2	2
Linear trend model	3	4
Classical exponential model	5	5
Modified exponential model	4	3

The authors concluded that "the consensus was the best for one-year-ahead earnings-per-share forecasts for both target years" (p. 22). The difference between the consensus and each of the other four forecast methods was statistically significant at the .05 level in both years. The increasing coverage of firms by services such as IBES and Icarus means that consensus measures of earnings-per-share forecasts are available for a sizable number of listed securities.

B. Aggregating Across Forecasting Approaches

One of the most promising research areas is combining the forecasts made by diverse forecasting approaches to obtain composite forecasts. Early work in this area also focused on the forecasts of macroeconomic variables. For example, Cooper and Nelson (1975) illustrate how combining the forecasts of econometric models and Box-Jenkins time-series models can lead to improved forecasts of variables such as GNP and the unemployment rate. The conclusion was that "no single model or predictor can be said to dominate the others in the sense of subsuming their information content; rather, each generally contains a marginal increment of information which may be usefully exploited" (p. 30). More evidence supporting this result is in Makridakis and Winkler (1983). This study examined forecasts made by (1) purely judgmental approaches, (2) causal or explanatory (for example, econometric or regression) methods, and (3) extrapolative (time-series) methods. The conclusion was that "using averages of forecasts provides considerable practical benefits in terms of improved forecasting accuracy and decreased variability of accuracy" (p. 995).

A financial statement application of this approach would be to combine both time-series and security analyst forecasts into a composite forecast of earnings per share, earnings, and so on. As noted in Table 8.3, each has its pros and cons, and the combination of the two potentially offers the promise of improved forecast accuracy.

8.7 SOME GENERAL COMMENTS

1. Early research on earnings forecast errors made by management or security analysts focused on distribution statistics such as the mean or median forecast error. Subsequent research has examined the determinants of the magnitude

of forecast errors. (A detailed review of this literature is in the appendix to Brown, Foster, and Noreen, 1985.) The most general approach would be a model that posits that the magnitude of the forecast error is a function of N variables such as the following:

$$\text{FE}_{i,t} = f(\text{T}_i, \text{I}_i, \text{S}_i, \text{LOB}_i, \text{V}_i, \text{Y}, \text{A}, \text{F}, \ldots) \tag{8.10}$$

where

$\text{FE}_{i,t}$ = forecast error of ith firm in period t

T_i = time yet to elapse before the earnings of firm i for the period being forecast is announced

I_i = industry of firm i

S_i = size of firm i

LOB_i = number of lines of business of firm i

V_i = variability measure of past earnings series of firm i

Y = calendar year being forecast.

A = a coding of accounting method changes made by firm i during the forecast year

F = individual forecaster (for example, management or a security analyst) coding

Research to date has concentrated on individually exploring one of these variables, typically without controlling for the effect of the other $N - 1$ variables. The most consistent finding from this literature is that the time yet to elapse before the announcement of the earnings being forecast (T) is an important variable in (8.10).

There are several limitations when the explanatory variables on the right-hand side of (8.10) are individually examined rather than simultaneously examined in a multivariate research design. One limitation is that interaction effects among the variables are not captured. A second limitation is that correlations between the independent variables are not taken into account. A study may report three correlated variables (for example, S_i, LOB_i, and V_i) as individually significant determinants of forecast errors, when in fact all three are proxying for the same underlying factor.

2. Much of the early literature on forecasting financial statement variables focused on univariate forecasting approaches. Increasing attention is now being paid to multivariate forecasting approaches. An illustrative study is Ang, Chua, and Fatemi (1983). Five forecasting models were examined: an ordinary least squares econometric model, two time-series models (univariate and multivariate), and two combined models (combinations of the econometric model and one of the time-series models). Forecasts were made for monthly observations of seven accounting variables (for example, cash, net sales, cost of goods sold, and gross profit) for a firm in the rubber and plastics industry. The authors reported that for monthly observations over a 14-month period

a. Comparing time-series models, the multivariate model produced better forecasts than did the univariate model

   b. Comparing combinations of a time-series model and the ordinary least squares model, the OLS multivariate model performed better than did the OLS univariate model

   c. Overall, the multivariate model produced better forecasts than did the other four models. (p. 310)

Two similar studies are Downs and Rocke (1983) and Hillmer, Larcker, and Schroeder (1983). Using a municipal budget data base, Downs and Rocke (1983) report that "unlike univariate time-series methods, multivariate models can use relationships among budget variables as well as relationships with economic and demographic indicators. Although available budget series are shorter than what is usually believed necessary for multivariate modelling, the forecasts seem to be of higher quality than those from univariate models" (p. 377). Hillmer, Larcker, and Schroeder (1983) used data for three accounting series "from a manufacturing division of a large corporation." The conclusion was that multivariate time-series models yield smaller forecast variances than do univariate models. An important challenge facing work in this area is to exploit economic analysis when selecting independent variables to include in a multivariate model. One has more confidence in a forecasting model when there are some economic rationales for the variables included (and ideally in their structural relationships with the forecast variable).

   3. Research into the properties of consensus security analyst forecasts typically has used the arithmetic mean or the median of the forecasts of the individual analysts examined. Ideally, given a stationary set of data from N individual forecasters, weights could be applied to maximize an objective function (for example, minimize the mean squared forecast error); more weight (than $1/N$) might be given to an individual analyst who has both minimal bias and low dispersion in his or her forecast errors.

   Figlewski and Urich (1983) discuss the weighting issue in a study of forecasts of the weekly changes in the money supply; they outline "aggregation methods which adjust for additive bias, differences in individual accuracy, and correlation among forecasts" (p. 695). However, they conclude that the complex weighting schemes they examined "cannot improve on the accuracy of a simple average" (p. 695). Similar issues are important as regards aggregating security analyst earnings forecasts. The stationarity assumption underlying estimation of complex weighting schemes appears questionable at best for many series, especially given the high turnover in security analysts at some institutions. An additional factor is that the forecast from one institution may itself be a consensus of individual analysts; many of the gains from aggregating over diverse information sets may already be embedded in the forecast published by a single institution.

   Several services, such as IBES and Icarus, publish their own consensus forecast measures (mean and median) that are derived from individual analyst information included in their data bases. Conversations with individuals at these services indicate that their "ideal" measure would access a data base that

   a. Includes all analysts forecasting earnings per share for a specific company

b. Has each analyst instantaneously revising his or her forecast as new information becomes available

c. Has each analyst instantaneously reporting his or her revision to the service

d. Has each analyst forecasting the same earnings variable, for example, primary earnings per share before extraordinary items, where all analysts agree as to the meaning of an extraordinary item.

Clearly, this ideal world does not exist. However, we know little in a systematic way as to how (a)–(d) are not descriptive, for example, the nature of timing difference between an analyst revising a forecast and its inclusion in the IBES or Icarus system. Departures from conditions (a)–(d) could well be another reason why complex weighting schemes to compute consensus earnings forecasts may not yield significant gains over simpler schemes such as equal weighting.

4. An important research area is the cues that security analysts use when revising their earnings forecasts. An understanding of the important cues would help to structure the information collection and monitoring activities of investment firms. The typical analyst reports a forecast revision three to five times each year. Between successive revisions, many potential revision cues will have been published, for example, firm-oriented releases such as earnings, dividends, sales, and production reports; industry releases (including the releases of competing firms); and economywide releases such as money supply, inflation, and international trade balance reports. The relative importance of each of these and other possible cues is currently not well understood.

Discussions with analysts indicate that forecast revisions made by other analysts are important revision cues. Individuals in some industries develop reputations as "lead analysts" and much interest attaches to the direction of their forecast revisions. Analysts also report that high penalties are placed on taking positions that diverge markedly from the consensus when the consensus subsequently turns out to be "correct." The result can be that analysts make forecasts that diverge less from the consensus than what they would report in the absence of these penalties.

One variable that appears to be important in analyst forecast revisions is security returns. Brown, Foster, and Noreen (1985) examined abnormal security returns in the 12 months *preceding* the month (termed month 0) consensus security analyst forecast revisions were reported by IBES. The results were

Period Used to Cumulate Abnormal Security Returns	One-Year-Ahead EPS Revised Down in Month 0	One-Year-Ahead EPS Revised Up in Month 0
Months (-12, -10)	-1.25%	.51%
Months (-9, -7)	-1.58	1.18
Months (-6, -4)	-2.36	1.78
Month (-3)	-1.18	.85
Month (-2)	-1.54	1.05
Month (-1)	-1.41	1.02
Months (-12, -1)	-9.32	6.39

FIGURE 8.6 Security Analyst Consensus Forecast Revisions (IBES Data Base) and the Behavior of Security Returns

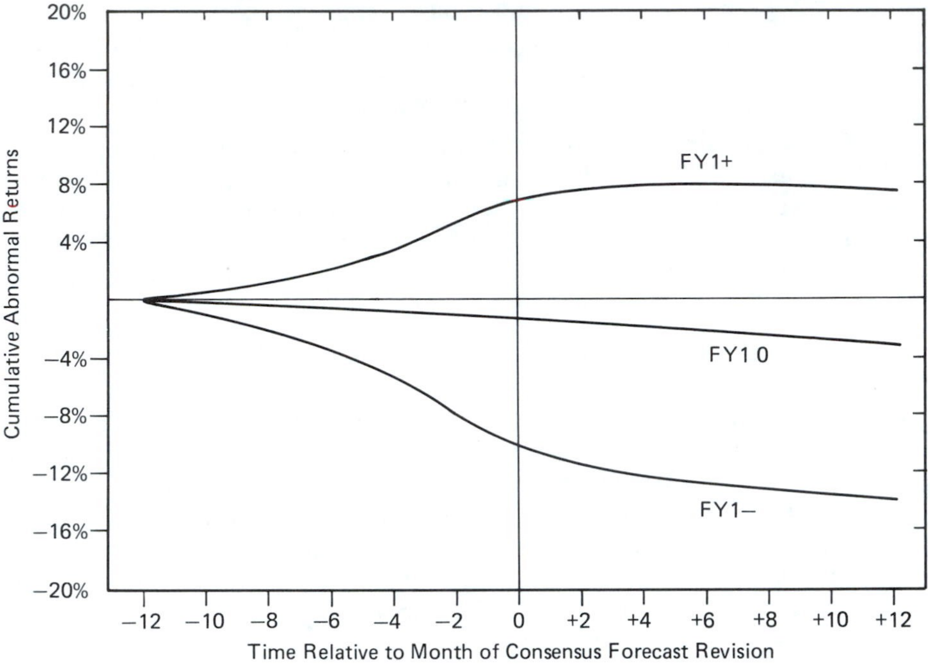

Source: Brown, Foster, and Noreen (1985, Figure 4.1): p. 72.

Downward consensus forecast revisions by analysts are preceded by a 9.32% decline in security returns, whereas upward forecast revisions are preceded by a 6.39% increase in security returns. Figure 8.6 presents the behavior of cumulative security returns for both the revised down and revised up consensus forecast revision groups. Finn (1984) presents similar evidence for earnings forecast revisions made by security analysts at an Australian institutional investment fund. One explanation for this finding is that analysts monitor security returns and use these as a prompt to their earnings forecasts revisions. The motivations for using security returns as an information base include (a) the aggregate capital market potentially is a more efficient processor of publicly available information than are individual security analysts, and (b) capital markets can impound information to which analysts do not yet have access (insider trading by management is one mechanism by which information internal to the firm is impounded). The traditional belief that security analyst opinions lead security price changes, rather than vice versa, may be in need of reconsideration.

8.8 SUMMARY

1. Forecasts of earnings and other related variables are important to many users of financial statement data. Forecasting approaches available to users differ

on important dimensions such as the information set examined and the explicitness of the link between the data inputs and the derived forecast.

2. There is considerable evidence on the properties of forecasts by security analysts and management and of mechanical time-series models. The increasing scope of data bases in this area is expanding the evidence available and decreasing the cost of obtaining that evidence.

3. A major limitation of much of the existing evidence is the absence of an explicit linkage to contexts such as investment decisions, credit decisions, and takeover/divestiture decisions. However, this limitation is no different from that for many other data reduction devices such as financial ratios and trend statements. The appropriate perspective is to understand this limitation and to attempt to appreciate how the data reduction devices can be used in actual decisions. Subsequent chapters of this book contain a more detailed analysis of investment, credit, merger, and other such decisions and of the role of forecasts in those decisions.

QUESTIONS

QUESTION 8.1: EPS Forecasting for Softcorp

Softcorp is a rapidly growing company specializing in the manufacture of software computer programs. The earnings-per-share (EPS) figures reported by the company in its first four years of existence were

Year 1	Year 2	Year 3	Year 4
($0.20)	$0.30	$1.10	$1.50

The company has a December 31 fiscal year.

Part A.   On March 25 of year 5, management issued a public press release forecasting EPS for the current fiscal year of $2.00. On September 15 another press release was issued updating the management earnings forecast to $2.20 per share. Forecasts made by security analysts for this same fiscal year included

- Analyst #1: $3.10 (March 10), $2.80 (July 18), and $2.50 (September 20)
- Analyst #2: $1.80 (April 1), $2.00 (June 11), and $2.10 (September 18)
- Analyst #3: $2.00 (March 28) and $2.20 (September 20)

On January 26 of year 6, Softcorp reported that EPS for year 5 was $2.40.

REQUIRED

1. Evaluate the relative accuracy of the management and security analyst EPS forecasts for year 5.

2. What factors could explain differences in the EPS forecasts made by management and security analysts?

3. What factors could explain differences in the EPS forecasts made by each of the three security analysts?

Part B. In year 6, Softcorp issued a press release on March 28 forecasting EPS for the current fiscal year of $3.50. On November 16 of the same fiscal year, management issued a press release forecasting EPS for the current fiscal year of $1.90. The press release cited problems due to new products not being as successful as management had anticipated and large write-downs associated with excessive inventories of products no longer high in demand. Its stock price dropped from $60 on November 15 to $35 on November 17. (It had been as high as $82 in August of that year.) Forecasts made by security analysts for this same fiscal year included

- Analyst #1: $3.80 (March 10), $4.00 (August 12), $3.60 (October 25), $2.00 (November 17)
- Analyst #2: $3.20 (March 30), $3.60 (August 20), $3.30 (November 10), $1.60 (November 17)
- Analyst #3: $3.50 (April 2), $3.70 (August 25), $1.85 (November 18)

On February 10 of year 7, Softcorp reported that EPS for year 6 was $1.75.

REQUIRED

1. Evaluate the relative accuracy of the management and security analyst EPS forecasts for year 6.

2. Analyst #2 made a company visit two weeks prior to the November 16 EPS forecast and interviewed senior management at Softcorp. Management did not convey to him the negative news released in the November 16 press release. How should he respond to the trenchant criticisms, made by several of his clients, of his November 10 report?

3. You have been hired as an expert witness by a group of institutional investors who bought sizable amounts of Softcorp stock in the six months prior to the November 16 press release. What information would you gather to determine whether (a) the actual results for the first three quarters of year 6 were overstated and (b) shareholders were damaged by material nondisclosures by the management of Softcorp?

QUESTION 8.2: Development and Use of Consensus EPS Forecast Data Bases

Investment Management Advisors is a consulting company that provides advice to clients developing and marketing products in the investment industry. A client (Rothschild & Partners) based outside North America reads the following information on the IBES service in a brochure from Lynch, Jones & Ryan:

> The I/B/E/S database contains statistical data relating to earnings-per-share estimates of over 3,300 publicly traded companies in the United States and Canada.

These estimates are made for one and two years in the future, one and two quarters in the future, plus a five-year growth forecast. Approximately 115 institutional brokerage firms provide the estimates and update them continually. The estimates, when given as summary statistics, are gathered together for each company. Historical monthly data is available back to January 1, 1976.

The brochure noted that the printed reports available to subscribers included:

Monthly Detail Reports include one and/or two year earnings forecasts in addition to long-term growth rate estimates for the companies you designate. Note that all estimates are identified by broker and analyst. Summary and historical statistics provide necessary perspectives.

Weekly Earnings Estimate Monitor tracks significant revisions in earnings in the periods between Monthly Detail Reports. Key summary statistics are updated to reflect changes in the basic data.

Monthly Digest ranks the universe on the percent change in consensus estimates which have occurred since last month. Since prices often react to changes in earnings expectations, subscribers find this report extremely valuable.

Monthly Summary Data published in indexed catalogue form, provides consensus earnings estimates for more than 3,300 companies in the IBES system.

I/B/E/S Monthly Comments offers interpretive analyses and amplification of IBES Summary Data pointing to developing trends and significant changes in analysts expectations for companies and industries.

Weekly Earnings Estimate Summary presents significant changes in consensus earnings estimates occurring between Monthly Summary Data volumes.

Investment Management Advisors is asked to examine a set of issues related to the development and marketing by Rothschild of a consensus forecast data base for EPS forecasts made by security analysts for non-North America-based companies. (Most of these security analysts are based outside of North America.)

REQUIRED

1. What are the pros and cons for the clients of Rothschild & Partners having access to consensus EPS forecasts when making their investment decisions?

2. What problems are likely to be faced by Rothschild when collecting and aggregating EPS forecasts made by analysts based at different investment/brokerage institutions? How would you attempt to reduce these problems?

3. Outline alternative ways of weighting (aggregating) individual analyst forecasts when computing consensus EPS forecasts for each company. How would you recommend that Rothschild decide the set(s) of weights to use in its proposed service?

QUESTION 8.3: Performance Evaluation for Security Analysts

Deborah Regent, the Director of Research at a large investment firm, is concerned with evaluating the performance of individual analysts. The approach that has been adopted for some time has been for the director to read the reports of each analyst and grade each from A (superb) to F (unsatisfactory). Informal feedback from salespeople as to which analyst's reports were most in demand by the firm's clients was also considered.

Part A. Regent decides to examine the use of more quantitative inputs into the evaluation process. The first area explored is the "quality of each analyst's earnings forecasts."

REQUIRED

1. What attributes of each analyst's earnings forecasts would you recommend be examined? Specify also how you would quantify each attribute.

2. Regent computes the mean absolute forecast error for the stocks followed by three analysts in each of the past four years. All forecasts made by each analyst are examined and given equal weight. Analyst #1 covers food-related consumer product companies, #2 covers natural resource companies (oil and gas, metals, etc.), while #3 tracks automobile and automobile parts manufacturing companies. The following error measure is used:

$$\frac{|\text{ Actual EPS } - \text{ Forecast EPS }|}{\text{Actual EPS}}$$

The mean absolute forecast errors for this four-year period are

Analyst #1:   6%
Analyst #2:   17%
Analyst #3:   13%

What factors would you consider in determining which of the three analysts has the best ability to forecast EPS?

Part B. Deborah Regent reads a monograph that reported that downward (upward) consensus analyst earnings forecast revisions are *preceded* by decreases (increases) in security returns in the 12-month period prior to the revision. She is dismayed by this result, which she interprets to mean that analysts are merely recoding information (that is, security returns) already in the public domain. She examines security price returns in the 12 months preceding forecast revisions by the analysts at her firm. Fixing the month of each analyst forecast revision as month 0, the following is found:

	Analyst Revises Forecast Down	*Analyst Revises Forecast Up*
Months $(-12, -10)$	-1.06%	.60%
Months $(-9, -7)$	-1.42	.92
Months $(-6, -4)$	-2.17	1.47
Months $(-3, -1)$	-4.30	3.86
Months $(-12, -1)$	-8.95	6.85

REQUIRED

1. What alternative explanations are there for the finding that in the 12 months *prior* to an analyst's revising an EPS forecast down (up), security returns

had already declined 8.95% (increased 6.85%)? How would you distinguish between these alternative explanations?

2. Given the foregoing finding, what changes would you recommend in the approaches used by the security analysts to forecast EPS?

REFERENCES

ANG, J. S., J. H. CHUA, and A. M. FATEMI. "A Comparison of Econometric, Time Series, and Composite Forecasting Methods in Predicting Accounting Variables." *Journal of Economics and Business* (August 1983): 301–311.

ARNOLD, J., P. MOIZER, and E. NOREEN, "Investment Appraisal Methods of Financial Analysts: A Comparative Survey of U.S. and U.K. Practices," working paper. University of Manchester, U.K., 1983.

BAREFIELD, R. M., and E. E. COMISKEY. "The Accuracy of Bank Earnings Forecasts." *Business Economics* (May 1976): 59–63.

BROWN, P., G. FOSTER, and E. NOREEN. *Security Analyst Multi-Year Earnings Forecasts and the Capital Market*. Sarasota, Fla.: American Accounting Association, 1985.

BROWN, L., P. GRIFFIN, R. HAGERMAN, and M. ZMIJEWSKI. "The Existence and Potential Sources of Analyst Forecast Superiority," working paper. State University of New York at Buffalo, 1984.

BROWN, L. D., and M. S. ROZEFF. "Univariate Time-Series Models of Quarterly Accounting Earnings per Share: A Proposed Model." *Journal of Accounting Research* (Spring 1979): 179–189.

BUCHENROTH, S., and R. JENNINGS. "A Descriptive Analysis of the Time-Series Behavior of Financial Analyst Earnings Forecasts," working paper. Indiana University, Bloomington, 1984.

COGGIN, T. D., and J. E. HUNTER. "Analysts' EPS Forecasts Nearer Actual than Statistical Models." *The Journal of Business Forecasting* (Winter 1982–1983): 20–23.

COLLINS, W. A., and W. S. HOPWOOD. "A Multivariate Analysis of Annual Earnings Forecasts Generated from Quarterly Forecasts of Financial Analysts and Univariate Time-Series Models." *Journal of Accounting Research* (Autumn 1980): 390–406.

COOPER, J. P., and C. R. NELSON. "The Ex Ante Prediction Performance of the St. Louis and FRB-MIT-PENN Econometric Models and Some Results on Composite Predictors." *Journal of Money, Credit and Banking* (February 1975): 1–32.

CRICHFIELD, T., T. DYCKMAN, and J. LAKONISHOK. "An Evaluation of Security Analysts' Forecasts." *The Accounting Review* (July 1978): 651–668.

DEMSKI, J. S., and G. A. FELTHAM. "Forecast Evaluation." *The Accounting Review* (July 1972): 533–548.

DOWNS, G. W., and D. M. ROCKE. "Municipal Budget Forecasting with Multivariate ARMA Models." *Journal of Forecasting* (October–December 1983): 377–387.

ELTON, E. J., M. J. GRUBER, and M. GULTEKIN. "Professional Expectations: Accuracy and Diagnosis of Errors." *Journal of Financial and Quantitative Analysis* (December 1984): 351–363.

FIGLEWSKI, S., and T. URICH. "Optimal Aggregation of Money Supply Forecasts: Accuracy, Profitability and Market Efficiency." *The Journal of Finance* (June 1983): 695–710.

FINN, F. J. *Evaluation of the Internal Processes of Managed Investment Funds.* Greenwich, Conn.: JAI Press, 1984.

FOSTER, G. "Quarterly Accounting Data: Time-Series Properties and Predictive-Ability Results." *The Accounting Review* (January 1977): 1–21.

GRIFFIN, P. A. "The Time-Series Behavior of Quarterly Earnings: Preliminary Evidence." *Journal of Accounting Research* (Spring 1977): 71–83.

HAGERMAN, R. L., and W. RULAND. "The Accuracy of Management Forecasts and Forecasts of Simple Alternative Models." *Journal of Economics and Business* (Spring 1979): 172–179.

HASSELL, J. M., and R. H. JENNINGS. "Relative Forecast Accuracy and the Timing of Earnings Forecast Announcements," working paper. Florida State University, 1984.

HILLMER, S. C., D. F. LARCKER, and D. A. SCHROEDER. "Forecasting Accounting Data: A Multiple Time-Series Analysis." *Journal of Forecasting* (October–December 1983): 389–404.

HOPWOOD, W. S. "The Transfer Function Relationship Between Earnings and Market-Industry Indices: An Empirical Study." *Journal of Accounting Research* (Spring 1980): 77–90.

HOPWOOD, W. S., P. NEWBOLD, and P. A. SILHAN. "The Potential for Gains in Predictive Ability Through Disaggregation: Segmented Annual Earnings." *Journal of Accounting Research* (Autumn 1982): 724–732.

IMHOFF, E. A. "The Representativeness of Management Earnings Forecasts." *The Accounting Review* (October 1978): 836–850.

LEES, F. *Public Disclosure of Corporate Earnings Forecasts.* New York: The Conference Board, 1981.

LEVENBACH, H. "Time-Series Forecasting Using Robust Regression." *Journal of Forecasting* (July–September 1982): 241–255.

MAKRIDAKIS, S., and R. L. WINKLER. "Averages of Forecasts: Some Empirical Results." *Management Science* (September 1983): 987–996.

MANEGOLD, J. G. "Time-Series Properties of Earnings: A Comparison of Extrapolative and Component Models." *Journal of Accounting Research* (Autumn 1981): 360–373.

MOIZER, P., and J. ARNOLD. "A Survey of the Methods Used by U.K. Investment Analysts to Appraise Investments in Ordinary Shares," working paper. University of Manchester, U.K., 1982.

PENMAN, S. H. "An Empirical Investigation of the Voluntary Disclosure of Corporate Earnings Forecasts." *Journal of Accounting Research* (Spring 1980): 132–160.

RULAND, W. "The Time Series of Earnings for Forecast Reporting and Nonreporting Firms." *Journal of Business Finance and Accounting* (Summer 1979): 187–201.

SCHREUDER, H., and J. KLAASSEN. "Confidential Revenue and Profit Forecasts by Management and Financial Analysts: Evidence from the Netherlands." *The Accounting Review* (January 1984): 64–77.

SILHAN, P. A. "Simulated Mergers of Existent Autonomous Firms: A New Approach to Segmentation Research." *Journal of Accounting Research* (Spring 1982): 255–262.

WATTS, R. "The Time-Series Behavior of Quarterly Earnings," working paper. University of Newcastle, Australia, 1975.

WAYMIRE, G. "Additional Evidence on the Accuracy of Analyst Forecasts Before and After Voluntary Management Earnings Forecasts," working paper. Washington University, St. Louis, 1984.

WAYMIRE, G. "Earnings Volatility and Voluntary Management Forecast Disclosure." *Journal of Accounting Research* (Spring 1985): 268–295.

WHEELWRIGHT, S. C., and S. MAKRIDAKIS. *Forecasting Methods for Management,* 4th ed. New York: John Wiley, 1984.

ZARNOWITZ, V. "The Accuracy of Individual and Group Forecasts from Business Outlook Surveys." National Bureau of Economic Research, Cambridge, Mass., December 1982.

9

CAPITAL MARKETS AND INFORMATION EFFICIENCY

9.1 INTRODUCTION

Financial statement information plays several important roles in capital markets:

- *Individual Investor Role.* The focus here is on selecting a portfolio of equity securities, bonds, and other investments for an individual, firm, or institution.
- *Aggregate Market Role.* The focus here is on the equilibrium pricing of equity securities, bonds, and other investments. This role includes both the absolute and the relative pricing of equities, bonds, and other investments.

This chapter discusses three topics important to an understanding of both roles: informational market efficiency, active versus passive investment styles, and portfolio theory. Subsequent chapters further discuss topics related to these two roles: capital asset pricing and risk estimation (Chapter 10), capital asset pricing and information releases (Chapter 11), equity security pricing (Chapter 12), acquisitions, divestitures and other forms of corporate restructuring (Chapter 13), and debt security evaluation (Chapter 14).

9.2 MARKET EFFICIENCY

Market efficiency is a term that is used in many contexts with many different meanings. Section 9.2.A outlines the definition adopted in this book. Mechanisms by which markets may become efficient (as defined shortly) are discussed in Section 9.2.B. Section 9.6 examines alternative definitions as well as problems that arise in empirical tests of market efficiency.

A. Definitional Issues

A capital market is termed efficient with respect to an information item (termed ϕ^a) if the prices of capital market securities fully impound the return implications of that item. Notationally, this definition can be expressed as

$$f(R_{i,t}, R_{j,t} \ldots \mid \phi_{t-1}^M) = f(R_{i,t}, R_{j,t} \ldots \mid \phi_{t-1}^M, \phi_{t-1}^a) \qquad (9.1)$$

where

$f(\cdot)$ = a probability distribution function

$R_{i,t}$ = the return on security i in period t

ϕ_{t-1}^M = the information set used by the market at $t - 1$

ϕ_{t-1}^a = the specific information item placed in the public domain at $t - 1$

There are several important implications of equation (9.1). First, an investor cannot use ϕ_{t-1}^a to earn nonzero abnormal returns consistently. Chapter 10 discusses alternative models used to estimate abnormal returns. Using the arbitrage pricing model, an abnormal return occurs when a zero net investment portfolio yields a nonzero return. Using the two-parameter capital asset pricing model, an abnormal return occurs when the relative risk-adjusted return on an investment is nonzero. A second implication of (9.1) is that in an efficient market, when a new information item is added to ϕ^M, its revaluation implications for $f(R_{i,t}, R_{j,t}, \ldots)$ are instantaneously and unbiasedly impounded into the current market price.

This approach to defining capital market efficiency adopts an investment perspective. The definition in (9.1) will be used in Sections 9.3 to 9.5 to gain insight into alternative investment styles and the assumptions they make about market efficiency. Three important aspects of this approach to defining market efficiency are

1. The focus is on aggregate market variables such as security price or security return, and not on the behavior of individual participants. Issues such as the volume of securities purchased or sold and the extent to which any one investor's portfolio is nondiversified are not of concern when determining whether a capital market is efficient with respect to ϕ_{t-1}^a. (This does not imply these topics are not interesting in their own right.)

2. The focus is on the ex ante link between the distribution of security returns and information. Investment choice is a decision made under uncertainty. After-the-fact occurrences such as security frauds or large price drops due to unexpected business difficulties can occur under the (9.1) definition of an efficient market. Security prices are unbiased estimates of future returns (based on the information available at the time the estimates are made) rather than omniscient predictors of those future returns.

3. Market efficiency is defined with respect to a specific information item or set of items (ϕ_{t-1}^a). Using this approach, one cannot address the question, "Is the market efficient?" without specifying ϕ_{t-1}^a. It is quite possible that market efficiency holds with respect to ϕ_{t-1}^a but not with respect to ϕ_{t-1}^b. Indeed, one objective of some investment styles is to identify (or create) items not in ϕ_{t-1}^M and then exploit them to earn abnormal returns.

B. Mechanisms by Which Efficiency Is Attained

Why might capital markets be informationally efficient? What factors might help to identify cases where market information inefficiencies are likely to exist? The following two are the major explanations offered in the academic literature or the financial press:

1. One explanation for market efficiency is the competitive activities of security analysts. Each analyst is seeking to detect mispriced securities and (if possible) create perfectly hedged portfolios with zero net investment but nonzero expected returns. Although each analyst may engage in an intensive examination of the available information set, the large number of analysts

examining this same set increases the likelihood that significant information items will be rapidly impounded into security prices. An extension of this explanation is the conjecture that market efficiencies are most likely for stocks followed by large numbers of analysts and least likely for stocks with limited coverage by analysts. Consider the following comment in a brochure circulated by Equity Research Associates, an investment company that focuses on so-called "junior companies":

> The larger and more visible a company, the more "perfect" its market is likely to be—"perfect" meaning that most of the likely factors affecting the price of its securities are presumably known to the market. Conversely, the smaller a company is, the less visible it is to the investing public and the more "imperfect" the market price for its shares is likely to be.

This explanation for market efficiency rests upon a paradox frequently noted in competitive markets; that is, if markets are efficient because of the activities of analysts, what are the incentives of those analysts to continue security analysis?

2. A second explanation rests on the law of large numbers. Each individual analyst can make mistakes of judgment or estimation. However, to the extent that these mistakes are independent across analysts, they will be diversified away in the price determination process. Given a large number of analysts and independence in their mistakes, the consensus can impound a broader information set than that possessed by even the most "sophisticated analyst." Under this explanation, the larger the number of analysts and the lower the correlation between the mistakes of judgment or estimation made by the individual analysts, the more efficient will be the market. Research on the properties of consensus earnings forecasts discussed in Chapter 8 is consistent with this explanation; consensus forecasts typically have a lower error rate than the average error rate of the individuals comprising the consensus.

In addition to these two explanations, several factors have been cited as important in explaining the broadness of the information set impounded into security prices. One factor cited is the information disclosed by firms; for example, "adequate disclosure of information minimizes ignorance in the market and causes the market price to reflect the true value of the security" (Singhvi and Desai, 1971, p. 136). This factor is often presented (at a heuristic level) by advocates of government mandates for increased disclosure by firms. It is also alluded to in studies comparing the relative efficiency of different capital markets. For instance, in a survey of market efficiency studies across world stock exchanges, Dawson (1984) noted: "Common explanations for the less frequent findings of market efficiency (in the less developed exchanges) include less stringent information disclosure requirements, less information released by companies, and less rigorous accounting regulations" (p. 153).

A second factor cited as important when explaining the broadness of the information set impounded into security prices is legal prohibitions against "insider trading." The argument is that inside information will be more rapidly incorporated into price when such prohibitions are lifted. For example, according to Kripke (1980),

> If market participants are legally restricted from using inside information, market prices cannot impound it. Furthermore, in the absence of differences in information conveyed to different investors, there will be no arbitrage opportunities, and securities markets will necessarily be thin. Thus inhibitions on the use of inside information impair both the speed and accuracy of the market. (p. 20)

One factor not considered by this argument is the incentives of the lesser informed outside parties to set up mechanisms to protect themselves when trading with insiders. In the limit, they could simply refuse to trade in markets known to have few restrictions against insider trading (or limited policing of laws against such trading).

These explanations for market information efficiency are best viewed as untested hypotheses. They are not necessarily the only possible explanations, nor need they be mutually exclusive. For instance, it is quite possible that the relative degree of information efficiency of a market is a function of several variables, for example, the competitive activities of security analysts, the number of market participants making assessments about security prices, and the quantity and quality of information disclosed by firms.

C. Capital Market Inefficiency Perspectives

The efficient markets model is like any other economic model. It is an abstraction of reality. One does not expect that every observation will be consistent with it. Many well-conducted empirical studies have provided evidence supporting it. (For an economic model this is a major achievement! As one financial economist put it, "The efficient markets model has done pretty well. Most economic models barely make it to the next set of data.") However, there is not universal (or perhaps even widespread) acceptance of the model. This subsection outlines several areas where market inefficiency assumptions are either explicitly or implicitly made.

Sizable sections of the investment community, by word or by their actions, reject the efficient markets model as descriptive of capital markets. The following statement by Kirby (1979), the Chairman of the Board of Capital Guardian Trust Company, is illustrative:

> The supposition that actively traded common stocks are efficiently priced at any given time, since virtually all relevant information about their companies is known to the investment community and reflected in the market, is preposterous. Extensive and detailed current information on publicly held companies is available—if one is willing to dig it out. However, most people are too lazy to dig it out, and whether adequate information is at hand or not, they make most investment decisions on emotional, not logical grounds. As long as this is true (and it is likely to be true forever), people armed with adequate information, adequate experience and the courage of their convictions will encounter periodic opportunities to buy from (or sell to) emotional sellers (buyers) substantially undervalued (overvalued) investment positions and to secure thereby consistently superior returns. (p. 22)

Section 9.4 describes three specific investment approaches that explicitly or implicitly assume that substantial market information inefficiencies exist and can be exploited for investment purposes.

Security Returns and Reported Earnings per Share

Two commonly exposited assertions or hypotheses about the relationship between security returns and reported earnings per share (EPS) (or reported earnings) are inconsistent with an efficient market that has access to many competing sources of information:

1. The mechanistic hypothesis, which states that the capital market is fixated on reported EPS, without any consideration paid to the accounting methods used to compute EPS, or the sources of gain or loss underlying EPS
2. The myopic hypothesis, which states that the capital market has a short-run focus on the current quarter's or the current year's reported EPS, rather than having a focus on a multiyear horizon period.

One example of the mechanistic hypothesis is Briloff's (1972) "Ajax Aero Computer" scenario, which was given to illustrate the "dirty pooling" alternative when accounting for acquisitions. Under pooling accounting, the full year's earnings of the acquired company are added to the earnings of the acquiring company in the year of acquisition rather than just the earnings accrued since the date of the acquisition. Prior to a merger, Ajax had a price-to-earnings ratio of 30. The reported earnings per share for Ajax in $t - 1$ was \$4; with a PE multiple of 30, it sold for \$120. During the period $t - 1$ to t, Ajax acquired another company and accounted for it on a pooling-of-interest basis. The reported earnings per share in t was \$5 (this included the whole year's earnings of the company acquired). Briloff hypothesized that the market took the \$5 at face value without any consideration as to how it was computed: "The tape watchers remember Ajax's P/E ratio of 30—Ajax shares get marked up to \$150" (p. 62).

The financial press frequently gives examples of the myopic hypothesis. For example,

- Being private lets long-run decisions override short-term consideration. It relieves us of the pressure to show increased earnings per share each period. (Executive of Days Inns of America)
- About 75% of all stock today is controlled by the money managers, who are short-term in the extreme. Their method of valuing equity is on a current times-earnings basis. And they're all sheep. Our stock is valued at about \$1.2 billion right now, but we've built facilities in the last four years that are worth more than that. It used to be that you'd buy some shares for your old aunt. But there are no long-term investors anymore. (Chairman of Champion International Corp.)

Further examples of the mechanistic and myopic hypotheses are given in Question 9.2. Chapters 11 and 12 contain further discussion of, and evidence relating to, the mechanistic hypothesis and the myopic hypothesis.

9.3 ALTERNATIVE INVESTMENT STYLES

One useful way of categorizing investment styles is into active or passive approaches:

- *Active investment style*. This assumes both (a) that the capital market mis-prices assets and (b) that the investor adopting this style perceives he or she has the ability to detect and exploit this mispricing. (Whether (a) and (b) are descriptively valid assumptions is an empirical issue.)
- *Passive investment style*. This assumes either (a) that the capital market does not misprice securities or (b), if it does, that the investor does not have the ability to detect and exploit this mispricing. Note that if (a) holds, there is ''price-protection'' to individual investors who may not have access to the full-information set impounded into security prices; that is, such inves-tors are not disadvantaged by their lack of full access to, or knowledge about, this information set.

Section 9.4 discusses three different active investment approaches: (A) tech-nical analysis, (B) market timing, and (C) fundamental analysis. Each approach assumes that market inefficiencies exist with respect to varying subsets of the available information. Section 9.5 discusses important components of a passive investment style.

Individual investors or institutions need not adopt one of the foregoing two investment styles to the exclusion of the other. For instance, an institution may allocate 60% of its portfolio to a passive investment style and 40% to an active style. Over time, the realized returns and costs (for example, transactions costs and management fees) of each style should be an important input into decisions about possible changes in the mix of funds allocated between active and passive investment styles.

9.4 ACTIVE MANAGEMENT-INVESTMENT APPROACHES

A. Technical Analysis

This approach assumes that there are systematic dependencies in security market returns that can be exploited to yield abnormal returns. Technical analysis is a general term that embraces a variety of specific tools. For instance, *trend analysis* relies on the sequencing of movements (so-called ''head and shoulders movements'') in security returns on individual stocks. *Relative strength analysis* relies on movements in the returns on individual stocks vis-à-vis returns on the market. Technical analysis assumes that the capital market is inefficient and that there is information in the past sequence of prices that is ignored by the capital market when assessing the distribution of security returns. Financial statement data of specific firms rarely play any role in this approach to investment selection.

Evidence pertaining to the success of technical analysis can be classified into two categories:

1. Evidence on systematic dependencies in security returns (for example, autocorrelations of security returns)
2. Evidence on the returns earned by trading rules that are designed to exploit possible dependencies in security returns.

(The phrase "abnormal return" is used to describe the difference between the returns from an investment strategy and the returns predicted to be earned, using an equilibrium model of security expected returns. Chapter 11 provides further discussion of "abnormal return" computation.)

Evidence on Systematic Dependencies

There is no shortage of studies or reviews of studies in this topic area. This is not surprising, given the ready availability of computer data bases and the possible gains from detecting systematic dependencies. Much evidence up to the early 1970s reported that daily or weekly security returns could be well described by a random walk model. (See Appendix 7.B for a discussion of the random walk model.) For instance, Kendall (1953) reported the following conclusion for weekly changes in 19 indices of British industrial share prices and in spot prices for two commodities:

> In series of prices which are observed at fairly close intervals, the random changes from one term to the next are so large as to swamp any systematic effect which may be present. The data behave almost like wandering series. . . . Investors can, perhaps, make money on the Stock Exchange but not, apparently, by watching price-movements and coming in on what looks like a good thing. (pp. 11, 18)

Fama (1965) examined the sample autocorrelations of daily returns for each of the 30 Dow Jones Industrials over the 1957–1962 period. The median autocorrelations across the sample were

r_1	r_2	r_3	r_4
.015	$-.033$	$-.020$	.011

The largest r_1 in the sample was .118 (Alcoa). This r_1 implies that only 1.39% of the variability in $R_{i,t}$ of Alcoa can be explained by the linear relationship between $R_{i,t}$ and $R_{i,t-1}$. Fama concluded that a random walk model provided a good approximation of the process generating daily security returns of the Dow Jones stocks. After a review of studies covering security returns in the United Kingdom, United States, Greece, and Australia, Granger (1972) concluded that "the majority of studies find the random-walk hypothesis, in one form or another, to give at least an extremely good approximation to whatever may be the truth" (p. 478).

By the early 1970s, a study reporting that the random walk model was descriptive for yet another security-return series was neither particularly newsworthy nor easily publishable. More recent publications have focused on documenting departures from the random walk model, for example, those relating to seasonality in monthly security returns and those relating to reversals in consecutive transaction data.

Seasonality.   Several authors have produced strong evidence of a January seasonal pattern in the security returns of U.S. companies. For instance, Keim (1983) reports that "daily abnormal return distributions in January have large (positive) means relative to the remaining eleven months" (p. 13). Evidence also exists of a second form of seasonality in U.S. security returns, a day-of-the-week seasonal pattern. For instance, Gibbons and Hess (1981) report "strong and persistent negative mean returns on Mondays for stocks" (p. 594). Chapter 10 discusses these findings in more detail.

Transaction-to-Transaction Dependencies.   Evidence of serial dependencies in consecutive security price changes within a trading day has been reported in several studies. For instance, Patell and Wolfson (1984) report that "in consecutive price changes, reversals occur slightly more than twice as often as continuations" (p. 241). They note, however, that as the sampling interval increases, the data better approximate the random walk model reported as descriptive of daily security returns in many prior studies: "As the sampling interval increases, the reversal frequency decreases markedly; 56.8 percent of the one-hour price changes are reversals in comparison to only 50.5 percent of the three-hour price changes" (p. 241).

This evidence is interesting in its own right. However, it is the departure from the previously overwhelming evidence supporting the random walk model that has given the seasonality and transaction-to-transaction findings added publicity.

Evidence on Returns from Trading Strategies

The evidence on the returns from trading strategies designed to exploit systematic dependencies in security returns is mixed. Several studies based on short time periods or small samples of firms, such as Levy (1967), have reported finding "abnormal returns" from trading strategies such as investing in stocks that have high price appreciations in the prior six months. In contrast, studies that (1) examine large samples of firms and extended time periods and (2) pay considerable attention to experimental research design issues typically have reported that technical analysis schemes do not outperform the returns from "benchmark" strategies (for example, Jensen and Bennington, 1970, and Ball, 1978).

The academic literature on security-return trading strategies was voluminous in the late 1960s and early 1970s. The absence of an active literature in this area since then largely reflects a belief, among academics at least, that the burden of proof has now shifted to those advocating technical analysis to provide evidence of its profitability.

B. Market Timing

Market timing is a variant of technical analysis in which the aim is to identify turning points and other systematic patterns in the overall market. An investor employing a market timing approach can invest in index funds covering alternative investments (stocks, bonds, etc.) as well as utilize futures markets in those investment media. Financial statement data of specific firms typically do not play a major role in this approach to investment selection.

Many indicators have been proposed to predict the "peaks" and "troughs" in the market. For example, an investment newsletter devoted to market timing (*Switch Fund Advisory*) included the following:

> Formula timing plans are the systematic methods we use to tilt the market cycles in our favor. . . . The method of analysis leading to our stock market forecasts is as follows.
>
> 1. Analysis of numerous fundamental/technical indicators as to the quantitative historical relationship between the indicator reading (magnitude and direction) at one period and the subsequent stock market movement,
>
> 2. Graphical depiction of the indicator readings versus the average subsequent stock market movement, then curve fitting to delineate the resultant forecaster model for future use, and
>
> 3. Summation of the matrix of selected forecaster models using current data to produce one quantitative composite forecast.

The variables used to predict market returns typically are based on correlation evidence without any attempt to discuss causality.

One tongue-in-cheek market timing proposal (based on correlation rather than causality) linked U.S. football results with the returns of the New York Stock Exchange composite index. An analyst in February 1984 predicted that the win by the Los Angeles (Oakland) Raiders in Super Bowl XVIII meant that the stock market would close out 1984 lower than it did in 1983. The support for this prediction was a formula that had held true for each of the last 17 years. If the Super Bowl winner in January is a team that once belonged to the American Football League, the stock market will finish that calendar year lower than it began; if any other team wins, it will finish higher. (In 1984 the NYSE composite closed at 96.38, whereas in 1983 it closed at 95.18.)

A detailed study of the market timing ability of 116 open-end U.S. mutual funds over the 1968–1980 period is in Henriksson (1984). Results for each fund were analyzed over the entire period and for two subperiods. The conclusion was that "on average, the funds appear to do slightly worse than a passive strategy, which is consistent with the hypothesis of no forecasting ability and the use of returns that are net of management costs and fees. Four funds were able to reject the null hypothesis of no forecasting ability at the 95% confidence level for the entire (period). However, only one fund was able to reject the null hypothesis in both subperiods'' (p. 89).

C. Fundamental Analysis

This approach to investment choice assumes that each security has an intrinsic value that can be determined on the basis of such fundamentals as earnings, dividends, capital structure, and growth potential. An analyst determines the intrinsic value on the basis of these fundamentals and compares this value with the current market price to determine if the security is under- or overvalued. Based on interview and questionnaire evidence, fundamental analysis is the primary approach used by security analysts, for example, see Arnold and Moizer (1984); Arnold, Moizer, and Noreen (1983); and Chugh and Meador (1984).

Two individuals who played a major role in the development of fundamental analysis are Graham and Dodd. In the final edition of their classic text on security analysis (1962), they (along with coauthor Cottle) drew the following distinction between current market price and intrinsic value:

> A general definition of intrinsic value would be "that value which is justified by the facts," e.g., assets, earnings, dividends, definite prospects, including the factor of management. The primary objective in using the adjective "intrinsic" is to emphasize the distinction between *value* and *current market price*, but not to invest this "value" with an aura of permanence. In truth, the computed intrinsic value is likely to change at least from year to year, as the various factors governing that value are modified. But in most cases intrinsic value changes less rapidly and drastically than market price, and the investor usually has an opportunity to profit from any wide discrepancy between the current price and the intrinsic value as determined at the same time.
>
> The most important single factor determining a stock's value is now held to be the *indicated average future earning power*, i.e., the estimated average earnings for a future span of years. Intrinsic value would then be found by first forecasting this earning power and then multiplying that prediction by an appropriate "capitalization factor." (p. 28)*

A detailed analysis of accounting statements was proposed as one means of detecting differences between current market price and intrinsic value. They gave the example of a "clearly undervalued common stock," the detection of which turned on the earnings of an unconsolidated subsidiary. The stock was the Hoover Company:

> In addition to its domestic (U.S.) business, it controls three foreign subsidiaries of which the most important is the 53 percent-owned Hoover Ltd. of England. The American company has a substantial equity interest in the undistributed earnings of the English affiliate. Since this equity is not reported directly in either the income

account or the balance sheet, the parent company's earnings and asset value are both understated.

The Hoover American shares appeared undervalued at the end of 1957 because they were selling at only 4.3 times their *full* 1957 earnings and less than 7 times their 10-year average earnings. (p. 31, emphasis added)

By "full 1957 earnings," Graham et al. meant the 1957 American earnings plus adjustments they made for Hoover's equity in the English company's 1957 earnings. The adjustments to the reported U.S. earnings proposed by Graham et al. involved publicly available information: the percentage ownership of the English affiliate and the annual report of the English affiliate. The argument that one can detect an undervalued security by these accounting adjustments assumes that publicly available information pertinent to security price determination is overlooked by the capital market.

One implication of an efficient capital market is that capital asset prices adjust rapidly to new information. Comments in Graham et al. (1962) explicitly assume a very different speed of adjustment. In discussing one limitation of the capitalization of earnings approach to detecting mispriced securities, they note the following:

Assuming that profits develop as anticipated, there remains . . . doubt as to whether the multiplier, or capitalization rate, will prove correctly chosen. A valuation may be very skillfully done in the light of all the pertinent data and the soundest judgement of future probabilities; yet *the market price may delay adjusting itself to the indicated value for so long a period* that new conditions may supervene and bring with them a new value. (p. 30, emphasis added)

That is, Graham et al. posit the existence of lags in the adjustment of security prices to publicly available information.

Graham et al. focused much of their analysis on corporate financial statement information. However, they and more recent advocates of fundamental analysis also stress the importance of understanding the economics of each firm's industry. In some fundamental analysis approaches, the primary focus is on issues such as the likely introduction of new successful products and the likely discovery of lower-cost production technologies. After developing predictions on such issues, a fundamentalist seeks to identify those cases where the market has not already fully impounded these implications into the current security price.

As with other active investment approaches, it is important that an analyst who believes he or she can detect divergences between current market price and intrinsic value assess the extent of his or her comparative advantage. The perceived potential gains from detecting over- or undervalued securities should be balanced against the costs of using the fundamental analysis approach to investment choice. Those costs can be substantial. For instance, there are costs of acquiring and analyzing information to obtain an estimate of intrinsic value. There are transaction costs in buying and selling securities perceived as "mispriced"; these costs have been described as a "lead anchor on performance." There are also costs of holding an undiversified portfolio if the market only rewards investors for incurring nondiversifiable risk. An undiversified portfolio is implicit in a fundamental security analysis approach. Those securities perceived to be undervalued/overvalued will be given a higher/lower weighting vis-à-vis their weighting in a portfolio that attempts to approximate the market portfolio.

9.5 PASSIVE MANAGEMENT-INVESTMENT APPROACHES

A. Elements of a Passive Approach

If an investor believes that the capital market is efficient with respect to the available information set, a passive management approach is appropriate. The aim of this approach is to construct a portfolio that "fits" the beliefs and preferences of an investor who perceives that the market fully impounds the price implications of the available information set. Important elements of a passive approach include the following:

Diversification.   This element aims to reduce uncertainty about the realized return. Portfolio theory illustrates how the variance of returns from a portfolio can be decreased by increasing the number of individual stocks in that portfolio; see Sharpe, 1985, and the appendix to this chapter for an overview of portfolio theory. One relatively cheap way of attaining a diversified equity investment portfolio is by investing in index funds. These funds attempt to match the return on a chosen index, for example, the Standard & Poor's 500 Index.

Risk control.   Investors differ in the risk-return trade-offs they prefer. An investor who seeks a portfolio with the same expected return as the market can invest in an index fund covering the whole market. An investor who seeks a different expected return must undertake additional activities; for example, if a higher expected return is desired, the additional activities can include short selling or constructing a less than fully diversified portfolio with risk higher than that of the market.

Taxation bracket–dividend payout alignment.   Where capital gains are taxed differently from dividends, investors have an incentive to align their tax bracket status with the dividend payout policies of the stocks in which they invest; for example, investors in high tax brackets will prefer low-dividend payout stocks if dividends are taxed at a higher rate than capital gains. A related issue is one where the returns from certain investment media are tax free (for example, interest on municipal bonds); such investments are most advantageous to those in the highest tax bracket.

Low transaction costs.   Transaction costs reduce the returns from investment. An investor in an efficient market typically will prefer a broker who charges only for "transaction services" rather than "transaction services plus active investment advice." Moreover, the concern will be to incur only those transactions necessary to achieve objectives such as diversification and risk control.

Issues related to diversification, risk control, taxation, and transaction cost reduction are extensively discussed in many investment texts. Suffice it to say that even if an investor believes that market efficiency is an acceptable characterization of the capital market, many important activities in portfolio construction still exist. Financial statement analysis can play a role in several of these activities, for example, in the estimation of the current risk and in the prediction of the future risk and dividend payout.

B. Nonimplications of Market Efficiency

The implications of efficient markets for investment choice are often misstated or misunderstood. Two typical assertions are

a. "Random selection of securities is as good as any other; therefore, practice your dart-throwing skill."
b. "A buy-and-hold policy is as good as any other."

Neither (a) nor (b) is implied by an efficient market.

A random selection of securities is not appropriate as investors differ on important dimensions such as risk-return preference and tax-bracket status. Differences on either or both of these dimensions imply that the same portfolio of investments need not be appropriate for each and every investor.

A buy-and-hold policy is not, in general, an appropriate investment strategy. It can result over time in a portfolio that is both inadequately diversified and not consistent with an investor's risk preferences. Consider an investor who wishes to maintain a portfolio with a relative risk (that is, beta; see Chapter 10) of twice that of the market portfolio. Over time, the relative weights of the stocks in the portfolio will change as each stock exhibits differential price behavior. It will only be by coincidence that these changing weights will result in the portfolio risk remaining twice that of the market. A related problem is that the risks of individual stocks in a portfolio may change, for example, due to changes in capital structure, in operating leverage, or in the mix of a firm's lines of business. The result is that portfolio rebalancing is necessary to maintain a portfolio that is both well diversified and consistent with an investor's objectives.

9.6 SOME GENERAL COMMENTS

1. The definition of market efficiency given in Section 9.2 focuses on the relationship between (a) an information item (ϕ_t^a) and (b) a capital market variable ($R_{i,t}$). The modifying term "informational" market efficiency is sometimes used when discussing this relationship. The phrase "market efficiency" has also been used in other contexts.

West (1975) distinguishes between the following two forms of efficiency when examining capital markets:

> *External efficiency.* This notion of efficiency implies that a market's equilibrium conditions are such that trading decisions based solely on existing information do not yield expected returns in excess of expected equilibrium returns.
>
> *Internal efficiency.* A well-organized, real-world securities market should not only establish price levels that are "right," in the sense that they fully reflect available information, but also should provide the types of transaction services buyers and sellers desire at prices as low as possible given the costs of providing these services. (pp. 30–31)

External efficiency as defined is akin to the definition of market informational efficiency given in Section 9.2.A of this chapter. Important issues to West concerning internal efficiency are the level of transaction costs and the spread between bid and ask prices.

Economists sometimes distinguish information efficiency (as defined in Section 9.2) from production efficiency. For example, Stiglitz (1981) includes the following in the criteria for production efficiency: (a) "If firms maximize their market value, will the resource allocation be Pareto optimal?" (b) "Would all shareholders wish firms to maximize their market value?" and (c) "Are there control mechanisms which ensure that the managers of firms will pursue the policies which are in the interests of shareholders?" (p. 237). A capital market can be informationally efficient but not productively efficient, as defined by (a) to (c).

Confusion caused by terminology in the literature concerning market efficiency is high. There is little prospect that this confusion will be reduced.

2. Three difficult issues that arise in empirically testing market efficiency with respect to a specific information item (ϕ_t^a) are

a. Specification of ϕ_t^a, including who has access to it and when
b. Specification of an accepted asset pricing model
c. Linking (a) and (b) to specify the appropriate asset price response to the disclosure of ϕ_t^a, so that the appropriate response can be compared to the observed response in the capital market.

This section discusses issues related to (a). Chapters 10 and 11 discuss issues related to (b) and (c).

Early theoretical discussions of market efficiency (for example, Fama, 1970) bypassed many problems that arise in empirical research by concentrating on an extreme set of conditions when discussing ϕ_t^a:

a. The information item is equally and instantaneously available to all market participants
b. Analysis of the information item is costless
c. All participants agree on the implications of that information item for the current price and the distribution of future prices of each security (the so-called homogeneous expectations assumption).

Given these assumptions, there was the unambiguous prediction that when ϕ_t^a is placed in the public domain, the capital market reaction will be instantaneous and unbiased. Once these assumptions are relaxed, even defining ϕ_t^a or "the public domain" becomes a difficult task.

Relaxing Equal Availability Assumption. Issues related to information differences across participants arise when this assumption is relaxed. One way to characterize this situation is via the following diagram:

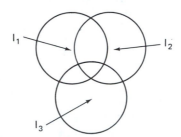

where I_i is the information set possessed by the ith participant. It is only for items in the intersection of the individual information sets that issues of differential information will not arise. For items not in this intersection, the theoretical literature provides empirical researchers with very little guidance on (a) predicting how an individual deals with uncertainty over how many other participants have access to a specific information item, or whether that item is already impounded into the current security price, and (b) predicting how an individual (say, I_2) who believes that he or she has access to superior information can exploit that information. If other individuals perceive that I_2 has superior information, they can take strategies to neutralize some of the information advantage possessed by I_2. For instance, they can refuse to trade with I_2.

Relaxing Costless Information Processing Assumption. Security analysts invest their time and resources on many aspects of information gathering and analysis. The object of this analysis is to combine individual information items to generate insights that are not already impounded into the current price. The following statement from an investment advisory firm illustrates this objective:

> We all know it is illegal to trade on confidential knowledge from company insiders . . . and numerous stock market studies at major universities have shown that investors are wasting their time seeking above-average profits using the same public information available to everyone. . . . What then is the intelligent and prudent way to manage your money? For sophisticated investors there is now a complete answer. A stock market advisory service which casts aside the quest for confidential knowledge and turns instead to the creation of private "inside information" from public data by means of extremely advanced statistical and computer techniques. . . . We have found that valuable private information can be created only by techniques so sophisticated as to be inaccessible to most market participants. *The Institute for Econometric Research* (undated)

At present, we do not have detailed models that predict either the competitive returns an analyst should expect from information analysis or the behavior of security prices in a world in which information analysis is costly. At best, we have cautions that positive information costs can result in less than complete or instantaneous impounding of all information. Tests of market efficiency with respect to the activities of security analysts are relatively ambiguous vis-à-vis tests of market efficiency where the costless information processing assumption appears reasonable.

Relaxing the Homogeneous Expectations Assumption. Participants in the capital market typically will have different backgrounds, will engage in different forms of information analysis, and will have different research budgets. Although each may observe the same company release (for example, earnings are up 20%), each can come to different conclusions as to the security price revaluation implications. The assessment implicit in security prices will be an aggregate or consensus of the assessments of each of the participants in the market. An investor seeking to earn abnormal returns in this context can adopt several strategies. For example, he or she might try to make assessments of the security price distribution that are more accurate or less dispersed than the distribution implicit in the current price. Alternatively, such an investor might attempt to speculate on the assessments made by other participants and form trading strategies designed to exploit these assessments. Predicting the net effect of these strategies is clearly a more challenging task than is predicting the reaction to an information release assuming homogeneous expectations.

There is now considerable awareness that testing the descriptive validity of the efficient markets model is a very difficult endeavor. A major reason for this difficulty is that our existing analytical models of efficient markets do not map well into the institutional domain in which actual capital markets operate. These actual markets are characterized by noninstantaneous availability of information to all participants, positive information analysis costs, and the existence of differential information across market participants. Several areas of empirical research (see Chapters 11 and 12) are currently reporting results inconsistent with the predictions of an efficient market model assuming instantaneous availability of information, zero information costs, and homogeneous expectations. These results have been labeled "market efficiency anomalies." Efficient market models based on a more realistic set of assumptions could well explain these empirical results. In the absence of such models, academics have much difficulty responding to assertions in investment publications that the "anomalies" evidence provides strong support for the adoption of active investment management styles.

3. In an important review article, Fama (1970) stated that a securities market is efficient if security "prices 'fully reflect' the available information" (p. 383). He classified the evidence on market efficiency into one of three categories, depending on the information set that is fully reflected in security prices:

a. *Weak form*. The information set is the past sequence of security prices.

b. *Semistrong form*. The information set is publicly available information.

c. *Strong form*. The information set is all information, including inside information.

Clear-cut distinctions do not exist among these three categories. For example, Fama did not provide operational guidelines on when information moves from being in the "all information set" (strong form) to being in the "publicly available information set" (semistrong form). No recognition was given by Fama to the costs of processing information or of possible heterogeneous expectations across investors. This classification scheme is best viewed as a convenient way of classifying pre-1970 empirical research rather than as a means of understanding how security prices reflect information in environments characterized by costly processing of information, heterogeneous expectations, and differential access to information by market participants.

4. Ambiguity over what is the information set available to the market is a source of much concern to security analysts (and a source of much revenue to lawyers specializing in "insider trading" litigation). Analysts, along with other parties, can face liability under various antifraud provisions of the U.S. federal securities laws (in particular, Rule 10b-5). There is not an operational definition in the federal securities law of either (a) "What is inside information?" or (b) "Who is an insider?" Insight into both (a) and (b) comes from case law.

An illustration of case law on "What is inside information?" is *Cady Roberts and Company*. This case involved a partner managing discretionary accounts in a brokerage house who obtained information about a proposed dividend cut from a director before the dividend cut was formally released by the company. A court held that trading on the basis of this dividend cut constituted the use of "inside information." According to this case, highly specific information (for example, a dividend or earnings announcement) is likely to fall in the domain of inside information (Loomis, 1972):

> The (SEC's) idea of highly specific information is a single concrete event or determination or fact, as opposed to a mosaic of general information, some of which is public and some of which isn't. Skillful assembly of a mosaic may lead an analyst to the conclusion that the company's stock is going up or down a point. We are trying not to inhibit securities research. That's one of the reasons why we refer to a specific event rather than the result of research. (p. 25)

Opponents of attempts by regulatory agencies to broaden the scope of what items fall under the "inside information umbrella" argue that the net effect of such broadening would be to decrease the speed with which new information is impounded into security prices.

Although case law does not restrict the term "insider" to internal management or directors, courts have been reluctant to adopt an open-ended definition of "insider." A celebrated case is *Dirks* v. *Securities and Exchange Commission*.

Raymond Dirks was an insurance security analyst. Gillis (1983) provides the following details of the case:

> In 1973, a former officer of an Equity Funding Corporation of America insurance subsidiary sought (Dirks) out and related the details of a massive fraud at Equity Funding that involved fictitious insurance policies, assets and activities. Dirks conducted an extensive investigation over the next several weeks, obtaining corroboration of the fraud from several former and present employees and other representatives of Equity Funding, although top management of the company denied the allegations of wrongdoing. The former Equity Funding officer proceeded to inform state insurance officials and Dirks informed *The Wall Street Journal* and the SEC, but no regulatory or media action ensued. After the New York Stock Exchange halted trading in Equity Funding stock because of unusually heavy volume and a precipitous price drop, Equity Funding was put in receivership. *The Wall Street Journal* published an article based largely on Dirks' information, and some 22 individuals were indicted and convicted on criminal activity. Because Dirks had communicated his knowledge to institutional investors who contacted him during his investigation, some of whom sold Equity Funding securities, the SEC censured him for violation of the federal securities laws. This finding was upheld through the courts until the Supreme Court reversed the judgement.
>
> In reversing the judgement, the Court noted that analysts commonly obtain information through interviews with corporate officers and other insiders and recognized that the nature of such information is such that it cannot be made available simultaneously to all the corporation's shareholders or to the public generally. If analysts are to continue to perform a vital role in the operation of healthy capital markets, a line between permissible and impermissible disclosure and use of information must be established. Toward that end, the Court's ruling eases considerably the ambiguities that have clouded analysts' use of information received from corporate officers and other insiders.

Gillis (1983) argued that based on the *Dirks* ruling, the test "now is whether the insider breached his duty in communicating the information, whether or not the information is material or non-public" (p. 6). In a further analysis of the case law, Gillis (1984) concluded that "there is no general duty to disclose before trading on material non-public information, and that a duty to disclose does not arise from mere possession of non-public material information" (p. 11).

5. An important task that the academic community largely has neglected is examining the investment styles of individuals or institutions with superior investment track records. (An exception is the Value Line Investment Survey; see Chapter 12.) By chance alone, a subset of individuals will have a superior investment track record even if they have no superior ability or insight. (To quote from Humphrey Neill, "Don't confuse brains with a bull market.") However, if a subset can be identified that adopted a similar investment style, consistently had invested in different securities, and had consistently superior performance over an extended period, the likelihood of this being due to superior ability or insight is much higher. Buffett (1984) presents interesting evidence on the track

record of a set of investors adopting Graham and Dodd's "look for values with a significant margin of safety relative to prices" approach to security analysis:

> A disproportionate number of successful coin flippers in the investment world come from a very small intellectual village that could be called Graham-and-Doddsville. . . . The children who left the house of this intellectual patriarch (Ben Graham) have called their "flips" in very different ways. They have gone to different places and bought and sold different stocks and companies, yet they have a combined record that simply can't be explained by random chance. . . . The common intellectual theme of the investors from Graham-and-Doddsville is this: they search for discrepancies between the *value* of a business and the *price* of small pieces of that business in the market. (pp. 4, 5, 6)

Buffett presented the results for each of the four individuals ("there were only four. I have not selected these names from among thousands") who worked at Graham-Newman Corporation from 1954 through 1956. Returns on portfolios managed subsequent to their leaving Graham-Newman were

Individual	Time Period for Measuring Performance of Managed Portfolio	Annual Compound Return of Managed Portfolio	Annual Compound Return on S&P 500 Index
Walter Schloss	1956–1984 (1st qtr)	21.3%	8.4%
Tom Knapp	1968–1983	20.0	7.0
Warren Buffett	1957–1969	29.5	8.0
Bill Ruane	1970–1984 (1st qtr)	18.2	10.0

Buffett noted that "throughout this whole period there was practically no duplication in these portfolios. These are men who select securities based on discrepancies between price and value but they make their selections very differently" (p. 11). Market inefficiency is but one explanation for the foregoing results. Other explanations include (a) the portfolios cited are of higher risk than is the S&P 500 Index (see Chapter 10), and (b) the returns are a chance phenomenon (they have gained publicity because they are the 4 in 1,000 (or even the 4 in 10,000, and so on) that have superior ex post performance).

9.7   SUMMARY

1. A capital market is efficient with respect to an information item if the prices of capital market securities fully impound the return implications of that item. Two important implications of an informationally efficient market are (a) an investor cannot use a publicly available information item to earn abnormal returns, and (b) the revaluation implications of new information items are rapidly impounded into the current market price. Increasing recognition is being given

to the difficulty of empirically testing the efficient markets model in environments characterized by noninstantaneous availability of information to all participants, positive information analysis costs, and the existence of differential information across market participants.

2. Markets may become informationally efficient through a variety of mechanisms, for example, due to the competitive activities of security analysts and due to the diversification of individual analyst mistakes associated with the law of large numbers.

3. Sizable segments of the investment community, by word or by action, assume that capital markets are not informationally efficient. Active investment strategies designed to exploit these inefficiencies include technical analysis, market timing, and fundamental analysis. An important task, to date largely neglected by academics, is analyzing the specific techniques used by investors with consistently superior performance records over extended time periods.

APPENDIX 9.A ELEMENTS OF PORTFOLIO THEORY

Portfolio theory is a normative approach to investment choice under uncertainty, having its roots in Markowitz's (1952) innovative research. It assumes that security returns are (multivariate) normally distributed and that investors are risk averse. These assumptions imply two features of investment decisions under uncertainty:

1. Two statistics are sufficient to describe the distribution of future returns of a portfolio, that is, the mean and variance of the distribution
2. Investors prefer higher expected returns to lower expected returns for a given level of portfolio variance and prefer lower variance to higher variance of portfolio returns for a given level of expected returns.

The assumption that investors are risk averse is an important one. It implies the reasonable prediction that investors will attempt to diversify their portfolio rather than hold the single asset with the highest expected return.

In portfolio theory, the concern of the investor is with the distribution of the return on the *portfolio*. The characteristics of *individual securities* are important only in terms of their effect on the distribution of the portfolio return. To model the relationship between the returns on a portfolio and the returns on the securities in that portfolio requires the use of some basic laws of probability theory. The results of these probability laws will be noted in the following discussion.

A. Expected Return on a Portfolio

Let R_i be the return on security i and $\tilde{R}_p$ be the return on a portfolio of securities. Then

$$E(\tilde{R}_p) = \sum_{i=1}^{n} X_{ip}E(\tilde{R}_i) \qquad \text{(9.A.1)}$$

where X_{ip} = the ith stock's proportionate weight in portfolio p. This result follows from the law of probability that the mean of the weighted sum is the sum of the weighted means that make up the sum.

Assume two securities with $E(R_1) = .12$ and $E(R_2) = .14$. If one invests 70% of funds in security 1 and 30% in security 2, then

$$E(\tilde{R}_p) = .7 \times .12 + .3 \times .14 = .126$$

That is, a portfolio's expected return is the weighted average of the expected values of its component securities—the weights are the current market values of these securities.

B. Variance of the Return on a Portfolio

The expression for the variance of the portfolio return is

$$\sigma^2(\tilde{R}_p) = E\{[\tilde{R}_p - E(\tilde{R}_p)]^2\} \qquad \text{(9.A.2)}$$

Given (9.A.2) and the probability law that

$$\sigma^2(X_{ip}\tilde{R}_i) = X_{ip}^2\sigma^2(\tilde{R}_i) \qquad \text{(9.A.3)}$$

then

$$\sigma^2(\tilde{R}_p) = E\left\{ \sum_{i=1}^{n} X_{ip}[\tilde{R}_i - E(\tilde{R}_i)]\right\}^2 \qquad \text{(9.A.4)}$$

The expression in (9.A.4) can be better understood by considering a two-security portfolio.

Two-Security Portfolio

For a two-security portfolio, on expansion (9.A.4) becomes

$$\sigma^2(\tilde{R}_p) = X_{1p}^2 E[\tilde{R}_1 - E(\tilde{R}_1)]^2 + X_{2p}^2 E[\tilde{R}_2 - E(\tilde{R}_2)]^2$$
$$+ 2X_{1p}X_{2p}E\{[\tilde{R}_1 - E(\tilde{R}_1)][\tilde{R}_2 - E(\tilde{R}_2)]\} \qquad \text{(9.A.5)}$$

The third component on the right-hand side of (9.A.5) includes the pairwise covariance between $\tilde{R}_1$ and $\tilde{R}_2$: $E\{[\tilde{R}_1 - E(\tilde{R}_1)][R_2 - E(\tilde{R}_2)]\}$. This covariance term measures the degree of covariation or comovement between the returns on security 1 and security 2.

The covariance between the returns on securities i and j is usually denoted σ_{ij}. By definition

$$\sigma_{ij} = r_{ij} \cdot \sigma_i \cdot \sigma_j \qquad \text{(9.A.6)}$$

where

r_{ij} = the correlation between the returns on security i and security j

σ_i = standard deviation of the returns on security i

A more succinct representation of (9.A.5), using (9.A.6), is

$$\sigma^2(\tilde{R}_p) = X_{1p}^2\sigma^2(\tilde{R}_1) + X_{2p}^2\sigma^2(\tilde{R}_2) + 2X_{1p}X_{2p}r_{12} \cdot \sigma(\tilde{R}_1) \cdot \sigma(\tilde{R}_2) \qquad \text{(9.A.7)}$$

Example One. Assume equal investment in two securities ($X_{1p} = .5$; $X_{2p} = .5$) with equal variances [$\sigma^2(\tilde{R}_1) = \sigma^2(\tilde{R}_2) = .03$].

$$\sigma^2(\tilde{R}_p) = (.5)^2 \times .03 + (.5)^2 \times .03 + 2 \times .5 \times .5 \times r_{12} \times \sqrt{.03} \times \sqrt{.03}$$
$$= .0075 + .0075 + .015r_{12}$$

The benefits of portfolio diversification can be illustrated by examining the effect on $\sigma^2(\tilde{R}_p)$ of different values of r_{12}.

One extreme case is where $r_{12} = 1$; that is, the two securities' returns are perfectly positively correlated:

$$\sigma^2(\tilde{R}_p) = .0075 + .0075 + .015 = .03$$

In this specific example, the variance of the portfolio is the same as the variance of either security. Consider now the case where $r_{12} = .1$; that is, the two securities' returns are weakly positively correlated,

$$\sigma^2(\tilde{R}_p) = .0075 + .0075 + .0015 = .0165$$

Note the reduction in $\sigma^2(\tilde{R}_p)$ relative to the case where $r_{12} = 1$. Finally, consider the other extreme case of $r_{12} = -1$; that is, the two securities' returns are perfectly negatively correlated:

$$\sigma^2(\tilde{R}_p) = .0075 + .0075 - .015 = 0$$

The portfolio variance is now zero. A perfectly hedged portfolio has been formed. This situation is where there is maximum benefit from diversification.

Example Two. Assume unequal investment in two securities ($X_{1p} = .6$; $X_{2p} = .4$) with unequal variances [$\sigma^2(\tilde{R}_1) = .04$; $\sigma^2(\tilde{R}_2) = .09$].

$$\sigma^2(\tilde{R}_p) = (.6)^2 \times .04 + (.4)^2 \times .09 + 2 \times .6 \times .4 \times r_{12} \times \sqrt{.04} \times \sqrt{.09}$$
$$= .0144 + .0144 + .0288r_{12}$$

When $r_{12} = 1$, then

$$\sigma^2(\tilde{R}_p) = .0144 + .0144 + .0288 = .0576$$

When $r_{12} = .1$, then

$$\sigma^2(\tilde{R}_p) = .0144 + .0144 + .00288 = .03168$$

Note the reduction in portfolio variance relative to where $r_{12} = 1$. Finally consider the case where $r_{12} = -1$:

$$\sigma^2(\tilde{R}_p) = .0144 + .0144 - .0288 = 0$$

As with Example One, it is possible to eliminate uncertainty about the portfolio return by creating a perfectly hedged portfolio.

An N-Security Portfolio

In the N-security portfolio,

$$\sigma^2(\tilde{R}_p) = \sum_{i=1}^{n} \sum_{j=1}^{n} X_{ip} X_{jp} \sigma_{ij} \tag{9.A.8}$$

By noting that when $i = j$

$$\sigma_{ij} = \sigma_i^2 = \sigma_j^2$$

(9.A.8) can be factored into an expression separately containing variance and covariance terms:

$$\sigma^2(\tilde{R}_p) = \sum_{i=1}^{n} X_{ip}^2 \sigma^2(\tilde{R}_i) + \sum_{\substack{i=1 \\ }}^{n} \sum_{\substack{j=1 \\ j \neq i}}^{n} X_{ip} X_{jp} \sigma_{ij} \tag{9.A.9}$$

In general, the number of variance terms in (9.A.9) is N and the number of covariance terms is $[N(N - 1)]/2$. Thus, for a 10-security portfolio, $\sigma^2(\tilde{R}_p)$ will contain 10 variance terms and 45 covariance terms. For a 100-security portfolio, $\sigma^2(\tilde{R}_p)$ will contain 100 variance terms and 4,950 covariance terms. Note that it does not necessarily follow that because there are numerically more covariance than variance terms in $\sigma^2(\tilde{R}_p)$ that the contribution of the covariance terms to $\sigma^2(\tilde{R}_p)$ is dominant. It also depends on the relative size of the variance and covariance terms. Empirically, however, covariance terms are the major contributors to $\sigma^2(\tilde{R}_p)$ in large, well-diversified portfolios. For instance, Fama (1976, Chap. 7) demonstrates that for a 50-security portfolio, the covariance terms constitute approximately 90% of $\sigma^2(\tilde{R}_p)$.

C. Efficient Portfolios and the Dominance Principle

The dominance principle in portfolio theory states that an investor will prefer the portfolio with the highest expected return for a given risk level and prefer the portfolio with the lowest risk level for a given level of expected return. To illustrate this principle, consider the second two-security example in the previous subsection, that is, where $\sigma^2(\tilde{R}_1) = .04$ and $\sigma^2(\tilde{R}_2) = .09$. Assume that

$$E(\tilde{R}_1) = .008$$
$$E(\tilde{R}_2) = .014$$
$$r_{12} = .1$$

For the case where $X_{1p} = .6$ and $X_{2p} = .4$

$$E(\tilde{R}_p) = .0104$$
$$\sigma^2(\tilde{R}_p) = .03168$$

Contrast this case with investing all funds in security 1:

$$E(\tilde{R}_1) = .008$$
$$\sigma^2(\tilde{R}_p) = .04$$

From a risk-averse investor's perspective, the two-stock portfolio *dominates* the single-stock portfolio—it has a higher expected return and a lower variance.

Portfolio theory analysis involves constructing the set of efficient portfolios and then choosing among these efficient portfolios on the basis of the investor's preferences as regards risk and return. An *efficient portfolio* is a portfolio that has the highest expected return for a given risk level; all securities with a given marginal contribution to the variance of the portfolio will have the *same* expected returns. The set of efficient portfolios forms the *efficient frontier*. Figure 9.1 illustrates these concepts. It is apparent that portfolio A dominates C and portfolio B also dominates C. No dominance relation exists between A and B as they are on different points of the efficient frontier. The choice between A and B (and other points on the frontier) will depend on the investor's preferences for risk versus return.

FIGURE 9.1 The Efficient Frontier

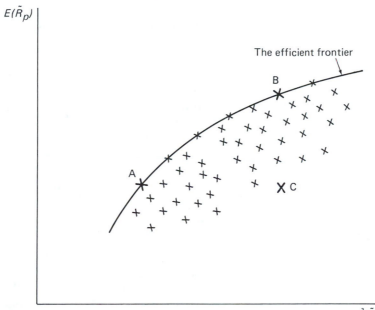

D. The Market Model

For even a moderately sized portfolio of N securities, (9.A.1) and (9.A.9) require estimation of a large number of inputs—N expected returns, N variances, and $[N(N - 1)]/2$ covariances. Concern with the computational burden in deriving these estimates led Sharpe (1963) to develop the following *market model:*

$$\tilde{R}_{it} = \hat{\alpha}_i + \hat{\beta}_i \tilde{R}_{mt} + \tilde{\epsilon}_{it} \qquad \textbf{(9.A.10)}$$

where

$\tilde{R}_{it}$ = return on security i in period t

$\tilde{R}_{mt}$ = return on the market portfolio in period t

The assumption was made that $E(\tilde{\epsilon}_{it}) = 0$ and $\tilde{\epsilon}_{it}$ and $\tilde{R}_{mt}$ are independent. The $\hat{\beta}_i$ term in (9.A.10) is termed the *beta* or *relative risk* of a security. The market model was initially proposed to reduce the number of inputs required in portfolio analysis. It can also be justified in the context of an equilibrium asset-pricing model; see Chapter 10 for discussion.

Given (9.A.10) and the foregoing assumptions, the expected return and variance of an equally weighted portfolio become

$$E(\tilde{R}_p) = \alpha_p + \beta_p \cdot E(\tilde{R}_m) \qquad \textbf{(9.A.11)}$$

$$\sigma^2(\tilde{R}_p) = \beta_p^2 \sigma^2(\tilde{R}_m) + \frac{1}{N^2} \sum_{i=1}^{N} \sigma^2(\tilde{\epsilon}_i) \qquad \textbf{(9.A.12)}$$

where $\alpha_p = (1/N) \sum_{i=1}^{N} \alpha_i$ and $\beta_p = (1/N) \sum_{i=1}^{N} \beta_i$.

An important result relating to (9.A.12) is that the second term on the right-hand side becomes relatively less important as N increases. In large, well-diversified portfolios, the $\beta_p^2 \sigma^2(\tilde{R}_m)$ component is the major contributor to $\sigma^2(\tilde{R}_p)$. This result is of fundamental importance in portfolio theory. An individual security may have a "large" variance, yet have a "low" covariance with the market portfolio. This security would then be viewed as a "low"-risk security when viewed as a component of a diversified portfolio.

This discussion covers only the basics of portfolio theory. Detailed coverage of theoretical and empirical issues related to portfolio theory is contained in many textbooks on investments.

QUESTIONS

QUESTION 9.1: Mechanisms for Attaining Market Efficiency

One entertaining piece of evidence that may provide insight into market efficiency is presented in Beaver (1981):

On Fridays during the 1966 through the 1968 football seasons, the *Chicago Daily News* reported the predictions of each of the members of the sports staff as to which team would win the weekend game. In addition to each individual forecast, there was a "consensus" forecast, which was determined by which team was favored by the majority of those forecasting. The forecasting accuracy (i.e., percentage of correct predictions) was also reported for each forecaster on a cumulative basis. (pp. 161–162)

Table 9.1 presents the results Beaver reported as of the "last Friday of November (essentially the end of each college season)" in 1966, 1967, and 1968.

REQUIRED

1. Evaluate the relative accuracy of the consensus forecast in Table 9.1.
2. How might evidence pertaining to the relative forecasting ability of individuals vis-à-vis a consensus forecast of football game outcomes provide insight into mechanisms by which capital markets become more (or less) informationally efficient?
3. An editorial in the *Financial Analysts Journal* made the following comment on the law-of-large-numbers explanation for capital markets being informationally efficient:

   > The key to the averaging process underlying an accurate consensus is the assumption of independence. If all, or even a substantial fraction, of these investors make the same error, then the independence assumption is violated, the market consensus can diverge significantly from "true" value, and the market ceases to be efficient in the sense of pricing available information correctly.

   Why might errors made by an individual analyst not be independent of those made by other analysts? Do you agree with this editorial comment?
4. What explanations, other than the law of large numbers, are there for markets being informationally efficient? Discuss how these explanations might lead to different predictions as to which markets are most likely to be informationally efficient.

TABLE 9.1 Forecasting Outcomes of Football Games

	1966	1967	1968
Total forecasters (including consensus)	15	15	16
Total forecasts made per forecaster	180	220	219
Rank of consensus forecast	1 (tie)	2	2
Median rank of forecasters	8	8	8.5
Rank of best forecasters			
J. Carmichael (1966)	1 (tie)	8	16
D. Nightingale (1966)	1 (tie)	11	5
A. Biondo (1967)	7	1	6
H. Duck (1968)	8	10	1

SOURCE: Beaver (1981, Figure 6.1): p. 162.

QUESTION 9.2: Managerial Behavior and the Mechanistic and Myopic Hypotheses

The following extracts raise issues associated with the mechanistic or the myopic hypotheses discussed in Section 9.2.C of this chapter:

- *Financial Press Discussion of Decision by Coca Cola to Sell Its Wine Division to Seagram:* A number of observers suggested that Coke's sale was at least partly prompted by pressure from Wall Street. "I think they were really influenced by Wall Street's desire for immediate returns, and that made Coke unwilling to make the kind of long-term investment spending that was necessary to build the brands," says the publisher of an industry newsletter. "If they had stayed in the business for the next five years, they would have been a key leader in a large and profitable industry, but they didn't have the courage or the guts."

- *Discussion by City Federal Savings & Loan on How They Structure Acquisitions:* We try to do things that are in the economic interests of the company, but we've got to make sure our acquisitions don't dilute earnings per share.

- *Financial Press Discussion of "What's Wrong with U.S. Management":* Amid today's takeover scramble, short-term performance is needed for survival. The financial community's stress on very, very short-range performance often can be ignored only at a company's peril, especially if it is contemplating equity or debt financing. It would be a very healthy change if quarterly reports were no longer required.

- *Financial Press Discussion of Corporate Raiders:* Power in corporate America has swung to institutional investors who can throw control of a company to a raider based on no consideration other than a quick profit. Today, the best defense against such raids is a high stock price. But money managers award high prices only to companies with high current earnings, not to those that sacrifice earnings to build for the future.

- *Discussion by Chairman of National Semiconductor on Long-Term Investment Spending:* Our concern is that in down periods, the Japanese continue spending at the same rate, but we can't match them. The capital marketplace doesn't allow you to match them in down years.

- *Financial Press Discussion of "Will Money Managers Wreck the Economy?":* The money managers' power acts as a Damoclean sword over companies today, forcing chief executives to keep earnings on a consistently upward track, quarter by quarter, even if it means frustrating their long-range plans. And because the low value assigned to their stocks closes equity markets to most companies, managements are borrowing more to operate their businesses.

- *Financial Press Discussion on a Leveraged Buyout Proposal for Harte-Hanks:* Harte-Hanks, the nation's eleventh largest newspaper and broadcast chain, said it decided to take the company private because the company's shares haven't been adequately "recognized by the stock market for a long time." By going private, Harte-Hanks said it also would be able to take advantage of investment opportunities without "the pressure for consistent and predictable quarterly earnings growth" expected of publicly held companies. "We'll now be able to expand in cable television and direct marketing without worrying about the dilutive earnings effects of such actions," said the president of Harte-Hanks.

REQUIRED

1. What is the mechanistic hypothesis? What is the myopic hypothesis?

2. Discuss the assumptions about information and capital markets implicit in the foregoing extracts.

3. What evidence would you examine to test the descriptive validity of the assumptions about information and capital markets implicit in the extracts?

4. What forces might operate to reduce the descriptive validity of the mechanistic and myopic hypotheses?

5. What noncapital market explanations might lead managers to have a short-run focus in their decision making?

QUESTION 9.3: Stock Prices and Information Dissemination by Security Analysts: "Wall Street Week" and "Heard on the Street"

Security analysts are believed to play an important role in the analysis and dissemination of information about securities. Individual analysts disseminate or distribute information about changes in their buy/sell recommendations and revisions in their earnings-per-share estimates in several ways:

1. Primary distribution to select clients—done via phone, telex, an on-line data base, or express mail

2. Primary distribution to general clients—typically done via first class mail

3. Primary distribution to the general investing population—an example is an interview with a security analyst on a nationally broadcast television program such as "Wall Street Week"

4. Secondary distribution—done when another (secondary) source summarizes the recommendations of the analyst and reports them—as in the "Heard on the Street" column of *The Wall Street Journal*.

This question examines the capital market reaction to examples of information dissemination in the (3) and (4) categories.

Stock Prices and the "Wall Street Week" Television Program

"Wall Street Week" is a nationally broadcast weekly television program that airs each Friday night. A regular feature on the program is an interview in which a security analyst is asked to name those stocks for which he or she is "currently issuing buy recommendations" or is "enthusiastic about." A study was conducted by the Institute for Econometric Research (1983) of the stock price behavior of 345 specific stock recommendations made by guests on the program. Security returns were measured net of the change in the equally weighted index of all NYSE stocks; the results were as follows:

	Security Return Performance of Recommended Stocks
Third week before show	− .3%
Second week before show	− .5
Week of show (first four days)	+ 1.0
Day of show (Friday)	+ .5
Day after show (Monday)	+ 1.1
Remaining four days of week after show	− .2
Second week after show	+ .3
Weeks 3 through 8 after show	− 1.3
Weeks 9 through 13 after show	+ .7
Weeks 14 through 26 after show	− 1.6

The president of the Institute concluded: "If you want to make money on Wall Street Week's recommendations, you can't do it by watching the show—you have to locate a forthcoming guest and find out what he will recommend. . . . The ultimate failure of the recommended stocks to retain the gains they made on the Monday following the show demonstrates that they were not undervalued to begin with."

Stock Prices and "Heard on the Street"

Each issue of *The Wall Street Journal* includes a "Heard on the Street" column. This column presents the opinion(s) of one or more security analysts. The opinions of the analysts often are published with comments solicited from the corporations whose stock is mentioned. The author of the column does *not* editorialize about the analyst's or the corporation's statements. A study by Davies and Canes (1978) examined a sample of 597 securities with buy recommendations cited in "Heard on the Street" and a sample of 188 with sell recommendations cited in "Heard on the Street." Security returns were measured net of the change in the equally weighted index of all NYSE and ASE stocks. (An adjustment for beta was also made; see Chapter 10.) The returns on each security were then centered on the announcement date in *The Wall Street Journal* (termed day 0). The buy recommendations had on average a .92% increase in security returns on day 0, while the sell recommendations had on average a 2.37% decrease in security returns on day 0. Both the buy and sell group mean returns were statistically significant from zero. The authors also noted that "there is no evidence that the [security prices] return to prepublication levels" in the 20-day trading period subsequent to the "Heard on the Street" publication date. Figure 9.2 presents the behavior of the daily abnormal security returns (see Appendix 11.A) of the two samples in the period surrounding publication of the column.

FIGURE 9.2 Daily Stock Returns of Stocks Cited in "Heard on Street" column of *The Wall Street Journal*

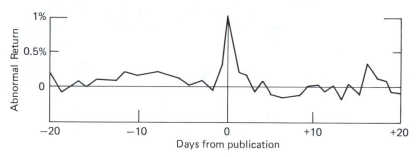

A. Purchase Recommendations

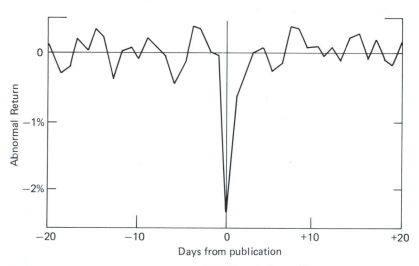

B. Sell Recommendations

Source: Lloyd-Davies and Canes (1978, Figure 1): p. 47.

REQUIRED

1. Would you expect security price changes to be associated with any one (or more) of the foregoing (1) to (4) ways in which security analysts disseminate information about their buy/sell recommendations or revisions in their EPS estimates? Give reasons. (Assume initially costless processing of information, homogeneous expectations, and information instantaneously available to all market participants, and then relax these assumptions.)

2. What way of information dissemination would you expect an analyst to adopt first (in time) for (1) to (4)? Why?

3. What factors might the editor of "Wall Street Week" consider in selecting security analysts to interview? What factors might the editor of "Heard on

the Street'' consider in selecting analysts' opinions to publish in *The Wall Street Journal?*

4. Assume that analysts always distribute their opinions first to select clients. What explanations are there for the security price changes on (a) Monday for stocks mentioned the prior Friday night on "Wall Street Week" and (b) the day that buy or sell recommendations are reported in "Heard on the Street"?

5. Assume that you are (in turn) (a) the executive in charge of selecting and scheduling analysts to appear on "Wall Street Week" and (b) the editor of "Heard on the Street" who has the task of selecting analysts to quote in the column. Should you or your friends be able to trade on this information before the TV show airs or the column is published?

QUESTION 9.4: Portfolio Risk and Return

Some relevant data pertaining to three stocks are

	$\sigma(\tilde{R}_i)$
A: Aluminum Company of America	.093
B: Eastman Kodak	.070
C: Union Carbide Corp.	.085

The pairwise correlations between the returns of these three securities are

$$r_{AB} = .137$$
$$r_{AC} = .476$$
$$r_{BC} = .422$$

These estimates are derived using monthly security return data over a five-year period.

REQUIRED

1. Compute the variance of equally weighted portfolios of the following stocks:
   a. A and B
   b. A and C
   c. B and C

   Why is $\sigma^2(\tilde{R}_p)$ for (b) $> \sigma^2(\tilde{R}_p)$ for (a)?

2. Given that $\sigma(\tilde{R}_B) = .070$ and $\sigma(\tilde{R}_C) = .085$, examine the effect on the $\sigma^2(\tilde{R}_p)$ of an equally weighted portfolio of B and C when
   a. $r_{BC} = 1$
   b. $r_{BC} = 0$
   c. $r_{BC} = -1$

   Comment on the results.

3. A portfolio manager of a pension fund for workers in the oil industry recently commented that she attempted to maintain a well-diversified portfolio. She also commented that she avoided investing in Exxon, Mobil, Shell, and other oil stocks. Oil stocks comprise over 20% of the market value of all stocks in Standard & Poor's 500 stock index. How do you reconcile these two comments by the portfolio manager?

REFERENCES

ARNOLD, J., and P. MOIZER. "A Survey of the Methods Used by UK Investment Analysts to Appraise Investments in Ordinary Shares." *Accounting and Business Research* (Summer 1984): 195–207.

ARNOLD, J., P. MOIZER, and E. NOREEN. "Investment Appraisal Methods of Financial Analysts: A Comparative Survey of U.S. and U.K. Practices," working paper. University of Manchester, U.K., 1983.

BALL, R. "Filter Rules: Interpretation of Market Efficiency, Experimental Problems and Australian Evidence." *Accounting Education* (November 1978): 1–17.

BEAVER, W. H. *Financial Reporting: An Accounting Revolution.* Englewood Cliffs, N.J.: Prentice-Hall, 1981.

BRILOFF, A. J. *Unaccountable Accounting.* New York: Harper & Row, 1972.

BUFFETT, W. "The Intelligent Investors of Graham & Doddsville," speech given at Columbia University, New York City, 1984.

Cady Roberts & Company, 40 Securities and Exchange Commission 907, 912 (1961).

CHUGH, L. C., and J. W. MEADOR. "The Stock Valuation Process: The Analysts' View." *Financial Analysts Journal* (November–December 1984): 41–48.

DAVIES, P. L., and M. CANES. "Stock Prices and the Publication of Second-Hand Information." *The Journal of Business* (January 1978): 43–56.

DAWSON, S. M. "The Trend Toward Efficiency for Less-Developed Stock Exchanges: Hong Kong." *Journal of Business Finance & Accounting*, (Summer 1984): 151–161.

FAMA, E. F. "The Behavior of Stock Market Prices." *The Journal of Business*, (January 1965): 34–105.

FAMA, E. F. "Efficient Capital Markets: A Review of Theory and Empirical Work." *The Journal of Finance* (May 1970): 383–417.

FAMA, E. F. *Foundations of Finance.* New York: Basic Books, 1976.

FOSBACK, N. G. *Stock Market Logic.* Fort Lauderdale, Fla.: The Institute for Econometric Research, 1976.

FOSTER, G. "Capital Market Efficiency: Definitions, Testing Issues and Anomalies." In M. J. R. Gaffikin, ed., *Contemporary Accounting Thought: Essays in honour of Raymond J. Chambers.* Melbourne: Prentice-Hall, 1984: 151–180.

GIBBONS, M. R., and P. HESS. "Day of the Week Effects and Asset Returns." *The Journal of Business* (October 1981): 579–596.

GILLIS, J. G. "Editorial Viewpoint: Dirks Redeemed." *Financial Analysts Journal* (July–August 1983): 6.

GILLIS, J. G. "Securities Law and Regulation: After Dirks." *Financial Analysts Journal* (January–February 1984): 11–14.

GRAHAM, B., D. L. DODD, and S. COTTLE. *Security Analysis: Principles and Techniques,* 4th ed. New York: McGraw-Hill, 1962.

GRANGER, C. W. J. "Empirical Studies of Capital Markets: A Survey." In G. P. Szego and K. Shell, eds., *Mathematical Models in Investment and Finance,* pp. 469–519. Amsterdam: North-Holland, 1972.

HENRIKSSON, R. D. "Market Timing and Mutual Fund Performance: An Empirical Investigation." *The Journal of Business* (January 1984): 73–96.

INSTITUTE FOR ECONOMETRIC RESEARCH. *Market Logic,* July 8, 1983.

JENSEN, M. C., and G. A. BENNINGTON. "Random Walks and Technical Theories: Some Additional Evidence." *The Journal of Finance* (May 1970): 469–482.

KEIM, D. B. "Size-Related Anomalies and Stock Return Seasonality: Further Empirical Evidence." *Journal of Financial Economics* (June 1983): 13–32.

KENDALL, M. G. "The Analysis of Economic Time Series—Part I: Prices," *Journal of the Royal Statistical Society,* Series A (1953): 11–25.

KIRBY, R. G. "Ethics, Gimmicks and Modern Portfolio Theory." *Financial Analysts Journal* (September–October 1979): 22.

KRIPKE, H. "Inside Information, Market Information and Efficient Markets." *Financial Analysts Journal* (March–April 1980): 20–24.

LEVY, R. A. "Relative Strength as a Criterion for Investment Selection." *The Journal of Finance* (December 1967): 595–610.

LOOMIS, P. "Loomis on Inside Information." *Financial Analysts Journal* (May–June 1972): 20–25, 82–88.

MARKOWITZ, H. "Portfolio Selection." *The Journal of Finance* (March 1952): 77–91.

PATELL, J. M., and M. A. WOLFSON. "The Intraday Speed of Adjustment of Stock Prices to Earnings and Dividend Announcements." *Journal of Financial Economics* (June 1984): 223–252.

SHARPE, W. F. "A Simplified Model for Portfolio Analysis." *Management Science* (January 1963): 277–293.

SHARPE, W. F. *Investments,* 3rd ed. Englewood Cliffs, N.J.: Prentice-Hall, 1985.

SINGHVI, S. S., and H. B. DESAI. "An Empirical Analysis of the Quality of Corporate Financial Disclosure." *The Accounting Review* (January 1971): 129–138.

STIGLITZ, J. E. "The Allocation Role of the Stock Market: Pareto Optimality and Competition." *The Journal of Finance* (May 1981): 235–251.

WEST, R. R. "On the Difference Between Internal and External Market Efficiency." *Financial Analysts Journal* (November–December 1975): 30–34.

WYATT, A. R. "Efficient Market Theory: Its Impact on Accounting." *The Journal of Accountancy* (February 1983): 56–65.

10

ASSET PRICING
AND FINANCIAL STATEMENT
INFORMATION

10.1 INTRODUCTION

Two attributes of equity securities that theory tells us are relevant to the equilibrium pricing of those securities, or options on those securities, are

1. The covariance of equity security returns with the return on the market portfolio
2. The variance of equity security returns.

Section 10.2 outlines two equilibrium theories of equity security expected returns: the capital asset pricing model of Sharpe (1964) and the arbitrage pricing model of Ross (1976). Section 10.3 outlines the option pricing model of Black and Scholes (1973). The intent of these two sections is to present a brief overview of models discussed in considerable detail in the finance literature. (Readers without prior exposure to these models should consult an investments textbook for more information.) Subsequent sections discuss economic determinants of, and techniques available for estimating, the covariance and variance attributes of securities. A major focus of this chapter is the role financial statement information can play in estimating these attributes.

The following notation is used frequently in this chapter. (It is useful to put a paper clip on this page to help in referencing back.)

- β_i refers to the beta of security i's returns, where beta is the standardized covariance of i's returns with respect to returns on the market portfolio (β_i is unobservable)
- $V(R_i)$ refers to the variance of security i's returns [$V(R_i)$ is also unobservable]
- $\hat{\beta}_i$ and $V(\hat{R}_i)$ refer to *estimates* of β_i and $V(R_i)$, respectively
- $\hat{\beta}_i^S$ and $V(\hat{R}_i^S)$ refer to *estimates* of β_i and $V(R_i)$, respectively, computed using only security return information.

$\hat{\beta}_i$ and $V(\hat{R}_i)$ refer to estimates based on any single information set or combinations of such sets. Examples include financial statement information, cost structure information, and security-return information. $\hat{\beta}_i^S$ and $V(\hat{R}_i^S)$ are based on a set of information (security returns) that is frequently used to estimate β_i or $V(R_i)$ in both investment analysis and academic research.

10.2 EQUILIBRIUM THEORIES OF EQUITY SECURITY EXPECTED RETURNS

Much of finance literature is concerned with developing and testing equilibrium theories of equity security expected returns. The two major theories are the capital asset pricing model (CAPM) and the arbitrage pricing theory (APT). A lucid discussion of this literature may be found in Sharpe (1985).

At a general level, each theory specifies a relationship for a security between expected return and one or more attributes of the security. The general form is

$$E(\tilde{R}_i) = f(a_{i1}, a_{i2}, \ldots) \tag{10.1}$$

where

$E(R_i)$ = the equilibrium expected return of security i

a_{i1} = attribute 1 of security i

a_{i2} = attribute 2 of security i

The theories discussed in this section add more structure to (10.1) to derive predictions about the expected returns of securities.

A. The Capital Asset Pricing Model (CAPM)

The original capital asset pricing model of Sharpe (1964) was derived as the equilibrium implication of investors using a mean-variance approach to portfolio construction. Two key assumptions about investor preferences underlie the CAPM:

1. Two statistics, the mean and variance, are sufficient to describe investor preferences over the distribution of future returns on a portfolio.
2. Investors prefer higher expected returns to lower expected returns for a given level of portfolio variance and prefer lower variance to higher variance of portfolio returns for a given level of expected returns.

Additional assumptions made in Sharpe (1964) include

3. All investors have the same expectations about means, variances, and co-variances of security returns.
4. All investors have a common time horizon (a single period) for investment decision making.
5. All investors can borrow and lend at the risk-free rate of interest (termed R_f).
6. Taxes are assumed to have no effect on asset pricing.
7. All assets are sold in complete and perfect markets (with zero transactions costs).

Given (1) to (7), the following asset pricing model can be derived:

$$E(\tilde{R}_i) = R_f + \beta_i[E(\tilde{R}_m) - R_f] \tag{10.2}$$

where

R_f = return on the risk-free asset

$\tilde{R}_m$ = return on the market portfolio, which is the combination of all assets

(stocks, bonds, real estate, stamps, etc., each weighted in proportion to its current market value)

$$\beta_i = \frac{\text{Cov}(\tilde{R}_i, \tilde{R}_m)}{V(\tilde{R}_m)}$$

β_i is a (standardized) measure of security i's responsiveness to movements in the market portfolio; $V(\tilde{R}_m)$ is the variance of the returns on the market portfolio and is an attribute that is used to standardize $\text{cov}(\tilde{R}_i, \tilde{R}_m)$ for each security. β_i is called the "beta" (or "relative risk" or "systematic risk") measure of security i. Note that when the CAPM is derived using assumptions (1)–(7), no assumptions are made about the nature of the interrelationships among security returns. (This is in marked contrast to the arbitrage pricing model described shortly.)

A numerical example will illustrate the predictions of the CAPM. Consider equation (10.2) and assume $E(\tilde{R}_m) = .01$ per month and $R_f = .002$ per month. Figure 10.1 displays the linear relationship between expected return and beta. For example, if

$$\beta_i = 0, \quad E(\tilde{R}_i) = .002 + 0 \times (.01 - .002) = .002$$
$$\beta_i = .5, \quad E(\tilde{R}_i) = .002 + .5 \times (.01 - .002) = .006$$
$$\beta_i = 1, \quad E(\tilde{R}_i) = .002 + 1 \times (.01 - .002) = .010$$
$$\beta_i = 1.5, \quad E(\tilde{R}_i) = .002 + 1.5 \times (.01 - .002) = .014$$

Efficient investment in the world portrayed in Figure 10.1 would include only the market portfolio and borrowing or lending at the risk-free rate.

The capital asset pricing model in (10.2) predicts that only one attribute of a security (β_i) determines differences across securities in their expected returns:

$$E(\tilde{R}_i) = f(\beta_i) \tag{10.3}$$

This model has had an important influence on the investment community. Section 10.5 of this chapter illustrates beta estimates from BARRA and several other commercial services. Chapter 12 illustrates the role of beta in a valuation model marketed by Wells Fargo Investment Advisors.

One extension of Sharpe (1964) is the zero beta version of the capital asset pricing model. Black (1972) derives a more general model than (10.2) in which R_f is replaced by $E(\tilde{R}_0)$; $E(\tilde{R}_0)$ is the expected return on a minimum variance portfolio whose returns are uncorrelated with those of the market portfolio (hence the term zero beta). In both Sharpe (1964) and Black (1972), the sole security-specific attribute explaining differences in equity security expected returns is beta.

Another extension of the original capital asset pricing model is to include attributes in addition to β_i. For instance, owing to capital gains being taxed differently from dividends, the dividend yield (DY_i) of a security may be an important attribute in an equilibrium theory:

$$E(\tilde{R}_i) = f(\beta_i, DY_i) \tag{10.4}$$

FIGURE 10.1 Relationship between Expected Return and Beta in a CAPM World

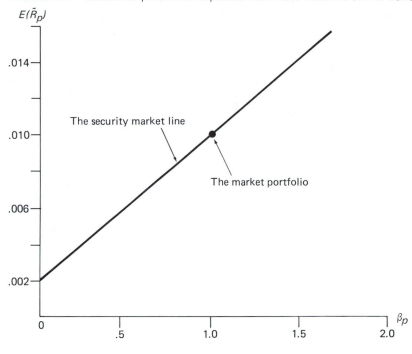

With two attributes in the equilibrium model, the "security market line" becomes a "security market plane." (Litzenberger and Ramaswamy, 1979, provide theory and empirical evidence pertaining to (10.4).)

B. The Arbitrage Pricing Theory (APT)

A factor model represents the relationship between security returns and the returns on one or more factors. The simplest model assumes that securities have a *single common factor*,

$$\tilde{R}_i = a_i + b_i \cdot \tilde{F} + \tilde{e}_i \qquad (10.5)$$

where

$\tilde{R}_i$ = the return on security i

a_i = constant

b_i = slope coefficient

$\tilde{F}$ = the value of the factor

$\tilde{e}_i$ = the security-specific return

The single factor in (10.5) could relate to expected movements in the macro-economy.

A multifactor model posits that comovements in security returns are related to several rather than to one factor:

$$\tilde{R}_i = a_i + b_{i1} \cdot \tilde{F}_1 + b_{i2} \cdot \tilde{F}_2 + \cdots + b_{ij} \cdot \tilde{F}_j + \tilde{e}_i \qquad (10.6)$$

The factors in (10.6) represent "pervasive" influences on $\tilde{R}_i$. Note that (10.6) does not specify the economic nature of the factors. At an intuitive level, they could relate to pervasive influences such as interest rates, energy prices, and gross national product. (A good introduction to the APT is in Bower, Bower, and Logue, 1984.)

The arbitrage pricing theory (APT) assumes that security returns are generated by an identifiable factor model. (Unlike the CAPM, the APT does not make strong assumptions about investor preferences.) The APT is based on the proposition that investment opportunities that provide "something for nothing" cannot exist in equilibrium; see Ross (1976). Arbitrage will ensure that all portfolios of a single factor or combination of the same factors will have the same expected return:

$$E(\tilde{R}_i) = R_f + b_{i1}\lambda_1 + b_{i2}\lambda_2 + \cdots + b_{ij}\lambda_j \qquad (10.7)$$

where

R_f = return on the riskless asset

b_{ij} = sensitivity of security i to factor j

λ_j = expected return premium (i.e., in excess of R_f) per unit of sensitivity to factor j

The equilibrium model in (10.7) predicts that security expected returns will be linearly related to the sensitivities of the pervasive factors, with a common intercept equal to the riskless rate of interest.

C.   Linkage Between CAPM and APT

Sharpe (1985) discusses linkages between the CAPM and the APT. The beta of a security (the only firm-specific variable in the original CAPM) is shown to be the weighted average of the betas of the relevant factors, with the security's sensitivities to the factors as weights,

$$\beta_i = b_{i1}\beta_{F1} + b_{i2}\beta_{F2} + \cdots + b_{ij}\beta_{Fj} \qquad (10.8)$$

where β_{Fj} is the beta value of factor j (standardized comovement of factor j with the market portfolio).

If returns are generated by a j factor model, equation (10.8) can be combined with the CAPM in (10.2) to yield

$$E(\tilde{R}_i) = R_f + b_{i1}[E(\tilde{R}_m) - R_f] \cdot \beta_{F1} + b_{i2}[E(\tilde{R}_m) - R_f] \cdot \beta_{F2}$$
$$+ \cdots + b_{ij}[E(\tilde{R}_m) - R_f] \cdot \beta_{Fj} \qquad (10.9)$$

The CAPM does not assume that returns are generated by a factor model. However, as demontrated by (10.9), the CAPM is not inconsistent with a factor model. The richness of the CAPM is that if it is assumed that returns are generated by a factor model, then the CAPM would make predictions about the factor-expected return premiums (the λ_j values) in (10.9), where

$$\lambda_1 = [E(\tilde{R}_m) - R_f] \cdot \beta_{F1}$$
$$\lambda_2 = [E(\tilde{R}_m) - R_f] \cdot \beta_{F2}$$
$$\vdots \qquad\qquad \vdots$$
$$\lambda_j = [E(\tilde{R}_m) - R_f] \cdot \beta_{Fj}$$

The CAPM predicts positive premiums for factors that move positively with the market portfolio and negative premiums for factors that move negatively with the market portfolio.

10.3 EQUILIBRIUM THEORY OF OPTION PRICING

A call (put) option on a security is a contract giving one party the right to buy (sell) a given number of shares of that security at a specified price up to some designated date (termed the expiration date). Organized exchanges have been set up in many countries to facilitate trading in option securities. An equilibrium theory of valuing (call) options may be found in Black and Scholes (1973). The valuation model is developed using arbitrage arguments; that is, prices will equilibrate so that opportunities to earn certain returns with no risk and no investment will not exist in equilibrium. The Black-Scholes model specifies that the value of an option is a function of five variables,

$$W_i = f[P_i, X, T, R_f, V(R_i)] \tag{10.10}$$

where

$$W_i = \text{current value of (call) option on stock } i$$
$$P_i = \text{current price of stock } i$$
$$X = \text{exercise price of the option}$$
$$T = \text{time to expiration of the option}$$
$$R_f = \text{continuously compounded risk-free rate of interest per period}$$
$$V(R_i) = \text{the variance of the continuously compounded returns on the stock per unit time}$$

Use of the Black-Scholes formula has been facilitated by the availability of tables illustrating how W_i varies with variation in one or more of the independent variables in (10.10). For this chapter, (10.10) is important in that $V(R_i)$, the variance of security returns, is specified as a variable in the equilibrium pricing of options on securities.

10.4   ECONOMIC DETERMINANTS OF BETA AND VARIANCE

The relationship between the underlying characteristics of a firm (for example, its financing, operating, and investment decisions) and the beta or variance of its security returns has been explored in many papers. This section highlights the findings of papers in which theory provided a major role in guiding the analysis. When interpreting these findings, it is useful to have evidence on cross-sectional differences in β_i and $V(R_i)$. Section 10.5 outlines several alternative approaches to estimating these parameters. Table 10.1 presents estimates of β_i and $V(R_i)$ based on past security returns of firms in 26 four-digit SIC industries. The $\hat{\beta}_i^S$ values are from the following market model regression, using monthly data over the January 1979 to December 1983 period:

$$\tilde{R}_{it} = \hat{\alpha}_i + \hat{\beta}_i^S \cdot \tilde{R}_{Mt} + \tilde{e}_{it} \tag{10.11}$$

where

R_{it} = return on security i in month t

R_{Mt} = return on an equally weighted index of all NYSE securities in month t

The $V(\hat{R}_i^S)$ values are based on the same 60 months of security return data.

The industries reported in Table 10.1 are those with ten or more firms on the 1984 Center for Research on Security Returns (CRSP) tape. Several features of the Table 10.1 data are noteworthy. First, there is considerable diversity across industries in their mean $\hat{\beta}_i^S$ and mean $V(\hat{R}_i^S)$ values. For both $\hat{\beta}_i^S$ and $V(\hat{R}_i^S)$, the mean of the industry with the highest estimated value exceeds the mean of the industry with the lowest estimated value by a factor of over 5. Second, there is considerable overlap in the rankings of industries by $\hat{\beta}_i^S$ and by $V(\hat{R}_i^S)$ at both the lower and upper ends of the spectrum. (The Spearman rank correlation between these two variables for the 26 industries in Table 10.1 is .86.)

Why might the differences observed in Table 10.1 for the values of $\hat{\beta}_i^S$ and $V(\hat{R}_i^S)$ exist? Variables hypothesized as economic determinants of β_i or $V(R_i)$ include (A) financial leverage, (B) operating leverage, (C) unexpected earnings variability or covariability, and (D) lines of business.

A.   Financial Leverage

Several studies have reported theoretical links between (1) financial leverage and β_i and (2) financial leverage and $V(R_i)$. The higher the financial leverage, the higher the theory predicts both β_i and $V(R_i)$; see Hamada (1969) and Bowman (1979, 1981). Most empirical studies have focused on β_i. An early empirical study by Hamada (1972) found statistically significant evidence of a positive relationship between financial leverage and $\hat{\beta}_i^S$ for a sample of 304 NYSE stocks over the 1948–1967 period; leverage "explained as much as 21 to 24 percent of the value

TABLE 10.1 Average Beta and Average Variance of Firms in Selected SIC Four-Digit Industries: Estimated Using Monthly Security Returns Over the 1979–1983 Period

SIC Code	No. of Companies	Industry Title	Average Beta	Average Variance of Monthly Returns
4911	63	Electric services (utilities)	.36	.0030
4931	30	Electric and other services combined	.39	.0031
4924	16	Natural gas distribution	.64	.0065
6723	41	Management investment companies (closed end)	.67	.0038
5411	18	Grocery stores	.74	.0103
2834	20	Pharmaceutical preparations	.81	.0072
6025	25	National banks (members FRS)	.88	.0080
5812	11	Eating places	.90	.0148
5311	26	Department stores	.93	.0107
3714	17	Motor vehicle parts	1.01	.0103
4923	16	Natural gas transmission	1.08	.0083
6711	66	Holding offices	1.09	.0110
2621	12	Paper mills	1.09	.0067
5912	11	Drugstores	1.10	.0104
3312	17	Blast furnances and steel	1.11	.0112
6799	28	Investors (not elsewhere classified)	1.15	.0135
3011	10	Tires	1.17	.0118
4011	12	Railroads	1.25	.0128
4511	17	Air transporation	1.30	.0197
2911	20	Petroleum refining	1.32	.0116
3662	20	Radio and T.V. transmitting equipment	1.47	.0145
1311	22	Crude petroleum and natural gas	1.47	.0153
3679	10	Electronic components	1.54	.0129
3573	23	Electronic computing equipment	1.64	.0209
6552	10	Land subdividers and developers	1.80	.0227
1381	12	Drilling oil and gas wells	1.90	.0192

SOURCE: Computed from 1984 CRSP data.

of the mean [beta]'' (p. 442). Mandelker and Rhee (1984) further examined this issue using a sample of 255 manufacturing firms in the 1957–1976 period. Using portfolios (grouped on $\hat{\beta}_i^S$), the authors reported a highly significant positive correlation between $\hat{\beta}_p^S$ and a financial leverage measure; the t statistic from a regression of $\hat{\beta}_p^S$ on the average financial leverage of the firms in the portfolio was 4.86 with an R^2 of .33. (One explanation for the higher R^2 is that the use of portfolios reduces measurement error when estimating the dependent and independent variables.) Results on the relationship between $V(\hat{R}_i^S)$ and financial leverage are reported in Christie (1982). Based on a "model of equity variance," Christie predicted that $V(R_i)$ "increases with leverage, but that it increases at a decreasing rate." Data for a sample of 379 firms strongly supported this prediction.

   The theoretical models underlying the prediction that capital structure is a determinant of β_i or $V(R_i)$ assume that both debt and equity are measured using current market values. Most empirical tests of this prediction use book values for all debt examined, in part due to the difficulty of obtaining market values for many classes of debt. Bowman (1980) collected (where available) market values for both debt and equity for a sample of 92 firms. He examined correlations between capital structure (alternatively measured using book or market values) and $\hat{\beta}_i^S$. Significant positive correlations across all measures of capital structure were found.

B. Operating Leverage

Operating leverage refers to the ratio of fixed to variable costs. Several authors have shown analytically that the higher the ratio of a firm's fixed to variable operating costs, the higher both β_i and $V(R_i)$. In an early study, Lev (1974) measured operating leverage via a regression of total operating costs on an output index (kilowatt hours for electric utilities, dollar volume of sales for steel manufacturers and oil producers). The coefficient on the output index (VC_i) was an estimate of the variable cost component of total costs. The following regressions were then run:

$$\hat{\beta}_i^S = \hat{\gamma}_1 + \hat{\gamma}_2 VC_i + e_i \tag{10.12}$$

$$V(\hat{R}_i^S) = \hat{\gamma}_1 + \hat{\gamma}_2 VC_i + e_i \tag{10.13}$$

The operating leverage hypothesis predicted that $\hat{\gamma}_2$ should be negative; the higher the variable cost component of total costs, the lower the $\hat{\beta}_i^S$ and $V(\hat{R}_i^S)$. The following results were obtained for firms in three industries over the 1949–1968 period:

	Equation (10.12)			Equation (10.13)		
	$\hat{\gamma}_2$	$t(\hat{\gamma}_2)$	R^2	$\hat{\gamma}_2$	$t(\hat{\gamma}_2)$	R^2
Electric utilities	−6.91	−2.06	.08	−.50	−1.99	.12
Steel manufacturers	−1.34	−2.41	.23	−.11	−3.38	.38
Oil producers	−.27	−1.16	.05	−.04	−3.26	.31

The overall results support operating leverage as an economic determinant of both β_i and $V(R_i)$. The Mandelker and Rhee (1984) study cited also reported a highly significant relationship (in the direction predicted) between operating leverage and $\hat{\beta}_i^S$ for a sample of 255 manufacturing firms over the 1957–1976 period. (Results pertaining to $V(\hat{R}_i^S)$ were not presented.)

One problem in empirically testing the operating leverage hypothesis is the difficulty of estimating the fixed and variable cost components of a firm. Information on these components is rarely disclosed in annual reports. Even using internal firm data, there are difficult estimation issues to address, for example, deciding on the relevant range, on the time period over which the cost relationship is constant, and on the appropriate measure of output for a multiproduct company (see Horngren, 1982).

C. Unexpected Earnings Covariability and Variability

Several authors have modeled the relationship between (1) uncertainty about the demand for the firm's output, the sales price per unit, and the variable operating cost per unit and (2) capital market variables such as $V(R_i)$ and β_i, for example, Pettit and Westerfield (1972), Rubinstein (1973), Myers (1977), Conine (1982), and Gahlon and Gentry (1982).

Most analytical models predict a positive relationship between uncertainty about the determinants of business risk (sales volume, unit sales price, and unit variable operating cost) and $V(R_i)$. Models that focus on β_i predict that it is only "systematic uncertainty" about the determinants of business risk that affects a firm's β_i. Thus, for instance, Conine (1982) derives a model linking a firm's β_i with its business risk determinants. Included in the model are terms representing the correlation between demand and the market portfolio and the correlation between contribution margins and the market portfolio. The intuition behind this result is that investors can diversify away that component of each firm's business risk that is not correlated with the market portfolio.

Empirical research in this area has focused on correlations between accounting earnings beta measures and $\hat{\beta}_i^S$. For example, Ball and Brown (1969) estimated an accounting beta (b_i) for each firm with the following single-factor model (see appendix to Chapter 6):

$$\Delta \tilde{E}_{it} = \hat{a}_i + \hat{b}_i \Delta \tilde{E}_{Mt} + \tilde{e}_{it} \tag{10.14}$$

where

$\Delta \tilde{E}_{it}$ = one-year change in earnings of ith firm in year t

$\Delta \tilde{E}_{Mt}$ = one-year change in an index of economywide earnings of firms in year t

For a sample of 261 NYSE firms over the 1946–1966 period, the Spearman rank correlation between $\hat{b}_i$ for each firm from (10.14) and $\hat{\beta}_i^S$ was .53. Similar significant results were also reported in several subsequent studies, for example, Beaver, Kettler, and Scholes (1970); Beaver and Manegold (1975); and Hill and Stone (1980).

D. Lines of Business

The beta or relative risk of a portfolio is the weighted average of the betas of the securities in that portfolio. By an extension of this result, it can be argued that the beta of a multiactivity firm's security is the weighted average of the betas of the individual activities,

$$\beta_i = \sum X_a \cdot \beta_a \tag{10.15}$$

where

X_a = "importance" of activity a in firm i

β_a = beta of activity a

Several investment consulting firms (e.g., BARRA and Wilshire Associates) use (10.15) in their beta estimation services. (See Section 10.5.C for further discussion.)

Portfolio theory predicts that the relationship between $V(R_i)$ of a multiactivity firm and the variance of the individual activities is more complex; it will depend on both the individual variances and the covariances between each of the individual activities. As yet, there is limited use of the approach in (10.15) to estimate $V(R_i)$ of the securities of multiactivity firms.

10.5 ESTIMATION OF BETA AND VARIANCE

Considerable resources have been spent in both the academic community and the investment community on the estimation of β_i or $V(R_i)$. There are several reasons for this allocation of resources. To illustrate, consider estimation of β_i for investment decisions in the following two contexts:

1. Assume that an investor does not have information superior to that implicit in current security prices. Under the assumptions underlying Sharpe's (1964) derivation of the CAPM (see Section 10.2), investors form portfolios via linear combinations of the risk-free asset (R_f) and the market portfolio (R_M); estimation of beta at the individual firm level is not required. However, once the stringent assumptions underlying the CAPM (for example, unlimited short sales, zero transaction costs, and all assets marketable) are relaxed, estimation of β_i can be required. Indeed, even several so-called index funds (funds that attempt to match the performance of a chosen index) use estimates of β_i in their portfolio construction activities. For instance, the Batterymarch Index Fund uses a stratified sample program, which includes estimates of individual firm betas, to select approximately half the number of stocks in their chosen index (the S&P 500 index); transaction cost minimization is an important factor behind Batterymarch not holding all 500 securities in its chosen universe.

2. Assume that an investor perceives that he or she has information superior to that implicit in current security prices. The resultant investment strategy typically will involve a less than fully diversified portfolio (for example, relative to the market weights, there will be higher proportional investment in "undervalued" stocks). Information on the $\hat{\beta}_i$ and $V(\hat{R}_i)$ of individual stocks will facilitate quantifying the expected costs of holding a nondiversified portfolio (and comparing them with the expected benefits from investing in the securities perceived as mispriced).

Estimates of β_i or $V(R_i)$ are used in many contexts other than security investment decisions, for example, cost of capital estimation for management decisions, legal testimony on allowable returns in rate regulation, and legal testimony on the security return effects of material nondisclosures in SEC Rule 10-b(5) legal cases. Suffice it to say that the derived demand for efficient estimates of these parameters has led to a very active level of research in both academia and investment firms.

A. Security Return-Based Estimation Approaches

Past security returns constitute the data base most frequently used to estimate β_i or $V(R_i)$. Table 10.2 presents security return-based estimates of β_i and $V(R_i)$ for ten securities plus an equally weighted portfolio of these ten securities. The $\hat{\beta}_i^S$ values are from the market model regression in (10.11). Both $\hat{\beta}_i^S$ and $V(\hat{R}_i^S)$ are computed using monthly security returns over the January 1979 to December 1983 period. At the individual security level, there is considerable uncertainty about the value of β_i or $V(R_i)$. Consider $\hat{\beta}_i^S$ for Security Pacific in Table 10.2; $\hat{\beta}_i^S = .94$ with a standard error of .21. This means that there is a 95% chance that the underlying β_i lies between .52 and 1.36. In contrast, typically there is much less uncertainty about the beta of a portfolio (β_p); $\hat{\beta}_p^S$ of the ten-security portfolio in Table 10.2 is .98, with a standard error of .09. This means that there is a 95% chance that the underlying β_p lies between .80 and 1.16. This range of uncertainty is considerably less than that for Security Pacific.

A variety of estimation issues arise when using security return data to estimate β_i or $V(R_i)$. There are three main choices of a time interval for analysis: daily, weekly, or monthly. Much initial work in this area used monthly data, in part because of the ready availability of this data. A recent trend is toward use of daily data; estimates of $V(R_i)$ provided in many options newsletters of investment firms are based on daily data. One advantage of using daily data is that more observations can be used in the estimation. Other things being equal, this will improve the efficiency of the estimation. A potential problem with the use of daily data is the so-called "nontrading" phenomenon. Assume that information

TABLE 10.2 Security Return Estimates of Market Model Parameters and $V(R_i)$, 1979–1983

Company	$\hat{\alpha}$	$t(\hat{\alpha})$	$\hat{\beta}_i^S$	$t(\hat{\beta}_i^S)$	S.E.$\hat{\beta}_i^S$	R^2	$V(\hat{R}_i^S)$
McDonald's Corp.	.01	.27	.38	2.58	.15	.10	.0037
Coca-Cola	.00	.04	.41	3.01	.14	.13	.0033
IBM	.00	.08	.54	4.43	.12	.25	.0030
Kellogg Co.	.00	.14	.57	3.95	.14	.21	.0041
Security Pacific	.00	.12	.94	4.44	.21	.26	.0086
Hewlett-Packard	.00	.09	1.10	5.89	.19	.37	.0086
United Airlines	−.02	−.33	1.35	4.63	.29	.27	.0178
Chrysler Corp.	.00	.05	1.45	3.64	.40	.19	.0300
Lockheed Aircraft	.01	.15	1.52	5.68	.27	.36	.0171
Boeing Airplane	−.02	−.39	1.54	6.46	.24	.42	.0148
Equally weighted portfolio of above ten companies	.00	.01	.98	10.78	.09	.67	.0038

SOURCE: Computed from 1984 CRSP data.

about a security arrives every day but that the security trades only every fifth day. This means that the listed price of the security will show zero returns for four days and (possibly) nonzero returns on the fifth day; however, the zero returns are an artifact of nontrading rather than of the nonarrival of new information. Scholes and Williams (1977) and Dimson (1979) provide a detailed discussion of this nontrading problem and outline econometric approaches to reduce its severity.

A second estimation issue with security return data is the choice of the time period for data analysis. There are two offsetting considerations in this choice. A longer time period means that more observations are available to estimate β_i or $V(R_i)$ efficiently. However, due to firms experiencing structural change, a longer time period can include observations that do not pertain to the current activities of the firm. When monthly data are used, 60 to 84 observations constitute the most commonly adopted time period. When weekly or daily data are used, a shorter calendar time period can be used, and there still will be a sizable data base to efficiently estimate β_i or $V(R_i)$; for example, over 250 daily observations are available to estimate β_i or $V(R_i)$, using the most recent one year's trading data.

When estimating β_i with security return data, it is important to recognize that the ordinary least squares (hereafter OLS) estimate may not be the best estimate of the underlying beta of a firm's securities. The average beta of all securities is 1. This average of 1 is the expected value of what an individual firm's security beta will be, without any knowledge of the characteristics of the firm, its industry, and so forth. Given this expected value of 1, it is reasonable not to place all weight on the estimate of a beta found in any one sample of security returns. Rather, if one estimates a beta of (say) 1.5 from a sample of 60 monthly security returns, it is probable that the underlying beta lies between 1 and the sample estimate of 1.5.

Evidence consistent with this argument is presented by Blume (1975). Using monthly data on the returns of 800 securities over the 1954–1968 period, Blume estimated (with OLS) two seven-year betas (1954–1961, 1961–1968). Then the betas covering the 1954–1961 period were ranked from highest to lowest and placed in eight portfolios of 100 securities. The first portfolio included the 100 securities with highest estimated betas; the eighth portfolio included the 100 securities with the lowest estimated betas. The average beta of each portfolio was estimated for both the 1954–1961 period and the 1961–1968 period. Results are presented in Table 10.3. If the 1954–1961 estimates of beta greater/less than 1 are overestimates/underestimates of the underlying beta, one would expect the 1961–1968 beta to be closer to 1 than the 1954–1961 beta. This pattern is strongly evident in the data in Table 10.3. After further analysis, Blume concluded that this reversion of estimated betas toward the mean of 1 was due to both (1) statistical factors (betas estimated over the 1954–1961 period via OLS to be greater/less than 1, being overestimates/underestimates of the underlying beta for 1954-1961) and (2) economic factors (firms taking on new projects with betas closer to 1 than

TABLE 10.3 OLS-Estimated Betas and Their Mean Reversion Tendencies

	Betas of Portfolios	
Portfolio	Grouping Period 7/54–6/61	First Subsequent Period 7/61–6/68
1	.37	.62
2	.56	.68
3	.72	.85
4	.86	.85
5	.99	.95
6	1.11	.98
7	1.23	1.07
8	1.43	1.25

SOURCE: Blume (1975, Table 1): p. 787.

their existing portfolio of projects, or the beta of the existing portfolio of projects moving closer to 1 over time).

Research in both universities and investment firms has produced a variety of techniques to estimate beta. We shall outline the technique developed by Merrill Lynch that first uses ordinary least squares to gain a preliminary estimate of beta ($\hat{\beta}_{i,p}^S$); 60 monthly security returns are used. It then adjusts $\hat{\beta}_{i,p}^S$ via the following formula:

$$\hat{\beta}_i^S = .35 + .65 \times \hat{\beta}_{i,p}^S \tag{10.16}$$

This adjustment has the effect of pulling the OLS-estimated beta toward the mean of 1. As an illustration, consider the OLS-estimated betas and the OLS-mean reversion-adjusted betas for four stocks in Table 10.2:

Stock	OLS	OLS–Mean Reversion Adjusted
Boeing	1.54	1.35
Chrysler	1.45	1.29
Kellogg	.57	.72
Coca-Cola	.41	.62

The OLS-adjusted estimates have all been pulled closer to the population mean of 1. (The exact weights in the Merrill Lynch formula can change over time.)

B. Financial Statement–Based Estimation Approaches

Section 10.4 outlined the results of studies examining correlations between several financial statement-based variables (for example, financial leverage and operating leverage) and security return-based estimates of β_i or $V(R_i)$. The variables examined in those studies were specified by some theory as to economic determinants of β_i or $V(R_i)$. These studies are part of a larger literature that has taken two main directions: (1) correlation analysis and (2) predictive analysis. Most studies have focused on β_i. The following discussion also will focus on β_i.

Correlation Analysis

The main issue addressed here is which financial statement-based variables are significantly correlated with security return estimates of β_i. Both univariate (each variable examined independently) and multivariate (n variables examined simultaneously) analyses have been conducted. Bildersee (1975) illustrates this approach. Other examples include Beaver, Kettler, and Scholes (1970) and Thompson (1976).

Bildersee's (1975) sample was 71 manufacturing and retail firms that had both common and nonconvertible preferred stocks traded on the NYSE over the 1956–1966 period. Correlations between the security-return estimates of beta (for the common stock) and 11 accounting variables were first examined on a univariate basis. Then, a multiple regression analysis was run. Bildersee used a stepwise regression program to choose those accounting variables that contributed most to explaining variations in the dependent variable ($\hat{\beta}_i^S$). The final regression reported by Bildersee (1975) contained the following six independent variables:

X_1 = Debt-to-common equity ratio

X_2 = Preferred equity-to-common equity ratio

X_3 = Sales-to-common equity ratio

X_4 = Current assets-to-current liabilities ratio

X_5 = Standard deviation of earnings-to-price ratio

X_6 = Accounting beta estimated from index model as in (10.14)

Market values were used for preferred and common equity measures (and for bonds where available); book values for all other variables were used. Panel A of Table 10.4 presents the correlation coefficient for each of these six variables with $\hat{\beta}_i^S$. The highest correlation was for X_1 with $r_1 = .36$. Variations in the debt-to-equity ratio explained 13% ($R^2 = .36 \times .36$) of variations in the security return estimate of beta. Panel B of Table 10.4 presents the estimated coefficients for the multiple regression model with all six independent variables; the adjusted $R^2 = .24$. Thus, the addition of the extra five variables to X_1 explained a further 11% of the variation in $\hat{\beta}_i^S$ of the 71 firms.

The multivariate model in Table 10.4 could be used to estimate the betas of firms that are newly listed. (A variant of the model also could be used to estimate the beta of privately held firms. This variant would require the model to be reestimated excluding the X_5 variable.)

TABLE 10.4 Contemporaneous Correlation Between Financial Statement-Based Variables and Security-Return Estimates of Beta

	Correlation Coefficient
A. Univariate Analysis	
X_1 (debt-to-common equity)	.36
X_2 (preferred equity-to-common equity)	.22
X_3 (sales-to-common equity)	.32
X_4 (current assets-to-current liabilities)	−.26
X_5 (standard deviation of earnings-to-price ratio)	.32
X_6 (accounting beta)	.13

B. Multivariate Analysis

$$\hat{\beta}_i^S = .92 + .42X_1 - .63X_2 + .02X_3 - .04X_4 + 4.03X_5 - .08X_6$$
$$t = 2.66 \quad t = -1.54 \quad t = 1.76 \quad t = -1.00 \quad t = 2.61 \quad t = -2.68$$
Adjusted $R^2 = .24$

SOURCE: Bildersee (1975, Tables 3 and 5): pp. 89 and 91.

Predictive Analysis

The aim of this research is to predict future betas of securities (or of portfolios), based on theory or observed empirical regularities between financial statement (and other) variables and security return estimates of beta. Important early studies are Beaver, Kettler, and Scholes (1970) and Rosenberg and McKibben (1973). A more recent study by Hochman (1983) examined data from 203 NYSE firms covering the 1964–1968 period. Hochman developed three different predictions of the (OLS–security-return) beta for the 1969–1973 period:

1. 1969–1973 $\hat{\beta}_i^S$ = unadjusted OLS $\hat{\beta}_i^S$ based on monthly security returns in the 1964–1968 period, using an equally weighted index of all NYSE stocks.
2. 1969–1973 $\hat{\beta}_i^S$ = OLS $\hat{\beta}_i^S$ from (1), adjusted for the mean reversion phenomenon documented in Blume (1975).
3. 1969–1973 $\hat{\beta}_i^S$ = fundamental $\hat{\beta}_i$ based on the following regression model estimated over the 1964–1968 period,

$$\hat{\beta}_i = .81 + .81\,\text{FL}_i - 70.38\text{DY}_i + .08\text{BR}_i \tag{10.17}$$
$$t = 11.69 \quad t = 5.44 \quad t = -3.59 \quad t = 5.14$$

where

$\hat{\beta}_i^S$ = OLS beta, as per (1) above.

FL_i = average annual financial leverage measure of firm i in 1964–1968 period, where the annual measure is (long-term debt + current liabilities + preferred stock)/(total senior securities + market value of equity).

DY_i = average dividend yield of firm i in 1964–1968 period, where the annual measure is (annual dividend)/share price at end of estimation period.

BR_i = measure of systematic business risk of firm i, based on a regression of seasonal change in (operating income after tax in quarter t/book value in quarter t) against economy index for same variable. The regression was estimated from a time series of 24 quarters (1963–1968) of data.

The test Hochman used for predictive ability was to regress the 1969–1973 beta realizations (A_i) on the prediction (P_i) from (1)–(3) above:

$$A_i = C_0 + C_1 \cdot P_i + e_i \qquad (10.18)$$

A perfect predictor will result in an intercept (C_0) of zero and a slope coefficient (C_1) equal to one. Results for each of the three prediction models were

	C_0	C_1	R^2
1. OLS, unadjusted	.39	.54	.30
2. OLS, adjusted	.13	.84	.26
3. Fundamental $\hat{\beta}_i$	− .01	.96	.28

The fundamental beta estimate best approximated the $C_0 = 0$ and $C_1 = 1$ condition. Based on the foregoing (and a variety of other tests), it was concluded that the "superiority of the [fundamental] beta as a predictor of next period's [beta] is clearly evident" (p. 140).

C. Commercial Service Products

The 1970s witnessed an upsurge in research by academics on techniques to estimate β_i and $V(R_i)$. An outgrowth of this research was the development of commercial products by investment and investment consulting firms. These firms subsequently have played an important role in continuing the research momentum in this area. This section illustrates a subset of the commercial products available from BARRA, a firm that had its impetus from the research of Barr Rosenberg and his associates. (The following is from information provided by BARRA in November 1984.)

The β_i and $V(R_i)$ estimates available to clients of BARRA are based on a set of over 60 independent variables (termed "fundamental and market-related descriptors"). These descriptors are classified into categories such as the following:

1. *Variability in markets,* for example, historical (security-return estimate of) beta and short-term daily standard deviation of security returns

2. *Success,* for example, IBES earnings increase, dividend cuts in past five years, and historical alpha

3. *Size,* for example, market capitalization and logarithm of total assets

4. *Trading activity,* for example, share turnover during last 12 months and IBES number of analysts

5. *Growth,* for example, IBES earnings increase and growth in earnings per share

6. *Earnings/price,* for example, typical earnings/price ratio over prior five years

7. *Book/price,* for example, book/price ratio

8. *Earnings variation,* for example, variance of earnings, earnings covariability, and variance of cash flow

9. *Financial leverage,* for example, debt/assets and uncovered fixed charges

10. *Foreign income,* for example, foreign operating income

11. *Labor intensity,* for example, net plant/gross plant and inflation-adjusted plant/equity

12. *Yield,* for example, dividend yield prediction.

Estimates of β_i and $V(R_i)$, based on these individual firm descriptors, are available from BARRA for a universe of over 6,000 securities.

There are several interesting features of the BARRA service. One feature is that it combines both security return-based information and financial statement-based information. As each may provide additional insight, combining the two offers the potential to increase substantially the efficiency of β_i or $V(R_i)$ estimation. For example, security return estimates of β_i or $V(R_i)$, based on monthly returns over the prior five years, may include the effect of a high-risk division recently divested or exclude the effect of a low-risk division recently acquired; descriptors based on the most recent set of financial statements may better capture both these events. A second feature of BARRA is the vast amount of econometric and data analysis underlying the specific techniques used. Great concern is given to exploiting documented empirical regularities for predictive purposes, even though there may be limited theory to explain the regularity.

An important development in the set of products available from BARRA relates to the individual activities of multiactivity firms. Using segment disclosures in each firm's annual report or 10-K, the activities of firms are classified in up to six industry groupings.

> Industry assignment for companies has traditionally forced every company into a single industry. The alternative is to apportion each company to multiple industries, based upon segment activity. We have used weights that reflect operating earnings and assets. In preliminary tests, this procedure yields satisfying results. A larger fraction of stock market returns (variance of return) is explained by the multi-segment allocation than by the principal-industry allocation. . . . Companies are priced as if they were a weighted average of multiple industries, rather than in a single industry.

Several examples of the segment information provided in the BARRA service are

Akzona		Armco		Brunswick Corp.	
Metals	46%	Oil services	36%	Producer goods	53%
Apparel	33	Steel	30	Health	29
Chemicals	14	Other industries	16	Leisure	18
Drugs	6	Producer goods	11		
Services	1	Coal, uranium	7		

There are 55 industry groupings in the BARRA service. These industry breakdowns can be used in several ways. For instance, details of industry risk factors are provided so that clients can compare the marginal contribution of investments across industry segments to the standard deviation of the returns on a portfolio. The industry breakdowns are also used to estimate the "intrinsic value" of securities based on (1) industry price-to-earnings multiples and (2) the earnings of each of the firm's activities.

Other Commercial Services

BARRA is but one of many commercial enterprises that provide estimates of β_i, $V(R_i)$ or other attributes thought to be relevant to (or requested by) their clients. There are considerable differences in the estimation techniques used by these institutions. Consider estimation of β_i. Some firms use only prior security returns (see Section 10.5.A), whereas others combine prior security return data with financial statement information. When using security return data, some firms use weekly data whereas others use monthly data; some use the prior two years of data, while others use the prior five years of data. Inevitably, not all services will agree as to their estimate of β_i. Table 10.5 presents estimates of β_i for six

TABLE 10.5 Beta Estimates by Commercial Services: Estimates as of August–September 1984 for Six Selected Stocks

Commercial Service	American Express	Anheuser-Busch	Apple Computer	Prentice-Hall	Quaker Oats	Resorts International
BARRA						
Historical Beta	1.04	.48	1.94	1.07	.73	1.61
Predicted Beta	1.21	.83	1.78	.93	.94	1.34
Drexel Burnham						
Exponentially weighted beta	1.64	.61	1.24	1.23	.63	1.92
Bayesian estimated beta	1.18	.65	1.07	.95	.64	1.45
Merrill Lynch beta	1.11	.48	1.99	1.02	.76	1.59
Value Line beta	1.30	.80	1.70	.90	.75	1.35
Wilshire Associates						
Five-year historical beta	1.24	.55	1.72	1.06	.43	1.30
Short fundamental beta	1.50	.86	1.86	1.27	.95	1.94
Long fundamental beta	1.50	.83	1.77	1.25	.91	1.91

selected stocks made by five commercial services in the August–September 1984 period. In some instances, differences across these services appear considerable; for example, the range of $\hat{\beta}_i$ for Apple Computer in Table 10.5 is from 1.07 to 1.99. While such differences may be disconcerting, they reflect (in part) the uncertainty investors face when attempting precisely to estimate β_i for individual securities. Fortunately, the beta of portfolios can be more efficiently estimated, and it is this level of analysis that is the central concern of investors holding a well-diversified security portfolio. (However, in a variety of other applications, the concern is with estimating β_i or $V(R_i)$ at the individual firm level. In these applications, analysts should recognize the (typically) large band of uncertainty surrounding their estimates.)

10.6 SOME GENERAL COMMENTS

1. The equilibrium theories of equity security expected returns discussed in Section 10.2 have been the subject of detailed empirical testing. Several severe problems arise in this testing that make it difficult to place heavy reliance on the results of any single study. *First,* both the CAPM and the APT refer to investor expectations (for example, expected risk and return), whereas only realized returns are used in the tests. It is possible that expectations can systematically differ from realizations over short time periods. Moreover, expectations can change over time; determining periods with constant expectations can be extremely difficult. A *second* problem is that measurement errors, at times substantial, can exist in the estimated parameters of the tested equilibrium model. For example, as discussed in Section 10.5.C, there is considerable uncertainty about the underlying beta of individual securities. A *third* problem is that data nonavailability may preclude a researcher from using the variables specified in the equilibrium theory. For example, the market index in the CAPM is a value-weighted index of all available assets, whereas most researchers have utilized indexes based on readily available data for stocks (or stocks and bonds). To the extent that the chosen indexes do not approximate the "true market index," misleading inferences may be drawn from the research.

Empirical tests of the CAPM have produced mixed results; the most consistent finding (albeit not always highly significant statistically) is that portfolios with higher estimated betas have higher realized returns; for example, see Black, Jensen, and Scholes (1972); Fama and MacBeth (1973); and Foster (1978). Other predictions of the original version of the CAPM are less consistently supported by the data. For example, the return on a zero beta portfolio (as described in Black, 1972) typically exceeds R_f, and variables in addition to beta (when beta is estimated using past security returns) have significant ability to explain differences across firms in their realized security returns. Testing methodologies in this area are undergoing reevaluation and refinement; see Gibbons (1982) for use of a multivariate testing approach.

Empirical tests of the APT are in their infancy. Two specific predictions of the model, important because they are rejectable, have not been the subject of detailed empirical testing:

a. The expected return on a security, after controlling for the pervasive factors (λ_1 to λ_j in (10.7)), should equal the riskless rate of interest

b. The security-specific component of a security's return ($\tilde{e}_i$ in (10.5)) should not explain differences across securities in their expected returns.

Most existing empirical research on the APT focuses on (a) determining the number of factors (F_j's) that may be empirically important in explaining differences in expected security returns (that is, factors that are "priced out") and (b) providing some economic interpretation to the F_j factors (see Roll and Ross, 1980; Chen, 1983; and Sinclair, 1984).

2. Three "puzzles" relating to the behavior of security returns are the subject of much current analysis and interest:

a. The differential positive returns for small firms vis-à-vis large firms

b. The differential positive returns in January vis-à-vis those in February to December

c. The differential negative returns for securities on weekends/Mondays vis-à-vis those on Tuesdays to Fridays.

Research to date has focused on documenting these differences. The challenge that remains is to explain what appear to be very systematic patterns over extended time periods. At this stage, advances in our empirical knowledge about security return behavior have outstripped the theorists' ability to provide credible explanations to account for them.

Firm Size Effects and Security Returns. There is considerable evidence, covering extended time periods, that the mean returns (and mean returns adjusted for beta) of small firms exceed those of large firms. This effect was first documented for U.S. markets. It subsequently has been observed in the equity markets of several other countries. A common methodology is to rank securities on market capitalization and form ten portfolios representing the deciles of the firm-size distribution; the mean returns of each portfolio in periods subsequent to their formation are then computed. The results of several studies using this methodology are summarized in Table 10.6. Note that across all the studies summarized in Table 10.6, the mean return for the smallest firm-size portfolio is the highest of all the firm-size deciles. Using firm-size quintiles, similar evidence exists for Canadian securities (Berges, McConnell, and Schlarbaum, 1984) and Japanese securities (Nakamura and Terada, 1984). Ibbotson (1984) reports yearly returns for a portfolio comprising the bottom 20% of firms on the NYSE and a portfolio comprising the S&P 500 stocks (these stocks include those with the largest market capitalization). Over the 1926-to-1983 period, the bottom 20% of NYSE firms had an annual average return of 17.05% vis-à-vis an average annual return of 11.26% for the S&P 500.

The small-firm effect exists with both (unadjusted) security returns and risk (beta) -adjusted security returns. Differences in the betas of firms across size categories do not appear to explain the results in Table 10.6. Further insight into the firm-size effect comes from evidence on the January effect.

January Effects and Security Returns.   A common finding across the stock exchanges of many countries is that mean returns in January exceed the mean returns in each of the other 11 calendar months. Keim (1983) reports that this January effect is not found across all firm-size categories. Figure 10.2 shows the average monthly security returns of the ten NYSE-AMEX firm-size categories over the 1963–1979 period. The January effect appears concentrated in the smallest firm-size decile. Indeed, if January returns are excluded, a sizable part of the firm-size effect just noted disappears. Roll (1983) examines daily data and finds that the small-stock effect is significant in the first four trading days of January and then becomes much less marked in the subsequent trading days in January.

Gultekin and Gultekin (1983) examine monthly security returns on 16 non-U.S. capital markets in the 1959–1979 period. In 13 countries, January has the highest average monthly return (Belgium, Canada, Denmark, France, Germany, Japan, the Netherlands, Norway, Singapore, Spain, Sweden, Switzerland, and the United Kingdom). For the other three countries, January has either the second-highest average monthly return (Australia and Italy) or the fifth-highest average monthly return (Austria). This evidence of January effects in security returns is striking indeed.

One explanation for the January effect in security returns is a "taxation-induced selling pressure" hypothesis. Investors in late December (the fiscal year end in many countries is December 31) are assumed to sell stocks with capital

TABLE 10.6 Mean Monthly Returns of Firm-Size Portfolios for Stocks Traded in Selected Countries

Country	United States 1955–1983	Australia 1958–1981	Finland 1970–1981	United Kingdom 1955–1984
Security-Return Measure	R_i	R_i	$R_i - R_m$	R_i
Firm size				
Smallest 10%	.0181	.068	.0072	.027
10–20%	.0156	.022	.0059	.019
20–30%	.0147	.017	.0057	.017
30–40%	.0138	.013	.0022	.017
40–50%	.0125	.015	.0039	.016
50–60%	.0122	.013	.0037	.015
60–70%	.0118	.011	.0006	.014
70–80%	.0114	.012	−.0007	.013
80–90%	.0099	.012	−.0015	.012
Largest 10%	.0082	.010	−.0018	.011

SOURCES: United States (computed from 1984 CRSP data); Australia (Brown et al., 1983); Finland (Wahlroos and Berglund, 1983); United Kingdom (Dimson and Marsh, 1985).

FIGURE 10.2 Mean Monthly Security Returns by Calendar Month for Ten NYSE-AMEX Firm-Size Portfolios, 1963–1979

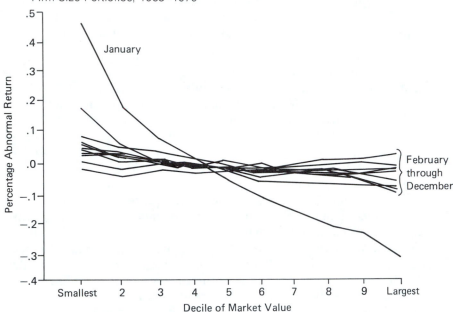

Source: Keim (1983, Figure 2): p. 21.

losses and temporarily depress their prices; in January these stocks are hypothesized to rebound to their equilibrium values. Preliminary tests of this hypothesis have produced mixed results (see Brown et al., 1983; Reinganum, 1983; and Gultekin and Gultekin, 1983).

Weekend/Monday Effects and Security Returns. Keim and Stambaugh (1984) report that this effect has persisted for over a 55-year period (1928–1982). Table 10.7 presents average returns on the S&P Composite Index for weekend/ Monday, Tuesday, Wednesday, Thursday, Friday, and (up to 1952) Saturday. All returns are measured from the close of the prior trading day to the close of the current trading day. The dramatic finding in Table 10.7 is that in each and every one of the 11 five-year subperiods examined, the return from the close of the prior trading day (Saturday up to 1952, Friday since 1952) to the close on Monday is negative. Moreover, in every five-year period, it is always the most negative of the days examined, and it is the only one with a negative average over the 1928–1982 period. The current literature is examining (a) how much of this negative return occurs over the weekend (that is, up to the opening on Monday) and (b) how much occurs from the opening of Monday to the close of Monday. Other research is examining whether the magnitude of the weekend/Monday effect is a function of firm size or calendar month of the year.

TABLE 10.7 Percent Returns ($\times$ 100) on the S&P Composite Index by Day of the Week

Time Period	Weekend to Monday	Tuesday	Wednesday	Thursday	Friday	Saturday
1928–1932	−.485	.038	.081	.165	.127	.006
1933–1937	−.223	.208	.139	.023	.020	.152
1938–1942	−.149	.096	−.044	−.057	−.137	.283
1943–1947	−.114	.048	.103	.096	.048	.139
1948–1952	−.149	−.012	.140	.102	.086	.145
1953–1957	−.220	.007	.148	.069	.145	—
1958–1962	−.165	.056	.080	.054	.128	—
1963–1967	−.137	.040	.103	.058	.096	—
1968–1972	−.164	−.004	.149	.002	.105	—
1973–1977	−.134	.006	.011	.051	−.107	—
1978–1982	−.102	.065	.130	−.021	.096	—
1928–1982	−.186	.048	.094	.050	.063	.147

SOURCE: Keim and Stambaugh (1984, Table 1): p. 821–823.

3. An active research area in which both academia and investment firms are making contributions is factor models of stock returns. Early research focused on a single-factor model, with that factor being the return on the market portfolio. Subsequent research has examined a broader set of factors. For example, Sharpe (1982) examined monthly security returns of 1,325 NYSE stocks over the 1931-to-1979 period. He reported finding five "common attributes" and "eight attributes representing 'sectors' of the economy" (p. 8). The five common attributes were

1. Dividend yield: "prior 12 months' dividends paid to common stockholders divided by the market value at the end of the prior month"
2. Firm size: "the logarithm (to base 10) of the market value (in billions of dollars) of the firm's equity at the end of the prior month"
3. Stock beta: the slope coefficient from a regression of "the excess returns on a stock over the prior 60 months on the Standard and Poor's stock index"
4. Alpha: the intercept from the regression used to calculate the stock beta factor
5. Bond beta: the slope coefficient from a regression of "the excess returns on stock over the prior 60 months on the excess returns on long-term government bond returns."

The "eight attributes representing 'sectors' of the economy" were

- Basic industries
- Capital goods
- Construction
- Consumer goods

- Energy
- Finance
- Transportation
- Utilities

For each month in the 1931–1979 period, Sharpe ran cross-section regressions of the realized returns against (a) the beta factor, (b) the five common factors, and (c) the five common and the eight sector factors. The mean R^2 over 588 cross-section regressions was

	Mean R^2
Beta	.037
Common factors	.079
Common and sector factors	.104

The conclusion was "in a typical month, about 10% of the variation in returns on individual securities could be attributed to our factors. While this may seem discouraging, recall that security-specific returns are much less important for portfolios than for individual securities, and that a much higher R-squared value would typically be observed if we were analyzing a group of diverse portfolios. . . . The four additional attributes collectively added 4.2% to the 3.7% explained by beta alone. The eight attributes added another 2.5%. Historic beta is clearly an important attribute, but it is not the only one worth considering" (p. 9).

   Multifactor models of security returns are now available from many investment institutions. For example, the Salomon Brothers model includes five factors: inflation, real economic growth, oil prices, defense spending, and real interest rates (see Estep, Hanson, and Johnson, 1983). One use of these factor models is in performance evaluation, where the focus is on the reasons for the security returns of an investment strategy being what they are (the so-called "performance attribution" stage of performance evaluation).

   4. An important area of investment analysis is performance evaluation; the aim is to *explain* the observed security returns of a chosen strategy so as to distinguish results due to chance from results due to superior insight or trading ability. There are several important choices in performance evaluation:

   (a) *Choice of the benchmark.* One approach is to use a specific theoretical asset pricing model (for example, the CAPM or the APT) as the benchmark and to compare the returns from a specific strategy with those predicted by the chosen asset pricing model. Another approach is to compare the observed returns from the chosen strategy with those earned by alternative strategies in the same period; for example, the returns of a mutual fund could be ranked vis-à-vis the returns of all other mutual funds in the same period.

(b) *Choice of the time period used to measure performance.* The shorter the time period examined, the more difficult it is to distinguish results due to chance from results due to superior insight or trading ability.

Consider the returns from the New Horizon Fund of T. Rowe Price. This fund is designed for investors who want "the long-term capital appreciation which can come from investments in small, rapidly growing companies." In a recent five-year period, the following was observed,

	Average Monthly Return
$R_i - R_f$	2.098%
$R_i - R_m$	1.597
$R_i - R_{\text{small}}$	−0.039

where

$$R_i = \text{return on New Horizon Fund}$$
$$R_f = \text{return on U.S. Treasury bills}$$
$$R_m = \text{return on S\&P 500}$$
$$R_{\text{small}} = \text{return on smallest 20\% of NYSE stocks}$$

The monthly return for R_i exceeded R_m in 40 of the 60 months in this period (66.7% of the time), which is a highly significant percentage under the null hypothesis that $R_i = R_m$. Using R_m as the benchmark, the New Horizon Fund had significantly superior return performance in this period. However, the monthly returns for R_i exceeded R_{small} in only 31 of the 60 months (51.7% of the time), which is consistent with R_i not significantly outperforming R_{small}. Over this period, much of the return performance of the New Horizon Fund (above the S&P 500) can be attributed to its choice of the sector of the market to invest (that is, small market capitalization stocks).

Important advances in this area are arising from the integration of research on multifactor models of security returns (see point (3)) into performance evaluation. Commercial services are now available that decompose the returns on a portfolio into that attributable to the choice of parameters such as beta, dividend yield, and firm size and that attributable to residual components. Sharpe (1985, Chap. 21) provides an introduction to work in this area.

10.7 SUMMARY

1. Much work in finance has been devoted to developing equilibrium theories of expected returns on equity securities and to developing theories of the price of options on those securities. Substantial empirical work has been con-

ducted to test the descriptive validity of predictions from these theories. Both theory and empirics can play central roles in guiding decisions about the attributes or parameters of securities that analysts should estimate.

2. Two parameters that have been the focus of both theoretical and empirical analysis are β_i and $V(R_i)$. Financial statement information can be an important data base in the estimation of these parameters. One approach to exploring how best to use financial statement information is guided by theory on the economic determinants of β_i and $V(R_i)$. Factors such as financial and operating leverage, unexpected earnings covariability/variability, and lines of business are highlighted using this approach. A second approach is to document empirical relationships that appear pervasive rather than due to chance. This approach can range all the way from economic intuition to brute empiricism (data mining). Work on both ends of this spectrum (and in between) can be observed in academia and in investment institutions.

3. Current research on asset pricing is being driven by ever increasingly rich data bases and more powerful computers and statistical tools of analysis. This research has discovered empirical regularities not easily explainable by existing theories, for example, the small-firm effect, the January effect, and the weekend/Monday effect. Knowledge of these relationships is important when making inferences from the behavior of past security returns about investment ability or the gains from specific forms of information analysis.

QUESTIONS

QUESTION 10.1: The Fundamental Analystics Contest

Fundamental Analystics, a firm that sells recommendations on stocks, advertises that a contest is to be held. Investors will be allowed to enter two equally weighted portfolios of 25 NYSE stocks each. Fundamental will choose one portfolio of 25 NYSE stocks. This portfolio will consist of those 25 stocks that they think have the greatest price appreciation potential over the next six months. Their choice of stocks will be based on "fundamental analysis" in the best traditions of Graham and Dodd. (The beta of a portfolio of their most recently chosen 25 stocks was 1.16; the annualized dividend yield on this portfolio was 2%.) Fundamental will award $100 to each portfolio that beats its portfolio over the next six months. The portfolio that beats Fundamental's portfolio by the largest amount will be awarded $100,000.

The rules of the contest are

1. Each participant is to print the names of the stocks in the two portfolios and deliver them to Fundamental by January 10. An equal amount will be as-

sumed invested in each stock in each portfolio at the close of the market on January 15.

2. Six months later, on July 15, the closing prices for each stock will be adjusted for stock splits, stock dividends, and other capital changes. No adjustment will be made for cash dividends paid in the six months. Then the percentage change in the price of each stock will be calculated. The total change in each portfolio will be determined by averaging the percentage changes of all 25 stocks.

REQUIRED

1. Assume that you are attempting to win a $100 prize. Describe how you would select the 25 stocks in each portfolio. Make explicit any assumptions that underlie your stock selections.

2. Assume you are attempting to win the $100,000 prize. Repeat the analysis in (1).

QUESTION 10.2: Multiactivity Firms and Risk Estimation

Part A. Justin Richman is a security analyst who for the last five years (termed 19X1 to 19X5) has tracked Dart Industries, a multiactivity firm with $2.403 billion of sales in 19X5. Table 10.8 presents the line-of-business disclosures from the 19X5 Annual Report.

Richman reads a newsletter from an investment consulting firm (Advanced Modern Portfolio Theory, AMPT) announcing a new beta (β_i) estimation service for multiactivity firms. AMPT will utilize the LOB disclosures in the annual reports of firms, as well as information about average industry betas, to estimate the betas of multiactivity firms. To date, Richman has estimated beta using a market model-based regression of the prior 60 months' security returns of Dart on the S&P 500 index.

TABLE 10.8 Dart Industries Line-of-Business Disclosures

	Sales					Earnings				
Segment	*19X1*	*19X2*	*19X3*	*19X4*	*19X5*	*19X1*	*19X2*	*19X3*	*19X4*	*19X5*
Direct selling	$ 459	$ 512	$ 576	$ 664	$ 728	$108	$133	$146	$186	$190
Mallory[1]	—	—	—	35	440	—	—	—	1	25
Consumer products	247	251	221	233	271	12	22	24	26	29
Chemicals, plastics	382	497	553	596	627	44	49	42	47	111
Glass containers	199	229	260	299	320	30	30	22	37	35
Resort development	10	10	16	29	34	(17)	(15)	(2)	2	5
Adjustments	(17)	(23)	(25)	(23)	(17)	(21)	(28)	(32)	(42)	(53)
Total	$1,280	$1,476	$1,601	$1,833	$2,403	$156	$191	$200	$257	$342

[1]Mallory (maker of Duracell batteries) was acquired in late 19X4. Results for 19X4 are for December only.

REQUIRED

1. Outline alternative ways of estimating beta for a multiactivity firm. How might the new risk estimation service provide better estimates of Dart's beta than the estimates currently used by Richman?

2. What problems might AMPT encounter in constructing beta estimates for Dart and other multiactivity firms?

3. A well-respected security analyst (David Norr) made the following comment:

> Probably segment reporting has been the most meaningful advance in analysis in the postwar period. . . . Management is in the best position to classify its segments. But, in view of the poor response in recent years, I believe we have no choice; we must go to a standardized or uniform industry classification (SIC) system with an increased number of segments . . . to be disclosed in interim and annual reports.

How might LOB disclosure along SIC codes "facilitate risk assessment" by external analysts? Why might companies strongly oppose a regulatory mandate that SIC codes be used for their line of business disclosures?

Part B. In late September of 19X6, Dart merged with Kraft in a tax-free exchange of stock. Kraft's 19X5 sales of $6.433 billion were derived from processed foods (80%, for example, cheese products, margarine, and salad dressings), dairy products (16%, for example, milk, ice cream, and frozen desserts), and nonfood products (4%, for example, chemicals, housewares, and toys). Both Dart and Kraft became wholly owned subsidiaries of Dart and Kraft, Inc.; all shares of Kraft's common stock, Dart's common stock, and Dart's $2.00 cumulative convertible preferred stock then outstanding were converted into an identical number of shares of Dart and Kraft common stock.

Justin Richman looks at his "to-do" items in early October 19X6 and notes that on December 2, 19X6, he has to provide his research director with an estimate of the beta of Dart and Kraft. He decides to gather some source data for a first pass. He collects (1) five years of premerger data on six items from a recent Value Line report on Dart and a recent report on Kraft, (2) December 31 market capitalizations of both companies in the prior five years, and (3) Value Line's beta estimates for both companies as of December of each year from 19X1 to 19X5. Table 10.9 presents this data. He notes with much interest that in December 19X5, Value Line estimated Dart's beta to be 1.20 and Kraft's to be .70. Market capitalizations of the two companies' equity securities on the day prior to the merger in September 19X6 were Dart, $1,099 million, and Kraft, $1,284 million; the market capitalization of Dart's cumulative convertible preferred stock on this same day was $114 million.

REQUIRED

1. What alternative approaches to estimating the beta of Dart and Kraft are available to Richman? Be specific.

2. What problems exist in implementing these approaches, given his December 2, 19X6, deadline? How would you reduce the severity of these problems?

TABLE 10.9 Dart Industries and Kraft Financial Data 19X1–19X7

Company/Financial Item	19X1 (actual)	19X2 (actual)	19X3 (actual)	19X4 (actual)	19X5 (actual)	19X6 (estimate)	19X7 (estimate)
A. *DART INDUSTRIES*							
Sales ($ millions)	$1,280	$1,476	$1,601	$1,833	$2,403	$2,400	$2,650
Net profit ($ millions)	79	102	109	127	172	165	185
Long-term debt ($ millions)	214	255	252	300	284	290	325
Net worth ($ millions)	684	765	846	932	1,059	1,170	1,300
Net profit margin	6.2%	6.9%	6.8%	7.0%	7.1%	6.9%	7.0%
Average annual P/E ratio	7.2	8.0	7.8	7.9	6.1	—	—
Market capitalization ($ millions)	607	774	862	925	927	—	—
Beta	1.25	1.25	1.25	1.25	1.20	—	—
B. *KRAFT*							
Sales ($ millions)	$4,857	$4,977	$5,239	$5,670	$6,433	$7,100	$7,800
Net profit ($ millions)	140	136	154	184	188	220	246
Long-term debt ($ millions)	215	221	344	307	312	280	300
Net worth ($ millions)	938	1,016	1,107	1,218	1,324	1,455	1,605
Net profit margin	2.9%	2.7%	2.9%	3.3%	2.9%	3.1%	3.2%
Average annual P/E ratio	7.9	9.1	8.5	7.0	7.0	—	—
Market capitalization ($ millions)	1,182	1,292	1,248	1,245	1,334	—	—
Beta	.75	.75	.75	.70	.70	—	—

SOURCE: Value Line Investment Surveys.

3. Describe how you would decide which of the approaches you outline provides the "best" estimate of Dart and Kraft's beta. Be specific.

QUESTION 10.3: Investment Choice by the Acorn Fund

The Acorn Fund is a no-load mutual fund based in Chicago that "invests with the objective of capital growth." Table 10.10 presents their annual investment performance (capital gains + dividends) over a 13-year period. Also included in Table 10.10 are the annual observations of a series of investment indexes and economic indicators over this same period. Over the 13-year period covered in Table 10.10, Acorn consistently has publicized that its focus will be on "smaller public companies":

19X1 Annual Report

Acorn Fund [chooses to] invest in many companies which are not widely known by the average investors. . . . Acorn chooses to work primarily with stocks in which values are more attractive and the facts about the company are not universally known.

TABLE 10.10 Annual Investment Returns ($\times$ 100) of Acorn Fund and Selected Market Indexes

Year	Acorn Fund	S&P 500	Small Stocks (smallest 20% of NYSE)	Long-Term Corporate Bonds	Long-Term Government Bonds	U.S. Treasury Bills	Consumer Price Index
19X1	31.0%	14.3%	16.5%	11.0%	13.2%	4.4%	3.4%
19X2	9.0	19.0	4.4	7.3	5.7	3.8	3.4
19X3	−24.0	−14.7	−30.9	1.1	−1.1	6.9	8.8
19X4	−28.0	−26.5	−19.9	−3.1	4.3	8.0	12.2
19X5	30.0	37.2	52.8	14.6	9.2	5.8	7.0
19X6	65.0	23.8	57.4	18.6	16.7	5.1	4.8
19X7	18.0	−7.2	25.4	1.7	−.7	5.1	6.8
19X8	17.0	6.6	23.5	−.1	−1.2	7.2	9.0
19X9	50.0	18.4	43.5	−4.2	−1.2	10.4	13.3
19X10	31.0	32.4	40.0	−2.6	−3.9	11.2	12.4
19X11	−7.0	−4.9	13.9	1.0	1.8	14.7	8.9
19X12	18.0	21.4	28.0	43.8	40.3	10.5	3.9
19X13	25.0	22.5	39.7	4.7	.6	8.8	3.8

SOURCE: Ibbotson Associates, *Stocks, Bonds, Bills and Inflation 1984 Yearbook*, Ibbotson Associates, Chicago, IL, 1984. p. 6.

19X6 First Quarter Report

If you follow the reasoning of the efficient market hypothesis to its logical conclusion, you should not try to get above-average performance by selecting stocks from a list of the 200 or 300 major "blue-chip" companies on which most institutions concentrate.

As a portfolio manager, one cannot hope to know more about Eastman Kodak or Avon Products than other analysts know. The chance to make an above-average return on investments has to be in the less "efficient" part of the market, by studying companies which are not under minute and constant scrutiny by a large group of analysts. In the past five years, as security analysts concentrate more and more on fewer stocks, there are many more possibilities of finding a group of smaller companies with excellent prospects, but selling at prices which still offer a chance to make an above-average return on our total portfolio without greater risk.

Will the price of such stocks ever go up, or is it possible these stocks will stay ignored? In our opinion, the sound economic values of these companies get reflected in their stock prices sooner or later. There are four different ways in which a stock price can rise:

(1) Growth: As the company grows, the market price of the stock will go up in line with earnings, dividends, and book value.

(2) Acquisition: The company can be acquired by a larger company at a price well above the market.

(3) Repurchase: If a stock sells well below its economic value, the company may repurchase sizeable blocks of its own shares.

(4) Revaluation: As a company grows and prospers, it can cross the threshold of institutional interest, at which time the Ugly Duckling is pronounced a Swan, and its price-earnings ratio substantially increases.

Good-quality smaller companies can produce stock market profits by all four mechanisms, while the established favorite stocks have only the first—one out of four. We therefore spend our time looking at stocks which are not covered by a lot of analysts, so the price is not set by the "efficient" process. Most Acorn portfolio stocks will be in the "inefficient" market.

Not only are smaller companies the best place to look for profits in a theoretical sense, but often in a practical way as well. A small company can be more easily understood than a large company and can be more responsive to positive developments in a specific area. For instance, a gas discovery by Houston Oil and Minerals causes the stock to jump, while Exxon would not even quiver after a similar discovery. The management of a good small company tends to be aggressive, cost conscious, entrepreneurial, and responsive, compared with large companies which tend toward conservatism and bureaucracy.

19X12 Annual Report

The best business book of the year is *In Search of Excellence* by Peters and Waterman. The authors state that "Smallness works. Small is beautiful." So, if small is beautiful, Acorn stocks should be Miss America.

[Recent academic research has found that] portfolios of stocks of small companies (yes, such as Acorn Fund) outperform large companies, even after adjusting for the higher volatility of small companies. Some recent tests disclose that a high proportion of this superior performance of small companies occurs in the month of January. So far, no one has come up with a causal mechanism to explain the January effect. If you have an explanation, send it to us, but it is tricky to explain why something that happens only in January (tax-selling effects, earnings reports, pension funds funding) should affect small company stocks so much more than the averages.

What happens to Acorn in January?

	Acorn Fund	S&P 500	Ratio
Average January appreciation	4.0%	2.1%	1.9
Average of other months	1.2	.7	1.7

Acorn does extremely well in January as compared with its average month (4.0% versus 1.2%). Part of this may be compensation for spending January in Chicago writing the Annual Report. However, the S&P 500 outperforms the average month in January as well. The ratio column shows that Acorn did well against the S&P 500 average in January (1.9X) but almost as well during the other months (1.7X). The January effect is significant for the Acorn Fund, but our strategy has worked well throughout the whole year.

REQUIRED

1. Critically discuss the Acorn investment philosophy. Comment on the distinction Acorn draws between the top 200–300 major stocks and those stocks in "the less efficient part of the market."

2. How would you examine if "smaller companies can produce stock market profits by all four mechanisms [growth, acquisition, repurchase, and reval-

uation], while the established favorite stocks have only the first [growth]''? What problems would occur in making this examination?

3. Two factors discussed in Acorn's investment philosophy are (a) small firm size and (b) limited coverage by security analysts. How might the research director of an investment firm gain insight into whether a focus on (a) or (b) has the greatest potential for superior investment returns?

4. Evaluate Acorn's investment performance over the 19X1–19X13 period. Is there evidence that Acorn possessed superior investment skill in this period?

5. Do you agree with the following comment on the empirical puzzles (anomalies) associated with the small-firm effect and the January effect:

> What then do the anomalies mean? They mean that the theories of capital asset pricing (at least as they pertain to equity markets) have been toppled. They mean that the most interesting insights into the pricing behavior of stocks are being discovered by tedious and painstakingly thorough examination of data. They mean that, in the constant ebb and flow between theory and empirics, empirics currently holds the upper hand. Given the rapid technological advances in empirical research (computers, data bases, statistical software, etc.), perhaps the recent surge in knowledge generated by empirical methods is not surprising. While it would be foolish to proclaim that "theory is dead," the anomalies signal that, at least in studies of equity markets, empiricism is currently the king.

REFERENCES

BALL, R., and P. BROWN. "Portfolio Theory and Accounting." *Journal of Accounting Research* (Autumn 1969): 300–323.

BEAVER, W. H., P. KETTLER, and M. SCHOLES. "The Association Between Market-Determined and Accounting-Determined Risk Measures." *The Accounting Review* (October 1970): 654–682.

BEAVER, W. H., and J. MANEGOLD. "The Association Between Market-Determined and Accounting-Determined Measures of Systematic Risk: Some Further Evidence." *Journal of Financial and Quantitative Analysis* (June 1975): 231–284.

BERGES, A., J. J. McCONNELL, and G. G. SCHLARBAUM. "The Turn-of-the-Year in Canada. *The Journal of Finance* (March 1984): 185–192.

BILDERSEE, J. S. "The Association Between a Market-Determined Measure of Risk and Alternative Measures of Risk." *The Accounting Review* (January 1975): 81–98.

BLACK, F. "Capital Market Equilibrium with Restricted Borrowing." *The Journal of Business* (July 1972): 444–455.

BLACK, F., M. JENSEN, and M. SCHOLES. "The Capital Asset Pricing Model: Some

Empirical Tests." In M. C. Jensen, ed., *Studies in the Theory of Capital Markets,* pp. 79–121. New York: Praeger, 1972.

BLACK, F., and M. SCHOLES. "The Pricing of Options and Corporate Liabilities." *Journal of Political Economy* (May/June 1973): 637–654.

BLUME, M. E. "Betas and Their Regression Tendencies." *The Journal of Finance* (June 1975): 785–795.

BOWER, D. H., R. S. BOWER, and D. E. LOGUE. "A Primer on Arbitrage Pricing Theory." *Midland Corporate Finance Journal* (Fall 1984): 31–40.

BOWMAN, R. G. "The Theoretical Relationship Between Systematic Risk and Financial (Accounting) Variables." *The Journal of Finance* (June 1979): 617–630.

BOWMAN, R. G. "The Importance of a Market-Value Measurement of Debt in Assessing Leverage." *Journal of Accounting Research* (Spring 1980): 242–254.

BOWMAN, R. G. "The Theoretical Relationship Between Systematic Risk and Financial (Accounting) Variables: Reply." *The Journal of Finance* (June 1981): 749–750.

BROWN, P., D. B. KEIM, A. W. KLEIDON, and T. A. MARSH. "Stock Return Seasonalities and the Tax-Loss Selling Hypothesis." *Journal of Financial Economics* (June 1983): 105–127.

CHEN, N. "Some Empirical Tests of the Theory of Arbitrage Pricing." *The Journal of Finance* (December 1983): 1393–1414.

CHRISTIE, A. A. "The Stochastic Behavior of Common Stock Variances: Value, Leverage and Interest Rate Effects." *Journal of Financial Economics* (December 1982): 407–432.

CONINE, T. E. "On the Theoretical Relationship Between Business Risk and Systematic Risk." *Journal of Business Finance and Accounting* (Summer 1982): 199–205.

DIMSON, E. "Risk Measurement When Shares Are Subject to Infrequent Trading." *Journal of Financial Economics* (June 1979): 197–226.

DIMSON, E., and T. MARSH. "Risk, Return and Company Size Effects: The Thirty Year Record," working paper. London Business School, 1985.

ESTEP, T., N. HANSON, and C. JOHNSON. "Sources of Value and Risk in Common Stocks." *The Journal of Portfolio Management* (Summer 1983): 5–13.

FAMA, E. F., and J. D. MACBETH. "Risk, Return and Equilibrium: Empirical Tests." *Journal of Political Economy* (May–June 1973): 607–636.

FOSTER, G. "Asset Pricing Models: Further Tests." *Journal of Financial and Quantitative Analysis* (March 1978): 39–53.

GAHLON, J. M., and J. A. GENTRY. "On the Relationship Between Systematic Risk and The Degrees of Operating and Financial Leverage." *Financial Management* (Summer 1982): 15–23.

GIBBONS, M. R. "Multivariate Tests of Financial Models: A New Approach." *Journal of Financial Economics* (March 1982): 3–27.

GULTEKIN, M. N., and N. B. GULTEKIN. "Stock Market Seasonality: International Evidence." *Journal of Financial Economics* (December 1983): 469–481.

HAMADA, R. S. "Portfolio Analysis, Market Equilibrium and Corporation Finance." *The Journal of Finance* (March 1969): 13–31.

HAMADA, R. S. "The Effect of the Firm's Capital Structure on the Systematic Risk of Common Stocks." *The Journal of Finance* (March 1972): 435–452.

HILL, N. C., and B. K. STONE. "Accounting Betas, Systematic Operating Risk, and Financial Leverage: A Risk-Composition Approach to the Determinants of Systematic Risk." *Journal of Financial and Quantitative Analysis* (September 1980): 595–637.

HOCHMAN, S. "The Beta Coefficient: An Instrumental Variables Approach." In *Research in Finance,* Vol. 4, pp. 128–151. Greenwich, Conn.: JAI Press, 1983.

HORNGREN, C. T. *Cost Accounting,* 5th ed. Englewood-Cliffs, N.J.: Prentice-Hall, 1982.

IBBOTSON (R. G.) ASSOCIATES, INC. *Stock, Bonds, Bills and Inflation 1984 Yearbook.* Chicago: R. G. Ibbotson Associates, 1984.

KEIM, D. B. "Size-Related Anomalies and Stock Return Seasonality: Further Empirical Evidence." *Journal of Financial Economics* (June 1983): 13–32. North Holland Publishing Company, Amsterdam, 1983.

KEIM, D. B., and R. F. STAMBAUGH. "A Further Investigation of the Weekend Effect in Stock Returns." *The Journal of Finance* (July 1984): 819–835.

LEV, B. "On the Association Between Operating Leverage and Risk." *Journal of Financial and Quantitative Analysis* (September 1974): 627–641.

LITZENBERGER, R. H., and K. RAMASWAMY. "The Effect of Personal Taxes and Dividends on Capital Asset Prices: Theory and Empirical Evidence." *Journal of Financial Economics* (June 1979): 163–195.

MANDELKER, G. N., and S. G. RHEE. "The Impact of the Degrees of Operating and Financial Leverage on Systematic Risk of Common Stock." *Journal of Financial and Quantitative Analysis* (March 1984): 45–57.

MYERS, S. C. "The Relation Between Real and Financial Measures of Risk and Return." In I. Friend and J. L. Bicksler, eds., *Risk and Return in Finance,* Vol. I, pp. 49–80. Cambridge, Mass.: Ballinger, 1977.

NAKAMURA, T., and N. TERADA. "The Size Effect and Seasonality in Japanese Stock Returns." Tokyo: Nomura Research Institute, 1984.

PETTIT, R. R., and R. WESTERFIELD. "A Model of Capital Asset Risk." *Journal of Financial and Quantitative Analysis* (March 1972): 1649–1677.

REINGANUM, M. R. "The Anomalous Stock Market Behavior of Small Firms in January." *Journal of Financial Economics* (June 1983): 89–104.

ROLL, R. "Vas ist das?" *Journal of Portfolio Management* (Winter 1983): 18–28.

ROLL, R., and S. A. ROSS. "An Empirical Investigation of the Arbitrage Pricing Theory." *The Journal of Finance* (December 1980): 1073–1103.

ROSENBERG, B., and W. McKIBBEN. "The Prediction of Systematic and Specific Risk in Common Stocks." *Journal of Financial and Quantitative Analysis* (March 1973): 317–334.

ROSS, S. A. "The Arbitrage Theory of Capital Asset Pricing." *Journal of Economic Theory* (December 1976): 341–360.

RUBINSTEIN, M. E. "A Mean-Variance Synthesis of Corporate Financial Theory." *The Journal of Finance* (March 1973): 167–181.

SCHOLES, M., and J. WILLIAMS. "Estimating Betas from Nonsynchronous Data." *Journal of Financial Economics* (December 1977): 309–327.

SHARPE, W. F. "Capital Asset Prices: A Theory of Market Equilibrium Under Conditions of Risk." *The Journal of Finance* (September 1964): 425–442.

SHARPE, W. F. "Factors in NYSE Security Returns, 1931–1979." *The Journal of Portfolio Management* (Summer 1982): 5–19.

SHARPE, W. F. *Investments,* 3rd ed. Englewood Cliffs, N.J.: Prentice-Hall, 1985.

SINCLAIR, N. A. "Aspects of the Factor Structure Implicit in the Australian Industrial Equity Market: February 1958 to August 1977." *Australian Journal of Management* (June 1984): 23–36.

THOMPSON, D. J. "Sources of Systematic Risk in Common Stocks." *The Journal of Business* (April 1976): 173–188.

WAHLROOS, B., and T. BERGLUND. "The January Effect on a Small Stock Market: Lumpy Information and Tax-Loss Selling," working paper. Northwestern University, Evanston, Ill., 1983.

11

CAPITAL MARKETS AND CORPORATE INFORMATION RELEASES

11.1 INTRODUCTION

Financial statement information is one of many potential sources that capital markets may use in revising the prices of common stocks, preferred stocks, corporate bonds, and other traded securities. What evidence is there that financial statement information plays an important role in the capital market revaluation process? What evidence is there that the capital market reacts to reported accounting earnings in the mechanistic way suggested by some company officials and authors quoted in Chapter 9? What evidence is there about the timeliness of financial statement releases? These and related issues are discussed in this chapter.

These issues are important to many groups. Consider security analysts who adopt the fundamental analysis approach to investment choice (see Chapter 9). A major part of this analysis examines trends in the financial statements of corporations. If there is no association between such trends and stock market returns, then this analysis is likely to be unrewarding. Moreover, even if there is such an association, the question of the timeliness of accounting data is important. If competing information sources can fully provide the capital market with the information in annual reports at an earlier date, then a reevaluation of the fundamental analysis approach seems to be warranted.

Corporate management is also vitally interested in the issues discussed in this chapter. Management has discretion over the timing of many information releases (for example, an earnings report) and, in some cases, over whether even to issue a release (for example, a forecast of earnings). An understanding of how the capital market reacts to the content and timing of individual releases facilitates the development of an integrated corporate disclosure policy.

Other parties also have an interest in the issues discussed in this chapter. For example, auditors increasingly are the subject of lawsuits alleging that investors suffered capital market losses due to material nondisclosures by management or the auditors themselves. One important implication of the evidence discussed in this chapter is that auditors should monitor the security returns of their clients when deciding whether to make detailed investigations of accounting or reporting problems of those clients.

Regulatory agencies such as the FASB and the SEC make decisions that affect the content or the timing of information reported to the capital market. Arguments made in submissions to these agencies often make assumptions about the role of reported earnings in security price determination (for example, that there is a mechanistic relation between reported earnings and security prices). The evidence in this chapter suggests that some of the assumptions made in these submissions are not descriptive of those capital markets that have been the subject of research.

An important technique that is frequently cited in this chapter is the cumulative abnormal return (CAR) measure. The appendix to this chapter describes and illustrates the CAR measure. Readers not familiar with the CAR measure are advised to read this appendix prior to reading Sections 11.2 to 11.7.

11.2 CAPITAL MARKET REACTION TO FIRM-ORIENTED ANNOUNCEMENTS

This section examines the behavior of capital market variables at the time firm-oriented releases are publicly announced. The focus is on whether such releases are informative to either individual capital market participants or to the aggregate capital market.

One issue addressed is whether these releases are associated with increased trading volume activity (TVA) at the time of their announcement. The following measure has been used in several studies to examine this issue:

$$ \text{TVA}_{i,t} = \frac{\text{Number of shares of firm } i \text{ traded in time } t}{\text{Number of shares of firm } i \text{ outstanding in time } t} \qquad \textbf{(11.1)} $$

By examining the behavior of $\text{TVA}_{i,t}$ in the announcement period, relative to the average $\text{TVA}_{i,t}$ in a nonannouncement period, evidence on whether the release is associated with increased trading volume can be gathered. The foregoing $\text{TVA}_{i,t}$ measure is used to examine whether *individual investors* find the release informative, in the sense that it has led to their making an above-normal level of purchases or sales of shares.

A second issue addressed is whether these releases are associated with a change in the distribution of security returns at the time of their announcement. One measure used in several studies to examine security return variability (SRV) is

$$ \text{SRV}_{i,t} = \frac{U_{i,t}^2}{V(U_{i,t})} \qquad \textbf{(11.2)} $$

where

$U_{i,t}$ = the abnormal return of security i in time t (see the appendix to this chapter)

$V(U_{i,t})$ = variance of abnormal returns in a nonannouncement period

This measure examines whether there is increased variability in security returns at the time the release is announced.

Another measure used in research is $U_{i,t}$, as defined earlier; this measure examines whether there is a change in the mean of security returns at the time the release is announced. Both the mean ($U_{i,t}$) and variability ($\text{SRV}_{i,t}$) abnormal return measures examine whether the *aggregate market* finds the release informative, in the sense that it is associated with a change in the distribution of security returns at the time of its announcement. When the $U_{i,t}$ measure is averaged across observations, positive and negative values can cancel each other. When the $\text{SRV}_{i,t}$ measure is averaged across observations, no such cancellation occurs (all values of $\text{SRV}_{i,t}$ are nonnegative). The result is that if there is heterogeneity within a set of observations as to the direction of the security return impact of a release, the $\text{SRV}_{i,t}$ measure is more likely to detect that such an impact occurred. (However, the $\text{SRV}_{i,t}$ measure will not provide insight into the directional nature of that impact.)

A.   Factors Affecting Information Content

Three factors that can affect the information content of a release are:

1. *The capital market's expectation as to the content and timing of the release.* Typically, there will be uncertainty as to either the content or timing of corporate releases. As a general rule, the larger the extent of uncertainty, the greater the potential for any one release to cause a revision in security prices. An important factor affecting the capital market's expectation is the availability of competing information sources. Table 11.1 provides a coding of firm-oriented releases. The coding was developed to apply to a broad cross section of firms. For specific industries, the "other" item in several categories in Table 11.1 could be broken down to capture specific classes of releases that are encountered on a recurring basis for firms in that industry. In many cases, releases in one category in Table 11.1 (for example, marketing-production-sales) can affect the capital market's expectations as to the content or timing of releases in other categories (for example, earnings).

2. *The implications of the release for the future distribution of security returns.* As a general rule, the larger the relative revision in expected cash flows, the larger the security price revaluation implication of the release. The president of one company (Cibola Energy Corporation) describes this factor under the heading "Big Companies, Little Companies and the Big Bang Theory":

> Why invest in a small, publicly traded oil company? Today, I know of only one reason—the Big Bang Theory. A small company has the potential for explosive growth if it discovers a large oil or gas field on its acreage. On the other hand, a large company usually will not be substantially affected by such a discovery because of the smaller relative impact in proportion to its total reserves.

Many of the releases reported in publications such as *The Wall Street Journal* or *The* (London) *Financial Times* have such minimal effects on future cash flows (or other attributes valued by the capital market) that, using existing state-of-the-art research methodologies, we would classify them as not having information content.

3. *The credibility of the information source.* As a general rule, the more credible the source of an information release, the larger the revaluation implication

TABLE 11.1   Coding of Firm-Oriented Information Releases

1. *Earnings-Related Announcements*. (a) Preliminary annual figures, (b) annual report details, (c) preliminary interim figures, (d) interim report details, (e) accounting changes, (f) auditor qualifications or report, (g) other.
2. *Forecast Announcements by Company Officals*. (a) Earnings forecasts prior to fiscal year end, (b) earnings estimates after fiscal year end, (c) sales forecasts, (d) other.
3. *Dividend Announcements*. (a) Cash distributions, (b) stock distributions, (c) other.
4. *Financing Announcements*. (a) Equity-related announcements, (b) debt-related announcements, (c) hybrid security announcements, (d) leasing, (e) standby credit agreements, (f) secondary issues, (g) stock splits, (h) stock repurchases, (i) joint venture announcements, (j) other.
5. *Government-Related Announcements*. (a) Impact of (new) legislation, (b) investigations into firm's activities, (c) regulatory agency decisions, (d) other.
6. *Investment Announcements*. (a) Exploration, (b) new ventures, (c) plant expansion/contraction, (d) plant shutdowns, (e) R&D developments, (f) other.
7. *Labor Announcements*. (a) Negotiations, (b) new contracts, (c) strikes, (d) other.
8. *Legal Announcements*. (a) Lawsuits against company or its officials, (b) lawsuits by company or its officials, (c) other.
9. *Marketing-Production-Sales Announcements*. (a) Advertising, (b) contract details, (c) new products, (d) price changes, (e) product recalls, (f) production reports, (g) product safety reports, (h) sales reports, (i) warranty details, (j) other.
10. *Management–Board of Director Announcements*. (a) Board of directors, (b) management, (c) organization structure details, (d) other.
11. *Merger-Takeover-Divestiture Announcements*. (a) Merger reports, (b) equity investment reports, (c) takeover reports–acquiror, (d) takeover reports–acquiree, (e) divestiture reports, (f) other.
12. *Securities Industry Announcements*. (a) Annual meeting reports, (b) changes in stockholdings, (c) "Heard on the Street" item, (d) "insider" trading report, (e) price/trading volume report, (f) trading restriction or suspension, (g) other.
13. *Miscellaneous*.

of that release. The truthfulness of an information release may be questioned on several grounds; for example, items included in the release are incorrect, or items excluded from the release are material to the interpretation of those included. One ground for questioning the veracity of a release is if the source has a track record of prior incorrect or misleading releases. While legal and other penalties (for example, reduced employment opportunities) create incentives for executives and other parties to make truthful and complete disclosures, a continuing saga of individuals making incorrect or misleading releases appears to accompany all markets in which securities are traded.

B. Effect of Earnings Releases on Trading Volume and Variability of Security Returns

One of the most robust findings in the financial statement research area is that the release of interim and annual earnings is associated with both increased trading volume and increased security return variability. An early classic study is Beaver (1968). A major strength of this study was the concern with methodological issues. Consider examining trading volume at the time of earnings releases. Trading can occur for a variety of factors:

1. Investors purchasing/selling to coordinate their income-earning and income-spending activities

2. Investors purchasing/selling to maintain a diversified portfolio

3. Investors purchasing/selling due to (a) changes in the risk of their portfolio or (b) changes in their own risk preferences

4. Investors purchasing/selling due to taxation reasons (for example, a differential tax on capital gains vis-à-vis other income)

5. Investors purchasing/selling due to new information causing a revision of their probability assessments of the distribution of returns.

Beaver devoted much effort to controlling for nonearnings-related factors inducing trading volume at the time of earnings releases. A sample of 143 firms over the 1961–1965 period was studied. This sample was restricted to non-December 31 fiscal year firms, thus minimizing the effect of December–January tax-induced trading volume. (This restriction also reduced the clustering of observations in a short calendar-time period due to many firms having a December 31 fiscal year end.) The sample was also restricted to firms that had no dividend announcement in the week of the annual earnings announcement; thus, the effect of one potentially important nonearnings impetus to trading volume was minimized. Similarly, Beaver examined trading volume in the earnings announcement period relative to that in the nonannouncement period; thus, trading volume due to factors that induce continuous trading was taken into account in the experiment.

The $TVA_{i,t}$ measure of (11.1) was used by Beaver to examine weekly trading volume. Results for the 17-week period surrounding (and including) the earnings announcement week are presented in panel A of Figure 11.1. The dashed line denotes the average $TVA_{i,t}$ in the nonreport period. Beaver reported that there was a "rather dramatic increase in volume in the announcement week (week 0). The mean volume in week 0 is 33 percent larger than the mean volume during the nonreport period and it is by far the largest value observed during the 17 weeks. Investors do shift portfolio positions at the time of the earnings announcement and this shift is consistent with the contention that earnings reports have information content" (p. 74). A second phase of Beaver's (1968) research examined the variability of security returns in the same 17-week period surrounding annual earnings announcements; the $SRV_{i,t}$ measure of (11.2) was used in this phase of the research. Panel B of Figure 11.1 plots the behavior of $SRV_{i,t}$ for the same 17-week period discussed. Security return variability was 67% higher in the earnings announcement week than in a nonearnings announcement period.

Firms listed on the New York Stock Exchange (NYSE) or the American Stock Exchange (ASE) typically first release their earnings figures on the Broad Tape. Using this tape, the hour and minute of each earnings news release can be identified. Patell and Wolfson (1984) used this information to examine the intraday behavior of security returns in the period surrounding earnings announcements.

FIGURE 11.1   Capital Market Reaction to Annual Earnings Announcements

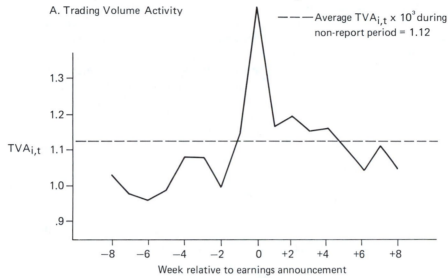

A. Trading Volume Activity

$- - -$Average $TVA_{i,t} \times 10^3$ during non-report period = 1.12

TVA$_{i,t}$

Week relative to earnings announcement

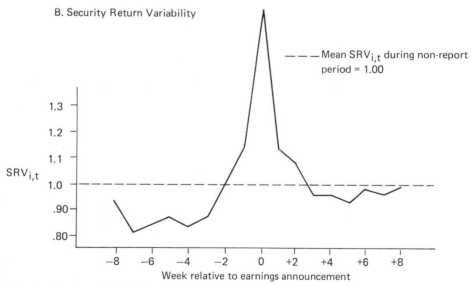

B. Security Return Variability

$- - -$Mean $SRV_{i,t}$ during non-report period = 1.00

SRV$_{i,t}$

Week relative to earnings announcement

Source: Beaver (1968, Figures 1 and 6): pp. 89, 91.

The sample was 96 firms that were listed on the NYSE or ASE in the 1976–1977 period (and which also had options traded on the Chicago Board Options Exchange in the same period). Part of their research focused on the number of extreme security price changes in a 26-hour trading period surrounding each announcement. An extreme price change was "one that falls in either of the five-percent tails of the distribution [of price changes] for the appropriate one-hour or overnight trading period'' (pp. 237–238). A period in which no earnings announcements were made was used to assess the expected distribution of security price changes. Results are reported in Figure 11.2. The conclusion was that there is ''a very strong reaction at the announcement, the major portion of which decays within two hours, but with detectable traces that linger into the following day'' (p. 240).

Foster (1981) also reported results using the $SRV_{i,t}$ measure in (11.2) for a sample of interim and annual earnings announcements by 53 U.S. firms over the 1963–1978 period. The conclusion was that in the two-day trading period up to and including the report of earnings in *The Wall Street Journal,* there was a 78% increase in security return variability relative to the variability of two-day security returns in nonearnings announcement periods. The sample was then partitioned on an industry basis; the focus of this analysis was whether differences in $SRV_{i,t}$ existed across industries in the sample. The mean $SRV_{i,t}$ for firms in each of the eight industries represented in the sample was

Industry (SIC Code)	Mean $SRV_{i,t}$
Photographic equipment and supplies (3861)	2.85
Flat glass (3210)	2.79
Motor vehicles and car bodies (3711)	2.75
Bakery products (2050)	1.65
Banks, New York City (6021)	1.60
Bottled and canned soft drinks (2086)	1.53
Savings and loan associations (6120)	1.26
Radio and T.V. broadcasters (4830)	1.19

FIGURE 11.2 Intraday Security Return Variability and Earnings Releases

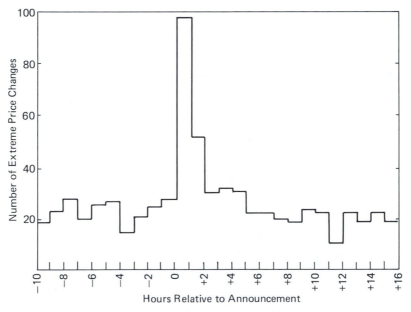

Source: Patell and Wolfson (1984, Figure 2): p. 240.

Firms included in each of these industries were required to have at least 50 percent of their annual revenues from the one "industry" line of business. Based on the foregoing (and similar) results, industry membership appears to be an important variable explaining differences across firms in the magnitude of the $SRV_{i,t}$ statistic at the time of the earnings release.

Several variables (in addition to industry membership) have been identified that explain differences in the magnitude of the security return variability associated with earnings releases. Richardson (1984) examined a sample of 153 NYSE and ASE firms. Focusing on annual earnings reports made in the 1976–1978 period, and using the $SRV_{i,t}$ measure in (11.2), he reported a 40% increase in the variability of security returns in the earnings announcement week. Richardson then partitioned his sample into firm-size deciles (based on market capitalization) and examined the mean $SRV_{i,t}$ and the mean of other variables for each decile. The other variables included the following:

1. Measures of extent of information available to market participants, for example, (a) the presence or absence of analyst earnings forecasts reported in *The Earnings Forecaster* and (b) the natural log of the number of *Wall Street Journal* news items in the 12 months prior to announcement. The motivation for these two measures was that "less analyst and press following could potentially result in systematically less information impounded in stock price" (p. 13).

2. Measure of extent of information available from macro sources. The proxy used for this variable was the R^2 from a regression of each firm's earnings on an economywide earnings index (see Chapter 6). The motivation for this measure was that "earnings reports for low R^2 firms tend to be less prompted by macro information sources, making earnings a relatively more important source of information for investors interested in such firms, compared to high R^2 firms" (p. 15).

Table 11.2 presents a subset of the results in Richardson (1984). Although there is not a monotonic relationship between the variables in Table 11.2, patterns in the results are observable. Firms with higher security return variability in the week of their annual earnings release typically

- Are of smaller size
- Have a lower frequency of a forecast being reported in *The Earnings Forecaster*
- Have fewer items reported in *The Wall Street Journal*
- Have a lower percentage of their earnings variability explained by an economy variable.

As is apparent in Table 11.2, these four variables are not independent of each other.

Other Exchanges and Other Countries

Most research using U.S. firms has concentrated on NYSE- or ASE-listed firms (in part due to the greater accessibility of security return data for these

TABLE 11.2   Security Return Variability, Earnings Releases, and Firm-Related
Characteristics

Firm-Size Decile (natural log of market value)	Security-Return Variability ($SRV_{i,t}$)	Presence (1) or Absence (0) of Forecast in S&P's Earnings Forecaster	Natural Log of Number of Annual WSJ Announcements	Macro Source of Information Measure
1. (7.6)	1.06	.98	3.2	.302
2. (6.5)	1.26	.83	3.0	.259
3. (5.9)	.79	.83	2.8	.224
4. (5.3)	1.06	.82	2.8	.260
5. (4.8)	1.26	.80	2.7	.223
6. (4.1)	1.49	.54	2.5	.240
7. (3.6)	1.84	.24	2.2	.195
8. (3.1)	1.83	.15	2.2	.178
9. (2.3)	1.95	.04	2.0	.136
10. (1.3)	1.62	.00	1.8	.099

SOURCE: Richardson (1984, Table 2): p. 20.

firms). A subset of studies has examined securities traded on the over-the-counter
(OTC) market. Grant (1980) reports results for a sample of 747 annual earnings
announcements from 211 OTC firms. The mean value of the $SRV_{i,t}$ measure in
(11.2) in the week of the earnings announcement was 2.596. The mean $SRV_{i,t}$ in
the eight weeks preceding and the eight weeks subsequent to the announcement
week was 1.054. Based on a control group of 101 NYSE firms, the conclusion
was that the $SRV_{i,t}$ measure "for the OTC sample in week zero is significantly
greater than that observed for the NYSE firms" (p. 265). It was hypothesized
that this result was due to OTC investors having "fewer alternative sources from
which to acquire information on firms prior to the release of the annual earnings
number" (p. 267). Morse (1981) examined the behavior of $TVA_{i,t}$ in (11.1) and
$SRV_{i,t}$ in (11.2) for a sample of 25 NYSE/ASE stocks and 25 OTC stocks in the
1973–1976 period. Increased trading volume activity and increased security return
variability at the time of earnings releases was observed for both samples. In
contrast to Grant (1980), Morse (1981) reported no significant difference between
the NYSE/ASE and OTC samples for either $TVA_{i,t}$ or $SRV_{i,t}$. (However, Morse's
sample of OTC stocks was drawn from a population of actively traded securities.)

Maingot (1984) reports results using the $SRV_{i,t}$ measure in (11.2) for 100
firms listed on the London Stock Exchange. The time period was 1976 to 1978.
The sample included only firms that had one dividend announcement in the week
of the annual earnings announcement: "U.K. earnings and dividends are announced at the same time. Therefore, one can only examine the joint impact of
both earnings and dividends" (p. 53). The mean $SRV_{i,t}$ in the announcement week
was 4.033 compared to a mean of .553 for the eight weeks preceding and the eight
weeks subsequent to the earnings/dividend announcement week. The conclusion
was that "the annual earnings numbers released by UK companies do possess

information. However, while the maximum response did take place at week 0, there did appear to be some anticipatory reaction in the week preceding [week − 1] the announcement week'' (p. 56).

C. Effect of Earnings Releases on Mean Security Returns

Considerable evidence exists about factors explaining the *direction* and *magnitude* of the capital market reaction to earnings announcements by firms. Two (related) variables that have support from many studies are

1. The sign and magnitude of the unexpected component of the earnings change
2. Firm size.

Results from Foster, Olsen, and Shevlin (1984) illustrate the importance of these two variables for interim and annual earnings releases of 2,053 NYSE and ASE firms in the 1974–1981 period. The forecast error of firm i in period $t(\text{FE}_{i,t})$, from using a time-series–based forecast model, was defined as actual earnings − forecast earnings. The magnitude of the unexpected earnings (forecast error) was computed as

$$\text{UE}_{i,t} = \frac{\text{FE}_{i,t}}{\sigma(\text{FE}_{i,t})} \qquad \textbf{(11.3)}$$

where $\sigma(\text{FE}_{i,t})$, the standard deviation of the forecast error, was computed using forecast errors made over the prior 20 quarters. Each earnings release was assigned to one of ten portfolios with portfolio 1 being the decile with the 10% most negative unexpected earnings observations; portfolio 10 was the decile with the 10% most positive unexpected earnings observations. Abnormal security returns were measured over the trading day preceding and the trading day that earnings were announced in *The Wall Street Journal*. Panel A of Figure 11.3 presents the full sample results for the ten unexpected earnings change portfolios. The mean abnormal security returns underlying panel A are

Unexpected Earnings Change Portfolios

	1	*2*	*3*	*4*	*5*	*6*	*7*	*8*	*9*	*10*
All firms	− 1.34%	− .88	− .49	− .25	.19	.44	.73	.81	1.03	1.26

These results provide strong evidence that the sign and magnitude of the unexpected earnings change is positively correlated with the sign and magnitude of security returns in the two trading days immediately surrounding the earnings announcement. Panels B and C of Figure 11.3 present results for two firm-size categories. Panel B reports firms in the largest 20% (based on market capitalization) of firms on the NYSE, while panel C reports firms in the smallest 20% of firms on the NYSE. The mean abnormal returns underlying panels B and C are

A. Full Sample

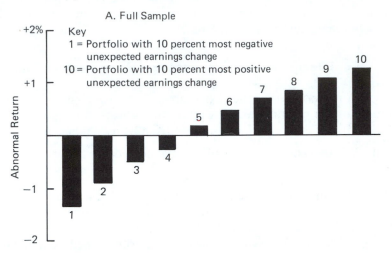

B. Large-Firm Sample (20 percent largest)

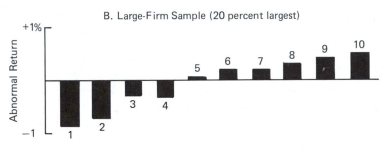

C. Small-Firm Sample (20 percent smallest)

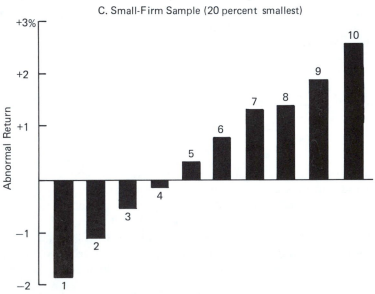

Source: Foster, Olsen, and Shevlin (1984, Tables 4 and 6): pp. 587, 596.

Unexpected Earnings Change Portfolios

	1	2	3	4	5	6	7	8	9	10
Largest 20% of firms	−.81%	−.71	−.26	−.31	.05	.20	.19	.36	.41	.50
Smallest 20% of firms	−1.83%	−1.07	−.50	−.09	.38	.81	1.36	1.41	1.91	2.58

The pattern observed in panel A for the full sample holds for both the largest- and smallest-firm subsamples. However, the magnitudes of the abnormal returns are larger for the smallest-firm subsample.

Another variable explaining differences in the sign and magnitude of abnormal security returns in the period surrounding earnings releases is the timeliness of the release. (Timeliness here is operationally defined as the difference between the actual release date and the expected release date.) Chambers and Penman (1984) examine a sample of 100 NYSE firms over the 1970–1976 period. Using each firm's historical reporting date sequence, these authors develop predictions for the release date of each interim and annual earnings release in this period. An early/late reporter was a firm that reported its earnings before/after the predicted date. Table 11.3 reports mean abnormal security returns in the two-day trading period up to and including the announcement of earnings in *The Wall Street Journal*. The most striking result in Table 11.3 is that firms that report their earnings releases earlier than expected have positive abnormal security returns in the period surrounding their actual release date; this is consistent with unexpectedly early reports conveying good news. The interpretation of the capital market reaction to late reports is more ambiguous. At the actual announcement date, the abnormal returns are typically negative (especially for interim reports);

TABLE 11.3 Security Returns in (−1, 0) Period Surrounding Earnings Announcements: Effect of Timeliness—Early (Late) Reporter Means Firm Reports Before (After) Expected Release Date

Interim Earnings Releases			*Annual Earnings Releases*		
Days Early	*Mean Abnormal Return*	*t Statistic*	*Days Early*	*Mean Abnormal Return*	*t Statistic*
≥ 9	1.29	2.48	≥ 23	1.53	1.95
6 to 8	1.00	1.16	16 to 22	4.21	2.77
4 to 5	.35	.62	10 to 15	.01	.00
2 to 3	−.18	−.45	7 to 9	.16	.33
0 to 1	.16	.64	3 to 6	.76	1.04
−1 to −2	−.26	−.74	0 to 2	.35	.86
−3 to −4	−.08	−.29	−1 to −3	−.61	−.89
−5 to −6	−.77	−1.51	−4 to −7	1.01	1.83
≤ −7	−.72	−1.26	≤ −8	−1.10	−1.44

SOURCE: Chambers and Penman (1984, Table 3): p. 28.

this is consistent with unexpectedly late reports conveying bad news. However, the very act of delaying a report appears to convey negative information to the capital market. Chambers and Penman report that in the period between the expected release date and just prior to the actual release date, the late reporters typically experience negative abnormal returns. In a study of 297 NYSE and ASE firms over the 1977 to 1980 period, Kross and Schroeder (1984) report similar results.

D. Effect of Other Releases on Security Returns

The information content of many of the firm-oriented releases outlined in Table 11.1 has been studied. Prior sections focused on interim and annual earnings releases. This section further illustrates this research by discussing the information content of management earnings forecast releases and dividend releases.

Management Earnings Forecasts

A subset of firms voluntarily release management forecasts of earnings (see Chapters 2 and 8 for further discussion). There is considerable evidence that the capital market views these forecasts as conveying information relevant to security price revaluation. Waymire (1984) examined a sample of 479 point projections of annual earnings per share by management reported in *The Wall Street Journal*. For these 479 firms, a consensus security analyst forecast was calculated as the average of all analyst forecasts of annual earnings per share in the issue of *The Earnings Forecaster* published immediately preceding the management forecast disclosure. This consensus forecast was used as the proxy for expected earnings. The management earnings forecast deviation (FD_i) was calculated as

$$FD_i = \frac{\text{Management forecast} - \text{Consensus analyst forecast}}{\text{Consensus analyst forecast}} \tag{11.4}$$

The sample contained 261 good-news management forecasts (that is, a positive forecast deviation) and 181 bad-news forecasts. Waymire examined the security return behavior in the three-day trading period surrounding *The Wall Street Journal* announcement date of the management forecast (termed $[-1, +1]$). The FD_i measure for each management forecast was ranked from most negative to most positive and 25 equal-sized portfolios were formed. The Spearman rank correlation between the median FD_i of each of the 25 portfolios and the mean portfolio abnormal security return in the $[-1, +1]$ period was .75 (significant at the .01 level). Summary results from combining the 25 portfolios into 5 portfolios are

Group	Median FD_i of Group	Abnormal Security Return in $(-1, +1)$ Period
I (20% lowest FD_i)	−.083	−1.70%
II	−.018	.24
III	.010	.88
IV	.040	.91
V (20% highest FD_i)	.127	2.47

The conclusion was that a "significant positive association exists between magnitude of forecast deviation and magnitude of abnormal returns in the period immediately around forecast disclosure date" (pp. 1–2).

Dividend Announcements

The release of earnings forecasts is one mechanism that management can use to signal its beliefs about the future profitability of the firm. An alternative signaling mechanism is via a change in dividend policy. Many studies have examined the behavior of security prices at the time of dividend releases; for example,

- Asquith and Mullins (1983) examined a sample of NYSE/ASE firms that either paid their first dividend in their corporate history or initiated dividends after omitting them for at least a ten-year period. The time period covered was 1954 to 1980.
- Brickley (1983) examined a sample of specially designated dividends (SDDs) labeled by management as "extra," "special," or "year end." The sample was 165 SDDs made by NYSE/ASE firms in the 1969 to 1979 period.
- Dielman and Oppenheimer (1984) examined a sample of NYSE firms that made large dividend changes in the 1969–1977 period; the sample was 39 resumptions of dividend payments, 51 dividend increases of 25% or more, 59 dividend decreases of 25% or more, and 53 dividend omissions.

Table 11.4 presents the mean daily abnormal returns in the period surrounding each release for the dividend categories in the preceding studies; day 0 is *The Wall Street Journal* date for each release. Each of the categories in Table 11.4 shows statistically significant abnormal returns in the $[-1, 0]$ announcement period. Firms that increase dividends, announce special or extra dividends, or initiate dividend payments for the first time experience positive abnormal returns.

TABLE 11.4 Security Returns of Dividend Change Categories Surrounding Announcement Date

Event Day	Asquith-Mullin (1983) Initiating Dividend Payment	Brickley (1983) Specially Designated Dividends	Dielman and Oppenheimer (1984)			
			Dividend Resumption	Dividend Increase > 25%	Dividend Decrease > 25%	Dividend Omission
−5	.60	−.01	.74	.30	.60	.36
−4	.10	−.08	1.22	−.12	−.53	−.14
−3	−.20	.55	.10	−.25	−.20	−.17
−2	.20	.21	−.16	.38	−.53	−.66
−1	2.50	.90	.02	.39	−.25	−.35
0	1.20	1.21	2.21	1.19	−3.99	−5.66
1	.20	.42	1.31	.95	−3.68	−2.48
2	−.20	.07	−.67	.59	.36	1.21
3	.50	.34	−.11	.06	.29	.62
4	−.00	.29	−.66	.27	−.66	−.12
5	.40	−.10	.73	−.06	−.77	.13

Firms that decrease or omit dividend payments experience significant negative abnormal returns. These results are consistent with the capital market using dividend releases as a signal from management about the future earnings prospects of the firm.

E.   Effect of Information Releases on Security Returns of Nonannouncing Firms

Information transfers between firms arise when the information releases of firm j $(k, \ldots, z)$ are used to make inferences about the share price of firm i. Information transfers could be associated with earnings releases for several reasons. One reason is that firm j's release could convey information about how movements in key variables are affecting profitability of firms in an industry; for example, changes in new housing starts are important in explaining changes in the profitability of homebuilders. A second reason is that firm j's release could convey information about competitive shifts within the industry; for example, a report by a major firm that it had significantly increased its sales and earnings (in an industry with minimal overall growth) could convey positive information for that firm but negative information for other firms in the industry.

Foster (1981) examined information transfers between firms in the same industry at the time of earnings announcements. For each interim and annual earnings announcement of 75 firms in the 1963–1978 period, the $SRV_{i,t}$ measure of stock return variability was computed for the day preceding and the day of the announcement in *The Wall Street Journal,* (termed $(-1, 0)$). Each earnings release was assigned to one of six groups, based on the magnitude of $SRV_{i,t}$. Then the $SRV_{i,t}$, of the nonannouncing firms in the same industry were computed over the same $(-1, 0)$ period that the announcing firm reported its earnings. Results for the announcing and nonannouncing samples are

	Mean $SRV_{i,t}$	
Group Assignment of Earnings Release Based on $SRV_{i,t}$ for Announcing Firm	Announcing Firm	Nonannouncing Firm
A. Greater than 6	12.89	1.76
B. Between 4 and 6	4.83	1.40
C. Between 3 and 4	3.45	1.25
D. Between 2 and 3	2.47	1.30
E. Between 1 and 2	1.42	1.06
F. Between 0 and 1	.27	.93

Those earnings releases that were associated with the largest increase in security return variability for the announcing firm also were associated with the largest increase in security-return variability for the other firms in its industry. Further analysis revealed that earnings releases that were associated with positive/negative price changes for the announcing firm in the $(-1, 0)$ period were also associated with positive/negative price changes for the other nonannouncing firms in the same industry. These results are consistent with the capital market viewing earnings releases as being informative not only for the announcing firm itself but also for other firms in its same industry. Clinch and Sinclair (1984) report similar results for a sample of 328 earnings announcements by 47 Australian firms in ten industries in the 1977–1981 period.

11.3 ASSOCIATION BETWEEN SECURITY RETURNS AND ACCOUNTING EARNINGS

In this section, we discuss evidence on the association between accounting earnings changes and security price changes in the period up to and including the earnings announcement date. Whereas Section 11.2 examined the behavior of capital market variables in the time period immediately surrounding the announcement of the firm-oriented release, Section 11.3 focuses on a much longer time period. The concern of this section is whether changes in accounting earnings are correlated with the information cues the capital market uses in revising security prices.

A. Early Evidence

The seminal paper on this issue is Ball and Brown (1968), which examined the security return behavior of firms in the 12-month period up to and including the month annual earnings were announced. Two portfolios of firms were examined: (1) firms whose earnings increased vis-à-vis the prior year and (2) firms whose earnings decreased vis-à-vis the prior year. The sample examined was 261 NYSE firms over the 1957–1965 period. Firms that reported earnings increases/decreases experienced a 5.6%/–11.3% abnormal return in the 12 months up to and including the earnings announcement month. Figure 11.4 plots these results. Note that most of the change in the abnormal security return occurs *prior* to the month that annual earnings are announced. Ball and Brown, after further analysis, concluded the following about the "content and timeliness" of annual income numbers:

> Of all the information about an individual firm which becomes available during a year, one half or more is captured in that year's income number. Its content is therefore considerable. However, the annual income report does not rate highly as a timely medium, since most of its content (about 85 to 90 percent) is captured by more prompt media which perhaps include interim reports. Since the efficiency of the capital market is largely determined by the adequacy of its data sources, we do not find it disconcerting that the market has turned to other sources which can be acted upon more promptly than annual net income. (pp. 176–177)

Other data sources the capital market can use to infer the direction of the annual earnings change include many of the releases outlined in Table 11.1 (for example,

FIGURE 11.4   Association Between Annual Earnings Changes and Security Returns

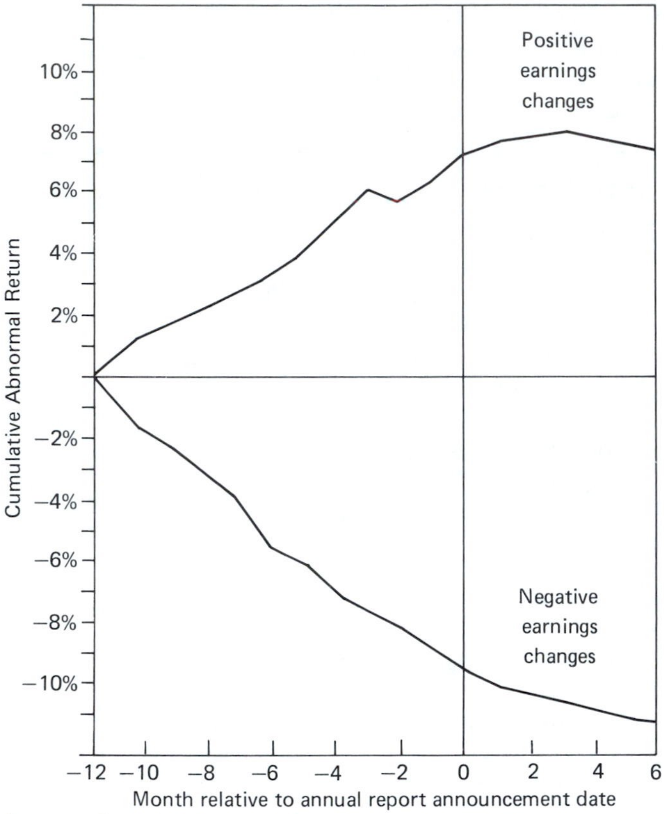

Source: Ball and Brown (1968, Figure 1): p. 696.

interim earnings releases, dividend releases, production reports, and reports by other firms in the same industry). Note, however, that while the capital market has anticipated much of the information content of the annual earnings report prior to its release, the evidence discussed in Section 11.2 indicates that full anticipation does not occur. At the hour (day, and even week) of the announcement, there is still an observable association between the sign and magnitude of the unexpected earnings change and the sign and magnitude of the hourly (daily, weekly) security return.

B.   Subsequent Evidence

The Ball and Brown (1968) study opened up an important research area in the accounting and finance literatures. One issue addressed in subsequent research is the determinants of the sign and magnitude of abnormal security returns in periods preceding interim or annual earnings releases. McEnally (1971) and Beaver, Clarke, and Wright (1979) report significant contemporaneous correlations between the magnitude and sign of unexpected annual earnings changes and the magnitude and sign of abnormal returns in the period preceding the annual earnings release. Foster, Olsen, and Shevlin (1984) extended these results to interim earnings and also to an analysis of the effect of firm size. Figure 11.3 reported results for this sample in the $(-1, 0)$ trading day period surrounding each interim and annual earnings release. Figure 11.5 presents abnormal returns for the 61 trading days up to and including the earnings announcement date, termed the $(-60, 0)$ period. Panel A of Figure 11.5 presents results for all firms partitioned into one of ten unexpected earnings change portfolios: 1 = 10% most negative unexpected changes, 10 = 10% most positive unexpected changes. The mean abnormal returns for the $(-60, 0)$ period underlying panel A are

Unexpected Earnings Change Portfolios

	1	*2*	*3*	*4*	*5*	*6*	*7*	*8*	*9*	*10*
All firms	-5.94%	-3.95	-2.37	$-.32$	.93	1.51	2.38	2.75	3.78	4.83

Panels B and C of Figure 11.5 presents results for the two firm size categories of the largest 20% of firms on the NYSE and the smallest 20% of firms on the NYSE, respectively. The mean abnormal returns for the $(-60, 0)$ period underlying panels B and C are

Unexpected Earnings Change Portfolios

	1	*2*	*3*	*4*	*5*	*6*	*7*	*8*	*9*	*10*
Largest 20% of firms	-3.43%	-2.20	-1.05	$-.16$	$-.38$	.74	.99	2.10	2.13	1.96
Smallest 20% of firms	-7.26%	-4.83	-3.26	$-.50$	1.98	2.60	4.14	4.29	6.50	9.38

All three panels in Figure 11.5 report that one determinant of abnormal security returns in the $(-60, 0)$ period is the sign and magnitude of the unexpected earnings change announced on day 0. In addition, panels B and C indicate that firm size is also a determining variable, with the smallest-firm sample having the largest downward price revaluation for bad news (portfolio 1) and the largest upward price revaluation for good news (portfolio 10).

Other Exchanges and Other Countries

Considerable evidence now exists that similar results to Ball and Brown (1968) hold for earnings releases of U.S. firms listed on the over-the-counter market and for firms listed on non-U.S. capital markets. Foster (1975) reported results for 63 U.S. insurance companies listed on the over-the-counter market. In the 12 months up to and including the earnings announcement month, firms that had unexpected increases/decreases in underwriting earnings had a 5.0% increase/5.2% decrease in abnormal security returns.

FIGURE 11.5 Security Returns in (−60, 0) Period Surrounding Earnings Announcements: Effect of (1) Sign and Magnitude of Forecast Error and (2) Firm Size

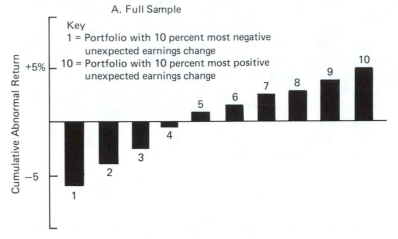

A. Full Sample

Key
1 = Portfolio with 10 percent most negative unexpected earnings change
10 = Portfolio with 10 percent most positive unexpected earnings change

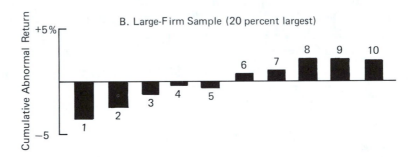

B. Large-Firm Sample (20 percent largest)

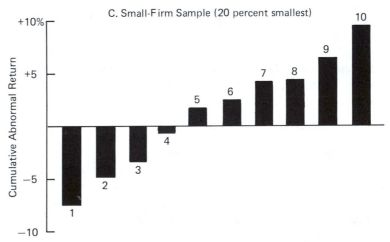

C. Small-Firm Sample (20 percent smallest)

Source: Foster, Olsen, and Shevlin (1984, Tables 4 and 6): pp. 587, 596.

Similar results have been reported in Australia and New Zealand. Brown (1970) reported results for a sample of 118 Australian companies over the 1959–1968 period; in the 12 months up to and including the earnings announcement month, firms that had unexpected increases/decreases in earnings had a 5.0% increase/9.0% decrease in abnormal security returns. Emanuel (1984) reported results for a sample of 1,196 earnings announcements by New Zealand companies in the 1967–1979 period. The magnitude of the unexpected earnings change was computed and six portfolios formed, based on ranks of observations from the most negative to the most positive unexpected earnings release. The cumulative abnormal returns in the 50 weeks up to and including the earnings release were

	Unexpected Earnings Change Portfolio					
	1	*2*	*3*	*4*	*5*	*6*
Cumulative abnormal returns	−11.2%	−4.4	−3.6	.2	3.8	12.8

New Zealand firms typically release dividend information with earnings information. Emanuel examined combinations of earnings changes and dividend changes in the same period and reported that security returns were positively correlated with the sign and magnitude of *both* unexpected earnings and unexpected dividend information.

11.4 EVIDENCE SUPPORTING A NONMECHANISTIC RELATIONSHIP BETWEEN SECURITY RETURNS AND REPORTED EPS

Chapter 9 outlined two commonly exposited assertions about the relationship between security returns and reported earnings, namely, the mechanistic hypothesis and the myopic hypothesis. Considerable evidence exists that is inconsistent with these hypotheses. This section describes a subset of the evidence relating to the mechanistic hypothesis (that is, the hypothesis that the capital market is fixated on reported earnings, without any consideration paid to the accounting methods used to compute earnings). Further evidence on both hypotheses is presented in Chapter 12.

A. EPS Estimate Announcements by Company Officials

The Beaver (1968) results and similar findings described in Section 11.2 are consistent with at least two propositions:

Proposition A: Investors react to the earnings announcement per se
Proposition B: Investors react to the information contained in the announcement.

Sterling (1970), for instance, would argue that proposition A may be the descriptively valid one:

> Accounting reports have been issued for a long time, and their issuance has been accompanied by a rather impressive ceremony performed by the managers and accountants who issue them. The receivers are likely to have gained the impression that they ought to react, and have noted that others react, and thereby have become conditioned to react. (p. 453)

Using the results in Foster [1973], it is possible to discriminate between these two propositions. This paper examined the trading volume and security price reaction to estimates of earnings per share (EPS), announced by company officials *after* the end of the fiscal year, but *before* the actual earnings announcement. The sample included 68 estimates made over the 1968–1970 period. The accuracy of the estimates was examined by computing the mean absolute percentage error:

$$\frac{\mid \text{Estimated EPS} - \text{Actual EPS} \mid}{\text{Estimated EPS}}$$

The average absolute error was only 1.8%. In contrast, if EPS was predicted to be the same as the previous year's EPS, the average absolute error was 26.7%. The trading volume reaction to the actual earnings announcements of a set of 68 firms with no EPS estimate by a company official was also examined.

The trading volume reaction to the following three announcements was examined:

> *Group I firms (no EPS estimate group)*
> (1) Actual earnings announcement
> *Group II firms (EPS estimate group)*
> (2) EPS estimate by company official
> (3) Actual earnings announcement

Proposition A would predict a significant volume reaction—$TVA_{i,t}$ in (11.1)—at least to announcements (1) and (3). Proposition B would predict a significant volume reaction, at least to announcements (1) and (2). For Group I, there was a 47% increase in $TVA_{i,t}$ in the actual earnings announcement week relative to the average of the 16 weeks surrounding that announcement. For Group II, there was a 51% increase in $TVA_{i,t}$ in the week the estimate was made, relative to the average $TVA_{i,t}$ for the 16 weeks surrounding the EPS estimate; for this same group of firms, there was only a 1% increase in $TVA_{i,t}$ at the week the actual earnings report was released. The security return analysis reinforced these findings. These results are consistent with proposition B; that is, the market reacts to the information contained in the announcement rather than to the announcement per se. If that information has already been conveyed to the market by a more timely medium, then there will be little reaction at the actual announcement date.

B. Accounting Changes

Under the mechanistic hypothesis, firms are able to increase their stock price by reporting increases in EPS, irrespective of whether that increase arises from an accounting change or from a factor such as increased operating efficiency. A subset of the literature has examined the behavior of security returns in the period surrounding accounting change announcements (or announcements of earnings in which a new set of accounting methods is employed). The early literature in this area assumed that the substantive effect of the accounting change was zero (that is, the accounting change was viewed as cosmetic). To reject the mechanistic hypothesis under this assumption, it was sufficient to find that positive/negative abnormal returns were not associated with positive/negative unexpected earnings for firms with accounting method changes. (Ideally, the focus would be on the component of unexpected earnings associated with the accounting method change and not the total unexpected earnings figure.)

Ball (1972) examined the capital market rection to 267 changes over the 1947–1960 period. These changes included 85 inventory changes, 75 depreciation changes, and 52 subsidiary accounting changes. Ball assumed that the net effect of these changes was no real increase in the value of the firms. Based on a detailed analysis of security returns of the changing firms, his conclusion was

> The year of the accounting change does not appear to exhibit any unusual behavior for the average firm. The average [abnormal return] in the month of accounting change is 0.12 of 1 percent. Hence, there is little unusual price behavior in that month, indicating that there is little market adjustment of a consistent sign associated with the release of the income report. In the 19 months after the accounting change there is little abnormal price movement. In short, changes in accounting techniques do not appear to be associated with market adjustments in a consistent direction for the average firm. (pp. 22–23)

Ball also computed the chi-square statistic (χ^2) between the sign of the earnings change and the sign of the abnormal return in the announcement month for the 267 accounting change observations. The higher this statistic, the higher the agreement between the sign of the earnings change and the sign of the abnormal return. The resultant χ^2 was insignificantly different from zero ($\chi^2 = .05$), which is consistent with the observed agreement being no higher than that expected when there is no relationship between the two variables. (This χ^2 differs strongly from that typically found for random samples of firms. For instance, the comparable χ^2 for the firms in Ball and Brown, 1968, was 28.0.) This result is strong evidence against a mechanistic relationship between reported accounting earnings and stock prices. One interesting finding in Ball (1972) was that firms making accounting changes were not a random sample of the population; typically, they were firms that had experienced negative abnormal security returns in the one-year (and also the nine-year) period preceding the accounting change.

The subsequent literature has hypothesized that accounting changes are associated with factors that have cash flow consequences, for example, taxation payments, borrowing costs, management compensation costs, and political costs.

Several of these studies are discussed in Section 11.6. At present, there is little in the form of a developed theory to predict the magnitude and timing of the capital market reaction to the hypothesized cash flow consequences of accounting changes. The result is that many recent accounting change/capital market studies are more difficult to interpret than were the early studies that focused on the more testable mechanistic hypothesis.

11.5 MARKET EFFICIENCY ANOMALIES

In an efficient market, security prices will instantaneously adjust to new information when it is placed in the public domain; it will not be possible to develop trading strategies, based on publicly available information, that yield abnormal returns (see Chapter 9 for further discussion). In an early review paper on market efficiency, Fama (1970) concluded that "the evidence in support of the efficient markets model is extensive, and (somewhat uniquely in economics) contradictory evidence is sparse" (p. 416). This conclusion no longer holds. There are now a sizable number of studies, in a diverse set of areas, that are inconsistent with the efficient markets model. This section will describe three such areas.

A. Postearnings Announcement Anomaly

In an efficient market, once earnings releases are announced, it should not be possible to develop a profitable trading strategy based on the magnitude of unexpected earnings. At least ten studies covering different time periods and different securities and using different methodologies have reported evidence of unexpected good/bad news portfolios having positive/negative security returns in the three-month period *subsequent* to the earnings announcement. Rendleman, Jones, and Latane (1982) examined quarterly earnings announcements over the 1971–1980 period. Using a standardized unexpected earnings (SUE) measure, each observation was placed into one of ten SUE categories (category 1 = most negative, category 10 = most positive). Summary results from Table 4 of this study are

Standardized Unexpected Earnings Category	Average Abnormal Return (day 0)	Cumulative Abnormal Return (days 1 to 90)
1 (most negative)	−1.4%	−4.0%
2	−1.0	−3.2
3	−.7	−3.3
4	−.2	−1.8
5	.1	−.8
6	.3	.5
7	.6	1.2
8	.8	1.6
9	1.3	3.4
10 (most positive)	1.3	4.3

The authors concluded that their "results are remarkably consistent in suggesting that the market does not assimilate unexpectedly favorable or unfavorable quarterly earnings information by the day of earnings announcement" (p. 283).

Foster, Olsen, and Shevlin (1984) report results for a SUE measure similar to that employed by Rendleman, Jones, and Latane. Using a sample of over 2,000 companies, the quarter-by-quarter results for a 60-day period subsequent to each earnings announcement were examined: $(+1, +60)$. Thirty-two quarters from 1974 to 1981 were examined. The postannouncement drifts in the $(+1, +60)$ period averaged -3.08% for the most negative unexpected earnings portfolio (30 out of 32 quarters were negative) and 3.23% for the most positive unexpected earnings portfolio (31 out of 32 quarters were positive). These results are inconsistent with a market that fully impounds the information in an earnings release at the time of its public release.

B. Price-to-Earnings Ratio Anomaly

In an efficient market, a publicly observable variable cannot be used to discriminate between securities with subsequent differential abnormal returns. A consistent finding across many studies (dating back to at least 1960) is that securities with low PE ratios outperform those with high PE ratios, in the period subsequent to the release of the earnings figure used to compute the PE ratio. Basu (1983) is a representative study documenting the PE anomaly. The sample was approximately 1,300 NYSE firms over the 1963–1980 period. Each year PE ratios of all firms were ranked and placed into one of five quintiles (1 = lowest, 5 = highest), and the security returns and abnormal security returns for the subsequent 12 months were calculated. Results for the 1963–1979 period were

PE Quintile	Median PE	Average Monthly Security Returns	Average Monthly Abnormal Security Returns
1	7.09	1.38%	.36%
2	10.31	1.14	.17
3	12.50	.87	−.09
4	15.87	.70	−.26
5	25.64	.72	−.27

The conclusion was that there is a "significant relation between [PE] ratios and risk-adjusted returns for NYSE firms" (p. 143) in the 12 months subsequent to the formation of the PE quintile-based portfolios. This result is inconsistent with an efficient market that precludes the formation, based on publicly available information, of portfolios that yield significant and predictable differences in subsequent abnormal returns.

C. The Briloff Phenomenon

The assumptions typically made in expositions of the efficient markets model (for example, zero transactions costs and all information is available cost-free to all market participants) leave no economic rationale for information intermediaries. Given these assumptions, there should be no reaction to releases made by intermediaries who restrict their activities to restatements of information already available at no cost to all market participants.

Abraham Briloff is a noted critic of contemporary financial reporting standards. Using what appears to be information already in the public domain, he makes detailed analyses of the accounting method choices and corporate disclosure policies of firms. The main theme underlying his articles is that management uses the flexibility in generally accepted accounting principles (GAAP) to show a smooth increasing EPS path over time; front ending of revenues and delayed recognition or understatement of costs is a frequent theme in his individual company critiques. In a subset of articles, Briloff also criticizes business judgments made by management. Management integrity is also the subject of adverse comments in some articles. Foster (1985) examines the daily security return behavior of companies criticized by Briloff in 21 articles published in *Barron's* in the 1968–1984 period; see Figure 11.6. On average, there is an 8.11% drop in security price on the day the Briloff critique first becomes available to the capital market. Using a postannouncement period benchmark of 30 trading days, this drop is a permanent

FIGURE 11.6 Security Returns Surrounding Publication of Abraham J. Briloff Articles

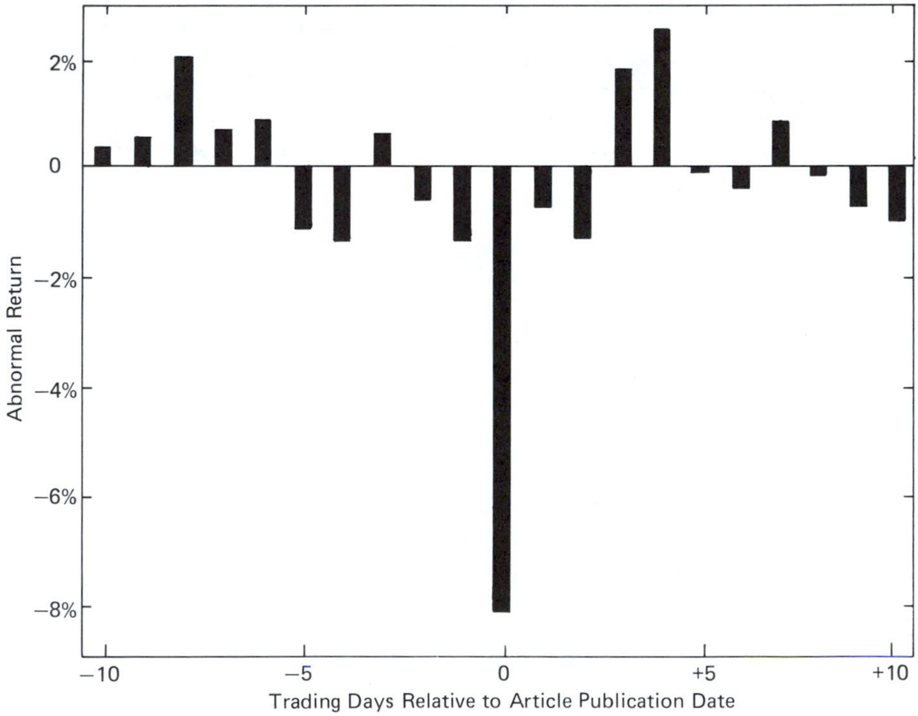

Source: Foster (1985, Figure 1): p. 15.

one. Although there are many nonmarket inefficiency explanations for the 8.11% decline (see Foster, 1979, 1985), there is little evidence to conclude that any one is more supportable than the market inefficiency explanation.

D. Overview on Anomalies

The foregoing three examples of evidence anomalous with respect to the efficient markets model are a subset of those documented in the accounting and finance literature (see Foster, 1984). Notwithstanding this evidence, the efficient markets model continues to play an important role in the literature. One reason is that competing models are not well articulated. A second reason is that non-market inefficiency explanations for the anomalous evidence exist. An active area of current research is examining these competing explanations. These include (1) the anomalies are concentrated in a specific time period or in a specific subset of firms, (2) the specific asset pricing model used in the research is not descriptively valid, and (3) biased or inefficient estimates of the parameters of the chosen asset pricing model are used in the research.

11.6 SOME GENERAL COMMENTS

1. Much progress has been made in identifying variables that are correlated with security return variability ($SRV_{i,t}$), or mean abnormal security returns ($U_{i,t}$), in the period surrounding the announcement of interim or annual earnings. For example,

$$U_{i,t} = f(UE_i, FS_i, TIME_i, IND_i \ . \ . \ .) \tag{11.5}$$

where

UE_i = unexpected earnings measure
FS_i = firm-size measure
$TIME_i$ = timeliness of announcement measure
IND_i = industry coding

Several of the independent variables identified in the literature are positively correlated with each other. One challenge facing research in this area is to develop and test models predicting which of these, or other possible variables, are the underlying determinants of the sign and magnitude of $U_{i,t}$ (or $SRV_{i,t}$).

McNichols and Manegold (1983) tested a model that predicts that "the marginal information content of an annual report is greater when it has not been preceded by interim reports and that greater variability will be observed at the annual report announcement date" (p. 49). The sample was 34 firms listed on the American Stock Exchange for which the date that interim reports were first publicly released could be identified. The finding was that the $SRV_{i,t}$ measure at the annual earnings release period was larger for years when no interim reports were issued than in later periods when those reports were issued. The conclusion was that the "evidence supports an ordinal relationship between disclosure and price variability" (p. 67). Pincus (1983) also reports results that probe the predictions of an analytical model. One hypothesis examined was that "earnings announcements ranked as hard to predict will have greater variability of unexpected returns at the time of the announcement than announcements ranked as easy to predict" (p. 161). Data for a sample of 136 NYSE firms in the 1978–1979 period supported this hypothesis.

One factor limiting progress in this model testing area is the failure of existing models to capture much of the richness of the institutional environment in which interim or annual reports are produced. For instance, most existing analytical models are developed with no recognition given to either competing information sources to earnings releases or to the role played by auditors with respect to the earnings releases issued by firms.

2. A frequent criticism of historical cost–based net income numbers is that they do not take account of changing price levels for inventories/cost of goods sold (COGS) and plant and equipment/depreciation. One proposed alternative is to use replacement cost or current cost to compute net income. Starting in 1976, a subset of large U.S. firms was required by the SEC (under ASR 190) to make supplemental replacement cost disclosures for inventories/COGS and plant and equipment/depreciation. Several studies were conducted on the capital market reaction to the ASR 190 disclosures; see the August 1980 issue of *Journal of Accounting and Economics* for three such studies. The consistent conclusion across these studies was that there was no stock price reaction to the ASR 190 data at the time of the initial disclosures. Explanations for this result include

a. Replacement cost data are perceived to be irrelevant to security price determination (in general, or at least for the samples examined)

b. Replacement cost data are perceived to be relevant, but (i) security prices already reflect this information via competing information sources, (ii) the magnitude of the security price adjustment is not detectable using the research methods adopted, or (iii) the specific ASR 190 disclosures contain so much measurement error that they provide no new information to the capital market

c. Replacement cost is an unfamiliar concept to the capital market, and some learning is necessary before security prices respond to such disclosures.

In 1979, the FASB (in *FASB Statement No. 33*) required some U.S. firms to report supplemental current cost and general price level-based income numbers in their annual reports. Capital market research was conducted using the *FASB Statement No. 33* data by Beaver and Landsman (1983) and Olsen (1984). Beaver and Landsman (1983) used several research methods to examine the information content of the *FASB Statement No. 33* data. The basic findings were

1. [FASB] 33 earnings provide no explanatory power with respect to differences in

    annual security returns across firms over and above that provided by historical cost earnings.

2. Historical cost earnings do provide explanatory power over and above that provided by any one of the [FASB] 33 variables. (p. 73)

The Beaver-Landsman sample of firms, from a diverse set of industries, ranged from 392 in 1979 to 297 in 1981. Olsen (1984) focused on a sample of 96 utility firms over the same 1979–1981 period. A similar conclusion of no incremental information content for the *FASB Statement No. 33* disclosures was reported. The set of previously outlined explanations for the ASR 190 disclosures not having information content apply to the *FASB Statement No. 33* disclosures. Over time, the learning effect explanation becomes less likely if the results found in the later years of the *FASB Statement No. 33* disclosures are the same as in the early years of these disclosures.

    These studies are part of an already large (and growing) literature on the capital market effects of mandated accounting disclosures and other forms of regulatory interventions. Review papers in this area include Foster (1980), Schwert (1981), Lev and Ohlson (1982), and Chow (1983). Concern with the internal validity of early research has prompted much effort on developing more reliable research designs; for example, see the "price-reversal" research designs in Noreen and Sepe (1981) and Collins, Rozeff, and Salatka (1982).

    3. The null hypothesis in early capital market studies of accounting changes was that the change would have no security price effect due to its having no cash flow implications for the firm (that is, it was a "cosmetic" change, with implications only for reported accounting numbers). Subsequent studies have hypothesized cash flow implications of accounting changes resulting from a diverse set of sources.

    Studies on LIFO/FIFO accounting changes relied on taxation effects of the change to motivate cash flow consequences. Under a U.S. tax law introduced in the 1930s, a firm electing to use LIFO for tax purposes must also use LIFO for financial reporting. If a company has rising input prices and constant or rising quantities of inventories, use of LIFO vis-à-vis FIFO will reduce reported income (ceteris paribus). The reduced income figure will mean lower income taxation payments. Several capital market studies have examined firms changing from FIFO to LIFO, hypothesizing that a capital market focusing on future cash flows, rather than reported accounting earnings, will revise upward the security prices of those firms. To date, the results of this research have been inconsistent. The most detailed study is by Ricks and Biddle (1985), which examines a sample of 607 LIFO adoptions by NYSE or AMEX firms in the 1973–1980 period. Results were reported for changes made in 1974 (415 firms) and changes made in other years (192 firms; termed non-1974 LIFO adopters). The conclusion was that for the "non-1974 LIFO adopters, neither their excess [security] returns nor their [earnings] forecast errors were significantly different from zero. The 1974 LIFO adopters experienced a significant negative market reaction near their annual earnings announcements. For 1974 LIFO adopters, analysts appeared to have systematically underestimated the earnings impact of LIFO adoption, resulting in a significant upward bias in their earnings forecasts. This bias appeared to explain much of the negative return behavior near the earnings announcements. Although the net market reaction to the earnings announcements was negative, once forecast errors were controlled for, there was a positive association between returns and the effects of LIFO adoption for 1974 change firms'' (p. 28).

Other capital market studies hypothesizing cash flow consequences from accounting changes have focused on variables such as management compensation costs, borrowing costs, and political costs. At present, empirical research has not been able to document that the cash flow consequences associated with these variables are statistically significant. For instance, in a study of depreciation changes made by 125 firms in the 1955–1978 period, Holthausen (1981) concluded: ''The evidence from both price and nonprice data is not consistent with the general hypothesis that bond covenants and management compensation contracts are important determinants of the decision to change depreciation techniques'' (p. 73).

At present, it is difficult to draw any reliable conclusions from the many capital market studies testing links between security returns and cash flow consequences of accounting changes. One reason is the difficulty of predicting the *timing* of the capital market reaction to any cash flow consequences associated with the change. For instance, the capital market may observe prices for some commodities in futures markets and may revise upward its probability that firms using these commodities will switch to LIFO. Immediately prior to the change, the remaining uncertainty about LIFO adoption may be relatively low (especially if many other firms in the industry have already changed). The result will be minimal security price reaction associated with the firm's formal announcement of the accounting change. A second reason for these studies having inconsistent or insignificant findings is the problems in measuring key variables. At present, there appear to be sizable measurement problems in capturing the accounting change–induced effects associated with management compensation costs, borrowing costs, political costs, and so on. Review papers discussing these and related research problems include Ball and Foster (1982), Lev and Ohlson (1982), Ricks (1982), Holthausen and Leftwich (1983), and Kelly (1983).

11.7 SUMMARY

1. A rich body of evidence exists on the relationship between security returns and corporate information releases. This evidence supports four major conclusions regarding accounting earnings:

   a. There is a positive contemporaneous association between the sign and magnitude of the accounting earnings change and the sign and magnitude of the security price change.

b. Much of the market's reaction to accounting earnings is anticipatory; more timely information sources than the earnings announcement are used in the security price revaluation process.

c. Notwithstanding (b), there is a significant security price and trading volume reaction to the information contained in interim and annual earnings announcements.

d. There is not a mechanistic relationship between reported accounting numbers and stock returns; this is consistent with the market using a broad-based information set in interpreting the information content of reported accounting numbers.

2. Notwithstanding the considerable increase in our knowledge on the relationship between security returns and corporate information releases, important puzzles remain to be solved. For instance, anomalies with respect to the efficient markets model have been reported in a diverse set of areas (see Section 11.5). The challenge facing research in this area is to determine whether findings such as the postearnings announcement anomaly and the price-to-earnings ratio anomaly reflect (a) experimental deficiencies in research designs, (b) inadequacies in our knowledge about asset pricing, or (c) the capital market *not* instantaneously and unbiasedly impounding information releases at the time they are placed in the public domain.

APPENDIX 11.A   THE CUMULATIVE ABNORMAL RETURN MEASURE

The cumulative abnormal return (CAR) measure is frequently used when examining the reaction of security prices to news releases and other types of announcements by firms. The CAR is used to control for factors affecting security returns that are not related to the information release of interest. This appendix discusses the estimation of abnormal returns and issues involved in the cumulation and interpretation of these abnormal returns.

Estimating Abnormal Returns

An abnormal return ($U_{i,t}$) is the difference between an actual return ($R_{i,t}$) and a benchmark or normal return ($R_{i,t}^{N}$):

$$U_{i,t} = R_{i,t} - R_{i,t}^{N} \tag{11.A.1}$$

The most appealing approach to deriving a benchmark or normal return is to use a theoretical asset pricing model. An example is the two-parameter capital asset pricing model (CAPM) described in Chapter 10. The CAPM specifies that the expected return on a security is a function of three variables (β_i, R_f, and R_m):

$$E(\tilde{R}_i) = R_f + \beta_i[E(\tilde{R}_m) - R_f] \tag{11.A.2}$$

Consider the following data for Company XYZ in a three-month period:

	R_i for XYZ	R_f	R_m
May	.0610	.0081	.0562
June	.0170	.0061	.0296
July	.0430	.0053	.0676

Assume that the beta (β_i) of XYZ's securities is estimated to be 1.60. The CAPM predicts the following returns to be "normal" returns for XYZ in this period:

May: $E(\tilde{R}_i \mid \beta_i, R_f, R_m) = .0081 + 1.60\,(.0562 - .0081) = .08506$

June: $E(\tilde{R}_i \mid \beta_i, R_f, R_m) = .0061 + 1.60\,(.0296 - .0061) = .04370$

July: $E(\tilde{R}_i \mid \beta_i, R_f, R_m) = .0053 + 1.60\,(.0676 - .0053) = .10498$

The use of these expected returns as the benchmark or normal return when computing $U_{i,t}$ for Company XYZ yields

Month	$U_{i,t} = R_{i,t} - R_{i,t}^N$
May	$U_{i,t} = .0610 - .08506 = -.02406$
June	$U_{i,t} = .0170 - .04370 = -.02670$
July	$U_{i,t} = .0430 - .10498 = -.06198$

In each of these three months, XYZ experienced negative abnormal returns; that is, its returns were below those predicted by the CAPM, conditional on realizations of R_f and R_m and the estimate of its β_i.

In some studies, the benchmark chosen for $R_{i,t}^N$ has been a market index (R_m). Using the foregoing data for XYZ, this approach yields the following $U_{i,t}$ values:

Month	$U_{i,t} = R_{i,t} - R_{i,t}^N$
May	$U_{i,t} = .0610 - .0562 = .0048$
June	$U_{i,t} = .0170 - .0296 = -.0126$
July	$U_{i,t} = .0430 - .0676 = -.0246$

The rationales for this approach have included simplicity (fewer variables to estimate) and prior research that in some contexts this approach yields similar inferences to the CAPM approach (for example, in large samples of firms whose average β_i is close to one).

Research on the properties of the foregoing and other alternative measures of abnormal returns includes Brown and Warner (1980), Beaver (1981), Shevlin (1981), and Brown and Warner (1985).

Cumulating Abnormal Returns over Time

A commonly used approach to cumulating abnormal returns is the arithmetic (additive) form:

$$CAR_i = \sum_{t=1}^{T} U_{i,t} \qquad (11.A.3)$$

Use of (11.A.3) in the example (where $U_{i,t}$ is calculated using the CAPM to estimate $R_{i,t}^N$) yields

$$CAR_i = \sum_{t=1}^{T} U_{i,t}$$
$$= (-.02406) + (-.0267) + (-.06198) = -.11274$$

The main attraction of the arithmetic form is its simplicity of calculation. Alternative cumulation approaches are available that provide more insight into the returns from implementable (or more realistic) trading strategies; see Roll (1983) for a discussion of the arithmetic, buy-and-hold, and rebalanced approaches to cumulating abnormal returns.

Drawing Inferences from CAR Measures

Many studies use the CAR measure to provide insight into the information content of news releases by firms; information content in this context means that the news release leads to a revision in the distribution of security returns. It is important to recognize the following four possible outcomes when using the CAR measure in this context:

1. News release leads to a revision in the security return distribution and the CAR measure reports a significant effect
2. News release does not lead to a revision in the security return distribution and the CAR measure reports no significant effect
3. News release leads to a revision in the security return distribution, but the CAR measure reports no significant effect
4. News release does not lead to a revision in the security return distribution, but the CAR measure reports a significant effect.

Considerable discussion exists in the literature about the design of experiments that increase the likelihood of outcomes 1 or 2 and to detect cases where outcomes 3 or 4 are likely to arise; for example, Foster (1980), Lev and Ohlson (1982), and Bowman (1983). The term "confounding events" is often used to describe factors that result in outcomes 3 or 4 arising. In general, outcomes 1 or 2 are most likely where the study includes a large sample of observations, drawn from a broad cross section of firms over many different time periods, and where the news release or announcement of interest contains only the item under study (for example, an interim earnings report). Many of the studies on earnings releases, earnings forecasts, and dividend releases discussed in Section 11.2 of this chapter have research designs that considerably reduce problems arising from confounding events.

QUESTIONS

QUESTION   11.1:   Stock Returns and Corporate Releases: Large Effects

Firms typically release many types of announcements. Only a subset of these have any detectable effect on security returns. Consider the following two:

1. Announcement by Texas Instruments (TI) on Friday, June 10, 1983, after the close of trading, that it would post a second-quarter loss of $100 million (over $4.20 per share). On the following Monday, the stock price of TI declined over 25%. It closed on Friday, June 10 at $157⅞ and closed on Monday, June 13 at $118⅜. TI cited slowing retail orders and industry price cutting for the loss in its home computer division. The home computer division was included in the digital products segment of TI's business. The percentage contribution of this segment to total net sales and income before "eliminations," "corporate items," and "income taxes" was

Percentage Contribution of Digital Products Segment to	1980	1981	1982
Net sales	25.8%	26.9%	27.1%
Income	12.7	7.8	7.4

One financial commentator observed that "Wall Street analysts said they are baffled by the events that reversed TI's fortunes. At the annual shareholders meeting in April, Company President J. Fred Bucy projected that 1983 'holds the promise of being a significantly better year for TI than 1982.'" The May 13, 1983, issue of the Value Line investment survey included the following information on TI's quarterly EPS up to March 31, 1983, as well as Value Line's EPS forecasts (designated F) for the remaining three quarters of 1983:

Calendar	Quarterly Earnings per Share				Full Year
	Mar. 31	June 30	Sept. 30	Dec. 31	
1979	$1.68	$1.95	$1.92	$2.03	$7.58
1980	2.20	2.40	2.30	2.32	9.22
1981	1.47	0.44	1.15	1.56	4.62
1982	1.17	1.56	1.57	1.80	6.10
1983	0.30	1.80(F)	2.35(F)	2.95(F)	7.40(F)

2. Announcement by ITT Corp. on Tuesday, July 10, 1984, after the close of trading, that it was cutting its quarterly dividend from 69 cents a share to 25 cents a share. Quarterly dividends paid over the 1980–1984 period were $0.60 for each quarter in 1980, $0.65 for each quarter in 1981, $0.67 for each quarter in 1982, and $0.69 for each quarter in 1983 and each of the first two quarters of 1984. On Wednesday, July 11, 1984, the stock price of ITT declined over 30%. It closed

on Tuesday, July 10, at $31 and closed on Wednesday, July 11, at $21⅛. The chairman of ITT (Rand Araskog) was quoted in the financial press as saying that "the company's dividend-to-earnings ratio had become inconsistent with the intensely competitive high technology environment. . . . Directors approved the dividend reduction so that ITT could continue its current rate of investment in high technology products and services at over $2 billion annually. . . . ITT wishes to increase its flexibility to consider new business opportunities that may come along in the future." Araskog also stated that "earnings for the current year aren't expected to equal the $4.50 a share attained in 1983. . . . He expects sales and revenue for 1984 to increase more than 10% from 1983."[1] *The Wall Street Journal* on July 11, 1984, stated that "analysts weren't surprised by ITT's estimate of lower earnings, but several were surprised by the slash in the dividend."

REQUIRED

1. What factors could explain (a) the 25% security price decline for Texas Instruments on Monday, June 13, and (b) the 30% security price decline for ITT on Wednesday, July 11?

2. How would you determine whether the magnitude of each price decline was appropriate or whether the capital market overreacted to the negative information?

3. Why might both Texas Instruments and ITT have released their respective news items after the NYSE had ceased trading rather than during trading hours? What are the benefits to this delayed release?

4. What other classes of corporate releases would you predict to have large stock price changes (say, ± 10%) in the announcement period? Give reasons.

QUESTION 11.2: Determinants of Capital Market Reaction to Earnings Announcements

Considerable evidence exists that there is both increased security return variability ($SRV_{i,t}$) and trading volume activity ($TVA_{i,t}$) in the period surrounding the release of interim or annual earnings announcements. One factor hypothesized to be a determinant of $SRV_{i,t}$ or $TVA_{i,t}$ for firm i is the level of competition in its industry. For example, Zeghal (1983) stated

> The amount and availability of information are the bases of a competitive system. The larger they are, the greater the number of participants in the market. Further, the characteristics, functioning and impersonal mechanisms of such a market favor the disclosure and dissemination of new information.

> By contrast, the firms in oligopolistic industries are interdependent, and their interdependence has several implications for the production and dissemination of information. First, oligopolistic firms cannot conclusively evaluate the effect of new information on their decisions without knowing or anticipating the decisions of rival

[1] *The Wall Street Journal*, July 11, 1984. Reprinted by permission of *The Wall Street Journal*. © Dow Jones & Company, Inc., 1984. All rights reserved.

firms. This can only but discourage these firms from the disclosing of information that is considered useful to their rivals. Similarly, the interdependence of firms makes it difficult for the outside observer to evaluate the effect of new information on the market and the decisions of participating firms.

Finally, it should be noted that as the number of participants in a market increases, the market moves closer to a competitive system. More precisely, as the number of sellers increases and the share of industry output supplied by a representative firm decreases, the likelihood that individual producers will ignore the effect of their price and output decisions on rival actions and the overall level of prices increases. (pp. 116–117)

The $SRV_{i,t}$ measure computed by Zeghal was the ratio of the variance of abnormal returns during the announcement period to the variance of abnormal returns in nonearnings announcement periods. The announcement period was defined to be the three-day period surrounding the publication day of the earnings release in *The Wall Street Journal* $(-1, +1)$. The $TVA_{i,t}$ measure was computed as the ratio of the mean volume of transactions during the three-day announcement period to the mean volume of transactions in nonearnings announcement periods.

The data base, consisting of firms in 210 four-digit SIC industries, was classified according to the number of firms in each industry:

No. of Firms in Each Industry	No. of Earnings Announcement Observations
≥3	2,796
≥6	1,823
≥9	1,316
≥12	1,083
≥15	1,045

To be included in the ≥3 category, firm i had to be in a four-digit SIC industry with three or more firms; to be included in the ≥15 category, firm i had to be in an industry with 15 or more firms.

The Herfindhal index, applied to the size of firms as measured by the market value of common stock, was used to measure the level of concentration in each industry; this index is frequently used in the economics literature, with size being measured by the sales of each firm in a given industry. The index classifications employed were

- Low concentration (less than .18)
- Medium concentration (between .18 and .40)
- High concentration (greater than .40).

Zeghal stated that market value (rather than sales) was used to compute the Herfindhal index due to the focus being on the market reaction to earnings announcements.

Results for the $SRV_{i,t}$ and $TVA_{i,t}$ measures for the combinations of industry size and concentration levels were

No. of Firms in Industry	$SRV_{i,t}$ (security-return variability)			
	Low Concentration	Medium Concentration	High Concentration	Total
≥3	1.58	1.76	1.78	1.71
≥6	1.45	1.73	1.83	1.67
≥9	1.41	1.73	1.84	1.66
≥12	1.40	1.60	1.89	1.63
≥15	1.39	1.51	1.82	1.58

No. of Firms in Industry	$TVA_{i,t}$ (trading volume activity)			
	Low Concentration	Medium Concentration	High Concentration	Total
≥3	1.23	1.35	1.37	1.31
≥6	1.15	1.36	1.38	1.30
≥9	1.10	1.33	1.43	1.29
≥12	1.10	1.27	1.40	1.26
≥15	1.10	1.20	1.36	1.22

REQUIRED

1. Critique the $SRV_{i,t}$ and $TVA_{i,t}$ measures as indicators of whether there is abnormal security return variability and abnormal trading volume activity at the time of earnings releases.

2. Do the results reported by Zeghal support the hypotheses that higher $SRV_{i,t}$ and $TVA_{i,t}$ values are associated with (a) industries with lower number of firms and (b) industries with higher concentration levels?

3. What problems arise in testing the hypotheses in (2)? How might more powerful tests be devised?

4. What other variables have been hypothesized or found to be determinants of the magnitude of $SRV_{i,t}$ or $TVA_{i,t}$ at the time of earnings releases? How should these variables (if at all) be taken into account in the research?

QUESTION   11.3:   Exploiting the Low Price-to-Earnings Ratio Anomaly

Hobie Leland, Jr., is in charge of an investment division of the EL Camino Bank. For some detailed empirical work, he develops a data base that contains all NYSE stocks that were continuously listed from 1949 to the present date. The data base contains the following items for all companies with December 31 fiscal years:

1. Monthly security returns

2. December 31 closing security prices

3. Annual earnings per share (restated to take account of prior mergers, divestitures, etc.).

The monthly security returns on Standard & Poor's Composite Index are also included in the data base. Dividends for each security and for the Standard & Poor's index were not collected.

A recently hired employee named Oscar decides to use the data base to test the performance of the following investment approach: rank the stocks in terms of their PE ratios and invest in those in the lowest PE decile. Oscar computes the PE ratios of all stocks in 1949 (that is, December 31, 1949, price-to-annual earnings per share in 1949), ranks them from highest to lowest, and assumes equal investment in those in the lowest decile. He holds each stock for one year and then assumes sale at the December 31, 1950, price. The average return is calculated as the average of the percentage gain on each stock in the lowest decile portfolio. This procedure is repeated for each subsequent year in the data base. Oscar is ecstatic when he reads the computer printout of the results:

Average annual return on the lowest PE decile portfolio = 21%

Average annual return on the Standard & Poor's Composite Index = 10%.

Oscar takes the results to Hobie and recommends the bank adopt the low PE decile strategy for its discretionary accounts. Hobie is skeptical of Oscar's results and seeks your assistance.

REQUIRED

1. What problems exist in drawing inferences from Oscar's results about the performance of the low PE decile strategy?
2. Devise a more refined test of whether the bank can earn abnormal returns using the low PE decile strategy.

QUESTION 11.4: Briloff and the Capital Market: Anacomp

In the period from 1968 to 1981, the security prices of firms cited in 16 *Barron's* articles by Abraham Briloff declined an average of 8.45% on the day of publication of the relevant article. On August 2, 1982, *Barron's* published an article by Briloff titled "Anacomp's Accounting: A Critic Finds Plenty to Fault It With." On the day of publication of this article, Anacomp's security price declined over 14%. The article is reproduced in Appendix A. The security return and trading volume of Anacomp in the period surrounding release of the article is in Table 11.5. Table 11.6 presents summary financial data relating to Anacomp.

REQUIRED

1. Using the "as reported" financial data in Table 11.6, what inferences would you draw about Anacomp's financial position and earnings-generating ability in the 1978–1982 period?
2. Describe and critically evaluate the criticisms Briloff makes of Anacomp's accounting. How would these criticisms affect the inferences drawn in question 1?

TABLE 11.5 Security Return and Trading Volume Behavior
Surrounding Publication of Anacomp Article (August 2,
1982)

Trading Day 1982	Anacomp Closing Price	S&P 500 Composite Closing	Anacomp Trading Volume (000s)
7/1	12 5/8	108.71	86
7/2	12 7/8	107.65	256
7/5	HOLIDAY	—	—
7/6	12 5/8	107.29	130
7/7	12 4/8	107.22	172
7/8	12 4/8	107.53	201
7/9	12 3/8	108.83	426
7/12	12 3/8	109.57	639
7/13	12 7/8	109.45	366
7/14	13 5/8	110.44	408
7/15	13 5/8	110.47	556
7/16	12 7/8	111.07	532
7/19	12 6/8	110.73	107
7/20	12 4/8	111.54	799
7/21	12 3/8	111.42	240
7/22	12 4/8	111.47	93
7/23	12 4/8	111.17	109
7/26	12 4/8	110.36	216
7/27	12 4/8	109.43	116
7/28	12 4/8	107.73	127
7/29	12 3/8	107.72	390
7/30	12 2/8	107.09	139
8/2	10 4/8	108.98	920
8/3	10 1/8	107.83	682
8/4	9 7/8	106.14	305
8/5	10 3/8	105.16	287
8/6	10 6/8	103.71	220
8/9	10 4/8	103.08	301
8/10	10 4/8	102.84	132
8/11	10 1/8	102.60	181
8/12	10	102.42	379
8/13	10	103.85	109
8/16	10 2/8	104.09	205
8/17	10 3/8	109.04	116
8/18	10 2/8	108.53	344
8/19	10 1/8	109.16	109
8/20	10 3/8	113.02	125
8/23	10 6/8	116.11	207
8/24	11 1/8	115.34	241
8/25	11 3/8	117.58	92
8/26	11	118.55	367
8/27	11	117.11	277
8/30	11 2/8	117.66	82

TABLE 11.6 Anacomp: Selected Financial Data ($ millions, as reported)

Financial Item	Fiscal Year to June 30				Nine Months to March 1981	Nine Months to March 1982
	1978	1979	1980	1981[2]		
1. Cash and marketable securities	3.721	3.159	4.558	29.392	29.607	54.149
2. Accounts receivable	3.321	7.052	15.408	23.216	23.985	20.909
3. Unbilled revenues	1.011	3.391	9.400	15.863	9.991	21.312
4. Inventories	.671	.970	2.336	3.014	2.875	4.156
5. Other current assets	.341	.716	1.072	3.968	5.502	9.811
6. Property and equipment	2.176	7.214	12.351	14.930	14.266	18.060
7. Goodwill[1]	.211	1.960	21.429	24.291	23.602	24.240
8. Other assets	.677	3.257	7.548	16.124	10.470	24.332
9. Total assets	12.130	27.719	74.104	130.798	120.298	176.969
10. Current liabilities	2.708	10.019	19.798	18.616	16.959	15.948
11. Convertible subordinated debentures	2.298	1.421	1.084	43.340	43.340	87.039
12. Other long-term liabilities	.752	6.103	8.958	7.251	7.251	4.860
13. Deferred income taxes	.082	.264	.453	4.460	.453	6.945
14. Minority interest	.044	.165	.111	.667	.578	.483
15. Stockholders' equity	6.246	9.747	43.699	56.464	52.173	61.694
16. Revenues	21.619	38.118	67.076	106.368	66.374	80.290
17. Operating income	3.082	4.614	7.051	12.311	9.293	7.626
18. Interest expense	.389	.755	1.218	4.090	2.787	4.982
19. Provision for income taxes	1.619	2.419	3.320	6.115	4.165	4.147
20. Net income	1.558	2.653	4.810	8.010	5.217	6.045
21. Dividends declared	.233	.380	.692	.956	.681	.824
22. Equity market capitalization	20.903	41.180	82.396	176.907	144.058	98.778

[1]Goodwill is excess of purchase price over net assets of business acquired less accumulated amortization.
[2]Fourth quarter of fiscal 1981 (1980) had revenues of $29.850 million ($20.944 million) and net income of $2.722 million ($1.771 million).

3. What sources of information does Briloff use in his analysis? Are these sources all "publicly available"?

4. How would you explain the drop in the stock price of Anacomp over the July 26–August 13 period? Be specific.

5. You are in the senior management of Anacomp. What options would you consider in responding to Briloff's criticisms? Which would you recommend?

Appendix A: "Anacomp's Accounting: A Critic Finds Plenty to Fault It With"[2]

It was the closest thing to a hot deal that Wall Street had seen in quite a while. The offering, which closed last Wednesday, involved units in CIBS Partners Ltd., a new

[2] Abraham Briloff, Barron's, August 2, 1982. Reprinted by permission of Barron's. © Dow Jones & Company, Inc., 1982. All rights reserved.

R&D partnership offered by Shearson/American Express on behalf of a New York Stock Exchange–listed computer service company, Anacomp, Inc. Shearson raised $26.25 million and, it claimed, could have sold another $8.75 million worth. The funds are earmarked for development of what Anacomp describes as a "state-of-the-art, proprietary software system" for banks with large international operations.

Anacomp is no stranger to R&D partnerships. In recent years it sponsored four others. Demand for CIBS Partners Ltd. doubtless was spurred by the success of an earlier deal, which the company bought from the partnership just last month; apart from sizable tax benefits, it returned to the partners in three years $6 for every $1 invested.

Serving mostly financial institutions with a growing array of computer-related and microfilm services, Anacomp built up sales from $1 million in 1972 to $106 million in the fiscal year ended June 30, 1981. During this stretch, earnings climbed from nothing to $8 million, or 88 cents a share. In the first nine months of fiscal 1982, net hit 65 cents vs. 58 cents in the comparable year-earlier stretch.

What intrigues me about Anacomp is less its impressive growth than the use the company has made of generally accepted accounting principles. To be sure, Anacomp's books are duly certified by the prestigious accounting firm of Coopers & Lybrand. However, in my study of Anacomp's financials, I found manifestations of front-end loading of revenues, the inclusion of questionable items of revenues, the avoidance of proper recognition of costs, and the deferral of recognized costs for inordinately long periods.

Accounting practices implemented by Anacomp over the past several years have had a salutary impact on reported earnings. In a telephone conversation with the company's vice-president-controller, Robert L. Parke, in which we discussed aspects of its accounting, he remarked that he "had a tiger by the tail."

As good a place as any to begin an analysis of Anacomp's financial practices is its accounting for acquisitions, of which there were no fewer than 16 in the three years ended June 30, 1981. Of these, 13 were booked under the so-called purchase method of accounting for business combinations, the rest as pooling of interests. At times, I believe, both alternatives can lead to serious distortions of the bottom line. In Anacomp's case, the purchases in the aggregate cost $31.6 million ($21.8 million in cash and notes, $9.8 million in stock). Of this amount, $7.2 million was booked as net assets (calculated at fair values), and $24.4 million went into the balance sheet under the rubric "excess of purchase price over net assets of business acquired," more commonly referred to as "goodwill." That latter figure is equal to almost 40% of shareholders' equity.

Were these companies so good as to warrant all that goodwill, there'd be no grounds for complaint. And I am not complaining, though the numbers do boggle the mind. For example, in fiscal 1980, of total purchases costing $23.7 million, $19.4 million went into goodwill. However, a footnote to the annual report discloses that had these acquisitions been effected so that they were included for a full 12 months in fiscal 1979, net that year would have been $400,000 less. Moreover, had they been taken into account for all of fiscal 1980—under purchase accounting, results are consolidated only from the date of acquisition—Anacomp's reported income would have been reduced by $100,000. In other words, in the aggregate they would have lost money.

What's more, the former shareholders of one Anacomp-acquired enterprise, Arthur S. Kranzley & Co., Inc., of Cherry Hill, N.J., are entitled to an additional $2.8 million pursuant to a five-year earn-out. Reviewing the data for this company alone, we find Anacomp paid $900,000 in the form of shares valued at $9 a share. Of this amount, after some adjustments, $251,000 went into net assets, leaving $649,000 as goodwill. In fiscal 1981, the erstwhile management was paid $400,000 on the earn-out commitment. Presumably, this should be considered compensation; instead, that additional sum was put into goodwill to be spread over an extended period.

According to the company, the excess of purchase price over net assets acquired is amortized over the estimated useful life, if determined, and over 40 years if an indeterminate life is expected. My computations indicate that Anacomp is using an average life of about 30 years for this intangible. To my mind, such a protracted life span is absurd. Especially for a company in an industry as dynamic as Anacomp's and where the technology is changing rapidly.

In fiscal '81, Anacomp issued a total of 279,035 shares, with an aggregate market value of about $5.25 million, for three entities booked as pooling of interests. Combined, they had $2.9 million in assets and $2 million in liabilities; a net equity, in other words, of less than $1 million. Hence, Anacomp managed to avoid booking an actual cost of more than $4 million.

In its third fiscal quarter ended March 31, 1982, Anacomp reported net of $3.5 million, down from $4.4 million in the like '81 period. However, results in the latest quarter were bolstered importantly by two transactions. In one, negotiations were completed with two suppliers, resulting in the recovery of previously recorded expenses; this reduced direct operating costs by $1.9 million.

The other involved the sales of assets and the business of two computer centers for $300,000 in cash and $3.2 million in installment notes due 1988. Anacomp will manage the centers on a cost-plus incentive basis. According to Anacomp's books, the cost basis of the centers was just $500,000—producing a gain of approximately $2.9 million. What is especially intriguing about this gain was that it was derived principally from sale of a center that just happened to be one acquired the preceding year in a pooling transaction and in which costs were suppressed.

Clearly, without these two transactions, which contributed $4.8 million, Anacomp would have reported a loss for the third quarter of fiscal 1982.

Anacomp also has been playing a most exhilarating game of put-and-take with Kalvar Corp., a faded glamor company of the 1960s, now, as then, a manufacturer of micrographic equipment. Beginning in 1977, Anacomp carried out a series of complex transactions with Kalvar. First, it entered into a management agreement with Kalvar, which included the granting to Anacomp of a warrant to buy 51% of Kalvar's common. For over two years, Anacomp managed Kalvar's business, marketing its film and providing substantial loans to Kalvar.

Then, in March of '79, both companies sold certain assets to a third party, Xidex Corp., of California. At the same time, Kalvar and Anacomp terminated their marketing and financing pact. Anacomp returned the warrant and received, instead, a seven-year $150,000 note, 100,000 restricted shares of Kalvar common and an option to purchase 750,000 shares. The management provisions of the 1977 agreements remained in force.

In early 1980, there were additional transactions in which stock, options, convertible preferred shares and cash changed hands. June 1981 saw further dealings between the two. Kalvar bought back preferred stock, $400,000 in notes and an option on 755,000 shares of its common: for these, it paid Anacomp 745,000 shares of common and promissory notes in the principal amount of $1 million at a rate two points below prime.

In May 1982, Anacomp purchased for cash DSI Corp., a Nashville company that transfers computer tapes onto microfilm. As part of the deal, and to win Justice Department approval of the acquisition, Anacomp and Kalvar agreed to split. But not before Kalvar bought 10 computer service centers from DSI, and sold centers in St. Louis and Omaha to Anacomp. Kalvar also conveyed to Anacomp 20,000 shares of non-voting preferred stock and $4 million in 16% income bonds, due 1997.

The upshot was that, in fiscal 1980, Anacomp picked up capital gains of $1,567,000, equal to 20% of pre-tax earnings. The following year, such gains amounted to $898,000, or 6%. However, the Kalvar-derived profits had an even more dramatic impact on the quarters in which they were taken. Thus, in the third quarter of fiscal 1980, they equaled 50% of pre-tax net, in the fourth quarter of fiscal 1981, 20%.

Further, in fiscal 1981, the company's thrift plan exercised an option, granted by Anacomp in March of 1980, to acquire 162,500 shares of Anacomp's common at $6.08 a share (the market price the day of the grant). The plan was amended so that the excess of the market value over the option price on date exercised would go to reduce or eliminate Anacomp's portion of the contributions that would otherwise be required. That neat device saved Anacomp approximately $1.26 million pre-tax, or 7 cents a share after tax, in fiscal 1981. Per-share net that year was up only 14 cents.

Turning now to Anacomp's balance sheet, one discovers an intriguing asset, to wit: unbilled revenues. This item, $3.4 million on June 30, 1979, grew to $8.6 million by June 30, 1980 (restated), $15.9 million 12 months later and to $21.3 million on March 31, 1982.

What is an unbilled revenue? According to note 1 of the latest audited balance sheet, under certain circumstances, Anacomp has decided to account for projects on a percentage-of-completion basis. The method traditionally has been used by contractors engaged in long-term projects—building bridges, dams, tunnels or airplanes.

Anacomp may well take comfort from, or cite as authority for its accounting treatment, a 1981 position statement of the Accounting Standards Executive Committee of the American Institute of Certified Public Accountants. The statement was entitled "Accounting for Performances of Construction-Type and Certain Production-Type Contracts."

Nonetheless, I believe that other parts of the position statement should have restrained the company and its auditors from using this revenue-anticipating procedure. (The company says that unbilled revenues generally are realized in the succeeding fiscal year, which suggests that the performance of the contracts is of short duration.) This asset category has been rising in absolute amounts and, more disturbing, has been accelerating as a percentage of annual revenues, from 8.2% in 1979, 12% in 1980 and 14.9% in fiscal 1981.

Experience informs me that percentage-of-completion accounting practices, regardless of the guise, all too often lead to rude awakenings and should be avoided, except where the usual standard for revenue recognition would produce a clear distortion.

As it happens, R&D partnerships occupy a singular position in the scheme of things at Anacomp. Over the years, as noted, Anacomp has sponsored four of them—EFT

Partners Ltd., CEFT Partners Ltd., CBS Partners Ltd., and RTS Associates—not including last week's CIBS Partners Ltd. Of these, the oldest and the only one to close was RTS, which was formed in November 1979. The partners contributed $1.44 million and signed up for bank letters of credit for $3.25 million. Anacomp agreed to lend the partnership $2.2 million. Noteworthy, too, was that various Anacomp officers and directors were personally involved in RTS as limited partners, accounting for 40.5% of the partnership.

R&D partnerships have proved felicitous to Anacomp in several ways. Through them, the company avoids current deductions for the related R&D expenses. In addition, Anacomp derives revenues and potential income from charges for R&D activities performed on behalf of the partnerships. And when the project is completed, Anacomp, which usually has a buyout arrangement, winds up with a capitalized asset that can be written off over an extended period. Furthermore, by use of the partnerships, Anacomp is able to obtain "off-balance-sheet financing."

All that is apart from the benefits derived by management participants in the partnership, who (a) get a tax-shelter, (b) share in the buyout, if one comes about and (c) via compensation arrangements, can participate in Anacomp's enhanced profits flow.

In that light, the RTS enterprise is especially intriguing. The financial statements tell us that, in fiscal 1980, Anacomp garnered $2.3 million in revenues and $300,000 in pre-tax income from its contracted services to RTS. Anacomp bought out the partnership for a nice round $16 million. The partner's out-of-pocket investment three years ago, as noted, was just $1.44 million; eliminating outstanding liabilities, they should reap a capital gain of about $7.5 million.

But Anacomp will benefit on yet another count. The company picked up $2.3 million of the $6-million development contract it signed with the partnership. Hence, if the acquisition was consummated before June 30, another $3.7 million would be recorded as revenues in the fourth quarter. At this point, it's impossible to determine how much of that will wind up on the bottom line. The company, meanwhile, acquires a $16-million asset that will find its way over the years into income as a depreciation charge against operations.

And let's not overlook how certain insiders benefit. Upon Anacomp's purchase of RTS, the partners received a profit I estimate at around $3 million. Anacomp's chairman and president, Ronald D. Palamara, owned 15% of RTS, and thus personally—apart from tax benefits—stands to reap over $1 million. Moreover, Mr. Palamara's compensation agreement calls for a base salary of $125,000, plus 3.54% of Anacomp's earnings in excess of $1 million.

This spring, the Financial Accounting Standards Board promulgated an exposure draft of a proposed statement entitled "Research and Development Arrangements." If adopted, the rules would be tightened somewhat and in some cases (like that of RTS) the corporate sponsor would have to book the R&D costs as expenses when incurred. However, the new rules would apply to partnerships started after Sept. 30. And, to my mind, there are enough qualifications to allow astute management to flout the objectives of the FASB.

Since Anacomp's independent auditors have given it a "clean" certifying opinion, there's little doubt that Anacomp can rationalize everything in its financial statements as being "in conformity with generally accepted accounting principles." But as one eminent jurist in a landmark case points out, it's one thing to be in conformity with generally accepted accounting principles, but quite another to assure that the financial statements are inherently fair.

REFERENCES

ASQUITH, P., and D. W. MULLINS. "The Impact of Initiating Dividend Payments on Shareholders' Wealth." *The Journal of Business* (January 1983): 77–96.

BALL, R. J. "Changes in Accounting Techniques and Stock Prices." *Empirical Research in Accounting, Selected Studies,* Supplement to *Journal of Accounting Research* (1972): 1–38.

BALL, R., and P. BROWN. "An Empirical Evaluation of Accounting Income Numbers." *Journal of Accounting Research* (Autumn 1968): 159–178.

BALL, R., and G. FOSTER. "Corporate Financial Reporting: A Methodological Review of Empirical Research." *Studies on Current Research Methodologies in Accounting: A Critical Evaluation,* Supplement to *Journal of Accounting Research* (1982): 161–234.

BASU, S. "The Relationship Between Earnings' Yield, Market Value and Return for NYSE Common Stocks: Further Evidence." *Journal of Financial Economics* (June 1983): 129–156.

BEAVER, W. H. "The Information Content of Annual Earnings Announcements." *Empirical Research in Accounting: Selected Studies,* Supplement to *Journal of Accounting Research* (1968): 67–92.

BEAVER, W. H. "Econometric Properties of Alternative Security Return Methods." *Journal of Accounting Research* (Spring 1981): 163–184.

BEAVER, W. H., R. CLARKE, and W. F. WRIGHT. "The Association Between Unsystematic Security Returns and the Magnitude of Earnings Forecast Errors." *Journal of Accounting Research* (Autumn 1979): 316–340.

BEAVER, W. H., and W. R. LANDSMAN. *Incremental Information Content of Statement 33 Disclosures.* Stamford, Conn.: FASB, 1983.

BOWMAN, R. G. "Understanding and Conducting Event Studies." *Journal of Business Finance and Accounting* (Winter 1983): 561–584.

BRICKLEY, J. A. "Shareholder Wealth, Information Signaling and the Specially Designated Dividend." *Journal of Financial Economics* (August 1983): 187–209.

BROWN, P. "The Impact of the Annual Net Profit on the Stock Market." *The Australian Accountant* (July 1970); 277–282.

BROWN, S. J., and J. B. WARNER. "Measuring Security Price Performance." *Journal of Financial Economics* (September 1980); 205–258.

BROWN, S. J., and J. B. WARNER. "Using Daily Stock Returns: The Case of Event Studies," *Journal of Financial Economics* (March 1985): 3–31.

CHAMBERS, A. E., and S. H. PENMAN. "Timeliness of Reporting and the Stock Price Reaction to Earnings Announcements." *Journal of Accounting Research* (Spring 1984): 21–47.

CHOW, C. W. "Empirical Studies of the Economic Impacts of Accounting Regulations: Findings, Problems and Prospects." *Journal of Accounting Literature* (Spring 1983): 73–109.

CLINCH, G., and N. A. SINCLAIR. "Intra-Industry Information Transfers Associated With Earnings Releases: A Recursive Systems Approach," working paper. Monash University, Australia, 1984.

COLLINS, D. W., M. S. ROZEFF, and W. K. SALATKA. "The SEC's Rejection of SFAS No. 19: Tests of Market Price Reversal." *The Accounting Review* (January 1982): 1–17.

DIELMAN, T. E., and H. R. OPPENHEIMER. "An Examination of Investor Behavior During Periods of Large Dividend Changes." *Journal of Financial and Quantitative Analysis* (June 1984): 197–216.

EMANUEL, D. M. "The Information Content of Sign and Size of Earnings Announcements: New Zealand Evidence." *Accounting and Finance* (November 1984): 25–43.

FAMA, E. F. "Efficient Capital Markets: A Review of Theory and Empirical Work." *Journal of Finance* (May 1970): 383–417.

FOSTER, G. "Stock Market Reaction to Estimates of Earnings per Share by Company Officials." *Journal of Accounting Research* (Spring 1973): 25–37.

FOSTER, G. "Accounting Earnings and Stock Prices of Insurance Companies." *The Accounting Review* (October 1975): 686–698.

FOSTER, G. "Briloff and the Capital Market." *Journal of Accounting Research* (Spring 1979): 262–274.

FOSTER, G. "Accounting Policy Decisions and Capital Market Research." *Journal of Accounting and Economics* (March 1980): 29–62.

FOSTER, G. "Intra-Industry Information Transfers Associated with Earnings Releases. *Journal of Accounting and Economics* (March 1981): 201–232.

FOSTER, G. "Capital Market Efficiency: Definitions, Testing Issues and Anomalies." In M. J. R. Gaffikin, ed., *Contemporary Accounting Thought,* pp. 151–180. Melbourne: Prentice-Hall, 1984.

FOSTER, G. "Briloff and the Capital Market: Further Evidence," working paper. Stanford University, Stanford, Calif., 1985.

FOSTER, G., C. OLSEN, and T. SHEVLIN. "Earnings Releases, Anomalies and the Behavior of Security Returns." *The Accounting Review* (October 1984): 574–603.

GRANT, E. B. "Market Implications of Differential Amounts of Interim Information." *Journal of Accounting Research* (Spring 1980): 255–268.

HOLTHAUSEN, R. W. "Evidence on the Effect of Bond Covenants and Management Compensation Contracts on the Choice of Accounting Techniques: The Case of the Depreciation Switch-Back." *Journal of Accounting and Economics* (March 1981): 73–109.

HOLTHAUSEN, R. W., and R. W. LEFTWICH. "The Economic Consequences of Accounting Choice: Implications of Costly Contracting and Monitoring." *Journal of Accounting and Economics* (August 1983): 77–117.

KELLY, L. "Positive Theory Research: A Review." *Journal of Accounting Literature* (Spring 1983): 111–150.

KROSS, W., and D. A. SCHROEDER. "An Empirical Investigation of the Effect of Quarterly Earnings Announcement Timing on Stock Returns." *Journal of Accounting Research* (Spring 1984): 153–176.

LEV, B., and J. A. OHLSON. "Market-Based Empirical Research in Accounting: A Review, Interpretation, and Extension." *Studies on Current Research Methodologies in Accounting: A Critical Evaluation,* Supplement to *Journal of Accounting Research* (1982): 249–322.

McENALLY, R. W. "An Investigation of the Extrapolative Determinants of Short-Run Earnings Expectations." *Journal of Financial and Quantitative Analysis* (March 1971): 687–706.

McNICHOLS, M., and J. G. MANEGOLD. "The Effect of the Information Environment on the Relationship Between Financial Disclosure and Security Price Variability." *Journal of Accounting and Economics* (April 1983): 49–74.

MAINGOT, M. "The Information Content of UK Annual Earnings Announcements: A Note." *Accounting and Finance* (May 1984): 51–58.

MORSE, D. "Price and Trading Volume Reaction Surrounding Earnings Announcements: A Closer Examination." *Journal of Accounting Research* (Autumn 1981): 374–383.

NOREEN, E., and J. SEPE. "Market Reactions to Accounting Policy Deliberations: The Inflation Accounting Case." *The Accounting Review* (April 1981): 253–269.

OLSEN, C. "Valuation Implications of SFAS 33 Data for Electric Utility Investors," working paper. University of Texas at Austin, 1984.

PATELL, J. M., and M. A. WOLFSON. "The Intraday Speed of Adjustment of Stock Prices to Earnings and Dividend Announcements." *Journal of Financial Economics* (June 1984): 223–252. North-Holland Publishing Company, Amsterdam, 1984.

PINCUS, M., "Information Characteristics of Earnings Announcements and Stock Market Behavior." *Journal of Accounting Research* (Spring 1983): 155–183.

RENDLEMAN, R. J., C. P. JONES, and H. A. LATANE. "Empirical Anomalies Based on Unexpected Earnings and the Importance of Risk Adjustments." *Journal of Financial Economics* (November 1982): 269–287.

RICHARDSON, G. D. "The Information Content of Annual Earnings for Large and Small Firms: Further Empirical Evidence," working paper. University of British Columbia, February 1984.

RICKS, W. "Market Assessment of Alternative Accounting Methods: A Review of the Empirical Evidence." *Journal of Accounting Literature* (Spring 1982): 59–102.

RICKS, W. E., and G. C. BIDDLE. "LIFO Adoptions and Stock Price Reactions:

A Comparison of Methods and Results," working paper. Duke University, Durham, N.C., 1985.

ROLL, R. "On Computing Mean Returns and the Small Firm Premium." *Journal of Financial Economics* (November 1983): 371–386.

SCHWERT, G. W. "Using Financial Data to Measure Effects of Regulation." *Journal of Law and Economics* (April 1981): 121–158.

SHEVLIN, T. J. "Measuring Abnormal Performance on the Australian Securities Market." *Australian Journal of Management* (June 1981): 67–107.

STERLING, R. R. "On Theory Construction and Verification." *The Accounting Review* (July 1970): 444–457.

WAYMIRE, G. "Additional Evidence on the Information Content of Management Earnings Forecasts." *Journal of Accounting Research* (Autumn 1984): 703–718.

ZEGHAL, D. "Industry, Market Structure, and the Informational Content of Financial Statements." *Journal of Accounting and Public Policy* (Summer 1983): 115–131. Published by North-Holland Publishing Company, Amsterdam, 1983.

12

EQUITY SECURITIES
AND FINANCIAL STATEMENT
INFORMATION

12.1 INTRODUCTION

This chapter discusses the use of financial statement information in the pricing of equity securities. Areas where this topic is important include the following:

1. *Active investment approaches.* One widely employed approach estimates the intrinsic value of a security and then makes recommendations based on divergences between this intrinsic value and the current market price. Examples of this approach are given in Section 12.3 of this chapter. (See also the discussion of fundamental analysis in Chapter 9.)

2. *Management decision making.* The following comment by Boise Cascade is typical of that found in the annual reports or other public releases of some companies:

   > The criterion underlying the analysis of the alternative investment and financial strategies at all stages of the planning process is the addition of value to our shareholders' investments in Boise Cascade. We believe that shareholders want management to attempt to responsibly optimize the long-term return on their investment, consistent with a prudent level of risk.

   To implement strategies that "add value" to shareholders' investments, management needs to understand the determinants of the market value of their firm. For instance, without such an understanding, they could unwittingly make acquisitions that dilute the market value of the shares held by the existing owners.

3. *Valuation of privately held companies.* There are many contexts in which estimates need to be placed on the value of companies that are not traded on organized markets, for example, (a) when determining the value of an estate of a deceased shareholder, (b) when determining the price at which a company could go public, (c) when estimating the value of dissenting minority shareholder interests in "squeeze out" merger contexts, and (d) when estimating the value of stock options in the executive compensation plan of a privately held company.

4. *Academic research.* Several areas of research in the accounting, business strategy, economics, and finance literatures use market values of equity securities. An understanding of the determinants of these market values facilitates the construction of better research designs in these literatures and the more careful drawing of inferences from the research results.

12.2 SOURCES OF VALUE AND EQUITY-VALUATION MODELS

Equity valuation models can focus on at least one or more of the following four attributes:

A. Stream of future earnings
B. Stream of future cash flows
C. Stream of future dividends
D. The values of the individual assets and liabilities owned or controlled by the firm.

These four attributes obviously are not independent of each other. However, valuation approaches that focus singly on one of these attributes can be found in the literature and in practice.

A.   Stream-of-Future-Earnings Approaches

The simplest form of a valuation model is for the certainty case in which all assets yield a uniform earnings stream in perpetuity. Given appropriate assumptions about capital markets (for example, perfect capital markets), the equilibrium market value of an (all-equity) firm is

$$V_{i,t} = \frac{X_i}{r} \tag{12.1}$$

where

$V_{i,t}$ = market value of firm i at the end of period t
X_i = uniform certain earnings stream of firm i
r = market rate of interest for riskless investments

Earnings as used in (12.1) is a generic label for the flows generated by the existing assets of firm i. (It need not be the same as earnings computed using generally accepted accounting principles.)

Extensions of (12.1) have relaxed either (1) the uniform earnings per period assumption or (2) the certainty assumption. An example of (1) is the following valuation model for a firm with constant growth in earnings:

$$V_{i,t} = \frac{X_{i,t+1}}{r} + \frac{X_{i,t+1}}{r} \left[\frac{k(r^* - r)}{r - kr^*} \right] \tag{12.2}$$

where

$V_{i,t}$ = market value of firm i at the end of period t
$X_{i,t+1}$ = earnings generated by firm i in period $t + 1$
r = market rate of interest for riskless investments
k = proportion of the firm's earnings invested each year (assumed constant)
r^* = rate of return on the investment

In this formulation, $V_{i,t}$ is a function of both a no-growth component (first term on the right-hand side, RHS) and a growth component (second term on the RHS).

Growth in (12.2) means investment in projects with returns exceeding their cost of capital (r in a certainty world). If $r^* = r$, the second term on the RHS of (12.2) becomes zero, and $V_{i,t}$ is determined as per (12.1).

Another extension of the model in (12.1) is to recognize the risk associated with uncertainty. This risk can be recognized (1) via the discount rate used or (2) by including a separate variable in the valuation equation. An example of (1) is Modigliani and Miller (1958), who develop the notion of a "risk class." Two firms are in the same risk class if investors perceive that whatever values their earnings and investment outlays take, they will always be proportionate by a factor (that is, they are perfectly correlated). Using assumptions such as rational investors, perfect markets, and no taxes, Modigliani and Miller derive the following valuation model for a no-growth (all-equity) firm in risk-class k:

$$V_{i,t} = \frac{E(X_i)}{r_k} \tag{12.3}$$

where

$\quad V_{i,t}$ = market value of firm i at the end of period t

$\quad E(X_i)$ = expected level of annual earnings generated by the assets that firm i currently holds

$\quad r_k$ = cost of capital of firms in risk-class k

The market's capitalization rate for the stream of future earnings is $1/r_k$. The more risky the "risk class," the higher is r_k and, thus, the lower the capitalization rate for each dollar of expected earnings. In empirical applications of this risk-class model, firms operating in "relatively homogeneous" industries have been said to constitute a risk class. Industries examined have included electric utilities (Miller and Modigliani, 1966) and railroads (Brown, 1968).

A second approach to recognizing risk is to include a separate risk term in the valuation equation. Litzenberger and Rao (1971) illustrate this approach in an empirical test of a valuation model derived from the two-parameter capital asset pricing model (see Chapter 10). The valuation model examined included a separate earnings and a separate risk term. Given the risk-aversion assumption underlying the two-parameter model, the coefficient on the risk term was predicted to be negative; the greater the riskiness of the earnings stream, the more negative the adjustment made for risk in the valuation model. More recent applications of this approach include Bowen (1981) and Daley (1984). (Sections 12.5.A and 12.6 provide further discussion of and evidence relating to the Litzenberger and Rao model.)

B.   Cash Flow-Based Approaches

Chapters on capital budgeting in corporate finance textbooks invariably advocate that management should use a discounted cash flow (DCF) approach to project selection rather than a maximize accounting earnings approach. Rationales for preferring DCF include

1. DCF takes into account the timing with which cash inflows and outflows occur
2. Accounting earnings are affected by arbitrary choices in such important areas as cost of goods sold, depreciation, and pension expense.

These arguments also have been used to support a DCF approach to equity valuation. As noted in Section 12.2.A, equation (12.1) does not specify that X_i is accounting earnings. Thus, if cash flows are predicted to be constant, (12.1) could be used to derive the estimate of equity value.

At an empirical level, most applications of (12.1), (12.2), and (12.3) have used accounting earnings (variously adjusted) as the proxy for the X_i series. A subset of authors and practitioners have criticized these applications for reasons (1) and (2) just given. For instance, Stern (1980) argues that "investors discount expected future 'free cash flow,' the expected future stream of cash flows that remains after deducting the anticipated future capital requirements of the business. It is free cash flow that is important to the market. EPS is immaterial" (p. 45).

C. Dividend-Based Approaches

Assuming an infinite holding period in a certainty setting, the formula for the market value of an equity security based on the future dividend stream is

$$V_{i,t} = \frac{d_{t+1}}{(1 + r_{t+1})} + \frac{d_{t+2}}{(1 + r_{t+1})(1 + r_{t+2})}$$

$$\cdots \frac{d_{t+n}}{(1 + r_{t+1})(1 + r_{t+2}) \cdots (1 + r_{t+n})} \quad \text{(12.4)}$$

where

$V_{i,t}$ = the market value of firm i at the end of period t
d_t = the dividend paid in period t
r_t = the market rate of interest in period t for riskless investments

One issue that arises with (12.4) is estimating $r_{t+1}, r_{t+2}, \ldots, r_{t+n}$ (the term structure of interest rates). Most institutions that utilize dividend-based valuation models (see Section 12.3 for an example) assume a flat term structure (that is, $r_1 = r_2 = r_3 \cdots = r_n$). With this assumption, (12.4) becomes

$$V_{i,t} = \frac{d_{t+1}}{(1 + r)} + \frac{d_{t+2}}{(1 + r)^2} + \cdots + \frac{d_{t+n}}{(1 + r)^n} \quad \text{(12.5)}$$

The typical rationale offered for this flat term structure assumption is the difficulty of estimating the pattern of interest rates over an n year horizon.

Attempts to relax the certainty assumption in (12.4) and (12.5) typically do so via an adjustment to the discount rate. When uncertainty is recognized in this way, the discount rate reflects both the time preference of investors plus the assessed risk associated with the dividend series of firm *i*.

D.   Individual Asset and Liability-Based Approaches

The individual assets and liabilities underlying a security can play an important role in the market valuation of that security. An extreme case is a no-load, open-end mutual fund where the assets underlying a share in the fund are equity securities. The market value of a share is based on the market value of the individual securities held by the fund. Many funds update these values on a daily basis and provide facilities for new purchases or redemptions based on these values.

An analysis of investment newsletters reveals several different perspectives on how to value the assets and liabilities of firms. One perspective is from a replacement viewpoint. For instance, some oil and gas stock acquisitions are portrayed as "asset plays," because it is (allegedly) cheaper for a company to acquire the proved oil and gas reserves of another company than it is to replace its own reserves via exploration. Another perspective is to adopt a market selling price (realization) viewpoint. A sale in the ordinary course of business or in a liquidation mode can be considered. An illustration of the latter is in an investment newsletter headed "Better Dead than in the Red—Let's Liquidate." Weinger and Metz (1982) screened companies to identify cases where their estimates of liquidation value (obtained by multiplying individual balance sheet items by a "conservative" discount, for example, gross plant $\times$ .2) exceeded the current market value of the firm. They concluded that "a surprising number of public companies are worth more dead than alive" and suggested that "investors use this data in conjunction with our other valuation screens as a starting point in the search for undervalued situations."

E.   Overview

The foregoing discussion outlined four different approaches (earnings, cash flow, dividends, and individual net assets) that can be used to obtain an estimate of equity security value. The rationale for outlining each approach individually is that examples of the use of each can be found in the academic literature or in practice. Analytical research can (and has, to a limited degree) examined conditions under which these four approaches will result in equivalent valuations. At an empirical level, however, such equivalence is rarely obtained. Indeed, some active investment approaches utilize divergences between the values given by two or more of the preceding approaches as a key input into decisions about which securities are hypothesized to be under- or overvalued by the capital market.

12.3   INVESTMENT COMMUNITY EQUITY-VALUATION MODELS

The investment community has developed many different valuation models to use in security selection decisions. A common feature of almost all these models is the use of financial statement data. An assumption underlying the use of these models is that the capital market misprices securities and that these models can be used to detect this mispricing. These models are examples of the fundamental approach to active investment analysis described in Chapter 9.

A.   Continual Change in Models or Their Inputs

When examining models of investment institutions, it is important to recognize that continual change in either the structure of the model, or its inputs, is the norm rather than the exception. The sources of these changes include

1. *New analytical insights.* Developments such as the capital asset pricing model (Sharpe, 1964), the option pricing model (Black and Scholes, 1973), and the arbitrage pricing model (Ross, 1976) have led to changes in the models used in the investment community.

2. *New empirical insights.* Empirical research is continually reporting new results and overturning results previously believed valid. Chapter 11 of this book presents a subset of the empirical evidence that has had an important effect on the investment community.

3. *New data bases.* As computer-based data analysis becomes more important in investment research, there are strong incentives for institutions to develop new data bases, and to market them to the investment community. Chapter 8 discussed the IBES and Icarus earnings forecast data bases; both have been incorporated into models used by several institutions. New data bases can also expand the set of securities that can be included in the investment universe that is researched; for example, new data bases covering over-the-counter securities have reduced the cost of examining the smaller firms traded on this market.

4. *New disclosures by firms.* Firms are continually changing the information they disclose, whether done voluntarily or due to a regulatory mandate. Investment institutions can use these new disclosures when changing their existing procedures. New disclosures related to line-of-business information, lease obligations, and pension obligations currently are being used by some firms in their methods for security risk estimation.

5. *New securities.* Changes in the set of securities traded are continually occurring, for example, expanded coverage of put and call options and the introduction of market index futures. In some cases, analysts can use these newly traded securities to expand the set of information they report about existing securities. For instance, the advent of organized options markets

has enabled analysts to estimate the market consensus implied variability of returns for the underlying equity security (via the Black-Scholes, 1973, option pricing model).

6. *New statistical tools.* Research on techniques such as factor analysis and nonlinear regression has the potential to provide institutions with new statistical ways of analyzing data.

7. *New developments in computer technology.* The developments here can be many; for example, reduced hardware costs can make large-scale data analysis more cost-effective, and the advent of the personal computer can dramatically change the perception of some analysts about computer capabilities.

Pressure for continual change in the models used by investment institutions also comes from marketing forces. When one institution develops a "new product," there are pressures on its competitors also to provide this product to their clients. Establishing property rights over many ideas associated with investment analysis is very difficult. A sizable part of applied investment research consists of developing in-house replications (clones) of products already available from other investment firms. Hawkins and Campbell (1978) provide examples of equity valuation products developed in the 1960s or 1970s. The next two subsections describe two currently available equity valuation products—Wells Fargo's security market plane and Value Line's investment survey.

B. Wells Fargo Model

The model used by Wells Fargo Investment Advisors combines both traditional valuation theory with developments in asset pricing theory. There are two steps in implementing the model:

1. Estimate the expected internal rate of return of each security—$E(\text{IRR}_i)$. This estimate is based on a dividend discount equity valuation model:

$$P_{i,t} = \frac{d_{i,t+1}}{(1 + \text{IRR}_i)} + \frac{d_{i,t+2}}{(1 + \text{IRR}_i)^2} + \frac{d_{i,t+3}}{(1 + \text{IRR}_i)^3} + \cdots + \frac{d_{i,t+n}}{(1 + \text{IRR}_i)^n} \quad \textbf{(12.6)}$$

where

$P_{i,t}$ = market price of security i at end of period t

$d_{i,t}$ = dividends paid by firm i in period t

IRR_i = implied internal rate of return of firm i

2. Estimate the equilibrium rate of return of each security—$E(\text{R}_i)$. This estimate is based on a capital asset pricing model.

A stock's measure of relative mispricing (MRM_i) currently is calculated as

$$\text{MRM}_i = E(\text{IRR}_i) - E(\text{R}_i) \quad \textbf{(12.7)}$$

The more positive (negative) the MRM_i value, the more under- (over-) valued the security. For each security in the Wells Fargo universe of stocks, the following inputs are used:

1. Estimated dividends per share for each of the next five years ($d_{i,t+1}$, $d_{i,t+2}$, . . .)
2. Estimated earnings per share for the fifth year ($E_{i,t+5}$)
3. Estimated earnings per share growth rate for the fifth year ($G_{i,t+5}$)
4. Estimated dividend payout ratio for the fifth year ($P_{i,t+5}$)
5. Year (T) in which a steady state growth rate ($G_{i,t+5}$) and dividend payout ratio ($P_{i,t+5}$) will be realized
6. Pattern of growth in earnings per share to be expected between the fifth year and year T. One of three patterns is assumed: "slow decay," "linear decay," or "rapid decay."

Inputs 2–6 are used to estimate the dividend sequence in years 6 to T. Using the relationship between the predicted dividend sequence for years 1 to T and the current $P_{i,t}$ in (12.6), an estimate of IRR_i is obtained.

The model used to estimate $E(R_i)$ has undergone several modifications to capture changing perceptions as to the factors affecting equilibrium security returns. The initial model incorporated the single factor (beta or relative risk) specified by the before-tax version of the two-parameter capital asset pricing model. The equation used to estimate MRM_i was

$$MRM_i = \begin{matrix} \text{internal rate} \\ \text{of return from} \\ \text{valuation model} \end{matrix} - \begin{matrix} \text{risk adjustment} \\ \text{using before-tax} \\ \text{version of CAPM} \end{matrix}$$

The second iteration (starting in February 1977) added an additional factor relating to liquidity:

$$MRM_i = \begin{matrix} \text{internal rate} \\ \text{of return from} \\ \text{valuation model} \end{matrix} - \begin{matrix} \text{risk adjustment} \\ \text{using before-tax} \\ \text{version of CAPM} \end{matrix} + \begin{matrix} \text{liquidity} \\ \text{adjustment} \end{matrix}$$

Stocks with below-average liquidity were assumed to require an above-average expected return in their equilbrium pricing. The third iteration (starting in September 1978) was motivated by Wells Fargo adopting an after-tax version of the CAPM. With this model, adjustments are made for both beta and dividend yield. An internal memorandum provided the following details:

> The Security Yield Line is derived by holding risk constant and allowing yield to vary. The slope of the Security Yield Line represents the average trade-off between expected return and yield. This line has a positive slope since current yield is taxed at a higher rate than are capital gains. To offset this tax differential, taxpaying investors should demand a higher expected return from higher-yielding stocks, and be willing to accept a lower expected return from lower-yielding issues, other things being equal.

The fourth iteration (starting in June 1980) was the dropping of the liquidity factor. Since June 1980, the equation used to estimate relative mispricing has been

$$\text{MRM}_i = \begin{matrix} \text{internal rate} \\ \text{of return from} \\ \text{valuation model} \end{matrix} - \begin{matrix} \text{risk and dividend yield} \\ \text{adjustment using after-} \\ \text{tax version of CAPM} \end{matrix}$$

Wells Fargo called the risk and dividend yield adjustment the market plane adjustment. Risk (beta) estimates are based on an OLS regression of monthly security returns against the S&P 500 index. Dividend yield is calculated as annual dividends divided by the current market price.

Wells Fargo presents estimates of relative pricing at both the individual security level and at the industry level. The following estimates for selected industries were made in October 1984:

Industry	$E(IRR_i)$	$-$	$E(R_i)$	$=$	MRM_i
Finance companies	20.37		17.93		2.44
Food stores	16.86		15.86		1.00
Construction equipment	17.17		17.04		.13
Beverages	14.45		15.71		−1.26
Electric utilities	14.73		17.00		−2.27

The prediction in October 1984 was that finance companies (as a group) were undervalued, while electric utilities were overvalued by the capital market. The Wells Fargo system represents an interesting blend of theory and pragmatism. Financial statement information potentially can be used in estimating both the $E(\text{IRR}_i)$ and $E(R_i)$ parameters.

Wells Fargo was an early proponent of combining traditional valuation theory with asset pricing theory in an attempt to detect mispriced securities. By the early 1980s, many other investment institutions were offering similar products to their clients, for example, Bache, Drexel Burnham Lambert, and Kidder Peabody. (Kidder Peabody calls its *Security Valuation System,* "SALUS." In Roman mythology, Salus was the goddess of good fortune, health, and prosperity.) Useful discussion of the problems of using this class of investment equity valuation models is in Michaud and Davis (1982).

C. Value Line Model

The Value Line model is of considerable interest due to some evidence of its success in detecting under- or overvalued securities. Each stock is placed in one of five categories based on its estimated price performance in the next 12 months. The basic approach is to measure each stock's price and earnings characteristics against the comparable characteristics of the other Value Line stocks. Each stock is ranked on its expected "relative price performance in the next 12 months" based on a combination of three criteria. Value Line provided (in November 1984) the following description of these three criteria:

Criterion 1: The Nonparametric Value Position

The non-parametric value position of a stock is a function of the "order" of its latest relative reported earnings and relative price in relation to the past 10 years' experience. Relative earnings and relative prices are defined as the stock's latest 12-months' earnings and price divided by the average earnings and prices of all Value Line stocks for the same period. If a stock's relative earnings are currently the highest in the past 10 years, its earnings rank is 10; if lowest, 1. The same applies to the latest 12 months' average price. The higher the earnings rank relative to the price rank, the more undervalued is the stock on the basis of its latest 12 months' earnings. The process of assigning an order or rank to relative earnings tends to tame and normalize the earnings data that, in their original form, particularly as far as highly cyclical stocks are concerned, are all too often unmanageable.

In addition to the current earnings and price ranks, a price momentum factor is included in order to help predict future relative price action. The price momentum factor for a stock is determined by dividing the stock's latest-10-week average relative price by its 52-week average relative price.

An electronic computer was used to test the discriminating ability of these variables. A multiple regression analysis was performed covering some 13,000 observations and 12 years of market experience. The results clearly indicated that these factors were significantly related to relative price movement in the year ahead. A formula was produced combining earnings rank, price rank, and price momentum into a composite number which could then be ranked from 1700 to 1, 1700 being the best. The number 1700 is used because it represents the number of stocks regularly reviewed by the Value Line Investment Survey.

Criterion 2: Earnings Momentum

The second component of the Value LIne next-12-months' Ranking System is a function of the year-to-year change in quarterly earnings per share of each stock relative to that of all stocks under regular review. Numerous tests with past data demonstrate conclusively that this "earnings momentum" factor has an important bearing on the subsequent price performance of individual securities and helps refine the selection of favorably situated stocks. No attempt is made to rank all stocks successively from 1700 to 1, based on the exact earnings changes from a year ago (the implied accuracy would be far greater than could be obtained in practice). Rather, all stocks reporting earnings on a quarterly basis are assigned to one of three equal categories—and ranked 1200, 800 or 400 respectively—depending upon the relative "earnings momentum" of the latest quarter. The most favorable quarterly earnings comparisons (the top one third) are assigned the number 1200; the middle third, 800; and the lowest third, 400. (The scaling of these numbers is chosen to maintain comparability with the ranking method applied to the "non-parametric" value criterion.) In assigning ranks, allowance is made, whenever possible, for "special" factors affecting earnings in a specific quarter, such as strikes, accounting adjustments, special tax credits, other nonrecurring income and expenses, etc.

Criterion 3: Earnings Surprise Factor

The third component of the Value Line Ranking System is an earnings surprise factor. Tests have indicated that when a company reports quarterly earnings significantly different from those estimated in the Survey, sharp price movements in the direction of the surprise tend to follow. In the Value Line Ranking System, this factor is treated as follows:

Deviation between Actual & Value Line's Estimated Quarterly Earnings	Assigned Numbers
−30% or more	−400
−15 to −29%	−200
−14 to +14%	0
+15% to +29%	+200
+30% and over	+400

As in the case of earnings momentum, the number assigned to the quarterly earnings deviations between actual and estimate is chosen to maintain comparability with the ranking method applied to the "non-parametric" value and earnings momentum criteria.

Final Ranking

After all stocks have been classified on the basis of each of the above criteria, the individual ranks are summed and the composite numbers arranged into five categories as follows:

Top 100	−Rank 1
Next 300	−Rank 2
Middle 900	−Rank 3
Next 300	−Rank 4
Bottom 100	−Rank 5

In the mid-1970s, Value Line had a fourth factor—"an analyst judgment factor"—that took account of "backlog trends, incoming order rates, facilities utilization, competitive factors, labor problems, product quality and numerous other non-quantifiable variables." This factor was deleted in mid-1979. An official of Value Line commented that "its contribution was statistically insignificant and hence it was a negative since it was causing unnecessary rank changes."

Figure 12.1 presents the record of the Value Line groups over the 1965–1984 period. The returns for Group 1 assume that an investor buys an equal dollar amount of every stock ranked in Group 1 (highest) for price performance at the beginning of each year. The investor holds that list unchanged for a whole year and then at the end of the year revises the list, dropping out all stocks no longer ranked 1 and replacing them with stocks that have taken their place in the group 1 rankings. The same procedure was repeated for stocks in the other four groups. (The returns in Figure 12.1 do not take into account transaction costs of changing portfolios at each year end.) Note that the price performance of each group appears consistent with Value Line's prediction; for example, group 1 has the highest price appreciation and group 5 has the greatest price depreciation. Eisenstadt (1982) noted that "academia has had a long, if not always friendly, interest in the Value Line ranking system. Can you imagine using known earnings and price

FIGURE 12.1 Price Performance of Value Line Groups, 1965–1984 (1 = Group with Highest Predicted Price Performance; 5 = Group with Lowest Predicted Price Performance)

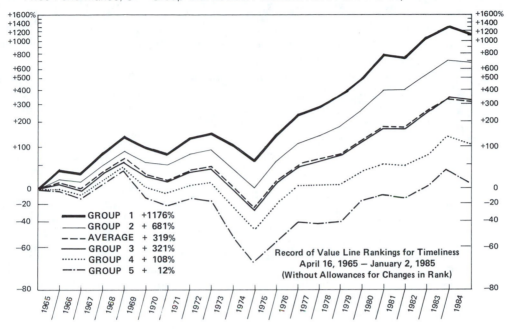

Record of Value Line Rankings for Timeliness (Without Allowance for Changes in Rank)
April 16, 1965 – January 2, 1985

Group	1965*	1966	1967	1968	1969	1970	1971	1972	1973	1974	1975
1	+33.6%	− 3.1%	+39.2%	+31.2%	−17.7%	− 8.9%	+26.5%	+10.1%	−17.1%	−23.1%	+51.6%
2	+18.9	− 6.0	+31.9	+26.3	−16.3	− 4.0	+17.4	+ 7.5	−26.2	−27.8	+53.0
3	+ 8.9	− 9.7	+30.1	+21.4	−20.7	− 5.5	+12.2	+ 6.2	−27.0	−28.5	+52.9
4	+ 0.8	− 7.2	+25.1	+25.1	−26.8	−11.7	+14.2	+ 3.2	−29.1	−33.6	+48.4
5	− 1.2	−12.4	+28.4	+25.9	−35.7	−13.1	+10.5	+ 2.9	−43.1	−36.8	+42.1
AVG	+10.1	− 7.9	+29.9	+24.6	−22.1	− 7.5	+14.9	+ 5.5	−27.7	−29.6	+51.2

Group	1976	1977	1978	1979	1980	1981	1982	1983	1984	1965 through 1984
1	+35.3%	+15.8%	+19.8%	+25.6%	+50.2%	− 1.9%	+33.7%	+25.2%	− 8.6%	+1176%
2	+36.3	+12.7	+16.1	+30.8	+37.4	+ 0.7	+29.0	+22.2	− 0.1	+ 681
3	+33.8	+ 5.2	+ 9.2	+27.6	+20.8	+ 2.7	+25.5	+26.7	− 1.6	+ 321
4	+36.1	− 0.2	+ 2.4	+23.1	+13.2	− 0.9	+18.5	+35.2	−12.3	+ 108
5	+38.2	− 2.8	+ 4.0	+39.9	+ 8.4	− 4.2	+19.9	+30.0	−17.1	+ 12
AVG	+35.1	+ 5.8	+ 9.6	+28.0	+23.4	+ 0.9	+25.0	+27.5	− 4.7	+ 319

Dow Jones Industrials   + 31
N.Y. Stock Exchange Composite   + 101

*April through December

Source: Value Line Selection and Opinion (January 18, 1985): p. 962.

data, not forecasts, to predict successfully relative price performance in the next 6 to 12 months? Small wonder, then, that Value Line results are greeted with a great deal of skepticism in an environment where efficient market theory is second only to the Bible as Gospel truth'' (p. 1).

Not surprisingly, academics have examined the Value Line rankings using their own performance benchmarks. An early study by Black (1973) covered the 1965–1970 period; five portfolios were constructed that represented the five groupings with stocks assigned to a group based on Value Line's code in the prior month. The conclusion was that ''the success of the rankings was very consistent over time . . . when the portfolio was revised on a monthly basis, the extra returns earned by the Rank 1 and Rank 5 stocks were, respectively, 10 percent per year and − 10 percent per year. . . . the possibility that this performance could have occurred by chance is one in 10,000'' (pp. 12–14). Copeland and Mayers (1982) examined Value Line rankings over the 1965–1978 period. Security returns in the 26-week and 52-week periods following publication of the Value Line codings were examined. The conclusion was that ''Value Line rankings do exhibit abnormal performance. . . . It is considerably less than that reported by Black (1973), but the possibility of economic significance for some investors remains'' (p. 291). Copeland and Mayers examined three subperiods (November 1965 to February 1970, May 1970 to May 1974, August 1974 to May 1978). Evidence of abnormal performance was most marked in the 1965–1970 subperiod with ''the excess rate of return [being] less with each succeeding subhistory'' (p. 313).

D. Equity Valuation Models and Financial Statement Analysis

The premise underlying the development of equity valuation models by the investment community is that they can be used to earn abnormal returns. There are several steps in examining if a link exists between financial statement analysis and abnormal returns.

1. Break down the investment system into its constituent parts; for example,
    a. Inputs: This can be further broken down into (i) the data (both its content and timeliness) used in the estimation of the inputs and (ii) the models or procedures used to transform this data into valuation model inputs.
    b. Valuation model: If this model is decomposable into separate factors (for example, a risk factor, a dividend yield factor, and a liquidity factor), the opportunity exists to examine the contribution of each factor.
    c. Buy-sell-retain decisions using predictions of the valuation model: This part can include both (i) the procedures within an investment firm or its client by which a purchase or sale decision is approved and (ii) the procedures by which the actual purchases or sales are made.
2. Estimate the probability that abnormal returns are currently being earned by the investment system. Chapter 10 discussed some of the difficult issues that arise with this step. The existence of abnormal returns does not nec-

essarily imply a superior investment system. (A small subset of systems will show abnormal returns by chance.)

3. If there is a high probability that abnormal returns are being earned, attempt to determine if sources within the investment system are associated with those abnormal returns. If there is a high probability that abnormal returns are not being earned, attempt to locate areas where changes in the existing approach could give rise to abnormal returns.

The overall process can be characterized as

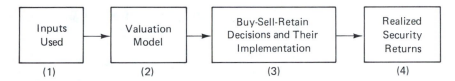

Inputs Used	Valuation Model	Buy-Sell-Retain Decisions and Their Implementation	Realized Security Returns
(1)	(2)	(3)	(4)

More reliable inferences generally can be drawn about the link between (3) and (4) than about either of the indirect links between (1) and (4) or (2) and (4). For instance, it is relatively easy to examine the effect on (4) of reducing the buy-sell approval process by two weeks or of reducing brokerage costs by a stipulated amount. In contrast, more difficult issues arise when examining the links between earlier components of the investment process and realized security returns.

Assume that abnormal returns are being earned by an investment system using earnings forecast inputs. There are at least two (both imperfect) approaches to examining if the earnings forecasts are the "cause" of the abnormal return:

1. Examine the effect of using alternative earnings forecasts. If one found that abnormal returns were not earned with alternative forecasts, the likelihood of "better quality" earnings forecasts being one source of abnormal returns would be increased.

2. Examine the individual nonearnings forecast components in the system to see if any one is a source of abnormal returns. If the evidence was that none of these components yield abnormal returns, the likelihood of "better quality" earnings forecasts being a source would be increased.

Each approach has its limitations. For instance, the first approach (1) is contingent upon the competing earnings forecast models examined. Chapter 8 illustrated that some forecasting models are known to provide less accurate and more dispersed forecasts than others. The use of a known inferior forcasting model could lead to misleading inferences about the quality of the existing earnings forecasts. The second approach (2) ignores the possibility that it is the interaction of the individual components that is the source of the abnormal returns. At present, little research has been conducted on the problems of implementing either approach. This topic area remains an important but relatively unexplored research area of financial statement analysis.

12.4 PRICE-TO-EARNINGS RATIOS

One of the most frequently cited financial indicators about a publicly traded company is the price- (P) to-earnings (E) ratio. This ratio typically is calculated using data on a per share basis:

$$\text{PE ratio} = \frac{\text{Market price per equity share}}{\text{Earnings per equity share}} \tag{12.8}$$

The PE ratio in (12.8) can be given a theoretical foundation via an equity valuation model of the form:

$$P_i = \frac{E_i}{r} \tag{12.9}$$

Key assumptions underlying this theoretical foundation include

1. Differences across firms in their riskiness either are irrelevant in the determination of P_i (as would be the case in a risk-neutral market), or these differences can be fully captured by the r term (as in the risk-class model described in Section 12.2.A)
2. The future earnings stream can be fully represented by a single number (a scalar). One such case is where the future stream is constant.

Where these assumptions are not met, the PE ratio should not be imbued with any theoretical importance. In most contexts, it is best viewed as a summary indicator of the capital market's perception of earnings generating power in the same way that many financial ratios are viewed as indicators of attributes such as liquidity, profitability, and leverage.

A. Computation Issues

Computation issues that arise when computing PE ratios include

1. *Choice of the date to measure the numerator.* The two main options are (a) use the fiscal year-end (fiscal quarter-end) price or (b) use the price immediately after the public release of the earnings figure in the denominator. The benefit of using (b) is that the numerator can then reflect the information content of the denominator.

2. *Choice of the time period to use for the denominator.* Assume that a firm has reported annual earnings of $6 per share for year t and has just reported first-quarter results for year $t + 1$ of $2:

	Year t			Year t + 1
Q1	*Q2*	*Q3*	*Q4*	*Q1*
$1.00	$1.30	$1.40	$2.30	$2.00

When computing the PE ratio after release of the $2 first-quarter figure, it is preferable to use a "rolling" 12-month reporting period (annual earnings for Q2, Q3, and Q4 of year t plus Q1 of year $t + 1 = \$7$) rather than the fiscal 12-month period chosen by the firm. Use of the "rolling" time period for the denominator incorporates more of the information impounded into the numerator of the PE ratio.

Several financial services report PE ratios using security analyst EPS forecasts for the current period. This denominator potentially could reduce diversity across the PE ratios of firms induced by the past EPS series having a sizable transitory component of earnings (see Section 12.4.B); this assumes that analysts adjust for these transitory earnings when forecasting EPS. (Note that use of analyst EPS forecasts as a denominator can cause circularity if analysts use PE ratios when making their EPS forecasts.)

3. *Choice of the earnings per share measure to use in the denominator.* For example: (a) primary *or* fully diluted and (b) preextraordinary items *or* postextraordinary items. In cases where this choice affects the observed PE ratio, the decision context can provide some guidance; for example, a banker may choose a fully diluted EPS concept due to a desire to adopt a conservative viewpoint of earnings per share. Unfortunately, no tight theory exists to guide choices on (a) or (b).

4. *Treatment of negative earnings per share figures.* The typical treatment when this problem arises is to delete negative numbers and compute PE ratios only for firms with positive earnings. However, if the perspective is taken that the PE ratio is but one of several inputs used to infer the market's expectations of future earnings, the rationale for deleting negative numbers is less clear. There is no presumption that, even for firms with positive earnings, the best estimate of future earnings is the earnings numbers used in the denominator of the PE. This book recommends computing PE ratios for negative earnings firms and including them in the sample when assessing the distribution of PE ratios across firms. A negative PE ratio is a very informative data item. It is a signal that the market's expectation of future earnings is different from that reported for the most recent period.

B. Permanent and Transitory Components of Reported Earnings

A useful dichotomy of reported earnings (E_i^R) is into a permanent component (E_i^P) and a transitory component (E_i^T):

$$E_i^R = E_i^P + E_i^T \tag{12.10}$$

Assume a valuation model of the following kind,

$$P_i = M_i \cdot E_i^P \tag{12.11}$$

where P_i is the price of one equity share of firm i and M_i is the multiple applied to the permanent earnings component of E_i^R. A permanent component of E_i^R is one for which $M_i \neq 0$. A transitory component is one for which $M_i = 0$. In practice, M_i need not assume only one of two values (M_i^P and 0). Rather, there may be a spectrum of values associated with different permanent components of the reported earnings series.

There are several reasons for expecting the concept of earnings implicit in security prices (E_i^P) to differ from the concept of earnings implicit in generally accepted accounting principles (E_i^R):

1. The concept of earnings implicit in GAAP is based on accounting notions such as realization and conservatism. With these notions, there are restrictions on both

   a. The events that are reflected in the reported earnings series; for example, periodic changes in the market value of debt associated with interest rate changes typically are excluded from being recognized in GAAP-based earnings numbers.

   b. The timing with which events are reflected in the reported earnings series; for example, when an oil and gas company makes a significant oil discovery, the recognition of that discovery in GAAP earnings numbers is delayed until the oil is extracted and sold to an external party.

   The capital market faces no such restrictions when assessing the period-by-period earnings of a company.

2. The time focus of GAAP earnings is for a *past* period, whereas the time focus of the earnings concept implicit in security prices is for a *future* period(s). This difference can give rise to two types of divergence:

   a. Past events that are reflected in reported GAAP earnings but are not expected to occur in the future, for example, motor-carrier rights written down due to Congress passing a deregulation act.

   b. Events that did not occur in the past but that are expected to occur in the future, for example, revenues from a newly adopted corporate policy of licensing products to companies in foreign markets.

   Both (a) and (b) can cause a divergence between E_i^R and E_i^P.

The existence of transitory components in reported earnings means that two firms with the same reported earnings (E_i^R) can have different PE ratios. Panel A of Figure 12.2 presents the case where Firms A and B have the same E_i^R in period t of $2 per share, but

$$\frac{P_A}{E_A^R} > \frac{P_B}{E_B^R}$$

due to $E_A^P > E_B^P$.

The valuation model in (12.9) assumes that permanent earnings can be represented as a scalar (single value). A more general case permits E_i^P to vary over time. Panel B of Figure 12.2 presents the case where Firms A and B have the

FIGURE 12.2 Alternative Earnings Patterns and PE Ratio Implications

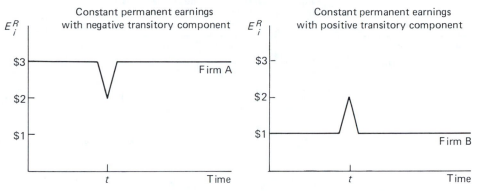

A. Constant Permanent Earnings

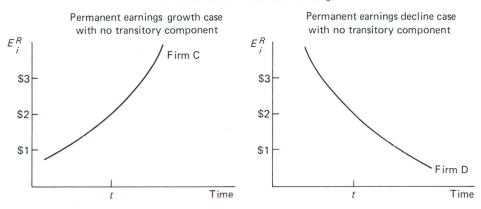

B. Nonconstant Permanent Earnings

same E_i^R in period t of \$2 per share, but

$$\frac{P_C}{E_C^R} > \frac{P_D}{E_D^R}$$

due to $E_C^P > E_D^P$ in periods beyond the current one.

C. Explaining Diversity in PE Ratios

Table 12.1 presents time-series and cross-sectional data for selected deciles of the distribution of PE ratios over the 1964–1983 period. Possible explanations for the considerable variation at a point in time include differences across firms in

   a. The sign and magnitude of the one-year transitory component in reported earnings

TABLE 12.1   PE Ratios of Compustat Firms: Time-Series and Cross-Sectional Differences

			Panel A: Time-Series Data for 1964–1983			
Year	*.1 Decile*	*.3 Decile*	*.5 Decile*	*.7 Decile*	*.9 Decile*	*No. of Firms*
1964	8.2	11.6	14.8	18.3	24.9	1,227
1965	9.2	12.4	15.0	18.2	27.5	1,273
1966	6.6	9.1	11.6	14.8	22.7	1,357
1967	9.7	12.6	15.5	22.0	40.8	1,414
1968	12.4	15.6	19.5	26.8	51.2	1,537
1969	8.5	11.2	14.2	20.2	37.6	1,639
1970	6.5	11.2	13.8	18.6	31.2	1,710
1971	7.7	11.5	14.8	20.5	37.2	1,822
1972	7.8	10.5	13.2	18.2	35.1	1,930
1973	3.6	5.5	7.5	10.2	21.5	1,991
1974	1.6	3.6	4.9	6.5	12.5	2,035
1975	1.5	5.2	6.9	9.1	16.2	2,054
1976	3.7	6.4	8.0	9.8	15.5	2,087
1977	3.8	6.1	7.4	9.1	13.8	2,121
1978	3.8	5.5	6.8	8.4	13.5	2,163
1979	3.7	5.5	6.8	9.2	15.9	2,196
1980	4.0	6.1	7.8	11.5	22.6	2,242
1981	3.0	5.9	7.4	10.2	19.3	2,307
1982	−3.8	6.6	9.5	13.3	27.0	2,323
1983	−4.0	7.7	10.8	14.5	27.2	2,140

	Panel B: Cross-Sectional Data for 1983						
		Deciles of Distribution					
SIC Code	*Short Industry Title*	*.1*	*.3*	*.5*	*.7*	*.9*	*No. of Observations*
1311 Oil, crude producers		−13.18	.30	12.50	17.14	32.16	67
2300 Textile apparel manufacturing		−2.90	8.27	9.22	11.12	20.50	37
2600 Paper and allied products		−28.50	11.22	14.38	18.37	27.34	24
2830 Drugs		8.92	11.45	12.92	15.48	32.77	28
2911 Petroleum refining		−2.29	7.41	8.67	12.53	17.99	41
3310 Steel and blast furnaces		−41.38	−7.16	−3.49	2.81	28.92	29
3560 General industrial machinery		−30.34	−4.53	12.59	20.54	131.73	26
3662 Radio and T.V. transmitting equipment		−15.42	13.68	17.31	21.70	49.92	34
3679 Electronic components		−3.29	12.96	22.27	27.11	35.23	22
4511 Air transport		−16.98	−3.57	−.88	8.16	18.71	22
4924 Natural gas		6.13	6.99	7.38	8.23	11.13	42
4931 Electric and other services		4.73	5.97	6.58	7.24	8.10	48
5411 Retail food chains		7.45	9.56	10.27	12.62	19.09	30
6312 Life insurance		6.64	7.67	8.32	8.69	11.52	26
6798 Real estate investment trusts		−6.87	8.99	10.80	12.11	18.36	44

SOURCE: Computed from 1983 Compustat annual industrial file.

b. Expected (permanent) earnings growth

c. Risk

d. Accounting methods.

Evidence on the relative importance of several of these explanations can be found in Beaver and Morse (1978). For a sample of U.S. firms with a December 31 fiscal year, the PE ratio (December 31 price to EPS before extraordinary items) was calculated. Then firms were ranked based on their PE ratio and placed into 1 of 25 portfolios. Table 12.2 (panel A) presents, for 6 of the 25 portfolios, the average PE ratio at the year of formation and for each of the ten subsequent years. One striking feature in Table 12.2 is the reversion over time in the PE ratio of portfolio 1, which comprises the top 4% of the population in terms of PE ratios; PE = 50.00 at the year of formation, 22.7 one year later, and 16.4 two years later. Portfolio 25 also reverts to the middle-portfolio PE ratios, but in a less dramatic fashion: from 5.8 at the year of formation, to 6.9 one year later, to 8.0 two years later. The sizable mean reversion in year 1 is consistent with part of the diversity in PE ratios being due to earnings having a transitory component. Firms with high PE ratios in any one year, on average, have negative transitory components in reported earnings for that year, and vice versa.

TABLE 12.2 Explaining Diversity in PE Ratios

	Panel A. PE Ratios of Portfolios Subsequent to Year of Formation (year 0)										
	Years After Formation										
Portfolio	*0*	*1*	*2*	*3*	*4*	*5*	*6*	*7*	*8*	*9*	*10*
1 (high PE)	50.0	22.7	16.4	13.8	12.3	13.2	13.5	13.2	17.2	14.9	13.0
5	20.8	17.5	16.9	15.9	15.9	13.7	13.0	12.8	12.5	11.8	11.9
10	14.3	11.9	11.5	11.1	10.3	10.1	9.4	9.0	10.0	10.0	9.9
15	11.1	10.8	10.4	10.8	10.0	10.0	9.4	9.7	9.3	9.5	8.6
20	8.9	9.1	9.6	9.3	9.4	9.3	9.3	9.0	8.8	8.8	9.0
25 (low PE)	5.8	6.9	8.0	7.8	7.9	7.9	8.2	8.8	8.3	8.5	7.8

	Panel B. Earnings Growth of PE Portfolios Subsequent to Year of Formation (year 0)										
	Years After Formation										
Portfolio	*0*	*1*	*2*	*3*	*4*	*5*	*6*	*7*	*8*	*9*	*10*
1 (high PE)	−4.1%	95.3%	37.2%	28.2%	16.4%	18.9%	18.1%	19.7%	13.1%	14.8%	15.3%
5	10.7	14.9	12.1	13.1	14.2	10.9	10.4	11.8	10.5	11.6	8.0
10	9.6	12.9	11.5	12.3	12.6	9.2	10.1	10.8	12.8	8.3	12.9
15	10.0	8.8	8.5	8.1	8.2	14.3	11.6	5.4	13.3	10.3	11.0
20	10.8	5.2	9.3	12.6	12.4	6.0	8.4	13.0	10.2	11.3	11.1
25 (low PE)	26.4	−3.3	7.5	10.8	8.3	12.9	17.1	13.6	18.0	12.8	16.7

SOURCE: Beaver and Morse (1978, Table 3, p. 68 and Table 5, p. 70).

While the one-year transitory component in reported earnings is important, it does not appear to be the sole explanation for differences across firms in their PE ratios. Notwithstanding the one-year mean reversion, differences in the PEs of portfolios exist for at least ten years subsequent to their formation; for example, in the tenth year after their formation, portfolio 1 in Table 12.2 has an average PE of 13.00 vis-à-vis an average of 7.8 for portfolio 25. To probe the (permanent) earnings growth explanation, Beaver and Morse examined the annual earnings growth rates of the 25 portfolios subsequent to their formation. Results are presented in Table 12.2 (panel B). Portfolio 1 shows the highest growth rate for each portfolio in Table 12.2 for each of the seven years subsequent to its formation. However, it is only in the first three years that its growth rate appears significantly different from that of the other portfolios. Portfolio 25 shows the lowest growth rate in only the first two years subsequent to its formation. Beaver and Morse concluded that "some of the initial dissipation of the PE ratio in the first three years after formation can be explained by differential growth in earnings. Beyond that, however, there clearly exists a PE differential that cannot be explained by differential earnings growth" (p. 70).

Beaver and Morse also examined the relative risks (beta) of the 25 portfolios ranked in terms of PE ratios. The results were

Portfolio	PE Ratio at Time of Formation	Average Beta
1	50.0	1.22
5	20.8	1.01
10	14.3	1.05
15	11.1	.96
20	8.9	1.03
25	5.8	1.04

The relationship between betas and PE ratios was described as "U shaped." It was concluded that beta "explains little" of the diversity across firms in their PE ratios.

Differences in Accounting Methods

One explanation for diversity in PE ratios is differences across firms in their accounting methods. This explanation has not been the subject of detailed testing. In a preliminary study, Beaver and Dukes (1973) examined the PE ratios of (1) 54 firms that used straight-line depreciation for reported earnings (mean PE = 15.08) and (2) 69 firms that used accelerated depreciation for reported earnings (mean PE = 16.61). The authors then adjusted the reported earnings of the straight-line set of firms to that which would be shown under accelerated depreciation; the revised mean PE was 16.20. The reduction in mean difference in PE ratios between the two groups, when a uniform depreciation method is used, is consistent with the capital market recognizing differences across firms in their depreciation methods when setting the PE ratios of those firms. The next section of this chapter discusses more recent evidence on whether the capital market makes any adjustment to the reported earnings of firms. (However, this evidence does not directly address the issue, still largely unresolved, of how much of the cross-sectional diversity in observed PE ratios is due to market recognition of diversity across firms in the accounting methods used to compute reported earnings.)

12.5 EQUITY VALUATION MODELS AND REPORTED EARNINGS

This section presents evidence relating to two commonly posited hypotheses about the relationship between equity security prices and reported earnings:

1. *The mechanistic hypothesis*, which states that the capital market is fixated on reported earnings, without any consideration paid to the accounting methods used to compute reported earnings, or to the sources of gain or loss underlying reported earnings
2. *The myopic hypothesis,* which states that the capital market has a short-run focus on the current quarter's or the current year's reported earnings, rather than a focus on a multiyear horizon.

A. The Mechanistic Hypothesis

Chapter 11 (Section 4) presented evidence inconsistent with the mechanistic hypothesis. Additional evidence inconsistent with this hypothesis comes from research using the following theoretically based equity valuation model (see Litzenberger and Rao, 1971):

$$V_i = f(E_i, R_i, G_i) \tag{12.12}$$

where

V_i = market value of firm i

E_i = expected permanent earnings of firm i

R_i = nondiversifiable risk of permanent earnings stream of firm i

G_i = expected growth of firm i where growth means investment in projects with returns exceeding their cost of capital

The research design in several studies examined whether the reported (GAAP) measure of earnings, or a nonreported measure of earnings, better explained cross-sectional differences in V_i. Both economic and statistical criteria were used to rank alternative earnings measures in terms of their ability to explain differences across firms in V_i.

1. Dukes (1976) examined the valuation of firms in three industries (chemicals, drugs, and electronics) that had a high research and development budget.

Earnings, both with R&D expensed, and with R&D capitalized, were examined using (12.12). The conclusion was that ''reported earnings are systematically adjusted before they are impounded into security prices, that the adjustment is largely industry specific, and that, for this sample of firms, the adjustment appears to be directly related to the research intensity of the industry. The evidence is consistent with the hypothesis that investors *do not* naively use the information signals certified by the accountant'' (pp. 53–54).

2. Foster (1977) examined the valuation of property-liability companies, using three different earnings measures: (a) underwriting earnings, (b) underwriting + investment earnings, and (c) underwriting + investment + capital gains on marketable equity securities. Earnings measure (c), which was computed using information about marketable securities reported in the footnotes to the financial statements, was the most highly associated with the V_i's of property-liability companies. This finding is inconsistent with a capital market mechanistically focused on reported earnings.

3. Bowen (1981) examined whether different multiples were placed on components of the reported earnings of electric utility companies. The focus was on whether the AFC (allowance for funds used during construction) component of reported earnings was given a lower multiple than the non-AFC or operating component of reported earnings. The AFC component is a non-cash credit to income based on capitalizing interest payments associated with debt used to finance long-term construction projects. Bowen reported that ''the AFC component was less valuable per dollar [had a lower earnings multiplier] than was operating earnings'' and that the ''cross-sectional valuation model was improved by separating utility earnings into operating and AFC components'' (p. 19).

Each of these studies reports results consistent with the capital market making adjustments to the reported earnings figure when setting equilibrium market prices. While these results reject the mechanistic hypothesis, they in no way imply that the capital market does (or should) fully adjust for all differences across firms in their accounting methods or for all differences across firms in the ''quality'' of the components of their reported earnings.

B. The Myopic Hypothesis

Evidence on the length of the horizon used by the capital market when setting equilibrium prices can be found in Brown, Foster, and Noreen (1985). One data base examined (IBES) included security analyst consensus earnings forecasts for 500 securities for each year of a two-year horizon. The conclusions of the research included

1. There is a significant association between (a) one-year-ahead (FY1) earnings forecast errors (revisions) and (b) security returns in the period up to and including the month the actual FY1 earnings are announced

2. There is a significant association between (a) two-years-ahead (FY2) earn-

ings forecast errors (revision) and (b) security returns in the period up to and including the month the actual FY1 earnings are announced

3. The association for the FY2 earnings forecast variable is significant, even when the research design takes into account the positive correlation between the sign and magnitude of contemporaneous FY1 and FY2 forecast errors (revisions).

Results were reported for a cross-sectional regression in which the dependent variable was security returns in the 11-month period up to and including the announcement of FY1 earnings; the independent variables included the FY1 and FY2 earnings forecast errors. The percentage of the variance in security returns that FY1 and FY2 individually explained are

	1977	1978	1979	1980
FY1	5.7%	12.2%	9.0%	10.6%
FY2	10.7	10.4	9.9	22.3

The significant percentages found for FY2 are inconsistent with the hypothesis that the capital market is myopically focused on only the current year's earnings. These percentages related to a regression in which the positive correlation between the FY1 and FY2 forecast errors is attributed to FY1. The following percentages were found for a regression in which the positive correlation was attributed to FY2:

	1977	1978	1979	1980
FY1	0.1%	0.0%	0.1%	8.5%
FY2	16.3	22.5	18.8	24.5

These results provide strong support for the capital market having a multiyear earnings forecast horizon.

One set of tests in Brown, Foster, and Noreen (1985) focused on observations for which the consensus forecast for FY2 was revised up or down from the prior month's forecast but for which the forecast for FY1 was unchanged. A capital market that focused on only one-year-ahead (FY1) earnings forecasts would treat all these observations as equivalent. Statistically significant evidence was reported that the capital market values downward (upward) the security prices of those companies for which the FY2 earnings forecasts are revised downward (upward), even when the FY1 forecast is unchanged.

12.6 SOME GENERAL COMMENTS

1. There is a long tradition of empirical work that examines the determinants of security prices. Regression analysis is the statistical technique most commonly

TABLE 12.3 Cross-Sectional Regression Studies of Firm or Equity Valuation Against Expected Earnings (and Other Independent Variables)

	Miller and Modigliani (1966)	Brown (1968)	Litzenberger and Rao (1971)	McDonald (1971)
Sample	63 electric utility firms	45 railroad firms	87 electric utility firms	102 public utility firms
Time period	1954, 1956, 1957	1954, 1956, 1957, 1960, 1963	1960–1966	1958–1969
Range of coefficient on earnings term	16.0 to 19.2	9.1 to 15.3	16.7 to 20.2	11.1 to 21.0
Range of t statistic on earnings term	36.4 to 44.6	13.0 to 30.3	16.5 to 48.1	29.1 to 56.3
Range of R^2	.56 to .77	.73 to .92	.50 to .57	.44 to .60

used. Table 12.3 summarizes results from four early studies that paid considerable attention and care to model specification and econometric issues: Miller and Modigliani (1966), Brown (1968), Litzenberger and Rao (1971), and McDonald (1971). Each study found that cross-sectional differences in expected earnings were an important factor in explaining cross-sectional differences in firm or equity valuation. The equity valuation studies discussed in Section 12.5.A (Dukes, 1976; Foster, 1977; and Bowen, 1981) also found the earnings variable to be highly significant.

Many studies in this literature have regressed market price (or price to book value) against numerous independent variables in an attempt to detect empirical regularities. In general, beyond documenting the importance of the earnings variable, the results have been disappointing. Granger's (1972) summary is as appropriate today as it was in 1972:

> There is no stability in the estimates of the coefficients of a model derived from a sequence of cross-sectional data sets through time. This is an extremely damaging observation, throwing considerable doubt both on the reality of the model and also on its usefulness as a predictive tool. . . . What causes this coefficient instability? A whole variety of technical statistical reasons can be proposed but the most important reason is likely to prove to be model misspecification. (pp. 503–504)

The problems of conducting quality empirical work in this area include obtaining "good" proxies for unobservables, such as expected earnings and growth, and dealing with econometric issues associated with cross-sectional correlation of residuals, heteroscedasticity, and multicollinearity.

2. One area of equity valuation where important unresolved questions exist is the link between the level of equity security prices and the values of the individual assets and liabilities owned or controlled by the firm. To illustrate, con-

sider the following two examples:

   a. With rare exceptions, over the last 40 years the market value of a closed-end mutual fund has been less than the aggregate of the market values of the individual net assets owned by the fund. For instance, Wiesenberger (1984) reported that the average year-end discount on nine closed-end mutual funds was over 10% in 9 of the 11 years in the 1973–1983 period and over 20% in 6 of those years.

   b. With rare exceptions, the market capitalization of natural resource companies is less than estimates of the aggregate of the market values of the individual net assets controlled by these companies. For instance, Herold (1984) reported that the ratio of the market price per share to the appraised worth of net assets per share (including oil and gas reserves) of the eight largest international oil companies ranged from only .33 (Chevron) to .58 (Exxon).

The most frequently given explanations for the foregoing and similar examples are that the valuations made of individual assets are overstated or individual liabilities are understated and that the share is currently mispriced by the capital market. Little research has been conducted to improve our understanding about why such divergences occur and persist for such extended time periods.

   3. There is considerable debate in the finance literature concerning the behavior of security prices in an inflationary period. One of the most provocative arguments in this area is advanced by Modigliani and Cohn (1979) and Cohn and Modigliani (1985). In the latter paper they analyze the behavior of earnings-to-price ratios and inflation rates over the 1963–1983 period and report an "unmistakable positive correlation between the E/P ratio of the Standard & Poor's 500 Stock index, based on reported earnings, and the inflation rate. Since the relationship between E/P ratios and inflation is a direct one, the relationship between the price-earnings (P/E) ratio and inflation is inverse" (p. 353). These authors posit two factors of a market myopia kind to explain this empirical relationship:

   a. The market underestimates the numerator of the PE ratio by not recognizing that firms with long-term debt gain under inflation via a decline in the real cost of repaying interest and principal on that debt

   b. The market overestimates the denominator of the PE ratio by capitalizing earnings at the nominal rather than the real rate.

These arguments imply a substantial degree of irrationality on the part of the capital market and have led to considerable debate in the literature about their validity; for example, see "Comments on Modigliani-Cohn" in the May–June 1981 issue of the *Financial Analysts Journal* and Goeltz (1985). Alternative explanations offered for the decline in PE ratios observed by Modigliani and Cohn include (a) a decline over time in the relative profitability of U.S. corporations, (b) an increase over time in the real rate of interest due to an increase in the riskiness of business activity, and (c) taxation-related effects (e.g., the taxation of nominal capital gains rather than real gains leads investors to demand an increase in the real pretax rate of return).

4. The evidence examined in this chapter (and in Chapter 11) is consistent with the capital market using a broad-based information set when pricing equity securities. One of the most interesting research areas is exploiting this broad base of information implicit in price to forecast future earnings. Beaver, Lambert, and Morse (1980) is an innovative study in this area. The time period examined was 1957 to 1974. The one-year-ahead forecasting accuracy of two models was compared:

Model A—based on information implicit in security prices (as reflected by the PE multiple)

Model B—the random walk plus drift time-series model that is discussed in Chapter 7.

Model A was developed using the current period's (t) earnings for firms and the past earnings growth rate observed for firms that were in the same PE ratio decile as firm i in period t. To illustrate, assume that the object is to forecast EPS in 1975. Beaver, Lambert, and Morse ranked stocks on the basis of their PE ratios each year from 1957 to 1973 and placed them into ten portfolios. The median one-year-ahead earnings growth for each portfolio was then calculated; thus, for portfolios formed in 1957 (1958, . . . , 1973), the 1958 (1959, . . . , 1974) growth rates were calculated. Then, for each PE decile from 1957 to 1973, a median earnings growth rate was calculated and used to forecast the 1975 earnings growth. Assume that a stock in 1974 fell into the highest PE decile and had a 1974 EPS of $1.00 and that the median one-year growth rate for that decile was 64%. The 1975 EPS forecast would be $1.64.

Forecasts from Models A and B were compared for 6,840 firm/year combinations. Model A was more accurate 54.9% of the time, which was a highly significant difference in accuracy from Model B. Across the ten deciles, the results were:

		% of Times PE-Based Forecast Model More Accurate	Mean Absolute Forecast Error	
Deciles			PE-Based Model	Random Walk + Drift Model
(Highest PE)	1	60.0%	.442	.462
	2	61.2	.291	.304
	3	58.5	.345	.355
	4	57.0	.337	.348
	5	53.3	.331	.329
	6	57.4	.354	.356
	7	49.0	.313	.379
	8	49.1	.428	.422
	9	49.4	.355	.354
(Lowest PE)	10	54.5	.470	.496
Total sample		54.9%	.373	.380

Model A's superiority is most marked for the stocks with PE ratios in deciles 1 and 2: these two deciles contain stocks for which a high proportion are likely to have a negative transitory component in reported earnings.

An interesting extension of this research would be to examine alternatives to the PE decile approach of extracting earnings forecast information from security prices; one alternative would be to rank securities based on their recent security-return performance. Another extension would be to examine earnings forecasts for time horizons longer than one year ahead.

12.7 SUMMARY

1. Equity valuation can be approached by focusing on flow variables, such as earnings, cash flows or dividends, or on a stock variable such as individual assets and liabilities. In practice, these alternative approaches rarely give equivalent values.

2. The investment community is continually searching for new ways of detecting mispriced securities. Change in the models used in this search can occur for a variety of reasons: new analytical or empirical insights, new data bases, new disclosures by firms, new statistical tools, and new developments in computer technology. Change can also be induced by the need to develop in-house replications of products already available from competitors.

3. The price-to-earnings ratio can be used to gain insight into the relationship between current earnings and the capital market expectation of future earnings. When using price-to-earnings ratios, it is important to distinguish between the permanent and the transitory components of reported earnings.

4. When pricing equity securities, the capital market appears to have a multiyear rather than a single-year horizon and makes adjustments for the fact that reported earnings are (in part) a function of the accounting methods used in their computation.

QUESTIONS

QUESTION 12.1: Equity Valuation Models and Financial Statement Analysis

Wells Fargo Investment Advisors hires you as a consultant. You are to provide expert advice on the use of financial statement information in its equity valuation model service. Section 12.3.B outlines this service. The two key components are (1) the estimates of expected internal rate of return, based on a dividend discount model, and (2) the estimates of the equilibrium rate of return, based on the two-parameter capital asset pricing model.

REQUIRED

1. Assume that the stocks coded as undervalued/overvalued by Wells Fargo experience positive/negative abnormal returns in the 12 months subsequent to publication of the coding. What factors could give rise to these abnormal returns? Be as specific as possible.

2. Assume that the director of research at Wells Fargo is concerned with finding more information about the link between financial statement analysis and the subsequent security performance of recommended stocks. Two areas of concern are

   a. How effective has the past analysis of financial statement information at Wells Fargo been?

   b. What additional use of financial statement information could be made in the equity valuation service?

   Write a memorandum to the director of research that outlines how you will address these two concerns.

Question 12.2: Intraindustry and Interindustry Diversity in PE Ratios

At any point in time, intraindustry and interindustry differences in price-to-earnings (PE) ratios can be observed. Table 12.1 presents time-series and cross-sectional data pertaining to firms on the 1983 Compustat tape. The PE ratio is calculated as the market price per share at 1983 fiscal year end, divided by 1983 net income before extraordinary and discontinued items. (The data presented in Question 12.3 may be useful in examining the issues raised in this question.)

REQUIRED

1. Alternative denominators that could be used to compute a price-to-earnings ratio include

   a. EPS for the most recent fiscal year with financial results reported

   b. EPS for the most recent 12-month period with financial results reported

   c. EPS forecast for year $t + 1$ made by the "leading" analyst for each firm (where "leading" is based on a survey such as that published annually in the *Institutional Investor*)

   d. Consensus EPS forecast for year $t + 1$, as reported by a consensus forecasting service (e.g., IBES or Icarus).

   Assume that you are computing PE ratios for a broad cross section of firms in September of year t. What are the pros and cons of each of the foregoing denominators?

2. What factors could explain the time-series differences in PE ratios observed in panel A of Table 12.1? Do you agree with the following: "Nobody really knows why the market has sold at a particular PE multiple in different periods

of history. There are so many arguments why it should sell at 6 times or 20 times earnings that, from a short-range viewpoint, the reasons are almost entirely emotional.''

3. What factors could explain the cross-sectional differences in PE ratios observed in panel B of Table 12.1?

4. How would you gain insight into the relative importance of the factors you cite in your answers to 2 and 3?

5. Comment on the following extract from the annual report of Borg-Warner:

> The price-to-earnings multiple (Borg-Warner's is now about 7) accorded any company generally results from the market's perception of four major characteristics:
>
> - future growth of the market(s) served,
> - how a company is positioned in its market(s),
> - consistency and predictability of profits,
> - management's ability to maximize profit potential.
>
> The more narrow a company's focus, the easier it is to understand; the market is able to match real value and market value more closely. Diversified companies are harder to understand. They generally sell at a discount; and the greater the complexity, the greater the discount.
>
> There are exceptions, of course. Most often they are the multi-industry companies closely identified with a single market that is enjoying a premium price/earnings multiple.
>
> For Borg-Warner, the situation is reversed. Through origin and history we have long been identified as an automotive parts supplier (even though not more than one quarter of our total earnings during the last five years has come from automotive business). Today, Wall Street accords the auto industry and its original equipment suppliers a below-average price/earnings multiple. And when investors look at Borg-Warner, they tend to see the historical image—not the current reality—let alone tomorrow's potential.

QUESTION 12.3: Price-to-Book Value Ratios and Management Decisions

Part A.   A key variable in the eyes of many managers is the price-to-book value ratio. Table 12.4 presents the .1, .3, .5, .7, and .9 deciles of the distribution for Compustat firms over the 1964–1983 period. Security price per share is calculated as the closing market price at fiscal year end. Book value per share is based on shareholders' equity per share as reported in each company's annual report; it is the difference between the book value of the individual assets and the book value of the individual liabilities. Also presented in Table 12.4 are several macroeconomic and capital market series over the 1964–1983 period. (The data presented in Question 12.2 may be useful in examining the issues raised in this question.)

REQUIRED

1. Why might the price-to-book value ratio of a company not equal unity (1)?

TABLE 12.4 Price-to-Book Value Ratios of Compustat Firms, 1964–1983

Year	Deciles of the Distribution					Total Corporate Profits ($ billions)	Profit to Stockholders' Equity: Manufacturing	S&P 500 Composite Stock Index	U.S. Treasury Bill Rate (3-month)	Consumer Price Index (annual change)
	.1	.3	.5	.7	.9					
1964	.75	1.25	1.70	2.37	3.81	66.0	.116	81.37	.035	.012
1965	.94	1.43	1.93	2.53	4.21	76.0	.130	88.17	.040	.019
1966	.72	1.14	1.54	2.12	3.61	80.9	.134	85.26	.049	.033
1967	1.00	1.46	2.03	3.12	6.35	78.1	.117	91.93	.043	.030
1968	1.25	1.76	2.42	3.46	6.87	84.9	.121	98.70	.053	.047
1969	.83	1.23	1.65	2.46	5.08	80.8	.115	97.84	.067	.061
1970	.70	1.07	1.40	1.95	3.80	68.9	.093	83.22	.065	.055
1971	.74	1.14	1.51	2.20	4.50	82.0	.097	98.29	.043	.034
1972	.70	1.07	1.43	2.11	4.55	94.0	.106	109.20	.041	.034
1973	.36	.60	.84	1.24	2.77	105.6	.128	107.43	.070	.088
1974	.22	.39	.55	.77	1.61	96.7	.149	82.85	.079	.122
1975	.33	.54	.75	1.00	2.07	120.6	.116	86.16	.058	.070
1976	.46	.72	.94	1.25	2.19	151.6	.139	102.01	.050	.048
1977	.47	.71	.93	1.21	2.07	178.5	.142	98.20	.053	.068
1978	.48	.69	.89	1.19	2.07	205.1	.150	96.02	.072	.090
1979	.50	.74	.96	1.40	2.55	209.6	.164	103.01	.100	.133
1980	.51	.74	1.03	1.67	3.50	191.7	.139	118.78	.115	.124
1981	.50	.73	.98	1.43	2.55	197.6	.136	128.05	.140	.089
1982	.58	.83	1.09	1.57	2.86	156.0	.092	119.71	.107	.039
1983	.74	1.00	1.29	1.79	3.03	192.0	.106	160.41	.086	.038

SOURCES: Price-to-book value data computed from 1983 Compustat annual industrial file; macroeconomic data from *Economic Report of the President, 1985.*

2. What factors could explain the sizable differences in the median price-to-book value ratio over the 1964–1983 period?

Part B.   Marakon Associates (1980), a consulting firm specializing in the application of financial theory to management decision making, presented the following discussion of the behavior of the price-to-book value ratio over time:

> One of the lesser known, but most interesting, principles of economics is that whenever a company consistently earns a rate of return on equity capital (ROE) which exceeds its cost of equity capital (K_e), the company's stock price will trade above book value—its market-to-book ratio (M/B) will exceed 1.0. Conversely, whenever a company consistently earns an ROE less than K_e, its M/B ratio will be less than 1.0. Finally, the common stock of those companies which are just able to earn the cost of equity capital year in and year out will trade at book value and M/B will equal 1.0.

> Using this simple framework leads us to the fundamental explanation for the market's behavior (that is, the decline in the average M/B ratio over time): the difference, or spread, between the rate of return on equity capital produced by U.S. business and the cost of equity capital—the rate of return expected (or demanded) by investors for bearing the risk of common stock ownership—has narrowed substantially [since 1965].

Marakon then analyzed inflation rates, the return on total investment ratio, and the earnings before interest and taxes to sales ratio since 1965. Its conclusions included

> There is a rational explanation for the decline of stock prices relative to both earnings and book value during the past fourteen years. Increasing inflation has driven the cost of equity capital higher, while management has been able to produce only a modest improvement in the return on equity capital by increasing financial leverage. This squeeze in the return-cost spread has resulted in the systematic markdown of equity values so apparent to all of us since 1965.

> Management strategies designed to stem [the decline in price-to-book value ratio] or reverse the tide must be focused on producing one or more of the following results:

> - An increase in operating margins, which can only be generated by increasing product prices relative to unit costs, or reducing unit costs relative to prices;

> - An increase in net asset turnover, which can be accomplished by reducing the amount of working capital and/or fixed assets required per dollar of sales; and

> - A further increase in financial leverage, which is probably a short-run solution, at best.

> The strategies designed to produce these results must, of course, be specific to each business unit in a company's portfolio.

REQUIRED

1. Discuss the Marakon (1980) argument and the recommendations they make for management decision making.

2. Comment on the following rationale for repurchasing stock given by Olympia Brewing Company in its annual report:

> The price of Olympia Brewing Company stock for the past year has declined in the marketplace, but I must confess that it is a mystery to us, particularly in view of the results we have attained and the fact that our Quarterly Reports indicate progress for the Company. Articles have been written in all media relative to the brewing industry with the large versus the smalls and regionals. Olympia is a large regional and I see no reason why we cannot compete and continue to make money and prosper. Our facilities are modern and efficient and our product well-established and respected. When the price of our stock fell below book value, the Board of Directors felt that the purchase of some of our own stock would be a good investment. You will note that during [the past year] 17,500 shares of its $10 Par Value Common Capital stock were purchased. The Board felt this was the best investment the Company could make and, in so doing, the shareholders' equity in the Company was increased.

What other motivations are there for a company repurchasing its own stock?

QUESTION 12.4: EPS Forecasts Based on PE Multiple Ranks

Justyn Shevlin was recently appointed the quantitative analyst in the research department of Graham and Partners, a major brokerage firm with a tradition in fundamental analysis. During his first two months, Shevlin attended numerous meetings. At these meetings, one or more analysts would forecast the future EPS series of a company independent of its price, derive an estimate of intrinsic value, and then compare this value with the current market price. Shevlin believed that the approach of his colleagues was outdated. In a recent meeting he commented that "this whole approach needed to be turned on its head." His colleagues did not take kindly to his attempt at a one-liner at their expense. (They had long viewed Shevlin's appointment as merely a public relations move, made only after several competitors had appointed quantitative analysts to their research departments.)

Part A. Shevlin decided to show his colleagues that he would indeed gain new insights by flipping the approach of his colleagues on its head. Whereas his colleagues forecasted earnings and then inferred "intrinsic value," he decided to use the current price to forecast earnings. Let $X_{i,t}$ be the PE ratio of firm i in year t (defined as closing share price on fiscal year end divided by annual earnings per share before extraordinary and nonrecurring items). The steps he took were as follows:

1. Calculate $X_{i,t}$ for all firms ($i = 1$ to N) on the Compustat tape for each of 20 years ($t = 1$ to 20).

2. For each year, rank $X_{i,t}$ in descending order and form deciles or portfolios ($p = 1$ to 10); portfolio 1 includes the 10% of firms with the highest PE ratios in year t; portfolio 10 includes the 10% of firms with the lowest PE ratios in year t.

3. Compute the one-year-ahead growth rates in EPS for firms in each portfolio for the year subsequent to their portfolio assignment. Thus, for firms placed into portfolio 1 in year t, the growth in EPS from year t to $t + 1$ was

calculated. The median growth rate in EPS for firms in each portfolio was used as the growth rate in EPS for that portfolio.

The EPS growth rates in the year subsequent to their portfolio assignment for selected years were

Portfolio Formed in Year t	Growth Rate in EPS from Year t to Year t + 1 for Portfolio (P) Formed in Year t									
	P = 1	P = 2	P = 3	P = 4	P = 5	P = 6	P = 7	P = 8	P = 9	P = 10
t = 1	.12	.06	.05	.05	.04	.06	.07	.06	.04	.02
t = 5	.06	.05	.04	.05	.02	.05	.00	−.06	−.01	−.13
t = 10	.14	.13	.10	.08	.06	.03	.06	−.01	.02	−.07
t = 15	.54	.21	.19	.13	.09	.10	.10	.11	.10	−.12
t = 18	.11	.05	.10	.06	.04	.01	−.01	−.07	−.06	−.21

Thus, the growth rate in EPS for year $t = 10$ to year $t = 11$ ranged from .14 for portfolio 1 (the 10% of firms with the highest PE ratios in year $t = 10$) to −.07 for portfolio 10 (the 10% of firms with the lowest PE ratios in year $t = 10$).

Shevlin then used the last ten years of data on the Compustat tape to evaluate the accuracy of the earnings forecasts derived from the foregoing information. Each firm forecast was computed as follows.

1. Determine the PE portfolio that firm i falls into in year t (say, $p = 1$).
2. Determine the median EPS growth rate for that portfolio for *prior* years with available data (say, .20).
3. Multiply the year t EPS for firm i (say, $2.00) by the median EPS growth rate of its PE portfolio (.20) to calculate the expected EPS growth in year $t + 1$. EPS growth is predicted to be $0.40 in $t + 1$, with EPS predicted to be $2.40.

Shevlin compared the accuracy of the one-year-ahead EPS forecast of this model with that of a random walk with a drift model (see Chapter 7 for evidence that this is a robust mean-median time-series model). The percentage of times that the PE-based earnings forecast model was more accurate than the random walk model, and the mean absolute forecast error of each model, was

	Deciles	% of Times PE-Based Forecast Model More Accurate	Mean Absolute Forecast Error	
			PE-Based Model	Random Walk + Drift Model
(Highest PE)	1	74.2%	.505	.571
	2	68.7	.378	.400
	3	65.2	.342	.357
	4	63.1	.304	.315
	5	59.6	.288	.294
	6	61.6	.314	.320
	7	58.4	.325	.327
	8	57.6	.345	.345
	9	55.1	.343	.349
(Lowest PE)	10	56.5	.509	.534
Total sample		61.9	.363	.379

REQUIRED

1. What factors might explain the differences across the ten portfolios in their EPS growth rates from year t to $t + 1$?
2. Compare the forecasting accuracy of the PE-based model and the random walk plus drift model. Are Shevlin's results consistent with those reported in the Beaver, Lambert, and Morse (1980) study discussed in Section 12.6?
3. What uses could be made by the other security analysts at Graham and Partners of the EPS forecasts generated by Shevlin's PE-based model?

Part B. Shevlin made a presentation to the other security analysts at Graham and Partners. He was somewhat surprised that several analysts became excited at his results and asked some very penetrating questions. These included

1. How were firms with negative EPS handled? Shevlin responded that if EPS of firm i was negative in year t or year $t + 1$, firm i was dropped from the sample. Questions were raised by his audience as to the other approaches available for handling this class of observations.
2. Why were medians of EPS growth rates consistently used in the research? Shevlin responded that this was done to avoid outliers having an undue influence on the results. Questions were raised by his audience as to the other approaches available for computing EPS growth rates.
3. What would be the effect of using "EPS after extraordinary items and non-recurring items" as the denominator of the PE ratio?
4. If one assumes that the security price captures a rich set of information, what alternatives to the PE rank approach exist to exploit this information to forecast EPS?

After his presentation, Shevlin met with William Lambert and Rick Morse, the co-directors of research at Graham and Partners. They expressed their enthusiasm for his research and said that they thought he should prepare a memorandum responding to the four questions raised during his presentation.

REQUIRED

Prepare a memorandum to be circulated to the security analysts at Graham and Partners that addresses the four questions raised during Shevlin's presentation.

REFERENCES

BEAVER, W. H., and R. E. DUKES. "Tax Allocation and Depreciation Methods: Some Empirical Results." *The Accounting Review* (July 1973): 549–559.

BEAVER, W., and D. MORSE. "What Determines Price-Earnings Ratios?" *Financial Analysts Journal* (July–August 1978): 65–76.

BEAVER, W., R. LAMBERT, and D. MORSE. "The Information Content of Security Prices." *Journal of Accounting and Economics* (March 1980): 3–28. Published by North-Holland Publishing Company, Amsterdam, 1980.

BLACK, F. "Yes, Virginia, There Is Hope: Tests of the Value Line Ranking System." *Financial Analysts Journal* (September–October 1973): 10–14.

BLACK, F., and M. SCHOLES. "The Pricing of Options and Corporate Liabilities." *Journal of Political Economy* (May/June 1973): 637–654.

BOWEN, R. M. "Valuation of Earnings Components in the Electric Utility Industry." *The Accounting Review* (January 1981): 1–22.

BROWN, P. *Some Aspects of Valuation in the Railroad Industry*, Ph.D. dissertation, University of Chicago, 1968.

BROWN, P., G. FOSTER, and E. NOREEN. *Security Analyst Multi-Year Earnings Forecasts and the Capital Market.* Sarasota, Fla.: American Accounting Association, 1985.

COHN, R. A., and F. MODIGLIANI. "Inflation and Corporate Financial Management." In E. I. Altman and M. G. Subrahmanyam, eds., *Recent Advances in Corporate Finance*, pp. 341–370. Homewood, Ill.: Richard D. Irwin, 1985.

COPELAND, T. E., and D. MAYERS. "The Value Line Enigma (1965–1978): A Case Study of Performance Evaluation Issues." *Journal of Financial Economics* (November 1982): 289–321.

DALEY, L. A. "The Valuation of Reported Pension Measures for Firms Sponsoring Defined Benefit Plans." *The Accounting Review* (April 1984): 177–198.

DUKES, R. E. "An Investigation of the Effects of Expensing Research and Development Costs on Security Prices." In M. Schiff and G. Sorter, eds., *Proceedings of the Conference on Topical Research in Accounting*, pp. 147–193. New York: New York University Press, 1976.

EISENSTADT, S. "An Update on the Value Line Performance Rankings." New York: Value Line, 1982.

FOSTER, G. "Valuation Parameters of Property-Liability Companies." *The Journal of Finance* (June 1977): 823–836.

GOELTZ, R. K. "Comments on the Modigliani and Cohn Paper and Inflation and Corporate Financial Management." In E. I. Altman and M. G. Subrahmanyam, eds., *Recent Advances in Corporate Finance*, pp. 371–394. Homewood, Ill.: Richard D. Irwin, 1985.

GRANGER, C. W. J. "Empirical Studies of Capital Markets: A Survey." In G. P. Szego and K. Shell, eds., *Mathematical Methods in Investment and Finance*, pp. 469–519. Amsterdam, North-Holland: 1972.

HAWKINS, D. F., and W. J. CAMPBELL. *Equity Valuation: Models, Analysis and Implications*. New York: Financial Executives Research Foundation, 1978.

HEROLD, J. S. *Oil Industry Comparative Appraisals*. Greenwich, Conn.: John S. Herold, November 1984.

LEV, B., and J. A. OHLSON. "Market-Based Empirical Research in Accounting: A Review, Interpretation, and Extension." *Studies on Current Research*

Methodologies in Accounting: A Critical Evaluation, Supplement to *Journal of Accounting Research* (1982): 249–322.

LITZENBERGER, R. H., and C. U. RAO. "Estimates of the Marginal Rate of Time Preference and Average Risk Aversion of Investors in Electric Utility Shares: 1960–66." *Bell Journal of Economics and Management Science* (Spring 1971): 265–277.

MARAKON ASSOCIATES. "Profitability and Stock Prices: 1965–1978." San Francisco: Marakon Associates, 1980.

McDONALD, J. G. "Required Return on Public Utility Equities: A National and Regional Analysis, 1958–1969." *Bell Journal of Economics and Management Science* (Autumn 1971): 503–514.

MICHAUD, R. O., and P. L. DAVIS. "Valuation Model Bias and the Scale Structure of Dividend Discount Returns." *The Journal of Finance* (May 1982): 563–573.

MILLER, M. H., and F. MODIGLIANI. "Some Estimates of the Cost of Capital to the Electric Utility Industry." *American Economic Review* (June 1966): 333–391.

MODIGLIANI, F., and R. A. COHN. "Inflation, Rational Valuation and the Market." *Financial Analysts Journal* (March–April 1979): 24–44.

MODIGLIANI, F., and M. MILLER. "The Cost of Capital, Corporation Finance and the Theory of Investment." *American Economic Review* (June 1958): 261–297.

OHLSON, J. A. "Risk, Return, Security-Valuation and the Stochastic Behavior of Accounting Numbers." *Journal of Financial and Quantitative Analysis* (June 1979): 317–336.

ROSS, S. A. "The Arbitrage Theory of Capital Asset Pricing." *Journal of Economic Theory* (December 1976): 341–360.

SHARPE, W. F. "Capital Asset Prices: A Theory of Market Equilibrium Under Conditions of Risk." *The Journal of Finance* (September 1964): 425–442.

SHEVLIN, T. "Further Evidence on Forecasting Annual Accounting Earnings," working paper. Stanford University, Stanford, Calif., 1983.

STERN, J. M. *Analytical Methods in Financial Planning*. New York: Stern, Stewart, Putnam and Macklis, 1980.

WEINGER, N., and E. M. METZ. "Better Dead than in the Red—Let's Liquidate." New York: Oppenheimer and Co., June 29, 1982.

WIESENBERGER INVESTMENT COMPANIES SERVICE. *Investment Companies 1984*. New York: Wiesenberger Financial Services, 1984.

13

CORPORATE RESTRUCTURING AND FINANCIAL INFORMATION

13.1 INTRODUCTION

Many different activities can be found under the corporate restructuring umbrella:

- *Merger*: A combination of two (or more) firms in which one firm survives under its own name while the other ceases to exist as a legal entity.

- *Consolidation*: A combination of two or more firms in which all firms cease to exist as legal entities and a new corporation is created.

- *Acquisition*: One firm purchases a complete or partial ownership in either some or all of the stock of another firm or some or all of the assets of another firm. Acquisitions of stock can occur via a merger (see above) or a tender offer. Mergers typically are negotiated directly with the management of the target firm; the approval of the target's board of directors is generally given before the merger offer is sent to the target's shareholders for approval. In a tender offer, the offer to buy stock is made directly to the shareholders of the target firm. Acquisitions of some or all of the assets of another firm typically are negotiated directly with the management of the firm selling those assets.

- *Divestiture*: A transaction in which one firm sells a subset of its assets (for example, a single division or line of business) to another firm.

- *Going Private*: A transaction in which the public stockholders of a firm are bought out by private owners. In some cases, the private owners will include the existing management.

- *Leveraged Buyout* (LBO): A transaction in which a substantial proportion of the current equity shareholders are bought out using cash raised by an increase in debt. In many cases the debt is secured by the assets of the LBO firm.

- *Spinoff*: A transaction in which a firm issues to its present stockholders separate shares for a subpart of the current firm. The single firm becomes two (or more) separate firms, whose shares can trade independently of each other.

Financial statement information can be a key input into many important decisions relating to the foregoing activities. The following are illustrative:

- Management placing a value on another company (or part thereof) as part of a corporate acquisition strategy

- Management placing a value on its own company for (say) determining the equity securities to offer for another company in a tender offer or for determining the amount they are willing to bid in a leveraged buyout of the nonmanagement shareholders

- Security analysts attempting to predict merger candidates (to profit from merger premiums) as part of an active investment strategy

- Investment banks and consulting firms making a presentation on the financial statement and capital market consequences of a spinoff as opposed to a divestiture of an existing division by one of their clients
- Judicial officials placing a value on the shares of a minority shareholder when a company compulsorily acquires those shares in a "freeze-out" merger context.

This chapter discusses the role of financial statement and other information in the preceding and related decisions.

13.2 EXPLAINING CORPORATE RESTRUCTURING BEHAVIOR

Why do firms undertake corporate restructuring? There are two main perspectives:

1. To maximize the market value of equities held by existing shareholders
2. To maximize the welfare of existing management.

Clearly, these two perspectives do not always coincide. For instance, management may prefer a growth policy and implement it by acquiring firms in diverse lines of business. Growth may be preferred because executive compensation is frequently correlated positively with firm size; diverse lines of business may be preferred because in the resulting conglomerate, management's own human capital is more fully diversified. A delightful characterization of these motivations is in Berkshire Hathaway's 1981 Annual Report; see Table 13.1. Neither diversification nor growth (in assets, sales, or even earnings) are attributes that necessarily maximize the market value of the firm. Given that shareholders can create diversified portfolios themselves, a market premium for firms providing this attribute is unlikely. If growth is achieved by management paying excessive merger premiums, reductions in the market value of the firm can occur.

Stated motives for corporate restructuring cover a wide variety of objectives. Baker, Miller, and Ramsperger (1981) report results from a questionnaire sent to the chief executives of 347 firms that had engaged in merger activity. The motives ranked 1 to 6 by firms making horizontal mergers (within the same line of business) and conglomerate mergers (unrelated lines of business) are presented in Table 13.2. As with any questionnaire study, issues of nonresponse bias (the response rate was 43%) and biased responses by executives arise in interpreting the rankings. However, they do illustrate the diverse set of considerations that potentially underlie merger decisions and, by inference, the diverse nature of the information that is used in those decisions. An alternative approach to gaining insight into motives for corporate restructuring is to examine statements by management at the time of restructuring activity. As an illustration, Table 13.3 reports the motives that management gave at the time of voluntary spinoff announcements (as reported by Schipper and Smith, 1983).

TABLE 13.1 Motivations for High-Premium Takeovers as Perceived by Berkshire Hathaway

We suspect three motivations—usually unspoken—to be, singly or in combination, the important ones in most high-premium takeovers:

(1) Leaders, business or otherwise, seldom are deficient in animal spirits and often relish increased activity and challenge. At Berkshire, the corporate pulse never beats faster than when an acquisition is in prospect.

(2) Most organizations, business or otherwise, measure themselves, are measured by others, and compensate their managers far more by the yardstick of size than by any other yardstick. (Ask a *Fortune* 500 manager where his corporation stands on that famous list and, invariably, the number responded will be from the list ranked by size of sales: he may well not even know where his corporation places on the list *Fortune* just as faithfully compiles ranking the same 500 corporations by profitability.)

(3) Many managements apparently were overexposed in impressionable childhood years to the story in which the imprisoned handsome prince is released from a toad's body by a kiss from a beautiful princess. Consequently, they are certain their managerial kiss will do wonders for the profitability of Company T(arget).

Such optimism is essential. Absent that rosy view, why else should the shareholders of Company A(cquisitor) want to own an interest in T at the 2X takeover cost rather than at the X market price they would pay if they made direct purchases on their own? In other words, investors can always buy toads at the going price for toads. If investors instead bankroll princesses who wish to pay double for the right to kiss the toad, those kisses had better pack some real dynamite. We've observed many kisses but very few miracles. Nevertheless, many managerial princesses remain serenely confident about the future potency of their kisses—even after their corporate backyards are knee-deep in unresponsive toads.

SOURCE: Berkshire Hathaway 1981 Annual Report.

The appendix to this chapter summarizes evidence from selected studies on the capital market impact of a diverse set of corporate restructuring announcements. The overall tenor of these studies is that the capital market perceives many restructuring decisions to either increase market value or (at least) to have no significant negative effect on market value. This finding is in contrast to many articles and statements in the financial press alleging that management takes actions that increase its own welfare but decrease shareholders' wealth. One explanation for this finding is that the interests of management and shareholders are congruent, especially if management has a sizable proportion of its own wealth

TABLE 13.2 Chief Executive Rankings of Motivations for Mergers

Horizontal Merger Motives	*Conglomerate Merger Motives*
1. To effect more rapid growth	1. To effect more rapid growth
2. To gain economies of scale	2. To spread risk through diversification
3. To increase market share	3. To increase market value of stock
4. To expand geographically	4. To expand/improve the product mix
5. To increase market value of stock	5. To counter cycle of seasonal sales
6. To expand/improve product mix	6. To enhance power/prestige of firm

SOURCE: Baker, Miller, and Ramsperger (1983, Table 2, p. 26).

TABLE 13.3 Stated Motivations by Management for Voluntary Spinoffs

Motive	Number of Firms with Stated Motive	
1. Loosen constraints of institutional or regulatory environment (taxation, price, or other regulation)		18
2. Improve managerial efficiency		
• Separate subsidiary so that management can concentrate on primary line(s) of business	8	
• Remove subsidiary which does not fit with other lines of business and/or long-run strategy of parent	11	
• Facilitate growth of subsidiary as an independent concern	5	
• Improve management incentives (usually mentioned in context of dissimilar lines of business)	6	
Subtotal		30
3. Other		
• Enhance investor evaluation of parent and subsidiary by separating them	7	
• Remove a source of fluctuation in net income	3	
Subtotal		10
Total		58

SOURCE: Schipper and Smith (1983, Table 8): p. 452.

dependent on the market value of the firm's equity securities. Another explanation is that although management does take actions that maximize its own welfare at the expense of shareholders, the dollar effect of those actions is minor relative to the market capitalization of the firm. For example, a $10 million diversion of wealth in a firm with a market capitalization of $1 billion is unlikely to show up in the research summarized in the appendix.

13.3 SOURCES OF VALUE IN CORPORATE RESTRUCTURING

There are many potential sources of value (whether to the shareholders or to other parties such as management) from corporate restructuring. It is important to stress that these are "potential sources." In any specific instance, only a subset may be applicable (and after the fact, an even smaller subset may be achieved). Appreciation of the diverse nature of such sources of value is important when designing an information system to estimate their magnitude and also when understanding the role that financial statement information can play in corporate restructuring decisions.

A. Strategic Opportunities

One motivation for mergers is to purchase options on future growth prospects that may have explosive upside potential. For example, acquisitions of biotechnology start-up ventures can be an integral part of a drug company's strategy in seeking future growth. Given that a firm has decided to expand its business in a specific industry, there can be important strategic reasons for acquiring an existing firm in that industry rather than relying on internal development. These reasons include (1) gaining an ongoing operation with a developed research department, (2) gaining a timing advantage, as delays due to plant construction time are avoided, and (3) making a preemptive move that can preclude a competitor from gaining a similar position in the industry.

Another potential strategic opportunity in corporate restructuring is the use of market power. For instance, two firms may merge and adopt a pricing policy that enables them to earn above competitive rates of return. Government regulations (for example, antitrust laws) often exist to prevent mergers where this possibility exists. However, there are many covert and overt ways for firms to exploit any potential for market power. For example, one approach is to redefine the marketing/distributing rules of the game in an industry so that it becomes more heavily segmented into submarkets that, on average, have a higher profit margin.

Numerous information sources are likely to be used in exploring strategic opportunities. Financial statements can play a key role in a subset of these explorations. For example, earnings data can be used when assessing the current profitability of individual firms in an industry and when assessing changes in the profitability of industries that have undergone significant corporate restructuring.

B. Synergy and Reverse Synergy

Many statements made at the time of acquisitions make reference to synergistic gains from combining two entities. The following two comments from the financial press are illustrative:

- "The chairman of the acquiree expressed enthusiasm for the merger, calling it a 'remarkable fit.' This is really a situation where two plus two makes five."
- "The chairman said that 'We expect that by combining their skills and our skills, we can add two and two and get five or six.'"

Even a popular song extolls the benefits of synergy ("Come on, baby, merge with me and feel the surge of synergy").

Table 13.4 gives examples of synergy in the functional areas of production, marketing/distribution, finance, and personnel. The type of synergy anticipated will guide the information sources used when placing a dollar value on the expected gains. For instance, when estimating the gains from better plant utilization, an analyst may want to examine the correlation between profitability and plant utilization rates of other firms in the industry. Estimating the gains from integrating diverse R&D departments will include analysis of the costs of duplicate activities in those separate departments. The achievement of synergistic gains requires that particular attention be paid to integration of the two entities. Problems due to (say) clashes in corporate cultures and managerial resignations can result in sy-

TABLE 13.4 Examples of Potential Synergy in Corporate Acquisitions

Functional Area	Source of Synergy
Production	Economies of scale Access to new technologies Reduced likelihood of supply shortages Exploitation of unused production capacity
Marketing/distribution	Economies of scale Access to new markets Exploitation of existing distribution networks Increased power in product markets
Finance	Utilization of unused tax loss carryforwards Exploitation of unused debt capacity Reduction of likelihood of bankruptcy Reduction of capital rationing
Personnel	Acquisition of key managerial talent Integration of diverse R&D departments

nergies not being achieved or taking longer to achieve than was anticipated in the premerger analysis.

The typical synergy argument used for mergers is of the "2 + 2 = 5" kind. A subset of arguments for divestitures and spinoffs is of the "5 − 2 = 4" kind. It is sometimes argued that large diversified firms impose bureaucratic rules on individual subsidiaries and that those rules impede the decision making by management at those subsidiaries. The alleged result is an inability to respond quickly to changing market conditions. A related argument is that subsidaries can differ in the type of appropriate management incentive schemes in a way that large corporations find difficult to accommodate. By creating separate firms for these diverse subsidiaries, management will be more strongly motivated due to their new incentive schemes that better reflect the nature of their business.

C. Increase in Managerial Effectiveness

A third potential source of gains from corporate restructuring is an increase in managerial effectiveness. One instance is where existing management is performing in a substandard manner and is replaced after an acquisition by a more effective team. Indeed, one argument for promoting an active market in acquisitions is the discipline it imposes on management. Existing managers are less likely to give substandard performance if there is a nontrivial probability that such performance is likely to induce another company to make an acquisition and then replace them with a new set of managers. Useful analysis in this context is to examine (1) where on the industry distribution of the accounting rate of return the takeover prospect lies and (2) the dispersion of that distribution. The lower the firm lies in the distribution, and the more dispersed is that distribution, the greater the gains to a new management who believes that it can be in (say) the top decile category for the accounting rate of return.

Corporate restructuring can also result in an increase in managerial effectiveness if there is a better alignment of management's self-interest with that of existing shareholders. An extreme example is a leveraged buyout where the existing management has a large component of its wealth dependent on the financial success of the firm. In this context, management is likely to be highly focused in its efforts to maximize the market value of the company.

D. Exploiting Capital-Market Mispricing

A fourth class of gains arise if individuals are able both to detect and exploit capital market mispricing of securities. The financial press frequently carries stories about individuals who acquire a company, sell off a subset of assets that cover the total purchase price, and, in effect, obtain the remaining assets at zero cost. (Stories in which individuals sell off all the assets for less than the purchase price are rarely given much publicity, in part because those individuals do not want to publicize their failures.) The market mispricing story is apparently one widely believed by corporate executives. A *Business Week* (February 20, 1984) survey reported the following response to the question ''Do you feel that the current price of your company's stock is an accurate indicator of the real value of your company?'':

Yes	32%
No, overvalues	2%
No, undervalues	60%
Not sure	6%

Investment bankers are very active in promoting capital market mispricing stories; for example, that it is cheaper for companies to acquire proved oil and gas reserves via a takeover than it is to discover them via an exploration program. Investment bankers have a conflict of interest in both advising management and taking fees based on management's restructuring decisions. It is important that their advice be treated with healthy skepticism. Note that if the capital market does misprice securities, then companies wishing to exploit that mispricing via acquisitions need to examine potential mispricing of their own company as well as that of the potential acquiree, especially if the mode of payment involves equity securities.

E. Other Sources

Many parties potentially are affected by corporate restructuring, for example, shareholders, bondholders, workers, and consumers. In any single restructuring, the bargaining power of the parties affected will influence how any value increase from corporate restructuring will be distributed. The appendix to this chapter summarizes empirical evidence in this area. A striking result is that in the merger area, the shareholders of the acquired firm appear to capture a sizable part of the value increment from the merger.

Even if a corporate restructuring does not increase market value, it can result in a redistribution of that value. Consider the effect on stockholders and bondholders of a merger that does not increase cash flow but that decreases the likelihood of bankruptcy (due to the events causing bankruptcy for the previously separate firms being less than perfectly correlated). If the merger is financed by an equity issue, bondholders will gain and the stockholders will lose because their debt is now less risky than it was before the merger. In a study of 39 pure exchange mergers, Eger (1983) reported results consistent with this redistribution argument.

An explicit motive for a corporate restructuring can be to redistribute wealth between various parties. Consider a highly profitable multiactivity firm with one division experiencing low profitability due to high wage contracts (relative to the workers at competitors of that division). The profitability of the multiactivity firm may make it difficult to negotiate with labor unions. Spinning off the low-profitability division as a separate company can be one means of "forcing" labor unions to agree on the necessity to bring their labor costs in line with the industry norm. The net effect can be a decrease in the wages of the employees of the spun-off company and an increase in the market value of the shares held by the shareholders of the two separate companies.

13.4 INFORMATION SOURCES ABOUT FIRM VALUE

This section discusses four sources of information that may be used in corporate restructuring decisions. Each source is not independent. In some contexts, information from only a subset may be available.

A. Organized Securities Markets

Organized securities markets such as the New York Stock Exchange (NYSE) and the London Stock Exchange (LSE) can provide direct and indirect information about firm value. Direct information is obtainable when the firm being valued is publicly traded. As a general rule, the current market price represents a minimum price that a potential bidder will have to pay to acquire control of the company. There are several reasons why another company (or the existing management of the company) may bid at a price greater than the current market price:

1. The acquisition or buyout is expected to create additional value due to (say) synergy or increased managerial effectiveness

2. The bidding party may have access to private information they perceive is not reflected in the current market price

3. The market has ignored information in the public domain and the takeover or buyout is an attempt to exploit capital market undervaluation

4. The bidding company has made errors in its valuation analysis or is pursuing a strategy aimed at (say) maximizing firm size rather than market capitalization.

W. T. Grimm (1984) reports the following average premiums paid over market price in acquisitions of publicly listed U.S. companies:

1978	1979	1980	1981	1982	1983
46.2%	49.9%	49.9%	48.0%	47.4%	37.7%

These premiums are consistent with several of the foregoing factors being important in decisions about how much to bid for a company.

Organized markets such as the NYSE and LSE can also provide indirect evidence about firm value. By "indirect" is meant that a set of comparable publicly traded companies is used to make inferences about the market value of another entity. For instance, a firm considering the divestment of a division may use the market prices of publicly listed firms in that division's industry to get an initial estimate of its value. Typically, this process will involve

1. Determining the appropriate set of "comparable" firms (see Chapter 6 for a discussion of issues in this step)

2. Estimating the relationship between the market price of these companies and their financial statement and other characteristics

3. Using the relationship from (2) and information about the potential divestment candidate to predict the market price of the division.

A key assumption in this process is that the chosen comparables are appropriately priced (or mispriced by a known amount). A similar process can be used in non-divestment contexts (e.g., in the valuation of a privately held company) and in "self-valuation" by a company to determine if its current market price is out of alignment with the market price of other firms in its industry.

B. Market for Corporate Control

Whole companies or parts thereof are bought and sold (via acquisitions, mergers, divestitures, etc.) in what has been called the market for corporate control. Direct information to value a company comes from this market when there is already a good-faith bid for the entity being valued. For instance, if there is already one bid outstanding for a company, that bid reveals information about (at least) the minimum value another company places on the acquisition candidate. Note that bids by other companies will reflect the value of the potential acquisition to them. If there are differences across bidders in the potential value increments from the acquisition, this factor should be considered in using bid information from the corporate control market.

Indirect information from the corporate control market emerges when comparable firms or parts thereof are traded. For instance, in industries that have a high rate of acquisition activity, the prices paid for those acquisitions can provide useful information about likely future premiums. Note, however, that it is important to analyze whether (and how) firms previously acquired differ systematically from those not acquired when making inferences about likely future takeover premiums; for example, if one adopted a market mispricing perspective, those acquired first may well be the most undervalued firms in the industry.

C. Individual Asset and Liability Values

In a limited number of cases, the value of a firm can be deterministically derived from the values of the individual assets and liabilities. For example, some mutual funds will redeem shares at the market value per share of the stocks in their portfolios. More typically, this deterministic relationship will not exist. However, with full recognition of its limitations, an analysis of individual assets and liabilities can be an important information source about firm value. These limitations include: (1) not all assets and liabilities relevant to a potential buyer are included in a firm's balance sheet (for example, the loyalty of customers is excluded from the balance sheet) and (2) there are several ways to value assets and liabilities (for example, historical cost, replacement cost, current cost, and resale price), and no single technique is appropriate in each and every corporate restructuring decision context. (See Chapter 12 for further discussion.)

D. Multiple-Based Analysis

In some contexts, rules of thumb have been developed in negotiations on acquisitions or divestitures. For example,

- The buying price of cable television companies is often expressed in terms of a standard multiple of the number of subscribers to the cable service
- The buying price of a rental apartment complex is often expressed in terms of a standard multiple of the annual rental payments.

Several firms collecting data on merger activity report summary statistics on merger prices as a multiple of current earnings. W. T. Grimm (1984) reports the following data on price-to-earnings ratios paid in acquisitions over the 1978–1983 period:

	1978	1979	1980	1981	1982	1983
Mean	14.3	14.3	15.2	15.6	13.9	16.7
Median	11.5	11.6	11.3	12.7	12.1	14.5

As with most benchmarks, multiple-based statistics such as these should not be the only data item used in a valuation exercise.

13.5 GENERATING A DISTRIBUTION OF FIRM VALUE

Assume that a manager wishes to undertake corporate restructuring decisions that maximize the market value of shareholders' equity. When analyzing how a specific transaction might change market value, an assumption must be made as to how the capital market prices equity and other securities. This assumption will influence the analyst in two ways:

1. Specifying the attributes to include in the valuation exercise. For instance, if it is assumed that the capital market values cash flow for a multiyear horizon, the focus of the valuation should be on this variable rather than (say) one-year-ahead earnings per share.

2. Specifying the attributes to exclude from the valuation exercise. A commonly cited motivation for acquisition is to provide greater diversification. From the existing shareholders' viewpoint, this assumes that the capital market provides a value increment to firms for providing diversification. This assumption does not underlie all the capital asset pricing models proposed in the finance literature. For instance, in the two-parameter capital asset pricing model described in Chapter 10, there is no value increment to a firm that provides diversification. Under the assumptions of this model, investors can form perfectly diversified portfolios by purchasing securities or other assets on their own account. (From a manager's viewpoint, however, diversification can be a desired object. For instance, it can reduce the fluctuations of reported earnings which may be important in the determination of management bonuses.)

The most commonly recommended approach for estimating the value of an acquisition or divestiture is the discounted cash flow (DCF) method. Implementation of this method involves

1. Choice of a horizon period to forecast cash flows
2. Estimation of the cash flows over this horizon (including the residual values of assets at the end of the horizon)
3. Discounting the period-by-period cash flows using a discount rate (or set of discount rates if period-by-period differences are recognized).

DCF methods are described in considerable detail in most corporate finance and cost accounting textbooks. Many computer software packages are available to implement the DCF method, with several providing considerable flexibility as to assumptions about discount rates, taxation consequences, and methods of financing.

This book advocates that the DCF method *not* be used in an exclusive or mechanical way for the following reasons:

1. Important unresolved theoretical issues exist with the DCF method such as the treatment of uncertainty and inflation, the definition and estimation of the cost of capital, and the treatment of dependencies in the opportunity set over multiple periods.

2. A desired number for the value of a company can be derived with ease by the "appropriate" set of estimates. (Warren Buffett of Berkshire Hathaway expressed this very aptly: "While deals often fail in practice, they never fail in projections—if the CEO is visibly panting over a prospective acquisition, subordinates and consultants will supply the requisite projections to rationalize any price.")

The DCF method should be used in conjunction with the information sources outlined in Section 13.4. Given the current state of the art in the finance literature (see Chapter 10), the analyst must learn to live with considerable uncertainty about the asset pricing model implicit in the capital market's pricing of securities. When this uncertainty is combined with uncertainty as to the inputs of any given model (e.g., future cash flows), the potential for individual analysts to arrive at very different estimates of firm value is apparent.

Almost all valuation exercises will contain an element of estimation error. It is important to recognize this error component before making inferences about capital market under- or overvaluation of companies. Suppose that one were valuing 100 oil and gas companies using the DCF method. Assume that the error component of the valuation exercise were random across companies. However, if one were to rank the 100 firms on their ratio of estimated DCF to current market capitalization, it is likely that those with the higher/lower ratios would have over-estimates/underestimates of DCF. The challenge facing an analyst in this context is to determine how much of the high ratio for an individual firm is due to DCF estimation error and how much is due to market undervaluation.

13.6   FINANCIAL VARIABLES AND PREMERGER ANALYSIS: CHARACTERISTICS OF ACQUIRED AND NONACQUIRED FIRMS

Research focusing on the characteristics of acquired and nonacquired firms has been conducted in two related areas: (A) ex post classificatory analysis and (B) ex ante predictive analysis. In the first, the focus is on the financial and other characteristics of acquired companies vis-à-vis nonacquired companies. The comparison has been made at both a single-variable (univariate) and a multiple-variable (multivariate) level. Examples include Simkowitz and Monroe (1971); Belkaoui (1978); Boisjoly and Corsi (1982); Harris, Stewart, Guilkey, and Carleton (1982); Dietrich and Sorensen (1984); Palepu (1985a); and Rege (1984).

In predictive analysis, the focus is on predicting which firms will subsequently become acquisition targets and (in some cases) developing trading strategies based on these predictions. Examples include Palepu (1985b) and Wansley, Roenfeldt, and Cooley (1983).

A. Classificatory Analysis

The Palepu (1985a) study is a good illustration of classificatory analysis. It also illustrates the joint analyses of financial statement and other firm- or industry-oriented data in an acquisition context. The focus of this paper is the relationship between financial characteristics of a firm and its acquisition likelihood in a given period. The results were based on a pooled sample of 163 targets that were acquired during the period 1971–1979 and a random sample of 256 control firms that were not acquired during this period. Both the target and control firms belonged to the manufacturing or mining sectors and were listed on either the New York or the American Stock Exchange. The first stage of Palepu's work was to compare the targets and controls on a univariate basis. Table 13.5 presents the ten variables examined. These variables were selected to probe several hypotheses as to the

TABLE 13.5 Characteristics of Targets and Controls, 1971–1979

Variable		Targets	Controls	t Statistic
X_1:	Average excess security return per day over prior four years	.0767	.1295	2.63*
X_2:	Average market-adjusted security return per day over prior four years	.0121	.0285	2.34*
X_3:	0/1 dummy variable with 1 for low-growth/high-liquidity/low-leverage combinations and high-growth/low-liquidity/high-leverage combinations and 0 for all other combinations	.4110	.2969	2.38*
X_4:	Average annual sales growth rate over prior three years	12.65	16.38	2.63*
X_5:	Ratio of net liquid assets to total assets averaged over prior three years	29.63	29.68	.05
X_6:	Ratio of long-term debt to total equity averaged over prior three years	46.20	62.05	1.44
X_7:	0/1 dummy variable with 1 if there is at least one acquisition in a firm's four-digit SIC industry in prior year	.2270	.3750	3.32*
X_8:	Net book assets of firm ($ millions)	134.9	818.0	4.62*
X_9:	Ratio of firm's market price to book value of common equity in prior year	1.077	1.091	.04
X_{10}:	Ratio of firm's price to earnings at end of fiscal year of prior year	10.97	8.39	1.75

* Indicates that the mean value of the targets and controls are significantly different at .05 level.
SOURCE: Palepu (1985a, Table III): p. 26.

causes of merger activity. The main conclusions drawn by Palepu were

1. The targets have lower stock returns during the four years prior to their takeover; see X_1 and X_2 in Table 13.5. This is consistent with acquisitions being a mechanism to replace inefficient managements.

2. The targets exhibit "higher growth-resource mismatch" (e.g., low growth and excess resources) compared to the controls; see X_3 to X_6 in Table 13.5. These variables captured some notions in the financial press and academic literature as to likely targets, for example, that cash-rich firms with limited internal investment opportunities are "natural acquisition targets."

3. Targets are not predominantly located in industries in which acquisitions occurred in the prior year. The X_7 variable in Table 13.5 indicates that 22.7% of the targets have at least one firm taken over from their industry in the year prior to their acquisition. In contrast, 37.5% of the controls belong to industries in which at least one acquisition occurred.

4. The average target is smaller in size than the average control firm.

5. Neither the average market-to-book ratio nor the price-to-earnings ratio of the targets and controls is significantly different from each other.

The second stage of Palepu's work was to compare the targets and controls on a multivariate basis. Using combinations of the ten variables in Table 13.5, four multivariate models were examined using logit. This statistical method yields a likelihood ratio index, which is an indicator of the overall explanatory power of the model. (It is analogous to the R^2 of a multiple regression model.) Palepu summarized the results of the logit analysis as follows:

> The likelihood ratio index for the estimated models ranges from 9.93% to 12.45%. . . . Collectively, the variables included in the models provide significant explanation of a firm's acquisition likelihood. (p. 18)

The author stressed that while the likelihood ratio index was statistically significant, its explanatory power was relatively low.

Harris et al. (1982) report a similar finding to Palepu (1985a) when using probit to classify a sample of 61 U.S. firms acquired in 1976 and 1977, 45 U.S. firms acquired in 1974 and 1975, and 1,200 nonacquired U.S. firms. Harris et al. note that despite the statistical significance of their multivariate model, "only a very small portion of the factors contributing to acquisition is captured by the statistical models based only upon acquired firm characteristics. The models give some insights into the factors contributing to merger, but are far short of providing a good explanation of merger activity" (p. 165).

B. Predictive Analysis

One motivation for research on acquisition candidates has been to develop investment strategies to exploit predictions of likely candidates. For example, the Dreyfus organization, in a prospectus for a "Merger and Acquisition Fund," stated that its objective was "investment in the equity securities of companies which are, or are believed to have the potential to become, subjects for acquisition by third parties.'' Given the sizable premiums paid in many acquisitions, the potential gains are large. Note, however, that to earn abnormal returns in this area, the prediction model must detect movements in acquisition likelihood that are not fully impounded in the prices of capital market securities. Management is also interested in predictions about the probability of acquisition. This information may be used either to seek an acquiring company that will maximize the wealth of the existing shareholders or to prepare a more elaborate defense against an unwanted suitor.

Results reported in Wansley, Roenfeldt, and Cooley (1983) directly test the ability to earn abnormal returns using predictions of acquisition likelihood. The first stage of their analysis was to develop a multivariate model to predict potential acquisition status. The sample consisted of 44 firms that merged during 1975–1976 and 44 randomly selected nonmerged firms that had fiscal years matching those of the acquired firms. The statistical method used was discriminant analysis. The means of the five independent variables included in the model were

Variable	Merged Firms	Nonmerged Firms
Price-to-earnings ratio	7.295	14.666
Long-term debt to total assets	.151	.220
Natural log of net sales (millions)	4.652	5.953
Compound growth in net sales	.147	.114
Market value of equity to total assets	.440	.563

The authors reported a total classification accuracy of 75% for the 88 firms; 32 of the 44 acquired firms were correctly classified as were 34 of the nonmerged firms.

The second stage in the Wansley, Roenfeldt, and Cooley (1983) study was to use the discriminant model built on 1975–1976 data to predict the acquisition status of Compustat firms in 1977, based on information from fiscal years *prior* to 1977. Using a sample of 754 Compustat firms, the 25 firms and the 50 firms with the ''highest posterior probabilities of belonging to the merged group (greatest resemblance to acquired firms)'' (p. 155) were selected. Investment in these 25- and 50-firm portfolios was assumed on March 31, 1977, and held to December 31, 1978. Results are presented in Figure 13.1. Abnormal returns were measured after controlling for both the market portfolio returns (R_m) and the beta of each security. The authors reported that ''an investor who purchased these firms on March 31, 1977, and held them for 12 to 21 months would have earned abnormal returns ranging from about 14 to 28 percent depending on the holding period'' (p. 156). The results in Figure 13.1 were marginally significant statistically for the top 25-firm portfolio but not for the top 50-firm portfolio. Two of the variables included in the discriminant model (firm size and the price-to-earnings ratio) meant that the portfolios comprised small firms with low price-to-earnings ratios. These variables are associated with either capital asset pricing puzzles (see Chapter 10) or market efficiency anomalies (see Chapter 11). Thus, interpretation of the CAR

FIGURE 13.1 Cumulative Abnormal Returns from Investing in Firms with High Likelihood of Acquisition

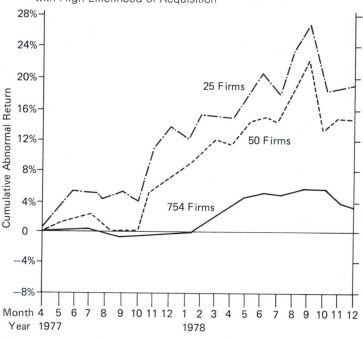

Source: Wansley, Roenfeldt, and Cooley (1983, Figure 2): p. 160.

results in Figure 13.1 is somewhat ambiguous. In addition, the authors examined only one time period (March 1977 to December 1978) and reported that not one of the firms in either the 25- or 50-firm portfolios actually was acquired during this period. The importance of the Wansley, Roenfeldt, and Cooley (1983) study is not the significance of the results reported. (They are marginally significant at best.) Rather the paper is important because it is an explicit attempt to test the hypothesis that abnormal returns can be earned by using research results on the profiles of acquisition candidates.

13.7 FINANCIAL VARIABLES AND POSTMERGER ANALYSIS: PERFORMANCE OF ACQUIRING FIRMS

Prior to the early 1970s, a large segment of empirical research in the corporate restructuring area examined the postacquisition performance of acquiring firms using data from financial statements. The benchmark used to assess performance was either the preacquisition period performance of the acquiring firm or the performance of a control group of nonacquisition-oriented firms. Dodd (1976, Table 1) summarizes results from 13 studies covering the 1893–1970 period;

9 reported that acquiring firms had lower profitability, 3 reported higher profitability, and 1 reported inconclusive results.

An example of research in this area is Meeks's (1977) study of the profitability of U.K. firms engaged in mergers in the 1964–1972 period. One variable examined by Meeks for the acquiring firms was a standardized profitability measure (E), the "profitability of the amalgamation (standardized for industry and year) less three-year average premerger profitability of the amalgamation (similarly standardized)" (p. 21). Table 13.6 presents the values of this E measure for the year of the acquisition (y) and for each of the seven subsequent years ($y + 1$ to $y + 7$). A positive/negative E value implies increased/decreased profitability relative to the average in the three years prior to the merger. Each firm in the sample had no merger in the three years prior to year y, and the E measure was computed only for those years subsequent to y in which no additional merger was made. Two values of E were reported: average E for all observations and average E with outliers removed. An outlier was defined as "a change in profitability greater than 200% of the level recorded by the industry; and it involved the exclusion of 20 of the original 233 cases" (p. 22). Based on the results in Table 13.6 and much subsequent analysis, Meeks concluded that "in all subsequent years [to the merger year] an average decline is reported. The scale of the decline is considerable, amounting in some years to more than half the level of profitability achieved by the industry. . . . The results with the outliers removed are much weaker in terms of the absolute value of the change, but much stronger in terms of statistical significance. The proportions experiencing declines in profitability

TABLE 13.6 Average Change in Standardized Profitability After Merger for U.K. Firms, 1964–1972

Year	All Observations			Outliers Omitted		
	E	%E < O	Number of Observations	E	%E < O	Number of Observations
y	.038	.38	233	.114**	.37	213
$y + 1$	− .168	.58	211	−.053**	.58	192
$y + 2$	− .503	.57	191	−.035*	.55	174
$y + 3$	− .369	.56	161	−.069**	.54	146
$y + 4$	− .197	.68	113	−.099**	.67	103
$y + 5$	− .567	.66	73	−.109**	.63	67
$y + 6$	− .659	.60	50	−.068	.54	44
$y + 7$	− .082	.61	23	−.073	.62	21

E – Profitability of the amalgamation (standardized for industry and year) less three-year average pre-merger profitability of the amalgamation (similarly standardized).
Outlier – Value of E greater than 200% of the level recorded by the industry.
* Significantly different from O at the 5% level (using a t-test).
** Significantly different from O at the 1% level.
SOURCE: Meeks (1977, Table 3.B): p. 21.

are little affected by the exclusion of outliers" (pp. 21, 22). Meeks aptly titled his study "Disappointing Marriage: A Study of the Gains from Merger."

A detailed review of evidence on the effect of mergers on accounting profitability measures of the acquiring firm is in Mueller (1980). Results from studies of mergers in Belgium, the Federal Republic of Germany, France, the Netherlands, Sweden, the United Kingdom, and the United States are summarized. The general conclusion was

> No consistent pattern of either improved or deteriorated profitability can be claimed across the seven countries. Mergers would appear to result in a slight improvement here, a slight worsening of performance there. If a generalization is to be drawn, it would have to be that mergers have but modest effects, up or down, on the profitability of the merging firms in the three to five years following merger. Any economic efficiency gains from the mergers would appear to be small. (p. 306)

At present, the literature contains little evidence of mergers that have significantly improved the relative profitability of the acquiring firm.

13.8 SOME GENERAL COMMENTS

1. Progress has been made in documenting the capital market's expectations about the often sizable gains from restructuring; see the appendix to this chapter. W. T. Grimm (1984) reports that merger premiums have averaged at least 30% for each year since 1970. However, little progress has been made in finding empirical support for factors hypothesized as the source of these expected gains. Empirical research has reported results that would support exclusion rather than inclusion of many individual factors as the source of gains. For instance, the available evidence (e.g., a comparison of accounting rate of return in the pre- and postmerger periods) does not support increases in managerial efficiency as a major source of gains in mergers; see Section 13.6. Similarly, the available evidence does not support increases in market power in the product markets as a source of the expected gain; see Eckbo (1983) and Stillman (1983). An important research area is constructing research designs that give insight into the potential contribution of factors such as strategic opportunities and synergy.

2. One motive for acquisitions given in the literature is to exploit undervaluation of assets by the capital market. Several studies have been conducted to probe the importance of this motive. An illustrative example is Bartley and Boardman (1984). One focus of this study was whether differences across firms in the ratio of their market value to the current replacement cost of their individual assets and liabilities explains differences in the likelihood of being an acquisition target. This ratio is known as the q ratio. The Bartley and Boardman sample included 33 nonregulated and nonfinancial firms that were subject to takeover

attempts during 1978. Each target was matched with a nontarget firm in the same or a similar industry. Replacement cost data for each firm were taken from the mandated disclosures that firms reported under Accounting Series Release 190 of the SEC. Using the market value of equity as the numerator (as of eight months prior to the takeover attempt), the authors reported the following mean q ratios:

Target Firms	*Nontarget Firms*
.57	.75

These means were significantly different from each other at the .05 level (t = 2.25). Other variables examined by the authors included the compound growth rate of earnings, dividend payout, price-to-earnings ratio, leverage, liquidity, profitability, and the ratio of the market value of the firm to the historical cost book value of its individual assets and liabilities. It was reported that the q ratio "was found to be the most important financial variable for discriminating between takeover target and nontarget firms" (p. 21). Other studies in this area include Bartley and Boardman (1983) and Chappell and Cheng (1984).

Research on this topic has produced results that, on balance, are consistent with the q ratio having some explanatory power in explaining merger activity. However, there are difficult problems in this research arising from the estimation of the replacement cost of individual assets and liabilities, for example, how to account for technological change and how to value assets for which there is excess industry capacity. Studies estimating replacement costs at the individual firm level (for example, Bartley and Boardman (1983, 1984)) potentially can make adjustments for such problems at this individual firm level. However, the individual firm disclosures used in several studies were mandated by the SEC or FASB, and many firms providing this information stressed its inherent lack of reliability (see Chapter 2). Studies estimating replacement costs for large aggregates of firms (for example, Chappell and Cheng (1984)) typically assume a high degree of uniformity as to how changes in construction costs, technological change, and so on affect individual firms.

3. The financial press frequently makes reference to the importance of managerial motives in corporate acquisitions and how these motives can conflict with shareholder wealth maximization. Executive compensation is often cited as an illustration of this conflict. The argument is that larger firms pay higher executive compensation and that management is willing to make acquisitions that decrease shareholder wealth to increase their own compensation. Lambert and Larcker (1984) provide evidence on this issue in a study of executive compensation paid by firms that made large acquisitions in the 1976–1981 period. The dollar magnitude of each acquisition was required to be at least 20 percent of the market value of equity of the acquiring firm in the year prior to the acquisition. Only firms that made one "major" acquisition in the 1976–1981 period were examined. Thirty-five acquisitions were included in the study. The mean (median) sales of

the acquired firm relative to the sales of the acquiring firm in the year prior to the acquisition was 31.70% (19.01%).

Lambert and Larcker examined the cash (salary plus bonus) portion of executive compensation. The benchmark used for compensation was "the salary and bonus paid to other executives in the same industry for firms . . . of the approximate size of the postacquisition firm in the absence of the acquisition" (p. 11). Results were presented for the full sample and for two subsamples, those acquisitions with a positive security return on the announcement of the merger (defined as day −1 to day +2) and those with a negative security return on the announcement of the merger. The *change* in executive compensation (adjusted for inflation) in the two years subsequent to the acquisition for the three samples was

Executives	Change for Full Sample	Change for Acquisitions with Positive Market Reaction	Change for Acquisitions with Negative Market Reaction
Top three executives	$23,618	$39,462	$13,056
CEO	10,254	21,640	2,636

After conducting significance tests on these and other aspects of the data, the authors concluded that "managers of acquiring firms experienced increases in their relative level of real cash compensation (inflation-adjusted change in cash compensation relative to industry norms). . . . However, this increase is obtained primarily by managers selecting acquisitions which increased shareholder wealth. Managers selecting acquisitions which decreased shareholder wealth experienced little change in real cash compensation. . . . Therefore, our results provide no evidence that executives can increase their compensation by selecting acquisitions which have an adverse impact on shareholder wealth" (p. i).

This study is but one of several that probe issues related to shareholder versus managerial conflicts associated with corporate restructuring. At present, the general tenor of the results is that many of the actions taken by management do not lead to reductions in shareholder wealth; see Jensen and Ruback (1983). However, several notable exceptions have been reported. For instance, both announcements of privately negotiated or targeted stock repurchases (typically at a premium) and standstill agreements (a contract in which a third party agrees to limit its holdings in the firm and, therefore, not to mount a hostile takeover attempt) on average decrease shareholder wealth; see Dann and DeAngelo (1983) and Bradley and Wakeman (1983).

13.9 SUMMARY

1. Corporate restructuring covers a diverse set of activities such as mergers, acquisitions, divestitures, leveraged buyouts, and spinoffs. The potential sources

of value believed to be important in specific decisions in this area will guide the information analysis conducted.

2. Information sources available in corporate restructuring decisions include organized securities markets, the market for corporate control, and markets for the individual assets and liabilities of the firm. Financial statement data typically play a key role in each source. Where possible, a broad set of information should be consulted so that the limitations of any one source are reduced.

3. Many studies have been conducted on the announcement effects of mergers, acquisitions, spinoffs, and so on. The overall tenor of the results from these studies is that the capital market perceives many restructuring decisions to increase market value. An unresolved issue in these studies is the source of these perceived gains.

APPENDIX 13.A   CAPITAL MARKETS AND CORPORATE RESTRUCTURING ANNOUNCEMENTS

Research on the effect of corporate restructuring decisions on capital market variables could focus on one or more of the following:

1. The impact on security returns of the announcement of (say) a proposed merger or divestiture
2. The impact on security returns of a completed transaction for a merger or divestiture, prior to the integration of the companies or the divestiture
3. The long-run impact on security returns of a merger or divestiture.

A key difference among (1), (2), and (3) is the time period examined, with (1) being the shortest and (3) the longest. For instance, (1) could focus on a one-day period (the day of the announcement), whereas (3) could focus on the five-year period following the announcement. Most research studies have examined (1), in part because the shorter the time period, the less likely that events unrelated to corporate restructuring will affect security returns. Clearly, the issues raised in the three time frames are not independent. One factor that will affect the capital market's reaction to a merger announcement is the predicted long-run effect of that merger on cash flows, risk, and so forth.

When interpreting the results from event studies, such as the effect on daily security returns of the announcement of a proposed merger, it is important to consider how the announcement changes the capital market's probability assessment of an outcome and the economic consequences of that outcome. For instance, if the capital market assessed a high probability of a merger bid before the formal announcement, there might be very little effect on security returns in the formal announcement period. The following subsections cite results from a representative set of studies in the corporate restructuring area. More detailed reviews of this literature include Dodd (1983), Jensen and Ruback (1983), Lev (1983), and Weston and Chung (1983).

Announcement Effects of Merger Proposals

A merger is a transaction in which approval is given by the management and stockholders of both the acquiring and the acquired firms. The acquired firm ceases to exist as a publicly traded entity subsequent to the acquisition. Dodd (1980) reports results for 151 U.S. merger proposals made over the 1971–1977 period. Of these 151 proposals, 71 were completed and 80 were canceled after the initial announcement. Part of Dodd's study focused on the date that the merger was first announced in *The Wall Street Journal* (termed day 0). The cumulative abnormal returns for the 151 target companies in the 40 trading days before and after the announcement were

	Cumulative Abnormal Returns		
Cumulation Period	Full Sample (N = 151)	Completed Mergers (N = 71)	Canceled Mergers (N = 80)
(−1, 0)	13.04%	13.41%	12.73%
(−40, 0)	23.42	24.01	24.51
(+1, +40)	−1.99	3.96	−8.86

There is a highly significant increase in the stock prices of targets in both the (−40, 0) and (−1, 0) trading day periods. After the merger proposal, the sample that completes the transaction experiences positive abnormal returns while the sample in which the merger is canceled experiences negative abnormal returns. The Dodd (1980) results for the target firms are consistent with those reported in many other similar studies.

There is less agreement in the literature on the effect of the merger proposal on the security returns of the bidding firm. The results from the Dodd (1980) study are

	Cumulative Abnormal Returns		
Cumulation Period	Full Sample (N = 126)	Completed Mergers (N = 66)	Canceled Mergers (N = 60)
(−1, 0)	−1.16%	−1.09%	−1.24%
(−40, 0)	5.37	4.89	5.80
(+1, +40)	−.20	1.18	−1.46

Focusing on the immediate announcement period, Dodd finds a small negative security return. Other studies using similarly large samples have reported either zero or small positive security returns for bidding firms at the time of merger proposal announcements (for example, Asquith, 1983). One problem in contrasting the acquiring and acquired firm results is that the acquiring firm typically is much larger than the acquired firm. Even if the acquiring firm captures part of the gains from the merger, its effect on total market capitalization may be small.

A subset of research in this area consists of case studies of a single merger. For instance, Ruback (1982) reported the following abnormal return on the day that DuPont made a $87.50-per-share bid for 40% of Conoco:

$$\text{Conoco daily abnormal security return} = 11.87\%$$

$$\text{DuPont daily abnormal security return} = -8.05\%$$

Individual case studies permit the researcher to make a detailed analysis of the merger examined. However, one must be careful when generalizing from such research. Most case studies have focused on instances where the bidding firm has a large negative security return on the announcement date. It may well be that case study researchers chose such instances because they make for a more interesting article rather than because they are representative of larger samples. For example, managerial motives are easier to discuss when there is a decline in the market value of the acquiring firm. The 8.05% drop in the market value of DuPont translates to a drop of $641 million in market capitalization!

Announcement Effects of Proposed Tender Offers

A tender offer is a transaction in which approval is given by the managers of the bidding firm and the stockholders of the target firm. In many cases, the bidding firm is seeking less than 100% of the target's shares outstanding. Bradley, Desai, and Kim (1982) report the following results for 394 successful tender offers made in the 1962–1980 period:

Cumulation Period	Cumulative Abnormal Returns	
	Target	Bidder
(−1, 0)	16.11%	.90%
(−20, 0)	22.94	2.86
(+1, +20)	8.92	.63

In a related study, Bradley, Desai, and Kim (1983) examine the returns realized by the stockholders of firms that were the targets of unsuccessful tender offers. They find that a subset is subsequently taken over at sizable premiums to shareholders. Those firms not taken over in the five years subsequent to the unsuccessful tender offer on average do not earn abnormal returns in the period from six months prior to the tender offer to five years subsequent to the tender offer.

Announcement Effects of Proposed "Going Private" Transactions

A going private transaction is one in which a "control group" of shareholders purchases the shares of other shareholders and withdraws that stock from those publicly traded on organized capital markets. There are several means of structuring such transactions. One is when the incumbent management seeks complete equity ownership of the surviving private company. Another approach is via a leveraged buyout, in which a party of investors (often including existing management) seeks to share equity ownership in the surviving private company. The potential gains from going private include (1) avoidance of the costs of being a publicly traded company (for example, stock exchange listing fees, SEC filing charges) and (2) an increase in managerial efficiency due to better alignment of management and shareholder interest. DeAngelo, DeAngelo, and Rice (1982) report the following CAR results for 72 firms making "going private" proposals in the 1973–1980 period:

Cumulation Period	Cumulative Abnormal Returns Full Sample (N = 72)
(−1, 0)	22.27%
(−40, 0)	30.40
(+1, +40)	−1.87

Eighteen of the 72 firms subsequently withdrew their "going private" proposals. These 18 firms had an average CAR of −8.88% in the (−1, 0) event time period surrounding the withdrawal announcement.

Announcement Effects of Proposed Voluntary Spinoffs

A spinoff is a transaction in which one firm is divided into two (or more) separate entities and shareholders receive a pro rata distribution of shares in each entity. Schipper and Smith (1983) examined the market reaction to the announcement of a proposed spinoff by 93 firms in the 1963–1981 period. The CAR results were

Cumulation Period	Cumulative Abnormal Returns Full Sample (N = 93)
(−1, 0)	2.84%
(−40, 0)	2.13
(+1, +40)	−1.98

The positive CAR on (−1, 0) of 2.84% is highly significant statistically ($t = 6.61$). The two most common motives given by firms in the sample for the spinoffs were (1) to loosen constraints of an institutional or regulatory kind (for example, taxation and rate regulation) and (2) to remove a subsidiary that does not fit with other lines of business and/or the long-run strategy of the parent.

Announcement Effects of Proposed Voluntary Divestitures

A divestiture is a transaction in which one firm sells a subset of its assets to another firm (for example, a subsidiary or separate line of business). Linn and Rozeff (1984) report CAR results for 77 divestiture announcements in the 1977–1982 period:

Cumulation Period	Cumulative Abnormal Returns Full Sample (N = 77)
(−1, 0)	1.46%
(−40, 0)	5.40
(+1, +40)	.61

The 1.46% increase on (−1, 0) is significantly different from zero ($Z = 5.35$). The authors concluded "that on average voluntary sell-offs create value for the selling firm's stockholders. These results are consistent with the hypothesis that the motive for the sell-off is the elimination of diseconomics for the selling firm and/or the unit being sold is more valuable in the hands of the buyer than if retained by the seller" (p. 17).

QUESTIONS

Question 13.1: Cities Service Company: Alternative Valuation Approaches

Cities Service Company is an integrated oil and gas company. Table 13.7 presents summary information for Cities Service covering the 19X1–19X5 period. The Annual Report for 19X5 disclosed the following information on the percentage of sales, operating profit, and identifiable assets in the segments of Cities' business:

	Sales	Operating Profit	Identifiable Assets
Oil and gas production	18%	83%	54%
Refining, marketing, and transmission	66	(2)	24
Natural gas transmission	10	15	13
Minerals	3	1	6
Other	3	3	3

In 19X5, Cities discontinued its plastics operations and incurred a one-time after-tax charge of $290 million.

Cities reported its proved oil and gas reserves on its balance sheet using the successful-efforts method, which is based on the historical cost of finding or pur-

TABLE 13.7 Cities Service Company, 19X1–19X5

Data Items	19X1	19X2	19X3	19X4	19X5
Income statement data ($ millions)					
Gross revenue	4,195	4,494	6,058	7,557	8,643
Operating profit	717	756	1,070	1,325	1,161
Income from continuing operations	204	121	361	489	286
Income from discontinued					
operations	6	(3)	(13)	(11)	(335)
Net income (loss)	210	118	348	478	(49)
Balance sheet data ($ millions)					
Working capital (CA − CL)	459	462	501	449	241
Long-term obligations	938	1,055	1,027	1,175	1,702
Total assets	3,740	4,005	4,773	5,358	6,049
Net book value	1,938	1,971	2,227	2,579	2,107
Shares outstanding (millions)	82.848	83.001	83.193	83.278	83.349
Reserves data (millions)					
Net oil reserves (barrels)	364	614	535	512	439
Net gas liquid reserves (barrels)	304	293	276	269	277
Net gas reserves (million cubic					
feet)	3,650	3,567	3,484	3,210	3,075

chasing those reserves. (Question 5.3 includes a discussion of the successful-efforts method.) John S. Herold, in its "Oil Industry Comparative Appraisals" service, provides estimates of the proved oil and gas reserves of Cities using the discounted cash flow method. Herold provided the following description of this method in March of 19X6:

> Estimated oil and gas reserve quantities are generally those provided by the company being appraised. Oil, gas and gas liquid reserves are appraised by the discounted cash flow method. Estimated future cash realization or operating profits (sales price less operating costs, including overhead and taxes levied directly against production) are, effective March 1, 19X6, discounted to a present worth basis at a 15% rate after deduction of estimated development costs. Prior to March 1, 19X6, a 10% rate was employed. (This 10% rate was used in each year of the 19X1-19X5 period.) Changing conditions necessitate revision of our basic appraisal assumptions from time to time. In our appraisal of U.S. oil reserves, we have assumed that the current average price received by each individual company will increase to $100 per barrel by the year 19X24, and remain constant thereafter. (Price per barrel in March 19X6 was $35.) The "windfall profit" tax has been calculated in accordance with the tax law and is considered to be an operating expense. Unit operating costs are escalated at a rate for each individual company which is dependent on the number of years to exhaust the reserves, and the unit price of oil or gas at the time of exhaustion.

Adding its own appraised value of Cities' oil and gas reserves to the other assets and liabilities of Cities Service, Herold reported an appraised estimate of its net worth. The Herold net worth estimate for Cities Service and the reported net book value figure from the annual reports of Cities Service were (in millions of dollars):

	19X1	19X2	19X3	19X4	19X5
Herold appraised net value	$3,646	$3,926	$6,605	$6,507	$7,532
Net book value per annual report	1,938	1,971	2,227	2,579	2,107

In its annual reports for years 19X3 to 19X5, Cities Service provided estimates of the net present value (using the discounted cash flow method) of its proved oil and gas reserves using the reserve recognition accounting (RRA) method prescribed by the SEC. The RRA method uses a discount rate of 10%. Future net revenue estimates are "based on projected production at year-end prices, less lifting costs (including the windfall profits tax), future development and reclamation costs, all projected at year-end levels." A critical assumption in developing RRA values is that no change would occur in year-end revenue per barrel and production cost per barrel over the period used to discount future cash flows. The estimated net worth of Cities Service when the RRA values were used for its proved oil and gas reserves (and balance sheet values used for all other assets and liabilities) was (in millions of dollars):

19X3	19X4	19X5
$4,479	$5,428	$4,819

The market capitalization on the New York Stock Exchange of the equity securities of Cities Service over this period was (in millions of dollars):

Dec. 19X1	Dec. 19X2	Dec. 19X3	Dec. 19X4	Dec. 19X5	Apr. 19X6
$1,474	$1,491	$2,316	$3,977	$3,834	$2,563

There were 78.271 million shares outstanding in April 19X6.

Other Information

1. In April 19X6, Value Line estimated 19X6 earnings for Cities Service as $210 million and the 19X6 "cash flow" as $532 million. It noted that "19X6 will be a dark year for earnings. We're estimating earnings for 19X6 will be more than 20% below last year's earnings from continuing operations. With only moderate improvement expected in 19X7, this stock will probably lag well behind the market over the next twelve months—unless last year's takeover rumors come true in 19X6. Management has firmly resisted merger proposals in the past. And merger seems less likely now, given the depressed outlook for the oil industry, and antitrust laws that make takeover by another oil company dubious."

2. In April 19X6, Value Line reported the following average annual price-to-earnings ratio for the aggregate of its integrated petroleum industry sample:

19X1	19X2	19X3	19X4	19X5
6.7	6.2	3.7	5.3	5.7

3. In April 19X6, Value Line reported the following ratios of December 19X5 market capitalization to RRA-adjusted 19X5 net book value for integrated oil and gas companies with large international operations: Exxon (.3), Gulf Oil (.2), Mobil (.2), Chevron (.4), and Texaco (.2). The comparable ratios reported for integrated oil and gas companies with a heavy focus on U.S.-based operations were Atlantic Richfield (.4), Cities Service (.5), Phillips Petroleum (.3), Shell Oil (.5), Amoco (.3), Sohio (.3), Sun Company (.4), and Union Oil (.4).

4. W. T. Grimm reported that in 19X5, 76 merger or acquisition transactions were made in the oil and gas industry. Summary information relating to these 76 transactions and the two largest transactions was

	Price-to-Earnings Paid	Premium Paid over Premerger Stock Price
Average for 76 transactions	15.9	40.8%
DuPont acquisition of Conoco	10.6	88.1
U.S. Steel acquisition of Marathon	18.6	70.6

5. In May 19X5, the Nu-West Group of Calgary, Canada, bought 6.3% of the shares outstanding of Cities Service for $250 million and, in June, increased this to 7.2%. Nu-West was attempting to negotiate for the acquisition of the Canadian properties of Cities Service. In September 19X5, Cities Service bought back Nu-West's 7.2% investment for $307 million. (Buyback price per share was approximately 20% above the then current market price.)

6. J. S. Herold estimated the "oil finding cost per barrel" of Cities Service and the industry as a whole to be:

	19X2	19X3	19X4	19X5
Cities Service	$5.18	$8.32	$17.28	$20.09
Industry	$5.42	$9.78	$ 7.96	$10.27

REQUIRED

1. You are hired by Cities Service in April 19X6 to advise the board of directors on the possible range of values that a third party would place on Cities Service. What approaches would you examine in this assignment?

2. Compare and contrast the three estimates available for the proved oil and gas reserves for Cities Service in 19X5 (book value, RRA value, and J. S. Herold value).

3. What factors could explain the low ratio of the market capitalization of Cities Service to the J. S. Herold appraised value?

4. Given only the information provided, what range of values would you report

to Cities Service's board of directors? Show your calculations and key assumptions.

QUESTION 13.2: Cities Service Company: Analysis of Security Returns in Periods Surrounding Acquisition Announcements

Question 13.1 provided background information on Cities Service Company as of April 19X6. On April 30, 19X6, Cities' stock closed on the New York Stock Exchange at 32¾, implying a market capitalization of $2.563 billion. The period from May to August 19X6 was a tumultuous one for the management of Cities Service. In May, Cities Service believed that Mesa Petroleum was preparing to make a takeover bid for Cities. On May 28 it announced its own bid for Mesa Petroleum. Table 13.8 presents 11 key event dates for Cities in the May-to-August period. The four major players in the events of this period were Cities Service, Mesa Petroleum, Gulf Oil, and Occidental Petroleum. Also included in Table 13.8 is the mean daily abnormal security return for the common stocks of these four companies on the day of each of the cited announcements. The source of Table 13.8 is Ruback (1983). Ruback summarized the results for each company as follows:

Firm	Holding Period	Cumulative Abnormal Return (percent)	Cumulative Abnormal Equity Value Change ($ millions)
Cities Service	May 28 to August 26	12.45%	$352
Mesa Petroleum	May 28 to June 21	− 5.90	− 64
Gulf Oil	June 17 to August 26	− 17.56	− 1,131
Occidental Petroleum	August 13 to August 26	− .25	− 4

Ruback noted that Mesa Petroleum realized a gain of about $80 million from selling its Cities Service shares at $55 each. Shareholders of Gulf incurred large losses in the period from June 17 to August 26. Most of these losses occurred in response to Gulf's initial offer for Cities Service. The Federal Trade Commission (FTC) reviewed Gulf's bid in the June-to-August period. The FTC was concerned that the proposed merger could lessen competition. When withdrawing its offer, Gulf cited its failure to overcome the FTC's objections to the merger. Cities Service asserted that Gulf did not attempt to resolve the FTC's objections and that Gulf refused a Cities offer to renegotiate the merger in light of the antitrust objections. Cities considered the cancellation to be a breach of contract and filed a $3 billion lawsuit against Gulf.

TABLE 13.8 Major Events in the Cities Service Takeover and Corresponding Percentage Abnormal Returns of Participating Firms

Date	Event	Cities Service	Mesa Petroleum	Gulf Oil	Occidental Petroleum
1. May 28[a]	Cities Service believes that Mesa Petroleum intends to bid for Cities.	5.23%[b]	5.91%[b]	1.10%	1.04%
2. June 1	Cities bids $17 per share for 51% of Mesa. Mesa offers to acquire Cities for $50 per share.	3.56	16.69[b]	1.82	.90
3. June 8	Cities bids $21 per share for 51% of Mesa.	−1.46	3.43	2.62	.03
4. June 17, 18	Gulf Oil agrees to acquire Cities for $63 a share.	43.38[b]	.32	−14.19[b]	.23
5. June 21	Cities repurchases stock held by Mesa at $55 a share. Cities and Mesa drop hostile bids for each other.	.95	−15.83[b]	.56	.79
6. August 2	Federal Trade Commission obtains a temporary restraining order on Gulf acquisition.	−20.97[b]	.21	−.66	1.02
7. August 6, 9	Gulf terminates its offer for Cities.	−28.50[b]	−1.29	3.67	.07
8. August 16, 17	Occidental Petroleum bids $50 for 50% of Cities. Cities rejects Occidental merger proposal.	4.87	−8.02[b]	−.40	−3.77
9. August 18, 19	Occidental announces tender offer for 49% of Cities at $50 per share.	12.97[b]	−.32	−.65	3.99
10. August 23	Mobil decides not to bid for Cities.	−10.82[b]	−3.04	−2.26	.48
11. August 25, 26	Cities accepts revised bid by Occidental. The bid includes $55 per share for 45% of Cities.	−1.40	3.25	−.66	2.70

[a] The dates listed are the trading days that the information reached the market. Multiple days are listed when the day on which the information reached the market is ambiguous or when trading in one of the firms was suspended.
[b] Indicates abnormal return significantly different from zero at .10 level (two-tailed test).
SOURCE: Ruback (1983, Table 1): pp. 322–323.

REQUIRED

1. Discuss the pattern of abnormal security returns reported in Table 13.8 for Cities Service, Mesa Petroleum, Gulf Oil, and Occidental Petroleum. What inferences can you draw from the information in Table 13.8?

2. Why might Gulf bid $63 a share for Cities in June 19X6 when it traded for

$32.75 in April 19X6? What could be the possible sources of the gain to Gulf to justify paying such a premium?

3. Many academic studies focus on the market reaction to an announcement using a very short time period, for example, the $(-1, 0)$ trading day period surrounding a morning newspaper announcement. What are the pros and cons of using such a short time period to examine if a management action (such as a takeover bid) was in the best interest of existing shareholders?

4. One explanation cited in the financial press for the "perceived" undervaluation of Cities Services (and other integrated oil and gas companies) was its heavy involvement in the downstream (transportation, refining, and marketing) end of the business. Consider the following comment made in the financial press:

> On the average, shares in integrated oil companies are priced at a mere 45% of their asset value, compared with an average of 88% for the smaller independent oil companies specializing in the upstream end of the business. In this context, asset value of the proved oil and gas reserves is based on their estimated future cash flows discounted back to their present value.

How would you gain evidence into possible explanations for the difference between the 45% figure for the integrated oil companies and the 88% figure for the smaller independent oil companies specializing in upstream activities?

QUESTION 13.3: Merger Activity, Market Values and the Replacement Cost of Individual Assets

The ratio of the market value of firms to the replacement cost of their assets is frequently discussed in the academic literature, in investment publications, and in the financial press. This ratio (often called Tobin's q) was developed in the early 1960s by the economist James Tobin. Table 13.9 presents estimates of Tobin's q for U.S. manufacturing corporations in the 1968–1983 period. These estimates are based on research by Von Furstenberg (1977). The numerator of the q ratio was obtained by adding estimates of the market value of debt, preferred stock, and common stock. The denominator of the q ratio was obtained by adding the net noninterest-bearing financial assets to the replacement cost of net fixed capital, inventories, and land. Replacement cost data were based on estimates by the U.S. Bureau of Economic Analysis. Von Furstenberg noted that the Bureau data "may not be entirely suitable for the purpose at hand since they do not reflect the current cost of putting a given number of efficiency units in place but instead measure the current cost of the same amount of resources as was previously used to produce capital goods; thus 'costless' technological progress is ignored" (p. 358). The replacement cost estimates in Table 13.9 are derived from aggregates of firms and *not* from individual firm estimates. Table 13.9 also presents summary statistics W. T. Grimm (1984) reports for merger activity in the 1968–1983 period.

The following extracts include comments on Tobin's q measure, merger activity, and the role of replacement cost data in merger decisions:

TABLE 13.9 U.S. Statistics on Mergers and Acquisitions, 1968–1983

Year	q Ratio (Von Furstenberg Series)	Net No. of Merger and Acquisition Announcements	Total Dollar Value Paid ($ billions)	Method of Payment				Average PE Paid	Average Premium Paid over Market	S&P 500 Stock Index (1926 = 1.00)
				Cash	Stock	Combination	Debt			
1968	1.022	4,462	43.0	29%	62%	9%	0%	24.6	25.0	65.6
1969	.825	6,107	23.7	32	57	11	0	21.0	25.0	60.1
1970	.720	5,152	16.4	29	52	16	3	23.1	33.4	62.5
1971	.747	4,608	12.6	32	49	17	2	24.3	33.1	71.4
1972	.869	4,801	16.7	34	51	14	1	21.4	33.8	85.0
1973	.766	4,040	16.7	41	44	14	1	18.9	44.5	72.5
1974	.558	2,861	12.5	48	33	16	3	13.5	50.1	53.3
1975	.606	2,297	11.8	48	27	23	2	13.3	41.4	73.1
1976	.690	2,276	20.0	52	26	20	2	15.1	40.4	90.6
1977	.606	2,224	21.9	54	26	18	2	13.8	40.9	84.1
1978	.582	2,106	34.2	46	30	23	1	14.3	46.2	89.6
1979	.675	2,128	43.5	53	26	20	1	14.3	49.9	106.1
1980	.732	1,889	44.3	47	31	21	1	15.2	49.9	140.5
1981	.671	2,395	82.6	42	34	23	1	15.6	48.0	133.6
1982	.705	2,346	53.8	37	29	31	2	13.9	47.4	162.2
1983	.700	2,533	73.1	32	35	33	0	16.7	37.7	198.7

SOURCE: Von Furstenberg (1977, Table 1, pp. 354–355 and correspondence) and Grimm (1983, p. 100).

1. "Merger Mania and the High Turnover Premiums," *The Wall Street Journal*, July 20, 1981. Reprinted by permission of *The Wall Street Journal* © Dow Jones & Company, Inc., 1981. All rights reserved.

There are reasons to suspect that, in many cases, increasingly high premiums may be a rational response to current economic signals. [There] is a common perception that stock prices in many industries are so low that assets can be bought on the cheap through acquisition. Perhaps the most dramatic evidence on an economy-wide basis is a series of statistics compiled by the Council of Economic Advisors and known as Tobin's *q*. One might expect the ratio to be at least 1:1, as it was during most of the 1960s. Since 1972, however, it has dropped steeply. . . .

On the denominator side, the declining *q* ratio reflects the accelerating costs of new plant and equipment in a period of high inflation. On the numerator side, the decline reflects the havoc wrought on share prices by high inflation combined with high rates of corporate and personal taxation, all in a period of increasing economic volatility and decreasing forecasting confidence. The decline in the *q* ratio might also be partly attributed to the growth of major liabilities that aren't recorded on balance sheets.

Whatever the reasons, the decline in the ratio means that it is often as cheap to pay twice the market price for an existing company as to construct one's own assets. This might give a special impetus to natural resource acquisitions; fuel or mineral reserves are threatened less by technological obsolescence than are manufacturing facilities.

2. "The Q-ratio: Fuel for the Merger Mania," *Business Week*, August 24, 1981.

What is gripping Wall Street is not merger mania but what might be called "Q-mania." The Q-ratio relates the market value of a company's physical assets to the cost of replacing those assets.

When stock prices are low and Q is less than 1, companies are not inclined to invest much because the markets are saying that each dollar plowed back into the company is worth less than a dollar in the revenue returns that it can generate. The market's message is that the company would be better off buying financial assets such as Treasury bills or distributing profits to its stockholders.

But a low Q has perhaps an even more important effect: It makes it much cheaper for companies to merge or to acquire the physical assets of other companies rather than make new capital investments. Thus, while the stock market is in the doldrums and capital investment is flagging, merger activity is booming. And the current merger boom, say economists, is largely the result of the unprecedented low value of Q.

3. "How Much Is a Company Worth?" 1984 semiannual report of the Acorn Fund.

Corporate takeovers are fueled by a divergence in stock valuation between two different valuation models (Dividend Discount Model and Replacement cost of Individual Net Assets Model). Security analysis techniques frequently generate low values compared to the asset values which business executives place on a company, and the exciting part for stockholders is when a stock pops up from a depressed price to a takeover price.

Most security analysts use a version of a Dividend Discount Model to make valuation judgments about stocks. A Dividend Discount Model uses the metaphor that a stock is nothing but a financial claim on the future dividend stream of a company, rather in the same way that a bond is valued as the present value of a future income stream of the bond. Because the Dividend Discount Model is related to bond values, this model uses the current interest rate as a key input, and as interest rates rise, the model says that the stock values must drop. Our Dividend Discount Model currently says that the stock market as a whole is worth about eight-times earnings. If you prefer to talk about a price-to-book value ratio instead of a price-earnings ratio, the market's worth is close to stated book value (book value is defined as total assets minus all liabilities; since plant and equipment assets are carried at a depreciated cost, in an inflationary period book value understates the replacement value of assets).

Businessmen, using a different metaphor, tend to think about corporate assets in terms of their replacement cost. They compare the cost of buying an existing factory with the cost of building a new one, and in many cases, the comparison favors buying the existing plant. For instance, Worthington Industries is a steel processing company. They were pleased to buy National Rolling Mills. For $20 million, Worthington bought a mill with a replacement value of $68 million. By buying an existing facility, they brought in trained employees, management, and customers. The National Rolling Mill product line makes a good fit for Worthington, extending their market into thin-gauge steel sheet. Manufacturers like to buy an operating factory instead of building a new mill for themselves because they gain market share without increasing industry capacity. The problem with increasing industry capacity is it might put downward pressure on prices and profits. Finally, by buying an existing plant, Worthington is able to be in business immediately, avoiding years of the construction cycle.

REQUIRED

1. Comment on the extracts and the potential role of the q ratio in explaining differences over time in merger and acquisition activity.

2. The estimates of the replacement cost of assets underlying the q ratio series in Table 13.9 are derived by applying indexes of replacement cost to data for aggregates of firms. Discuss the pros and cons of this approach to developing the q ratio index vis-à-vis an approach based on estimating a q ratio for each firm and then averaging these individual q ratios.

3. Why might the q ratio of a firm diverge from unity (1.0)?

4. What factors could explain the behavior of the q ratio series in Table 13.9 over the 1968–1983 period?

5. Design an empirical test to examine the relative importance of the "cheaper to acquire on Wall Street than build from scratch" motive (vis-à-vis other motives) in explaining differences over time in merger and acquisition activity.

REFERENCES

Asquith, P. "Merger Bids, Uncertainty, and Stockholder Returns." *Journal of Financial Economics* (April 1983): 85–119.

Baker, H. K., T. O. Miller, and B. J. Ramsperger. "A Typology of Merger Motives." *Akron Business and Economic Review* (Winter 1981): 24–29.

Bartley, J. W., and C. M. Boardman. "The Use of SFAS 33 Data to Identify Investment and Takeover Targets," working paper. University of Utah, Salt Lake City, 1983.

Bartley, J. W., and C. M. Boardman. "The Replacement-Cost Adjusted Valuation Ratio as a Discriminator Among Takeover Target and Nontarget Firms," working paper. University of Utah, Salt Lake City, 1984.

Belkaoui, A. "Financial Ratios as Predictors of Canadian Takeovers." *Journal of Business Finance & Accounting* (Spring 1978): 93–107.

Benston, G. J. *Conglomerate Mergers: Causes, Consequences and Remedies.* American Enterprise Institute for Public Policy Research, Washington, D.C.: 1980.

Boisjoly, R. P., and T. M. Corsi. "A Profile of Motor Carrier Acquisitions 1976 to 1978." *Akron Business and Economic Review* (Summer 1982): 30–35.

Bradley, M., A. Desai, and E. H. Kim. "Specialized Resources in the Market for Corporate Control: The Case of Tender Offers," working paper. University of Michigan, Ann Arbor, 1982.

Bradley, M., A. Desai, and E. H. Kim. "The Rationale Behind Interfirm Tender Offers: Information or Synergy?" *Journal of Financial Economics* (April 1983): 183–206.

Bradley, M., and L. M. Wakeman. "The Wealth Effects of Targeted Share Repurchases." *Journal of Financial Economics* (April 1983): 301–328.

Chappell, H. W., and D. C. Cheng. "Firms' Acquisition Decisions and Tobin's q Ratio." *Journal of Economics and Business* (February 1984): 29–42.

Dann, L. Y., and H. DeAngelo. "Standstill Agreements, Privately Negotiated Stock Repurchases, and the Market for Corporate Control." *Journal of Financial Economics* (April 1983): 275–300.

DeAngelo, H., L. DeAngelo, and E. M. Rice. "Going Private: Minority Freezeouts and Stockholder Wealth," working paper. University of Rochester, New York, 1982.

Dietrich, J. K., and E. Sorensen. "An Application of Logit Analysis to Prediction of Merger Targets." *Journal of Business Research* (September 1984): 393–402.

Dodd, P. "Company Takeovers and the Australian Equity Market." *Australian Journal of Management* (October 1976): 15–35.

Dodd, P. "Merger Proposals, Management Discretion and Stockholder Wealth." *Journal of Financial Economics* (June 1980): 105–137.

DODD, P. "The Market for Corporate Control: A Review of the Evidence." *Midland Corporate Finance Journal* (Summer 1983): 6–20.

ECKBO, B. E. "Horizontal Mergers, Collusion, and Stockholder Wealth." *Journal of Financial Economics* (April 1983): 241–273.

EGER, C. E. "An Empirical Test of the Redistribution Effect in Pure Exchange Mergers." *Journal of Financial and Quantitative Analysis* (December 1983): 547–572.

GRIMM, & Co. W. T. *Mergerstat Review 1983*. Chicago: W. T. Grimm & Co., 1984.

HARRIS, R. S., J. F. STEWART, D. K. GUILKEY, and W. T. CARLETON. "Characteristics of Acquired Firms: Fixed and Random Coefficients Probit Analyses." *Southern Economic Journal* (July 1982): 164–184.

HITE, G. L., and J. E. OWERS. "Security Price Reactions Around Corporate Spin-Off Announcements." *Journal of Financial Economics* (December 1983): 409–436.

JENSEN, M. C., and R. S. RUBACK. "The Market for Corporate Control: The Scientific Evidence." *Journal of Financial Economics* (April 1983): 5–50.

LAMBERT, R. A., and D. F. LARCKER. "Executive Compensation Effects of Large Corporate Acquisitions," working paper. Northwestern University, Evanston, Ill., 1984.

LEV, B., "Observations on the Merger Phenomenon and a Review of the Evidence." *Midland Corporate Finance Journal* (Winter 1983): 6–28.

LINN, S. C., and M. S. ROZEFF. "The Effect of Voluntary Divestiture on Stock Prices: Sales of Subsidiaries," working paper. University of Iowa, Iowa City, 1984.

MEEKS, G. *Disappointing Marriage: A Study of the Gains from Merger*. Cambridge: Cambridge University Press, 1977.

MUELLER, D. C. "A Cross-National Comparison of the Results." In D. C. Mueller, ed., *The Determinants and Effects of Mergers,* pp. 299–314. Cambridge, Mass.: Oelgeschlager, Gunn & Hain, 1980.

PALEPU, K. "The Determinants of Acquisition Likelihood," working paper. Harvard University, Cambridge, Mass., 1985a.

PALEPU, K. "Predicting Takeover Targets: A Methodological and Empirical Analysis," working paper. Harvard University, Cambridge, Mass., 1985b.

REGE, U. P. "Accounting Ratios to Locate Take-over Targets." *Journal of Business Finance and Accounting* (Autumn 1984): 301–311.

RUBACK, R. S. "The Conoco Takeover and Stockholder Returns." *Sloan Management Review* (Winter 1982): 13–33.

RUBACK, R. S. "The Cities Service Takeover: A Case Study." *The Journal of Finance* (May 1983): 319–330.

SCHIPPER, K., and A. SMITH. "Effects of Recontracting on Shareholder Wealth: The Case of Voluntary Spin-offs." *Journal of Financial Economics* (December 1983): 437–467. Published by North-Holland Publishing Company, Amsterdam, 1983.

SIMKOWITZ, M., and R. J. MONROE. "A Discriminant Analysis Function for Conglomerate Targets." *Southern Journal of Business* (November 1971): 1–16.

STILLMAN, R. "Examining Antitrust Policy Towards Horizontal Mergers. *Journal of Financial Economics* (April 1983): 225–240.

VON FURSTENBERG, G. M. "Corporate Investment: Does Market Valuation Matter in the Aggregate?" *Brooking Papers on Economic Activity* 2 (1977): 347–397.

WANSLEY, J. W., R. L. ROENFELDT, and P. L. COOLEY. "Abnormal Returns from Merger Profiles." *Journal of Financial and Quantitative Analysis* (June 1983): 149–162.

WESTON, J. F., and K. S. CHUNG. "Do Mergers Make Money?" *Mergers & Acquisitions* (Fall 1983): 40–48.

14

DEBT RATINGS, DEBT SECURITIES, AND FINANCIAL INFORMATION

14.1 INTRODUCTION

Debt securities cover a broad range of borrowing instruments used by companies, municipalities, and governments and their agencies. This chapter discusses two areas where financial statement information can play an important role in the analysis of debt securities: (1) in the rating of debt securities by agencies such as Moody's and Standard & Poor's and (2) in the pricing of debt securities by the capital market.

14.2 RATINGS OF DEBT SECURITIES

A. Descriptions of Debt Ratings

Ratings for the debt securities of many companies, municipalities, or governments are issued by at least five firms in the United States and by a smaller number of firms in each of several other countries. Table 14.1 presents summary information pertaining to a selected set of firms publishing ratings of debt securities. ''In-house'' debt-rating systems have also been developed by several banks and other financial advisory firms; see Hawkins, Brown, and Campbell (1983, pp. 105–130).

Firms differ in the wording used to describe what a rating represents. For example,

- Ratings are designed exclusively for the purpose of grading bonds according to their investment qualities.   Moody's (1984, p. 2)
- A Standard & Poor's corporate or municipal debt rating is a current assessment of the credit worthiness of an obligor with respect to a specific obligation.   Standard & Poor's (1984, p. 10)
- A corporate credit rating provides lenders with a simple system of gradation by which the relative capacities of companies to make timely repayment of interest and principal on a particular type of debt can be noted.   Australian Ratings (1984, p. 2).

As a generalization, a debt rating is an indicator of the likelihood of timely repayment of principal and interest by a borrower. The more likely the borrower will repay both the principal and interest, in accordance with the time schedule in the borrowing agreement, the higher will be the rating assigned to the debt security. Table 14.2 presents the descriptions that Standard & Poor's provides for the ten categories it uses to rate corporate and municipal debt. These descriptions (and the gradations they represent) are representative of those available from several other firms.

TABLE 14.1 Summary Data on Selected Debt Rating Firms

Rating Firm	No. of Full-Time Analysts	Institutions Whose Issues Rated		Major Corporate Issues Rated	Bond Rating Categories
Duff & Phelps, Chicago Since 1974	60 (cover equity and debt issues)	Companies Municipalities Countries	500 0 2	Bonds Preferred stock Commerical paper	1, 2, 3, . . . , 16, 17
Fitch Investors Services, New York Since 1922	23	Companies Municipalities Countries	550 55 6	Bonds Preferred stock Commerical paper	AAA, AA, A, BBB, BB, B, CCC, CC, C, DDD, DD, D
McCarthy, Crisanti & Maffei, New York Since 1978	16	Companies Municipalities Countries	500 0 0	Bonds Preferred stock Short-term debt	AAA, AA, A, BBB, BB, B, DP, DD
Moody's Investors Services, New York Since 1909	175	Companies Municipalities Countries	2,000 13,000 12	Bonds Preferred stock Commercial paper	Aaa, Aa, A, Baa, Ba, B, Caa, Ca, C, D
Standard & Poor's, New York Since 1923	220	Companies Municipalities Countries	2,000 8,000 13	Bonds Preferred stock Commercial paper	AAA, AA, A, BBB, BB, B, CCC, CC, C, D
Australian Ratings, Melbourne Since 1981	7	Companies Municipalities Countries	250 15 0	Bonds Commercial paper Unsecured debt	AAA, AA, A, BBB, BB, B, CCC, CC, C
Canadian Bond Rating Service, Montreal Since 1972	5	Companies Municipalities Countries	250 175 0	Bonds Preferred shares Commercial paper	A++, A+, A, B++, B+, B, C, D, S
Dominion Bond Rating Service, Toronto Since 1976	5½	Companies Municipalities Countries	200 0 0	Bonds Preferred shares Commercial paper	AAA, AA, A, BBB, BB, B, CCC, CC, C
Mikuni & Co., Tokyo Since 1983	8	Companies Municipalities Countries	638 0 1	Bonds	AAA, AA, A, BBB, BB, B, CCC, CC, C, D
Simon & Coates/Extel, London Since 1978	Quantitative model	Companies Municipalities Countries	500 0 0	Debentures Loan stocks	A, B, C, D, E

SOURCE: Correspondence with firms (January–February 1985).

499

TABLE 14.2 Standard & Poor's Corporate and Municipal Debt-Rating Definitions

AAA. Debt rated AAA has the highest rating assigned by Standard & Poor's. Capacity to pay interest and repay principal is extremely strong.

AA. Debt rated AA has a very strong capacity to pay interest and repay principal and differs from the higher-rated issues only in small degree.

A. Debt rated A has a strong capacity to pay interest and repay principal although it is somewhat more susceptible to the adverse effects of changes in circumstances and economic conditions than debt in higher-rated categories.

BBB. Debt rated BBB is regarded as having an adequate capacity to pay interest and repay principal. Whereas it normally exhibits adequate protection parameters, adverse economic conditions or changing circumstances are more likely to lead to a weakened capacity to pay interest and repay principal for debt in this category than in higher-rated categories.

BB, B, CCC, CC. Debt rated BB, B, CCC, and CC is regarded, on balance, as predominantly speculative with respect to capacity to pay interest and repay principal in accordance with the terms of the obligation. BB indicates the lowest degree of speculation and CC the highest degree of speculation. While such debt will likely have some quality and protective characteristics, these are outweighed by large uncertainties or major risk exposures to adverse conditions.

C. The rating C is reserved for income bonds on which no interest is being paid.

D. Debt rated D is in default, and payment of interest and/or repayment of principal is in arrears.

Plus (+) or Minus (−). The ratings from "AA" to "B" may be modified by the addition of a plus or minus sign to show relative standing within the major rating categories.

Source: Standard & Poor's, *Bond Guide* (January 1985, p. 10).

Increasing attention is being given to the default rate experience of corporate debt, in part because of the publicity given in the financial press to debt rated below BBB or Baa. (Debt rated below BBB or Baa has been called variously high-yield, low-grade, or junk debt.) Altman and Nammacher (1985) present the following statistics (derived from prior studies plus their own analysis) for corporate debt default rates:

1900–1909	.90%	1930–1939	3.20%	1960–1967	.03%
1910–1919	2.00	1940–1949	.40	1968–1977	.16
1920–1929	1.00	1950–1959	.04	1978–1984	.07

Altman and Nammacher also report that few defaults occurred for debt rated in the top four investment-grade categories; "out of 130 defaulting issues from the 15-year period 1970–1984, only four had a rating of BBB/Baa or higher six months prior to default" (p. 3). Focusing on low-rated debt (less than BBB or Baa), they report that in the 1974–1984 period, the default rate ranged "from .155 of 1% in 1981 to 4.488% in 1977, with the average annual rate being 1.60% of par value" (p. 6). Other studies on low-grade bonds include Blume and Keim (1984) and Drexel, Burnham, and Lambert (1985).

Although most rating agencies stress that a mechanical relationship between financial ratios and debt ratings does not exist, systematic patterns in the average ratios of different rating categories are observable. For instance, Standard & Poor's (1983a, p. 26) reports the following averages for the financial ratios of industrial companies whose debt is rated in the AAA to BBB categories:

	AAA	AA	A	BBB
Pretax interest coverage	14.44	7.61	5.47	3.26
Cash flow/long-term debt	2.51	1.10	.68	.39
Pretax return on average long-term capital employed	.290	.249	.197	.160
Operating income/sales	.166	.144	.124	.096
Long-term debt/capitalization	.116	.196	.257	.359

Other factors considered by rating agencies include the provisions of indenture agreements, the protection afforded by existing assets, and the quality of management.

B. Function of Debt Ratings

At least six functions have been attributed to debt ratings (or debt rating firms):

1. *Superior information source on the ability of corporations, municipalities, or governments to make timely repayment of principal and interest on borrowings.* This superiority could arise from greater ability to analyze public information or from access to confidential information. (Some parties disclose confidential information to rating firms on the condition that its confidentiality be respected.)

2. *Low-cost source of credit information pertaining to a broad cross section of firms, municipalities, and governments.* The gathering of information about numerous firms, municipalities, or governments can be a very costly activity. For many investors, it is cost effective to have a single agency collect, process, and summarize this information in a readily interpretable format (such as a nine-point rating scale).

3. *Source of "legal insurance" for an investment trustee.* By restricting investments to debt securities in only the highest-rated categories (for example, BBB and above), a trustee can reduce exposure to legal suits claiming mismanagement of investment funds. (This "legal insurance" operates via increasing the costs of third parties proving mismanagement.)

4. *Source of additional certification of the financial and other representations of managements.* When a debt rating firm assigns a given rating, its own reputation is at risk. The rating firm has an incentive to pursue, with the institution whose debt securities are being rated, concerns as to the completeness or timeliness of the financial statements and other data on which the ratings are based. In this context, the rating firm can serve as certifier on the quality of information provided by the issuer of a rated debt security. (As discussed in Chapter 1, external auditors also perform a certification role.)

5. *Monitor of the actions of management.* Chapter 1 describes conflicts of interest that may arise between management and other parties. Management that intends not to take actions at variance with the interests of shareholders

or bondholders has an incentive to hire a body such as a debt rating agency. The hiring itself is a signal that management is prepared to expose its actions to external scrutiny.

6. *Facilitate a public policy that restricts speculative investments by institutions such as banks, insurance companies, and pension funds.* The social costs can be high when such institutions become bankrupt. To reduce the likelihood of bankruptcy, legislation or regulations exist in some countries that preclude such institutions investing in debt securities that are "distinctively or predominantly speculative." One means of implementing this public policy is to use debt ratings as a means of distinguishing nonspeculative from speculative investments. For example, a U.S. Bank Examination Procedure (quoted in *Moody's Investor Service* publications) restricts bank investments to Group 1 securities: "Group 1 securities . . . includes general market obligations in the four highest [rating] grades and unrated securities of equivalent value."

There is no unanimity about the relative importance of these (and possibly other) functions of debt rating services. For instance, whereas the rating firms themselves (not unexpectedly) argue that the superior information source function is important, some others view it as nonexistent. For example, Wakeman (1981) comments that "rating change announcements provide no new information to the capital markets" (p. 19). He argues that rating firms perform the following functions: "They attest to the relative quality of the bond issue and to the accuracy of the accompanying information about the issuing company; and they further monitor that bond's risk over the life of the bond" (p. 22).

C. Quantitative Models of Debt Ratings

Models developed to predict the ratings assigned to debt securities have generally taken the following form:

$$Z_i = f(X_{i1}, X_{i2}, \ldots, X_{in}) \tag{14.1}$$

where

Z_i = rating assigned to debt security i

X_{ij} = value of the jth variable pertaining to debt security i

Discriminant analysis is the statistical technique used most frequently for estimating (14.1). The appendix to this chapter discusses and illustrates discriminant analysis. Readers not familiar with this technique should read this appendix before proceeding.

Models to explain or predict debt ratings can be useful to the rating agencies themselves. It is important to these agencies that there be consistency at a point in time of the ratings assigned to individual debt issues. The incorporation of a model into the rating process is one way of reducing inconsistencies across individual ratings. The model could be used in an initial stage of the analysis to form a preliminary rating of the debt issue. Then individual raters could exercise judgment on factors or interrelationships not captured by the model to decide the final rating of the debt issue. Moreover, the model could provide important information to rating agencies on the judgment process of their raters. It is a frequent finding in the human judgment literature that individuals overestimate the weight actually given to minor cues and underestimate the weight given to major cues; see Slovic and Lichtenstein (1971) and Slovic, Lichtenstein, and Fischhoff (1983). Developing a model that examines whether this finding occurs for the judgment of debt-security raters could provide valuable information when deciding on the scope of, and variables examined in, future rating engagements. Finally, a bond rating model can also be useful to agencies in their ongoing activity of reevaluating currently rated debt issues. The model could be used as a screening device to signal changing economic conditions of companies, municipalities, or governments.

Rating models can also be important to investors. Not all debt securities are rated by firms such as those described in Table 14.1. For example, a sizable number of privately placed debt issues are not rated. A quantitative model such as (14.1) could be useful in screening which private placements have investment value equivalent to those in the higher rating grades. (A problem could arise in using a model estimated with rated bonds to predict the ratings of privately placed bonds, if there are substantive economic differences between the two groups of bonds, that is, if there is a self-selection bias in having as an estimation sample only those companies which applied for a rating.)

Another use of a debt-security rating model is to highlight to management those variables that are (or are correlated with those that are) important to rating firms. Management can then factor into their decisions the likely consequences for their debt-security ratings of alternative actions they are considering (for example, whether to acquire another firm via a debt-financed cash offer or via an equity offer).

One of the problems in developing quantitative models in this area is selecting the set of independent variables. An explicit and testable statement of what a bond rating represents, or of the variables that should be examined, is not provided in this literature or by rating firms. Not surprisingly, there is much diversity across studies developing quantitative models in their approaches to variable selection. Ideally, there should be some underlying "economic rationale" for the variables included in the model. One has more confidence that variables will possess some predictive value when there is such a rationale for their inclusion.

Although most bonding rating schemes are judgmental, a subset are directly based on quantitative models. For instance, Simon and Coates (1980) give the following details of their British Bond Rating Service (BBRS):

> The ratings are based upon objective criteria, and subjective criteria have been excluded. To this extent, the system must be regarded as simplified and not all-embracing. In judging the yield appropriate to a given bond the investor will also

need to consider factors not built into the system. The ratings contain no element of judgment or opinion on the part of Simon & Coates, their servants or agents. . . . The financial information within this service is collected and analysed, on our behalf, by Extel Statistical Services Ltd. (p. i)

The variables examined in the BBRS service include company size, a leverage ratio, and an interest coverage ratio. Many of the "in-house" debt rating systems described in Hawkins, Brown, and Campbell (1983) likewise rely exclusively on quantitative models to derive individual debt-security ratings.

D. Quantitative Models of Corporate Debt Ratings

For many years, rating firms focused on corporate bond and municipal bond securities. With the increasing diversity of corporate debt securities, ratings for a broader set of debt securities are now issued. For example, securities rated by Moody's include corporate bonds, convertible bonds, commercial paper, medium-term notes, and preferred stock. This section illustrates rating models of corporate debt securities via a discussion of Belkaoui's (1983) study of the bond ratings of industrial companies.

Bond Ratings of Industrials

The bond ratings examined in Belkaoui (1983) included an estimation sample of 266 industrial bonds and a validation sample of 115 industrial bonds, all rated B or above by Standard & Poor's in 1981. Nine independent variables were used in a linear multiple discriminant analysis model:

X_1 = Total assets

X_2 = Total debt

X_3 = Long-term debt/total invested capital

X_4 = Short-term debt/total invested capital

X_5 = Current assets/current liabiities

X_6 = Fixed charge coverage ratio

X_7 = Five-year cash flow divided by five-year sum of (1) capital expenditure, (2) change in inventories during most recent five years, and (3) common dividends

X_8 = Stock price/common equity per share

X_9 = Subordination (0–1 dummy variable), 1 if the bond being rated is subordinated (that is, ranked lower in security) to other debt issues

These variables were selected by Belkaoui, based on an analysis of the variables that determine "the investment quality of a bond" (p. 90). (Prior research had indicated the X_9 variable to be highly important; see, for example, Pinches and Mingo, 1975). One benchmark rule used in prior research was that when a firm has both subordinated and nonsubordinated bonds, the subordinated bond is rated one grade lower than the nonsubordinated bond.)

The classification matrices for the estimation and validation samples in Belkaoui (1983) are in Table 14.3. For the estimation sample, the discriminant model correctly classifies 72.9% (194/266) of the bond ratings. In the validation sample, the model correctly classifies 67.8% (78/115) of the bond ratings. Both percentages are significantly greater than the percentages expected by chance alone.

These percentages of correct classification compare favorably with those reported in prior studies of industrial bond ratings. For example,

- Horrigan (1966) reported a 58% success rate for 70 bonds rated by Moody's and a 52% success rate for 60 bonds rated by Standard & Poor's in the 1961–1964 period

- Pinches and Mingo (1973) reported a 65% success rate in classifying a validation sample of 48 bonds rated by Moody's in the 1967–1968 period

- Kaplan and Urwitz (1979) reported a 71% success rate in classifying a validation sample of 67 bonds rated by Moody's in the 1971–1972 period.

TABLE 14.3 Actual and Predicted Ratings for Industrial Bonds

		\multicolumn{7}{c}{*Panel A. Estimation sample of 266 industrial bonds*}
		\multicolumn{7}{c}{*Actual Rating*}
		AAA	*AA*	*A*	*BBB*	*BB*	*B*	*Total*
Predicted	AAA	10	6	1	1	0	0	18
Rating	AA	2	38	10	1	0	0	51
	A	1	7	90	12	0	0	110
	BBB	0	0	10	28	2	0	40
	BB	0	0	1	6	5	8	20
	B	0	0	0	3	2	22	27
	Total	13	51	112	51	9	30	266

		\multicolumn{7}{c}{*Panel B. Validation sample of 115 industrial bonds*}
		\multicolumn{7}{c}{*Actual Rating*}
		AAA	*AA*	*A*	*BBB*	*BB*	*B*	*Total*
Predicted	AAA	2	5	0	0	0	0	7
Rating	AA	4	12	0	0	0	0	16
	A	0	0	25	3	0	0	28
	BBB	0	0	0	21	4	0	25
	BB	0	0	10	6	13	2	31
	B	0	0	0	0	3	5	8
	Total	6	17	35	30	20	7	115

SOURCE: Excerpted from Ahmed Belkaoui, *Industrial Bonds and the Rating Process,* Quorum Books, a Division of Greenwood Press, Westport, CT, 1983. Used with permission of the publisher. Exhibits 4.8 and 4.9, pp 104–105.

All three studies and Belkaoui (1983) report much higher percent-correct classifications when the criterion is "predict within one rating class" of the actual rating class. For instance, using this criterion, the success rate in Belkaoui (1983) is 96.2% for the estimation sample and 91.3% for the validation sample.

Other Debt Securities

The foregoing methodology has also been applied to other debt securities. For example, Peavy and Edgar (1983) examined the 1980 ratings by Moody's of the commercial paper of 83 bank holding companies. A five-variable linear model was used to predict commercial paper ratings; the five variables were (1) net income, (2) common stockholder equity/total assets, (3) growth rate of assets in last five years, (4) return on equity, and (5) reserves for loan losses/loans. This model was able to predict the actual Moody rating category with an 88% success rate. (This percentage is for a validation sample, based on the Lachenbruch procedure. Under this procedure, each observation is held out and classified by the discriminant function formed using the remaining observations.) A related study is Peavy and Edgar's (1984) analysis of the commercial paper ratings of 244 industrial firms.

E. Quantitative Models of Municipal Debt Ratings

The debt securities issued by municipalities fall into two main categories:

1. *General obligation bonds*. These bonds are issued by a governmental unit that has the power to levy taxes. They are secured by the issuers' unconditional promise to pay the principal and interest expense payments in a timely manner. General obligation bonds mandate the issuer to use its ability to levy taxes for the repayment of the bonds. Variables said to be important in rating these bonds include the debt burden of the governmental unit, the breadth and viability of its economic base, the quality of its administration, and the current and prospective revenues of the unit.

2. *Revenue bonds*. These typically are issued to finance a project that will generate income (for example, an airport, bridge, housing development, tollway, or an electric power plant). The revenue generated by the project is used to pay the interest and principal on the bond. Variables said to be important in rating these bonds include the expected revenues of the project and the quality of its management.

Quantitative models of muncipal bonds have concentrated on the general obligation bonds of local government units. This section illustrates rating models of municipal securities via a discussion of Raman's (1982) study of the ratings of 236 U.S. cities. Raman examined a sample of 236 U.S. cities (population 50,000 and above) in Moody's four highest-rating categories that had their ratings unchanged in the 1975–1979 period. The independent variables, chosen based on an analysis of the municipal bond-rating literature, were

$$X_1 = \text{General obligation debt per capita}$$

$X_2 = $ General obligation debt to general revenues

$X_3 = $ Short-term debt to general revenues

$X_4 = $ Log of per-capita income

$X_5 = $ Net change in working capital from operations

$X_6 = $ Net change in working capital from all sources

$X_7 = $ General revenues from own sources to general revenues

$X_8 = $ Property taxes to general revenues

$X_9 = $ Log of general obligation debt outstanding

$X_{10} = $ Log of gross debt outstanding

Table 14.4 presents the classification matrix for the 1977–1978 ratings reported in the study. (These classification rates are based on the Lachenbruch technique). The overall classification success rate in 1977–1978 was 54.5%. For other years, this figure range from 51.3% to 55.6%. In each period examined, the success rate was significantly higher than that expected by chance.

The classification success rates in several other studies of general obligation municipal bond ratings are

- Carleton and Lerner (1969) reported a 35% success rate in classifying a validation sample of 200 general obligation bonds rated Aaa to Ba by Moody's in 1967
- Michel (1977) reported a 58% success rate in classifying a validation sample of 225 general obligation bonds of U.S. cities rated Aaa to Baa by Moody's in the 1967–1971 period
- Westcott (1984) reported a 58% success rate in classifying the bond ratings (Aaa to Baa) Moody's assigned to 110 cities in the 1972–1977 period.

TABLE 14.4 Actual and Predicted Ratings for General Obligation Bond Ratings of U.S. Cities

		Actual Rating				
		Aaa	Aa	A	Baa	Total
Predicted Rating	Aaa	11	8	1	0	20
	Aa	13	60	37	5	115
	A	4	33	55	6	98
	Baa	0	0	0	2	2
	Total	28	101	93	13	235

SOURCE: Raman (1982, Table 3, p. 151): Reprinted by Permission from the *Journal of Accounting Auditing and Finance,* Winter 1982. Published by Warren, Gorham & Lamont, Inc., 210 South St., Boston, MA. Copyright © 1982. All rights reserved.

The consistent finding in these and similar studies is that the classification success rates for quantitative models of municipal bond ratings are lower than are those for models of corporate bond ratings (see section 14.2.D).

Various explanations have been offered for the greater difficulty of modeling municipal bond ratings relative to corporate bond ratings:

1. Municipal bonds are more heterogeneous (for example, differences across samples in legal restrictions on repayment may be more marked than with corporate bonds)

2. Uniformity in financial reporting is at a lower level (for example, considerable diversity exists in how municipalities account for pension costs)

3. Financial reports for municipalities are of lower quality (for example, audited statements are less frequent and time delays more frequent with municipal reports)

4. Rating lag problems are more severe with municipals (that is, rating firms take a longer time to revise their ratings of municipals after underlying conditions have changed)

5. Rating firms are more inconsistent in rating municipal bonds than they are in rating corporate bonds.

At present, these and other explanations are best viewed as untested hypotheses for differences in the ability of models to predict the ratings of corporate and municipal bonds.

14.3 PRICING OF DEBT SECURITIES

A. Debt-Security Yields and Debt-Security Ratings

The current yield and the yield to maturity are two terms frequently used in the bond investment literature. The current yield of a bond is the coupon rate of the bond, expressed in dollars, divided by the current market price. Assume a 7% coupon bond (interest paid semiannually) with par value of $1,000, 30 years to maturity, and a current market price of $857. The current yield of this bond is

$$\frac{\$70}{\$857} = 8.17\%$$

This yield calculation is analogous to the dividend yield calculation for common stocks.

The yield to maturity of a bond is calculated to take the following into account: even though the above bond is selling for $857 now, it will be worth $1,000 at maturity. The yield to maturity is equivalent to the rate of interest, compounded semiannually, at which you would need to invest the $857 market price now to "guarantee" $35 every half-year and have $1,000 at the maturity date of the bond. In terms of present value calculations, it is the rate of interest that makes

Present value of $1,000, 30 years hence

+ present value of a 30-year semiannual annuity of $35 = $857.

For this bond, the yield to maturity is 8.3%. In practice, most calculations of yield to maturity are made by reference to a yield book. In Section 14.3.B, evidence on factors that determine differences in the yield to maturity of different bonds is examined.

An interesting issue is the relationship between debt-security ratings and debt-security yields. Empirically, they are highly correlated. Table 14.5 presents the average yield to maturity of industrial, public utility, and municipal bonds in each of Moody's top four rating classes over the 1975–1984 period. The lower average yields of municipals vis-à-vis industrials and public utilities reflect (in part) the tax-exempt feature of interest on municipal bonds. The general pattern in Table 14.5 is that the lower the debt rating, the higher the average yield of that category.

It is sometimes argued that the relationship between debt-security ratings and debt-security yields is a causal one. That is, the rating given a security will "determine within limits" the interest rate that an issuer must pay on the debt issue. An alternative explanation of the data in Table 14.5 is that debt ratings and debt yields are correlated because they are both influenced by the same underlying economic factors (for example, interest coverage and profitability of the company issuing the debt security). Section 14.4 discusses this correlation versus causality issue further.

B. Determinants of Differences in Corporate Bond Yields

The first detailed empirical analysis of factors explaining differences in corporate bond yields is Fisher (1959). To control for nonfirm factors that may influence bond yields, Fisher examined risk premiums rather than yields to maturity. "The risk premium on a bond . . . [is] the difference between its market yield to

TABLE 14.5 Rating Classes and Debt-Security Yield Averages

Year	Industrial Bonds				Public Utility Bonds				Municipal Bonds			
	Aaa	Aa	A	Baa	Aaa	Aa	A	Baa	Aaa	Aa	A	Baa
1975	8.51	8.99	9.23	10.33	9.07	9.51	10.11	10.79	6.50	6.94	7.78	7.96
1976	7.81	8.04	8.43	9.03	8.15	8.45	8.62	9.21	5.07	5.50	6.42	6.73
1977	8.04	8.25	8.49	8.90	8.34	8.55	8.64	9.08	5.07	5.23	5.46	5.79
1978	8.98	9.10	9.35	9.79	9.34	9.56	9.70	10.08	5.91	6.01	6.51	6.76
1979	10.51	10.82	11.12	11.61	10.96	11.47	11.79	12.51	6.50	6.69	6.89	7.42
1980	12.79	13.18	13.43	14.98	13.62	14.37	14.63	15.29	9.44	9.64	9.80	10.64
1981	13.93	14.77	15.21	16.07	14.52	15.23	16.29	17.02	11.70	12.16	12.60	13.30
1982	11.34	12.12	12.88	13.58	12.32	12.76	14.43	14.69	9.34	9.85	10.24	10.80
1983	12.14	12.36	12.88	13.27	13.00	13.14	13.52	14.23	9.34	9.58	10.08	10.29
1984	11.76	12.23	12.72	13.34	12.49	12.76	13.11	13.46	9.54	9.88	10.19	10.45

SOURCE: *Moody's Bond Record* (issues from 1976 to 1985).

maturity and the corresponding pure rate of interest" (p. 221). The pure rate of interest was defined as "the market yield on a riskless bond maturing on the same day as the bond under consideration" (p. 221). Both *default risk* and *marketability risk* were hypothesized to be the determinants of risk premiums. The three variables used as proxies for default risk were

X_1 = Earnings variability, measured as the coefficient of variation on earnings after tax of the most recent nine years

X_2 = Solvency, measured as the length of time since one of the following events occurred: "firm was founded, the firm emerged from bankruptcy, or a compromise was made in which creditors settled for less than 100% of their claims" (p. 224)

X_3 = Equity/debt ratio, measured as the "ratio of market value of the firm's equity to the par value of its debt" (p. 224)

The coefficient on X_1 was predicted to be positive whereas the coefficients on X_2 and X_3 were predicted to be negative. The variable used as a proxy for marketability risk was

X_4 = Total market value of the publicly traded bonds the firm has outstanding.

The coefficient on X_4 was predicted to be negative. Cross-section regressions were run for 71 firms in 1927, 45 firms in 1932, 89 firms in 1937, 73 firms in 1949, and 88 firms in 1953. Results when all 366 bonds were pooled were

$$Y_i = .987 + .307X_{1i} - 2.53X_{2i} - .537X_{3i} - .275X_{4i} \qquad \textbf{(14.2)}$$
$$t = 9.59 \quad t = -7.03 \quad t = -17.32 \quad t = -13.10$$

where Y_i = the risk premium of corporate bond i. All four variables were statistically significantly different from zero, and in the direction hypothesized. Moreover, the R^2 of (14.2) was .75, implying that the preceding variables explained considerable variation in risk premiums on bonds.

The variables examined by Fisher (1959) are a subset of those potentially important in explaining differences across securities in their yields. For instance, other variables could include the provisions in the bond indenture agreement (for example, subordination status) and the call status of the bond. An extension of Fisher's research on corporate bonds is provided in Johnson (1967). Little subsequent research on this topic appears to have been done.

C.   Determinants of Differences in Municipal Bond Yields

Regression analysis has also been used in research on municipal bond yields. Ingram and Copeland (1984) examined risk premiums on the general obligation bonds of 76 municipalities in the 1976–1979 period. The risk premium on each bond was the dependent variable; it was "derived by subtracting from the yield to maturity of each municipal issue a corresponding yield to maturity of a U.S.

Treasury bond with the same maturity and coupon characteristics'' (p. 24). The focus of their research was whether differences in financial ratios across municipalities could explain differences in the risk premiums on the bonds of those municipalities. The financial ratios examined as independent variables, the predicted sign of their coefficient in the regression, and the sign of their estimated coefficient were (from Table 4 and Table 8)

Financial Ratios Included as Independent Variables	Predicted Sign of Regression Coefficient	Estimated Sign of Regression Coefficient
1. Short-term debt/total revenue	+	−
2. Bond funds/total debt	−	−
3. Percentage change in long-term debt	+	+
4. Vital expenditures/total expenditures	+	−
5. Percentage change in personal expenditures	+	−
6. Total revenue per capita	+	+
7. Revenue mix	−	−
8. Property tax/total revenue	+	+
9. Total revenues/total expenditures	−	−
10. Percentage change in (revenue − expenditure)	−	−

These financial ''ratios were developed to capture different aspects of default and marketability risk. Each ratio demonstrates the potential effect of variations in economic conditions on a municipality's ability to generate resources and provide essential services while making timely payments on debt and interest'' (p. 29). The R^2 from the regression was .243. The authors concluded, ''This study provides evidence consistent with the contention that municipal accounting information can be useful to market participants'' (p. 35).

Each of the variables was derived from the financial statements of the municipality. An interesting extension would be to examine the effect on the R^2 of including variables not based on financial statements, for example, the default history of the municipality, and a measure of the diversification of the economic base of the municipality. Early research by Hastie (1972) would indicate that these, and other nonfinancial statement variables, could substantially increase the power of the model to explain differences in risk premiums across municipalities.

D. Determinants of Bond Prices and Bond Returns

Much recent research on bond securities has focused on bond prices or bond returns rather than on yields to maturity. Two factors found to be important determinants of corporate bond prices are

1. The time stream of the coupon payments on the bond
2. The characteristics of the bond (for example, current yield, the call provisions, the conversion provisions, and its liquidity).

An illustrative study is Boardman and McEnally's (1981) analysis of the prices of "515 randomly chosen seasoned corporate bonds at four different points in time—year-end 1972, 1973, 1974, and 1975" (p. 215). A separate regression was run for each of the Aaa, Aa, A, and Baa bond rating categories. The independent variables included

- Net present value of the coupon sequence
- Log of the market value of all bond issues outstanding (a measure of marketability)
- Bond beta (a measure of risk)
- Sinking fund dummy variable (1 = presence of a sinking fund/0 = absence)
- Security status dummy variable (1 = presence of a claim on assets/0 = absence)
- Exchange listing dummy variable (1 = traded over the counter, 0 = traded on major exchange)
- Industry dummy variable (1 = industrial bond, 0 = nonindustrial bond).

The explanatory power (R^2) of the variables in regressions for each year were

	1972	1973	1974	1975
Aaa bonds	.997	.998	.998	.997
Aa bonds	.983	.997	.971	.983
A bonds	.991	.988	.969	.971
Baa bonds	.982	.933	.895	.897

The authors noted that the lower explanatory power for Baa bonds "is consistent with the standard observation that lower-quality bonds are less homogeneous than those in the higher-quality groups" (p. 217).

At present, empirical research on debt securities has been hampered by the limited progress in modeling the pricing of debt securities. Overviews of research on such modeling include Courtadon and Merrick (1983) and Schaefer (1984). Models that link the price of a debt security to variables such as the call feature, the tax status of the interest coupons, and the covenants in the debt agreements are not well developed. Moreover, the trend in corporate finance is toward more rather than less heterogeneity in the debt securities issued by the firms. In addition, it is only in recent years that reliable data bases, covering large numbers of corporate or municipal securities, have become available. Relative to empirical research on equity securities, empirical research on debt securities is in its infancy and shows few signs of a rapid advancement to maturity.

14.4 SOME GENERAL COMMENTS

1. The criterion used in the literature to judge the success of quantitative models of debt-security ratings is their ability to predict the ratings assigned by

TABLE 14.6 Relative Timing of Rating Changes by Moody's and Standard & Poor's for Public Utility Bonds that Had Rating Changes by Both Firms in 1960–1979 Period

Total number of observations	133
Number of instances when Standard & Poor's changed rating earlier	58
Number of instances when Moody's changed rating earlier	53
Number of instances when both changed rating in same month	22
Average monthly timing difference for all changes	11.5 months
Median monthly timing difference for all changes	7 months

SOURCE: Altman, Avery, Eisenbeis, and Sinkey (1981, Table V. 2): p. 217.

firms such as Moody's or Standard & Poor's. Note, however, that the failure of a linear model to predict a bond rater's judgment may say as much about the consistency or quality of the rater's judgment as about any misspecification in the linear model. Some insight into this possibility is the frequency of the so-called mixed rating phenomenon (that is, when firms differ in the rating assigned to a specific debt issue). Table 14.6 presents data (from Altman et al., 1981) on the timing of rating changes on bonds changed by both Moody's and Standard & Poor's in the electric public utility sector from 1960 to 1979. Simultaneous rating changes by the two agencies took place in only 17% (22/133) of the cases examined. Inconsistency by individual raters and rating lag (that is, the failure of a rating firm to change its rating in a timely manner) are two possible explanations for this low percentage. Another explanation is access to differential information.

An alternative approach to evaluating quantitative models of debt-security ratings would be to select an observable event (for example, default on a debt security) and then compare the timing of rating revisions made by a rating firm with the rating revision implied by the quantitative model. (Ideally, the rating revision of a composite of the rating firm and the quantitative model would also be examined.) To date, this approach has not been used extensively in the literature. Note that this approach assumes that the ex post default rate is a good proxy for the ex ante unobservable default rate at the time of the rating.

2. The problem of operationalizing specific variables in debt-security rating models is often a difficult one. Consider modeling the terms of a bond indenture agreement. These agreements are reported to be important in bond rating. Given the numerous terms and covenants in these agreements and the diverse remedies provided for lack of compliance, devising a single variable (or set of variables) to capture differences across firms seems monumental. Not surprisingly, only the crudest modeling has been employed (for example, use of a dummy variable to

capture the subordination status of the bond). Consider also modeling the economic diversification of a municipality. This variable is frequently cited as important in municipal bond rating. The measure used to represent this variable in several studies (logarithm of the size of population) appears to be relatively crude. One can think of large municipalities heavily dependent on one industry, and smaller municipalities having at least four or five separate industries providing employment opportunities, taxation revenues, and so on. Yet, one important test, when evaluating these measures/proxies for variables, is whether models incorporating them led to better decisions than models excluding them. On this test, even crude measures of variables may be warranted in a specific decision context.

3. An interesting issue is whether the predictive ability of debt rating models can be improved by adjustments to the accounting principles used by companies or municipalities in their financial statements. Two studies, relating to adjustments in the pension accounting area, will be used to illustrate research; Martin and Henderson (1983) and Copeland and Ingram (1983).

Martin and Henderson (1983) examined the incremental explanatory power of variables relating to unfunded pension benefits in models of corporate bond rating. The sample was 129 industrial bonds rated B or above by Moody's in the 1979–1980 period. The basic model included five variables (four accounting ratios and a 0/1 dummy for the subordination status of the bond). This model correctly classified 50.4% of the bonds. The augmented model included the five variables in the basic model and five additional variables relating to pension accounting, for example, (a) unfunded past-service costs per employee and (b) pension-related debt equivalent to stockholder's equity. This augmented model correctly classified 54.3% of the bonds. Thus, the incremental explanatory power of the pension variables was minimal in this bond prediction context.

Copeland and Ingram (1983) reported a similar finding for predicting the ratings of 62 municipal general obligation bonds. The basic model had nine accounting ratios derived from the financial statements of each municipality. The classification success rate of the basic model was 56.5%. The augmented model included the nine accounting ratios and three additional pension variables, for example, (a) the ratio of pension receipts to pension payments and (b) total pension fund investment balance divided by the current total pension expenditure. The classification success rate of the augmented model was 61.3%. The authors concluded that "the pension ratios are associated with a marginal 4.8 percentage-point difference in the classificatory accuracy . . . ; an amount that is not significant at the 0.20 level" (p. 159).

There are several alternative explanations for the results in the Martin and Henderson (1983) and Copeland and Ingram (1983) studies: (a) pension accounting information is not relevant to classifying bonds into different rating categories; (b) pension accounting information is relevant, but the variables used in the studies include sizable measurement error; and (c) pension accounting information is relevant, but bond-rating firms have not yet incorporated this information into their rating decisions.

4. Two areas of financial reporting where there has been little systematic research are

a. Whether and how newly mandated disclosures are incorporated into the bond rating process

b. The recognition of and adjustments made by bond-rating agencies for off-balance-sheet financing by entities whose securities are being rated.

Statements made by rating agencies provide some insight into both areas. Consider the following statements by Standard & Poor's relating to mandated disclosures on changing prices and on the proved reserves of oil and gas companies:

- *Changing Prices:* A quantitative tool that S & P is beginning to use in evaluating earnings protection is the supplemental information on inflation and changing prices that public corporations are now required to report. For industrial companies, the current cost method, which attempts to adjust costs for changes in specific prices, is viewed as more useful than the constant dollar method. . . . It is especially interesting to compare current cost profits as a percentage of historical profits and price-adjusted returns on assets for companies in the same industry.   Standard & Poor's (1983a, p. 21)

- *Value-Based Disclosure of Proved Oil and Gas Reserves:* "Value" as a percentage of debt outstanding has become an important ratio. It provides a missing link by quantifying a previously subjective element. It recognizes that all reserves do not have the same value. . . . Smaller independent companies have benefited the most from increased disclosure. Some are now being accorded higher ratings to the extent their future cash flows show relative strength, which information was previously unavailable.   Standard & Poor's (1983b, p. 19)

Off-balance-sheet financing is frequently discussed by rating agencies. The following statements by Duff and Phelps in its *Credit Decisions* series are illustrative:

- Forms of off-balance-sheet financing that are currently in use include:
  1. The wholly or partly owned but unconsolidated subsidiary.
  2. Systematic sale of receivables to a third party.
  3. Production payments.
  4. Take or pay contracts.
  Failure to adjust [for the above] fouls the ratios that are so heavily relied upon in the quantitative part of credit analysis.   (March 26, 1984)

- Duff and Phelps usually adjusts the balance sheet to reflect off-balance-sheet obligations. For industrial companies, the most frequent adjustment is capitalizing operating leases, placing this figure on the balance sheet, and increasing fixed charges over those reported by the portion of operating lease payments estimated to be interest expense.   (November 26, 1984)

Research on quantitative models of bond rating decisions has yet to incorporate adjustments for off-balance-sheet financing into the variables examined.

5. There is dispute in the literature over whether debt-security ratings convey new information to capital market participants (that is, beyond that already in the public domain from other sources). One approach has been to examine

bond returns, bond yields, or stock returns at the time of announcements of rating changes. The assumption in this research is that no capital market reaction at the time of the rating change is consistent with the ratings conveying no new information. Studies to date have examined monthly data in the period surrounding the announcement of a rating change. A consistent set of findings has not emerged from this literature. Using monthly bond returns, Katz (1974) found evidence of a detectable immediate reaction to the announcement of a rating change. Katz also found that the adjustment continues for some time (an average of a six- to ten-week lag) after the announcement of the rating change. In contrast, Weinstein (1977) reported no bond price reaction at the time of a rating change and no postannouncement price adjustment. Pinches and Singleton (1978) and Griffin and Sanvicente (1982) report conflicting results for the impact of a bond rating change announcement on the monthly stock returns of the bond issuing company.

The problems of research in this area are many. For instance, most studies have focused on the announced rating changes of one firm (say, Moody's), without analysis of all the other firms that issue ratings on the debt security examined. What is termed a preannouncement for one rating firm may well be the announcement period of another rating firm. A second problem is that most announcement effect studies in this area have used monthly data, which increases the likelihood of other information releases creating noise in the research. At this stage, the unresolved issue is not what rating changes are likely to have the largest capital market effects, but rather whether any rating change announcements per se have a detectable effect on bond or stock returns.

14.5 SUMMARY

1. Firms rating debt securities are an important user of financial statement information. Published statements by these firms cite financial statement variables as key items examined in the debt rating process. Quantitative models of ratings also find financial statement variables to have significant ability to discriminate between debt securities in different rating categories.

2. The possible functions of debt security ratings and rating firms include the provision of superior or low-cost information about debt securities, the provision of legal insurance for an investment trustee, the certification of the financial and other representations of management, a monitor of the actions of management, and the facilitation of a public policy that restricts speculative investments by institutions such as insurance companies and pension funds.

3. Variables representing default risk and marketability have been found to explain significant differences across debt securities in their prices, returns, or yields. Other variables such as subordination status, tax, and call provisions also appear important in the pricing of debt securities. However, advances in our

understanding of these and other variables have been limited by the meager progress made in modeling debt securities, and by the slow development of extensive and reliable data bases on the prices or returns of debt securities.

APPENDIX 14.A   DISCRIMINANT ANALYSIS MODELING OF BOND RATINGS

Discriminant analysis is a classificatory technique that has a wide number of uses in financial analysis. This appendix illustrates the linear discriminant analysis technique. The following description is intended to convey some intuitive understanding of the technique. Several assumptions underlie the following example:

1. There are two discrete and known groups (Z_i)
2. Each observation in each group has a set of two characteristics (variables X_i and Y_i)
3. The two variables arise from multivariate normal populations. The variance/covariance matrix of the two variables is assumed to be the same for each group, but the means of the two variables in each group are different.

Given these assumptions, the following linear discriminant function can be used for classificatory purposes:

$$Z_i = aX_i + bY_i \qquad (14.A.1)$$

The analysis is restricted to a two-group/two-variable example for exposition. Research typically has examined n-group/m-variable contexts where $n > 2$ or $m > 2$.

The example used for illustrative purposes is the classification of ten municipal bonds into two groups: (1) those rated A or above by Moody's and (2) those rated Baa or below by Moody's. The two variables used in the analysis are

X_i = Assessed property valuation per capita of municipality i

Y_i = General obligation bonded debt per capita of municipality i

The ten municipalities, their values for the two variables, and the actual ratings for their general obligation bonds are detailed in Table 14.7. The municipalities used to estimate the discriminant function are termed the *estimation sample*. The steps in using a discriminant model are illustrated next.

Step One: Estimate Discriminant Function.   In the two-group case with the foregoing assumptions, the discriminant function that "best" distinguishes between the two groups is found by maximizing the ratio of the *between*-group sum of squares of the Z_i scores to the *within*-group sum of squares of the Z_i scores.

TABLE 14.7 Discriminant Analysis Example: Financial Data for Estimation Sample

Municipality	Assessed Property Valuation per Capita	General Obligation Bonded Debt per Capita	Moody's Bond Rating
1. Arlington, Mass.	$ 6,685	$116	Aa
2. Highland Park, Ill.	6,360	87	Aa
3. Springdale, Ohio	11,806	272	Aa
4. El Cerrito, Calif.	2,957	53	A
5. La Grange, Ga.	3,183	47	A
6. Pampa, Tex.	2,408	188	A
7. Coon Rapids, Minn.	2,703	613	Baa
8. Hot Springs, Ark.	1,212	43	Baa
9. Mauldin, S.C.	1,054	366	Baa
10. Pascagoula, Miss.	2,684	149	Baa

The coefficients of this function are calculated as follows:

$$a = \frac{\sigma_y^2 \cdot d_x - \sigma_{xy} \cdot d_y}{\sigma_x^2 \cdot \sigma_y^2 - \sigma_{xy} \cdot \sigma_{xy}} \tag{14.A.2}$$

$$b = \frac{\sigma_x^2 \cdot d_y - \sigma_{xy} \cdot d_x}{\sigma_x^2 \cdot \sigma_y^2 - \sigma_{xy} \cdot \sigma_{xy}} \tag{14.A.3}$$

where

σ_y^2 = variance of Y_i

σ_x^2 = variance of X_i

σ_{xy} = covariance of X_i with Y_i

d_x = difference between the mean X_i for group 1 and the mean X_i for group 2

d_y = difference between the mean Y_i for group 1 and the mean Y_i for group 2

For the data in Table 14.7,

$$\sigma_x^2 = \frac{1}{N-1} \sum (X_i - \overline{X})^2 = \$10,861,900$$

$$\sigma_y^2 = \frac{1}{N-1} \sum (Y_i - \overline{Y})^2 = \$32,790$$

$$\sigma_{xy} = \frac{1}{N-1} \sum (X_i - \overline{X})(Y_i - \overline{Y}) = -\$16,187$$

$$d_x = \$5,566 - \$1,913 = \$3,653$$

$$d_y = \$127 - \$292 = -\$165$$

Substituting these values in (14.A.2) and (14.A.3) yields

$$a = .000329$$
$$b = -.004887.$$

Thus, the estimated discriminant function is

$$Z_i = .000329X_i - .004887Y_i \qquad \text{(14.A.4)}$$

This function implies that the higher the assessed property valuation per capita, the higher the bond rating, and the higher the general obligation bonded debt per capita, the lower the bond rating. These implications are consistent with pre-scriptions given in the municipal bond rating literature.

Given the ratios in Table 14.7 and the discriminant function (14.A.4), the estimated Z_i scores are calculated as

Arlington, Mass.: $Z = .000329 \times 6,685 - .004887 \times 116 = 1.632$

Highland Park, Ill.: $Z = .000329 \times 6,360 - .004887 \times 87 = 1.667$

The Z_i score for all ten municipalities (ranked from highest to lowest Z_i) is presented in Table 14.8. The mean Z scores for the two categories of bonds are

Bonds rated A or above	1.210
Bonds rated Baa or below	$-.801$

Step Two: *Choose Cutoff Point for Discriminant Function.* It is apparent from Table 14.8 that the discriminant function does not correctly rank the municipalities according to their bond ratings. One A-rated bond (Pampa) is given a Z score below that of two Baa-rated bonds (Hot Springs and Pascagoula). The choice of the cutoff point for predicting (1) bonds rated A and above and (2) bonds rated Baa or below will depend on the probability of bonds being misclassified and the cost of the misclassifications associated with each cutoff point considered.

A frequently used criterion in choosing the cutoff point is to minimize the

TABLE 14.8 Discriminant Analysis Example: Z Scores for Estimation Sample

Municipality	Predicted Z Score	Moody's Bond Rating
Springdale, Ohio	2.555	Aa
Highland Park, Ill	1.667	Aa
Arlington, Mass.	1.632	Aa
La Grange, Ga.	.817	A
El Cerrito, Calif.	.713	A
Hot Springs, Ark.	.188	Baa ⎫
Pascagoula, Miss.	.154	Baa ⎬ Misranked municipalities
Pampa, Tex.	$-.126$	A ⎭
Maudlin, S.C.	-1.441	Baa
Coon Rapids, Minn.	-2.106	Baa

total number of misclassifications in the estimation sample. (This criterion assumes that the costs of misclassification are the same for each observation.) We shall assume that the only cutoff points considered in this criterion are the midpoints of the Z scores of adjacently ranked bonds. Thus, for instance, the only cutoff point between Arlington and La Grange that is considered is 1.2245 (midpoint between 1.632 and .817). The total number of misclassifications for several alternative cutoff points in Table 14.8 are

Cutoff Point	Total Number of Misclassifications
Predict $\geq A$ if $Z_i >$ 1.2245	3
Predict $\geq A$ if $Z_i >$ .7650	2
Predict $\geq A$ if $Z_i >$ .4505	1
Predict $\geq A$ if $Z_i >$ .1710	2
Predict $\geq A$ if $Z_i >$ .0140	3
Predict $\geq A$ if $Z_i >$ $-.7835$	2
Predict $\geq A$ if $Z_i >$ -1.7735	3

Thus, the cutoff point that minimizes the total number of misclassifications in the estimation sample is to predict a bond rating of A or above if the municipality's Z score exceeds .4505. Only Pampa is incorrectly predicted to be a Baa or below with this cutoff point.

Step Three: *Examine Predictive Ability of Discriminate Model on Validation Sample.* The estimates of a and b in (14.A.4) will reflect not only any underlying population differences between bonds rated $\geq A$ and bonds rated $\leq$ Baa, but also specific characteristics of the firms in the estimation sample. Moreover, in many cases the variables used in the final discriminant function are selected from a larger set initially considered. The final set chosen is comprised of those that work best (for example, result in minimum misclassifications) on the estimation sample. In this context, there is a search bias in the estimation sample that leads to an

TABLE 14.9 Discriminant Analysis Example: Financial Data and Z Scores for Validation Sample

Municipality	Assessed Property Valuation per Capita	Genera Obligation Bonded Debt per Capita	Predicted Z_i Scale	Moody's Bond Rating
Palo Alto, Calif.	$ 6,114	$ 110	1.474	Aa ⎫
Homewood, Ill.	4,134	34	1.194	A ⎪ Predicted
Portland, Maine	11,271	562	.962	Aa ⎬ as $\geq A$
East Lansing, Mich.	2,835	64	.620	A ⎭
Dodge City, Kan.	2,781	98	.436	A ⎫
Flagstaff, Ariz.	1,616	50	.287	Baa ⎪
Cambridge, Mass.	3,270	278	$-.282$	Aa ⎪ Predicted
Bogalusa, La.	1,796	333	-1.036	Baa ⎬ as $\leq$ Baa
Aspen, Colo.	11,274	1,159	-1.954	Baa ⎪
Cape Coral, Fla.	25,763	2,304	-2.783	Baa ⎭

overestimate of the predictive ability of the model on samples independent of that used to select the final variables.

In this situation, it is advisable to examine how well the estimated discriminant function performs on a new sample of rated municipal bonds. This new sample is generally referred to as a *validation or holdout* sample. Table 14.9 presents values of X_i, Y_i, the predicted Z_i score, and the actual bond rating for ten new municipalities. Similar to the sample used to estimate the model, the predicted Z_i scores do not perfectly rank the municipalities by actual bond rating. How would the cutoff point of .4505 perform on the new sample? Two bonds (Dodge City and Cambridge) are misclassified as Baa or below.

A convenient way to summarize the predictions of a discriminant model is via the following classification matrix:

		Actual rating	
		≥ A	≤ Baa
Predicted rating	≥ A	a_{11}	a_{12}
	≤ Baa	a_{21}	a_{22}

If the discriminant model correctly predicts the group to which each observation belongs, all observations will be on the main diagonal of the matrix (that is, in the a_{11} and a_{22} elements). The percentage correctly classified is calculated as

$$\frac{a_{11} + a_{22}}{a_{11} + a_{12} + a_{21} + a_{22}}$$

TABLE 14.10 Discriminant Analysis Example: Classification Matrices

		Actual rating	
Panel A Estimation Sample		≥A	≤Baa
Predicted rating	≥A	5	0
	≤Baa	1	4

Percentage correct = 90%.

		Actual rating	
Panel B Validation Sample		≥A	≤Baa
Predicted rating	≥A	4	0
	≤Baa	2	4

Percentage correct = 80%.

Table 14.10 illustrates the classification matrices for the municipal bond rating example. A cutoff point of predict A or above if $Z > .4505$ is assumed in Table 14.10.

This example illustrates *linear* discriminant analysis for classifying observations into one of *two* groups on the basis of *two* variables. Many extensions of this example are possible: for example, one could classify observations into one of n groups on the basis of m variables. When the equal variance/covariance matrix assumption of *linear* discriminant analysis appears inappropriate, techniques such as *quadratic* discriminant analysis may be applied. Where the normality assumption appears to be strongly violated, statistical tools such as logit or probit can be used. The reader should be aware that the technical literature on classificatory techniques (of which discriminant analysis is but one) is a vast and expanding one. An excellent compilation of research in this area is in Altman et al. (1981).

QUESTIONS

QUESTION 14.1: Quantitative Models of Debt-Security Ratings

The following comments have been made by the executives of debt-security rating firms:

- [Bond-rating] is not a numbers game. You couldn't rate bonds on a computer. It would blow a gasket. Bond-rating is a comprehensive analysis of the position of a company in whatever industry it is in.

- [Bond-rating] is a question of examining each area of information, and their inter-relationships, and making a judgment modified as necessary by evidence and experience. There is no way to cram them all into a single formula, which invariably produces the right answer. The stumbling block is weighting, and most disagreements on ratings spring from different weights attached to the factors in analysis by different analysts.

- Can a reasonably accurate classification of utilities into their observed bond-rating categories be made using only published financial data plus a multivariate model? . . . I came to the conclusion that ignoring basic fundamentals, and using only the financial data published by a rating agency, could result in some very dangerous assumptions, no matter what set of ratios or type of model was used. Furthermore, unless the fundamentals, their trends, and management's approach to these developments were analyzed, the probability of accurately predicting future rating changes would be something less than the flip of a coin.

- Since ratings involve judgments about the future, on the one hand, and since they are used by investors as a means of protection, on the other, the effort is made when assigning ratings to look at "worst" potentialities in the "visible" future, rather than solely at the past record and the status of the present. Therefore, investors using the rating should not expect to find in them a reflection of statistical factors alone, since they are an appraisal of long-term risks, including the recognition of many non-statistical factors.

REQUIRED

1. What does a debt rating represent?

2. What purposes could the statistical debt-rating models examined in Chapter 14 serve for the following parties: a debt-rating agency, investors, and management?

3. Comment on the foregoing statements by executives of debt-security-rating firms.

4. It has been argued that "there is no way of demonstrating whether the rating agencies are right or wrong" in their rating decisions. Do you agree? How would you gain insight into the relative abilities of each rating agency?

5. Until 1968, rating agencies derived revenues solely from the sale of bond-related services and publications; issuers of debt securities were not charged a rating fee. In 1968, Standard & Poor's broke with this tradition and started charging issuers a rating fee. Nowadays, a rating fee is charged by many rating firms. What are the pros and cons of such firms charging issuers of debt a rating fee? Do you agree that "it's like an artist paying an art critic for a review"?

QUESTION 14.2: Debt-Security Ratings and Debt-Security Yields

It is commonly argued that there is a causal link between debt ratings and debt yields. For example,

- Ratings normally are assigned to large, widely known issues of municipal bonds prior to public sale by the issuer. Investors are so accustomed to the system that almost automatically, a rating will determine within certain limits the interest rate the issuer must pay on its bonds.   Goodman (1968, p. 60)

- Bond ratings are widely publicized and are, therefore, critically important. A bond's rating affects investors' purchase decisions and, consequently, the issuing firm's cost of debt.   Martin and Henderson (1983, p. 463)

- The rating assigned to an issue influences the cost of the issue, as investors require a return commensurate with the rater's judgment of the potential risks, and one which falls within a range established by current issues of the same quality.   Hawkins, Brown, and Campbell (1983, p. 15)

REQUIRED

Design an empirical study that would provide evidence on whether the interest rate on a bond can be influenced by the ratings assigned to it by rating agencies.

QUESTION 14.3: Rating General Obligation Municipal Bonds

Part A.   Hobie Leland, Jr., has just been appointed to the municipal investment division of the Down-Under Bank. His first task is to build a linear discriminant model for predicting whether bonds will be rated (1) A or above or (2) Baa or below. His superior provides him with details (from *Moody's Municipal and Government Manual*) of the population, general obligation debt, assessed property valuation, and the current *Moody's* rating for 12 general obligation bonds. Hobie calculated the following financial ratios for each municipality:

$X_{1,i}$ = General obligation debt per capita of municipality i

$X_{2,i}$ = Assessed property valuation per capita of municipality i

$X_{3,i}$ = General obligation debt to assessed property valuation

of municipality i

The values of X_1, X_2, and X_3, and the current rating for each municipal bond, are presented in Table 14.11 (panel A). After trying all combinations of X_1, X_2, and X_3 in linear discriminant models, Hobie chooses the following discriminant

TABLE 14.11 Municipal Bond Rating: Estimation and Validation Samples

City	General Obligation Debt per Capita (X_1)	Assessed Property Valuation per Capita (X_2)	General Obligation Debt to Assessed Value $\times 10^2$ (X_3)	Moody's Bond Rating
A. Estimation Sample				
Austin, Tex.	$192	$5,905	3.25	Aa
Corpus Christi, Tex.	266	4,188	6.35	Aa
Fresno, Calif.	52	3,011	1.73	Aa
East Cleveland, Ohio	32	2,286	1.40	A
Franklin, Tenn.	41	2,428	1.69	A
Rome, Ga.	160	4,515	3.54	A
Crowley, La.	100	870	11.49	Baa
Franklin, Pa.	157	2,478	6.34	Baa
Great Bend, Kan.	144	2,597	5.54	Baa
Hamtramck, Mich.	62	4,725	1.31	Baa
Midfield, Ala.	360	1,652	21.79	Baa
Vicksburg, Miss.	128	2,137	5.99	Baa
B. Validation Sample				
Bristol, Conn.	$269	$4,687	5.74	Aa
Monterey, Calif.	44	4,977	.88	Aa
Anaheim, Calif.	49	4,378	1.12	A
Jonesboro, Ark.	91	956	9.52	A
Peekskill, N.Y.	113	2,945	3.84	A
Scottsdale, Ariz.	98	3,141	3.12	A
Tempe, Ariz.	165	2,924	5.64	A
Barstow, Calif.	148	2,423	6.11	Baa
Dayton, Kentucky	120	2,445	4.91	Baa
Escondido, Calif.	136	4,230	3.22	Baa
Port Needles, Tex.	262	4,117	6.36	Baa
Ruston, La.	187	1,035	18.07	Baa

model:

$$Z_i = -.00435X_{1,i} + .00064X_{2,i}$$

He chooses the cutoff point that minimizes the total number of misclassifications. The potential cutoff points are the midpoints between the Z scores of the adjacently ranked bonds.

REQUIRED

1. Given a criterion of minimizing the total number of misclassifications, what cutoff point should Hobie choose? Present the classification matrix for the model with this cutoff point.

2. Under what circumstances would a criterion different from minimizing the total number of misclassifications be appropriate for Down-Under?

3. What problems may occur in measuring the municipal variables chosen by Hobie's superior?

Part B. Hobie remembers that it is advisable to use a validation or holdout sample to test the predictive ability of the discriminant function chosen. He collects information for another 12 general obligation municipal bonds (see Table 14.11, panel B).

REQUIRED

1. Examine the predictive ability of the cutoff point chosen in Part A on the validation sample of 12 municipal bonds. Present the classification matrix for this validation sample.

2. Hobie is disappointed by the results for the validation sample. What factors may explain these results?

3. Hobie's superior is disillusioned by the performance of Hobie's model on the validation sample. He examines discriminant functions using all combinations of the variables in Table 14.11 (panel B) and reports that the following model has fewer misclassifications than does Hobie's model:

$$Z_i = -.00023X_{2,i} - .2166X_{3,i}$$

Can you defend Hobie's model choice vis-à-vis the model chosen by his superior?

QUESTION 14.4: Evaluating the Debt Securities of Sovereign Countries

Part A. Sovereign governments are an important issuer of debt securities. There are several sources of information on the creditworthiness of such debt: (a) debt-rating firms, (b) *Euromoney,* (a financial magazine) and (c) the *Institutional Investor* (a financial magazine).

(a) Debt-Rating Firms

The debt of some countries is rated by several U.S. rating firms. In 1984, Standard & Poor's (with ratings for 13 countries) and Moody's (with ratings for

12 countries) had the broadest coverage of sovereign debt issues. Examples of ratings in 1984 were Australia (Aaa), Canada (Aaa), Denmark (Aa), and the United Kingdom (Aaa). Standard & Poor's (1984) presents the following information on the rating of sovereign governments:

> The objective in assigning a credit rating to a debt instrument issued by a sovereign government is to determine the likelihood of timely repayment of interest and principal. . . . In the case of external obligations issued by a sovereign government, the rating process must address the question of country risk. Broadly defined, country risk is the probability of incurring a loss on a cross-country claim due to events which are, to a certain extent, under the control of the government. . . . The assessment of a government's willingness to repay its debts assumes greater importance with external obligations because the enforceability of a legal claim against a sovereign government by a foreign investor is very limited. . . . Although the probability of outright default is quite low for sovereign governments, the possibility of other types of disruptions in the debt service schedule is somewhat greater. For example, the more likely occurrence of external debt restructurings and reschedulings involves at the very least an opportunity cost to investors, and in some cases actual losses due to repayment delays. (p. 25)

Factors considered by rating firms include political risk (political system, social environment, and external relations) and economic risk (debt burden, international liquidity, balance-of-payments flexibility, economic diversification, growth performance, and track record of economic management).

(b) *Euromoney* Country Risk Ratings

Each year, *Euromoney* publishes "country risk league tables" based on a statistical modeling technique:

> The *Euromoney* country risk league tables measure one thing, and one thing only: the reality of the market place. They do not measure opinions, or views, or expectations. They are, purely and simply, a statistical ranking of the spreads and maturities that the sovereign borrowers of the world obtained in the largest part of Euromarkets—the syndicated bank loan market. As such, they are the visible manifestations of the interaction of the market place. A country's placing will depend, therefore, on a host of factors such as the number of times it taps the market in any one year (the less often it comes to market, the better should be its rating), the skill of its negotiators, its economic performance, its perceived political stability, its record of servicing debt, the level of its existing debt, and traditional relationships. (February 1981)

Euromoney includes three variables in its statistical formula for computing the score of each country:

1. *Access to Market* (50% weight). "Does a sovereign borrower have access to the LIBOR (London Interbank Borrowing Rate) market? If so, could it obtain a U.S. prime option? Does it have access to the bond markets?"
2. *Terms Obtained* (30% weight). "In the case of the syndicated loan market, the *Euromoney* system differentiates between loans in different currencies priced at variable rates over LIBOR. In the case of the bond markets, sov-

ereign issues are graded according to any premium paid over that for prime supranational borrowers, such as the World Bank."

3. *Selling Down or Success of Syndication* (20% weight). "A country that pushed its bankers to the limit by demanding the finest spreads and fees would not necessarily be welcomed by the markets in general in open syndication. On the other hand, a sovereign borrower that conceded relatively generous terms to its bankers, and enjoyed an excellent syndication as a result, merits points in the system for doing so." (September 1982)

In October 1984, the three top-ranked countries were (1) the United States, (2) Germany, and (3) Japan, and the three bottom-ranked countries were (114) Sudan, (115) El Salvador, and (116) Uganda.

(c) *Institutional Investor*'s Country Credit Ratings

Every six months, the *Institutional Investor* publishes country credit ratings based on a polling of bankers' opinions:

> The country-by-country credit ratings are based on ratings provided by leading international banks. Bankers are asked to grade each of the countries on a scale of zero to 100, with zero representing the least creditworthy countries and 100 representing the most creditworthy countries and the ones with the least chance of default. The sample for the study, which is updated every six months, ranges from 75 to 100 banks, each of which provides its own ratings. All participants in the survey are assured that their responses and the fact of their participation are kept strictly confidential. Banks are not permitted to rate their home countries. The individual responses are weighted, using an *Institutional Investor* formula that properly gives more weight to responses from banks with largest worldwide exposure and the most sophisticated country analysis systems. (September 1984)

In September 1984, the three top-ranked countries were (1) the United States, (2) Japan, and (3) Switzerland, while the three bottom-ranked countries were (107) Nicaragua, (108) Uganda, and (109) North Korea.

REQUIRED

1. Outline the major differences among (a) debt-rating firm, (b) *Euromoney*, and (c) *Institutional Investor* approaches to evaluating the creditworthiness of the debt securities of sovereign countries.
2. Discuss the strengths and weaknesses of (a), (b), and (c).
3. What approaches could be used to evaluate the quality of the ranking information provided by (a), (b), and (c)?

Part B. In 1983, the following countries restructured loans with foreign banks (the month refers to month in 1983 the rescheduling agreement was either signed or reached in principle):

Argentina, January (refinancing)
Brazil, February (refinancing)
Chile, July (refinancing)

TABLE 14.12 Debt-Security Rankings of Nine Countries with Rescheduled Debt in 1983

A. *Euromoney Country Risk Rankings*

Country (month of rescheduling)	Oct. '79	Feb. '80	Oct. '80	Feb. '81	Oct. '81	Feb. '82	Sept. '82	Feb. '83*	Oct. '83
Argentina, January	26	37	25	23	29	38	69	N/R	65
Brazil, February	42	47	23	52	49	62	59	N/R	87
Chile, July	37	41	40	37	26	34	49	N/R	81
Nigeria, July	45	55	48	40	32	43	38	N/R	62
Uruguay, July	31	53	37	35	27	33	62	N/R	66
Mexico, August	28	34	20	13	23	27	65	N/R	60
Costa Rica, September	44	48	49	55	N/R	N/R	97	N/R	93
Yugoslavia, September	36	46	44	48	46	58	74	N/R	70
Ecuador, October	40	50	41	41	25	39	60	N/R	78
No. of countries ranked	66	75	67	67	58	69	106	N/R	116

B. *Institutional Investor's Country Credit Rankings*

Country (month of rescheduling)	Sept. '79	Mar. '80	Sept. '80	Mar. '81	Sept. '81	Mar. '82	Sept. '82	Mar. '83	Sept. '83
Argentina, January	38	31	30	30	42	48	64	70	70
Brazil, February	33	43	50	54	50	49	42	42	51
Chile, July	50	52	46	47	46	44	44	47	62
Nigeria, July	51	49	49	45	43	43	46	49	55
Uruguay, July	67	66	67	68	65	63	58	57	64
Mexico, August	25	25	22	23	25	29	37	58	60
Costa Rica, September	65	68	69	70	73	81	91	90	90
Yugoslavia, September	46	51	53	52	54	61	60	66	66
Ecuador, October	55	54	52	48	49	50	52	67	71
No. of countries ranked	93	96	98	100	104	104	107	107	107

* N/R – Not reported. Starting in 1983, *Euromoney* reported rankings on an annual rather than on a semiannual basis.

SOURCE: *Euromoney* and *Institutional Investor* (various issues).

Nigeria, July (rescheduling)

Uruguay, July (rescheduling)

Mexico, August (rescheduling)

Costa Rica, September (rescheduling)

Nigeria, September (rescheduling)

Yugoslavia, September (refinancing)

Ecuador, October (rescheduling)

None of these countries restructured any loans with foreign banks in the 1978–1982 period. Table 14.12 presents the *Euromoney* country risk rankings and the *Institutional Investor* country credit rankings of the listed countries in the 1979–1983 period. None of the countries cited had debt rated by a debt-rating firm such as Moody's or Standard & Poor's.

REQUIRED

1. Evaluate the relative ability of the *Euromoney* and *Institutional Investor* rankings to anticipate the 1983 debt schedulings of the foregoing countries.

2. What additional information would you analyze to examine whether these rankings provide useful information about the relative likelihood of timely repayment of interest and principal?

REFERENCES

ALTMAN, E. I., R. B. AVERY, R. A. EISENBEIS, and J. F. SINKEY. *Application of Classification Techniques in Business, Banking and Finance*. Greenwich, Conn.: JAI Press, 1981.

ALTMAN, E. I., and S. A. NAMMACHER. "The Default Rate Experience on High Yield Corporate Debt." *Financial Analyst Journal* (July-August 1985): 25–41.

AUSTRALIAN RATINGS. *An Introduction to Australian Ratings*. Melbourne: Australian Ratings, 1984.

BELKAOUI, A. *Industrial Bonds and the Rating Process*. Westport, Conn.: Quorum Books, 1983.

BLUME, M. E., and D. B. KEIM. "Risk and Return Characteristics of Lower-Grade Bonds," working paper. University of Pennsylvania, 1984.

BOARDMAN, C. M., and R. W. McENALLY. "Factors Affecting Seasoned Corporate Bond Prices." *Journal of Financial and Quantitative Analysis* (June 1981): 207–226.

CARLETON, W. T., and E. M. LERNER. "Statistical Credit Scoring of Municipal Bonds." *Journal of Money, Credit and Banking* (November 1969): 750–764.

COPELAND, R. M., and R. W. INGRAM. "Municipal Bond Market Recognition of Pension Reporting Practices." *Journal of Accounting and Public Policy* (Fall 1983): 147–165.

COURTADON, G. R., and J. J. MERRICK. "The Option Pricing Model and the Valuation of Corporate Securities." *Midland Corporate Finance Journal* (Fall 1983): 43–57.

DREXEL BURNHAM LAMBERT. "The Case for High Yield Bonds." New York: Drexel, Burnham and Lambert, 1985.

DUFF and PHELPS. "An Introduction to Duff and Phelps Fixed Income Rating Service." Chicago: Duff and Phelps, September 1980.

FISHER, L. "Determinants of Risk Premiums on Corporate Bonds." *Journal of Political Economy* (June 1959): 217–237.

GOODMAN, R. M. "Municipal Bond Rating Testimony." *Financial Analysts Journal* (May–June 1968): 59–66.

GRIFFIN, P. A., and A. Z. SANVICENTE. "Common Stock Returns and Rating Changes: A Methodological Comparison." *The Journal of Finance* (March 1982): 103–119.

HASTIE, K. L. "Determinants of Municipal Bond Yields." *Journal of Financial and Quantitative Analysis* (June 1972): 1729–1748.

HAWKINS, D. F., B. A. BROWN, and W. J. CAMPBELL. *Rating Industrial Bonds.* Morristown, N.J.: Financial Executives Research Foundation, 1983.

HORRIGAN, J. "The Determination of Long-Term Credit Standing with Financial Ratios." *Empirical Research in Accounting: Selected Studies,* Supplement to *Journal of Accounting Research* (1966): 44–62.

INGRAM, R. W., and R. M. COPELAND. "The Association Between Municipal Accounting Numbers and Credit Risk and Return." In *Advances in Accounting, Vol. 1,* pp. 19–40. Greenwich, Conn.: JAI Press, 1984.

JOHNSON, R. E. "Term Structure of Corporate Bond Yields as a Function of Risk of Default." *The Journal of Finance* (May 1967): 313–345.

KAPLAN, R. S., and G. URWITZ. "Statistical Models of Bond Ratings: A Methodological Inquiry." *The Journal of Business* (April 1979): 231–261.

KATZ, S. "The Price Adjustment Process of Bonds to Rating Reclassifications: A Test of Bond Market Efficiency." *The Journal of Finance* (May 1974): 551–559.

MARTIN, L. J., and G. V. HENDERSON. "On Bond Ratings and Pension Obligations: A Note." *Journal of Financial and Quantitative Analysis* (December 1983): 463–470.

MICHEL, A. "Municipal Bond Ratings: A Discriminant Analysis Approach." *Journal of Financial and Quantitative Analysis* (November 1977): 587–598.

MOODY'S INVESTOR SERVICE. *Moody's Bond Record.* New York: Moody's Investor Service, December 1984.

PEAVY, J. W., and S. M. EDGAR. "A Multiple Discriminant Analysis of BHC Commercial Paper Ratings." *Journal of Banking and Finance* (June 1983): 161–173.

PEAVY, J. W., and S. M. EDGAR. "An Expanded Commercial Paper Rating Scale: Classification of Industrial Issuers." *Journal of Business Finance and Accounting* (Autumn 1984): 397–407.

PINCHES, G. E., and K. A. MINGO. "A Multivariate Analysis of Industrial Bond Ratings." *The Journal of Finance* (March 1973): 1–18.

PINCHES, G. E., and K. A. MINGO. "The Role of Subordination and Industrial Bond Ratings." *The Journal of Finance* (March 1975): 201–206.

PINCHES, G. E., and C. SINGLETON. "The Adjustment of Stock Prices to Bond Rating Changes." *The Journal of Finance* (March 1978): 29–44.

RAMAN, K. K. "Financial Reporting and Municipal Bond Ratings." *Journal of Accounting, Auditing and Finance* (Winter 1982): 144–153.

SCHAEFER, S. M. "Immunisation and Duration: A Review of Theory, Performance and Applications." *Midland Corporate Finance Journal* (Fall 1984): 41–58.

SIMON & COATES. *British Bond Rating Service*. London, United Kingdom: 1980.

SLOVIC, P., and S. LICHTENSTEIN. "Comparison of Bayesian and Regression Approaches to the Study of Information Processing in Judgment." *Organizational Behavior and Human Performance* (November 1971): 649–744.

SLOVIC, P., S. LICHTENSTEIN, and B. FISCHHOFF. "Decision Making," working paper. Decision Research, Eugene, Oregon, 1983; forthcoming in R. C. Atkinson, R. J. Herrnstein, G. Lindzey, and R. D. Luce, eds., *Stevens' Handbook of Experimental Psychology*.

STANDARD & POOR'S. *Credit Overview: Industrial Ratings*. New York: Standard & Poor's, 1983a.

STANDARD & POOR'S. *Credit Overview: Corporate and International Ratings*. New York: Standard & Poor's, 1983b.

STANDARD & POOR'S. *Credit Overview: Corporate and International Ratings*. New York: Standard & Poor's, 1984.

STANDARD & POOR'S. *Bond Guide*. New York: Standard & Poor's, January 1985.

WAKEMAN, L. M. "The Real Function of Bond Rating Agencies." *Chase Financial Quarterly* (Fall 1981): 18–25.

WEINSTEIN, M. I. "The Effect of a Rating Change Announcement on Bond Price." *Journal of Financial Economics* (December 1977): 329–350.

WESCOTT, S. H. "Accounting Numbers and Socioeconomic Variables as Predictors of Municipal General Obligation Bond Ratings." *Journal of Accounting Research* (Spring 1984): 412–423.

15

DISTRESS ANALYSIS AND FINANCIAL INFORMATION

15.1 INTRODUCTION

Prediction of the financial distress of corporations, municipalities, universities, and other institutions is a subject of much interest and research. This chapter outlines the role that financial statement and other information can play in distress prediction. Parties that can utilize the models discussed in this chapter include

- *Lenders*. Research on financial distress prediction has relevance to lending institutions, both in deciding whether to grant a loan (and its conditions) and in devising policies to monitor existing loans.

- *Investors*. Distress prediction models can be of assistance to investors in debt securities when assessing the likelihood of a company experiencing problems in making interest or principal repayments. Investors adopting an active investment approach (see Chapter 9) may develop strategies based on the assumption that distress prediction models can provide earlier warnings of financial problems than is implicit in the existing security price. (The validity of this assumption is an empirical issue. Evidence presented in Section 15.6 indicates that early warning signals of subsequent distress are recognized by the capital market.)

- *Regulatory Authorities*. In certain industries, regulatory bodies have the responsibility of monitoring the solvency and stability of individual companies. Financial institutions such as banks, building societies, insurance companies, and savings and loan associations are subject to overview by regulatory bodies in many countries. An important subset of the models discussed in this chapter have been motivated by such regulation-based applications.

- *Government Officials*. Government subsidies (bailouts) to financially distressed firms occur in many countries with varying degrees of frequency. Models that predict the likelihood of survival of a potential bailout candidate can be an important data item in weighing the economic, political, and social considerations in this area. The prediction of financial distress is also important to government officials in antitrust regulation. One defense against violating U.S. antitrust laws is the failing company doctrine. This doctrine can apply where one of the two merging companies is likely to fail and where the ''failing'' company has received no offer to merge from a company with which a merger would not have violated existing antitrust guidelines.

- *Auditors*. One judgment auditors must make is whether a firm is a going concern. This judgment affects the asset and liability valuation methods that are deemed appropriate for financial reporting. Financial distress prediction models can be a useful aid to the auditor in making a going-concern judgment.

- *Management*. Bankruptcy can mean that a firm incurs both direct and indirect costs. Direct costs include fees to professionals such as accountants and lawyers. Indirect costs include the lost sales or profits due to the constraints imposed by the court or the court-appointed trustee. Altman (1984b) estimated that for a sample of 19 industrial firms that went bankrupt, "bankruptcy costs ranged from 11% to 17% of firm value up to three years prior to bankruptcy" (p. 1087). It may well be that if early warning signals of bankruptcy were observed, these costs could be reduced by management arranging a merger with another firm or adopting a corporate reorganization plan at a more propitious time.

15.2   PROBLEMS IN OPERATIONALIZING FINANCIAL DISTRESS

Financial distress is used in this chapter to mean severe liquidity problems that cannot be resolved without a sizable rescaling of the entity's operations or structure. Operationalizing this notion raises difficult problems. Financial distress is best viewed as an economic notion for which there are many points on a continuum. Empirical research in this area has sought objective criteria to categorize firms. Filing for bankruptcy is the criterion used in most studies; this event is a legal one that can be heavily influenced by the actions of bankers or other creditors. Even if the financial distress notion were binary, there need not be a one-to-one correspondence between the nondistressed/distressed categories and the nonbankrupt/bankrupt categories:

	Nonfinancially Distressed	Financially Distressed
Nonbankrupt	I	II
Bankrupt	III	IV

Consider firms that fall in II, that is, nonbankrupt but financially distressed. These firms may resolve their liquidity problems via a dramatic rescaling of their operations (for example, the sale of 80% of their asset base) or via a merger with another company. Consider firms that fall in III, that is, nonfinancially distressed but bankrupt. Firms may voluntarily enter bankruptcy to force unions to accept lower hourly wage rates or to reduce the size of a potential lawsuit against them. Ambiguity caused by firms falling in categories II and III is an inherent limitation when generalizing many of the research studies discussed in this chapter.

The problem of defining financial distress in the not-for-profit sector of the economy is an especially difficult task (see Schipper, 1977). Suppose that a private university is having extreme difficulty meeting running expenses out of tuition fees, grants, and endowment income. Several options may be open to the university trustees. One is to close the university formally and sell its physical facilities. A second option is to seek a merger with another university. Yet another option is to reduce drastically research grants and library acquisitions and to increase existing faculty teaching loads. The last option may result in important changes in the "mission, role, or scope" of the university. In an empirical study, it would be relatively easy to use the first option (closure) as a sign of financial distress. It would be considerably more difficult to set up criteria for classifying universities that chose the last option (change in mission, role, or scope) as being in a financially distressed or nondistressed category.

15.3 INDICATORS OF FINANCIAL DISTRESS

There are several indicators of, or information sources about, the likelihood of financial distress. One source is a *cash flow* analysis for the current and future periods. One benefit of using this information source is that it focuses directly on the financial distress notion for the period of interest. The estimates of cash flow included in this analysis are critically dependent on the assumptions underlying preparation of the budget.

A second source of information about financial distress is a *corporate strategy* analysis. This analysis considers the potential competitors of the firm or institution, its relative cost structure, plant expansions in the industry, the ability of firms to pass along cost increases, the quality of management, and so on. Ideally, these considerations also will underlie the cash flow analysis. However, a separate focus on strategy issues can highlight the consequences of sudden changes occurring in an industry. For example, an examination of break-even points and cost structures of oil rig operators can provide insight into potential financial distress candidates should there be a dramatic drop in the demand for oil rigs.

A third source of information about financial distress is an analysis of the *financial statements* of the firm and those of a comparison set of firms. This analysis can focus on a single financial variable (univariate analysis) or on a combination of financial variables (multivariate analysis). Sections 15.4 and 15.5 provide a detailed description of this information source.

A fourth source of information comes from *external variables* such as security returns and bond ratings. These variables potentially can encode information about future cash flow and corporate strategy and information from the financial statements of the firm or institution. Moreover, they can incorporate relatively complex interactions between individual items. Section 15.6 provides a description of this information source.

15.4 UNIVARIATE MODELS OF DISTRESS PREDICTION

A univariate approach to predicting financial distress involves the use of a single variable in a prediction model. There are two key assumptions in this approach:

1. The distribution of the variable for distressed firms differs systematically from the distribution of the variable for the nondistressed firms

2. This systematic distribution difference can be exploited for prediction purposes.

The univariate approach will be illustrated by the following case study.

A.   Case Study of U.S. Railroad Bankruptcies

In 1970, several large U.S. Class I railroads filed for bankruptcy under provisions of the National Bankruptcy Act, for example, Boston and Maine Corporation and the Penn-Central railroad complex. How well did the financial statements issued in the year prior to 1970 predict this bankruptcy? To examine this question, a sample of ten railroads was chosen to build a univariate prediction model. (A detailed analysis of the prediction of U.S. railroad bankruptcies is in Altman, 1973.) The following two ratios were calculated for each company from the 1969 statements filed by these railroads with the Interstate Commerce Commission:

1. *Transportation expenses to operating revenue* (*TE/OR*). Transportation expenses are primarily the actual cost of train operations and include the wages of train crews and fuel costs. Operating revenues comprise mostly freight revenues. They also include passenger revenues and revenues from miscellaneous sources such as mail express.

2. *Times interest earned* (*TIE*). Interest charges are for fixed interest obligations. Earnings are before interest and tax. A negative value of this ratio implies that the company had negative earnings (a loss) before interest and tax payments.

For simplicity, it is assumed that these two ratios are normally distributed. Table 15.1 details the ten railroads and the 1969 values of the two ratios for each railroad. This sample is used to build several univariate prediction models and is referred to as the estimation sample.

Distribution Differences Between Ratios of Bankrupt
and Nonbankrupt Railroads

The first assumption in the univariate approach is that the distribution of the ratio differs between the bankrupt and nonbankrupt railroads. The assumption of normality for each ratio implies that either the mean or the variance of the distribution differs between the two groups of railroads. In this section we shall concentrate on differences in means. For the TE/OR ratio, the means of the two groups are

Nonbankrupt railroads   .356
Bankrupt railroads   .473

TABLE 15.1 Railroad Bankruptcy Prediction Example:
Estimation Sample

Railroad	TE/OR	TIE
Nonbankrupt in 1970		
1. Ann Arbor Railroad	.524	− 1.37
2. Central of Georgia Railway	.348	2.16
3. Cincinnati, New Orleans, and		
Texas Pacific Railway	.274	2.91
4. Florida East Coast Railway	.237	2.82
5. Illinois Central Railroad	.388	3.10
6. Norfolk and Western Railway	.359	2.81
7. Southern Pacific Transportation Co.	.400	3.56
8. Southern Railway Company	.314	3.93
Bankruptcy filings in 1970		
9. Boston and Maine Corporation	.461	− .68
10. Penn-Central Transportation Co.	.485	.16

That is, the bankrupt group spends more (on average) of each dollar of operating revenue on transportation expenses such as train crew wages and fuel costs. The means for the TIE ratio of the two groups are

Nonbankrupt railroads   2.49

Bankrupt railroads   − .26

Thus, the nonbankrupt group evidences a greater ability (on average) to generate revenues sufficient to cover fixed interest obligations. On balance, these differences suggest that at least one year prior to bankruptcy, the financial ratios of the bankrupt and nonbankrupt railroads appear to be markedly different. A statistical significance test (student t), used to determine the difference between the means of the two groups, supported this conclusion at the .05 level for each ratio.

Predictive Ability Tests

An important issue is whether one can use the noted differences in mean values of the ratios for predictive purposes. The univariate approach to prediction that will be outlined is a dichotomous classification test. This approach involves ranking the railroads by the value of a ratio and then visually inspecting the data to determine an "optimal" cutoff point for predicting a railroad as bankrupt or nonbankrupt. The rankings of companies for each ratio are presented in Table 15.2. For simplicity, it will be assumed that the only cutoff points considered are the midpoints between the adjacently ranked ratios; for example, for the TE/OR ratio, the first cutoff point considered is .5045, which is midway between the .524 of Ann Arbor Railroad and the .485 of Penn-Central. A Type I prediction error occurs when a bankrupt (B) railroad is predicted to be nonbankrupt (NB). A Type

TABLE 15.2   Railroad Bankruptcy Prediction Example: Dichotomous Classification Test for Estimation Sample

Railroad	Ratio	Actual Status in 1970
1. Ranking on TE/OR ratio		
Ann Arbor Railroad	.524	NB
Penn-Central Transportation	.485	B
Boston and Maine	.461	B
Southern Pacific Transportation	.400	NB
Illinois Central Railroad	.388	NB
Norfolk and Western Railway	.359	NB
Central of Georgia Railway	.348	NB
Southern Railway	.314	NB
Cincinnati, New Orleans, and Texas Pacific	.274	NB
Florida East Coast Railway	.237	NB
2. Ranking on TIE ratio		
Southern Railway	3.93	NB
Southern Pacific Transportation	3.56	NB
Illinois Central Railroad	3.10	NB
Cincinnati, New Orleans, and Texas Pacific	2.91	NB
Florida East Coast Railway	2.82	NB
Norfolk and Western Railway	2.81	NB
Central of Georgia Railway	2.16	NB
Penn-Central Transportation	.16	B
Boston and Maine	− .68	B
Ann Arbor Railroad	− 1.37	NB

NOTE: NB–Nonbankrupt.
      B–Bankrupt.

II error occurs when a nonbankrupt (NB) railroad is predicted to be bankrupt (B).

The Type I, Type II, and the total number of errors (misclassifications) from using several alternative cutoff points of the TE/OR ratio are

Cutoff Point	Number of Type I Errors	Number of Type II Errors	Total Number of Errors
Predict B if TE/OR > .5045	2	1	3
Predict B if TE/OR > .4730	1	1	2
Predict B if TE/OR > .4305	0	1	1
Predict B if TE/OR > .3940	0	2	2
Predict B if TE/OR > .3735	0	3	3

The cutoff point that minimizes the total number of misclassifications (errors) is predict B if a railroad's TE/OR ratio >.4305. Only one railroad is misclassified using this cutoff, that is, Ann Arbor Railroad. For the TIE ratio, the cutoff point that minimizes the total number of misclassifications is predict B if a railroad's TIE $<$ 1.16. This cutoff also misclassifies only one railroad.

The technique of choosing the cutoff based on the ten railroads in the estimation sample runs the danger that specific characteristics of the firms in the two categories will overly influence the value of the cutoff point. Ideally, one wants any difference between the bankrupt and nonbankrupt firms that are incorporated into the univariate prediction model to reflect only the underlying population differences between these two groups. Therefore, it is important to examine the predictive ability of the univariate model on an independent sample of railroads. This independent sample is termed the validation (or holdout) sample. During 1971, only one U.S. Class I railroad filed for bankruptcy—Reading Company. This railroad and nine other nonbankrupt railroads in 1971 were used as a validation sample. Details of these companies and the 1970 values of their TE/OR and TIE ratios are in Table 15.3.

Table 15.4 summarizes the prediction results for the validation sample. Use of the .4305 cutoff point for the TE/OR ratio results in no Type I errors and two Type II errors: Erie-Lackawanna and Chicago, Milwaukee, St. Paul, and Pacific. For the TIE ratio, the 1.16 cutoff point results in no Type I errors and three Type II errors; Erie-Lackawanna; Chicago, Milwaukee, St. Paul, and Pacific; and Bangor and Aroostook. (The Erie-Lackawanna Railroad filed for bankruptcy in 1972.)

General Comments on the Railroad Example

1. The criterion used for choosing the cutoff points for each ratio was minimization of the total number of misclassifications. This criterion will not always lead to a unique cutoff point. Consider the following ranking of five companies:

Railroad	TE/OR	Actual Status
V	.50	B
W	.49	NB
X	.48	B
Y	.47	NB
Z	.46	NB

A cutoff point of predict B if TE/OR $>$ .495 and predict B if TE/OR $>$ .475 will both lead to one company being misclassified. In general, the choice of the cutoff point will depend on the probability of firms being misclassified and the cost of the misclassifications associated with each cutoff point considered.

2. The dichotomous classification test described is but one of several univariate approaches to predicting bankrupt firms. An alternative approach to deriving a cutoff point is to use the mean or median values of the ratio in the estimation sample. The mean TE/OR ratio for the ten railroads in the estimation sample is .356. Using a mean ratio univariate model implies predicting bankruptcy if the ratio $>$.356 and predicting nonbankruptcy if the ratio $<$.356. (How does this model perform on the estimation and validation samples?)

TABLE 15.3 Railroad Bankruptcy Prediction Example: Validation Sample

Railroad	TE/OR	TIE
Nonbankrupt in 1971		
1. Akron, Canton, and Youngstown Railroad	.382	1.85
2. Alabama Great Southern Railroad	.305	4.05
3. Atchison, Topeka, and Santa Fe Railway	.373	4.72
4. Bangor and Aroostook Railroad	.341	.88
5. Burlington Northern Incorporated	.425	2.73
6. Chesapeake and Ohio Railway	.395	3.12
7. Chicago, Milwaukee, St. Paul, and Pacific Railroad	.437	.27
8. Erie-Lackawanna Railway Co.	.469	.22
9. St. Louis Southwestern Railway Co.	.352	46.70
Bankruptcy filing in 1971		
10. Reading Company	.451	.40

TABLE 15.4 Railroad Bankruptcy Prediction Example: Dichotomous Classification Test for Validation Sample

Railroad	Ratio	Actual Status in 1970	
1. Ranking on TE/OR ratio			
Erie-Lackawanna	.469	NB	Predicted bankrupt
Reading Company	.451	B	
Chicago, Milwaukee, St. Paul, and Pacific	.437	NB	
Burlington Northern	.425	NB	
Chesapeake and Ohio	.395	NB	
Akron, Canton, and Youngstown	.382	NB	Predicted nonbankrupt
Atchison, Topeka, and Santa Fe	.373	NB	
St. Louis Southwestern	.352	NB	
Bangor and Aroostook	.341	NB	
Alabama Great Southern	.305	NB	
2. Ranking on TIE ratio			
St. Louis Southwestern	46.70	NB	
Atchison, Topeka, and Santa Fe	4.72	NB	
Alabama Great Southern	4.05	NB	Predicted nonbankrupt
Chesapeake and Ohio	3.12	NB	
Burlington Northern	2.73	NB	
Akron, Canton, and Youngstown	1.85	NB	
Bangor and Aroostook	.88	NB	
Reading Company	.40	B	Predicted bankrupt
Chicago, Milwaukee, St. Paul, and Pacific	.27	NB	
Erie-Lackawanna	.22	NB	

NOTE: NB–Nonbankrupt.
    B–Bankrupt.

3. If several univariate models are used, it is possible that they may yield conflicting predictions for a firm. Consider the Bangor and Aroostook Railroad in the validation sample (Tables 15.3 and 15.4). Based on its TIE ratio of .88, it would be incorrectly predicted to be bankrupt in 1971. Yet, its TE/OR ratio of .341 gives the opposite prediction. The multivariate prediction models examined in Setion 15.4 are motivated, in part, by attempts to resolve such conflicting predictions.

B. Differences in Financial Variable Distributions

Comparisons of the mean ratios of distressed and nondistressed firms have a long history in the published literature. An important study is Beaver (1966), which included a comparison of the mean financial ratios of 79 failed firms and 79 nonfailed firms. A firm was designated as failed when any one of the following events occurred in the 1954–1964 period: bankruptcy, bond default, an overdrawn bank account, or nonpayment of a preferred stock dividend. The 79 nonfailed firms were selected using a paired-sample design. For each failed firm, a nonfailed firm of the same industry and asset size was selected. The equally weighted means of 30 financial ratios were computed for each of the failed and nonfailed groups in each of the five years before failure. Beaver called this comparison of mean ratios a profile analysis. It examines if there are observable differences in the mean ratios of the two sets of firms. Results for five financial ratios are presented in Figure 15.1. In general, there is a marked difference in the behavior of the mean financial ratios of the two groups. The cash flow-to-total debt ratio and the net income-to-total assets ratio appear to exhibit marked differences as early as five years before failure.

One limitation of the comparison of the mean financial ratios test is that it examines only one point on the distribution. Differences between the means could be induced by several extreme observations in either one of the groups examined. Apart from these extreme observations, there could be almost complete overlap in the distribution of the ratio of both groups. There are several options one can use to increase confidence that there are distribution differences in the ratios of distressed and nondistressed firms. One option is to plot selected points of the distribution (say, the .1, .3, .5, .7, and .9 fractiles) of the two samples and examine the overlap. A second option is to use a formal statistical significance test for a difference in the distributions. Yet another option is to conduct a univariate predictive test of the kind outlined in the railroad bankruptcy prediction example presented earlier in this chapter.

C. Univariate Prediction Tests

The dichotomous classification test outlined earlier was first used extensively by Beaver (1966). The sample was the 79 failed and 79 nonfailed firms described in the prior section. The cutoff point was chosen by arraying the values of each ratio and choosing the value that minimized the total misclassification

FIGURE 15.1 Profile Analysis: Mean Ratios of Failed and Nonfailed Firms

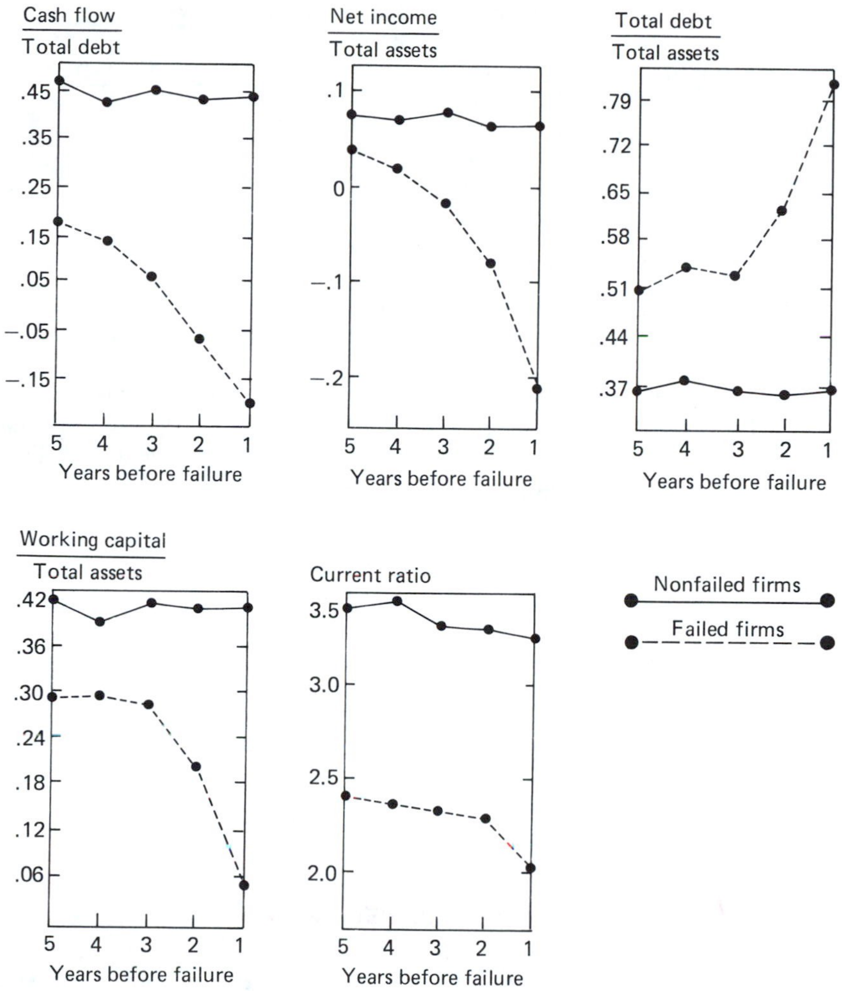

Source: Beaver (1966, Figure 1, adapted): p. 82.

percentage. The sample was randomly divided into two subgroups. The cutoff point chosen on the first subgroup (the estimation sample) was used to classify firms in the second subgroup (the validation sample) as failed or nonfailed. The percentage misclassification rates for five ratios for each of the five years before failure are presented in Table 15.5. These percentages are for the validation sample of firms. The cash flow-to-total debt and the net income-to-total assets ratios classified with similar success in each of the three years prior to "failure"; for example, both misclassify only 13% of the firms one year prior to "failure." One interesting result in Beaver (1966) was that the cutoff point that minimized the

TABLE 15.5   Univariate Failure Prediction:
Dichotomous Classification Test
and Percentage Misclassification Rates

Financial Ratio	Year Before Failure				
	5	4	3	2	1
Cash flow/total debt	.22	.24	.23	.21	.13
Net assets/total assets	.28	.29	.23	.20	.13
Total debt/total assets	.28	.27	.34	.25	.19
Working capital/total assets	.41	.45	.33	.34	.24
Current ratio	.45	.38	.36	.32	.20

SOURCE: Beaver (1966, Table 3): p. 85.

total number of misclassifications resulted in different percentages of Type I and Type II errors. In particular, nonfailed firms were correctly predicted to a greater extent than were failed firms. For instance, the Type I and Type II error percentages for the cash flow-to-total debt ratio were

Year Before Failure	Type I Error Percentage	Type II Error Percentage	Total Misclassification Percentage
5	.43	.05	.22
4	.47	.03	.24
3	.37	.08	.23
2	.34	.08	.21
1	.22	.05	.13

In a decision context, any differential penalty between Type I and Type II errors would explicitly need to be taken into account when choosing the cutoff point in a univariate prediction model.

D. Overview of Univariate Evidence

The number of individual financial ratios and other variables examined in distress prediction studies published in the last 20 years is well over 100. Zmijewski (1983) classified 75 of these into ten categories. Using a sample of 72 bankrupt and 3,573 nonbankrupt firms over the 1972–1978 period, he computed

- The means of these 75 variables in the year prior to bankruptcy
- A univariate F test for the hypothesis that the means of the two groups were the same
- The percentage correctly classified using a single-variable discriminant function.

Table 15.6 presents a subset of the results. The four categories of variables showing the most consistent difference between bankrupt and nonbankrupt firms were

TABLE 15.6 Mean Financial Ratios of Bankrupt and Nonbankrupt Firms: One Year Prior to Bankruptcy Filing

Financial Characteristic	Mean of Distribution		Univariate F Test	Percentage Correctly Classified
	Bankrupt	Nonbankrupt		
1. *Rate of return measures*				
• Cash flow/Net worth	.119	.316	77.18	93.64
• Net income/Net worth	−.591	.091	230.53	97.06
2. *Liquid asset composition*				
• Quick assets/Total assets	.258	.273	1.18	50.41
3. *Liquidity position*				
• Current assets/Current liabilities	1.860	2.381	1.97	46.69
• Quick assets/Current liabilities	.838	1.231	2.24	51.92
4. *Financial leverage*				
• MVE/(MVE + book value debt)	.995	.999	177.41	88.08
• Total debt/Total assets	.785	.476	276.45	86.02
5. *Activity/turnover*				
• COGS/Inventory	9.991	10.432	.11	21.29
• Accounts receivable/Sales	.188	.147	3.92	66.43
• Total assets/Sales	.836	.783	.51	68.52
6. *Fixed payment coverage*				
• Funds from operations/Total debt	−.049	.249	88.92	84.39
7. *Trends and dispersions*				
• Standard deviation of net income/Net worth	3.330	.179	78.17	97.03
• Break in trend of net income	2.403	1.610	43.23	80.49
8. *Firm size*				
• Total assets	153.76	769.05	4.11	27.84
9. *Stock return and volatility*				
• Common stock return	−.045	.003	73.46	72.21
• Total stock return variance	.011	.004	160.81	86.81

SOURCE: Zmijewski (1983, Table 3): pp. 28–30.

- Rate of return—bankrupt firms were less profitable
- Financial leverage—bankrupt firms were more highly leveraged
- Fixed payment coverage—bankrupt firms had lower coverage of their fixed payments by their earnings or cash flow
- Stock return volatility—bankrupt firms had lower mean stock returns and had higher stock return variability.

Consistent with many other research studies, Zmijewski reported that the liquidity and activity/turnover categories of variables exhibited limited differences between the bankrupt and nonbankrupt firms. (An issue not addressed in this literature is how the profiles of bankrupt firms differ from the profiles of highly successful nonbankrupt firms. For instance, it may be that both bankrupt firms and highly successful nonbankrupt firms have high financial leverage and high stock return variability.) The results in Table 15.6 pertain to the period one year prior to the bankruptcy filing. An interesting extension would be to examine which of the categories of variables remain significant in (say) the period three to five years prior to bankruptcy.

15.5 MULTIVARIATE MODELS OF DISTRESS PREDICTION

One limitation of the univariate approach is that different variables can imply different predictions for the same firm. It is not surprising that attempts have been made to combine the information in several financial variables into a single multivariate model. The dependent variable in these models is either a prediction as to group membership (for example, bankrupt or nonbankrupt) or a probability estimate of group membership (for example, the probability of being bankrupt). Independent variables examined typically have been financial ratios and other firm-oriented variables. Issues that arise in modeling in this area include

1. What variables should be included?
2. What forms should the model take (for example, variables entering in a linear additive fashion or in a nonlinear multiplicative fashion)?
3. What weights should be applied to the variables?

Ideally, some economic theory of financial distress should help guide decisions on (1), (2), and (3). Unfortunately, there is very little available theory that a model builder can access. It is not surprising that published analysis has relied on extensive data searching and the results of prior studies to guide variable choice.

The statistical techniques used in most research studies can be classified into one of three categories: (1) discriminant analysis where the aim is to classify observations into one of two groups, based on a set of predesignated variables (for example, Altman, Haldeman, and Narayanan, 1977); (2) logit or probit analysis where the aim is to estimate the probability that an event (for example, bankruptcy) will occur based on a set of predesignated variables (for example, Ohlson, 1980); and (3) recursive partitioning, which is a nonparametric classification technique, based on pattern recognition (for example, Marais, Patell, and Wolfson, 1984, and Frydman, Altman, and Kao, 1985). We shall illustrate multivariate modeling by reference to the railroad bankruptcy example discussed previously. Discriminant analysis will be used as the statistical technique in this illustration. (See the appendix to Chapter 14 for a description of this technique.)

A. Case Study of U.S. Railroad Bankruptcies

In this example, there are two discrete and known groups: railroad non-bankrupt in year t or railroad bankrupt in year t. Each railroad has two financial variables that will be used in the multivariate model: the transportation expense-to-operating revenue ratio (X_i = TE/OR) and the times interest earned ratio (Y_i = TIE). It is assumed that these two ratios come from a multivariate normal population and that the variance-covariance matrices of the two groups are equal.

The linear discriminant analysis model to be used for classificatory purpose is

$$Z_i = aX_i + bY_i \qquad (15.1)$$

Using the data for the estimation sample (Table 15.1), we obtained the following estimate of (15.1):

$$Z_i = -3.366X_i + .657Y_i \qquad (15.2)$$

The lower the Z_i score in (15.2), the more likely a railroad is to be bankrupt. A negative coefficient on X_i means that the higher the ratio of transportation expenses to operating revenues, the lower the Z_i score. A positive coefficient on Y_i means that the lower the number of times that earnings cover interest payments, the lower the Z_i score. To illustrate estimation of Z_i for each railroad, consider Penn-Central with TE/OR = .485 and TIE = .16:

$$Z_i = -3.366 \times .485 + .657 \times .16$$
$$= -1.527$$

Table 15.7 details the ten railroads in the estimation sample ranked on their Z_i scores. The cutoff point that minimizes the total number of misclassifications is $Z_i = -.640$ (midpoint between .247 and -1.527). This cutoff misclassifies only one firm (Ann Arbor Railroad).

The discriminant function estimated on the 1970 sample can now be used to predict the bankrupt/nonbankrupt status of railroads in 1971. The estimated Z scores for the 1971 sample from Table 15.3 are presented in Table 15.8. Use of the $Z_i = -.640$ cutoff point correctly classifies the status of eight out of ten railroads. Two nonbankrupt railroads are incorrectly predicted to be bankrupt in 1971: Chicago, Milwaukee, St. Paul, and Pacific and Erie-Lackawanna; as noted earlier, Erie-Lackawanna entered bankruptcy in 1972.

TABLE 15.7   Railroad Bankruptcy Prediction Example: *Z* Scores for Estimation Sample

Railroad	Z Score	Actual Status in 1970
Southern Railway	1.524	NB
Florida East Coast Railway	1.054	NB
Southern Pacific Transportation	.991	NB
Cincinnati, New Orleans, and Pacific	.989	NB
Illinois Central	.730	NB
Norfolk and Western	.637	NB
Central of Georgia	.247	NB
Penn-Central Transportation	−1.527	B
Boston and Maine	−1.998	B
Ann Arbor Railroad	−2.663	NB

NOTE: NB–Nonbankrupt.
       B–Bankrupt.

B. Performance of Selected Multivariate Models

The literature contains many studies reporting predictive ability results using multivariate models. Overviews of the research in this literature include Altman et al. (1981), Scott (1981), Ball and Foster (1982), Altman (1983), Zavgren (1983), and Zmijewski (1983, 1984). Generalizing from this research is difficult due to differences across individual studies with respect to statistical techniques employed, criteria used to assign firms to different categories, and samples examined. The Zmijewski (1983) study considerably reduces these problems. Multivariate models based on variables used in prior studies were individually examined using a common statistical technique (probit analysis), a common definition of group categories (bankrupt/nonbankrupt), and a common sample (72 bankrupt and 3,573

TABLE 15.8   Railroad Bankruptcy Prediction Example: *Z* Scores for Validation Sample

Railroad	Z Score	Actual Status in 1971	
St. Louis Southwestern	29.482	NB	
Atchison, Topeka, and Santa Fe	1.844	NB	
Alabama Great Southern	1.633	NB	Predicted nonbankrupt
Chesapeake and Ohio	.719	NB	
Burlington Northern	.362	NB	
Akron, Canton, and Youngstown	−.071	NB	
Bangor and Aroostook	−.570	NB	
Reading Company	−1.255	B	Predicted bankrupt
Chicago, Milwaukee, St. Paul, and Pacific	−1.294	NB	
Erie-Lackawanna	−1.434	NB	

NOTE: NB–Nonbankrupt.
       B–Bankrupt.

nonbankrupt firms in the 1972–1978 period). One interesting aspect of the Zmijewski (1983) paper was the analysis of how predictive ability varies with different assumptions as to the relative cost of Type I errors (bankrupt predicted to be nonbankrupt) and Type II errors (nonbankrupt predicted to be bankrupt). Results were presented for four cases: cost of Type I error equals 1 times, 2 times, 20 times, and 38 times the cost of a Type II error. Most prior studies assumed equality of Type I and Type II errors when making predictions.

Table 15.9 presents classification results for multivariate models based on variables included in the following seven studies:

1. Beaver (1966), 30 financial ratios
2. Altman (1968), 5 financial ratios
3. Blum (1974), 5 financial ratios, 6 trend and dispersion measures of financial variables, and 1 stock return variable
4. Altman, Haldeman, and Narayanan (1977), 5 financial ratios, 1 financial ratio dispersion variable, and 1 firm-size variable
5. Dambolena and Khoury (1980), 19 financial ratios and 19 financial ratio dispersion variables
6. Ohlson (1980), 6 financial ratios, 2 financial statement-based dummy variables, and 1 firm-size variable
7. Zmijewski (1983), 5 financial ratios and 1 financial ratio dispersion variable

Several important results are found in Table 15.9. First, with the cost of Type I error equal to the cost of Type II error assumption, all models have a relatively high percentage of correct classifications (the lowest being 97.9% for the total sample). In part, this finding is due to the high percentage of the population in the nonbankruptcy category. Indeed, a model that predicted all firms were nonbankrupt has a 98.0% correct classification rate (72 out of 3,645 misclassified) for the Zmijewski (1983) sample. Second, when the cost of a Type I error increases relative to a Type II error, there is an increase in the percentage of bankrupts correctly classified and a decrease in the percentage of nonbankrupts correctly classified. Third, the differences in the performance of the seven models become more marked as the relative cost of Type I error increases. For instance, when the cost of Type I and Type II errors are the same, the percentage-correct classifications of the seven models range from 97.9% to 98.9%. In contrast, when the cost of a Type I error is 38 times the cost of a Type II error, the percentage-correct classifications range from 83.5% to 91.7%.

The variables examined in these studies have been almost exclusively firm oriented, such as a profitability ratio or a coverage ratio. There is considerable evidence that failure rates in the economy are correlated with macroeconomic variables such as interest rate changes and unemployment rate changes; see Altman (1983, Chap. 2) and Rose, Andrews, and Giroux (1982). This evidence raises the possibility that multivariate models incorporating forecasts of macroeconomic aggregates could increase the predictive ability of models currently reported in the literature.

TABLE 15.9 Percentage Correct Classifications of Seven Multivariate Distress Prediction Models

Study Variables Derived from	Type I Cost = Type II Cost			Type I Cost = 2 × Type II Cost			Type I Cost = 20 × Type II Cost			Type I Cost = 38 × Type II Cost		
	NB	B	TS	NB	B	TS	NB	B	TS	NB	B	TS
1. Beaver (1966)	99.7	36.1	98.4	99.2	43.1	98.1	91.8	86.1	91.7	91.8	86.1	91.7
2. Altman (1968)	99.8	6.9	97.9	99.3	33.3	98.0	88.8	84.7	88.8	83.3	93.1	83.5
3. Blum (1974)	99.8	18.1	98.9	99.4	38.9	98.2	95.9	77.8	95.6	90.6	87.5	90.1
4. Altman et al. (1977)	99.8	4.2	97.9	98.9	38.9	97.7	91.4	81.9	91.2	84.0	94.4	84.3
5. Dambolena and Khoury (1980)	99.7	26.4	98.3	98.9	47.2	97.7	95.7	73.6	95.3	83.7	91.6	83.9
6. Ohlson (1980)	99.8	8.3	98.0	98.8	40.3	97.7	93.5	84.7	93.3	89.6	93.1	89.7
7. Zmijewski (1983)	99.7	9.7	98.0	99.3	37.5	98.1	95.5	75.0	95.1	86.0	91.2	86.0

NOTE: NB–Nonbankrupt firms.
    B–Bankrupt firms.
    TS–Total sample.
SOURCE: Zmijewski (1983, Tables 5 and 6): pp. 32–33.

International Evidence

Multivariate models of financial distress have been developed in many countries. Altman (1983, 1984) surveys models developed in the United States, Japan, Germany, Switzerland, Brazil, Australia, England, Ireland, Canada, the Netherlands, and France. One issue addressed in the survey was the similarity between the ratios of failed and nonfailed firms across national boundaries. Table 15.10 presents comparative average ratio results for several different countries. Also presented in Table 15.10 is the average Z_i score using the following multivariate model first published in Altman (1968):

$$Z_i = 1.2X_{1i} + 1.4X_{2i} + 3.3X_{3i} + .6X_{4i} + 1.0X_{5i} \qquad (15.3)$$

where

X_{1i} = (current assets − current liabilities)/total assets

X_{2i} = retained earnings/total assets

X_{3i} = earnings before interest and taxes/total assets

X_{4i} = market value of preferred and common equity/book value of total liabilities

X_{5i} = sales/total assets

Consider the following mean values for the bankrupt and nonbankrupt firms in Altman's (1968) estimation sample:

	Bankrupt Firms	Nonbankrupt Firms
X_{1i}	− .061	.414
X_{2i}	− .626	.355
X_{3i}	− .318	.154
X_{4i}	.401	2.477
X_{5i}	1.500	1.900

The resultant mean Z_i values for (15.3) would be − .258 for the bankrupt firm sample and 4.885 for the nonbankrupt firm sample. Altman (1984a) noted that "any firm with a Z-score below 1.8 is considered to be a prime candidate for bankruptcy, and the lower the score, the higher the failure probability" (p. 173). Table 15.10 presents means for the above five variables and the mean Z_i scores from (15.3). Across all five countries, there appear to be marked differences between the financial ratios of the failed and nonfailed groups of firms.

In some cases, the concern is with the financial distress of firms that do not have publicly traded securities. For many countries, such firms comprise a major component of corporate activity. Altman (1983, pp. 120–124) reestimated (15.3), with X_{4i} being the book value of preferred and common equity/book value of total liabilities. The coefficients for this revised model, which can be applied to both publicly traded and nonpublicly traded firms, are

$$Z_i = .717X_{1i} + .847X_{2i} + 3.107X_{3i} + .420X_{4i} + .998X_{5i} \qquad (15.4)$$

TABLE 15.10 International Comparison of Average Group Ratios

Financial Ratio	United States (Altman, 1968)	United States (Altman et al., 1977)	Australia (Castagna and Matolcsy, 1981)	Brazil (Altman et al., 1979)	Canada (Altman and Levallee, 1980)	Japan (Ko, 1981)
Failed groups						
X_1 = (Current assets − current liabilities)/Total assets	−.061	.150	.062	−.120	.100	−.181
X_2 = Retained earnings/Total assets	−.626	−.406	−.038	.010	N.A.	−.163
X_3 = Earnings before interest and taxes/Total assets	−.318	−.005	.002	.050	−.120	−.077
X_4 = Market value equity/Total liabilities	.401	.611	.800	.350	N.A.	.533
X_5 = Sales/Total assets	1.500	1.310	1.200	.880	1.480	1.052
Average Z_i score for multivariate model (15.3)	−.258	1.271	1.707	1.124	N.A.	.667
Nonfailed groups						
X_1 = (Current assets − current liabilities)/Total assets	.414	.309	.187	.230	.300	.107
X_2 = Retained earnings/Total assets	.355	.294	.220	.240	N.A.	.154
X_3 = Earnings before interest and taxes/Total assets	.153	.112	.086	.160	.040	.063
X_4 = Market value equity/Total assets	2.477	1.845	3.110	1.140	N.A.	.878
X_5 = Sales/Total assets	1.900	1.620	N.A.	1.230	2.310	.988
Average Z_i score for multivariate model (15.3)	4.885	3.878	4.003	3.053	N.A.	2.070

SOURCE: Altman (1984, Table 5): p. 195.
N.A.–Not available.

This revised model has a percentage-correct classification rate on the original estimation sample of 94% (62/66 correct) compared to 95% (63/66 correct) for (15.3). The cutoff points Altman reported for (15.3) and (15.4) were

	(15.3)	*(15.4)*
Assign to nonbankrupt group if $Z >$	2.99	2.90
Assign to bankrupt group if $Z <$	1.81	1.20
Gray area	1.81–2.99	1.20–2.90

The gray area refers to the Z score zone where misclassifications of firms arise. Altman (1983) noted that with (15.4) "the distribution of Z scores is now tighter with larger group overlap. The gray area (or ignorance zone) is wider. . . . All of this indicates that the revised model is probably less reliable than the original, but only slightly less" (p. 124).

C. Commercial Applications of Multivariate Models

An interesting commercial application of the research discussed in this chapter is the ZETA® CREDIT RISK reports produced by Zeta Services, Inc., of Hoboken, New Jersey. This service had its genesis in research reported in Altman, Haldeman, and Narayanan (1977). The multivariate model reported in this paper was based on the following seven variables:

1. Overall profitability: earnings before interest and taxes/total assets
2. Size: total assets
3. Debt service: earnings before interest and taxes/total interest payments
4. Liquidity: current ratio
5. Cumulative profitability: retained earnings/total assets
6. Market capitalization: five-year average of market value of common equity/five-year average of market value of total capital (includes preferred stock, long-term debt, and capitalized leases)
7. Earnings stability: normalized measure of the standard error of estimate around a ten-year trend in the overall profitability variable.

The coefficients on each variable are proprietary and are not disclosed.

Zeta Services provides the following information in its promotional literature:

ZETA is a risk evaluation model developed by Zeta Services Inc. For the development of ZETA, risk was defined as the inability of a company to meet its obligations. The ZETA SCORE tells a user how much a company resembles firms that have been poor credit risks, i.e., firms that have recently filed bankruptcy petitions. We are not interested in bankruptcy *per se* but we feel that it is an unequivocal credit standard. Prior to bankruptcy, companies have a strong tendency to pass common and preferred dividends, go into technical defaults and engage in forced sales of assets, all to the detriment of securities values. The ZETA model does not forecast failure or nonfailure and Zeta Services Inc. did not design it to do so. Rather, it compares a company's operating and financial characteristics to those of over 50 firms *which have already failed*. The test sample [used to develop the model] was composed of 53 industrial corporations which filed for bankruptcy or were taken over by their banks. No banks, finance companies, real estate companies or railroads were included. All firms were required to have at least $20 million in reported assets in the two years prior to bankruptcy. These firms were paired with other randomly selected, nonbankrupt firms in similar industries. The ZETA SCORE is the result of a linear combination of all seven variables (weighted by the discriminant analysis technique) plus a constant. Zero was the dividing line between nonfailing (positive scores) and failing firms (negative scores).

FIGURE 15.2   Performance of Zeta Credit Risk Model

A. Mean Zeta Credit Risk Score in Five-Year Period Prior to Bankruptcy

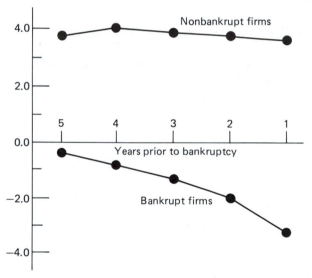

B. Distribution of Zeta Credit Risk Scores One Year Prior to Bankruptcy

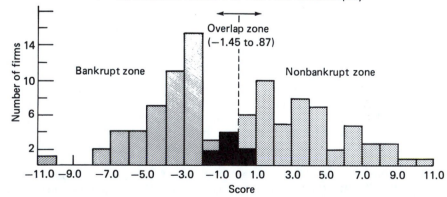

Source: Altman, Haldeman, and Narayanan (1977, Figures 1 and 2): p. 49.

ZETA™

CUSIP: 69805710
S & P'S RATING: B

PAN AMERICAN WORLD AIRWAYS INC
(PN)

SIC CODE: 4511
MOODY'S RATING: B

FISCAL YEAR END	ZETA		ADJUSTED PER SHARE DATA				UNFUNDED PENSION LIABILITIES AS A % OF NET ASSETS
	WEIGHTED SCORE	RELATIVE PERCENTILE	EARNINGS	DIVIDENDS	HIGH PRICE	LOW PRICE	
12/83	-3.28	7	-0.58	0.0	9.00	3.50	116
12/82	-4.17	4	-6.30	0.0	4.25	2.50	135
12/81	-2.04	10	-0.27	0.0	6.00	2.38	46
12/80	-1.00	16	1.13	0.0	6.13	3.75	28
12/79	-1.32	15	1.07	0.0	8.00	5.00	43
12/78	-1.34	15	2.31	0.0	10.75	4.75	44
12/77	-2.23	10	1.06	0.0	6.50	3.63	63
12/76	-2.10	11	2.27	0.0	7.88	4.25	59
12/75	-2.67	7	-1.11	0.0	5.75	2.00	29
12/74	-2.45	7	-2.00	0.0	5.50	1.75	11

MODEL VARIABLES - HISTORICAL ANALYSIS

FISCAL YEAR END	OVERALL PROFITABILITY		SIZE		DEBT SERVICE		LIQUIDITY		CUMULATIVE PROFITABILITY		MARKET CAPITALIZATION		EARNINGS STABILITY	
	INDEX	%-ILE	INDEX	%-ILE	INDEX	%-ILE	INDEX	%-ILE	INDEX	%-ILE	INDEX	%-ILE	INDEX	%-ILE
12/83	2	20	10	91	3	17	0	4	0	5	0	4	1	2
12/82	0	1	10	90	1	1	0	1	0	4	0	3	1	1
12/81	0	1	10	91	1	1	0	2	2	16	0	8	1	2
12/80	3	13	10	93	4	13	0	3	2	14	0	6	2	13
12/79	3	10	9	93	4	16	0	1	2	14	0	10	1	7
12/78	5	33	9	93	4	20	1	4	2	12	0	6	1	9
12/77	4	19	9	93	4	11	1	7	1	9	0	1	1	6
12/76	2	12	9	94	3	11	2	14	1	9	0	2	1	7
12/75	1	5	9	94	3	5	1	4	0	5	0	3	2	12
12/74	0	1	9	95	2	1	0	3	0	6	0	2	2	14

Zeta Services Inc., 1983
THIS REPORT HAS BEEN PREPARED FROM ORIGINAL SOURCES AND DATA WE BELIEVE RELIABLE BUT WE MAKE NO REPRESENTATIONS AS TO ITS ACCURACY OR COMPLETENESS.

PREPARED 5/84

FIGURE 15.3 Zeta Services Report for Pan American World Airways
Source: Zeta Services Inc., *Zeta Credit/Risk Evaluation* (Summer 1984).

Panel A of Figure 15.2 presents the mean ZETA® CREDIT RISK score for the two groups of firms in each of the five years prior to the year the bankrupt firm filed for bankruptcy. Over this period, the mean ZETA® CREDIT RISK score of the bankrupt group becomes more negative and the magnitude of the difference between the mean scores for the two groups becomes larger. Panel B of Figure 15.2 presents the distribution of ZETA® CREDIT RISK scores one year prior to bankruptcy for the firms used to develop the model. The area in which misclassifications of firms occur is from −1.45 to .87.

Figure 15.3 presents a Zeta Services report for Pan American World Airways. The ZETA® CREDIT RISK score for each year ranges from −1.00 in 1980 to −4.17 in 1982. Over the 1974–1983 period, Pan American has been in a continually distressed condition. One means it has used to survive in this period has been to sell major income-producing assets (for example, the Inter-Continental hotel chain) and to sell major real estate (for example, the Pan Am Building in New York City). The relative percentile in each report indicates where, on the population of ZETA® CREDIT RISK scores computed by Zeta Services, the ZETA® CREDIT RISK score of Pan American lies. For example, the relative percentile of 7 for the December 1983 fiscal year indicates that of all the companies rated in May 1984, 93% had ZETA® CREDIT RISK scores higher than Pan American. By reporting both the absolute ZETA® CREDIT RISK score and the relative percentile, the user can gain insight into how much of the change in a firm's ZETA® CREDIT RISK score is due to an overall economy change in the seven independent variables and how much is due to firm-specific changes in these seven independent variables.

Industry mean or median ZETA® CREDIT RISK scores can also be computed using the Zeta Services data base. Table 15.11 presents the ZETA® CREDIT RISK score and relative percentile for each of the four major U.S. automobile firms in the 1974–1983 period and the equally weighted mean for all four companies. Over this period, there was a marked increase in the financial distress level of this industry, as evidenced by the mean ZETA® CREDIT RISK score. (An analyst may also wish to value weight, say, by relative sales, the individual firm ZETA® CREDIT RISK scores when computing industry ZETA values.) Over the 1974–1983 period, the two most distressed automobile firms had external assistance to help weather their financial problems; American Motors had several large capital infusions from Renault, which gained a majority interest in this company, while Chrysler Corporation was provided with a U.S. government-backed loan guarantee. Table 15.12 presents the distribution of ZETA® CREDIT RISK scores in the 1974–1983 period for the population of firms monitored by Zeta Services.

Zeta Services is one of several firms that sell products that draw on, and now contribute to, research on financial distress analysis. Other firms in the United States include Advantage Financial Systems of Boston and the Trust Division of the First Union Bank, Charlotte, North Carolina. The Johannesburg stockbrokerage firm of Ivor Jones, Roy and Co. publishes a "financial ratings" service covering publicly traded South African companies. Financial distress anal-

TABLE 15.11 ZETA® CREDIT RISK Scores and Relative Percentile Values
of ZETA® CREDIT RISK Scores for U.S. Automobile Firms, 1974–1983

YEAR	American Motors		Chrysler Corp.		Ford Motor		General Motors		Mean ZETA Score for Four Companies
	ZETA SCORE	Relative Percentile	ZETA SCORE	Relative Percentile	ZETA SCORE	Relative Percentile	ZETA SCORE	Relative Percentile	
1974	2.23	41	1.82	37	4.72	64	6.63	79	3.85
1975	.05	24	1.37	36	4.27	63	6.52	81	3.05
1976	−.60	19	1.61	38	4.68	65	6.80	82	3.12
1977	−.22	21	1.05	31	4.52	62	6.71	80	3.01
1978	.48	27	.42	27	4.29	59	6.31	77	2.87
1979	1.10	33	−1.12	16	4.07	58	6.24	77	2.57
1980	−2.07	10	−3.55	5	2.26	41	4.51	61	.29
1981	−3.64	5	−3.68	5	1.77	35	3.91	55	−.41
1982	−4.54	4	−3.29	6	1.55	33	3.59	52	−.67
1983	−5.29	4	−2.38	9	2.03	38	3.99	55	−.41

SOURCE: Zeta Services, Inc.

TABLE 15.12 Distribution of ZETA® CREDIT RISK Scores in 1974–1983 Period for Population of Firms Monitored by Zeta Services

Year	*Percentiles of Distribution of ZETA® CREDIT RISK Scores*									
	5%	*15*	*25*	*35*	*45*	*55*	*65*	*75*	*85*	*95*
1974	− 3.61	− 1.37	.18	1.27	2.22	3.27	4.45	5.71	7.08	9.93
1975	− 3.99	− 1.39	.14	1.30	2.41	3.51	4.58	5.81	7.28	9.97
1976	− 4.27	− 1.28	.23	1.46	2.57	3.76	4.88	5.97	7.50	10.23
1977	− 4.58	− 1.35	.09	1.31	2.63	3.85	4.87	6.01	7.62	10.33
1978	− 4.41	− 1.46	.03	1.27	2.57	3.67	4.81	6.04	7.68	10.22
1979	− 3.78	− 1.18	.29	1.38	2.58	3.69	4.88	6.11	7.74	10.21
1980	− 3.87	− 1.18	.33	1.66	2.80	3.90	4.94	6.22	7.83	10.35
1981	− 4.12	− 1.00	.44	1.71	2.93	3.89	4.83	6.30	8.01	10.73
1982	− 4.92	− 1.29	.25	1.60	2.66	3.89	4.87	6.12	7.92	10.58
1983	− 4.88	− 1.55	.20	1.67	2.81	3.97	5.11	6.33	8.07	10.63

SOURCE: Zeta Services, Inc.

ysis for U.K. firms is provided by two commercial services, Datastream and Performance Analysis Services Ltd. See Taffler (1984) for a description of these two services and a detailed description of U.K. research on distress analysis.

15.6 CAPITAL MARKET REACTION TO FINANCIAL DISTRESS

Studies examining financial statement variables report that as early as three to five years prior to bankruptcy, the financial ratios of bankrupt firms start to exhibit behavior different from those of nonbankrupt firms. Studies examining the behavior of the security returns of bankrupt stocks likewise report that the capital market revises downward its valuation of these companies well before the date that the bankruptcy is announced, for example, Beaver (1968); Aharony, Jones, and Swary (1980); Pettway and Sinkey (1980); Shick and Sherman (1980); Altman and Brenner (1981); and Clark and Weinstein (1983). Results from two representative studies are

1. Aharony, Jones, and Swary (1980) compared the returns of 45 industrial U.S. companies that went bankrupt in the 1970–1978 period with 65 control firms (matched in industry and firm size). The average weekly risk-adjusted return for each group was calculated. Letting week 0 be the week that bankruptcy is declared, the mean risk-adjusted return difference between the bankrupt and nonbankrupt firms was

Time Period	*Average Weekly Return Difference*	t *Statistic*
− 312 to − 209 weeks	− .19%	− 1.32
− 208 to − 105 weeks	− .28	− 1.74
− 104 to − 53 weeks	− .31	− 1.54
− 52 to − 21 weeks	− .68	− 2.78
− 20 to − 1 weeks	− 1.30	− 2.38

The authors concluded "that investors adjusted gradually to the declining solvency position of the bankrupt firms over approximately a four-year period" (p. 1011). The sharpest decline in the average weekly return difference was in the seven weeks prior to bankruptcy.

2. Clark and Weinstein (1983) report results similar to those of Aharony, Jones, and Swary (1980) for 36 bankruptcy filings by NYSE-listed firms between 1962 and 1979 for the average daily return in the period immediately surrounding the filing of the bankruptcy petition. Observations on only a subset of the 36 firms were available, due to nontrading in the stocks of many companies in their sample.

Time Period	Average Daily Returns	Number of Observations
Day −3	−1.2%	42
Day −2	−3.1	31
Day −1	−8.2	23
Day 0	−28.5	12

The conclusion was that "although shareholders have suffered losses prior to event day −1, they typically suffer additional large losses in a very short period immediately surrounding a bankruptcy filing" (p. 496).

There are several reasons for expecting capital market variables to contain information about financial distress, over and above that in linear additive multivariate models based on financial statement data:

a. Capital markets can recognize nonlinear and multiplicative relationships between financial statement data and financial distress

b. Capital markets can access information not reflected in financial statements, for example, the recent entry of new competitors with lower-cost manufacturing plants.

For similar reasons, a variable such as a bond rating could contain information relevant to distress prediction. The challenge facing analysts is to exploit the incremental information in security return behavior and bond-rating changes when developing distress prediction models.

15.7 SOME GENERAL COMMENTS

1. Economic theory has played a small role in the development of univariate or multivariate distress prediction models. The few attempts at having theoretical analysis guide empirical model development have drawn on the statistics or mathematics literature. For instance, Wilcox (1973) and Vinso (1979) both used the gambler's ruin model from the statistics literature. More recent papers have used catastrophe theory models from the mathematics literature, for example, Ho and Saunders (1980) and Scapens, Ryan, and Fletcher (1981). The absence of an economic underpinning to modeling in this area has led to trenchant criticism of

research on financial distress. The position taken in this book is that the major contribution of the research to date is documenting empirical regularities. This documentation is important both for decision making by creditors and management and to researchers wishing to model economic aspects of financial distress.

2. One consequence of the lack of an economic theory to guide research is that individual authors have undertaken extensive "searching exercises" with the object of discovering models with significant predictive power. This searching can occur in several areas:

a. Searching over N different models, for example, linear additive versus non-linear multiplicative

b. Searching over N independent variables, for example, starting with 30 variables and choosing the subset that includes the "best" performers

c. Searching over N firms, for example, starting with data for 100 firms over 10 years and then excluding firms/years for which the model performs worst (typically with an ex post rationalization)

d. Searching over N estimation techniques, for example, linear discriminant analysis versus quadratic discriminant analysis.

When even a subset of combinations within (a) to (d) are examined, by chance alone one or more subsets of data can be statistically significant.

Given the potential for overfitting the data by "searching exercises," it is critical that researchers develop procedures to gain unbiased estimates of the predictive performance of the chosen multivariate model. One such procedure is to divide the initial sample into an estimation sample and a hold-out sample, with the hold-out sample only being used to provide estimates of the predictive ability of the model developed from the estimation sample. A variant of this approach is to use observations from one time period (say, 1980–1983) to develop the model and then to use observations from a subsequent time period (say, 1984–1986) to gain estimates of the predictive ability of the model. With this variant, any decrease in the predictive ability for the hold-out sample will reflect nonstationarity between the two periods as well as search bias on the estimation sample and random chance factors. A third approach, known as the Lachenbruch method, sequentially holds out each observation and predicts its status using a model estimated on the remaining observations. The overall predictive performance of the model is assessed by the percentage of the sequentially held-out observations whose status is correctly predicted. A detailed discussion of issues in this area is in Altman et al. (1981, Chap. 3).

The Zmijewski (1983) research described earlier used logit as the statistical technique for estimating each multivariate model. Many other studies have used linear or quadratic discriminant analysis. To date, research generally has concluded that the classification performance of multivariate models is not highly sensitive to the choice of the statistical technique. Hamer (1983), for example, compared the performance of failure-prediction models using four alternative variable sets on firms that failed from 1966 to 1975. The sets of variables were those found in four prior studies: Altman (1968), Deakin (1972), Blum (1974), and Ohlson (1980). For each variable set, a linear discriminant model, a quadratic discriminant model, and a logit model were developed. The conclusion was that "for a given variable set, the linear and logit models had comparable misclassification rates and performed at least as well as the quadratic model. Using linear discriminant analysis or logit analysis, all four variable sets performed comparably" (p. 289).

3. One limitation of much of the published research arises from the retrospective or ex post nature of the analysis; that is, the estimation and validation samples both include firms that are known to have "failed" or not "failed" on a set date. Thus, it is possible in the research to compare the financial ratios of failed and nonfailed firms one year, two years, and so on prior to failure. Yet, in decision-making contexts, one knows neither which firms will fail nor the date on which they will fail. To demonstrate that the results of this research have direct applicability to applied decision contexts, it would be necessary to make predictions about the failure (and its timing) of firms currently nonfailed. The existing literature has not yet addressed itself to the important task of including a time dimension in its failure predictions. One problem in this area when examining the timing of bankruptcies is that the exact date of the bankruptcy filing can be influenced by a diverse set of factors not easily factored into a model, for example, the willingness of a bank to restructure a loan, the bankruptcy of a major creditor, or the timing of a forthcoming labor contract renegotiation.

4. The sample selection criteria used in many studies make it difficult to draw inferences about the performance of multivariate functions for the general population. An extreme example is provided by studies that use samples of 50% failed and 50% nonfailed firms. In the Dun & Bradstreet (1985) survey of business failures in the 1925–1983 period, the failure percentages ranged from 1.54% in 1932 to .04% in 1945; the 1983 rate was 1.1%. One important strength of the Zmijewski (1983) study discussed previously in this chapter was the use of a sample that better approximated the general population.

The requirement of some studies that a firm have at least five years of financial data available omits from the analysis newly formed firms in which the incidence of corporate failure is relatively high. The Dun & Bradstreet (1985) survey notes that 47.0% of the failures that occurred in 1983 were businesses that had been in existence five years or less. This statistic suggests that age may well be an important variable when building a discriminant model to predict failure.

Zmijewski (1984) provides further discussion of methodological issues in this area, with specific attention to "oversampling" of distressed firms and the deletion of firms when certain data items for them are not available.

5. The use of a paired-sample design, where firms are matched on size and industry criteria, effectively precludes these variables as indicators of financial distress in the study. Yet there is considerable evidence that both size and industry groups contain important information on distress likelihood. For example, Dun & Bradstreet (1985) gives the following industry information on 1983 failure rates:

	Failure Rate per 10,000 Operating Concerns
Manufacturing	
Furniture	211
Transportation equipment	180
Textiles	126
Food	93
Paper	71
Retail	
Infant and children's wear	227
Sporting goods	116
Men's wear	112
Eating and drinking places	65
Department stores	34

Thus, differences do appear across industries in their observed failure rates. Incorporating these differences into a discriminant model could well improve its predictive ability.

6. Many studies report that financial statement-based variables of distressed firms behave over time differently from those of nondistressed firms. A natural extension is to ask if the results in these studies are sensitive to the use of alternative accounting methods. To date, there is very little evidence that making adjustments to place all firms on a consistent set of accounting methods, or using a nonreported accounting method, significantly improves the predictive ability of multivariate bankruptcy prediction models. For instance, Norton and Smith (1979) conclude that "in spite of the sizable differences in magnitude that existed between general price level and historical cost financial statements, little difference was found in the bankruptcy predictions. General price level data were shown to be consistently neither more nor less accurate than historical data for predictions of bankruptcy" (p. 72). Mensah (1983) examined "the usefulness of specific price-level–adjusted data for bankruptcy prediction." The conclusion was that specific price-level "data do not greatly improve bankruptcy prediction" (p. 228) vis-à-vis models estimated using historical cost-based variables.

Altman, Haldeman, and Narayanan (1977) went to much effort to use footnote data and to make several accounting adjustments to the firms in their sample; for example, they capitalized "all non-cancellable operating and finance leases," deducted goodwill and intangibles from assets and equity, and consolidated "captive finance companies . . . with the parent company accounts as well as the information would allow. The pooling of interest method was used" (p. 33). One motivation for these adjustments was to make the model more compatible with recent financial reporting requirements imposed by the FASB or the SEC. Unfortunately, the authors did not report how the results based on the adjusted data compared with models based on the (nonadjusted) numbers reported in the basic financial statements.

15.8 SUMMARY

1. Research on financial distress has benefited considerably from continued interaction between the academic and the business community. This interaction has been motivated, in part, by the many decisions in which information on financial distress likelihood is relevant. Most progress has been made in documenting empirical regularities in the profiles of financially distressed and nondistressed firms. Considerable refinement also has been made over time in the statistical techniques used and the research designs employed in model development.

2. From a pragmatic decision-making perspective, an important criterion when evaluating the literature discussed in this chapter is whether better decisions can be made using the documented empirical regularities vis-à-vis the decisions made ignoring these regularities. Using this criterion, the potential contribution of the financial distress analysis literature is substantial.

QUESTIONS

QUESTION 15.1: Profile Analysis for Failed and Nonfailed Firms

Table 15.13 presents the means of several financial statement items for a sample of 32 failed firms and a matched sample of 32 nonfailed firms. A firm was defined as failed if it experienced bankruptcy, insolvency, or was otherwise liquidated for the benefit of creditors during the 1964–1970 period. Each failed firm was matched with a nonfailed firm on the basis of industry classification, calendar year, and asset size as of five years prior to failure. Table 15.13 presents mean financial statement items for each of the five years prior to the bankruptcy, insolvency, or liquidation. These data are based on research conducted by E. Deakin.

REQUIRED

1. What are the problems in using bankruptcy, insolvency, or liquidation as the criterion for determining if a firm was distressed or nondistressed?
2. Use the data in Table 15.13 to determine which financial ratios exhibited the most marked differential behavior for the failed and nonfailed firms in the five-year period prior to failure? Use the graphical approach illustrated in Figure 15.1.
3. Compare the results from (2) with those in the Beaver (1966) study.

TABLE 15.13 Mean Financial Items of Failed and Nonfailed Firms ($000s)

PANEL A. FAILED FIRMS

	Years Before Failure				
Financial Item	*5*	*4*	*3*	*2*	*1*
Balance sheet data					
1. Cash and marketable securities	753	1,020	730	511	329
2. Accounts receivable	1,845	3,164	3,563	2,359	2,090
3. Inventories	2,827	6,064	7,390	2,525	2,378
4. Other assets	3,937	7,018	8,332	5,107	5,229
5. Total assets	9,362	17,266	20,015	10,502	10,026
6. Current liabilities	3,780	4,820	8,092	6,102	6,860
7. Other liabilities	2,149	8,617	9,784	3,537	3,408
8. Net worth	3,433	3,829	2,139	863	− 242
9. Liabilities and net worth	9,362	17,266	20,015	10,502	10,026
Income and funds statement data					
10. Sales	16,508	15,425	18,359	16,656	16,938
11. Net income	65	− 29	− 664	− 858	− 1,309
12. Cash flow	145	308	− 244	− 518	− 909

PANEL B. NONFAILED FIRMS

	Years Before Failure				
Financial Item	*5*	*4*	*3*	*2*	*1*
Balance sheet data					
1. Cash and marketable securities	981	1,086	1,107	1,304	1,365
2. Accounts receivable	1,716	1,730	1,837	2,146	2,358
3. Inventories	3,022	3,000	3,006	3,479	3,974
4. Other assets	3,678	3,995	4,225	5,243	5,565
5. Total assets	9,397	9,811	10,175	12,172	13,262
6. Current liabilities	2,023	2,251	2,370	2,920	3,305
7. Other liabilities	2,169	2,432	2,479	2,826	3,800
8. Net worth	5,205	5,128	5,326	6,426	6,157
9. Liabilities and net worth	9,397	9,811	10,175	12,172	13,262
Income and funds statement data					
10. Sales	16,989	16,395	17,610	20,445	22,426
11. Net income	206	46	211	426	480
12. Cash flow	523	381	577	865	941

4. In drawing inferences about the differential behavior of the ratios of failed and nonfailed firms, what problems arise from the matched sample selection criteria?

5. Comment on the following statements:

- Profile analysis can demonstrate that failed and nonfailed firms have dissimilar ratios, not that ratios have predictive power. But the crucial problem is to make an inference in the reverse direction, that is, from ratios to failures.

- This research does not deal with the prediction of business failures. It represents an autopsy of deceased firms.

QUESTION 15.2: Predicting Financial Distress of Property-Liability Insurers

Statutes in all states of the United States provide for an insurance department that has the responsibility of "supervising insurance companies and enforcing compliance with the law." The concerns of these insurance departments include

1. Solvency of insurers
2. Propriety of premium rates
3. Fair dealings with the policyholders
4. Uniform financial reporting

A number of techniques have been used in the solvency monitoring process: audits of annual statements, screening financial ratios and company data, observing consumer complaints, and actions by other state insurance departments or industry groups.

Research by Pinches and Trieschmann has examined univariate and multivariate financial distress prediction models that could be used in monitoring the solvency of property-liability insurers. A sample comprising both insolvent and solvent firms was used in their research. The selection criteria for the insolvent firms were

1. Involuntary receivership, rehabilitation, conservatorship, or liquidation
2. Asset size of at least $100,000
3. Availability of two years of financial data
4. No overlapping management between distress firms
5. No exchanges, bonding, fraternals, or guaranty firms
6. Reinsurance of less than 100% before distress.

These insolvent firms were matched with solvent firms from a set of companies that met the following criteria:

1. Property-liability firms licensed in the state of Missouri
2. Total asset size of less than $30 million
3. Not affiliated with or owned by another company with more than $30 million in assets.

This question uses 24 of the 52 firms in the Pinches and Trieschmann research. Twelve firms are used for an estimation sample and an additional 12 for a validation sample. Each sample includes six insolvent firms and six matched solvent firms. Three variables from the original set of 70 variables are examined:

X_1 = Book value (cost) of stocks/Market price of stocks

X_2 = Combined ratio

X_3 = Direct premiums written/Policyholders' surplus

The X_1 variable was developed to measure investment management performance. Pinches and Trieschmann argued that "since distressed firms have a higher ratio, one could assume that their stock investments have not increased in value to the same extent that solvent firms' stock investments have. Because market price is in the denominator, a lower ratio reflects better performance."

The X_2 variable (combined ratio) is the sum of the loss ratio and the expense ratio. These two ratios are frequently used in this industry to measure profitability. The two ratios are calculated as follows:

$$\text{Loss ratio} = \frac{\text{Loss and loss adjustment expenses incurred}}{\text{Net earned premiums}}$$

$$\text{Expense ratio} = \frac{\text{Underwriting expenses incurred}}{\text{Net written premiums}}$$

Pinches and Trieschmann hypothesized that "one would expect the distress firm's ratio to be higher than the solvent firm's ratio. This relationship would reflect on the greater profitability of solvent firms."

The X_3 variable was used as a measure of underwriting risk "where a high ratio indicates greater underwriting exposure and more risk." Pinches and Trieschmann cited research that reported that a sample of six failed automobile insurance companies had a higher average net premiums written to policyholders' surplus ratio than did a sample of ten surviving automobile insurance companies.

Table 15.14 (panel A) reports the twelve firms in the estimation sample and their values of the foregoing ratios. The ratios for the insolvent firms are taken from the last financial statement issued prior to "liquidation" or "receivership." The ratios for each solvent firm are taken from the same financial year that the ratios of the matched insolvent firm are taken from. Table 15.14 (panel B) provides similar details for the firms in the validation sample.

REQUIRED:

A. *Univariate Prediction Models*

   1. What evidence is there of differences in the mean ratio of the insolvent firms and the solvent firms for X_1, X_2, and X_3? Are these differences in the direction predicted by Pinches and Trieschmann?

   2. For each ratio, choose the cutoff point that minimizes the total number of misclassifications. The exact cutoff point is to be the midpoint between adjacently ranked ratios. If several cutoff points give the same total number of misclassifications, choose that cutoff (from these) that minimizes the number of Type I errors.

   3. For each ratio, evaluate the predictive ability of the cutoff point developed

TABLE 15.14 Property-Liability Insurers: Estimation and Validation Samples

PANEL A. ESTIMATION SAMPLE	X_1	X_2	X_3
Solvent firms			
1. LaSalle National Insurance Company	.398	.928	1.050
2. Maine Insurance Company	.757	.960	1.924
3. Wabash Fire & Casualty Insurance Company	.701	.983	2.963
4. Workmen's & Suffolk Mutual Insurance	.802	.730	1.768
5. Great Northern Casualty Mutual Company	.705	.965	1.386
6. Highway Insurance Company	.979	.964	4.161
Insolvent firms			
7. Pennsylvania Millers Mutual Insurance	1.545	1.318	7.815
8. Continental Western Insurance Company	.846	1.024	2.737
9. Mid-Continent Casualty Company	.773	1.296	2.869
10. Church Mutual Insurance Company	1.314	1.042	2.187
11. Protective Insurance Company	1.011	.990	9.221
12. Great Central Insurance Company	1.120	.975	8.989

PANEL B. VALIDATION SAMPLE	X_1	X_2	X_3
Solvent firms			
1. Knickerbocker Insurance Company	.600	1.120	.892
2. Mid-Central Mutual Casualty Company	.558	.816	.896
3. Mid-America Mutual Insurance Company	.382	.950	.240
4. State Fire & Casualty Company	.530	.956	2.684
5. St. Lawrence Insurance Company	.851	.890	1.946
6. Reliable Mutual Insurance Company	.602	1.008	4.905
Insolvent firms			
7. Square Deal Insurance Company	1.168	1.077	4.056
8. Druggists Mutual Insurance Company	1.072	1.014	11.720
9. Germantown Insurance Company	1.148	.765	12.643
10. Millers Mutual Fire Insurance Co. of Texas	.984	1.023	2.298
11. National Automobile & Casualty Insurance Co.	.780	1.048	5.475
12. Traders & General Insurance Company	1.000	.996	7.287

in (2) on the validation sample. Why is it important to examine the predictive ability of a univariate model on a validation sample?

4. Evaluate X_1 as a measure of the investment management performance of a property-liability insurer.

B. *Multivariate Prediction Models*

1. Consider the following linear discriminant function, which is based on the estimation sample data:

$$Z_i = -5.822X_{2,i} - .287X_{3,i}$$

Choose the cutoff point that minimizes the total number of misclassifications in the estimation sample. The exact cutoff point is to be the midpoint between adjacently ranked Z_i scores. Present the classification matrix for this discriminant function.

2. Evaluate the predictive ability of the model chosen in B.1 on the validation sample.

3. Discuss areas where multivariate models of solvency could be useful to an insurance regulator.

4. Suppose an insurance regulator decided to adopt a multivariate model for monitoring the solvency of property-liability insurers. Why might the regulator be reluctant to make public the full details of this model?

QUESTION 15.3: Multivariate Financial Distress Scoring Systems: Analysis of U.S. Airline Companies

Several commercial services are available that provide subscribers with numerical codings of the financial distress (or lack thereof) of broad cross sections of companies. Section 15.5.C. discussed Zeta Services, Inc., which provides individual reports for a broad cross section of U.S. companies. Table 15.15 presents ZETA® CREDIT RISK scores and the relative percentile figure of each ZETA® CREDIT RISK score for 12 U.S. airline companies over a ten-year period (1974–1983). Table 15.12 presents distribution statistics of ZETA® CREDIT RISK scores in the 1974–1983 period for the population of firms monitored by Zeta Services.

REQUIRED

1. Zeta Services stresses that "the ZETA® CREDIT RISK model does not forecast failure or nonfailure and Zeta Services Inc. did not design it to do so. Rather, it compares a company's operating and financial characteristics to those of over 50 firms which have already failed." What distinctions are being made in this statement? Why might Zeta Services not design its ZETA® CREDIT RISK model to forecast failure or nonfailure?

2. Using the data in this question, what inferences can you make about relative changes in the "financial health" of firms in the U.S. airline industry in the 1974–1983 period? Can the data referenced in this question provide any insight into the "financial health" of the airline industry vis-à-vis other industries?

3. What uses could the following parties make of the data in Tables 15.12 and 15.15 (and Figure 15.3):

   a. Management of individual airline companies

   b. Investors and security analysts

   c. Creditors

   d. Government officials

4. Why might a firm with a relatively low ZETA® CREDIT RISK score in each year over an extended time period (say, even ten years) be able to avoid becoming bankrupt?

5. *Business Week* recently published an article that discussed firms with high negative ZETA® CREDIT RISK scores. Scores for individual companies were reported. What might be the reaction of these companies to the publication of these scores? Is it responsible journalism to publish them?

TABLE 15.15 ZETA® CREDIT RISK Scores and Relative Percentile of ZETA® CREDIT RISK Scores for Selected U.S. Airline Companies

PANEL A. ZETA® CREDIT RISK Scores

Year	AMR (American)	Alaska Airlines	Braniff	Delta Airlines	Eastern Airlines	Northwest Orient	PSA	Pan American	UAL (United)	U.S. Air Group	Western Airlines	World Airways
1974	−.30	−7.28	.04	2.35	−2.14	4.06	−1.17	−2.45	.14	−2.89	−.50	1.98
1975	−.50	−5.55	.10	2.03	−2.80	3.71	−2.18	−2.67	−.44	−3.85	−.81	2.88
1976	−.31	−4.48	.63	3.06	−2.37	5.38	−1.22	−2.10	−.35	−3.21	−1.10	2.61
1977	−.43	−4.17	1.02	4.26	−2.60	6.57	−1.92	−2.23	.24	−2.76	−.82	2.82
1978	−.61	−3.11	1.21	5.40	−2.46	5.87	−1.96	−1.34	.97	−2.13	−.68	−1.04
1979	−.67	−3.69	−2.18	6.02	−1.92	4.81	−1.55	−1.32	−.57	−1.49	−.68	−1.35
1980	−1.78	−3.29	−3.40	4.30	−2.21	5.16	−2.42	−1.00	−.29	−.77	−2.21	−2.86
1981	−1.42	−2.95	−5.37	4.87	−2.49	5.79	−1.67	−2.04	−.77	−.06	−3.57	−3.27
1982	−1.45	−1.89	−15.42	2.81	−2.55	7.46	−1.81	−4.17	−.79	1.14	−3.85	−2.60
1983	.01	−1.11	Bankrupt	.57	−2.81	6.28	−2.34	−3.28	−.30	1.71	−4.78	−3.64

PANEL B. Relative Percentile of ZETA® CREDIT RISK Scores

Year	AMR (American)	Alaska Airlines	Braniff	Delta Airlines	Eastern Airlines	Northwest Orient	PSA	Pan American	UAL (United)	U.S. Air Group	Western Airlines	World Airways
1974	18	1	21	42	9	61	13	7	22	6	19	42
1975	19	2	24	42	7	56	9	7	20	4	18	48
1976	21	4	29	50	10	70	16	11	21	6	15	45
1977	20	5	31	59	9	79	11	10	25	8	18	46
1978	19	7	33	70	10	73	12	15	31	11	19	17
1979	19	6	11	74	12	63	14	15	20	14	18	14
1980	12	6	6	59	10	67	9	16	20	17	9	7
1981	13	7	3	64	8	71	12	10	17	21	5	6
1982	12	10	1	44	8	82	11	4	16	30	6	9
1983	23	16	Bankrupt	26	8	74	9	7	20	36	5	7

SOURCE: Zeta Services, Inc.

6. You are hired by Zeta Services to help develop the next set of products (or refinements of existing products) that it will develop and market. What areas would you think hold the most promise in the financial distress analysis area?

REFERENCES

AHARONY, J., C. O. JONES, and I. SWARY. "An Analysis of Risk and Return Characteristics of Corporate Bankruptcy Using Capital Market Data." *The Journal of Finance* (September 1980): 1001–1016.

ALTMAN, E. I. "Financial Ratios, Discriminant Analysis and the Prediction of Corporate Bankruptcy." *The Journal of Finance* (September 1968): 589–609.

ALTMAN, E. I. "Predicting Railroad Bankruptcies in America." *Bell Journal of Economics and Management Science* (Spring 1973): 184–211.

ALTMAN, E. I. *Corporate Financial Distress.* New York: John Wiley, 1983.

ALTMAN, E. I. "The Success of Business Failure Prediction Models: An International Survey." *Journal of Banking and Finance* (June 1984a): 171–198. Published by North-Holland Publishing Company, Amsterdam, 1984.

ALTMAN, E. I. "A Further Empirical Investigation of the Bankruptcy Cost Question." *The Journal of Finance* (September 1984b): 1067–1089.

ALTMAN, E. I., R. B. AVERY, R. A. EISENBEIS, and J. F. SINKEY. *Application of Classification Techniques in Business, Banking and Finance.* Greenwich, Conn.: JAI Press, 1981.

ALTMAN, E. I., T. BAIDYA, and L. M. RIBERIO-DIAS. "Assessing Potential Financial Problems of Firms in Brazil." *Journal of International Business Studies* (Fall 1979): 9–24.

ALTMAN, E. I., and M. BRENNER. "Information Effects and Stock Market Response to Signs of Firm Deterioration." *Journal of Financial and Quantitative Analysis* (March 1981): 35–51.

ALTMAN, E. I., R. G. HALDEMAN, and P. NARAYANAN. "Zeta Analysis: A New Model to Identify Bankruptcy Risk of Corporations." *Journal of Banking and Finance* (June 1977): 29–54. Published by North-Holland Publishing Company, Amsterdam, 1977.

ALTMAN, E. I., and M. Y. LEVALLEE. "Business Failure Classification in Canada." *Journal of Business Administration* (Fall 1980): 147–164.

BALL, R., and G. FOSTER. "Corporate Financial Reporting: A Methodological Review of Empirical Research." *Studies of Current Research Methodologies in Accounting: A Critical Evaluation,* Supplement to *Journal of Accounting Research* (1982): 161–234.

BEAVER, W. H. "Financial Ratios as Predictors of Failure." *Empirical Research in Accounting,* Supplement to *Journal of Accounting Research* (1966): 71–111.

BEAVER, W. H. "Market Prices, Financial Ratios, and the Prediction of Failure." *Journal of Accounting Research* (Autumn 1968): 179–192.

BLUM, M. "Failing Company Discriminant Analysis." *Journal of Accounting Research* (Spring 1974): 1–25.

CASTAGNA, A. D., and Z. P. MATOLCSY. "The Prediction of Corporate Failure: Testing the Australian Experience." *Australian Journal of Management* (June 1981): 23–50.

CLARK, T. A., and M. I. WEINSTEIN. "The Behavior of the Common Stock of Bankrupt Firms." *The Journal of Finance* (May 1983): 489–504.

DAMBOLENA, I. G., and S. J. KHOURY. "Ratio Stability and Corporate Failure." *The Journal of Finance* (September 1980): 1017–1026.

DEAKIN, E. B. "A Discriminant Analysis of Predictors of Business Failure." *Journal of Accounting Research* (Spring 1972): 167–179.

DUN & BRADSTREET. *The 1982–1983 Business Failure Record.* New York: Dun & Bradstreet, 1985.

FRYDMAN, H., E. I. ALTMAN, and D. L. KAO. "Introducing Recursive Partitioning for Financial Classification: The Case of Financial Distress." *The Journal of Finance* (March 1985): 269–291.

HAMER, M. M. "Failure Prediction: Sensitivity of Classification Accuracy to Alternative Statistical Methods and Variable Sets." *Journal of Accounting and Public Policy* (Winter 1983): 289–307.

HO, T., and A. SAUNDERS. "A Catastrophe Model of Bank Failure." *The Journal of Finance* (December 1980): 1189–1207.

KO, C. J. *A Delineation of Corporate Appraisal Methods and Classification of Bankruptcy Firms in Japan,* unpublished thesis. New York University, 1982.

LINCOLN, M. "An Empirical Study of the Usefulness of Accounting Ratios to Describe Levels of Insolvency Risk." *Journal of Banking and Finance* (June 1984): 321–340.

MARAIS, M. L., J. M. PATELL, and M. A. WOLFSON. "The Experimental Design of Classification Models: An Application of Recursive Partitioning and Bootstrapping to Commercial Bank Loan Classifications," in *Studies on Current Econometric Issues in Accounting Research*, supplement to *Journal of Accounting Research* (1984): 87–114.

MENSAH, Y. M. "The Differential Bankruptcy Predictive Ability of Specific Price Level Adjustments: Some Empirical Evidence." *The Accounting Review,* (April 1983): 228–246.

NORTON, C. L., and R. E. SMITH. "A Comparison of General Price Level and Historical Cost Financial Statements in the Prediction of Bankruptcy." *The Accounting Review* (January 1979): 72–87.

OHLSON, J. S. "Financial Ratios and the Probabilistic Prediction of Bankruptcy." *Journal of Accounting Research* (Spring 1980): 109–131.

PETTWAY, R. H., and J. F. SINKEY. "Establishing On-Site Bank Examination Priorities: An Early-Warning System Using Accounting and Market Information." *The Journal of Finance* (March 1980): 137–150.

PINCHES, G. E., and J. S. TRIESCHMANN. "The Efficiency of Alternative Models for Solvency Surveillance in the Insurance Industry." *Journal of Risk and Insurance* (December 1974): 563–577.

PINCHES, G. E., and J. S. TRIESCHMANN. "Discriminant Analysis, Classification Results, and Financially Distressed P-L Insurers." *Journal of Risk and Insurance* (June 1977): 289–298.

ROSE, P. S., W. T. ANDREWS, and G. A. GIROUX. "Predicting Business Failure: A Macroeconomic Perspective." *Journal of Accounting, Auditing & Finance*. (Fall 1982): 20–31.

SCAPENS, R. W., R. J. RYAN, and L. FLETCHER. "Explaining Corporate Failure: A Catastrophe Theory Approach." *Journal of Business Finance and Accounting* (Spring 1981): 1–26.

SCHIPPER, K. "Financial Distress in Private Colleges." *Studies on Measurement and Evaluation of the Economic Efficiency of Pubic and Private Nonprofit Institutions,* Supplement to *Journal of Accounting Research* (1977): 1–45.

SCOTT, J. "The Probability of Bankruptcy: A Comparison of Empirical Predictions and Theoretical Models." *Journal of Banking and Finance* (September 1981): 317–344.

SHICK, R. A., and L. F. SHERMAN. "Bank Stock Prices as an Early Warning System for Changes in Condition." *Journal of Bank Research* (Autumn 1980): 136–146.

TAFFLER, R. J. "Empirical Methods for the Monitoring of U.K. Corporations." *Journal of Banking and Finance* (June 1984): 199–227.

VINSO, J. "A Determination of the Risk of Ruin." *Journal of Financial and Quantitative Analysis* (March 1979): 77–100.

WILCOX, J. W. "A Prediction of Business Failure Using Accounting Data." *Empirical Research in Accounting: Selected Studies,* Supplement to *Journal of Accounting Research* (1973): 163–179.

ZAVGREN, C. V. "The Prediction of Corporate Failure: The State of the Art." *Journal of Accounting Literature* (Spring 1983): 1–38.

ZETA SERVICES. *Zeta Credit/Risk Evaluation.* Hoboken, N.J.: Zeta Services Inc., various editions.

ZMIJEWSKI, M. E. "Predicting Corporate Bankruptcy: An Empirical Comparison of the Extant Financial Distress Models," working paper. State University of New York at Buffalo, 1983.

ZMIJEWSKI, M. E. "Methodological Issues Related to the Estimation of Financial Distress Prediction Models." *Studies on Current Econometric Issues in Accounting Research,* Supplement to *Journal of Accounting Research* (1984): 59–82.

16

LOAN DECISIONS AND FINANCIAL INFORMATION

16.1 INTRODUCTION

This chapter examines the use and potential use of financial statement and other information in loan decisions. There are many aspects to such decisions. When a bank is approached by a new loan applicant, the decision is not simply to grant a loan or not grant a loan. In the grant loan alternative, decisions about the rate of interest to charge, the amount of the loan, and the restrictions to be placed on the borrower must be made. Having decided to grant an applicant a loan, the bank faces further decisions. The bank may attempt to design an early warning system to anticipate loan defaults. The design of such a system entails decisions about the model to use for predicting default, and about the variables to include in the model. If a loan actually defaults, decisions relating to the restructuring of the loan may be made. This chapter explores aspects of loan decisions, the benefits of using quantitative models in those decisions, and issues related to the analysis of financial statement information in those decisions.

16.2 INFORMATION SOURCES FOR LOAN DECISIONS

The information sources an analyst can access include

1. *Loan applicant.* Information requested from the applicant can include past financial statements, projections of financial statement items (for example, cash flow), descriptions of the assets offered as collateral, and details of business plans and management experience.

2. *Lending institution files and personnel.* If the applicant is already a client of the bank, information about the prior payment record, the past track record of management, and so on may be readily available. Even if the applicant is a new client, information in the loan institution's files about "comparable firms" (for example, those in the same industry) can be useful in decision making. This information can be accessed in a heuristic way or via the development of a distress prediction model, a numerical scoring system, or a similar computerized data analysis technique.

3. *External credit surveys.* Bond- and credit-rating services provide information on many potential clients of a lending institution. For example, reports on many small companies are available from Dun & Bradstreet (see Section 16.3.D). Another example is commercial applications of the financial distress prediction literature described in Chapter 15, for example, the ZETA® CREDIT RISK Reports from Zeta Services, Inc. (see Jaggi (1984) for a comparison of Dun & Bradstreet and ZETA).

4. *Factor, labor, and product markets.* Each of these three markets can be a rich information source about the ability of a firm to retain the support of

suppliers, customers, and so on. Issues relevant to loan analysis include the reliability of supply sources, the timing of wage contract negotiations, and the time trend of market share. Information about the competitors of the client, as well as about the client itself, can be critical in predicting the likely ability of a firm to make interest and principal repayments.

5. *Capital markets.* By explicitly incorporating capital market information in the loan decision process, analysts can exploit two important features of the capital market documented in prior chapters of this book: (a) its forward-looking orientation and (b) its utilization of information from a broad spectrum of sources. Even if the applicant is privately held, the loan analyst can still use capital market information relating to other firms in the industry to gain insight into expectations of future developments in that industry. Capital market variables can be especially useful as a monitoring device for an existing loan as they may capture adverse developments before they are reflected in financial statements. Specific capital market variables include security price movements, option price movements, and trading volume statistics. In addition, reports from brokerage firms can provide useful insights about likely future developments, the quality of management, and so on.

6. *Industry and economy reports.* An analyst can access numerous sources of information in this area, for example, industry trade group forecasts, forecasts made by economists or econometric models, and reports from government departments and agencies about money supply, gross national production, and taxation.

These information sources differ in several dimensions, for example, qualitative versus quantitative, past versus future oriented, and verifiable versus nonverifiable. The challenge facing a loan analyst is to exploit these diverse information sources in a cost-effective and efficient way. Several sections of this chapter discuss advances in statistical modeling that can make an important contribution to this challange.

16.3 DESCRIPTIVE ANALYSIS OF EXISTING LOAN DECISIONS

Figure 16.1 presents an overview of three stages in the commercial lending process (Cohen, Gilmore, and Singer, 1966, and Altman, 1980, present similar overviews):

1. Loan approval
2. Loan monitoring
3. Loan termination

There are two related reasons for studying how existing decisions are made in one or more of these processes. One reason is to gain insight into the role that financial statement and other information play in these decisions. A second reason

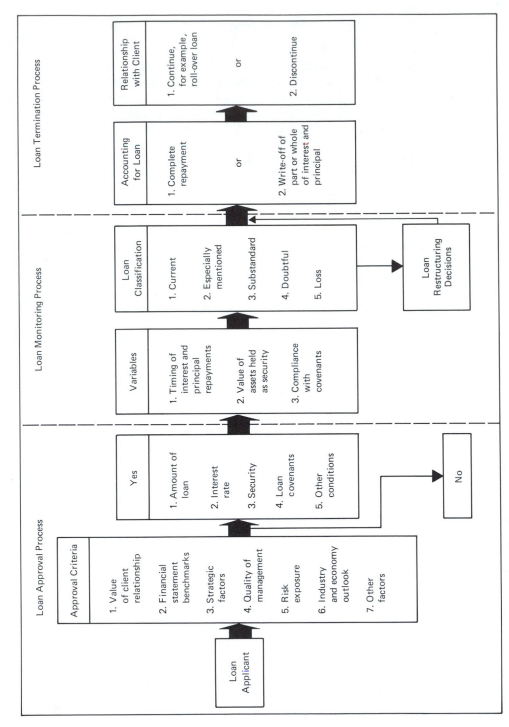

FIGURE 16.1 Commercial Lending Processes

is to examine areas where "innovations" can lead to improved loan decisions. An understanding of the current loan decision process facilitates placing a dollar magnitude on the expected gains from implementing improvements. These improvements could be manifested in several areas, for example, a reduction of current loan processing costs, an increase in the consistency with which analysts apply the bank's loan loss function, a reduction in loans made to clients that subsequently default, and an increase in loans made to clients that repay interest and principal in a timely manner.

A. Analysis of Loan Agreements

One information source on existing loan decision processes is loan agreements. These include details on the interest rate charged, the amount of the loan, and lending covenants. Castle (1980) provides a summary of "term loan covenants and other financial restrictions" in 37 term loan agreements written by the Chemical Bank of New York. These 37 loan agreements cover companies whose bonds were rated between Aaa and B by Moody's. Table 16.1 presents a representative example of the covenants in these 37 loan agreements. Many of the covenants included in Table 16.1 are designed to reduce the potential conflicts that can exist between lenders and borrowers, for example, a company obtaining a $10 million loan, declaring a $10 million dividend to shareholders, and then declaring bankruptcy. (Chapters 1 and 2 contain a description of such conflicts and mechanisms available that reduce their severity.) The set of monitoring procedures/covenants adopted in any loan will be influenced by the bargaining power of the two parties. For instance, if a bank is facing many potential competitors for the business of a client, it may be willing to "live with" a relatively small number of restrictions on that client's behavior.

One interesting insight from loan agreements is the incentive of lenders to adopt procedures that supplement perceived deficiencies in financial reporting. For instance, a frequent criticism of the use of historical cost-based reporting in the oil and gas industry is that for any single firm, the cost of discovering oil and gas reserves has no necessary relation to the "proved value" of those reserves. Not surprisingly, we find examples of loan agreements that focus directly on the "proved value" of oil and gas reserves rather than the historical cost-based numbers that appear in the financial statements. Foster (1980) includes several such examples in a discussion of why a proposed FASB requirement for full-cost (FC) companies to change to successful-efforts (SE) accounting may not affect selected lending agreements. Juniper Petroleum indicated that the FC to SE change was not "anticipated to have any material effect on the Company's borrowing arrangements since most of the Company's borrowings are related primarily to engineering projections of revenues from its producing properties." Houston Oil and Minerals noted that several loan clauses were based on the ratio of the "proved oil and gas reserves to the amount of secured indebtedness." The Left-

TABLE 16.1 Covenants and Restrictions in 37 Loan Agreements

	Rating of Bonds by Moody's (Sample Size)					
CATEGORIES OF COVENANTS	*Aaa* *(2)*	*Aa* *(3)*	*A* *(12)*	*Baa* *(11)*	*Ba* *(5)*	*B* *(4)*
A. AFFIRMATIVE COVENANTS						
1. Furnish annual audited financial statements	50%	66%	100%	100%	100%	100%
2. Furnish quarterly interim financial statements	—	33	100	100	80	50
3. Maintain system of accounting according to GAAP	—	—	17	9	40	50
4. Permit bank to have access to books/records	—	—	25	18	—	50
5. Maintain insurance	—	—	50	82	100	100
B. NEGATIVE COVENANTS						
1. Minimum working capital	—	67%	83%	91%	60%	75%
2. Minimum current ratio	—	—	33	27	60	100
3. Minimum tangible net worth	—	—	17	27	40	75
4. Limit on indebtedness	—	—	33	73	100	100
5. Limit on mergers and consolidations	50%	33	67	82	100	100
6. Limit on dividends	—	—	50	91	60	100
7. Limit on sale of stock and/or debt of subsidiaries	50	—	33	64	60	75
8. Limit on sale of all or substantial part of assets	—	67	67	82	100	100

SOURCE: Grover R. Castle, "Term Lending—A Guide to Negotiating Term Loan Covenants and Other Financial Restrictions," Copyright 1980 by Robert Morris Associates. Reprinted with Permission from *The Journal of Commercial Bank Lending*, November 1980. Tables 2 and 3, pp. 30–33.

wich (1983) study described in Section 16.5.B also includes evidence on departures by firms from GAAP in their loan agreements.

A major advantage of loan agreements as a source of information on existing loan procedures is that they are (relatively) explicit as to what is included. Moreover, both parties have an incentive to verify that the conditions included in those agreements represent their understanding of each party's rights and obligations. However, it is important to recognize that loan agreements (especially private agreements) are frequently revised. In addition, not every violation of individual clauses in an agreement causes the lender to pursue the legal steps set out in it. Loan agreements are best viewed as the opening rules of the game, with both the borrower and lender recognizing that many changes may be made in those rules before the final whistle is blown.

B. Interviews/Questionnaires with Loan Officers

Interviews with, or questionnaires sent to, loan officers can focus on more than just those items included in the final loan agreements. This section illustrates this expanded focus by discussing research on the financial ratios reported to be used by loan officers in their decisions. Backer and Gosman (1979) report the results of interviews at major U.S. banks, Dun & Bradstreet, investment banking firms, and bond-rating agencies. Opinions were solicited as to which "financial ratios have the highest priority in term loan decisions." The general finding was that as the length of the loan is increased, more emphasis is placed on leverage and profitability ratios and less on liquidity and turnover ratios. Addressing a similar issue, Gibson (1983) sent a questionnaire to the commercial loan departments of the 100 largest banks in the United States. The response rate was 44%. Each questionnaire included a listing of 59 financial ratios. One question related to the significance of each ratio in their decisions (0, 1, 2 = low importance; 3, 4, 5, 6 = average importance; 7, 8, 9 = high importance). Table 16.2 (panel A) presents the top ten ratios ranked in terms of average importance; the debt-to-equity ratio is the financial ratio ranked of highest importance. Another question relates to the frequency with which financial ratios are included in loan agreements. Table 16.2 (panel B) presents the ten ratios ranked from one to ten in terms of average percentage of inclusion. Again, the debt-to-equity ratio is ranked first.

C. Modeling Loan Officer Classifications

A third approach to gaining insight into how existing loan decisions are made is via modeling of the judgments of loan officers (or committees of loan officers). An important set of judgments in many banks is the classification of existing loans into loan categories. The categories that Dietrich and Kaplan (1982) describe for one bank are illustrative of those found in many financial institutions:

1. Current—normal acceptable banking risk.
2. Especially mentioned—evidence of weakness in the borrower's financial condition or an unrealistic repayment schedule.
3. Substandard—severely adverse trends or developments of a financial, managerial, economic, or political nature that require prompt corrective action.
4. Doubtful—full repayment of the loan appears to be questionable. Some eventual loss (as yet undetermined) seems likely. Interest is not accrued.
5. Loss—loan is regarded as uncollectable.

Several studies have examined the ability of statistical models to replicate the judgments of loan officers when assigning loans to one of the foregoing categories. (This research is part of a sizable literature on human judgment modeling. For a

TABLE 16.2 Financial Ratios as Perceived by Commercial Loan Officers

PANEL A. FINANCIAL RATIOS RANKED IN TERMS OF IMPORTANCE IN LOAN ASSESSMENT

Financial Ratio	*Average Rating Across Respondents*
1. Debt/equity	8.71
2. Current ratio	8.25
3. Cash flow/Current maturities of long-term debt	8.08
4. Fixed charge coverage	7.58
5. Net profit margin after tax	7.56
6. Net interest earned	7.50
7. Net profit margin before tax	7.43
8. Degree of financial leverage	7.33
9. Inventory turnover in days	7.25
10. Accounts receivable turnover in days	7.08

KEY: 0, 1, 2–low importance.
           3, 4, 5, 6–average importance.
           7, 8, 9–high importance.

PANEL B. FINANCIAL RATIOS RANKED IN TERMS OF PERCENTAGE INCLUSION IN LOAN AGREEMENTS

Financial Ratio	*Percentage Inclusion in Loan Agreements*
1. Debt/Equity	95.5%
2. Current ratio	90.0
3. Dividend payout ratio	70.0
4. Cash flow/Current maturities of long-term debt	60.3
5. Fixed charge coverage	55.2
6. Times interest earned	52.6
7. Degree of financial leverage	44.7
8. Equity/Assets	41.0
9. Cash flow/Total debt	36.1
10. Quick ratio	33.3

SOURCE: Gibson (1983, Tables 7 and 8): p. 26.

related issue, see the discussion in Chapter 14 on statistical models to replicate the judgment of bond-rating agencies.)

Dietrich and Kaplan (1982) examined a sample of "commercial loans of a large money-center commercial bank." The objective of the study was "to develop a simple linear model which can replicate the judgment used in classifying loan risk" (p. 19). The sample used to estimate the linear model comprised 140 loans with the following classifications: Current (109), Especially mentioned (16), Substandard (10), and Doubtful (5). No loans in the loss category were included in the research. A three-variable linear function was reported to have "important explanatory power'':

$$Y_i = -3.90 + 6.41 \times DE_i - 1.12 \times FCC_i + .664 \times SD_i \qquad \textbf{(16.1)}$$

where

DE_i = (long-term debt + current liabiities)/total assets

FCC_i = funds from operations/(interest expense + minimum rental commitment + average debt maturing within three years)

SD_i = number of consecutive years of sales decline

The higher the Y_i score, the higher the estimated risk of the loan. The signs of the coefficients on each variable follow intuition; a higher-risk loan is likely to have higher leverage, lower funds flow, and more years of consecutive sales decline.

The classifications made by the loan officers and the linear model in (16.1) are presented in panel A of Table 16.3. In only two cases did the loan officers and the linear function differ by more than one category in their classifications. Given that the choice of variables in (16.1) was influenced by an empirical search for that subset that performed best on the estimation sample, Dietrich and Kaplan (1982) analyzed a validation sample of 187 loans outstanding. Panel B of Table 16.3 presents the classification matrix for this sample. The percentage-correct rates for the two samples are

Loan Classification	Estimation Sample	Validation Sample
Current	93%	94%
Especially mentioned	44	29
Substandard	80	30
Doubtful	60	50

The linear model predicted the current category loans equally as well on both samples, but predicted the other three categories less well for the validation sample.

Marais, Patell, and Wolfson (1984) examined a sample of 716 loan classifications made by a large commercial bank. This sample also did not include loans in the loss category. Two loss functions were examined: a uniform loss function, in which all misclassifications were weighted equally, and a loss function provided by the bank in which the heaviest penalty was given to predicting an actually doubtful classified loan to be in the current classified category. Using 13 financial statement items as independent variables in a probit multivariate model, the following percentage-correct classifications were reported:

Loan Classification	Uniform Loss Function	Loss Function Supplied by Bank
Current (655)	99.5%	91.8%
Especially mentioned (29)	.0	37.9
Substandard (23)	.0	26.1
Doubtful (9)	11.1	.0

TABLE 16.3 Loan Officer Classifications: Predicted and Actual Classifications for Estimation and Validation Samples

PANEL A. ESTIMATION SAMPLE

		Actual Status				
		Current	Especially Mentioned	Substandard	Doubtful	Total
Predicted Status	Current	101	9	0	0	110
	Especially Mentioned	7	7	2	1	17
	Substandard	1	0	8	1	10
	Doubtful	0	0	0	3	3
	Total	109	16	10	5	140

PANEL B. VALIDATION SAMPLE

		Actual Status				
		Current	Especially Mentioned	Substandard	Doubtful	Total
Predicted Status	Current	152	8	3	0	163
	Especially Mentioned	9	4	2	0	15
	Substandard	0	2	3	1	6
	Doubtful	0	0	2	1	3
	Total	161	14	10	2	187

SOURCE: Dietrich and Kaplan (1982, Tables 1 and 2): pp. 25–26.

Marais, Patell, and Wolfson did not use separate estimation and validation samples, but adjusted for overfitting via their significance tests. As with Dietrich and Kaplan (1982), these authors found it considerably more difficult to predict classifications in the noncurrent categories. Note, however, that when the loss function supplied by the bank is used, there is a substantial increase in the percentage-correct classifications in these noncurrent categories (17/61 with loss function supplied by the bank vis-à-vis 1/61 with a uniform loss function).

When interpreting the percentages in Dietrich and Kaplan (1982) and Marais, Patell, and Wolfson (1984), it is important to consider the various explanations for a lack of perfect classification: for instance, (1) the loan officers consider more variables than the three included in (16.1), (2) the loan officers consider only those three variables but in a nonlinear or nonadditive manner, and (3) a consistent set of classifications is not made by the individual loan officers in the sample. A low percentage agreement in no way implies that the linear model is incorrect. Indeed, this line of research does not address the issue of whether the initial classification by a loan officer is "good" or "correct" in the sense of whether it maximizes a bank's expected return from the corporate lending function. Some indirect evidence that relates to this issue is provided by Spong and Hoenig (1979). They report that loan classifications are correlated with subsequent charge-offs. In a sample of approximately 700 charged-off loans from 13 banks, they found that 87 percent had been previously classified below the current category by the lending bank. These authors, however, did not report a breakdown of the time lag between the initial classification of each loan (as substandard, doubtful, etc.) and its subsequent charge-off.

D. External Data Sources Used in Existing Decisions

In many loan and trade credit decisions, information about the applicant can be purchased from a commercial service. One of the most widely used sources in existing decisions is Dun & Bradstreet (D&B). To illustrate the data available from such external sources, details of the D&B "Capital and Credit Rating" service will be presented. This rating, consisting of two parts (estimated financial strength and composite credit appraisal), can be purchased for a broad cross section of privately and publicly held U.S. firms. The main objectives of the D&B rating information are to help clients set credit guidelines and evaluate smaller and less risky orders and to serve as a quick reference guide for checking credit before a detailed credit analysis can be made. Dun & Bradstreet [1985] provides the following information in its promotional literature:

> Estimated Financial Strength is a size indicator, based on the net worth, or equity, of a business enterprise. It is derived, often without modification, from the most recent financial statement of that business. Sometimes there are modifications as the deducting of exempt real estate, or of intangibles such as goodwill, which is why the result on which Estimated Financial Strength is based is also referred to as tangible net worth. Composite Credit Appraisal is an indicator of a concern's stability and general credit worthiness. (p. 2)

Estimated financial strength ratings cover 15 categories of tangible net worth; for example,

Rating	Firm Size Category
5A	$50,000,000 and over
4A	$10,000,000 to $49,999,999

The lowest rating (HH) includes firms up to $4,999 in tangible net worth. Composite credit appraisal ratings cover four categories: high, good, fair, or limited. Figure 16.2 presents the factors (payments, finance, history, antecedents, and

FIGURE 16.2 Factors Considered by Dun & Bradstreet in Its Composite Credit Appraisal Ratings

	High Rating	Good Rating	Fair Rating	Limited Rating
	If **all** conditions listed below are favorable.	If **most** conditions listed below are favorable.	Still considered creditworthy, but with **some** of the following unfavorable elements.	Even greater elements of risk, creditworthiness limited.
Payments	Satisfactory. Suitable explanations for any slowness.	Generally satisfactory. Suitable explanation for slowness.	Significant slowness.	Significant, even chronic, slownesses.
Finance	*Statements regularly obtained. Usually comparative figures. Strong condition. Upward trend.	*Statement obtained. Sound condition. Trend usually favorable.	*Statement obtained. Condition unbalanced. Operating losses. Impaired cash flow. Heavy debt.	*Statement obtained. Condition unbalanced. Even heavier losses and debt.
History	One year old, at least; three years preferably. Adequate assurance of ownership.	No minimum years if other factors satisfactory. Adequate assurance of ownership.	Adequate assurance of ownership.	Adequate assurance of ownership.
Antecedents	Experienced in all aspects of business management. No recent business failures, felony convictions, etc., that would have serious impact on business.	If new, previous experience in line or in successfully managing a previous business. No recent business failures, felony convictions, etc., that would have serious impact on business.	May lack balanced experience or experience in line. Consider impact on business of any recent business failures or felony convictions.	May lack balanced experience or experience in line. Consider impact on business of any recent business failures or felony convictions.
Other	Other factors to be considered for their possible favorable or unfavorable influence on a business include: operation or location, bank record, public record information, general economic factors, industry or local conditions.			

*Book figures are required where tangible net worth is $50,000 or more. In cases where net worth is under $50,000, ratings can be assigned based on estimates, preferably signed by a principal.

Source: Dun & Bradstreet (1985): p. 4.

other) considered by Dun & Bradstreet in assigning one of these ratings to a firm. The final rating is assigned by a "D&B business reporter, with exceptional cases going to a National Rating Committee for review and approval."

16.4   QUANTITATIVE APPROACHES TO LOAN DECISIONS

Quantitative models are playing an increasing role in loan decisions. In the consumer loan area, the rating given by a quantitative model often is the major input into a loan approval decision. In the commercial loan area, the rating of a quantitative model is used by a small but growing number of institutions as one of several inputs into loan review decisions. This section discusses issues in the construction of such models, the benefits of a quantitative approach, and consumer and commercial loan applications of such models.

A.   Issues in Construction of a Quantitative Scoring Model

Key decisions in designing a quantitative scoring model for loan decisions include choices of (1) the loss function for model prediction errors, (2) the set of firms to include in the sample, (3) the population to which the model is to apply, (4) the independent variables to include in the model, (5) the treatment of missing data, and (6) stationarity of the time period for which the model is assumed valid. Consider each of these in turn.

Loss Function to Use for Model Prediction Errors

Two important parameters when processing loan applications are

- C1—the cost of predicting that a loan applicant will repay when it subsequently does not repay
- C2—the cost of predicting that a loan applicant will not repay when it subsequently could repay.

Included in C1 will be the loss associated with the interest and principal the bank does not receive when due, the opportunity cost of a loan officer's time in monitoring the loan, and the extra legal expenses associated with the loan write-down or write-off. Included in C2 will be the contribution margin on the loan that was foregone, assuming that applicants predicted not to repay are refused loans. If there is a restricted amount of loan funds available, C2 will be reduced by the return on the alternative use of the funds.

Some evidence on the magnitude of C1 is provided by Altman (1980). Data from the New York Federal Reserve Bank was used to estimate the recovery rates on loan losses. The median recovery rates for selected years were

1970	1972	1974	1976
26.5%	34.1%	25.5%	28.3%

The recovery rate is the ratio of the amount finally recovered to the amount outstanding at the time the loan is charged off. Note that this recovery rate ignores the time value of money (the amount recovered could be received several years later), and it does not include the extra costs that the lending institution incurs in monitoring the loan and in writing it off. For these reasons, the recovery rates may understate considerably the costs of predicting that a loan applicant will repay when it subsequently does not repay.

Very little analysis of the C2 cost has been reported in the literature. Altman, Haldeman, and Narayanan (1977) argue that its magnitude is "extremely small." Assuming that the lending institution has a restriction on the total loan funds available, they estimate the opportunity cost of not lending to a client who would have repaid (at interest rate R) as $R - R_f$, where R_f is the return on a riskless government security; $R - R_f$ they estimate to be 2%. Using estimates of C1 based on loan loss recovery statistics in the 1971–1975 period, they reported that a C1 error was 35 times more costly than was a C2 error.

Broadness of the Set of Firms to Include in a Sample

Loan analysts often face a trade-off between having a large enough set of observations to efficiently estimate a scoring model and having a set of firms that are homogeneous with respect to attributes relevant to their loan decisions. One possibility is to build separate scoring models for each individual industry in which loans are made. While this approach does control for industry differences in financial ratios, in many cases it will result in models being developed on very small data bases (especially in the "problem" loan categories).

An alternative approach is to control for the hypothesized source of heterogeneity across observations when estimating values of the variables of each firm. Consider the use of industry-relative ratios as a means of controlling for differences across industries in their average financial ratios. (This approach will reduce the contribution that industry membership can play in a scoring model.) The following example illustrates this approach for the long-term liability-to-equity ratio of four firms:

Firm #	Industry	Financial Ratio of Firm i	Median Ratio of Firm i's Industry	Firm i's Industry-Relative Ratio
1	Textile Apparel	.36	.27	1.33
2	Drugs	.42	.15	2.80
3	Steel	.30	.53	0.57
4	Air Transport	1.20	1.41	0.85

Izan (1984) illustrates this approach when building a failure classification model for a broad cross section of Australian firms.

Population to Which Model Is to Apply

The sample used in developing the model should correspond to the population to which the scoring model is to apply. In this regard, it is important to distinguish between two populations of interest to a lender:

1. The population of new applicants
2. The population of accepted applicants.

In many studies, a scoring model is based on a sample of accounts in a firm's files. This sample is appropriate if one is concerned with developing internal review procedures to monitor existing accounts. If, however, the concern is with building a model to process new credit applicants, a sample based only on accounts in a firm's files may not be representative. These accounts have already been screened as "good" credit risks by the existing system. Thus, it is possible that a variable currently used in evaluating new applicants may not show up as a significant discriminatory variable on a model built on only accepted applicants. This is known as the pre-screening problem. It is difficult to overcome this problem when estimating scoring models to process new applicants. One alternative is to accept every applicant for a time period and track their subsequent loan experience. (Clearly, this is potentially a costly way to gather information.) Another proposed alternative is to assume that the applicants rejected by the existing system would subsequently have been classified as "bad"; the assumption is that the existing system has no Type II errors. Yet another alternative is to estimate subjectively what would have been the credit experience of applicants who were rejected by the existing system.

Independent Variables to Include in a Model

The choice of variables to include in quantitative scoring models typically has been based on one or more of the following:

1. Past experience of the lending institution
2. Past research on distress prediction or loan classifications
3. Data-intensive search methods such as stepwise regression or stepwise discriminant analysis.

At present, there does not exist an underlying theory relating loan experience with the characteristics of borrowers and lenders (and possibly other variables representing, say, industry and economic factors) that model builders in this area can access. Pragmatic rationales (for example, to improve loan decision making) rather than attempts to test economic theories of loan behavior have been the prime concern of researchers in this area.

The variables included in the chosen scoring model are often a small subset of those initially considered by the model developer. In some cases, the model builder may believe that a variable should be included in a model but finds that it is not significant (or is even excluded from a scoring model). In this context, it is important to consider potential explanations for the variable being insignificant or excluded before deciding whether to reestimate the model with the variable included. Consider an internal bank study on accepted loan applicants that reported that a specific financial ratio was not a significant variable in discriminating between loans subsequently repaying principal and interest, and loans subsequently defaulting on principal or interest. At least six explanations exist for the insignificance of the ratio, with differing implications as to the design of a scoring model. Table 16.4 presents these six explanations and their potential implications. One important message from Table 16.4 is that many substantive issues need to be considered in the design and operation of a successful credit scoring model.

Treatment of Missing Data

In building numerical scoring systems and in processing applicants with these systems, the problem of missing observations can arise. For example, an applicant may only fill out answers to 39 of the 40 questions on an application form. In this case, a firm may not deem it cost effective to return the application form to the applicant seeking the missing information. Ewert (1977) encountered this problem in estimating a scoring model for processing trade credit applicants. None of the 100 variables examined was available for all firms in the sample. One solution adopted was that "if a few firms (approximately 10 percent or less of all the firms) were missing information for a given variable, the median value for the [combined good and bad] sample was substituted for the missing information" (p. 92).

Stationarity

Over time, changes can occur in the set of loan applicants being examined, in the characteristics of those applicants, or in the industry or economic environment. One approach when faced with such nonstationarities is to retain the existing set of independent variables but reestimate their coefficients and establish new cutoff points for classifying loans into various categories. Should the nonstationarities be especially marked, it may be necessary to develop a new scoring model in which independent variables, other than those currently included, are examined. (An alternate approach would be to identify the possible sources of nonstationarity and explicitly include them in the scoring model.) A possible example of nonstationarity is the increasing probability that large firms will become bankrupt. Prior to the late 1960s, this probability was extremely low. Since that period, however, firms with total liabilities in the billions have filed for bankruptcy, for example, Penn-Central Transportation in 1970 with liabilities of $3.3 billion and Itel in 1981 with liabilities of $1.7 billion.

B. Contributions of a Quantitative Scoring Model

A scoring model can make several important contributions in the credit decision-making area:

1. A scoring model can facilitate the monitoring of, and control over, the risk of incoming accounts. By comparing the characteristics of applicants on which the model was built with the characteristics of applicants currently applying for loans, it is possible to ascertain if there is some stability in the credit population. Moreover, by comparing the predictions of the scoring

TABLE 16.4 Explanations for Financial Ratios and Other Variables Not Being Significant in a Quantitative Scoring Model

EXPLANATION FOR INSIGNIFICANCE OF FINANCIAL RATIO	*IMPLICATION*
1. *Ratio "prescreened" out.* Applicants with "low" levels of ratio were rejected in initial loan application stage.	Scoring model applies only to accepted applicant pool. If lender wants to use it to cover all applicants, may want to accept applicants with greater variation in ratio.
2. *Applicants manipulate ratio.* Ratio is included in loan covenants, and clients manipulate their financing, investment, operating, or accounting method decisions to avoid violation of covenants.	Manipulation is not necessarily against lender's interest. Concern is with those manipulations that merely defer (or even increase likelihood of) default, for example, a client making a LIFO to FIFO change that increases tax liability but avoids a bond covenant violation. Lender may want to specify in covenants limits on accounting method changes and other decisions.
3. *Measurement error.* For example, due to differences in accounting methods in sample or model covering a broad cross section of industries in which industry norms differ significantly.	Depends on source of error and ability of bank to reduce it. For example, if due to model covering heterogeneous set of industries, bank could build separate models for subsamples more homogeneous in industry composition.
4. *Sampling phenomenon.* Ratio is significant variable in population of interest, but in subsample examined it is not significant. Sample selection may be nonrandom such as being first N files (these could be filed by industry or date of loan issue).	Use a larger sample and take care in selecting sample from the loan files, for example, by stratified sampling based on attributes perceived relevant to likelihood of default.
5. *Correlated variables.* Variables in scoring model highly correlated with excluded financial ratio.	If correlations are stable over time, predictive performance of model is likely not to be affected by exclusion of ratio. Factors such as extent of measurement error and ability to be manipulated need to be considered in choosing which of the highly correlated variables to include.
6. *Not relevant.* Attribute measured by financial ratio not relevant to predicting default on loan principal or interest.	Do not include financial ratio in scoring model.

model (for example, as regards the percentage of defaults) with its subsequent experience, it is possible to determine areas where revision of the model may be appropriate.

2. Decisions relating to C1 and C2 (see p. 585) are key inputs into a scoring model. By having senior management provide (or at least sign off on) estimates of these parameters, senior management can impose a consistent loss function on individual loan evaluation officers. One of the major limitations of the heuristic system used in some banks is that inconsistent decisions can be made by different loan officers of the same institution. (One reason for this inconsistency is that individual loan officers may use their own loss function, which may be more risk averse than that of the bank.)

3. A credit scoring system can be used to test which variables (financial or otherwise) are important in discriminating between "good" and "bad" credit risks. Collecting and processing financial information is a costly activity, and it is important not to devote resources to collecting information on variables that lack discriminatory power. Note that the importance of a variable should be considered from a multivariate rather than a univariate perspective.

4. Credit scoring systems can assist in the allocation of a loan officer's time and resources. For instance, applicants above a set score could be accepted without further analysis; those below the score could be subject to further credit analysis. Similarly, a credit scoring system could be used as a screening device for the existing set of loans. The financial statements and other variables of companies with bank loans could be regularly scored and only those failing to reach a certain level subjected to internal review procedures.

5. Credit scoring systems can assist in implementing lending policies consistent with federal or state laws, for example, an Equal Credit Opportunity law that prohibits discrimination on the basis of age, race or sex; see Hsia (1978). The use of a model not incorporating such variables can be one means by which a lender can document compliance with existing federal or state laws.

C. Consumer Loan Applications

An early example of a consumer credit scoring model is the system developed by Spiegel for its mail-order business; see Wells (1963). In 1934, Spiegel began handling new customers' applications by a vital question system. Four principal questions were scored, and if the customer's total score exceeded a stated total, he or she was given credit without further analysis. If the score did not exceed the stated total, the mail order was held for further credit analysis. Scoring models are now used by many financial and retail institutions, for example, in decisions to extend credit, to issue credit cards and other charge accounts, and to grant personal loans. Companies have the option of in-house development of these models or the use of outside consultants. Examples of research in this area include Durand (1941); Myers and Forgy (1963); Apilado, Warner, and Dauten (1974); Orgler (1975); and Wiginton (1980).

An illustrative study on consumer credit scoring models is Apilado, Warner, and Dauten (1974). Data were obtained "from the records of 307 commercial banking offices and eighteen finance companies located in a relatively highly industrialized southwestern state" (p. 276). The accounts were taken from the *closed loan files* of the banks and finance companies. A sample of 950 accounts was used in the analysis; one-half were "good" loans (paid as agreed) and one-half were "bad" loans (charged off). Thirteen variables relating to each account were initially examined, for example, discount of loan, age of borrower, marital status, home status, and gross monthly income. Based on a univariate analysis, the following variables were found to be the best predictors of credit risk:

1. Home status (own free and clear, buying, renting, or other)
2. Checking account (yes or no)
3. Purpose of loan
4. Terms of loan (number of monthly payments).

Among the variables least effective on a univariate basis were the sex of the borrower and the number of dependents of the borrower.

Multiple discriminant analysis was then applied to the initial sample of 950 accounts. The final discriminant function included 8 of the 13 variables. A stepwise discriminant procedure was used in choosing these variables. The final discriminant function included variables for home status, checking account, purpose of the loan, number of dependents, number of monthly payments, age of borrower, amount of loan, and marital status. On a validation sample of 835 accounts (404 "bad" and 431 "good"), 299 of the "bad" accounts were correctly classified (Type I error of 26%) and 313 of the "good" accounts were correctly classified (Type II error of 27.38%). These percentage errors are, to say the least, quite "high." One reason for these high error rates appears to be that the variables used were restricted to those on the initial loan application form. Information gained from credit references and other sources was excluded from the study.

D. Commercial Loan Applications

The literature on scoring models for commercial loans is small relative to the literature on the use of such models in the consumer credit area. One potential explanation is that commercial loans are relatively less homogeneous in relation to the applicant pool, the loan evaluation process, or the loan agreements (for example, size of loan, interest rate charged, covenants, and security). A second explanation is that the number of observations available for model building is much smaller in the commercial loan area.

A subset of banks does include quantitative models in their commercial loan decision processes. Makeever (1984) polled the 98 largest U.S. banks on whether "your bank uses a bankruptcy prediction or other numerical credit scoring model in the evaluation of commercial loans"; 19 responded yes, 75 responded no, and four did not respond. Of the 19 "yes" responses, seven were using the Zeta Service (see Chapter 15), one the Gambler's Ruin model (see Wilcox, 1971), and 11 were using internally developed systems.

The most frequent application of credit scoring in the commercial sector is with respect to trade credit. A study by Ewert (1977) is illustrative of research in this area. The data analyzed were taken from the credit records of a manufacturing company. The sample comprised 507 firms that obtained credit with this company; 298 of the accounts were "good" and 209 were "bad." A bad account was defined as one placed for collection with an outside agency or written off in the books of the manufacturing company. The 209 bad accounts were all the bad accounts of the manufacturer for which Ewert could obtain data. The 298 good accounts were randomly drawn from the approximately 15,000 accounts defined as good over the time period that the bad accounts were recognized as such. The following details on variable choice were given by Ewert:

> There was no shortage of variables to test. Since there is a proliferation of plausible hypotheses and an absence of a general theory about credit worthiness, virtually every piece of information available could be rationalized as a possible discriminator between the goods and the bads. Over 100 variables were tested. . . . Many variables which have been suggested as good indicators of credit worthiness could not be tested because the requisite information was not in the credit files. It was surprising to find the limited amount of information consistently available for most of the customers sampled. For instance, income statements were rarely found in the sample. Slightly less scarce were balance sheets from a year other than the current year. The paucity of data precluded testing income statement ratios and changes in balance sheet ratios. (pp. 89–90)

Of the 507 firm accounts, 307 were used in estimating a model to discriminate between good and bad accounts. A stepwise regression procedure was used in choosing the independent variables. The final regression function included 17 variables, including nine based on information provided by trade creditors to Dun & Bradstreet (for example, the percentage of the firm's suppliers who report it to be a slow payer of trade accounts). Financial statement-based variables included net worth, the current ratio, and the sales-to-working capital ratio. The validation sample included 100 good accounts and 100 bad accounts; 165 of these accounts were correctly classified with a Type I error of 18% and a Type II error of 17%.

One area where there has been growing interest in the use of quantitative models for commercial lending is for small firms. Cowen and Page (1982) examined the ability of a multiple discriminant model, using eight nonfinancial ratio variables, to predict the status (default/nondefault) of 60 minority small-business loans. The eight variables were the owner's age, education, and net worth; the firm's age and legal structure; and the length, size, and interest payment plan of the loan. The percentage-correct classification rate was 75%. Related research in this area includes studies on financial distress prediction models for small firms, for example, Edmister (1972) and Fulmer, Moon, Gavin, and Erwin (1984).

16.5   EXISTING LOAN DECISIONS AND ACCOUNTING ALTERNATIVES

The accounting literature includes the following criticisms of generally accepted accounting principles (GAAP):

1. Interfirm comparability is severely impeded due to the wide range of permissable alternatives within GAAP

2. Non-GAAP reporting systems are more informative than GAAP.

Lending officers have an incentive to use information that facilitates the making of better loan decisions. Moreover, they are under no regulatory mandate to stay within the GAAP framework and can request that loan applicants supplement or replace the historical cost-based numbers. In this context, the opinions and behavior of loan officers provide insight into whether criticisms associated with (1) or (2) are perceived by a set of financial statement users as being important.

A.   Diversity Within GAAP

Evidence on efforts by bank loan officers to make adjustments for accounting method differences is presented by Deitrick and Stamps (1981). A questionnaire was mailed to 100 "selected bankers" with a response rate of 42%. Each loan officer was instructed to assume that "he or she was evaluating a publicly held corporation within a nonregulated industry for the purpose of making a three- to five-year term loan." For each of 11 independent reporting situations, "the subjects were informed that because the company being evaluated uses an accounting method that is different from standard industry practice, the reported results are materially different from what would have been produced had the industry approach been adopted" (p. 57). Each officer was asked to indicate how much effort he or she would expend to adjust the published financial information in order to provide greater comparability in each situation (1 = no effort, 2 = minimum effort, 3 = moderate effort, 4 = fairly substantial effort, or 5 = very substantial effort). The results are presented in Table 16.5. One important finding from Table 16.5 is that the adjustment effort is not uniform across all 11 reporting methods. For example, 61% reported they would make a very or fairly substantial effort to adjust for lease accounting differences, whereas only 17.5% reported they would make a very or fairly substantial effort to adjust for historical cost versus current replacement cost differences.

There are several explanations for loan officers not making a substantial effort to adjust for diversity in some of the accounting methods used by applicants:

1. Inferences about trends in profitability, leverage, and so on are not perceived to be sensitive to the use of different accounting methods used by applicants.

2. Loan analysts lack the detailed experience or knowledge to make appropriate adjustments in some areas. For example, Deitrick and Stamps (1981) re-

TABLE 16.5   Effort Made by Loan Officers to Adjust Net Income When Accounting Method of Applicant Differs from Standard Industry Practice

REPORTING METHOD: COMPANY VERSUS INDUSTRY	AVERAGE ADJUSTMENT EFFORT
1. Different treatment of exploration costs in an extractive industry	3.65
2. Different treatment of similar leases	3.54
3. Different treatment of foreign currency translation gains and losses	3.43
4. Business combination: pooling of interest versus purchase	3.28
5. Different inventory cost flow assumptions	3.14
6. Different depreciation methods	2.80
7. Different periods for amortizing goodwill	2.71
8. Different treatment of investment tax credits	2.64
9. Different pension plan assumptions	
a. Excess of vested benefits over funding	2.62
b. Unfunded benefit adjustment	2.52
c. Pension expense adjustment	2.50
10. Different interim reporting philosophy	2.45
11. Capital asset values: historical cost versus current replacement cost	2.45

KEY: 1 = no effort, 2 = minimal effort, 3 = moderate effort, 4 = fairly substantial effort, 5 = very substantial effort.
SOURCE: James W. Deitrick and Jennifer L. Stamps, "The Use of Accounting Information by Bank Loan Officers," copyright 1981 by Robert Morris Associates. Reprinted with Permission from *The Journal of Commercial Bank Lending*, November 1980. Table 2, p. 58.

ported that only 9.5% of the loan officers in their sample stated that they had above-average or extensive knowledge of pension accounting alternatives.

3. Analysts can access competing sources of information that compensate for accounting method diversity. For example, Wells Fargo Bank requests that loan applicants submit sufficient information for them to develop "uniform cash flow" statements, along with their income statement and balance sheet. Wells Fargo believes that one advantage of its "uniform cash flow" approach is a reduction in comparability problems arising from interfirm diversity in accounting method choice.

B.   Non-GAAP Financial Reporting Alternatives

Lending officers can and do use non-GAAP-based alternatives when evaluating loan applicants or when writing loan agreements with accepted applicants. Leftwich (1983) presents evidence of such deviations from GAAP in an analysis of the "accounting measurement rules that are negotiated in private corporate lending agreements'' (p. 23). He reports that "virtually all lending agreements contain specific references to measurement rules that are to be used in calculating the accounting numbers for the purposes of the agreement" (p. 26). A subset of the "measurement rules" adopted was "entirely outside generally accepted accounting principles." For example,

- Contingencies—"All charges for contingencies must be made against income, not against reserve accounts."
- Foreign currency—"Foreign subsidiaries are seldom consolidated. Income from foreign investments is recognized only when it is actually received."
- Goodwill and intangibles—"Goodwill and intangibles are frequently excluded from the asset base against which firms may borrow. The accounting double entry is not preserved—goodwill is eliminated from balance sheet numbers, but amortization is required in the income statement."
- Income tax—"Deferred tax credits are not always classified as a liability. Deferred tax debits are excluded from the firm's asset base." (p. 39)

These deviations from GAAP were interpreted as evidence that "parties to lending agreements devise accounting measurement rules in a variety of ways to reduce the conflicts of interest between borrowers and lenders" (p. 37).

An interesting extension of the evidence would be to examine successive loan agreements over an extended period of time and to document changes in the accounting methods employed (and probable reasons for these changes). Such evidence would enable a better understanding of how institutions modify their accounting methods as knowledge about their benefits and costs is accumulated. For example, when a bank suffers large loan loss write-offs with a borrower who made discretionary accounting changes in the capitalize/expense area to avoid violating loan covenants, how quickly do they add restrictions in the capitalize/expense area in subsequent lending agreements?

Given that lending officers can request applicants to provide specific data items to supplement perceived deficiencies in GAAP, information about the perceived usefulness of non-GAAP data can be inferred from the opinions and behavior of lending officers. For instance, surveys of loan officers report limited interest (at best) by loan officers in general price-level accounting data; see Murdoch (1982) and McCaslin and Stanga (1983). One explanation offered for this finding of limited interest is loan officer nonfamiliarity with non-GAAP alternatives. This explanation is less than persuasive for several reasons. First, techniques for making general price-level adjustments have been available for over 50 years; see Zeff (1976). If there were important benefits to using such data, loan officers would have an economic incentive to request that information from clients or to estimate it internally. Second, starting in 1979, a large number of U.S. firms provided this information at zero cost to users in their annual reports. Surveys made several years after 1979 (for example, McCaslin and Stanga, 1983) report the same low level of interest in general price-level data as do surveys made prior to 1979 (for example, Epstein 1975).

C. Accounting Method Diversity and Quantitative Scoring Models

Diversity in accounting methods used by companies can create difficulties when using a quantitative scoring model in loan evaluation. In this context, it is useful to distinguish between

1. Cross-sectional diversity (differences in the accounting methods used by firms at a point in time)
2. Time-series diversity (differences in the accounting methods of the same firm over time).

Consider cross-sectional diversity. If, say, the scoring model is estimated on primarily a FIFO inventory/straight-line depreciation set of firms, then it is possible that a LIFO inventory/accelerated depreciation firm could be rejected for credit when it would have been extended credit had it used different accounting techniques. There are several alternatives one can adopt in this situation. One is to build a separate scoring model for each major combination of accounting alternatives. A second is to use adjustment techniques to place all applicants scored by the model on a similar basis as regards accounting methods. Time-series diversity in accounting methods can arise from voluntary or mandated (for example, by the FASB) accounting changes. If a model builder decides that the impact of such changes is significant, it may be appropriate to reestimate the model using data derived from the currently adopted set of accounting methods.

When faced with accounting diversity, a model builder may decide to include variables in the scoring model that are less affected by either cross-sectional or time-series diversity in accounting methods, for example, physical measures or capital market measures such as market value of debt to market value of equity. If one assumes capital market efficiency, capital market measures are also useful due to their impounding a very broad information set. Note, however, that capital market measures will only be available for publicly traded firms. For many small-loan applicants to banks, such measures would not be available.

16.6 SOME GENERAL COMMENTS

1. An important but little researched area is the integration of financial statement information with other information in loan decisions. The latter includes strategy information about the firm and its competitors and capital market information. For instance, strategy analysis could help flag potential problem situations such as

a. Loan applicant is currently profitable, but, due to several competitors constructing large-scale state-of-the-art plants, applicant will need to make sizable investments in a new plant to remain profitable
b. Loan applicant is experiencing rapid growth and high profitability, but both

these factors could be quickly eroded by a competitor's technological breakthrough.

Capital market information can be especially useful in the loan review process. Given the ability of capital markets to impound new information rapidly, lending institutions can use sudden drops in security price as a prompt for internal review of the loan. Little research has been published in this area, and at present most loan officer training programs do not include detailed segments on either strategy analysis or capital market analysis.

One example of progress in this area is Stein and Ziegler's (1984) analysis of corporate credit risks in Germany. This study integrated assessments of the quality of management with balance sheet variables and variables based on transactions made on the current bank account. It was reported that simultaneously combining these three sets of variables "avoids deficiencies of using only one of the components and improves the early detection of credit risks" (p. 249).

2. The published literature contains limited analysis of loans in the "loss" category. Several explanations could explain this situation:

a. Lending institutions do not want to publicize their "failures" to the outside world

b. Individual loan officers associated with the losses are either no longer employed or are unwilling to cooperate, because they believe the research will highlight factors that are critical with the benefit of 20/20 hindsight, but that at the time of their decisions, were only a few of many ambiguous items of information.

One benefit of making a detailed analysis of the loan-loss category is gaining insight into how loan review resources could be allocated: for instance, (a) the analysis may disclose that the existing procedures were not followed and, if they had been, earlier warnings of the loss would have been available, or (b) the analysis may highlight information areas not currently integrated into the existing procedures that could have provided earlier warning signals, or (c) the analysis may find that the loan loss could not have been prevented by any known form of loan review, given the risk profile of loans that the senior management of the lending institution had targeted.

3. The financial press continually stresses the many noneconomic factors underlying loan decisions. For example,

a. Corporate lenders have a "herd instinct" such that if $N - 1$ institutions are willing to join a loan syndicate, the nth institution feels pressure to join likewise, even if the loan does not pass its own lending criteria

b. Senior management of banks use their positions to maintain high international corporate or personal profiles (for instance, by making large loans to Third World countries when those loans do not pass existing loan criteria).

Attempts to model loan decision making have not yet explicitly recognized the importance of the above and similar factors. At present, it is difficult to know whether these so-called noneconomic forces are as pervasive as indicated by the financial press.

4. A sizable amount of research on loan decision making is conducted internally within lending institutions or by consulting firms. The incentives of these parties to publish detailed descriptions of any innovations appear to be minimal. Even when these parties cooperate with academics, difficult issues relating to the independence of the researcher or constraints on the issues to be examined can be encountered. For instance: (a) The lending institution may provide a subset of loan files to the researcher who is not in a position to verify their representativeness (for example, large losses may be deliberately omitted); (b) the lending institution may not disclose the names of the loan applicants, which precludes the researcher from using information about applicants not in the files (for example, security-return behavior); (c) the lending institution may only agree to cooperate with the researcher on the condition of less than full disclosure of the findings (for example, names of firms in the sample are not disclosed); and (d) the consulting firm may prevent publication of information that is informative to readers of academic journals but that may diminish the revenue base of the consulting firm (for example, the coefficients on the variables of a commercially sold distress prediction model may not be reported in a journal article).

16.7 SUMMARY

1. Many decisions in the commercial and consumer lending area use financial information as a key item. These decisions include the initial processing of a loan applicant, the ongoing monitoring of accepted loans, and the restructuring of loans for companies that have failed to meet obligations in their lending agreements.

2. An important gap in the published literature is detailed analysis of loans that fail to meet obligations in lending agreements. In many cases, these loans are restructured with a considerable reduction in the value of the loan to the lender. In other cases, the loans are completely written off by a lender. Although individual lenders may analyze these cases for internal review purposes, the research community typically has not been granted access to the source data necessary to conduct extensive analysis.

3. Financial statement information ideally should be part of a comprehensive set of information that also includes information from the factor, labor, and product markets; from the capital market; and from industry analysts. Quantitative scoring models have the potential to capture major subsets of the foregoing information. The benefits of using quantitative models in lending decisions include (a) senior management being able to provide key inputs into model development (for example, the costs of Type I and Type II errors), (b) lending officers being

able to allocate their resources to those applicants/accounts where there is the highest level of uncertainty, and (c) applicants and existing loans being processed in a consistent and timely way. Quantitative models comprise the major input for many decisions in the consumer lending area. For commercial loan decisions, these models are but one of many sources examined.

QUESTIONS

QUESTION 16.1: Quantitative Scoring Models for Commercial Loan Decisions

Part A. Hobie Leland, Jr., had been examining the potential of several discriminant models to make decisions on new loan applicants superior to those that were at present being made by the commercial loan officers of the El Camino Bank. His data base was the first 100 accepted applicants in the loan files of the bank. He classified each loan into one of two populations:

a. Subsequently went into "default" (10 loans)
b. Did not go into "default" (90 loans)

The initial application form for each loan contained 20 financial items from which the loan officers computed 15 financial ratios. Hobie included these 15 ratios plus another three he thought could be important in his analysis. He put all 18 variables into a forward stepwise linear discriminant package. The minimum misclassification rate percentage stabilized after eight variables had been added. Hobie was surprised when one of the ratios he thought should be important (the current ratio) was not included in the eight-variable function. He was delighted that two of the three "new" ratios he had added (cash flow-to-total debt and an earnings variability measure) were included in the eight-variable function. At this stage, he seeks your assistance in explaining these results.

REQUIRED

1. What explanations are there for the insignificance of the current ratio? Do these various explanations have different implications for the design of Hobie's study?
2. What factors could explain the significance of the cash flow-to-total debt ratio and the earnings variability measure?
3. It has been proposed that quantitative scoring models be used in commercial loan evaluations in place of loan evaluation officers. This proposal is consistent with the following recommendation made in the human judgment modeling literature: "Get the human decision maker out of the decision process at the earliest possible moment." What factors may underlie this

recommendation? Comment on its applicability to commercial loan evaluation.

Part B. Hobie then became concerned about the so-called "prescreening" effect. He read an early classic study on consumer credit discriminant models (Durand, 1941) and found the following comment:

> Perhaps the most serious limitation of the present study is that it is based upon data derived from applications that were carefully investigated and finally accepted. The findings therefore pertain to high grade, selected risks and not to risks in general. (p. 20)

Hobie wants to develop a model to process the population of new incoming applicants. He seeks your advice about what extra data (if any) to collect and what extra procedures (if any) to adopt in building and using a linear discriminant model.

REQUIRED

1. What is the "prescreening effect"?
2. What possible alternatives should Hobie consider when attempting to eliminate (reduce) this prescreening effect?
3. What are the pros and cons of each of the alternatives cited in (2)? Which alternative would you recommend that Hobie adopt?

QUESTION 16.2: Loan Syndication and Financial Analysis

Since leaving college eight years ago, Susan Teece has had a rapid career advancement, culminating in her recent appointment to head the energy loan division of Mountainfirst Bank. On her second day on the job, a close friend tells her that rumor has it that a large bank in Oklahoma is about to declare bankruptcy and that several other banks with participating loan agreements with that bank also are about to have severe problems. Teece looks at her files and discovers that Mountainfirst has participated in many loan syndicates for which First Bank of Oklahoma is the lead bank. Most loans are to oil and gas or real estate companies. In a loan syndicate, individual lending institutions each provide a designated percentage of the total amount being borrowed by a lendee. A lead bank in a loan syndicate does much of the initial evaluation of the loan applicant and then approaches other banks about their willingness to join a syndicate providing money to the applicant. In some cases, other banks lend money to the lead bank, which in turn lends it to the loan applicant. In other cases, each bank in the syndicate lends directly to the loan applicant; in these cases, the lead bank may collect interest and principal payments for all syndicate members and then send to the other banks their appropriate amounts.

Teece discovers that First Oklahoma is the only bank in Oklahoma with which Mountainfirst has syndicated loans,. (A sizable set of these loans are to First Oklahoma, which in turn lent the money to several rapidly growing oil and gas and land development companies.) After much analysis, she finds that important loan procedures of Mountainfirst were not always followed on the First Oklahoma loans. She wonders how her predecessor ever approved so many loans being placed with this one bank, especially given that it was not in the top ten banks in terms of firm size. Teece makes her own investigation and learns that the president of First Oklahoma is ''charisma personified'' and that he had secured the participation of many large banks in First Oklahoma syndications. She also learns that her own predecessor was very impressed by the prestige of the banks joining First Oklahoma loan syndicates.

Two weeks after her friend's first call, Teece receives a second call. Her friend tells her that the Oklahoma bank in trouble is Penn Square and that the national T.V. news would carry the story the following night. Her friend's information turns out to be correct. Although Teece feels a sense of relief that First Oklahoma was not the bank mentioned in the rumor, she is still deeply worried. This worry was not reduced after reading the following release from Seafirst Corporation, a major West Coast bank with headquarters in Seattle.

> Our provision for loan losses was increased $125 million in second quarter to cover possible charge-offs of Penn Square-related and other energy loans. Penn Square was geographically close to an area of energy development known as the Anadarko Gas Basin, where significant concentrations of untapped natural gas existed. Penn Square was considered knowledgeable in this area and was known to have connections with developers. Penn Square provided loans to developers and then sold all or portions of these loans to other banks. It was understood that it was Penn Square's responsibility to document such loans and to help manage the borrower/lender relationship. Despite assurances to the contrary by outside examiners and auditors, Penn Square's procedures were grossly inadequate and provided the major reason for the bank being closed by regulators. As is the case with all lending, it is our responsibility to ensure that loans we purchase meet our lending standards, are appropriately collateralized and properly approved. In the case of some Penn Square loans, certain important loan procedures were not followed including management of the overall size and rate of growth of loans purchased from Penn Square. Our auditing and examining procedures did not uncover these problems at first because the surge in loans with Penn Square occurred suddenly at the end of last year and the beginning of this year. In addition to these management shortcomings, the gas exploration activity virtually collapsed with the glut of oil and gas brought on by the recession and conservation nationally. The individuals directly responsible for these activities have either resigned or retired.

> Management changes have been announced and other actions taken to correct these problems and recover possible losses. A number of these programs were already in progress as we became aware of the magnitude of possible losses. We have reemphasized the importance of credit quality among our loan officers and have added new checks and review points for all new loans. To recover losses, we have dispatched a team of credit personnel to meet with customers and to check collateral. We are taking aggressive actions to get this problem behind us.

Teece decides to take both short-run and long-run actions. Her short-run actions will focus on the current exposure of Mountainfirst to losses should First Oklahoma encounter severe financial problems in the near future. Her long-run actions will focus on designing an information system to monitor the financial solvency of lead banks that syndicate loans to Mountainfirst. A key feature of this monitoring system will be the richness of the information sources examined. She calls her uncle, a noted accounting expert at a major business school, to inquire about research on failure prediction for financial institutions. Her uncle promises to send an executive brief on financial distress research relating specifically to banks. Table 16.6 is the information Teece receives from her uncle.

REQUIRED

1. What actions would you recommend Teece take to understand, and if possible limit, Mountainfirst's exposure to any financial problems at First Oklahoma? What information sources should she use in this analysis?

2. Teece considers using the following information in the proposed monitoring system:

   a. Financial statements of lead bank and other banks

   b. Security returns of lead bank and other banks

   c. Bond ratings of lead bank and other banks

   Outline the pros and cons of each of these three information sources, as regards a monitoring system for the solvency of banks. What alternative ways of incorporating information about (a), (b), and (c) into the monitoring system should she consider?

3. Teece reads Table 16.6 and finds the attempts to utilize quantitative scoring models in financial distress analysis very appealing. However, she is worried that several studies had small samples and that most had a retrospective bias (that is, they focused on failed firms after the fact). She suspects that other limitations may exist in the research designs. From Teece's perspective, what are the three major limitations of the results of this research? How would you overcome (or minimize) these three limitations if you are designing a study to guide the development of a monitoring system for Mountainfirst?

4. One factor that worries Teece is the ability to obtain early warning signals of fraud at lead banks. She remembers that many banks that regulatory authorities fail to classify as "problem banks" until the very last minute involve management fraud or embezzlement. What advice would you give her to reduce Mountainfirst's exposure to bankruptcies arising from these factors?

QUESTION 16.3: Cash Flow Analysis and Corporate Lending Decisions

The importance of cash flow as a measure of corporate performance and as a variable to analyze in loan decisions has been supported by several influential persons or organizations. For example,

1. Harold Williams (when chairman of the SEC) made the following comments

TABLE 16.6 Selected Research on Financial Distress in the Banking Industry

---

1. *Hanweck* (1977). Aim was to examine bank failures in the 1973–1976 period to develop a successful bank "screening" program for the Board of Governors of the Federal Reserve System. A failed bank was defined as one that was either closed by the chartering authority or merged for recognized financial difficulty. The estimation sample consisted of 20 failed banks and 177 nonfailed banks. The prediction model included seven publicly available data items as independent variables (e.g., ratio of net operating income to assets and loan to capital ratio). On the hold-out sample, 8 of the 12 failed banks and 176 of the 177 nonfailed banks were correctly classified, an overall accuracy of 97% with a Type I error of 33%.

---

2. *Pettway* (1980). Examined the weekly security returns of seven failed banks in the period prior to three critical dates: the starting date of the examination that led to the bank being classified as a problem bank, the date the bank was placed on the FDIC's problem-bank list, and the bank's failure date. Security returns were measured two ways: adjusted for general market returns and the risk of each bank and adjusted for changes in an index of bank stock returns. Both measures indicated that security returns declined prior to each of the three critical dates. Pettway concluded that examining security returns for banks with actively traded securities could aid in identifying potential bankruptcy.

---

3. *Pettway and Sinkey* (1980). Aim was to develop an early warning technique using accounting and capital market data. The accounting screen used a two-variable, linear discriminant function (total operating expenses/total operating income and investments/total assets) and was based on prior failure-prediction research by Sinkey. The capital market screen included a runs test; a run was defined as at least six successive negative market- and risk-adjusted security returns with each return being less than the cumulative return previously observed (that is, no reverses of the trend). A screening system utilizing both screens identified six of the largest U.S. bank failures at least one full year before the beginning of the time the bank was placed on the problem-bank list by the Federal Deposit Insurance Corporation.

---

4. *Shick and Sherman* (1980). Examined the feasibility of developing an early warning system based on bank stock prices. Results presented for 25 large banks that experienced a change as evidenced by a change in their regulatory agency rating. (This change was not made public.) In the 20 months up to and including the month of the regulatory agency rating change, the cumulative abnormal return (CAR) was $-.3525$. Selected CAR values over this time period were $(-20, -16$ months$) = -.0982; (-15, -11$ months$) = -.1035; (-10, -5$ months$) = -.0241; (-5, -1$ month$) = -.0847; (0$ month$) = -.0420$. Author concluded that "stock prices would have signaled problems long before the examiners confirmed their existence by an examination" (p. 145).

---

5. *Sinkey, Dince, and Terza* (1985). Used a Zeta Service, Inc., approach (including all seven variables from the ZETA® CREDIT RISK model; see Chapter 15). Model estimated using 1980–1982 period and observations from 1983 used as a hold-out sample. Model estimated from a paired-sample in which a failed commercial bank was paired with a nonfailed bank on the basis of location, approximate size and regulatory jurisdiction. The hold-out sample included 35 failed and 253 nonfailed banks. For the hold-out sample, the Type I error was 11.43% six months prior to failure, 28.57% 18 months prior to failure, and 25.71% 30 months prior to failure; the Type II error was 25.51% six months prior to failure, 27.38% 18 months prior to failure, and 46.64% 30 months prior to failure.

in a speech to the Financial Executives Research Foundation:

> Corporate earnings reports communicate, at best, only part of the story. And, their most critical omission—in recognition that insufficient cash resources are a major cause of corporate problems particularly in inflationary times—is their failure to speak to a corporation's cash position. Indeed, in my view, cash flow from operations is a better measure of performance than earnings-per-share.
>
> [What should be considered is] more revealing analytical concepts of cash flow or cash-flow-per-share, which reflect the total cash earnings available to management—that is, earnings before expenses such as depreciation and amortization are deducted. An even more sophisticated—and, in my opinion, more informative—analytical tool is free cash flow, which considers cash flow after deducting such spiralling corporate costs as capital expenditures. This technique allows [evaluation of] the costs of maintaining the corporation's present capital and market position—costs which are, in essence, expenses and cash flow obligations that should be considered in determining the corporation's financial position. *Arthur Young Views* (January 1981)

2. Robert Morris Associates (1982), a national association of bank loan and credit officers, advocates the use of cash flow analysis as "a tool necessary to evaluate, understand, and accurately determine a borrower's ability to repay loans":

> Banks lend cash to their clients, collect interest in cash, and require debt repayment in cash. Nothing less, just cash. Financial statements, however, usually are prepared on an accrual, not on a cash basis. And projections? Same thing. Projected net income, not projected cash income. Yet, cash repays loans. Therefore, we are compelled to shift our focus if we truly wish to assess our client's ability to pay interest and repay debt. We must turn our attention to cash, working through the roadblocks thrown up by accrual accounting, to properly evaluate the creditworthiness of our client.

RMA provides teaching tools (based on material developed by Wells Fargo) that outline a step-by-step approach to deriving "cash flow" statements for loan applicants.

Casey and Bartczak (1984) present evidence that, they argue, calls into question the enthusiasm many exhibit for cash flow analysis. They examined 290 companies, 60 of which had been declared bankrupt, and found that operating cash flow data for a five-year span could not distinguish between the healthy enterprise and the one that would fail. An operating cash flow (OCF) variable was less accurate a predictor of failure than a combination of six conventional accrual-based measures, including debt-to-equity and profitability ratios. Casey and Bartczak gave the following example to illustrate the OCF measure used in their research:

	Net income	$ 100
Plus	depreciation	100
Equals	"traditional" cash flow	$ 200
Plus	other expenses not affecting working capital (e.g., deferred taxes)	100
Less	other revenues not affecting working capital (e.g., equity earnings)	(50)
Equals	working capital provided by operations	$ 250
Less	increase in accounts receivable	(500)
Less	increase in inventories	(500)
Plus	increase in accounts payable	300
Plus	increase in accrued liabilities	200
Equals	OCF	$(250)

They selected 60 companies that had "filed petitions for bankruptcy during the period 1971–1982 and matched them with 230 viable (or at least 'non-bankrupt') companies chosen at random from similar industry groupings on the Compustat Industrial Tape" (p. 62). Three variables were computed:

$$OCF = \text{Operating cash flow}$$

$$OCF/CL = \text{Operating cash flow/Current liabilities}$$

$$OCF/TL = \text{Operating cash flow/Total liabilities}$$

The authors report that none of the three variables "could discriminate between the bankrupt and nonbankrupt companies with reasonably good accuracy. In fact, overall accuracy for OCF was only slightly better than chance (50%) for the first and second years before failure and was worse than chance for the remaining years" (p. 62). The means of the two groups of firms in the five-year period prior to bankruptcy were

Year Prior to Failure	OCF ($ millions) Bankrupt	Nonbankrupt	OCF/CL Bankrupt	Nonbankrupt	OCF/TL Bankrupt	Nonbankrupt
Year 5	$4.6	$33.3	.12	.35	.05	.19
Year 4	4.5	34.9	.12	.37	.07	.21
Year 3	2.5	35.4	.09	.28	.15	.15
Year 2	− 3.0	34.0	− .01	.32	− .01	.17
Year 1	− 3.9	56.1	.03	.44	.02	.25

Although the means of the two groups were statistically significantly different, none of the three OCF variables was reported to be able to "discriminate between the bankrupt and healthy companies with reasonably good accuracy. The poor predictive accuracy was due to the many inaccurate classifications of nonbankrupt companies as failures. . . . The distributions overlap considerably, making it difficult to distinguish between the two groups. . . . Although a large number of companies generate little operating cash flow, most of them do not file for bankruptcy'' (p. 66). Table 16.7 (Sections I–III) presents the percentage accuracy rates of classifications using the OCF, OCF/CL, and OCF/TL variables.

As a further test, Casey and Bartczak also constructed a multivariate prediction model that used six independent variables, all of which were derived from the conventional accrual accounting financial statements (net income/total assets, cash/total assets, current assets/current liabilities, net sales/current assets, current assets/total assets, and total liabilities/owners' equity). The model was estimated

TABLE 16.7 Percentage Accuracy for Classifying Bankrupt and Nonbankrupt Firms Using Operating Cash Flow and Accrual Accounting Based Variables

Years Prior to Failure	Overall Sample (N = 290)	Bankrupt Companies (N = 60)	Nonbankrupt Companies (N = 230)
I. OCF			
5	49%	85%	40%
4	46	88	35
3	47	83	63
2	54	92	44
1	60	90	53
II. OCF/CL			
5	62%	63%	62%
4	63	72	60
3	58	60	57
2	66	70	65
1	75	83	73
III. OCF/TL			
5	59%	53%	60%
4	59	70	56
3	59	58	60
2	68	72	67
1	72	82	69
IV. Accrual variable discriminant model			
5	61%	73%	58%
4	72	30	83
3	84	57	90
2	84	63	89
1	86	83	87

KEY: OCF–Operating cash flow.
    CL–Current liabilities.
    TL–Total liabilities.
SOURCE: Casey and Bartczak (1984, Exhibits I and II): p. 64.

using linear discriminant analysis. A separate model was estimated for each of the five years prior to bankruptcy. Table 16.7 (Section IV) presents the percentage accuracy of the classifications of this model. The authors concluded that the multivariate model results "show a significant improvement over the best performing operating cash flow ratio, the one incorporating current liabilities. The reason for the improvement is the increase in the percentage of accurately classified healthy companies" (pp. 64–65). The final test reported by the authors examined the incremental predictive ability from adding the three cash flow variables to the six variables in the multivariate model: "For each year we ran separate discriminant analysis including the six financial ratios and each of the operating cash flow variables. None of the results improved significantly on the percentage accuracy obtained using the combination of financial ratios alone" (p. 65). The authors concluded that "operating cash flow data are not the Holy Grail that some have made them out to be" (p. 62).

REQUIRED

1. What factors may have given rise to the increased attention paid in the last decade to cash flow measures? Do you agree with Harold Williams that "cash flow from operations is a better measure of performance than earnings-per-share"?

2. Evaluate the strengths and weaknesses of the evidence Casey and Bartczak present to support their conclusion that "operating cash flow information fails as a thermometer in gauging corporate health" (p. 61).

3. A major finding in the Casey and Bartczak evidence was that while operating cash flow variables could discriminate between the bankrupt and healthy companies with reasonably good accuracy, they produced many inaccurate classifications of nonbankrupt companies. What explanations could you give for these results?

4. An article in the financial press reported that "cash flow devotees remain skeptical of the Casey and Bartczak conclusions." What areas would you examine to gain further evidence on the value of using cash flow analysis in corporate lending decisions? Be both explicit and detailed in your suggestions.

REFERENCES

ALTMAN, E. I. "Commercial Bank Lending: Process, Credit Scoring, and Costs of Errors in Lending." *Journal of Financial and Quantitative Analysis* (November 1980): 813–832.

ALTMAN, E. I., R. G. HALDEMAN, and P. NARAYANAN. "Zeta Analysis: A New Model to Identify Bankruptcy Risk of Corporations." *Journal of Banking and Finance* (June 1977): 29–54.

APILADO, V. P., D. C. WARNER, and J. J. DAUTEN. "Evaluative Techniques in Consumer Finance: Experimental Results and Policy Implications for Financial Institutions." *Journal of Financial and Quantitative Analysis* (March 1974): 275–283.

BACKER, M., and M. L. GOSMAN. "The Predictive Value of Financial Ratios in Bank Term Loan Decisions." *The Journal of Commercial Bank Lending* (March 1979): 53–67.

CASEY, C. J., and N. J. BARTCZAK. "Cash Flow—It's Not the Bottom Line." *Harvard Business Review* (July–August 1984): 61–66. Copyright 1984 by the President and Fellows of Harvard College. All rights reserved.

CASTLE, G. R. "Term Lending—A Guide to Negotiating Term Loan Covenants and Other Financial Restrictions." *The Journal of Commercial Bank Lending* (November 1980): 26–39.

COHEN, K. J., T. C. GILMORE, and F. A. SINGER. "Bank Procedures for Analyzing Business Loan Applications." In K. J. Cohen and F. S. Hammer, eds., *Analytical Methods in Banking,* pp. 218–249. Homewood, Ill.: Richard D. Irwin, 1966.

COWEN, S. S., and A. L. PAGE. "A Note on the Use of Selected Nonfinancial Ratio Variables to Predict Small-Business Loan Performance." *Decision Sciences* (January 1982): 82–87.

DEITRICK, J. W., and J. L. STAMPS. "The Use of Accounting Information by Bank Loan Officers." *The Journal of Commercial Bank Lending* (November 1981): 51–62.

DIETRICH, J. R., and R. S. KAPLAN. "Empirical Analysis of the Commercial Loan Classification Decision." *The Accounting Review* (January 1982): 18–38.

DUN & BRADSTREET. *The D&B Rating.* New York: Dun & Bradstreet, 1985.

DURAND, D. *Risk Elements in Consumer Installment Financing.* New York: National Bureau of Economic Research, 1941.

EDMISTER, R. O. "An Empirical Test of Financial Ratio Analysis for Small-Business Failure Prediction." *Journal of Financial and Quantitative Analysis* (March 1972): 1477–1493.

EPSTEIN, M. J. *The Usefulness of Annual Reports to Corporate Shareholders.* Los Angeles: California State University, 1975.

EWERT, D. C. *Trade Credit Management: Selection of Accounts Receivable Using a Statistical Model.* Atlanta: Georgia State University, 1977.

FOSTER, G. "Accounting Policy Decisions and Capital Market Research." *Journal of Accounting and Economics* (March 1980): 29–62.

FULMER, J. G., J. E. MOON, T. A. GAVIN, and J. M. ERWIN. "A Bankruptcy Classification Model for Small Firms." *The Journal of Commercial Bank Lending* (July 1984): 25–37.

GIBSON, C. "Financial Ratios as Perceived by Commercial Loan Officers." *Akron Business and Economic Review* (Summer 1983): 23–27.

HANWECK, G. A. "Predicting Bank Failure," Research Papers in Banking and

Financial Economics, Financial Studies Section. Board of Governors of the Federal Reserve System, Washington, D.C., 1977.

HSIA, D. C. "Credit Scoring and the Equal Credit Opportunity Act." *The Hastings Law Journal* (November 1978): 371–448.

IZAN, H. Y. "Corporate Distress in Australia." *Journal of Banking and Finance* (June 1984): 303–320.

JAGGI, B. "Which Is Better, D&B or Zeta in Forecasting Credit Risk?" *Journal of Business Forecasting* (Summer 1984): 13–16, 22.

LEFTWICH, R. "Accounting Information in Private Markets: Evidence from Private Lending Agreements." *The Accounting Review* (January 1983): 23–42.

MAKEEVER, D. A. "Predicting Business Failures." *The Journal of Commercial Bank Lending* (January 1984): 14–18.

MARAIS, M. L., J. M. PATELL, and M. A. WOLFSON. "The Experimental Design of Classification Models: An Application of Recursive Partitioning and Bootstrapping to Commercial Bank Loan Classifications." In *Studies on Current Econometric Issues in Accounting Research,* supplement to *Journal of Accounting Research* (1984): 87–114.

MCCASLIN, T. E., and K. G. STANGA. "Accounting Information Adjusted for Changing Prices: How Do Users React?" *The Journal of Commercial Bank Lending* (July 1983): 50–60.

MURDOCH, B. "User Perceptions of the Usefulness of Historical Cost, Constant Dollar, and Current Cost Financial Information." *Akron Business and Economic Review* (Summer 1982): 36–42.

MYERS, J. H., and E. W. FORGY. "The Development of Numerical Credit Evaluation Systems." *Journal of the American Statistical Association* (September 1963): 799–806.

ORGLER, Y. E. *Analytical Methods in Loan Evaluation.* Lexington, Mass.: Lexington Books, 1975.

PETTWAY, R. H. "Potential Insolvency, Market Efficiency, and Bank Regulation of Large Commercial Banks." *Journal of Financial and Quantitative Analysis* (March 1980): 219–236.

PETTWAY, R. H., and J. F. SINKEY. "Establishing On-Site Bank Examination Priorities: An Early-Warning System Using Accounting and Market Information." *The Journal of Finance* (March 1980): 137–150.

ROBERT MORRIS ASSOCIATES. *RMA Uniform Credit Analysis.* Philadelphia, Robert Morris Associates, 1982.

SHICK, R. A., and L. F. SHERMAN. "Bank Stock Prices as an Early-Warning System for Changes in Condition." *Journal of Bank Research* (Autumn 1980): 136–146.

SINKEY, J. F., R. R. DINCE, and J. V. TERZA. "A Zeta Analysis of Failed Commercial Banks," working paper. University of Georgia, Athens, 1985.

SPONG, K., and T. HOENIG. "Bank Examination Classifications and Loan Risk."

Economic Review of the Federal Reserve Bank of Kansas City (June 1979): 15–25.

STEIN, J. H. V., and W. ZIEGLER. "The Prognosis and Surveillance of Risks from Commercial Credit Borrowers." *Journal of Banking and Finance* (June 1984): 249–268.

WELLS, H. L., "New Customer Credit Pointing System." In *Numerical Pointing Plans for Evaluating Consumer Credit Risks*. Philadelphia: Philadelphia Credit Bureau, 1963.

WIGINTON, J. C. "A Note on the Comparison of Logit and Discriminant Models of Consumer Credit Behavior." *Journal of Financial and Quantitative Analysis* (September 1980): 757–770.

WILCOX, J. W. "A Simple Theory of Financial Ratios as Predictors of Failure." *Journal of Accounting Research* (Autumn 1971): 389–395.

ZEFF, S. A., ed. *Asset Appreciation, Business Income and Price-Level Accounting: 1918–1935*. New York: Arno Press, 1976.

AUTHOR INDEX

SUBJECT INDEX

Moody's ratings, 498, 499, 502, 504–7, 509, 513, 514, 517–20, 577
Morgan Stanley, 33
Multiple regression model and financial ratio variables, 114–15
Multivariate models of distress prediction, 542, 546–62
Municipal bonds:
  ratings of, 506–9, 514
    linear discriminant analysis of, 517–22
  yields differences of, 510–11
Municipal debt ratings, 506–8
Mutual funds, 308–9, 311
Myopic hypothesis of equity valuation, 326–27, 443, 444–45

N

Net cash flow (NCF), 79–80
Net income before extraordinary items (NIBEI), 79, 216–*18*
Net return rating (NRR), 15
New Horizon Fund (T. Rowe Price), 361
New York Stock Exchange (NYSE), 14, 25, 26, 41–42, 308
  Company Manual, 28
  firms on: earnings releases, 378–87, 400
  firms valuation by, 467–68
  returns on securities traded on, 342, 350, 351, 356–62
New Zealand information sources rated, *12*–13
News releases, good and bad, 42–43
Newspapers, competitive disclosure, 38
Nu-West Corporation, 84–86

O

Off-balance-sheet financing methods, 76–77, 101, 515
Oil and gas industry:
  accounting method choice in, 167–70
  cross-sectional comparison of profitability, 201–4
  exploration: information demand of, 10, 14–15
    Reserve Recognition Accounting for, 27, 29, 486
    vs. takeover, 466
  using full-cost accounting, 143–45, 577
  value-based reserves disclosure by, 515, 577
  windfall profits disclosure by, 37
Operating cost, firm, and inventory decisions, 139
Operating leverage, 342, 344
Option pricing, equilibrium theory, 341
Ordinary least squares (OLS) estimated betas, 102, 104, 348–49, 351
Organizational changes and LOB data, 186
Outlier (data) observations, 99–101, 108
Over-the-counter (OTC) market and abnormal returns, 382, 391

P

Pabst Brewing Company:
  analysis of information of, 3–4, 58–62, 64–*75*
  corporate release by, 35
Partnership, joint, 4
Partnership, limited and general, 14–15
Pearson moment correlation statistic, 114
Pension benefits accounting (reporting), 152, 153, 514

Percentiles, distribution, 104, 178
Performance evaluation, security returns, 359–61
Personal computer data analysis, 428
Planning, budgeting, and goal setting (PBGS), 78, *79*
Political costs and accounting method choice, 140,
Political costs and disclosure, 37, 40–41
Pooling accounting, 304
Portfolio construction with CAPM, 337–39, 355, 360, 362
Portfolio efficiency theory, 311–12, 319–24
Portfolio risk, relative (Beta), 311, 312, 345–46
Post-earnings announcement anomaly, 396–97
Predictive analysis for acquisition, 473–75
Price-to-earnings (PE) ratio, 189, 190
  anomaly of, 397
  computation with, 436–43, 447–49
  market capitalization and, 74–75
  merger prices and, 469
Prices changing and alternative accounting, 150
Private companies, 182–83, 468
Processing costs and disclosure, 35–36
Product market information:
  analysis of, 73–74
    for loans, 574–75
  combined with statement data, 73–74
Prooduct substitutability, 177, 187
Profit impact of market strategies (PIMS) data base, 194
Profit-sharing plans, 4–5, 16–18, 141
Profitability, 81, 99
  of acquiring firms, 464, 475–77
  differences across firms, 193–94
  of government contracting, 41
  of mergers, 475–77
Profitability ratios, 67–68, 72, 77–79, 110–12, 116–18, 122, 152, 188–190, 192, 193–95, 198, 219–20, 230–38, 244–45, 543–44, 545, 551–52, 553–55, 580
Profitability variables, 476–77
Public utility bond ratings, 509, 513

Q

Quarterly reports filing, 31, 35, 184
Quartiles, distribution, 107, 179
Questionnaires:
  surveying financial ratios use, 78–79
  surveying information demands, 12–13
  about managerial accounting use, 157, *158*

R

Railroads, U.S., bankruptcy case study, 537–*48*
Random-walk model:
  of annual earnings-per-share, 232–33, 239–47
  of daily security returns, 306–7
Rating, debt securities, described, 498
Ratio form, 96 (*see also* Financial ratios)
Ratios:
  in annual reports, 64, 77–79
  cross-sectional aggregation of, 178–79
  See also Capital market ratios; Capital structure; Cash flow; Cash position; Debt service coverage; Firm size measures; Liquidity; Price-to-earnings; Profitability; Turnover; Working capital